THE COLLECTED WORKS OF
L. S. VYGOTSKY

Volume 3
Problems of the Theory and
History of Psychology
Including the Chapter on the Crisis in Psychology

COGNITION AND LANGUAGE
A Series in Psycholinguistics • Series Editor: R. W. RIEBER

Recent Volumes in this Series:

THE COLLECTED WORKS OF
L. S. VYGOTSKY

Volume 3

Problems of the Theory and
History of Psychology

Including the Chapter on the Crisis in Psychology

Translated and with an Introduction by
RENÉ VAN DER VEER

Department of Education
Leiden, University
Leiden, The Netherlands

Prologue by
ROBERT W. RIEBER and JEFFREY WOLLOCK

Editors of the English Translation
ROBERT W. RIEBER and JEFFREY WOLLOCK
John Jay College of Criminal Justice
and the Graduate Center
City University of New York
New York, New York

Solidarity Foundation
New York, New York

PLENUM PRESS • NEW YORK AND LONDON

The Library of Congress cataloged earlier volumes of this title as follows:

Vygotskii. L. S. (Lev Semenovich), 1896–1934.
The collected works of L. S. Vygotsky.

(Cognition and language)
Translation of: Sobranie Sochinenii.
Vol. 1– includes bibliographies and indexes.
Contents: v. 1. Problems of general psychology.
1. Psychology I. Rieber, R. W. (Robert W.) II. Carton, Aaron S.

BF121.V9413 1987   150   87-7219

ISBN 0-306-45488-2
90000

9 780306 454882

This volume is published under an agreement with the
Russian Authors' Society (RAO)

ISBN 0-306-45488-2

© 1997 Plenum Press, New York
A Division of Plenum Publishing Corporation
233 Spring Street, New York, N. Y. 10013

http://www.plenum.com

10 9 8 7 6 5 4 3 2 1

Printed in the United States of America

TRANSLATOR'S FOREWORD AND ACKNOWLEDGMENTS

The strength of a chess move in a certain position must be judged against the background of the statics and dynamics of the position and the moves made in similar positions in earlier periods of chess history. The same holds true when we want to evaluate Vygotsky's genuine contribution to psychology. We cannot reach a proper understanding of his work without knowledge of the situation in psychology in the 1920s and 1930s and the history of psychology. An adequate assessment of Vygotsky's achievements comes after our understanding of the finer details of these developments and situations. That is why I have tried to restore this historical landscape as far as possible by supplying historical notes, references, etc. Together with the notes to the Russian edition they should enable the reader to come to a historical understanding and evaluation of Vygotsky's works.

Various colleagues and friends have assisted me by finding references, clarifying parts of the Russian text, etc. These included Igor Arievich, Ellen Bakker, Guillermo Blanck, Peter Keiler, Siebren Miedema, Carl Ratner, Anna Stetsenko, and Jaan Valsiner. Igor Arievich suggested many improvements to the translation of the "Crisis" and clarified obscure passages in the text of the whole volume. Finally, Carl Ratner read a substantial part of the text in translation, corrected mistakes, and suggested changes which improved the readability of the text. I have not always followed his advice but am very grateful for the work he did.

After I had translated the whole volume I carefully checked my translation against the German and Spanish translations of the same volume (see Vygotsky, 1985, 1991). This saved me from making a number of mistakes. I found the necessary information for the notes in my own stock of old psychology books, in numerous libraries, and in the usual dictionaries and encyclopedias. Throughout the book I have checked Vygotsky's quotations of foreign and Russian authors and in the case of English or American authors I have not retranslated Vygotsky's translation but used the original texts. English translations (e.g., in the case of Pavlov) I have sometimes changed somewhat if this seemed necessary. Vygotsky's way of referring to other authors was very sloppy, and I have tried to supply book titles, page numbers, names of authors (in cases where Vygotsky referred to "a psychologist"), and (sometimes) information about authors. In addition, I tried to explain some terms. This resulted in the information given in square brackets in the text, in the notes to the English edition, and in a list of references which is three times as long as the original one.

I have not attempted to improve Vygotsky's style of writing although it was at times difficult to refrain from doing so. It is clear that Vygotsky—unlike, for example, William James—never rewrote a text for the sake of improving its style and readability. Hence the redundancy, the difficulty to follow the thread of his argument, the awkward sentences, etc. However, I feel there is a (sometimes vague) boundary between translating and editing a text and I have set myself the task of providing a scholarly translation and no more than that. The readers will judge to what extent I have succeeded.

Finally, let me end this foreword in a typically Vygotskian fashion by quoting "a well-known psychologist" who once apologized for his imperfect English in the following fashion: "It is needless to say that in spite of the helpful retouching of my language, the whole cast shows the style of the foreigner who is a beginner in the use of English and who must thus seriously ask for the indulgence of the reader."

René van der Veer
March 1994, Leiden

PROLOGUE

Vygotsky's "Crisis," and Its Meaning Today

R. W. Rieber
John Jay College of Criminal Justice

Jeffrey Wollock
Research Director, Solidarity Foundation

"The Historical Meaning of the Crisis in Psychology" was not published during Vygotsky's lifetime, and may not even be a finished work. It was long believed lost. Nevertheless the ideas it focuses on, reflected in other of Vygotsky's works, did have an influence even while he was alive (Yaroshevsky, 1989, pp. 197-198). History, moreover, has increased the significance of the work, for Vygotsky is not only a most perceptive witness to the professional crisis of his time, but also a prophet of the crisis of today.

At the end of the nineteenth century, Wilhelm Wundt wrote:

> Psychology, even in our own day, shows more clearly than any other experimental science traces of the conflict of philosophical systems. We may regret this influence in the interest of psychological investigations because it has been the chief obstacle in the way of an impartial examination of mental life. But in the light of history we see that it was inevitable (as quoted in Misiak, 1961, p. 127).

This statement was made at a time when the issue of conflicting philosophies had already been raised by Wilhelm Dilthey. Around the turn of the century, when psychology was first becoming professionalized and psychologists were filled with the hope of making it a science, the debate between Dilthey and Ebbinghaus (both at Berlin) was still going on. In taking the position that psychology is separate from philosophy—that it is a science, strictly speaking, Ebbinghaus, Ewald Herring, and others began the movement in that direction. The original crisis in psychology arose from conflicting answers to the question of how this should be done.

Vygotsky is looking at the same problem, but thirty years later, and the crisis he refers to is already a second one. Dilthey had long since been pushed aside (he died in 1911), and it was clear that Ebbinghaus had won the first battle. The first decade of the century had seen the rise of the structuralists under Titchener, the functionalists led by Dewey, James, and others, and the behaviorists under Watson. As the 1920s came in, all kinds of new schools were emerging—not only behaviorists, but also Freudians and neo-Freudians, Gestaltists, Marxists, and so on. In

America the Wundtians (introspection) fought the Deweyans; the behaviorists would watch these two kill each other off and eventually take over. This second crisis is succinctly reflected in two well-known books of the time, *Psychologies of 1925* and *Psychologies of 1930* (Murchison, 1926, 1930).

The root of the crisis has always been the question of the genuine relation of psychology to the entire field of knowledge, and the variety of answers has been the source of fragmentation within the profession. In reality the lines between psychology and other disciplines are thin; yet the mainstream of the profession, sociologically speaking, has a vested interest in maintaining tight boundaries in its relations with other fields. As the crisis was beginning in the West, there seemed to be an opportunity for unity, but the simultaneous process of professionalization was so mishandled as to make this goal impossible.

Thus, as Vygotsky shows, each field has a tendency to construct its own theory as "the" general science (pp. 235 ff)—transposing concepts and analogies indiscriminately; and this leads to pseudo-science.

> . . .a concept that is used deliberately, not blindly, in the science for which it was created, where it originated, developed, and was carried to its ultimate expression, *is blind*, leads nowhere, when transposed to another science. Such blind transpositions, of the biogenetic principle, the experiment and the mathematical method from the natural sciences, created the appearance of science in psychology which in reality concealed a total impotence in the face of studied facts (p. 280).

The same process of fragmentation and creation of pseudo-concepts takes place among the various schools within psychology itself.

Vygotsky's analysis of the problem is of particular interest not only for its clarity and fertility but also because of the special conditions under which he was working. For in Soviet psychology of the 1920s, the problem of professionalization posed itself in a particularly stark way. It was important not only for all the above reasons, but even more because the USSR was a revolutionary society, a society that was re-institutionalizing the professions under a brand-new system.

Thus, the crisis as Vygotsky saw it lay in the tendencies that were already beginning the proliferation of schools and incommensurate views (cf. Yaroshevsky, 1989, pp. 186 ff). Yet to him a solution seemed genuinely possible, for society was wiping the slate clean and starting anew. The Soviet Union in the 1920s was not yet what it was later to become; there was much variety, and experimentation was encouraged. Formulating a unified theory and applying it to build the society of the future seemed not merely hopes, but necessities. There was thus in Vygotsky an intensity of motivation that could not have emerged out of a mere mass of disparate, competing schools. Although we tend to see the Marxist blueprint as oppressive and totalitarian, for men like Vygotsky it represented a genuine opportunity for the formation of both a general science and a profession.

Vygotsky's main response to the "crisis" is epistemological, an analysis of the way various schools understood knowledge about the human mind. It is a keen critique based on common sense and clear thinking rather than party dogmatics, in which he pinpoints the lack of a general science as the main cause of the problem, and carefully discusses how a general science must be constructed. A unifying science would show the connections and relations between all the fields of knowledge, and it is the lack of a unifying general science of psychology that is the main focus of Vygotsky's critique throughout. He emphasizes (p. 281) that analysis of terminology is one of the best ways to get an idea of the extent of the crisis.

Before Vygotsky, the Russian psychologist Nikolai Lange (1914) had already indicated the crucial importance of terminology and the lack of a common system:

> Without fear of exaggeration it can be said that the description of any psychological process becomes different whether we describe and study it in the categories of the psychological system of Ebbinghaus or Wundt, Stumpf or Avenarius, Meinong or Binet, James or G. E. Muller. Of course, the purely factual element must remain the same. However, in science, at least in psychology, to separate the described fact from its theory, i.e., from these scientific categories by means of which this description is made, is very often difficult and even impossible, for in psychology . . . each description is already a certain theory . . . (quoted by Vygotsky, p. 289).

From this quotation alone, it is difficult to avoid the conclusion that Lange was a major inspiration for Vygotsky's entire approach to the problem—a point which Yaroshevsky (1989, pp. 170-199; on terminology, pp. 181-182; 1990, pp. 390-391) would also seem to support.

So the Soviet Union presented a special opportunity, for there the sought-for general science seemed not only a possible but an obligatory goal. In the Soviet Union, Marxism was that general science (cf. Yaroshevsky, 1989, p. 189). And it is true that Marxism is one of the few systems of modern thought that is *not* fragmentary and within which it is possible to make all kinds of connections between forms of knowledge and objects of knowledge. Marxism, moreover, at least from its own particular point of view of dialectical materialism and social struggle, is a radically humanist philosophy; radical in that it not only emphasizes the human, but by removing God from the traditional God/man nexus inevitably throws all emphasis on the human. Moreover, the emphasis placed on human society means that the latter virtually replaces God in explaining the end, nature, and motivating force of humanity. Finally, it is human society at any given historical moment, not God, that is seen as the final cause of nature itself, in the Hegelian sense that society is the highest development of the dialectic of nature and that man's knowledge of nature is a historically mediated social construct. In Marxism, therefore, the opposition between nature and society is transcended by the unity of the historical dialectic. Human psychology with a strong social emphasis would have to play a central role in such a world view. That this repositioning of man distorts the definition of humanity is another matter (for further discussion of this see Fromm, 1961).

Because Marxism sees history as a kind of experimental record of scientific sociology, it views itself as a science. Consistent with this, Vygotsky felt the goal of a scientific psychology should be to understand the human individual as a historically developing process—a process-oriented rather than entity-oriented approach that studies man experimentally at the "proximal zone of development," both in terms of the individual and the species. From this perspective, Dilthey's distinction between the human sciences and the natural sciences is a false solution, though not at all for the reason that the behaviorists believed it was. Indeed Vygotsky saw the "psychology of the mind" of Dilthey as the most dangerous opponent of the scientific study of consciousness (pp. 335-336; see also Yaroshevsky, 1989, pp. 195-196).

To see this more clearly, it is important to understand Vygotsky's relation to behaviorism, which, given his underlying Marxist perspective, does not conform to Dilthey's dichotomy between the human sciences and the natural sciences. The *ideology* of positivism has no place for human action or human history: when positivism is the generalizing principle, it tends to bifurcate history and nature, and for that reason above all Marxism has always been opposed to it (cf. pp. 286-287). On the other hand, Vygotsky admired behaviorism (reflexology) as a pure methodology, for Marxism, with its unifying principles, could comfortably assimilate the results of all forms of experimental psychology into dialectical materialism, both theory and praxis.

According to Vygotsky, an investigator proceeding from the perspective of the general science (Marxism)

> will see what and how much in the development of science depends on the good and bad intentions of its practitioners . . . and what from this intention itself should, on the contrary, be explained on the basis of the objective tendencies operative behind the backs of these practitioners . . . in Pavlov . . . reflexology is the 'ultimate science,' 'an omnipotent method,' which brings 'full, true and permanent human happiness.' And in their own way behaviorism and Gestalt theory cover the same route. Obviously, rather than the mosaic of good and evil intentions among the investigators we should study the unity in the processes of regeneration of scientific tissue in psychology, which determines the intentions of all the investigators (p. 257; the passage on pp. 277-278 to the words "are *different* facts" is really a criticism of behaviorism, or "reflexology," though he compliments Watson on p. 277).

Today's Crisis in Psychology

The crisis today, while formally similar, is substantially different from what it was in the 1920s. When Vygotsky was writing the "Crisis," psychology was only at the start of its popularization in Europe and America. Then as now the profession was chaotic, but for a different reason. At that time it was because the profession was everywhere undeveloped, though full of brilliant possibilities. Today it is because the field is overdeveloped and its general level is mediocre.

However, just as the profession began without a definite identity, so today there is a struggle on the part of psychologists who sought *some formal agreement* on the definition of the science and goal of psychology to benefit mankind.

In those days nearly all psychologists, including those in the Soviet Union, knew what was going on in foreign countries. The number of people involved in the profession was much smaller, making it more possible to keep abreast of their thinking; and the intellectual calibre of the profession was higher, which meant that more of its members were capable of following, of analyzing and synthesizing, developments in the field.

In the West, the need for a general science and the need for professionalization suggested that the general science should become the unifying factor for the professionalization. However, if the need for a general, unifying science was recognized by most Europeans and Americas in the 1920s, there was no general agreement on what it should be.

What most of the schools of the 1920s had in common, with the exception of personalism (see p. 245) and neo-scholasticism (which Vygotsky does not mention), was that they were based on materialistic presuppositions. Yet what was not then much in evidence (except among the neoscholastics) was any perception of positivism as a *threat* to psychology. On the contrary, positivism was seen as the way of insuring that psychology would become a real *science*.

After World War II, numerous variants of behaviorism started to emerge and gradually set up a more "scientific" methodology that conformed to positivistic principles, until they were challenged in the late 1960s by humanistic psychology. However, this challenge did not last very long—humanistic psychology was predominant for about ten years but itself split into too many different schools. Then emerged the latest crisis, with cognitive psychology, neuropsychology, developmental psychology, and artificial intelligence—all varieties of positivism—becoming the most active forms of psychology.

It might be said that positivism won because it was the most purely materialist approach to psychology. In giving the human sciences a materialist foundation,

Marxism at least embraced them and preserved the formal coherence of all intellectual disciplines. In contrast, positivism rejected the human sciences, giving them no foundation at all, and presented Western thought with an insoluble dichotomy and a dangerous incoherence.

Thus within a period of fifty years psychology had come full circle; it was the "in" profession of the 1980s. Indeed psychology is still growing by leaps and bounds, still highly successful in terms of quantity and productivity. Qualitatively, however, it's another story. The field has metastasized and there is neither the opportunity to start afresh, nor any agreed general science. Today the crisis is the chaos of overdevelopment and misdirection (see Bakin, 1996; Sarason, 1981).

In defining success, we have to avoid the idea that "bigger is better." We cannot ignore the great dissension of goals and shirking of responsibility that characterize the fields today. Today, however, the complaint that the positivist paradigm is simply unsuited to psychology is at least being taken more seriously in the field than it has been at any time since the end of World War II.

The critics of positivism all agree that positivism *removes the human from psychology*. But different philosophies differ on precisely why this is a problem. For Marxism, positivism's nonhuman character represents tacit support for the socioeconomic status quo. For many modern critics, on the other hand, the problem with positivism is rather that it denies the spiritual in man.* But when the status quo is one of materialism, when the ruling class denies (either positively or in its effect) the spiritual in man, there is a breakdown of values. Isn't it this that ultimately leads to social breakdown and social distress?

Officially the Soviet ideology was materialism, but personal consumption was so underemphasized and the great majority of people had so little in the way of material goods, that unofficially and for the majority there developed, paradoxically, a rather high level of intellectual and spiritual values. Under these conditions, the overall intellectual coherence of Marxism may have been a more significant influence than its spurious materialism. In the West, on the other hand, the official ideology champions freedom of religion, yet life has become so saturated with material values and pursuits that a materialist approach to life is the norm. The fragmentation of knowledge and of the professions only contributes to this tendency.

If psychology is going to find a new direction, it probably will have to embrace an epistemology similar to that of Vygotsky. It will have to allow for the understanding that we cannot divorce the subject from the object, especially when we study the social nature of the object. It will have to allow psychology to decide the best methodology for a particular problem, and not throw the baby out with the bathwater because of some ideological obligations, whether to post-modernism, Marxism, behaviorism, or any other "ism."

Because of Vygotsky's emphasis on the ultimate unity of the forms of knowledge, it is at least possible to integrate into his approach yet another kind of knowledge, that concerned with the uniquely human spirit. With behaviorism, this is impossible. To do so would of course require a far more comprehensive map of all forms of knowledge and a wider and more diverse definition of knowledge than even Vygotsky would allow. Here new questions arise: Are the intellectual foundations of the presently recognized boundaries of knowledge really valid? On what presuppositions do they actually rest? Are these presuppositions logically necessary or merely historical contingencies? Can we bring ourselves to be skeptical about

*We use the word *spiritual* here in the strictly traditional sense (extended metaphor) and not with any "New Age" or similar connotations.

our culture's faith in skepticism? These are some of the questions we must begin to face if we are to find the most useful path to a unified and integrated psychology.

References

Bakin, David (1996). The Crisis in Psychology. *Journal of Social Distress and the Homelessness. 5(4),* p. 335.

Fromm, Eric (1961). *Marx's Concept of Man.* New York: Frederick Ungar.

Misiak, Henryk (1961). *The Philosophical Roots of Scientific Psychology.* New York: Fordham University Press.

Murchison, Carl, ed. (1926). *Psychologies of 1925.* Worcester: Clark University Press.

Murchison, Carl, ed. (1930). *Psychologies of 1930.* Worcester: Clark University Press.

Sarason, Seymour (1981). *Psychology Misdirected.* New York: Free Press.

Yaroshevsky, Mikhail (1989). *Lev Vygotsky.* Moscow: Progress Publishers.

Yaroshevsky, Mikhail (1990). *A History of Psychology.* Moscow: Progress Publishers.

CONTENTS

SOME MAJOR THEMES IN VYGOTSKY'S THEORETICAL WORK. AN INTRODUCTION

René van der Veer

This is the translation of the first volume of the Russian edition of Vygotsky's *Collected Works*. It contains several of Vygotsky's major theoretical papers, a number of discussions of the work of outstanding contemporaries, and his manuscript on the crisis in psychology. Together these allow us to get a fairly adequate impression of Vygotsky the theoretical psychologist (as opposed to Vygotsky the educationalist, clinician, experimenter, etc.). Before we turn to a short overview of these texts, it is important to make a few remarks about the selection of texts for this volume (and for all six volumes in general) and their status. We believe that it is fitting to make these remarks in a volume that in the Russian edition formed the first of the whole series.

It must be realized that reliable archives of Vygotsky's writings open to the general public or interested expert do not exist. There is no Vygotsky Center which on demand sends facsimile copies of original manuscripts, papers, and letters to interested researchers. There is no Vygotsky Library where we can consult copies of Vygotsky's publications as well as those of his contemporaries. What exists are the family archives which by nature are accessible to only a very limited group of people and the private archives of different people interested in Vygotsky. This situation poses a problem to those who want to study Vygotsky's work thoroughly.

The fact that Vygotsky's original works and manuscripts have always been difficultly accessible has meant that two other problems have been less evident. These are the problem of the completeness of our list of his writings and the problem of the reliability of the texts that have been (or will be) published. The first problem is, perhaps, less important as the finding of a handful of unknown writings by Vygotsky will probably not substantially change our understanding of his work. But it must be said that we still do not know whether our record of Vygotsky's writings (especially for the period from 1916 to 1920) is complete, and it would come as no surprise if another dozen literary reviews would be discovered in the future. The problem of the reliability of Vygotsky's texts is more important. Here we can distinguish between (a) manuscripts not published during Vygotsky's lifetime, (b) works published posthumously, and (c) republications. As to (a) we can say that there has been virtually no scholarly work on the unpublished manuscripts. No one sorted out the manuscripts, ordered them, signalled variants of the same text, etc. In short, no philological or other work has been done on these manuscripts. The problem of (b) is perhaps more serious. Let us first look at some books that were

1

published in the 1930s. *Thinking and Speech* (1934) is least debatable, because here we know for sure that Vygotsky compiled the book himself and saw the ultimate or penultimate version of the book. More complicated are the cases of *Children's Mental Development in the Process of Education* (1935) and *Foundations of Pedology* (1935). The first book consists of several papers and lectures delivered at several institutes. The book was edited by Zankov, Shif, and El'konin, who explicitly state that the published lectures are based on shorthand reports and that they were not corrected by Vygotsky himself. The second book was edited by Levina and consists of lectures delivered by Vygotsky at the Herzen State Pedagogical Institute in Leningrad. The published text of these lectures was quite probably also based on shorthand reports made by students, and it is not likely that Vygotsky authorized the text. This circumstance does not make these posthumous publications totally unreliable as source material—cf. the case of George Herbert Mead, whose reputation is largely based on similar lecture notes—but we must keep this in mind when interpreting his ideas. Little can be said about posthumous publications made in later decades as these were based on material found in archives. They can be more or less reliable, but in view of the fact sketched above (of limited access) the general reader has no way of checking this. The problem of (c) republications is equally serious. Soviet republications of original texts published in the 1920s or 1930s tend to be notoriously sloppy and long lists of errors could be compiled. Most of these errors are of minor importance and regard, for example, the orthography. Others are more annoying and concern deleted references to authors now out of favor (e.g., Trotsky, Watson) and the suppression of unacceptable terms (e.g., pedology). Wherever possible, researchers should consult the original texts. This policy has also been followed for the present volume, which is based on (a) manuscripts not published during Vygotsky's lifetime and (c) republications. The latter have been checked against the original in the case of *The Methods of Reflexological and Psychological Investigation, Preface to Lazursky, Consciousness as a Problem for the Psychology of Behavior, Apropos Koffka's Article on Self-Observation, Preface to Leont'ev,* and *Preface to Köhler.* In other cases no originals were available. We may conclude that the status of works published under the name of Vygotsky has not always been sufficiently clear and that scholarly editions have been exceedingly rare.

The Russian editors of Vygotsky's *Collected Works* have done little to solve the problems listed above. They did not attempt to unearth thus far unknown writings by Vygotsky, did not question the reliability of the texts used, made use of unreliable republications (e.g., in the case of *Thinking and Speech*), and in republishing original publications introduced mistakes of their own. This does not diminish the value of the work they accomplished (e.g., the tremendous number of useful notes), but it should make us realize that the critical and scholarly reception of Vygotsky's writings is still in its infancy.

Finally, we must dedicate a few words to the problem of selection. After all, it is not for nothing that the present series of volumes is called *Collected Works* and not *Complete Works*. Limiting ourselves to books, we can make a list of the most important publications not included in the *Collected Works*. These include, in chronological order, *The Psychology of Art* (1925), *Educational Psychology* (1926), *Essays in the History of Behavior. Ape. Primitive. Child* (1930; with Luria), *Imagination and Creativity in Childhood* (1930), *Foundations of Pedology* (1935), *Children's Mental Development in the Process of Education* (1935), and various textbooks. Unfortunately, the editors of the Russian edition never justified their selection of texts nor did they discuss the criteria used to include or reject certain texts. We will not contest their choice here, but at the least one can say that on the basis of Vygotsky's books alone the present edition of the *Collected Works* could easily have contained several more volumes. Fortunately, the modern reader of English is now in a position to compile his own more or less complete edition of Vygotsky's *Complete Works* as several of the volumes mentioned above have recently been published or will be published shortly.

This brings us to the present volume which (judging by its subtitle) aims to give an overview of Vygotsky's writings as a theoretical psychologist. How well does it serve this goal? And how should we evaluate the texts included? We will first briefly answer the first question and then devote the rest of this introduction to a brief discussion of some major themes in Vygotsky's writings in this volume (and their place in his body of writings as a whole).

A fair judgment of this volume must first of all take into account that any division of Vygotsky's writings into theoretical, developmental, pedological, etc. works is largely arbitrary. We should also bear in mind that other volumes of the *Collected Works* contain or will contain other equally relevant theoretical writings. The first volume of the present American edition contained the major theoretical writings compiled in *Thinking and Speech* and future volumes will contain the book manuscripts *Tool and Sign in Child Development* (1930) and *The History of the Development of the Higher Mental Functions* (1931). Taking this into account, the present volume (together with the other volumes) presents a reasonably fair picture of Vygotsky's theoretical writings. The one thing that is underrepresented are his pedological writings (see several of the books mentioned above) and writings in which he distinguishes the pedological from the educational and psychological approach in child development.

The first major theme that is present in much of Vygotsky's theoretical writings in this volume is the theme of *continuity and change*. It is especially prevalent in his discussion of the various writings of Gestalt theorists and in his analysis of Bühler's conception. The key question can be formulated as follows: how is it possible that continuous development results in intermediate products or stages which are fundamentally distinct? The question recurs time and again and takes various disguises, e.g., how can we explain continuity in phylogenetic development without taking the viewpoint of either mechanism (which reduces all qualitatively distinct forms to the workings of some primordial mechanism) or vitalism (which creates a gap between lower and higher forms of development by introducing a mysterious principle which is only applicable to the latter)? How can we explain that the immediate evolutionary predecessors of humans, the anthropoid apes, seemingly have almost all of the prerequisites necessary for intelligent behavior (such as tool use and tool manufacture) but nevertheless seem fundamentally less intelligent than humans? How can we explain the development from instinct to intellect without either creating an unbridgeable gap between the two forms of behavior or invoking some mysterious purely mental acts? These are questions which have a long tradition in Western philosophical thought, and the reader will no doubt remember that basically similar questions were already posed in pre-Socratic philosophy (cf. Mourelatos, 1974). They are also questions which are still very much on the agenda of contemporary developmental psychology (cf. Beilin, 1993; Eldredge, 1993; Overton, 1993; Vonèche, 1993; Von Glasersfeld, 1993) and which we cannot avoid in dealing with, for example, the concept of stage.

What attracted Vygotsky in Gestalt theory was that it seemed to provide an explanation for qualitatively distinct stages in development without taking one of the extreme positions sketched above, i.e., Gestalt theorists did not accept fundamental gaps between qualitatively distinct stages of development but neither took recourse to irrational (nonbiological) principles to explain the very real differences that exist between species and between various stages of ontogenetic development.

There is a clear evolution in Vygotsky's evaluation of Gestalt theory's contribution to the solution of this problem. At first he believed that the principle of Gestalt was able to struggle at "two fronts" (i.e., to avoid both extremes in the explanation of continuity and change) and thus performed the magical trick of explaining one of the fundamental paradoxes of Western thought. Thus, in his discussions of Koffka (1926), Köhler (1930), and of Gestalt psychology as a whole, Vygotsky (1930) is inclined to regard the Gestalt concept as a major contribution to psychological thought because it was a form of monistic materialism as we find Gestalten in perception, cognitive development, and in inorganic nature. One and the same principle seemed thus capable of explaining different levels of development. But towards 1930 Vygotsky also begins to emphasize a theme that already surfaced in his analysis of the crisis of psychology: the primordial, universal, and therefore metaphysical character of the Gestalt concept. He now argues that it is not enough to posit the existence of Gestalten because their existence itself should be explained. In the background is his growing conviction that it will not do to explain development with the help of a single principle since development results from the contribution of fundamentally different factors: biology and history (in phylogeny) or maturation and culture (in ontogeny). In his discussion of Bühler (1930), Vygotsky makes it quite clear that he believes that the denial of this fact is equal to defending an antidialectical viewpoint. In his opinion, Bühler was wrong in attributing paramount importance to biological factors and in claiming that nature makes no leaps. The cognitive development from animal to human being cannot be viewed as ascending a "single biological ladder."

The same kind of reasoning was applicable to Gestalt theory, and Vygotsky's discussion of Koffka (1934) illustrates this very well. In fighting both Thorndike and Bühler (who in this connection play the role of representatives of, respectively, the mechanistic and vitalistic conceptions), Koffka argued that the Gestalt criterion for intelligent action (i.e., the development of a solution to the task that is in accord with the structure of the field) is equally applicable to both lower and higher forms of mental actions. But in so doing he refuted his own criterion since it now loses all discriminative power. Whereas the criterion was originally introduced by Köhler to designate the intelligent behavior of anthropoid apes, it now becomes a characteristic of virtually all mental processes regardless of their complexity. In Vygotsky's view such a criterion was useless for explaining specifically human capacities, and he now argues that the so-called intelligent behavior of chimpanzees is in actual fact much closer to instinct than it is to human intellect. Koffka's main flaw is that he attempts to understand animal and man by means of a single principle and thereby reduces human behavior to animal behavior. He thus "overcomes vitalism by making concessions to mechanism" and fails to solve the "most difficult task that research psychologists ever faced," i.e., to explain the origin and development of intelligence.

Vygotsky now also criticizes Gestalt theory for its view of perception and admirably demonstrates a regularity which he much earlier had described in his analysis of the crisis in psychology. This regularity says that explanatory principles tend to be extended beyond the original area in which they were first formulated and then become vulnerable to criticism. Later, they are not just contested as general principles or "world views" but also become the subject of criticism in the restricted domain in which they first originated. Similarly, Vygotsky first criticizes the Gestalt principle as a general principle to be found in both inorganic nature and child development and then switches to the field of perception in which the Gestalt principle emerged. He now contests Köhler's (1933) discussion of the role that knowledge plays in perception. Köhler had argued that perception was indisputably often co-determined by previous knowledge but that there is also something like a primitive organization of the visual field into figure-background, good forms, etc. that seems innate and independent of any knowledge the person may have acquired. This amounts to saying that Gestalten are prior to any experience and that knowledge ("meaning" in Vygotsky's terms) becomes fused with these primordial forms only at a later stage. To this he argued that there is no such thing as primitive pure perception independent of any knowledge or experience and that "the child begins to perceive the things with meaning and introduces elements of thinking into his immediate perceptions." His example of chess players of different strength who perceive different things while looking at the same stimulus configuration was meant to illustrate this point. The knowledge of each of these chess players fundamentally determines their perception of the situation on the board. Vygotsky was probably right in arguing that Gestalt theorists played down the factor of experience and in so doing biologized perception. Similar criticisms were voiced by Hamlyn (1969), who argued that the general theory of Gestalt does not allow for the effect of experience since it ultimately regards perception as a purely physiological process. In his view as well it is a "conceptual mistake to think that it is possible to isolate a pure perceptual experience, which is the end-product of a process of stimulation, albeit modified by autonomous neural processes" (Hamlyn, 1969, p. 74).

The fundamental role of word meaning (experience or knowledge) in all higher mental processes had now become a major theme in Vygotsky's thinking, and he goes on to demonstrate that word meaning fundamentally determines children's perception. In his view this does not mean that the structural principle is invalid but that it needs to be complemented by other more specific principles. The major shortcoming of Gestalt theory is that it lacks an adequate principle to explain development, i.e., it cannot explain why simple structures or Gestalten develop into complex structures. In other writings he explained that a major factor in human mental development is the introduction of word meanings or concepts in instruction. It is instruction in the school setting that propels child development along lines that are each time specific for a certain culture or society. In other words, the "biological" conception of Gestalt theory must be complemented by a sociocultural or sociohistorical view to get a complete view of human mental development. It must be said that as a solution to the classic problem of continuity and change this is not entirely satisfactory. After all, in the classic problem, as it is often stated in dialectical logic, it is small quantitative changes that lead to abrupt qualitative changes (e.g., the beloved example of water becoming steam after a gradual rise in temperature). Characteristic of these examples is that the set of relevant factors determining the process is constant and that the sudden change is not brought about by the introduction of a new factor. In Vygotsky's thinking, on the contrary, it is exactly the introduction of a new factor (i.e., culture in the form of word meanings) that announces a qualitatively new stage in development.

The second major theme that is present in Vygotsky's theoretical writings is the theme of the *systemic and semantic nature of mind* (cf. Vygotsky, 1930, 1934). Mind, in his view, was a hierarchically organized and dynamic system of functions. Development results first and foremost in the alteration of interfunctional connections, in different cerebral systems. This view implies that it is impossible to localize a mental function in some specific brain center and that the relationship between specific mental functions is never fixed. The interconnection of various mental functions and their position in the hierarchical system changes as the organism develops. It would be Luria who would use this aspect of Vygotsky's thinking in creating (together with Goldstein and many others) the science of neuropsychology. Toward the end of his career it was again the development of word meanings or concepts (and, more generally, speech) to which Vygotsky attached predominant importance in this connection. In his view, concepts form the key to understanding both cognitive and emotional development and mental disintegration. Mastering mature conceptual thinking is not confined to the cognitive domain but will at the same time lead to more mature aesthetic reactions and a more refined emotional life. In the case of serious pathology, such as in schizophrenia (Vygotsky, 1934c) or Pick's disease (Samukhin, Birenbaum, and Vygotsky, 1934), the thinking in concepts will be influenced adversely and several of the symptoms of these diseases can be understood as the result of the breakdown of conceptual thinking. It is a fascinating and controversial view that can be criticized on various grounds. From the present viewpoint, for example, the emphasis on (scientific) concepts as the prime movers of mental development seems to imply a somewhat static view on (scientific) thinking. In this view scientific views crystallize into scientific concepts (such as "energy" and "mammal") that subsequently must be transmitted to the next generation. Quite probably, this is a somewhat one-sided view that should be complemented by an approach in which children are taught certain heuristics, skills, and practices which may be flexibly used in broad contexts (cf. Van der Veer, 1994). Such criticisms, however, do not diminish the heuristic value of Vygotsky's broad view on the systemic nature of mind and the dominant role concepts play in its development. For him word meanings or concepts embodied the contribution of culture or society and as such formed co-constituents of human development in that specific culture or society.

A third major theme was the theme of *method or methodology* which concerned Vygotsky throughout his career. The problem of method or methodology can be analyzed at several levels. Vygotsky was concerned with the choice of appropriate research methods and techniques, with the selection of a general approach to psychological phenomena (e.g., objectivating or subjectivating), and with more general problems of epistemology. Thus, we can see him discuss introspection and the method of double stimulation as a specific research technique to disclose the development of mind (the most concrete level), the drawbacks and advantages of the behavioristic approach in psychology (the intermediate level), and the merits of general philosophical views such as materialism and empiricism (the most abstract level).

His famous "The historical meaning of the crisis in psychology" (1926), which was written under very difficult circumstances (see Van der Veer and Valsiner, 1991), dealt mainly with the latter two levels. From this essay, but also from his earlier and later writings, it becomes quite clear that Vygotsky advocated an objective, deterministic, causal psychology that uses objective means which yield replicable results. He argued that no third way besides objective and subjective psychology was possible, sharply criticized subjective approaches, and seemed to opt for a psychology inspired by the natural sciences. Whether psychology itself might be called a natural science he did not discuss since he felt that this is "a special and very deep problem, which does not, however, belong to the problem of the meaning of the crisis as a whole" (p. 303; this volume).

Vygotsky made it quite clear, however, that there can be no such thing as an a-theoretical psychology (or science at large), as the behaviorists seemed to imply. There is no such thing as objective registration of facts (this he regarded as a sensualistic prejudice) because our epistemological principles always co-determine our scientific facts. The positivistic idea that we merely have to register the objective facts and then through induction and mathematical elaboration can arrive at genuine scientific theories was very foreign to Vygotsky. He strongly condemned such an approach and argued that we need interpretation, abstraction, and analysis as the "salto vitale" for psychology. The psychologist may act as a "detective who brings to light a crime he never witnessed" (see "The methods of reflexological and psychological investigation," p. 49 of this volume). It is interesting to note that these ideas were written down in the very period that Carnap, Neurath, and others developed logical-positivism and that they in many ways anticipate much of the later criticism of this view.

The influence of theory or interpretation begins with the words we use to designate the facts or phenomena discovered in our research, and it is for this reason that Vygotsky attached such tremendous importance to the choice of a proper terminology in scientific research. Historically, there are quite strong links between Vygotsky's early interests in linguistic thinkers such as Potebnya and Shpet (and, through them, Von Humboldt) and his emphasis on the importance of words as proto-theories. Similarly, it is quite interesting to see how his analysis of the role that words play in the production of scientific facts (i.e., at the level of methodology) is transposed to the domain of ontogeny in the early 1930s when he seems to realize gradually that words or word meanings can be viewed as the vehicle of mental development.

Summarizing, we can say that the three interconnected themes of development, the systemic and semantic nature of mind, and method or methodology played a major role in Vygotsky's theoretical writings. In the final few years of his career it was the theme of language or word meaning that became quite dominant. Mental development was now largely seen as the result of the development of word meanings acquired in instruction. Likewise, the theme of the systemic structure of mind became actually a way to describe how word meanings gradually come to dominate all human mental processes. Finally, in the realm of epistemology he still held that scientific terms or words as proto-theories co-determine our view of reality. It seems, then, that Vygotsky arrived at a sort of "linguistic psychology" and that in the final analysis both opponents and adherents of Vygotsky's theories can adequately summarize these three themes and large parts of his theorizing by quoting one of Vygotsky's most beloved authors: "Words, words, words."

ON VYGOTSKY'S CREATIVE DEVELOPMENT [1]

A. N. Leont'ev

In the present *Collected Works*, the main works of the eminent Soviet psychologist Lev Semyonovich Vygotsky are presented for the first time with sufficient completeness. Vygotsky was a prolific writer: in less than 10 years of activity as a professional psychologist he wrote about 180 works. Of these, 135 have been published, and 45 await publication. [2] Many of Vygotsky's publications have become bibliographic rarities.

Not only psychologists, but also representatives of the humanities—philosophers, linguists, etc.—have pointed to the need for a new edition of Vygotsky's works. None of these scholars regard his works as belonging to history. Today, more than ever, they turn to Vygotsky's works. His ideas have become so firmly established in scientific psychology that they are mentioned as being generally known, without reference to the corresponding works or without even mentioning Vygotsky's name. [3]

This is the situation not only in Soviet but also in international psychology. In recent years the works of Vygotsky have been translated into English, French, German, Italian, Japanese, and other languages. And abroad as well he is not a historical figure, but a living, contemporary investigator.

It can be said that Vygotsky's scientific destiny developed fortunately and unusually for the 20th century, which is characterized by tempestuous scientific developments in which many ideas are already obsolete the day after they are first expressed. Psychology is, of course, no exception here and we can hardly find concrete investigations in the international psychology of the 20th century that have retained all their topicality 45-50 years after they were first published.

In order to understand the "phenomenon Vygotsky," the exceptionality of his scientific fate, it is essential to point to two aspects of his creative work. On the one hand, there are the concrete facts, the concrete methods and hypotheses of Vygotsky and his collaborators. Many of these methods and hypotheses have been brilliantly confirmed and were further developed in the works of contemporary psychologists. The methods elaborated by Vygotsky, the facts he found, are considered classic. They became very important component parts of the foundation of scientific psychology. And here contemporary psychology, having confirmed Vygotsky's thinking and relying upon it, went further in the plane of facts, methods, hypotheses, etc. But, on the other hand, there is still another aspect in Vygotsky's creative work—a theoretical methodological aspect. Being one of the greatest theoretical psychologists of the 20th century, he was truly decades ahead of his time. And the topicality of Vygotsky's works lies in the theoretical methodological plane. That is why we should not speak about his conceptions as if they were somehow completed. His concrete investigations were just the first stage in the realization of his theoretical methodological program.

1

Vygotsky's creative work was first of all determined by the time in which he lived and worked, the era of the Great Socialist October Revolution.

The deep, decisive reform which the revolution introduced in scientific psychology did not take place right away. As is well known, a spirit of idealism pervaded the official scientific psychology cultivated in the pre-revolutionary universities and gymnasia despite powerful materialistic and revolutionary democratic tendencies in Russian philosophy and psychology. Furthermore, from the scientific point of view it significantly lagged behind the scientific psychology of the leading European countries (Germany, France) and the US. Admittedly, around the turn of the century several experimental laboratories evolved in Russia, and in 1912 the first Psychological Institute of the country was created at Moscow University on the initiative of Chelpanov. But the scientific production of these centers was low and its content in many cases not very original.

Indeed, in the beginning of the 20th century in Europe were born such new psychological schools as psychoanalysis, Gestalt psychology, the Würzburg school, etc. The traditional subjective empirical psychology of consciousness obviously came to naught. In the US emerged a (for the time radical) current in psychology—behaviorism. International scientific psychology was in a frenzy; it went through an excruciating and intense period. In the same years Chelpanov and his co-workers were busy dealing with the replication of the experiments carried out in the Wundtian school. For them the latest news was still the works of James. In a word, they were at the periphery of international psychology and did not feel all the acuteness of the crisis which got hold of it. They lost touch with the most important problems of psychological theory. Psychology in Russia existed as a narrowly academic university science about the practical applications of which it was inconceivable to speak. And this at a time when in Europe and the US applied psychology or psychotechnics was rapidly developing, medical psychology made its first steps, etc.

The revolution brought radical changes for scientific psychology. Psychology was forced to regenerate in all respects, in its essence. A new science had to develop instead of the old psychology within a very short time frame.

The first requirement for scientific psychology was dictated by the life in the country itself, a country destroyed and ruined by the war. It was the requirement to proceed to the analysis of practical applied problems. Immediately after the revolution a new field of psychology—industrial psychology or psychotechnics—began to develop in Russia. This requirement of life was so much beyond doubt that even in the citadel of academic introspectionist psychology—the Psychological Institute headed by Chelpanov—a new section emerged: the section for applied problems.

But the main task for psychologists in these years was to elaborate a new theory instead of the introspective psychology of individual consciousness which was cultivated in the pre-revolutionary period and which rested upon philosophical idealism. The new psychology should proceed from the philosophy of dialectical and historical materialism—it was to become a Marxist psychology.

Psychologists did not immediately realize the need for such a reform. Many of them were students of Chelpanov. However, already in 1920, and more definitely in 1921, Blonsky began raising this matter (in his books *The Reform of Science* and *Outline of a Scientific Psychology*). But the decisive event of those years was Kornilov's well-known talk "Psychology and Marxism" at the First All-Russian Congress on Psychoneurology which took place in Moscow in January 1923. It formulated the line for a development of Marxist psychology with great clarity. In this talk several fundamental theses of Marxism were presented that have direct relevance for psychology (the primacy of matter above consciousness, the mind as a property of highly developed matter, the societal nature of man's mind, etc.). At the time, for many psychologists educated in the spirit of idealism, these theses were not only not obvious, but simply paradoxical.

After the congress a polemic broke out with the fervor characteristic of the revolutionary years of the 1920s. More correctly, it was a genuine struggle between the psychologists-materialists headed by Kornilov and the psychologists-idealists headed by Chelpanov. The overwhelming majority of scholars soon acknowledged that Kornilov was right in his struggle for the development of a Marxist psychology. An external expression of the victory of the materialistic current was the decision taken by the State Scientific Council in November 1923 to relieve Chelpanov of his duties as a director of the Psychological Institute and to appoint Kornilov in his place.

From the beginning of 1924 the reorganization of the Institute was rapid. New collaborators appeared. Some of the supporters of Chelpanov left the Institute. New sections etc. were created. Within a short period the Psychological Institute became fundamentally changed. It presented a very motley picture. Kornilov himself and his closest collaborators developed a reactological theory which did not become a generally accepted dominant current for the Soviet psychologists of those years. Many psychologists used the reactological terminology only superficially and shrouded the results of their own research in it, research which was very far from Kornilov's ideas. This research went in very diverse directions and could not be reduced to the investigation of the speed, form, and strength of the reaction in which Kornilov himself was interested. Thus, N. A. Bernstein, who in those years worked at the Institute, began his classic investigations of the "formation of movements." In the area of industrial psychology (psychotechnics), S. G. Gellerstein and I. N. Spielrein and their collaborators began their work. The young scholars of the Institute, A. R. Luria and A. N. Leont'ev, conducted investigations with the combined motor method. V. M. Borovsky, who in those years adhered to behaviorism, occupied himself with zoopsychology. B. D. Fridman attempted to develop psychoanalysis, and M. A. Rejsner, who worked in the area of social psychology, incredibly combined reflexology, Freudian theory, and Marxism. [4]

Despite this, many psychologists working in various fields and defending different positions agreed about the main thing. They attempted to develop a Marxist psychology and accepted this as the basic task of scientific psychology. But the concrete paths toward the development of a Marxist psychology were in that period still unclear. This completely new task did not have its analogues in the history of international psychology. Moreover, the majority of the Soviet psychologists of those years were not expert Marxists—they studied the rudiments of Marxism and its application to scientific psychology at the same time. It is not surprising that as a result they at times did no more than illustrate the laws of dialectics with psychological material.

A multitude of complex questions emerged: what was the connection of the various concrete psychological currents existing in the 1920s (reflexology, reactology,

Freudian theory, behaviorism, etc.) to the future Marxist psychology? Must a Marxist psychology study the problem of consciousness? Can a Marxist psychology use the methods of self-observation? Should Marxist psychology really emerge as the synthesis of empirical subjective psychology (the "thesis") and the psychology of behavior (the "anti-thesis")? How to solve the problem of the social determination of the human mind? And what place belongs to social psychology in the system of Marxist psychology?

A number of other questions emerged which were no less important and fundamental and which had to be solved to make further movement forward possible. The situation was complicated by the need to fight on two fronts: with idealism (Chelpanov, in particular, continued fighting the idea of a Marxist psychology) and with vulgar materialism (mechanism and Bekhterev's energism, physiological reductionism and the biologizing of the mind, etc.).

Nevertheless, the main, decisive step was taken at that time: the Soviet psychologists were the first in the world to consciously proceed to the development of a new, Marxist psychology. Exactly at that time, in 1924, Lev Semyonovich Vygotsky made his appearance in psychology.

2

In January 1924, Vygotsky participated in the Second All-Russian Psychoneurological Congress which took place in Leningrad. He presented several communications. His talk "The methods of reflexological and psychological investigation" (later he wrote an article with the same name) made a strong impression on Kornilov, who invited him to come and work at the Psychological Institute. The invitation was accepted and in 1924 Vygotsky moved from Gomel, where he lived at the time, to Moscow and began working at the Psychological Institute. From this moment Vygotsky's actual psychological career begins (1924-1934).

But although in 1924 the 28-year-old Vygotsky was still a beginning psychologist, he was already a mature thinker who had gone through a long spiritual development which logically led him to the need to work in the area of scientific psychology. This circumstance was of paramount importance for the success of Vygotsky's psychological investigations.

His scientific activity began when he was still a student at the Faculty of Law at Moscow University (simultaneously he studied at the Historical-Philological Faculty at Shanyavsky University). In this period (1913-1917) his interests were of an outspoken humanitarian nature. Thanks to his unique capacities for serious education Vygotsky was able to work in several directions at the same time: in the area of dramaturgy (he wrote brilliant theater reviews), history (in his native Gomel he led a circle on history for students of the highest classes of the gymnasium), in the area of political economy (he spoke splendidly at seminars on political economy at Moscow University), etc. Of special importance for his creative work was his thorough study of philosophy which began at the time. Vygotsky studied the classical German philosophy on a professional level. In his student years began his acquaintance with the philosophy of Marxism, which he studied mainly using illegal editions. At this time was born Vygotsky's interest in the philosophy of Spinoza, who would remain his favorite thinker for the rest of his life. [5]

For the young Vygotsky the most important place in all these diverse humanitarian interests was occupied by literary criticism (this became definitely clear around 1915). From his youth he passionately loved literature and very early he began to deal with it on a professional level. His first works as a literary critic (the manuscripts have unfortunately been lost) [6]—an investigation of *Anna Karenina*, an analysis of Dostoyevsky's creative work, etc.—grew directly from his interests as a reader. Incidentally, that is why Vygotsky called his works a "reader's critique." The crown of this line of his creative work became the famous analysis of Hamlet (there are two variants of this work, written in 1915 and 1916, respectively; the second variant was published in Vygotsky's book *The Psychology of Art* in 1968). [7]

All these works are characterized by a psychological orientation. One may approach a work of art from various sides. One can clarify the problem of the author's personality, try to understand his idea, study the objective orientation of the work of art (e.g., its moral or social-political meaning), etc. What interested Vygotsky was something else: how does the reader perceive a work of art, what is it in the text of the work of art that causes certain emotions in the reader, i.e., he was interested in the problem of the analysis of the psychology of the reader, the problem of the psychological influence of art. From the very beginning Vygotsky tried to approach this complex psychological problem objectively. He tried to suggest some methods for the analysis of an objective fact—the text of the work of art—and from that to proceed to its perception by the spectator.

The given period of Vygotsky's creative career reached its completion in his extensive work *The Psychology of Art*, which he finished and defended as a dissertation in Moscow in 1925. The ideas which he in 1916 in his analysis of *Hamlet* still expressed "in an undertone" now became a demand for the development of a materialistic psychology of art. [8]

Vygotsky tried to solve two problems—to give both an objective analysis of the text of a work of art and an objective analysis of the human emotions that arise during the reading of this work. He rightfully picked out the internal contradiction in the structure of a work of art as its central aspect. But the attempt to objectively analyze the emotions caused by such a contradiction were not successful (and could not be successful in view of the level of development of the psychological science at the time). This predetermined the somewhat unfinished and one-sided nature of *The Psychology of Art* (apparently, Vygotsky himself felt this as well. He had the opportunity to publish it during his lifetime but nevertheless refrained from doing so). [9]

The problems that revealed themselves during the work in the area of the psychology of art and the impossibility of solving them on the level of the scientific psychology of the 1920s made it inevitable that Vygotsky would move to actual scientific psychology. The transition took place gradually in the years 1922-1924. Toward the end of this period, Vygotsky, who in Gomel continued his work on *The Psychology of Art*, had already begun his investigations in the field of scientific psychology. As has already been said, the transition became complete with his move to Moscow in 1924.

3

Having arrived in psychology, Vygotsky immediately found himself in a special situation compared to the majority of Soviet psychologists. On the one hand, he clearly understood the need to build a new, objective psychology as he independently arrived at these ideas while working on his psychology of art. On the other hand, particularly for Vygotsky, with his primordial interest in the higher human emotions caused by the perception of a work of art, the deficiencies of the actually existing objective currents in the international and Soviet psychology of the 1920s (behaviorism, reactology, reflexology) were especially intolerable. Their main shortcoming was the simplification of mental phenomena, the tendency toward physiological reductionism, the inadequate description of the highest manifestation of the mind—human consciousness.

Vygotsky needed to clearly expose the symptoms of the disease from which the objective currents in psychology suffered and then find ways for their cure. His early theoretical works were dedicated to these goals: his talk "The methods of reflexological and psychological investigation," which he presented at the Second Psychoneurological Congress (1924), the article "Consciousness as a problem for the psychology of behavior" (1925) and the lengthy historical-theoretical work "The Historical Meaning of the Crisis in Psychology" (1926-1927), which is published for the first time in this volume. Various ideas that were in keeping with these works can also be found in other works, including his last. Many of Vygotsky's ideas which formed the key to his creative work as well as for much of Soviet psychology can be found in his work only implicitly or were expressed by him by word of mouth.

The shortcoming of the objective currents in psychology—their incapability of adequately studying the phenomena of consciousness—was seen by many psychologists. Vygotsky was merely one of the most active, but by far not the only participant in the struggle for a new understanding of consciousness in the Soviet psychology of the 1920s.

It is essential to note Vygotsky's unique position. He was the first who already in his article "Consciousness as a problem for the psychology of behavior" raised the problem of the need for a concrete psychological study of consciousness as a concrete psychological reality. He made the (for that time) bold claim that neither the "new" psychology—behaviorism, which ignored the problem of consciousness— nor the "old" psychology—subjective empirical psychology, which declared itself to be the science about consciousness—really studied it. This seems a paradoxical way to state the problem. For Kornilov, for example, the study of consciousness meant the return to some milder version of subjective empirical psychology. Next he envisioned a concrete task—combining the introspective methods of the "old" psychology with the objective methods of the "new" psychology. This he called a "synthesis."

Contentwise the "new" psychology could add nothing to the analysis of consciousness in the "old" psychology. It was simply a difference in appraisal. The "old" psychology saw the study of consciousness as its most important task and believed that it was really studying it. The "new" psychology saw no new methods whatsoever to study consciousness and farmed it out to "old" psychology. The representatives of the "new" psychology might evaluate the problem of consciousness as insignificant and ignore it, or consider it to be important and compromise with the "old" psychology in solving it (Kornilov's position).

For Vygotsky the problem looked quite different. He did not want to hear about a return to the "old" psychology. One must study consciousness differently from the way it was done (or, more correctly, "declared") by the representatives of the psychology of consciousness. Consciousness must not be viewed as a "stage" on which the mental functions act, not as "the general boss of the mental functions" (the viewpoint of traditional psychology), but as a psychological reality which has tremendous importance for all the vital activity of the person and which must be studied and analyzed concretely. In contrast to the other psychologists of the 1920s, Vygotsky managed to view in the problem of consciousness not just a problem of concrete methods, but first and foremost a *philosophical and methodological* problem of tremendous importance, the cornerstone of the future scientific psychology.

This new psychology which dealt with the most complex phenomena of the mental life of man, including consciousness, could only evolve on the basis of Marxism. In such an approach the perspective of a materialistic treatment of consciousness reveals itself and the concrete, and not declarative, tasks of a Marxist psychology take shape.

In speaking about the development of a Marxist psychology, Vygotsky managed to see the main error of the majority of the psychologists of the 1920s who set themselves this same task. It was that they saw this task as one of merely finding the proper methods. In addition, they approached this task from some concrete psychological theory and tried to combine this with the basic theses of dialectical materialism through simple addition. In his work "The Historical Meaning of the Crisis in Psychology," Vygotsky wrote directly about the fundamental incorrectness of such an approach. He pointed out that psychology is, naturally, a concrete science. Each psychological theory has its philosophical basis. Sometimes it is manifest, sometimes it is hidden. And in each case this theory is determined by its philosophical foundations. That is why we cannot take psychology's results ready-made and combine them with the theses of dialectical materialism without first having reformed its foundations. We must really *build* a Marxist psychology, i.e., we must begin with its philosophical foundations.

How can we concretely build a Marxist psychology proceeding from the theses of dialectal materialism? To answer this question Vygotsky suggests turning to a classical example—Marxist political economy, explained in *Das Kapital*, where a model is given of how to elaborate the methodology of a concrete science on the basis of the general theses of dialectical materialism. Only after the methodological basis of a science has been elaborated can the concrete facts be considered which have been gathered by researchers taking different theoretical positions. Then these facts can be organically assimilated and we do not become their victims. We do not become captivated by them and do not turn the theory into an eclectic conglomerate of diverse methods, facts, and hypotheses.

Thus, Vygotsky was the first among Soviet psychologists to pick out such an important stage in the creation of a Marxist psychology as the development of a philosophical and methodological theory of an "intermediate level."

In the same works of the years 1925-1927, Vygotsky made an attempt to determine a concrete path for the development of a theoretical methodological basis of Marxist psychology. Thus, the epigraph in the work "The Historical Meaning of the Crisis in Psychology" is the well-known saying from the gospel: "The stone which the builders rejected is become the head stone of the corner." He further explains that he is referring to the builders of scientific psychology. This "stone" is two-fold: on the one hand, the reference is to the philosophical and methodological theory of an "intermediate level"; on the other hand, to the practical activity of man.

The thesis about the extreme importance for psychology of man's practical activity was paradoxical for the international and Soviet psychology of the 1920s. At the time the dominating current studied the person's external motor activity by fragmentizing it into different elementary behavioral acts (behaviorism), motor reactions (reactology), or reflexes (reflexology), etc. No one dealt with the analysis of practical activity in all its complexity, if we do not count the specialists of labor psychology. But these and other psychologists treated it as a purely applied area and assumed that the fundamental regularities of man's mental life cannot be revealed when we analyze his practical labor activity.

Vygotsky held a diametrically opposed opinion. He emphasized that the leading role in the development of scientific psychology belongs to the psychology of labor, or psychotecnics. [10] Admittedly, he added that it is not a matter of psychotechnics itself with its methods, results and concrete tasks, but its general problem. Psychotechnics was the first to proceed to the psychological analysis of the practical, labor activity of man, although it did not yet understand the full importance of these problems for scientific psychology.

Vygotsky's idea was clear—the elaboration of the theoretical methodological foundations of a Marxist psychology must begin with a psychological analysis of the practical, labor activity of humans on the basis of Marxist positions. It is precisely in this plane that the basic regularities and primary units of the mental life of man lay hidden.

4

To realize the idea of which Vygotsky found the vague outlines was, of course, exceedingly difficult. But the idea of a reform of psychology was profoundly in keeping with the revolutionary era of the 1920s. Such ideas could not but draw talented youth toward Vygotsky. In these years Vygotsky's psychological school developed, which played a great role in the history of Soviet psychology. In 1924, his first collaborators became Leont'ev and Luria. Somewhat later they were joined by L. I. Bozhovich, A. V. Zaporozhec, R. E. Levina, N. G. Morozova, and L. S. Slavina. In the same years the following persons took active part in the investigations carried out under the guidance of Vygotsky: L. V. Zankov, Yu. V. Kotelova, E. I. Pashkovskaya, L. S. Sakharov, I. M. Solov'ev, and others. After that Vygotsky's Leningrad students started to work with him—D. B. El'konin, Zh. I. Shif, and others.

The bases for the work of Vygotsky and his collaborators were in the first place the Psychological Institute at Moscow University, the Krupskaya Academy for Communist Education, and also the Experimental Defectological Institute founded by Vygotsky. For Vygotsky the scientific contacts with the Clinic for Nervous Diseases at the First Moscow Medical Institute were of great importance (officially he began working there in 1929).

The period in Vygotsky's scientific activity which lasts from 1927 to 1931 was extremely rich and important for the subsequent history of Soviet psychology. In that period the foundations for the cultural-historical theory of the development of the mind were developed. Its basic theses are expounded in Vygotsky's works *The Instrumental Method in Pedology* (1928), *The Problem of the Cultural Development of the Child* (1928), *The Genetic Roots of Thinking and Speech* (1929), "Outline of the cultural development of the normal child" (1929, manuscript), *The Instrumental Method in Psychology* (1930), "Tool and Sign in the Development of the Child" (1930, first published in this series), *Studies in the History of Behavior* (1930, together with Luria), *The History of the Development of the Higher Mental Functions* (1930-1931, first part published in 1960 in the book of the same name, second part first published in this series), and some others. Many key ideas of the cultural-historical theory are stated in Vygotsky's most well-known book *Thinking and Speech* (1933-1934). Apart from these, important for the understanding of the cultural-historical theory are the works of his collaborators: *On the Methods of Investigating Concepts* by L. S. Sakharov (1927), *The Development of Memory* by A. N. Leont'ev (1931), *The Development of Everyday and Scientific Concepts* by Zh. I. Shif (1931), and others.

In keeping with his fundamental views, Vygotsky did not turn to the examination of mental phenomena in themselves, but to the analysis of labor activity. As is well known, the classics of Marxism saw this activity as first and foremost characterized by its tool-nature, the mediation of the labor process by tools. Vygotsky decided to begin his analysis of the mental processes with this analogy. He hypothesized: cannot we find the element of mediation in the mental processes of people through some unique mental tools? An indirect confirmation of this hypothesis he found in Bacon's (1620/1960, p. 39) well-known words, which he afterwards would often cite: "Neither the naked hand nor the understanding left to itself can effect much. It is by instruments and aids that the work is done." Of course, Bacon's idea is not at all unequivocal; it can be understood in different ways. But for Vygotsky it was important simply as one of the confirmations of his own hypothesis which rested upon Marx's theory of labor activity.

According to Vygotsky's idea, we must distinguish two levels in human mental processes: the first is mind left to itself; the second is mind (the mental process) armed with tools and auxiliary means. In the same way we must distinguish two levels of practical activity: the first is the "naked hand," the second the hand armed with tools and auxiliary means. Moreover, in both the practical and the mental sphere the second, tool level is of decisive importance. In the area of mental phenomena Vygotsky called the first level the level of "natural" and the second level the level of "cultural" mental processes. A "cultural" process is a "natural" process mediated by unique mental tools and auxiliary means.

It is not hard to see that the analogy Vygotsky drew between labor processes and mind is rather crude. The human hand is both the organ and a product of labor, as the Marxist classics have pointed out. Consequently, contraposition of the "naked hand" and the hand armed with tools in such a sharp form is not justified. Nor is sharp contraposition of "natural" and "cultural" mental processes justified. The terminology used by Vygotsky led to misunderstandings as the justified question was raised whether not all mental processes of modern humans are cultural processes. These weaknesses in Vygotsky's ideas caused justified criticism both during his lifetime and after his death.

At the same time, we must note that Vygotsky needed such contrasts in the first stage of his work in order to set off the basic thesis of his theory which regarded the decisive importance of psychological tools in the course of mental processes.

It is true that in the 1920s Köhler approached the problem of the role of tools in mental life from a totally different angle. At that time the results of his experiments with anthropoid apes were published. They showed, in particular, that external material objects—sticks, boxes, etc.—can play a nonpassive executive role in the apes' problem-solving process and are actively included in the structure of their mental processes (the introduction of sticks into the situation led to a restructuring of the animal's optical field, and for the Gestalt psychologist Köhler this meant that the structure of the mental process was changed as well).

Köhler's experiments greatly impressed psychologists and in the 1920s several scholars tried to transfer them to child psychology. These experiments proved in keeping with Vygotsky's thinking. He was the initiator of the translation into Russian of Köhler's *The Mentality of the Great Apes* and wrote a foreword to it. Afterwards, Vygotsky often (in *Thinking and Speech, The History of the Higher Mental Functions*, etc.) referred to the results of Köhler's investigations and to those scholars who attempted to conduct similar experiments in the field of child psychology (Bühler, Koffka, and others). Vygotsky, who was oriented toward the study of practical, objective activity, viewed in Köhler's experiments (which showed the active role of external tools in the restructuring of mental functions) an approach for the study of one of the aspects of this activity.

Köhler studied this issue merely on the experimental methodical level. His theoretical methodological starting points as a major Gestalt psychologist were opposed to Vygotsky's positions. Köhler was far from an understanding of the important role of labor activity and could not, of course, mark out the *tool* as the central aspect of the mediation of mental functions. It is a paradox that Köhler, who first described the restructuring of the mental process by an external tool, did not see the specific character of the tool and considered it as just one of the elements of the optical field. That is why he could not see the problem of activity which was central to Vygotsky. Vygotsky himself emphasized the specific character of the tool-level of the mediation of mental processes, particularly in the social-historical determination of the human being.

When we now evaluate the meaning of the analogy between labor and mental processes offered by Vygotsky and the two levels of mental processes he contrasted, we must not examine these views in themselves, but in the context of the assumptions and the further development of his whole theory, in connection with the results to which they led.

What did the hypothesis of the "psychological tools" and the two levels of mental functions concretely yield? This question, which to a significant degree served to verify the correctness of the hypothesis, was the question of the real analogues of the "natural" and "cultural" mental processes. And exactly the answer to this question showed to which degree the hypothesis was justified and fruitful for scientific psychology. As is well known, starting from completely different parameters (their degree of being meaningful and voluntary), psychologists had distinguished all mental functions into higher (thinking in concepts, logical memory, voluntary attention, etc.) and lower (imagistic thinking, mechanical memory, involuntary attention, etc.) ones. The fact of such a division itself was an important achievement of scientific psychology. However, later a number of questions arose about the nature of the relation between the higher and lower functions, about what makes for the presence of such specific qualities of the higher functions as their voluntary and conscious nature, etc. Each major theory had to give an answer to these questions one way or the other. But some currents (associative psychology, behaviorism) practically lost the qualitative distinction between higher and elementary functions when translating it into their own language, i.e., they both dissolved into some elementary component parts (such an approach Vygotsky called "atomistic"). [11] The obvious nature of the qualitative distinction between the lower and higher mental functions made the weakness of such approaches apparent.

The opposite currents ("understanding psychology"), on the contrary, regarded the qualitative distinction of the higher and elementary functions as a fundamental fact. They moved the integral nature of the structure and the goal-directed character of the mental processes to the forefront. These currents categorically protested against the "atomistic" approach. But they "threw away the baby with the bath water." The psychologists of this orientation occupied idealistic positions in the philosophical plane and entirely denied the possibility of a causal explanation of mental phenomena. They rejected natural scientific methods in psychology. For them psychology can at most strive for an understanding of the connections that exist between the mental phenomena and should not attempt to include them in the web of cause–result relations which covers events in the real physical world. As a result, the psychology of this orientation could not find the link between higher and lower mental functions.

The hypothesis proposed by Vygotsky offered a new explanation for the problem of the relation between the higher and the elementary mental functions. The lower, elementary mental functions he connected with the stage of the natural mental processes and the higher with the stage of the mediated, "cultural" ones. Such an approach explained both the qualitative difference between the higher and the elementary functions (it consisted in the mediation of the higher mental functions by "tools") and the connection between them (the higher functions develop on the basis of the lower ones). Finally, the properties of the higher mental functions (e.g., their voluntary nature) were explained by the presence of "psychological tools."

By means of the hypothesis about the mediation of mental processes through unique "tools," Vygotsky attempted to introduce the directives of Marxist dialectical methodology into scientific psychology in a nondeclarative and concrete methodical way. This was the basic property of all of his creative work to which he owes all his successes.

5

The question of methodology is all but the main question when we are dealing with Vygotsky's creative work. Internal dialectics, in principle, always formed the characteristic feature of his thinking. It suffices to think of his early works (e.g., *The Psychology of Art*). Thus, when he defines our perception of works of art Vygotsky is not afraid to single out the contradiction inherent in the work itself. The same position showed in his inclination to discern two polar, struggling sides in a phenomenon when he analyzed it and to regard this struggle as the moving force of development.

Historicism in the examination of the phenomenon is characteristic of Vygotsky's thinking (in this connection it is important to bear in mind the humanitarian roots of his creativity, particularly the great influence upon his school of Potebnya and the historical method in literary criticism that he developed). All these premises helped Vygotsky to understand Marxists dialectics and to master the Marxist historical method. The understanding of the foundations of Marxist dialectics lifted Vygotsky's thinking to a qualitatively new level.

The hypothesis about the mediated nature of mental functions implicitly contained elements of an *integral historical* method. They were precisely expressed and carried to their logical end by Vygotsky himself in such works as *The History of the Development of the Higher Mental Functions* and *Thinking and Speech*.

Vygotsky's fundamental idea that the mental functions are mediated by unique "psychological tools" only made sense insofar as the mental functions themselves were seen as integral formations with a complex internal structure. Such an approach immediately swept aside the "atomistic analysis," which for Vygotsky formed a particularly intolerable shortcoming of the materialistic currents in the psychology of the 1920s (behaviorism, reflexology, etc.). At the same time it opened the perspective of an *integrative materialistic and objective* approach to the analysis of the mental, which was conceived as a complex structured nonclosed system which was open to the outside world (for Vygotsky the closed nature of the mental formed the main shortcoming of the integrative idealistic views which were developed in, for example, "understanding psychology").

Naturally, in the 1920s and 1930s it was not only Vygotsky who tried to examine the mental functions as complex structured formations which are open to the outside world. Such views were held by the Gestalt psychologists as well. Their works, particularly Köhler's experiments, which investigated the intellect of anthropoid apes, made a great impression upon Vygotsky (see above). But to reveal the inner difference of his methodology from the positions of the Gestalt psychologists, it is important to take another aspect of his holistic theory into account: its historicism.

Generally speaking, the idea of historicism was foreign to the Gestalt psychologists, who attempted to study the situation "here and now." For Vygotsky, his very starting idea of the mediation of natural functions by unique "psychological tools" already contained the need to approach the cultural, higher mental functions as historical formations and, thus, the need to study them via the historical method. In principle, Vygotsky viewed three possible paths for the historical investigation of the formation of the higher mental functions: the phylogenetic and ontogenetic path plus pathology (tracing the loss of these functions in patients). Ontogenetic investigations occupied the most important place in his creative work (*The History of the Development of the Higher Mental Functions* and *Thinking and Speech*).

It is important to note that in Vygotsky the integrative approach and historicism were, in principle, inseparable. They are two dimensions of one idea—the idea of the mediated nature of mental processes *conceived from dialectical positions*.

Speaking about Vygotsky's historicism, it is essential to distinguish it from the historical approaches which could be found in the work of other psychologists of the 1920s and 1930s. It is well known that one of the distinguishing characteristics of the psychology of the 20th century was that it started to conceive itself as a historical science, as a science about development. Many psychological schools of that time which attempted to cover the sum total of the mental phenomena (depth psychology, the French school, etc.) described the mind as being organized according to the principle of system levels. But the question was: what was it in the various theories that acted as the determinants of the phylo- and ontogenetic development of the mind?

The idea of development (in the ontogenetic plane) was central for the child psychology which took shape toward the end of the 19th century (Darwin, Preyer, and others). From the very beginning it developed under the decisive influence of evolutionary theory, and the development of the child's mind was considered from the viewpoint of its adaptive meaning (the comparison of onto- and phylogenetic development was carried out in this connection—cf. Hall's law of recapitulation which is, in principle, very close to the biogenetic law). The idea of development, also understood in the biological evolutionary plane, was also central to zoopsychology, which developed in that same period.

The founder of descriptive psychology, Dilthey, and his followers tried to introduce the principle of historicism into psychology. Dilthey, as is well known, took idealistic positions and treated mental life as being purely spiritual. Speaking about history, he essentially had in mind the history of culture which he also considered from idealistic positions, i.e., merely as a manifestation of the spiritual activity of the person. That is why, when he criticized Dilthey's follower, Spranger, in his *The History of the Development of the Higher Mental Functions*, Vygotsky wrote that by bringing history and psychology closer together he, essentially, brings together the spiritual with the spiritual (this fully applies to Dilthey himself as well).

The French psychologists treated the principle of historicism in their own way and intimately connected it with the problem of the social determination of the mind. Thus, Durkheim, one of the founders of the French school, regarded society as the sum total of collective representations. Lévy-Bruhl, in his well-known works about the psychology of primitive people, expressed the idea that not only the content, but also the ways of human thinking themselves (human logic, more precisely—the relation of logical and pre-logical aspects in human thinking) is a historical, developing concept.

Toward the 1920s the leading position in the French school was occupied by the great scholar Janet, who tried to combine historicism with an activity approach. This allowed Janet to arrive at a number of profound ideas about the nature and development of the mind which exerted influence upon the subsequent development of scientific psychology. In particular, he proposed the hypothesis that the child in the process of development internalizes the social forms of behavior which were first used vis-à-vis the child itself by adults. This investigator attempted to investigate this process of internalization in detail in memory and thinking. But in doing so Janet, just like the whole French school, proceeded from the assumption that the person is initially asocial, that socialization is forced upon him from outside. In the analysis of human activity and social life Janet was very far from Marxism. He regarded the relation of cooperation as the basic social relation, which is only natural for a scholar who sees the external picture of the social connections, but does not attach fundamental importance to the economic relationships which form their basis.

Vygotsky's historicism has a fundamentally different character from the approaches examined above. His historicism is an attempt to apply Marx's historical method in psychology. Thus, for Vygotsky the determinants of human mental development are not biological maturation in ontogenesis and biological adaptation in the course of the struggle for life in phylogenesis (child psychology and zoopsychology in the evolutionary tradition), it is not the mastery by the human being of the ideas of the universal spirit [*Weltgeist*] embodied in the products of culture (Dilthey's "understanding psychology") and not the relation of social cooperation (Janet's theory), but human *tool-mediated labor activity*. It is this approach which was organically tied to the hypothesis of the mediation of mental processes by tools.

Before Vygotsky, the method for the ontogenetic investigation of the mind itself can be called the method of cross sections. At different ages the level of development and behavior and the condition of the different mental functions of the child were measured and then it was attempted to reconstruct the general picture of development judging by the results of the different measurements which gave discrete points on an age axis.

For Vygotsky the shortcomings of such an approach were obvious. He considered that the mediation hypothesis indicated the path toward another method of investigating the mental development in ontogenesis which allows us to model (to put it in the terminology of the 1960s) this process. And indeed, Vygotsky's historical-genetic method in a number of cases yielded results that were, in principle, inaccessible for the method of cross sections.

The study of the formation of the higher mental functions in ontogenesis and phylogenesis as structures which develop on the basis of elementary mental functions and are mediated by psychological tools became the major theme of the research of Vygotsky and his collaborators.

6

When we state the goal this way the central question becomes the question concerning psychological tools: what are they and what is the mechanism of mediation?

At first, when the idea of mediation was born, Vygotsky illustrated it with the example of a patient with Parkinson's disease who lay in Rossolimo's clinic. When the patient was asked to walk he could only respond with an increase in his tremor and could not walk. After that white pieces of paper were laid down before him on the floor and the request was repeated. Now the tremor decreased and he actually began to walk, stepping on each paper successively.

Vygotsky explained these experiments by saying that the patient is confronted with two series of stimuli. The first series consists of the verbal commands which are incapable of eliciting the adequate behavior in the patient. Then the second series of stimuli—the pieces of white paper—comes to the rescue. The patient's initial reaction is mediated by this series. It is the second series of stimuli which serves as the means to guide the behavior. That is why Vygotsky called them means-stimuli. [12] In this description, it seems as if Vygotsky's idea was close to the positions of behavioral psychology, but soon it will become clear that this affinity is purely terminological. For the behaviorist the matter ends with the investigation of behavior, but for Vygotsky this is just an example whose basic meaning is the study of the process of the mediation of mental functions by means-stimuli and not at all the study of behavioral reactions. And the circle of means-stimuli immeasurably widened. Thus, in the theses for his talk "The instrumental method in psychology" (1930), Vygotsky mentioned, as examples of stimulus-means language, different forms of numeration and counting, mnemotechnical adaptations, algebraic symbolism, works of art, writing, schemas, diagrams, maps, drawings, all sorts of conventional signs, etc. Here we must again take account of the scientific courage of Vygotsky, who dared to combine in one series objects which seem incompatible. The generally accepted viewpoint at the time was that the psychologist examines secondary adaptations which play an executive role (tying a knot to remember something), on the one hand, and fundamental psychological structures (e.g., speech), on the other hand.

What do these heterogeneous objects—from the word to the "knot to remember something"—have in common? First of all, they have all been artificially created by humanity and represent elements of culture (hence the name of Vygotsky's theory as "cultural-historical"). In addition, they are all means-stimuli, or psychological tools, and they are first directed outward, to a partner. Only afterwards are the psychological tools applied to the self, i.e., they become for the person a means to steer his own mental processes. Subsequently, the ingrowing of the means-stimuli proceeds. The mental function is mediated from inside and the need for an external (with respect to the given person) means-stimulus ceases to exist. This whole process from the beginning to the end Vygotsky called the "full circle of the cultural-historical development of mental functions."

In his article "The problem of the cultural development of the child" (1928), he described this process in detail using the example of the experiments with memorization of words which he and his collaborators carried out with children. Pictures formed the means-stimuli in these experiments. While in the first stage the experimenter had to present the pictures to the child, in the second stage the child already selected the corresponding pictures himself (applying the tool to himself), and in the third stage the ingrowing took place, i.e., the need for the picture no longer existed. In his article Vygotsky mentioned several different types of ingrowing: simple replacement of external stimuli by internal ones, the stitch type which combines in a single act parts of the process which were at first relatively independent, and the mastery of the structure (principle) of mediation itself (this is the most advanced type of ingrowing). [13]

Thus, the internal logic of the development of his theory closely led Vygotsky to the problems of internalization which were in those years being elaborated by the French psychological school. But there existed a difference in principle between the conception of internalization of this school and Vygotsky's. The first conceived of internalization as the forcing from outside upon the *primordially existing and primordially asocial individual consciousness* of some forms of societal consciousness (Durkheim), or of the elements of external social activity, social cooperation (Janet). For Vygotsky, consciousness is only formed in the process of internalization—there is no primordial asocial consciousness, neither phylogenetically nor ontogenetically speaking.

In these experiments Vygotsky's basic hypothesis was experimentally confirmed. Due to the mediation by psychological tools the mental process itself became changed, its structure became reformed (for example, logical memory was formed on the basis of sensory memory). Here we see another of Vygotsky's hypotheses in embryonic form: in the process of mediation thinking becomes attached to memory, which plays an enormous role in logical memory. Later this became the starting point for the ideas he developed about psychological systems (see below).

Vygotsky's historical-genetic method was of principal importance in the investigations of the process of mediation. Here the heuristic power of this method was revealed on concrete material. The facts which Vygotsky discovered were already partly known in scientific psychology. He himself in his article "The problem of the cultural development of the child" mentions, for example, Binet's experiments with memorization, which showed that a subject can apply certain methods to enhance the quantity of numbers he must memorize. However, neither Binet nor other psychologists who knew such facts perfectly well (there existed a well-known term "mnemotechnics") were able to interpret them adequately. They were seen as just a convenient technical trick for memorizing which had at best applied meaning, if not as simply a curiosity, a conjuring trick (Binet wrote about the simulation of memory by means of mnemotechnics).

No one was capable of seeing here the key to disclosing the fundamental regularities of mental life. We should realize that these investigations were carried out with adults and that the experimenters who studied, for instance, the span of attention, did not deal with the question of the onto- and phylogenetic development of the corresponding mental functions. One could only lay bare the fundamental meaning of the corresponding facts by following, just like Vygotsky, the path of historical-genetic investigation (historical-genetic investigation which permits us to follow the formation of some function and not just to investigate it by means of the cross-sectional approach).

For Vygotsky the hypothesis of the mediation of mental functions, combined with the historical-genetic method, opened new perspectives for his research. This approach allowed him to isolate the basic unity of mental life. Thus, in his articles "The instrumental method in psychology" and "The problem of the cultural development of the child," he examines it for the example of the processes of memorization. In the first article he writes: "In natural memorization a direct link is established between the stimuli A and B; in artificial mnemotechnical memorization of the same impression instead of this direct link A–B two new links A–X and X–B are established by means of the psychological tool X; each of these is as natural a conditional reflex process . . . as the link A–B; new, artificial, instrumental is the fact that the single link A–B is replaced by the pair A–X and X–B, which lead to the same result but via another path" (see Chapter 5 of the present volume).

In order to understand Vygotsky's idea properly we must take into account the following. The processes of memorization were for him just a model. According to his hypothesis, the processes of mediation are of paramount importance for any mental function. That is why the proposed schema has universal meaning. We are talking about the replacement of the bipartite schema, which was generally accepted in the 1920s, by a tripartite schema in which a third, intermediate, mediating part—the means-stimulus or psychological tool—is placed between the stimulus and the reaction. The crux of Vygotsky's idea is that only the tripartite schema which cannot be further decomposed can be the minimal unit of analysis which preserves the basic properties of the mental functions.

Thus, a decisive question arose: does the hypothesis of mediation suggested by Vygotsky really allow us to isolate a new and adequate universal unit of the structure of mental functions? If this were true, then Vygotsky might proceed to the solution of the problem of consciousness from the position of the historical-genetic method. But first this general hypothesis had to be verified. Models for such a verification became first memory and later attention ("The development of higher forms of attention in childhood," 1925). In the course of the experiments on attention, the mediation hypothesis was once again confirmed—the structure of the processes of attention also became restructured due to psychological tools.

The further program of investigations of Vygotsky and his collaborators concerned the verification of the mediation hypothesis on the example of such a fundamental mental process as thinking. These investigations, however, led to new and unexpected results.

7

It is well known that thinking is closely interwoven with speech. Some psychologists (e.g., Watson) drew the conclusion that thinking can simply be reduced to internal speech. Watson imagined the ontogenesis of thinking to proceed along the following line: loud speech–whispering–internal speech. However, the investigations of the Würzburg school carried out at the beginning of the century showed that thinking and speech do not at all coincide.

Thus, there were two viewpoints in this area: the claim that thinking and speech fully coincide and the claim that they are totally different. The one-sidedness of these positions led to the development of many compromising intermediate theories. From the very start Vygotsky did not agree with the way they were developed. It consisted of examining the process of verbal thinking in adult civilized persons, which psychologists then decomposed into its component parts. Thought was considered independent of speech, and speech independent of thinking. Then psychologists tried, in the words of Vygotsky, to picture the link between the one and the other as a purely external mechanical dependency between two different processes (*Thinking and Speech*, Chapter 1). Here he found the two main shortcomings of psychology in a most obvious form: analysis into elements and anti-historicism.

The true answer to the question of the relation between thinking and speech was, consequently, only to be found on the path of historical-genetic investigation. Psychology had already gathered some factual material for such an approach. Thus, in the 1920s Köhler's investigations had shed new light on these questions. On the one hand, he discovered in apes what he called instrumental intellect. It seemed likely that this instrumental intellect was linked to human (particularly, verbal) thinking. It could be seen as one of the levels which phylogenetically preceded human thinking. On the other hand, in the apes were discovered several analogues of human-like speech. But most interesting was that Köhler himself and other investigators who replicated his experiments agreed about the absence of a link be-tween the instrumental intellect and these rudiments of speech in apes. It turned out, consequently, that the genetic roots of human thinking and human speech were different and only crossed at a certain stage.

In light of these facts and in keeping with the general logic of his conception, Vygotsky came to the conclusion that speech is a psychological tool which mediates thinking in its early stage (by the early stage of thinking he meant practical activity). As a result of such mediation verbal thinking develops. Vygotsky expressed this idea in an aphoristic manner, paraphrasing the famous words from Faust. Instead of the biblical "In the beginning was the word" Goethe writes "In the beginning was the act." For Vygotsky, in the problem of the genesis of thinking the logical emphasis is transferred to the words "in the beginning." Thus, *in the beginning* was the act (practical activity), which became mediated by the word. [14] Vygotsky sug-gested that this was the kernel of the problem in the phylogenetic plane.

In principle, something similar must take place in ontogenesis as well. In the 1920s ontogenetic investigations of thinking and speech were carried out by Piaget. They made a strong impression on Vygotsky. Actually, the book *Thinking and Speech* is to a great extent structured as a polemic with Piaget, although it does not form, of course, the main part of the content of his work. (Interestingly enough, Piaget himself read *Thinking and Speech* only in the late 1950s and largely agreed with Vygotsky's critical remarks.) [15] Piaget managed to observe and describe the phenomenon of egocentric speech which he interpreted as the manifestation of the child's would-be primordial intrinsic asocial nature. In further development, as the child becomes socialized, egocentric speech gradually dies off.

In the course of the experiments Vygotsky convincingly showed that it is exactly the opposite. Egocentric speech is originally social. It does not fade away, but be-comes *internal* speech. It is internalized. It is the most important means of thinking which is born in the external, objective activity of the child. Verbal thinking develops insofar as activity is internalized. Here Vygotsky's hypothesis was again confirmed: the thinking which develops from practical activity is *mediated* by speech, by the word.

But a still more important verification of this hypothesis took place with the material of the investigations of the formation in children of such a product of verbal thinking as generalization. The task was to verify whether the word indeed is such a means, such a psychological tool, which mediates the process of gener-alization and the formation of concepts in children.

The investigations to which we refer were begun in 1927 by Vygotsky, together with his collaborator Sakharov, and after the latter's death (in 1928) they were continued from 1928 to 1930 by Vygotsky and Ju. V. Kotelova and E. I. Pash-kovskaya (the most detailed exposition of the methods and results of these inves-tigations are given in Vygotsky's work *Thinking and Speech* and in Sakharov's article "On the methods of investigating concepts"). [16]

For the investigation of the processes of generalization, Vygotsky and Sakharov developed a new variant of the method of double stimulation, which was in fact a particular version of the method of artificial words introduced by Ach at the be-ginning of the century for the study of concepts. The investigation was carried out along the same fundamental lines as the investigations of the other mental func-tions. The subject had to group a number of three-dimensional geometrical figures according to their features. The figures differed in size, form, and color. The role of the second series of stimuli—the means-stimuli—was to be carried out by mean-ingless artificial words introduced in the experiment.

In the course of the experiments an unforeseen result was found which changed the direction of the investigation. It turned out that for the subject the task of generalizing the figures by means of the means-stimuli turns into another task—of discovering the meaning of these means-stimuli by way of selecting the geometrical figures. Thus, the psychological tools, the means-stimuli, showed a new side—they turned into the bearers of certain meanings. These data permitted the investigators to change the terminology of the investigation. Psychological tools, or means-stimuli, came to be called *signs*. Vygotsky began using the word *sign* in the sense of "having meaning."

It must be said that Vygotsky was already interested in the question of the role of signs in the mental life of humans before he became involved in scientific psychology. The first time he faced this question was in the years he worked in the area of the psychology of art. Already in his book *The Psychology of Art* he wrote that human emotions are caused by certain signs and that his task was to proceed to the analysis of emotions on the basis of the analysis of these signs. Here by sign is also meant a symbol which has a certain meaning.

Such a viewpoint was traditional for literary criticism and dramaturgy, but unexpected for psychology or physiology (a reflexologist might also say that a sign causes an emotion, but he would mean that the sign is a conditional stimulus in the system of the conditional reflex). It is precisely the humanitarian (particularly, his semantic and semiotic) education that Vygotsky acquired in the years of work on *The Psychology of Art* which allowed him to resist the reflexological schemes in the analysis of his experiments on generalization and to view them as an entrance to the problem of meaning.

In this connection, it is interesting to note that already in the late 1920s to early 1930s Vygotsky had resumed the investigation of the role of signs in the psychology of art, i.e., he resumed his, in modern language, semiotic investigations (semiotics as a science did not yet exist at the time). Together with Eisenstein, he began working on the theory of film language (their collaboration was severed by Vygotsky's death; some material is preserved in the Eisenstein archives).

8

Thus, for Vygotsky the study of the problem of generalization, the development of concepts, the problem of word meaning became the path to investigate the ontogenesis of thinking, which became the nerve-center of his whole theory.

The experiments carried out with the method of double stimulation proved that, in their development, concepts (and words together with them) go through several stages.

The *first stage* (the early preschool period) is the stage of syncretic wholes. In this stage the word has no fundamental meaning for the child. Figures are combined according to accidental features (e.g., because they are spatially close or have some striking external feature, etc.). Such a combination based on accidental impressions was, of course, not stable.

The *second stage* is the stage of complexes. The complex-generalization has several different forms. They have in common that the child still combines objects on the basis of the immediate sensory experience, but according to *factual* connections. Each connection may serve as the basis for the inclusion of an object in a complex, provided it is present. In the process of the development of the complex these connections constantly change place as the basis of the grouping. They slip away, lose their contours, and the only thing they have in common is that they have been discovered through some single practical operation. In this stage children cannot yet examine some feature or connections between objects outside the concrete, present, visible situation in which these objects display their abundance of mutually intersecting features. That is why children slip from one detail to another and so on.

All features are equal in functional meaning, there is no hierarchy between them. A concrete object enters a complex as a real visual unit with all its inalienable factual features. In the formation of such a generalization a paramount role is played by the verbal sign. It functions as a *family* indication [17] of the objects, combining them according to some factual feature.

A special place amid the complexes is held by one of its forms—the pseudoconcept, which, in Vygotsky's words, forms "the most widespread form of complex thinking in the child of the preschool period which prevails above all other forms and is often almost exclusively present." (*Selected Psychological Investigations*, 1956, p. 177). According to its external features the child's generalization is a concept, but according to the process which leads to the generalization it is still a complex. Thus, the child can freely select and combine into a group all triangles independent of their color, size, etc. However, special analysis shows that this combination is carried out by the child on the basis of a visual comprehension of the characteristic visual feature of "triangularity" (closure, the characteristic intersecting of the lines, etc.) without any isolation of the essential properties of this figure as a geometrical figure, i.e., without the idea of a triangle. To the extent that such a grouping can be done by a person who has already mastered this idea, the pseudoconcept and the concept coincide as a product, but behind them are various working methods, various intellectual operations.

The *third stage* is that of the actual concept. It is formed on the basis of the selection of a group of objects which are combined according to one feature that has been abstracted. When the abstract features have been isolated and the different elements have been abstracted from the visual situation in which they are presented in the experiment, this is the first stage of concept formation. The concept itself develops when a number of abstracted features are again synthesized. The decisive role in the formation of concepts is played by the word as a means to guide attention to the corresponding features and as a means for abstraction. Here the role of the word (the meaning of the verbal sign) is totally different from its role at the level of complexes.

This investigation yielded a number of important results and raised a number of problems. In the context of Vygotsky's general theory, the discovery of the fact that the meaning of words-signs changes in ontogenesis is very important. Their function changes from a family indication to means of abstraction. Important is also that the method of double stimulation again justified itself and showed that the sign in the processes of generalization acts as a means of mediation (its role is different in the various stages).

However, with respect to the problem of concept formation and the problem of generalization itself, Vygotsky's investigation raised more new questions than it answered old ones. His most important achievement in this connection became the discovery of the level of complexes and, particularly, the pseudoconcepts. Here the natural question arises: why did traditional psychology before Vygotsky pass by and ignore the pseudoconcepts? The thing is that traditional psychology took the pseudoconcept to be a concept and did not have the means to distinguish them. Traditional psychology viewed generalization, the isolation of some common features, as the concept's only characteristic. In such an approach to the problem, the pseudoconcepts and the genuine concepts indeed become indistinguishable. [18]

It is important to keep in mind that such a characterization of concepts was not psychological, but formal logical. Its uncritical transferral from formal logic, where it really functioned, to psychology, where it was without content, did psychology harm of which the psychologists themselves were not aware. Such a treatment of the concept received its first blow by Jaensch's investigations in the 1920s, and Vygotsky's work put an end to it. [19] The fundamental psychological historical-genetic method of Vygotsky's investigations revealed the lack of content of the formal logical definition of the concept, which united psychologically diverse phenomena—the genuine concept and the pseudoconcept.

But the paradox of Vygotsky's discovery resided in the fact that he himself in his work on concepts went along the line of the development of generalizations which started from the visual situation and that at the end of his investigation, due to the historical-genetic method, he showed the psychological inadequacy of such a path. Of course, the object relatedness remains an indisputable aspect of the materialistic explanation of the concept, but it should not be confused with situational visuality. Vygotsky sensed that even the highest stage of generalizations of the visual situation is nevertheless not the highest stage of development of the concept itself. Despite all its abstractness the concept revealed in this way was related to the pseudoconcept and the complex. It formed with them a continuum. They were linked by the content of the generalization that lies behind them. In order to make one's way to the highest level of the concept, it was necessary to proceed from another principle of generalization, to approach the concept from another side.

Vygotsky's further search went this direction. He did not manage to accomplish very much, but the little he did (in the years 1930-1931 Shif worked on this problem under his guidance) left a fundamental trace in psychology and was widely practically applied subsequently.

Vygotsky distinguished two types of concepts: everyday concepts and scientific concepts. The everyday concepts are the concepts revealed in the experiments described above. It is the highest level to which a generalization can be elevated which proceeds from the visual situation, the abstraction of some visual characteristic. These concepts are general ideas which go from the concrete to the abstract. They are spontaneous concepts. They are the "generalization of things" as Vygotsky himself expressively said in his work *Thinking and Speech*.

Shif established in her investigations that the child develops scientific concepts in another way. They are the "generalization of ideas." Here a connection is established between concepts, and *systems* are formed. Then the child becomes aware of his own intellectual activity. Due to this the child develops a special relation to the object, which allows him to view in them what is inaccessible to empirical concepts (the penetration into the *essence* of the object). The path of the formation of the scientific concept is, Vygotsky showed, opposite to the path of the formation of the everyday, spontaneous concept. It is the path from the abstract to the concrete during which the child is more conscious of the concept than of the object from the very beginning.

Vygotsky could not fully investigate this process at the time, but his great scientific achievement was that he managed to experimentally establish the psychological difference between the processes of the formation of everyday and scientific concepts.

How can the development in the child of everyday and scientific concepts be connected? Vygotsky connected this problem with the broader problem of teaching

[20] and learning. In the process of his investigation he stumbled upon the fact that the development of scientific concepts proceeds faster than the development of spontaneous concepts (*Thinking and Speech*, Chapter 6). The analysis of this fact led him to the conclusion that the degree of mastery of the spontaneous concepts indicates the level of the child's actual development while the degree of mastery of scientific concepts indicates the child's zone of proximal development. With the introduction of the concept of the "zone of proximal development," Vygotsky rendered psychology and pedagogics a great service.

Everyday concepts indeed develop spontaneously. Scientific concepts are brought into the child's consciousness in the course of instruction. [20] "Scientific concepts stimulate a segment of development which the child has not yet passed through . . . . This allows us to begin to understand that instruction . . . plays a decisive role in the child's mental development" (ibid., p. 220). "Instruction is only useful when it moves ahead of development" (ibid., p. 212). Then instruction "calls into life a whole number of functions which are in a stage of maturation lying in the zone of proximal development" (ibid., p. 212). [21]

Thus, the zone of proximal development characterizes the difference between what the child is capable of himself and what he can become capable of with the help of a teacher.

Such a view was revolutionary for its time. It is well known that at the time dominated views according to which instruction [20] must follow development and strengthen what it has accomplished. It seemed impossible that instruction would move ahead of the child's development—we cannot teach something for which the basis has not yet matured in the child. It seemed natural to determine the level of development of the child by what he can do independently. Analysis of the child's development using the cross-sectional method could not, in principle, yield any other conclusion. But things changed radically after the application of Vygotsky's historical-genetic method, which allowed investigators to reveal the potential level of the child's cognitive development, the zone of proximal development.

The application of this concept had direct practical significance for the diagnosis of the cognitive development of children which now could be carried out both on the actual and the potential level.

After the hypothesis of the mediation of mental processes had been verified in the formation of various mental functions (thinking, memory, attention, etc.) and after the corresponding new methods for psychological investigation had been created, Vygotsky returned to his initial, fundamental problem for which the cultural-historical theory served as a prelude—the problem of consciousness. Vygotsky did not finish this work; it was broken off by his death. That is why his psychological theory cannot be regarded as completed. But he did nevertheless sketch some of the general contours of a theory of consciousness which are of great interest. Particularly important for the understanding of his approach to the problem are such works as *Thinking and Speech* (especially the last chapter), the talk "The problem of the development and loss of higher mental functions" (1934), the lecture "Play and its role in the child's mental development" (1933), the unfinished manuscript "Spinoza's and Descartes' theories about the passions in the light of modern psychoneurology" (1934), and the talk "Psychology and the theory of the localization of mental functions" (1934). Many ideas regarding this problem can also be found in his earlier works, especially *The History of the Development of the Higher Mental Functions*, and in his talk "On psychological systems" (1930).

What were the main conclusions at which Vygotsky arrived? Mental functions develop in the course of the historical development of mankind. The decisive factor in this development are signs. Vygotsky (1960, pp. 197-198) wrote that "In a higher structure the sign and the way it is used are the decisive functional whole or focus of the whole process." A sign is any conventional symbol which has a certain meaning. The word is the universal sign. A higher mental function develops on the basis of an elementary one which becomes mediated by signs in the process of internalization. Internalization is the fundamental law of development for the higher mental functions in onto- and phylogenesis. "Each function in cultural development . . . appears on the stage twice, in two planes. First as a social, then as a psychological function. First between people, as an interpsychological category, then . . . as an intrapsychological category" (*The History of the Development of the Higher Mental Functions*, 1960, pp. 197-198). Human consciousness is formed in the process of internalization.

Toward the end of the 1930s, Vygotsky's understanding of the process of internalization became fundamentally changed. He himself said this about it: "In the process of development . . . it is not so much the functions which change, as we studied this earlier (this was our mistake), not so much their structure . . . but it is *the relations, the connections between the functions* which become changed and modified. New groups develop which were unknown at the preceding stage" ("On psychological systems," p. 110). Here Vygotsky wants the listeners to pay close attention to the distinction between these two aspects of the problem and is being unfair to himself. Had he not begun his study of the fact that the structure of different functions changes under the influence of mediation with such a "mistake," he could never have arrived at the new conclusion that the connections between functions change in the course of development.

Speaking about the problem of interfunctional connections, Vygotsky turned to the works of the major Russian evolutionary theorist and zoopsychologist Vagner, in whose work he found the concept of evolution along mixed or pure lines which was very important for him. Evolution along pure lines is characteristic for the animal world, i.e., "the appearance of a new instinct, a variant of an instinct which leaves . . . unchanged the system of functions which developed before" ("The problem of the development and loss of higher mental functions," 1960, p. 368). In contrast, for the development of human consciousness, "most important . . . in the development of higher mental functions is not so much the development of each mental function . . . but the change of the interfunctional connections" (ibid.).

In connection with this turning point in his investigation of the interfunctional relationships, Vygotsky turned to the new concept of the *psychological system*. In various vague meanings it had been used in psychology already before Vygotsky, but he meant the system of interfunctional connections, the interfunctional structure responsible for a specific mental process (perception, memory, thinking, etc.). In his *Lectures on Psychology* (1932/1987, p. 324) he wrote that "the development of thinking is of central importance to the whole structure of consciousness, central to the entire system of mental functions." [22]

The concept of the psychological system proved very fruitful for Vygotsky's theory. [23] Thus, for example, psychologists had known for a long time that in the processes of logical memory not only memory but also thinking participates. But Vygotsky succeeded in showing, using the historical-genetic method, how the formation of a psychological system takes place in the process of the mediation of the elementary mental functions by signs. This fact already manifested itself during the experiments on the development of mediated memory ("The problem of the cultural development of the child"). But then it had meaning in the context of the mediation hypothesis. Now it has meaning in the investigation of psychological systems, and due to this fact Vygotsky arrives at a number of new interesting psychological problems.

The problem of the *localization* of higher mental functions was opened anew. It is well known that in the 19th century the theory of localization was confined to strict localizationism. The investigators (e.g., Broca and others) viewed it as their main task to find out which concrete part of the brain was responsible for some psychological process. In the 20th century this idea outlived its usefulness. Under the influence of the new successes of neurology and physiology such a statement of the problem came to be seen as incorrect. Such scholars as Goldstein, Sherrington, and others developed ideas about the complex character of mental activity, about the impossibility of strict localization. They did not, however, see a positive way out.

The conception of the psychological systems allowed Vygotsky to show the way out of the crisis of localizationism. He introduced a new approach to the problem of localization—a dynamic and historical-genetic approach which emphasized how the corresponding psychological system *develops*. But the investigatory path now did not go along the lines of ontogenesis and phylogenesis, but along the lines of the investigation of pathological cases—the disintegration of psychological systems (e.g., in the case of local brain damage). Here Vygotsky managed to discover an important regularity: damage to certain cortical zones in childhood influences the development of the higher cortical zones built upon them, whereas damage to the same area in adulthood, in contrast, influences lower cortical zones ("Psychology and the theory of the localization of mental functions"). This thesis and, most important, the application of the historical-genetic method to the material of the local brain damage became the starting point for the development of a new scientific field—neuropsychology.

Thanks to the concept of the psychological systems a new view on the problem of consciousness became possible. It became clear that in the analysis of consciousness we must not proceed from the examination of the different functions, but from the examination of psychological systems. But Vygotsky did not manage to develop such an analysis. There is every reason to assume that following the logic of his theory he would have placed *meaning* in the center of consciousness. In the last years of his life he worked intensively on this problem.

Vygotsky's approach to this problem requires special examination. Of course, by including consciousness in the world of such refined products of culture as the sign and meaning he seemed to have moved away from his initial psychological program which was first and foremost directed at the study of human practical, objective, labor activity. The latter was, in principle, the topic to which Vygotsky devoted all his efforts.

Vygotsky felt this acutely in his study of the fundamental problem of consciousness and activity when he wrote that "behind consciousness there is life." But how to force one's way to this life, in other words, to practical activity?

It must be said that several psychologists of the 1930s (e.g. Talankin, Razmyslov, and others) had already seen and noted this genuine weakness in the conception of the connection between consciousness and real life which manifested itself in the cultural-historical theory. [24] The problem was and remains a very complex one for psychology.

Vygotsky, who tried to add the category of practical activity to psychology in the 1920s, began a new series of investigations in the 1930s. Now he viewed the analysis of the emotional-motivational sphere as his main task, assuming that via this sphere activity determines mental processes or consciousness. At the end of his book *Thinking and Speech* he wrote: "Thought is not the last of these planes. It is not born of other thoughts. Thought has its origins in the motivating sphere of consciousness . . . . The affective and volitional tendency stands behind thought.

Only here do we find the answer to the final "why" in the analysis of thinking" (Vygotsky, 1934/1987, p. 282). [25] The work "Spinoza's and Descartes' theories about the passions in the light of modern neuropsychology," which he began in this connection, remained unfinished. Vygotsky basically managed to give an analysis of Descartes' creative work (this manuscript is published for the first time in the present series).

In his last works, Vygotsky pointed to yet another point where activity and consciousness meet (e.g., in his lecture "Play and its role in the mental development of the child," read in 1933). Whereas he demonstrated earlier that the child's activity determines the formation of his thinking in early childhood, he now attempted to show how external activity (play) determines mental development ("creates a zone of proximal development") and is a *leading* activity. In keeping with this new aspect of his interests, Vygotsky now started paying more attention to the affective-emotional aspect of play.

*   *   *

In one article it is hardly possible to give even a concise characterization of all the problems which Vygotsky dealt with and developed. He was one of the last persons of encyclopedic learning in scientific psychology. Thus, we left his defectological, pedagogical and other works out of consideration. These problems will be treated in the corresponding volumes of the present series. We saw it as our task to show the evolution of Vygotsky's general psychological theory, which is the most important part of his many-sided creative work. Vygotsky's goal was to build the foundations of a Marxist psychology, more concretely—a psychology of consciousness. He managed to see that for Marxist psychology human objective activity must become the central category. And although the term "objective activity" is not to be found in his works, this is the objective meaning of his works, these were also his subjective plans. [26] The first manifestation of this category in psychology was Vygotsky's cultural-historical theory with the idea of the mediation of mental processes by psychological tools—by analogy with the way the material tools of labor mediate human practical activity. Via this idea Vygotsky introduced the dialectical method into psychology and elaborated his historical-genetic method in particular.

These ideas of Vygotsky allowed him to arrive at a number of brilliant scientific achievements. At the same time, such a dimension of activity as the emotional-affective sphere appeared at the center of his attention. But this new program of investigations he could not realize.

Fifty years separate us from the ideas voiced by Vygotsky. But the central problems to the solution of which Vygotsky dedicated his life remain central to contemporary psychology as well, and their solution must rest upon the theoretical methodological principles he developed. This is his major achievement and the best assessment of the creative work of this great psychologist of the 20th century—Lev Semyonovich Vygotsky.

PART 1

PROBLEMS OF THE THEORY AND METHODS OF PSYCHOLOGY

Chapter 1

THE METHODS OF REFLEXOLOGICAL AND PSYCHOLOGICAL INVESTIGATION[*,1] [1]

The methods of the reflexological investigation of man have now reached a turning point in their development. The necessity (and inevitability) of a turnaround results from the discordance between, on the one hand, the enormous tasks which reflexology sets itself—that of studying the whole of man's behavior—and, on the other hand, those modest and poor means for their solution which the classic experiment of creating a conditional (secretory or motor) reflex provides. This discordance becomes more and more clear as reflexology[2] turns from the study of the most elementary links between man and his environment (correlative activity [2] in its most primitive forms and occurrences) to the investigation of the most complex and diverse interrelations necessary for the detection of the fundamental laws of human behavior.

Here, outside the domain of the elementary and primitive, reflexology was left with only its general bare claim—equally well applicable to all forms of behavior— that they constitute systems of conditional reflexes. But neither the specific properties of each system, nor the laws of the combination of conditional reflexes into behavioral systems, nor the very complex interactions and the reflections of some systems on others, were clarified by this general (far too general) statement, and it did not even prepare the way for the scientific solution of these problems. Hence the declarative, schematic character of reflexological works when they state and solve problems of human behavior that are somewhat more complex.

Classical reflexology sticks to its elaboration of the universal scientific principle, the law of Darwinian significance, and reduces everything to a common denominator. And precisely because this principle is too all-embracing and universal, it does not yield a direct scientific means for the study of its particular and individual forms. After all, it is for a concrete science of human behavior as impossible to confine itself to this principle as it is for concrete physics to confine itself to the principle of gravity. We need scales, we need our instruments and methods in order to identify the concrete, material, limited terrestrial world on the basis of this general principle. It is the same in reflexology (everything incites the science of human behavior to transcend the boundaries of the classic experiment and to search for other means of knowledge).

*First published as Vygotsky, L. S. (1926). Metodika refleksologicheskogo i psikhologicheskogo issledovanija. In K. N. Kornilov (ed.), *Problemy sovremennoj psikhologii* (pp. 26-46). Leningrad: Gosudarstvennoe Izdatel'stvo.

And now the tendency to broaden the reflexological methods has not only clearly revealed itself, but the line this broadening will follow has taken shape as well. This line is directed toward the increasing approximation of and eventual definitive merging with methods of investigation that were established in experimental psychology[3] a long time ago. Although this sounds paradoxical with regard to such hostile disciplines and although in this respect within the milieu of reflexologists themselves there is no complete unanimity and they assess experimental psychology completely differently—despite all this—we can talk about this merging, about the creation of unified methods for the investigation of human behavior, and therefore also about a unified scientific discipline, as if it were a fact that is realized before our eyes.

The short history of this approximation is as follows. Initially an electro-cutaneous stimulus was applied on the sole, which evoked a defensive reflex of the foot or the whole leg. Then Professor Protopopov[4] introduced a very essential change in the procedure—he changed the leg to the hand, reasoning that it is much more profitable to select the arm as a criterion for the reaction since it is the most perfect response apparatus, more finely tuned to the orienting reactions to the environment than the leg (cf. Protopopov, V. P., 1923, "The methods of the reflexological investigation of man," *Zhurnal Psikhologii, Nevrologii i Psikhiatrii,* 3. Moscow–Petrograd: Gosudarstvennoe Izdatel'stvo). He very convincingly argues the importance of a suitable choice of the responding apparatus for the reaction. Indeed, it is clear that if we choose the speech apparatus as the responding apparatus in the case of a stutterer or a mute, or with a dog that extremity of which the corresponding cortical motor center has been removed, or, in general, an apparatus that is little or not suitable for the corresponding type of reaction (the leg of a person for grasping movements)—that in all these cases we will learn very little about the speed, accuracy, and perfection of the animal's orientation, although the analyzing and synthesizing functions of the nervous system are completely preserved. Professor Protopopov (1923, p. 22) says:

> and indeed, the experiment proved that the formation of conditional reflexes in the hands is reached much faster, the differentiation is also reached faster and is more stable.

This change in the methods of the reflexological experiment makes it very similar to the psychological one. The hand of the subject is placed freely on a table and his fingers touch a plate through which runs an electric current.

Thus, if in the study of human reflexes we wish to go further than the establishment of a general principle and set ourselves the goal of studying the different types of reactions that determine behavior, the choice of the reacting organ is a factor of vital importance. Professor Protopopov (ibid., p. 18) says that

> man and animal have many responding apparatuses at their disposal, but undoubtedly they respond to the various environmental stimuli with those that are for them the most developed and most suitable for the given case . . . . Man runs away from danger with his legs, defends himself with his arms, etc. Of course, it is also possible to create a defensive synthesizing reflex in the foot, but if it is necessary to investigate not just the synthesizing function of the cerebral hemispheres as such (= the general principle, L. V.), but also the degree of rapidity, accuracy, and perfection of the orientation, then for this type of investigation it turns out not to be indifferent which type of responding apparatus we chose for observation.

But in for a penny, in for a pound. Professor Protopopov (ibid., p. 22) has to confess that the reform cannot stop here.

> Man has at his disposal an effector apparatus in that same motor area which is much more developed (than the arm), by means of which he can establish a much broader

link with the surrounding world—here I have in mind the speech apparatus I
think that it is already possible and useful to turn in reflexological investigations to
the use of the object's speech, considering the latter as a specific case of those
conditional links that determine the interrelation between man and his environment
through his motor area.

That speech must be regarded as a system of conditional reflexes hardly needs any
discussion. It is for reflexology almost a truism. The benefits that the use of speech
can bring to reflexology by broadening and deepening the circle of the phenomena
studied are also evident to everyone.

Thus, with respect to the reacting apparatus there is no longer a disagreement
and difference of opinion with psychology. Academician Pavlov[5] pointed to the suitability of the salivary reflex in the dog as being the least voluntary and conscious.
That was indeed extremely important as long as it regarded the solution of the
principle of the conditional reflexes as such, the "mental saliva" at the sight of
food. But new tasks require new means, the advance forward requires a changed
road map.

The second and more important circumstance is that the methods of reflexology stumbled upon "certain facts" that are well known to every child. The process
of stimulus discrimination is not quickly established in man. Much time is required
for the established reflex to turn from generalized into differentiated, i.e., for man
to learn to react only to the main stimulus and to inhibit his reactions to irrelevant
ones. And here

> it turned out (my emphasis, L. V.) that by influencing the objects with corresponding
> suitable speech it was possible to create both inhibition and excitation of the conditional
> reflexes (ibid., p. 16).

When we explain to a person that only one specific sound will be combined with
the electric current and no others, discrimination is realized immediately. Through
speech we can also evoke the inhibition of conditional reflexes to the *main* stimulus
and even of the unconditional reflex to an electric current. We just have to tell
the subject not to withdraw his hand.

Thus, "corresponding suitable speech" is included in the methods of the experiment in order to establish discrimination. But the same means cannot only be
used to evoke inhibition but also to stimulate the reflex activity. "If we verbally
suggest that the object withdraw his hand after some specific signal," then the result
will be nothing worse than in the case of a withdrawal of the hand after the electric
current passed through the plate. "We will always elicit the desired reaction" (ibid.).
Obviously, from the viewpoint of reflexology the withdrawal of the hand after verbal
instruction is a conditional reflex too. And the whole difference between this conditional reflex and the one established with a reflex to an electric current is that
here we have a *secondary* conditional reflex[6] and there a *primary* one. But Professor
Protopopov also acknowledges that this circumstance is rather to the credit of such
methods. He says (1923, p. 22)

> that there is no doubt that in the future the reflexological investigation of man must
> primarily be carried out by means of secondary conditional reflexes.

And, indeed, is it not obvious that in analyzing human behavior the most essential aspect—both quantitatively and qualitatively—is precisely the *superreflexes*
and that precisely they explain behavior in its statics and dynamics?

But with these two assumptions—(1) the stimulation and limitation (differentiation) of reactions by means of verbal instruction and (2) the use of all sorts of
reactions, including verbal, speech ones—we fully enter the area of the methods
of experimental psychology.

Twice in the quoted historical article Professor Protopopov raises this issue. He says that

> the setup of the experiments in the given case . . . is fully identical to the one used for a long time in experimental psychology in the investigation of a so-called simple mental reaction.

He further includes

> various modifications in the setup of the experiments. It is, for example, possible to use Jung's so-called associative experiment[7] for reflexological goals and, by means of it, to take account of not just the present object, but to detect the traces of earlier stimuli, including inhibited ones (ibid.).

Turning with such resolution from the classical experiment of reflexology to the very rich variety of psychological experimentation—so far forbidden for physiologists—and outlining with great courage new paths and methods for reflexology, Professor Protopopov, for all his high assessment of the psychological experiment, leaves *two extremely essential points* unsaid. The present article is devoted to the foundation and defense of these points.

The first point concerns the techniques and methods of investigation, the second one the principles and goals of the two (?) sciences. The two are intimately connected with each other and both are connected with an essential misunderstanding that obscures the problem. The acknowledgment of both of these remaining points is dictated both by the logically inevitable conclusions from the tenets already accepted by reflexology and by the next step, which is already implied by the whole line of development of these methods and which will be taken in the very near future.

What is left that prevents the final and complete coincidence and merging of the methods of the psychological and reflexological experiment? In Professor Protopopov's understanding of the problem, *only one thing*: the interrogation of the subject, his verbal account of the course of some aspects of the processes and reactions which cannot be perceived by the experimenters in another way, the utterance, the testimony of the object of the experiment himself. It would seem that the root of the difference of opinion is to be found here. Reflexologists are not against making this difference of opinion a principal and decisive one.

Thereby they connect it with the second question, that of the different goals of the two sciences. Not once does Professor Protopopov mention the interrogation of the subject.

Academician Bekhterev[8] frequently says that "from the standpoint of reflexology subjective investigation is permissible only on oneself" (V. M. Bekhterev, 1923, *General Foundations of the Reflexology of Man*, Gosudarstvennoe Izdatel'stvo; Chapter XVIII; [1932, pp. 61-62; p. 220]). [3] Meanwhile, *precisely from the viewpoint of the completeness of the reflexological investigation* it is necessary to introduce the interrogation of the subject. Indeed, human behavior and the creation of new conditional reactions is not just determined by the exposed (manifest), complete, fully disclosed reactions, but also by reflexes that are not demonstrated in their external part, that are half-inhibited, interrupted. Following Sechenov[9] [1866/1965, p. 86], Academician Bekhterev demonstrates that a thought is only an inhibited reflex, a reflex that is nonmanifest, interrupted after two-thirds. Verbal thinking, in particular, is the most frequent case of a nonmanifest speech reflex.

One may ask why it is allowed to study complete speech reflexes and even to pin great hopes on this area, and why it is forbidden to take account of these *same* reflexes when they are inhibited, not exposed in their external part, but nevertheless undoubtedly exist objectively. When I pronounce aloud, audible for the experimenter, the word "evening," then this word that comes to my mind by association is taken into account as a verbal reaction = a conditional reflex. But when I pronounce it inaudibly, for myself, when *I think it*, does it thereby really stop being a reflex and change its nature? And where is the *boundary* between the pronounced and the unpronounced word? When my lips started moving, when I whispered, but inaudibly for the experimenter, what then? Can he ask me to repeat this word aloud, or will that be a subjective method, self-observation and other forbidden things? If he can (and with this, probably, almost everybody will agree), then why can't he ask one to pronounce aloud a word that was pronounced *in thought*, i.e., without the movement of the lips and the whispering. After all, it still was and remains a motor reaction, a conditional reflex without which there would be no thought. And this is already an interrogation, an utterance of the subject, his verbal testimony and declaration about reactions that *undoubtedly objectively existed* but were not manifest, *not perceived by the experimenter's ear* (here we have the sole difference between thoughts and speech, only this!). We can convince ourselves in many ways that they existed, existed objectively with all the signs of material being. And what is most important, they themselves will take care to convince us of their existence. They will *express themselves* with such a force and vividness that they *force* the experimenter to take them into account, or to fully refrain from the study of such streams of reactions in which they pop up. And are there many of those processes of reactions, of those courses of conditional reflexes in which nonmanifest reflexes (= thoughts) will not pop up? Thus, either we refrain from the study of human behavior in its most essential forms, or we introduce the obligatory registration of these nonmanifest reflexes in our experiment. Reflexology must study both thought and the whole mind if it wishes to understand behavior. Mind is just inhibited movement, and what is objective is not just what can be felt and seen by everyone. That which is only visible through the microscope or telescope or with x-rays is objective too. Inhibited reflexes[10] are equally objective.

Academician Bekhterev [1932, p. 411] himself points out that the results of the Würzburg school[11] in the area of "pure thought," in the highest spheres of the mind, essentially coincide with what we know about conditional reflexes. And Professor Krol'[12] (Thinking and Speech, official talk at the State Institute in Minsk— "Trudy B.G.U.", Vol. II) openly says that the new phenomena detected by the Würzburg investigations in the area of imageless and nonverbal thinking are nothing other than Pavlovian conditional reflexes. And much sophisticated work in the study of reports and verbal testimonies of subjects was required in order to establish that the act of thought itself cannot be perceived through self-observation, that it is found ready-made, that one cannot account for it, i.e., that it is a pure reflex.

But it is evident that the role of these verbal reports, of this interrogation, and their meaning for both reflexological and psychological investigations does not fully coincide with the ones attributed to them at times by subjective psychologists. How do objective psychologists have to look at them and what is their place and meaning in the system of scientifically verified and rigorous experimentation?

Reflexes do not exist separately, do not act helter-skelter, but band together in complexes, in systems, in complex groups and formations that determine human behavior. The laws of composition of reflexes into complexes, the types of these formations, the kinds and forms of interaction within them and the interaction between whole systems—all these issues are of paramount importance for the most acute problems of the scientific psychology of behavior. The theory of reflexes is only in its beginning and all these areas are yet to be investigated. But already now we may speak, as if it were a fact, about the undeniable interaction of different systems of reflexes, about the *reflection* of some systems on others, and we can even in general and rough traits provide a preliminary clarification of the mechanism of this reflection. *The response part of each reflex (movement, secretion) becomes itself a stimulus for a new reflex from the same system or another system.*

Although I never came across such a formulation in any of the works of the reflexologists, its truth is so obvious that it is evidently only omitted because it is tacitly implied and accepted by everybody. The dog reacts to hydrochloric acid by salivating (a reflex), but the saliva itself is a new stimulus for the reflex of swallowing or rejecting it. In free association I pronounce "nasturtium" to the word-stimulus "rose"—this is a reflex, but it also is the stimulus for the next word "buttercup" (this is all within one system or between related, interacting systems). The howling of a wolf elicits, as a stimulus, the somatic and mimic reflexes of fear in me. My changed respiration, my palpitation, my trembling, my dry throat (the reflexes) force me to say: I am afraid. Thus, a reflex can play the role of stimulus with regard to another reflex of the same or another system and provoke it in the same way as an external (extraneous) stimulus. And in this respect the association of reflexes is evidently fully determined by all the laws governing the formation of conditional reflexes. A reflex is linked to another reflex according to the law of conditional reflexes and will under certain circumstances become its conditional stimulus. This is the obvious and basic first law of the association of reflexes.

This mechanism also leads us to a very rough and global understanding of the (objective) meaning that the subject's verbal reports may have for scientific investigation. Nonmanifest reflexes (tacit speech), internal reflexes which are not accessible to direct observation by the observer can often be exposed indirectly, in a mediated way, *via* the reflexes that are accessible to observation and for which they form the stimuli. Through the presence of a full reflex (a word) we judge the presence of a corresponding stimulus, which in this case plays a *double* role: that of stimulus for the full reflex and of reflex to a preceding stimulus. Taking into account the gigantic, colossal role that precisely the mind, i.e., the nonmanifest group of reflexes, plays in the system of behavior, it would be suicidal for science to refrain from exposing it through the indirect path of its reflection on other systems of reflexes. (Recall Academician Bekhterev's theory about the internal, external–internal, etc. reflexes. All the more as we often have internal stimuli hidden from us, hiding in somatic processes, but which can nevertheless be exposed via the reflexes they elicit. The logic is the same here, as is the line of thought and the proof.)

In such a conception the report of the subject is not at all an act of self-observation that, as it were, puts a spoke in the wheels of scientifically objective investigation. *No self-observation whatsoever.* The subject is not put in the position of an observer, does not help the experimenter to observe reflexes hidden from him. The subject *fully* remains—also in his own account—the *object* of the experiment, but in the experiment itself some changes, a transformation, are introduced through this interrogation. A new stimulus (the new interrogation), a new reflex is introduced that allows us to judge the unclarified parts of the foregoing. The whole experiment is, as it were, filtered through a double objective.

Indeed conscious awareness itself, or the possibility of becoming conscious of our acts and mental states, must evidently be understood, first of all, as a system of transmission mechanisms from some reflexes to others which functions properly in each conscious moment. The more correctly each internal reflex, as a stimulus, elicits a whole series of other reflexes from other systems, is transmitted to other systems—the better we are capable of *accounting* for ourselves and others for what is experienced, the more consciously it is experienced (felt, fixed in words, etc.). "To account for" means to translate some reflexes into others. The psychological unconscious stands for reflexes that are not transmitted to other systems. Endlessly varied degrees of conscious awareness, i.e., of interactions of systems included in the system of the acting reflex, are possible. Being conscious of one's experiences means nothing more than having them as an object (a stimulus) for other experiences. Consciousness is the experience of experiences in precisely the same way as experience is simply the experience of objects. But precisely this, the capacity of the reflex (the experience of an object) to be a stimulus (the object of an experience) for a new reflex (a new experience)—this mechanism of conscious awareness is the mechanism of the transmission of reflexes from one system to another.

It is approximately the same as what Academician Bekhterev [1932; p. 44; pp. 421-422] calls the accountable and nonaccountable reflexes. The results of the investigations of the Würzburg school speak, in particular, in favor of such an understanding of awareness. They established, among other things, the unobservability of the thought act itself—"one cannot think a thought"—which eludes perception, i.e., cannot itself be the object of perception (the stimulus), because here we speak about a phenomenon of a different order and a different nature than the other mental processes, which can be observed and perceived (= can serve as stimuli for other systems). And the act of thought, the act of consciousness is in our opinion not a reflex, i.e., it cannot also be a stimulus, but it is *the transmission mechanism between systems of reflexes*.

Of course, in such a conception, which makes a *principled* and radical methodological distinction between the verbal report of the subject and his self-observation, the scientific nature of the instruction and interrogation also changes in a most radical way. The instruction does not suggest that the subject do part of the observation himself, split his attention and direct it to his own experiences. *Nothing of the sort*. The instruction, as a system of conditional reflexes, as a preliminary, elicits the reflexes of the set necessary for the experiment, which determine the further course of the reactions, and the set reflexes of the transmission mechanisms, precisely those which must be used in the course of the experiment. Here the instruction regarding the secondary, reflected reflexes in principle differs *not at all* from the instruction regarding the primary reflexes. In the first case: say the word that you just pronounced for yourself. In the second: withdraw your hand.

Further: the interrogation itself is no longer the *questioning* of the subject about his experiences. Things are principally and radically changed. The subject is no longer the witness testifying about a crime that he witnessed as an eyewitness (his role earlier), but the criminal himself and—what is most important—at the very moment of the crime. No interrogation *after* the experiment, when the experiment is finished, but an interrogation as the continuation of the experiment, as its organic inherent part, as the experiment itself. Interrogation is *absolutely* inseparable from the first part and merely utilizes the experimental data in the process of the experiment itself.

The interrogation is no superstructure upon the experiment but the experiment itself, which has not yet been completed and still continues. The interrogation has to be composed, therefore, not like conversation, speech, an interrogation by the experimenter, but as a *system of stimuli* with an accurate registration of each sound, with the strictest choice of only those reflected systems of reflexes which in the given experiment can have an absolutely trustworthy, scientific and objective meaning.

This is why each system of modifications of the interrogation (to catch the subject unaware, a partial method, etc.) is very important. We must create a strictly objective system and methods of interrogation as parts of the stimuli introduced in the experiment. And, of course, nonorganized self-observation, as most of its testimony, can have no objective meaning. One must know what one can ask. If words, definitions, terms and concepts are vague, we cannot in an objectively trustworthy way connect the testimony of the subject about "a slight feeling of difficulty" with the objective reflex-stimulus that elicited that testimony. But the testimony of the subject—at the sound "thunder" I thought "lightning"—can have a perfectly objective meaning which can indirectly establish that to the word "thunder" the subject reacted with the nonmanifest reflex "lightning." Thus, a radical reform of the methods of interrogation and instruction is needed which will take into account the testimony of the subject. I claim that in each particular case such perfectly objective methods are possible, which will turn the interrogation of the subject into a perfectly accurate scientific experiment.

Here I would like to raise two points: one restricting what was said before, the other extending its meaning.

The restricted meaning of these claims is self-evident: this modification of the experiment is applicable to the adult, normal person who understands and speaks our language. Neither with the newly born infant, nor with the mental patient, nor with the criminal who hides something, will we conduct an interrogation. We will not do so precisely because with them the interlacing of the systems of reflexes (consciousness), the transmission of reflexes to the speech system, is either not developed, is disturbed by a disease, or is inhibited and suppressed by other, more powerful set reflexes. But for the normal adult person who has of his own free will agreed to the experiment this procedure is indispensable.

Indeed, in man a group of reflexes that we might justifiably call the system of reflexes of social contact (A. Zalkind[13]) easily stands out. These are reflexes to stimuli that in turn can be created by man. The word that is heard is a stimulus, the pronounced word a reflex that creates the same stimulus. These reversible reflexes, which create the basis for consciousness (the interlacing of the reflexes), also serve as the basis of social interaction and the collective coordination of behavior, which, incidentally, points to the social origin of consciousness. From the whole mass of stimuli one group clearly stands out for me, the group of social stimuli coming from people. It stands out because I myself can reconstruct these stimuli, because they very soon become reversible for me and thus determine my behavior *in another way* from all others. They make me comparable, identical with myself. The source of social behavior and consciousness also lies in speech in the broad sense of the word. Speech is, on the one hand, a system of reflexes of social contact and, on the other hand, primarily a system of reflexes of consciousness, i.e., for the reflection of the influence of other systems.

That is why the key to the solution of the problem of the other person's Ego, of the knowledge of another person's mind lies here. The mechanism of being conscious of oneself (self-consciousness) and of the knowledge of others is the same. We are conscious of ourselves because we are conscious of others, and by the same method by which we are conscious of others, because we are the same vis-à-vis ourselves as others vis-à-vis us. We are conscious of ourselves only to the extent that we are *another* to ourselves, i.e., to the extent that we can again perceive our own reflexes as stimuli. There is in principle no difference in mechanism whatsoever between the fact that I can repeat aloud a word spoken silently and the fact that I can repeat a word spoken by another: both are reversible reflex-stimuli. That is why in the social contact between the experimenter and the subject, when this contact proceeds normally (with persons who are adult, etc.), the system of the speech reflexes of the subject has all the trustworthiness of a scientific fact for the experimenter provided that all conditions have been observed and something absolutely correct has been selected, something absolutely needed and of which the connection with the reflexes under study has been taken into account by us beforehand.

The second, extended sense of what was said above can be most easily expressed as follows. The interrogation of the subject with the goal of a perfectly objective study and account of nonmanifest reflexes is *an essential part of each* experimental investigation of a normal person in the waking state. I am not referring here to the testimony of the self-observation of subjective experiences that Academician Bekhterev rightly considers to have only supplementary, secondary, subsidiary meaning, but to the objective part of the experiment that cannot be missed by *hardly any* experiment and that itself serves as a verifying instance which provides the sanction of trustworthiness to the results of the preceding part of the experiment. Indeed, compared to the complete reflexes, mind in general plays a larger and larger role in higher organisms and man, and to not study it is to refrain from the study (precisely the objective study and not its one-sided, subjective caricature) of human behavior. In experiments with intelligent persons *there is not one case* where the factor of inhibited reflexes, or mind, does not in one way or another determine the behavior of the subject and can be completely eliminated from the phenomena under study and ignored. There is no experimental study of behavior where the manifest reflexes are unaccompanied by reflexes that are not accessible to the eye or the ear. Therefore, there can be no case where we could refrain from this, albeit purely verificatory, part of the experiment. And in essence, it, this element, is introduced by experimenters (it cannot be not introduced) but precisely as speech, as a conversation which is not taken into account on the same scientific level as the other elements of the experiment.

When your subject tells you that he did not understand the instruction, do you really not take into account this speech reflex later as a clear testimony of the fact that your stimulus did not elicit the set reflexes you needed? And when you yourself ask the subject whether he understood the instruction, is not this natural precaution really an appeal to a complete reflecting reflex of the word "yes or no," as to testimony about a number of inhibited reflexes? And the declaration of the subject "I recalled something unpleasant" after a very delayed reaction, is it really not taken into account by the experimenter? etc. We could give thousands of examples of the *unscientific* use of this method, for the method cannot be avoided. And when a reaction is delayed unexpectedly and not in line with the other series of tests, would it really not be useful to turn to the subject ourselves with the question "Were you thinking of something else during the experiment?" and to receive the answer "Yes, I was the entire time calculating whether I received enough change in all the places I went today"? And not just in these cases, in these *accidents*, is it useful and essential to ask for testimony from the subject. In order to determine the reflexes of his set, to take into account the essential hidden reflexes elicited by us, to check whether there were no extraneous reflexes, yes for a thousand other reasons it is necessary to introduce scientifically elaborated methods of interrogation instead of the talk, the conversation that inevitably pops up in the experiment. But, of course, these methods are in need of complex modifications in each particular case.

Curiously enough, to finish this topic and switch to another one that is intimately connected with it, the reflexologists who have fully and entirely accepted the methods of experimental psychology omit precisely this point, evidently because they think it superfluous and in principle without anything to do with objective methods, etc. In this respect, Volume 4 of *New Ideas in Medicine* (Petrograd: Obrazovanie, 1923) is very interesting. In a number of articles a new line of development in methods is outlined that goes in the same direction as that of Professor Protopopov, and with the same peculiarity—the exclusion of the interrogation. Matters stand the same in practice. When it turned to experiments with humans, Pavlov's school reproduced all methods of psychology with the exception of interrogation.

Would not this partially explain the meagerness of the conclusions, the poverty of the results of the investigations that we witnessed at this congress during the presentations about these experiments? What can they establish other than the general principle that was established a long time ago more eloquently and the fact that in man reflexes can be created faster than in dogs? This is clear without any experiments. To assert the obvious and to repeat the fundamentals remains the inevitable fate of all experimenters who do not want to alter radically their research methods.

Here I have set myself the goal of creating a plan for the construction of a *unified* objective scientific system of methods for investigating and experimenting with human behavior and of defending this attempt theoretically.

But this technical problem is intimately connected, as I have said already, with another difference of opinion of a theoretical nature which the reflexologists emphasize even when they accept the methods of investigation shared with psychology. Professor Protopopov expresses himself as follows:

> the inclusion into these methods (of reflexology) of research methods already applied a long time ago in experimental psychology . . . formed the result of the natural development of reflexology and does not at all imply that reflexology is transformed into psychology. The gradual perfection of the reflexological methods *by accident* (my emphasis, L. V.) led to forms of investigation that *only seen from the outside look like* (my emphasis, L. V.) the ones applied in psychology. The foundations of principle, the subject matter and the goals of these two disciplines remain completely different. Whereas psychology studies mental processes as spiritual experiences from their objective side (ibid.).

And so forth, and so forth, the rest is well known to anyone who reads the booklets on reflexology.

It seems to me that it is not difficult to show that this rapprochement is *not accidental* and that the similarity in forms is *not just external*. To the extent that reflexology aspires to explain the *whole* behavior of man it will inevitably have to deal with the same material as psychology. The question is: can reflexology dismiss and fully ignore the mind as a system of nonmanifest reflexes and interlacings of different systems? Is a scientific explanation of human behavior possible without the mind? Does the psychology without a soul, the psychology without any metaphysics, have to be transformed into a psychology without a mind—into reflexology? Biologically speaking it would be absurd to suggest that the mind is completely unnecessary in the behavioral system. We would either have to accept that clear absurdity or to deny the existence of the mind. But for this not even the most extreme physiologists are prepared—neither Academician Pavlov nor Academician Bekhterev.

Academician Pavlov [1928/1963, p. 219] openly says that our subjective

> states are for us a reality of the first order, they give direction to our daily life, they determine the progress of human society. But it is one thing to live according to the subjective states and quite another to analyze their mechanism in a purely scientific way (*Twenty Years of Experience with the Objective Study of Higher Nervous Activity*, Petrograd, 1923).

Thus, there is a reality of the first order that gives direction to our daily life—this is most important—and yet the objective study of higher nervous activity (behavior) cannot ignore this reality that gives direction to our behavior, this mind.

Academician Pavlov [1928/1963, p. 80] says that

> only one thing in life is of actual interest to us—our psychical experience . . . . What interests man most of all is his consciousness, the torments of consciousness.

And Academician Pavlov himself acknowledges that

we cannot ignore them (the mental phenomena), because they are intimately connected with the physiological phenomena that determine the integral functioning of the organ (ibid.).

After this can we refrain from the study of the mind? Academician Pavlov [1928/1963, p. 113] himself very correctly defines the role of each science when he says that reflexology builds the foundation of nervous activity, and psychology the higher superstructure.

> And as the simple and elementary is understandable without the complex, whereas the complex cannot be explained without the elementary, it follows that our position is better, for our investigations, our success do not in any way depend on their investigations. On the contrary, it seems to me that our investigations should have great significance for psychologists, as they eventually will have to lay the main foundation of the psychological building.

Any psychologist will subscribe to that: reflexology is the general principle, the foundation. *Until now*, as long as the building of the foundation common to animals and man was in process, as long as we were talking about the simple and elementary, there was no need to take the mind into account. But this is a temporary phenomenon: when the twenty years of experience will have become thirty years the situation will change. That is what I said in the beginning, that the crisis of methods in reflexology begins precisely when they turn from the foundation, from the elementary and simple, to the superstructure, to the complex and subtle.

Academician Bekhterev [1932, p. 103] expresses himself even more decidedly and openly and, therefore, takes a view that is still more intrinsically inconsistent and contradictory. He says that

> it would be a big mistake to regard subjective processes as completely superfluous or subsidiary phenomena in nature (epiphenomena) for we know that everything superfluous in nature becomes atrophied and obliterated, whereas our own experience tells us that the subjective phenomena reach their highest development in the most complex processes of correlative activity (*General Foundations of the Reflexology of Man*, Gosudarstvennoe Izdatel'stvo, 1923).

Is it possible, one may ask, to exclude the study of *those* phenomena that reach their highest development in the most complex processes of correlative activity in *that* science that has precisely this correlative activity as its subject of study? But Academician Bekhterev does not exclude subjective psychology and draws a boundary line between it and reflexology. After all, it is clear to everyone that here only one of two things is possible: (1) a complete explanation of correlative activity without mind—this is accepted by Academician Bekhterev—and then mind is made into a superfluous, unnecessary phenomenon—which Bekhterev denies or (2) such an explanation is impossible—but can we then accept subjective psychology and separate it from the science of behavior, etc? Accepting neither of the two alternatives, Academician Bekhterev talks about the relation between the two sciences, about a possible rapprochement in the future

> but as for this the time has not yet come, we can for the time being defend the viewpoint of the close interaction of one and the other discipline (ibid., 1st edition).

Further, Academician Bekhterev [1932, p. 380] speaks about

> the possible and even inevitable future construction of a reflexology with particular consideration for subjective phenomena (ibid., 2nd edition).

But if the mind is inseparable from correlative activity and reaches its highest development precisely in its highest forms—how can we then study them separately? This is only possible when we assume that both sides of the matter are heterogeneous and essentially different, which for a long time has been defended by psychology. But Academician Bekhterev dismisses the theory of psychological parallelism and interaction and claims the unity of mental and nervous processes.

Academician Bekhterev often talks about the relation between subjective (mind) and objective phenomena and all the time implicitly defends a dualistic viewpoint. And, in essence, *dualism* is the real name of Academician Pavlov's and Bekhterev's point of view. For Bekhterev, experimental psychology is unacceptable precisely because it studies the internal world of the mind by the method of self-observation. Academician Bekhterev suggests that we examine its results irrespective of the processes of consciousness. And of methods he openly says [1932, p. 220] that reflexology "uses its own strictly objective methods" (ibid.). With regard to methods, however, we have seen that reflexology itself acknowledges that they completely coincide with the psychological methods.

Thus, two sciences with the *same* subject of investigation—the behavior of man—and that use the *same methods*, nevertheless, despite everything, remain different sciences. [4] What prevents them from merging? "Subjective or mental phenomena" the reflexologists repeat in a thousand ways. What are these subjective phenomena, this mind?

With regard to this question—the decisive question—reflexology defends purely idealistic points of view and a dualism that might more correctly be called an idealism turned upside down. For Academician Pavlov they are nonspatial and noncausal phenomena. For Academician Bekhterev they have no objective existence *whatsoever* as they can only be studied on oneself. But both Bekhterev and Pavlov know that they rule our life. Nevertheless they regard these phenomena, mind, as something different from the reflexes, something which must be studied separately, and independently of which we must study the reflexes. This is of course materialism of the purest order—to ignore mind—but it is materialism only in its own area; outside of it, it is idealism of the purest order—to isolate the mind and its study from the general system of human behavior.

Mind without behavior is as impossible as behavior without mind, if only because they are the same. Subjective states, mental phenomena exist, according to Academician Bekhterev, in the case of an electric potential, in the case of *reflexes* (NB!) of concentration connected with the inhibition of a nervous current, in the case where new connections are set going—what kind of mysterious phenomena are they? Is it not clear now that they can be completely and fully reduced to reactions of the organism, to reactions that are reflected by other systems of reflexes—by speech, by feelings (mimico-somatic reflexes), etc. Psychology must state and solve the problem of consciousness by saying that it is the interaction, the reflection, the mutual stimulation of various systems of reflexes. Conscious is what is transmitted in the form of a stimulus to other systems and elicits a response in them. Consciousness is a response apparatus.

That is why subjective experiences are only accessible to me—only I perceive my own reflexes as stimuli. In this sense James,[14] who showed in a brilliant analysis that nothing forces us to accept the existence of consciousness as something distinguished from the world, is profoundly right, although he denied neither our experiences nor the awareness of them ("Does consciousness exist?"). [5] The whole difference between consciousness and the world (between the reflex to a reflex and a reflex to a stimulus) is only in the context of the phenomena. In the context of stimuli it is the world, in the context of my reflexes it is consciousness. This window is an object (the stimulus for my reflexes), the same window with the same qualities is my sensation (a reflex transmitted to other systems). Consciousness is merely a reflex to reflexes.

In claiming that consciousness too has to be understood as a reaction of the organism to its own reactions, one must be a bigger reflexologist than Pavlov himself. So be it, if you wish to be consistent you sometimes have to raise objections to half-heartedness and be a bigger papist than the pope, a bigger royalist than the king. Kings are not always royalists.

When reflexology excludes mental phenomena because they do not fall under its jurisdiction from the circle of its investigations, it acts just like idealistic psychology which studied mind as having nothing whatsoever to do with anything else, as a secluded world. By the way, psychology in principle hardly ever excluded the objective side of mental processes from its jurisdiction and did not retire into the circle of inner life conceived as a desert island of the spirit. Subjective states in themselves—out of space and causality—do not exist. Therefore, a science studying them cannot exist either. But to study the behavior of man without mind as reflexology wishes to do is as impossible as to study mind without behavior. There is no place, consequently, for two different sciences. And it does not require great perspicacity to see that mind is also correlative activity, that consciousness is correlative activity within the organism itself, within the nervous system, correlative activity of the human body with itself.

The contemporary state of both branches of knowledge urgently raises the question of the necessity and fruitfulness of a complete merging of both sciences. Psychology is experiencing a most serious crisis both in the West and in the USSR. "A string of raw facts," it was called by James [see p. 401 of Burkhardt, 1984]. The contemporary state of the psychologist is compared by a Russian author to that of Priam on the ruins of Troy. Everything collapsed—that is the result of a crisis that was not confined to Russia (cf. Lange's[15] "Psychology" in *The Results of Science*). But reflexology, having built the foundation, reached a dead end too. The two sciences cannot manage without each other. It is imperative and vital to elaborate common scientifically objective methods, a common formulation of the most important problems that each of the sciences can no longer state, let alone solve separately. And isn't it clear that the superstructure cannot be built except on the foundation, but that the builders of the foundation too, having finished it, cannot lay another stone without checking it against the principles and the design of the building to be erected?

We have to speak openly. The enigmas of consciousness, the enigmas of the mind cannot be avoided with any methodological tricks or subterfuges of principle. You cannot cheat them. James asked whether consciousness exists and answered that breathing exists, of this he was convinced, but about consciousness he was in doubt. But that is an epistemological statement of the problem. Psychologically speaking, consciousness is an indisputable fact, a primary reality, a fact of the greatest importance, and not a secondary or accidental one. About this there is no dispute. Thus, we should have and might have *put aside* the problem, but not have *removed* it. As long as in the new psychology one does not make both ends meet, the problem of consciousness will not be stated clearly and fearlessly and it will not be solved in an experimentally objective way. On which level do the conscious characteristics of reflexes emerge, what is their nervous mechanism, the details of their course, their biological sense?—these questions we must pose, and we must prepare to work on their empirical solution. The only thing is to state the problem correctly and in a timely manner, and then the solution will sooner or later be found. Academician Bekhterev in his "energetic" enthusiasm talks to the point of panpsychism, stating that plants and animals are animated beings. Elsewhere he cannot bring himself to repudiate the hypothesis about a soul. [6] And in such primitive ignorance with respect to the mind reflexology will remain as long as it steers clear of the mind and isolates itself in the narrow circle of *physiological materialism*. To be a materialist in physiology is not difficult—try to be it in psychology and if you cannot, you will remain an idealist.

Quite recently the issue of self-observation and its role in psychological investigation sharpened acutely under the influence of two facts. On the one hand objective psychology, which apparently initially was inclined to sweep aside introspection completely and thoroughly as a subjective method, began recently to try to find the *objective* meaning of what is called introspection. Watson,[16] Weiss,[17] and others spoke about "verbalized behavior," and they linked introspection with the functioning of this verbal side of our behavior. Others talk about "introspective behavior," about "symptomatic-speech" behavior, etc. On the other hand, the new current in German psychology, the so-called *Gestalt-psychologie*[18] (Köhler,[19] Koffka,[20] Wertheimer,[21] and others), which exerted tremendous influence in the last three to four years, raised sharp criticisms on both fronts, accusing both empirical psychology[22] and behaviorism[23] of the same sin—of not being able to study the real, daily behavior of man with a *single* accepted (objective or subjective) method.

Both of these facts add new complications to the problem of the value of self-observation, and therefore compel us to carry out a *systematic* examination of those essentially different forms of self-observation that are used by the three sides in the debate. The following lines present an attempt to systematize this question. But first we make some general remarks.

The first thing which is remarkable in this new complication of the problem is that the attempts to solve it take place during an increasingly explicit crisis within empirical psychology itself. Nothing could be more false than the attempt to picture the crisis that is breaking up Russian science into two camps as a purely local Russian crisis. The crisis in psychology is now taking place on a worldwide scale. The emergence of the psychological school of *Gestalt-theorie*, which came from the depths of empirical psychology, clearly testifies to this. Of what do these psychologists accuse introspection? Essentially, that by using this method of investigation the mental phenomena inevitably *become* subjective because introspection, which requires analytical attention, always isolates contents from their own connections and inserts them into a new connection—"the connection of the subject, the Ego" [Koffka, 1924, p. 151]. [7] Using this method the experience inevitably *becomes* subjective. Koffka compares introspection, which can only study *clear* experience, with a pair of glasses and a magnifying glass, which we utilize when we cannot read a letter. But whereas a magnifying glass does not alter the object but helps to observe it more clearly, introspection *changes* the very object of observation. When we compare weights, Koffka [1924, p. 151] says, the real psychological description in this view should not be "this weight is heavier than that," but "my sensation of tension is now stronger than before." In this way such a method of study *transforms* that which is objective in itself into something subjective.

The new psychologists acknowledge both the heroic bankruptcy of the Würzburg school and the impotence of all empirical (experimental) psychology. It is true, these psychologists also acknowledge the futility of the purely objective method. These psychologists put forward a functional and integrative viewpoint. For them conscious processes "are only part-processes of larger wholes" [Koffka, 1924, p. 160] and therefore we may subject our ideas to a functional verification by the objective facts by following "the conscious part of a larger process-whole beyond its conscious limits" [Koffka, 1924, p. 160]. A psychology which accepts that self-observation is not the main, most important method of psychology speaks only about real, about reliable self-observation, which is verified by the consequences that functionally follow from it and is confirmed by the facts.

We thus see that while, on the one hand, Russian reflexology and American behaviorism attempt to find "objective self-observation," the best representatives of empirical psychology seek "real, reliable self-observation" as well.

In order to answer the question as to what it involves it is necessary to systematize all forms of self-observation and to examine each one separately.

We can distinguish five basic forms.

1. The instruction to the subject. This is, of course, partially introspection for it presupposes the internal conscious organization of the subject's behavior. Who attempts to avoid it in experiments with man is in error, for the subject's self-instruction will then take the place of the manifest and accountable instruction, a self-instruction which is suggested by the circumstances of the experiment, etc. Hardly anyone will now dispute the necessity of instruction.

2. The subject's statements about an external object. Two circles are shown: "this one is blue, that one is white." Such a form of introspection, in particular when it is verified by the functional change of a series of stimuli and a series of utterances (not one blue circle, but a series of blue circles that become gradually darker or lighter), can also be reliable.

3. The subject's statements about his own internal reactions: I have pain, I like it, etc. This is a less reliable form of introspection; however, it can be objectively verified and can be accepted.

4. The disclosure of a hidden reaction. The subject mentions a number he has thought of; tells how his tongue lies in his mouth; repeats a word he has thought of, etc. This is that form of indirect disclosure of a reaction which we defended in this article.

5. Finally, the detailed descriptions of his internal states by the subject (the Würzburg method). This is the type of introspection that is most unreliable and most difficult to verify. Here the subject is put in the position of an observer. He is the observer ("observer" as the English psychologists say), the subject, and not the object of the experiment. The experimenter only investigates and records what happens. Here instead of facts we get ready-made theories.

It seems to me that the question of the scientific reliability of self-observation can only be solved in a way similar to the practical value of the testimonies given by the victim and the culprit in an inquest. Both are partial, we know that *a priori*, and therefore they include elements of deception, maybe they are completely false. Therefore it would be madness to rely on them. But does this mean that in a lawsuit we do not have to listen to them at all and only have to interrogate the witnesses? This would be foolish as well. We listen to the accused and the victim, verify, compare, turn to the material evidence, documents, traces, testimonies of the witnesses (here too we may have false evidence)—and that is how we establish a fact.

We should not forget that there are whole sciences that cannot study their subject through direct observation.[24] [8] Using indirect methods the historian and the geologist reconstruct facts which no longer exist and, nevertheless, in the end *they study the facts that were* and not the traces or documents that remained and were preserved. Similarly, the psychologist is often in the position of the historian and the geologist. Then he acts like a detective who brings to light a crime he never witnessed.

Chapter 2

PREFACE TO LAZURSKY[*,1]

1

Professor Lazursky's[2] book comes out in a new edition at a time when both Russian psychological science and the teaching of the psychological disciplines in the higher educational institutions are suffering an acute crisis. On the one hand, through the methods of exact natural science the successes of physiological thought penetrated into the most complex and difficult areas of higher nervous activity. On the other hand, there was an ever growing opposition to the traditional systems of empirical psychology within the psychological science itself. These factors caused and determined this crisis. To this was added the fully inevitable and natural desire, common to almost the entire contemporary Russian cultural front, to reconsider the foundations and principles of psychology in light of dialectical materialism, to connect the scientific-investigative, theoretical elaboration and the teaching of this science with more general and fundamental premises of a philosophical character.

This whole complex situation—both the theoretical and the educational aspect—was created by the crisis and reform of psychology. It absolutely requires some preliminary explanations for each new work on these issues that comes out, particularly for previous courses now republished.

Professor Lazursky's course was composed fifteen years ago from lectures read to students at one of the institutes in St. Petersburg [1] and was meant as a textbook for this course at the institute. It served this goal completely satisfactorily. Written with singular simplicity, clarity, and easily understood, it combines merits that are essential for every textbook: the fully scientific nature of all the reported material and a didactically adequate, short and systematic exposition. Now the book has come out in a third edition and it should first of all, in our view, serve the same goal—to give our schools a guide to the course in psychology and thereby help both the teacher and the student to overcome the crisis which in practice is felt by the school earliest and most acutely through the absence of a textbook.

It was exactly this practical goal of the new edition that made it impossible to simply reprint the text of the book from the previous edition in the form in which it was written by the author himself. Republication demanded that the course be submitted to some critical editing, which for the present edition has been realized by the assistants of the Psychological Institute of the 1st Moscow State University:

*First published as Vygotsky, L. S. (1925). Predislovie. In A. F. Lazurskij, *Psikhologija obshaja i eksperimental'naja* (pp. 5-23). Leningrad: Gosudarstvennoe Izdatel'stvo (3d edition; first edition published in St. Petersburg in 1912 by M. K. Kostin).

V. A. Artemov,[3] N. F. Dobrynin,[4] A. R. Luria[5] and the writer of these pages. [2] The task was exceedingly difficult. On the one hand, it was necessary to preserve all faithfulness to the scientific and pedagogical legacy of such a great scholar as the honorable Professor Lazursky, to avoid all distortion and vulgarization of his thought, to preserve as far as possible both the spirit and even the letter of his book, and his way of expression—the intonation and the pauses of the course, as it were—in an untouched and exact form. On the other hand, it was necessary to give the student a textbook for a course in psychology that he attends in 1925, i.e., to take into account and put into the book all those necessary corrections for the time that had elapsed. Such changes always occur in academic literature over 10-15 years. However, they have increased particularly appreciably and obviously in the last decade—the years of the crisis.

It is obvious to anyone that this revision cannot be fully carried out. Therefore the present attempt must be viewed as a compromise, a sort of a half-hearted solution of the problem, which may create a temporary textbook of the transitional type but which cannot at all solve the problem entirely. It certainly is not the definitive creation of a new textbook of the type that would meet all requirements posed by the present state of the science. Such a textbook of the new type is a matter for the future. Professor Lazursky's course can, in our opinion, fully serve as a temporary textbook that forms the transition to such a textbook of the new type. The perfectly sound scientific ground on which the author in general stood in his pedagogical and scientific work and on which his course is built speaks in favor of this.

The course begins with the statement that

> the gradual transformation into an exact science, in the sense of the word used with respect to natural science, can be regarded as one of the most characteristic traits of contemporary psychology (Lazursky, 1912; p. 27).

This "gradual transformation" has led to such radical attempts to reform our science that the viewpoint of the author of the course can easily seem too moderate and "gradual." But he was no doubt one of those psychologists who were engaged in the transformation of psychology into an exact science. His general biological viewpoint on the mind treated all problems of psychology as problems of a biological order. His fundamental claim that "all mental functions have their physiological side as well," in other words, that purely mental processes do not exist in the organism; the conviction that mental activity is fully lawful; finally, the theory of the integral character of the personality, which claims that "our mental organization is given to us as an integral whole, as a connected, organized unity"—all this coincides to such an extent with the basic principles of biological and realistic psychology that it brings the book much closer to contemporaneity than quite a number of other university courses created even quite recently (incidentally, he says that "the creative process is like all other mental phenomena a psychophysiological process, i.e., it has a definite physiological correlate"). To this we should add a peculiarity that is relatively rare for a Russian university course, to wit the introduction into the course of the elements and data of experimental psychology, and the general sober and transparent spirit of the natural scientist and the realist that pervades the whole book.

These are the indisputable merits of the textbook, its points of contact with the newly emerging scientific psychology, which first had to be raised, emphasized, and made dominant in the book. But in order to guarantee their predominance we had to introduce with the greatest care some changes into the text itself. In general, all changes of the text, i.e., the technical side of the editing work that we did on the book, come down to the following.

Chapter XXI (in the second edition) "Religious feelings" has been removed from the book. This chapter is not organically connected with the course, does not form an indispensable composite part of the system of the course, and is not of any serious and original value in the scientific respect. It is no more than a small offshoot in the chapter on the psychology of feelings which is not at all indispensable or intrinsically essential. Besides, in hardly any other area do the theses of the author seem so questionable, his psychological analysis of faith so scientifically unfounded, and the religious ideas so conjectural and apocryphal, as in this chapter. It would, therefore, be extremely inadequate to retain in a textbook such questionable and one-sided material. Moreover, in recent years, in connection with the general cultural changes, it has lost almost all interest. In a contemporary university course such a chapter cannot, of course, be included. Neither should it, consequently, form part of the textbook that is destined to serve this course. [3]

Then we have deleted a page from Chapter 1 "The subject matter and aims of psychology," where the author, in contradistinction to his general viewpoint, defends the right of science to introduce hypotheses and claims that "in this sense the concept of the soul as the basis of the mental processes that we observe, is fully justified." Even in comparison to empirical psychology this throws us back so far into the past, that it would undoubtedly sound sharply dissonant in a course on scientific psychology.

In other respects the text is reprinted in its entirety from the second edition with insignificant deletions of various words, half-sentences, remarks and so on. These deletions were mostly called for by purely technical and stylistic demands connected with some additions that we introduced into the text. We considered ourselves entitled to do so, as we proceeded from the conviction that a textbook is not a song from which you cannot remove a word and that the deletion of one word or the replacement of one word by another that is more suitable in the context can in no way be considered a distortion. It has been done in extremely few cases— when it was absolutely essential and inevitable and where refraining from doing so would have been equivalent to not doing any editing of the text at all.

The corrections in the text and the additions entered are always given in square brackets and thereby they are separated from the text and marked as later additions. We had to resort to this because the character of a textbook itself does not allow for extensive comments, footnotes, references to the literature and to other authors. A textbook must remain a textbook, i.e., a book that coherently and systematically explains an academic scientific course.

The additions and corrections were nearly always dictated by the time that had elapsed since the text was written. Thus, always when the tasks, methods, and subject matter of psychology are mentioned, we have added the word "empirical" in square brackets, because both theoretically and historically speaking the claims of the author only retain their scientific validity with this correction. Previously, the term "empirical" was implied as well, but at the time it was unnecessary to mention it specifically because psychology other than empirical psychology did not exist for our academic courses. The majority of the corrections are, generally speaking, of this type. Now and then a word has been inserted to strengthen an idea, to connect it with the context or with an addition made before. Sometimes a word that was superfluous and caused confusion was left out. Sometimes it was replaced by another one, again in order to make the additions organically fit in with the general context.

Finally, the more extensive additions to some chapters, also given in brackets, seemed to us the minimum amount of necessary information that should be present in a textbook. Without it the use of the textbook would be positively impossible, because the course as read from the pulpit and the course as read in the book would then diverge completely and irremediably. Furthermore, these additions could never be given in the form of references, cursory remarks, and simple provisos concerning certain claims. We always had to reckon with the student and to explain in a few words the very essence of the matter. Each time we have made these additions with an eye to the historical perspective. They are always reported as a later scientific viewpoint. This seemed all the more fitting as Lazursky's book itself does not represent a strictly closed, centralized and original psychological system. Lazursky's original scientific contribution revealed itself in other branches of his work, but not in the elaboration of a general system, a theoretical psychology.

In the absence of a generally accepted system, so characteristic of the last decades of empirical psychology, the psychologists of various currents and schools almost always created their own original system of exposition of a course and interpreted the basic psychological categories and principles in their own way. In such a situation Professor Lazursky's book cannot be characterized as other than a compilation, which includes the elements of several systems, combines a multitude of different conceptions, and sketches a certain middle course which integrates various psychological currents. Furthermore, the author's personal viewpoint, which rather clearly proclaimed itself, of course, in the selection and combination of the material itself, may rather be called eclectic. This also allows us to think that the newly added claims and information will not be organically foreign to the system of the book, but will find their place among the other intersecting lines of the course.

In addition to this, we must keep in mind that a textbook, in general, should not be constructed dogmatically; rather it should have an informative and familiarizing character. In our time, however anti-pedagogical it may be, a psychological textbook must necessarily be more or less critical. That new system of scientific psychology which is capable of creating its course without in the least relying on previous ones has not yet been created. The basic viewpoints in our science are still to a large extent determined by purely negative characteristics. Very much in the new science still rests on opposition and critique. Psychology as a science, in the words of Thorndike [1906, p. 9],[6] is nearer to zero than to complete perfection. On the other hand, the need to use previous experience, realized in old terms, is still too great. The usual concepts and categories still rest on the common use of both everyday and scientific language.

All this made us from the very beginning reject the idea of translating the whole course into the language of the new psychology or even to introduce a parallel terminology, classification, and system. This would have meant writing a completely new book, instead of editing a new edition of Lazursky's book. Therefore, we had to consciously decide to publish a book which explains the system of empirical psychology in the terms of empirical psychology, with the traditional classification, etc. But all this we wished to refresh somewhat with new scientific material and to bring it somewhat closer to contemporaneity. The second task was to report some critical material of principal importance, to give a critical vaccination with the new viewpoint. [4]

The point is that by and large Professor Lazursky stands with both feet on the ground of traditional empirical psychology. He shares all its shortcomings and imperfections which force the developing scientific psychology to resist empirical psychology and oppose it. It was utterly impossible to reveal the main line of divergence with sufficient force and clarity in the additions, to present the new viewpoint in sufficient detail and convincingly, as they were always made in passing, on accidental grounds, and had a fragmentary nature. Therefore, it seemed adequate to us to do this in very few words in the second chapter of this foreword, which might give each person using this book some critical direction in his thinking, a necessary vaccination, and would place him in the right relation to the viewpoint which is represented with sufficient completeness in Lazursky's book. Thus, the second chapter is prescribed for each reader of the book as an introductory or supplementary chapter to the book.

   We fully realize that in so doing, although not at all digging into the text, we change the main tone and idea of the book to a much greater extent than by all those insignificant deletions, notes, and corrections that were made in the text and were mentioned above. But in the present case as well we reasoned that for the memory of Lazursky too it is more flattering to re-introduce his textbook, albeit in a critical revision, in our school, for which it was uniquely created, than to definitively commit it to the archives. This is especially so because undoubtedly neither would Lazursky, who himself was not only a scholar but also a person actively engaged in public life and a pedagogue, now himself repeat his second edition verbatim. This we can claim with confidence, although it is risky to guess which position he would have occupied now. And for the school it is more useful to use, albeit critically, suitable material rather than to remain completely without a textbook for the whole transitional period.

2

   It would be a big mistake to think that the crisis in psychological science began in the past few years with the emergence of the currents and schools which opposed empirical psychology and that before that everything was well in science. Empirical psychology, which replaced rational[7] or metaphysical psychology, carried out an essential reform in its subject matter. Having declared in the words of Locke[8] that the investigation of the essence of the soul is speculation, it evolved—in accordance with the general scientific spirit of the time—in the same direction until it was transformed into "a psychology without a soul," an empirical science of the phenomena of the soul, or states of consciousness, studied through internal perception or self-observation. However, in contrast to other sciences, psychology did not succeed in creating a generally accepted and obligatory system. The general state of this science toward the end of the 19th century can most accurately be characterized as the strongest disorder of scientific thought. Psychology was split into a variety of separate currents, each of which defended its own system and interpreted and understood the basic and fundamental categories and principles of the science in its own way. In this connection, Lange (1914, p. 43) said that

> one can say without fear of exaggeration that the description of any mental process looks differently if we describe and study it in the categories of the psychological system of Ebbinghaus[9] or Wundt,[10] Stumpf[11] or Avenarius,[12] Meinong[13] or Binet,[14] James or G. E. Müller.[15]

On the one hand, the deep crisis that split empirical psychology inevitably led to the lack of a unitary, generally accepted scientific system. On the other hand, it made inevitable the birth of new psychological currents, which tried to find a way out of the crisis by rejecting the fundamental assumptions of empirical psychology and turning to more firm, stable and scientifically reliable foundations and sources of knowledge.

Indeed, the basic theses of empirical psychology are still to such an extent impregnated with the legacy of metaphysical psychology, to such an extent intimately connected with philosophical idealism, to such an extent pervaded by subjectivism, that they do not form a good and convenient basis to create a unified scientific system for psychology as a natural science. The very concept of "phenomena of the soul" contains a whole number of elements that are irreconcilable with scientific natural science. The legacy of rational psychology and the incompleteness of its reform make themselves felt very clearly here. If we accept the phenomena of the soul as being utterly different, by their nature and essence, from absolutely all the rest of the world that is studied by science, and ascribe to them characteristics and properties that again appear in nothing else, never and nowhere in the world, we thereby exclude the very possibility of transforming psychology into an exact natural science.

Finally, the material of empirical psychology, which is always subjectively colored, procured from the narrow well of individual consciousness, and its basic method, which accepts the fundamental subjectivity of the knowledge of mental phenomena, restrict the science to such an extent and so limit its possibilities that thereby they forever condemn it to atomize mind, to fragment it into a multitude of separate, mutually independent phenomena which cannot be brought together. This psychology was powerless to answer the questions that are most basic and primary for any science. The subjective testimony of one's own experience could never stand its ground to genetic and causal explanations, to an exact and differentiated analysis of their composition, to a completely indisputable and objectively reliable establishment of their main characteristics.

All this was determined from within psychology by the need to stand on an objective viewpoint and thereby to determine the subject matter, the method and principles of its study so that the possibility of building an exact and rigorous scientific system would thereby be ensured. Despite the fact that this future system is very undetermined and vague, that the various currents of objective psychology frequently do not agree, that its most fundamental theses and points of departure remain frequently unclear, we can nevertheless attempt to provide a very concise sketch of some general ideas of this scientific psychology in light of which the psychologist of our days must critically interpret and digest the material of the previous psychology.

The behavior of man and animals is usually mentioned as the subject matter of scientific psychology, and by behavior one understands all those movements that are produced only by living beings and which distinguish them from inanimate nature. Each of such movements always represents a reaction of the living organism to some stimulation, which either reaches the organism from the external environment or arises in the organism itself. "Reaction" is a general biological concept— and we can equally well speak of the reactions of plants, when the stems of plants reach out for the light; about the reactions of animals, when the moth flies into the flame of a candle or the dog salivates when it is shown meat; or about the reactions of a person when, on hearing the doorbell, he opens the door. In all those cases, we have an entirely manifest process of a complete reaction which begins with some stimulation, an incitement, a stimulus (light, the flames of a candle, the sight of the meat, the bell), which then turns into some internal processes, which develop in the organism due to this incitement (chemical processes under the influence of light in the plant and moth; nervous excitation, perception, "remembering," "thought"—in dog and man). Finally, the end of the reaction is some response movement, an action, a change, an act in the organism (the bending of the stem, the flying of the moth, salivation, walking and opening the door). These three aspects—stimulation, its processing in the organism, and the response movement—are always inherent in any reaction, both in its most elementary and simplest cases and forms, where all of them can be easily detected and graphically shown, and in those cases where because of the extreme complexity of the process, or the collision of many stimuli and reactions, or the action of an invisible internal stimulus somewhere in the internal organs (the contraction of the walls of the intestines, the rush of blood to some organ), it is impossible to graphically reveal all these three aspects. In these cases as well, however, an exact analysis would each time reveal the presence of all composite parts of the reaction. Often reactions take such complex forms that they require very careful analysis to detect all three aspects. Sometimes the stimuli are so deeply hidden in the internal organic processes or so much removed in time from the moment of the response movement or get connected with such a complex compound of other stimuli that the bare eye cannot always notice and establish them. Often the response movement or the action of the organism is suppressed, abbreviated, unrevealed and hidden to such an extent that it may easily remain unadvertised and seem wholly absent. Such are the changes of respiration and blood circulation in some weak feelings or tacit thought, accompanied by inaudible internal speech. Starting with the simplest movements of unicellular animals which grow away from unfavorable stimuli and toward favorable ones, the reactions become more complex and assume ever higher forms eventuating in the intricately organized behavior of man.

Such a view of the fundamental mechanism of behavior is fully compatible with the "fundamental biological scheme of our mental life" which is mentioned in the present textbook:

> the perception of external impressions, their subjective processing and, as a result of this processing, some act upon the external world (Lazursky, 1912).

The other general claim of this course is also fully in accord with such an understanding.

> Each mental experience, whatever it may be—perception or judgment, volitional effort or feeling—is already a process or activity (ibid.).

Animal and human behavior form an extremely important form of the organism's biological adaptation to the environment. Adaptation is the fundamental and universal law of development and life of organisms and has two basic forms. One type of adaptation is formed by the change in the animals' structure, the change in their organs under the influence of certain environmental influences. Another type of adaptation, which is no less important than the first, consists in the change in the animals' behavior without a change in the structure of the body. Everyone knows the enormous importance of the instinct for the preservation of the individual and the species. It can be reduced to extremely complex adaptive movements of the animal, without which the existence of the animal and its species would be unthinkable. Hence the biological purpose of mind becomes understandable. By introducing tremendous complexity into man's behavior, by giving it endlessly varied forms and by providing it with enormous flexibility, mind turns out to be the most valuable biological adaptation. Mind is unequalled in the whole organic world and it is to mind that man owes his dominion over nature, i.e., the higher forms of his adaptation. Furthermore, in scientific research mind itself reveals its motor nature, its structure which fully coincides with the structure of a reaction, its meaning as a real vital adaptation of the organism, a special function which is in all respects similar in nature to the other adaptive functions. The most subtle phenomena of the mind are nothing other than especially organized and particularly complex forms of behavior and, consequently, mind fulfills the same adaptive function as all other forms of organisms' adaptation which do not change their organization.

Both types of adaptation, the change in the animals' structure and the change in their behavior without a change in the structure, can, in turn, be subdivided into hereditary and nonhereditary ones. The former develop through a very slow evolution, develop due to natural selection, become consolidated, and are transmitted by heredity. The latter represent more rapid and flexible forms of adaptation and develop in the process of the petty experience of the individual. Whereas the former enable one to adapt to slow changes in the environment, the latter respond to rapid and acute, sudden changes. Therefore, they secure much more varied and flexible forms of connection between the organism and the environment.

The behavior of animals and man also consists of inherited reactions and ones that are acquired in personal experience. The inherited reactions consist of reflexes, instincts, some emotional reactions and represent the shared inherited capital of useful biological adaptations of the organism. Their origin is, in general, the same as that of the inherited alterations of the organism's structure and can be entirely explained by the general theory of evolution, which was brilliantly elaborated by Darwin.[16] Only recently, due to the investigations of Academicians Pavlov and Bekhterev, did the theory of the conditional reflexes emerge, which reveals the mechanism of the origin and elaboration of acquired reactions.

The essence of this theory comes down to the following. If a stimulus acts upon the animal and elicits an innate reaction (a simple or unconditional reflex), and another, indifferent stimulus, which normally does not elicit this reaction, acts simultaneously (or somewhat earlier) upon the animal, and such a simultaneous action of both stimuli, concurrent in time, is repeated several times, then usually, as a result of this, the animal also begins to react to the formerly indifferent stimulus presented alone. For example, a dog is given meat. It salivates—this is a simple or unconditional reflex, an innate reaction. When simultaneously (or somewhat earlier) any other stimulus begins to affect the dog, for example, a blue light, the ticking of a metronome, scratching, etc., then after several of these simultaneous actions of both stimuli a conditional reflex is usually established in the dog, i.e., it begins to salivate only when the blue light is switched on or when it hears the ticking of the metronome. A new connection has thus been established between the reaction of the dog (the salivation) and the environment, which was not given in the inherited organization of its behavior and which developed due to certain conditions (the coincidence in time) in the process of the personal experience of the dog.

This mechanism of the formation of the conditional reflex explains a great deal of animal behavior. It is one of the most remarkable adaptive mechanisms. It is extremely flexible and allows the animal to establish extremely varied, complex and flexible connections with the environment and gives the animal's behavior a singular biological importance. The mechanism clearly reveals the basic law of behavior: acquired reactions (conditional reflexes) develop on the basis of inherited (unconditional) ones and represent, in essence, the same inherited reactions, but in a differentiated, combined form. They develop completely new connections with the elements of the environment. Furthermore, any reaction may become under certain conditions (sufficient force of the stimulation, coincidence in time with the unconditional stimulus) the excitation. In other words, due to this mechanism the organism can establish infinitely varied connections and relationships with the environment. This makes behavior in all (?) the higher forms we meet in man the most perfect means of adaptation.

Furthermore, the decisive factor in the establishment and formation of conditional reflexes turns out to be the environment as a system of stimuli that act upon the organism. It is the organization of the environment which determines and causes the conditions on which the formation of the new connections which form the animal's behavior depends. For each of us the environment plays the role of the laboratory which establishes conditional reflexes in the dog and which, by combining and linking the stimuli (meat, light, bread + metronome) in a certain manner, organizes the animal's behavior in a way that is each time different. In this sense the mechanism of the conditional reflex is a bridge thrown from the biological laws of the formation of hereditary adaptations established by Darwin to the sociological laws established by Marx. This very mechanism may explain and show how man's hereditary behavior, which forms the general biological acquisition of the whole animal species, turns into man's social behavior, which emerges on the basis of the hereditary behavior under the decisive influence of the social environment. Only this theory allows us to give a firm biosocial footing to the theory of the behavior of man and to study it as a biosocial fact. In this sense, Academician Pavlov [1928/1963, p. 113] is quite right in saying that this theory must form the foundation of psychology: psychology must begin with it.

The theory of the conditional reflexes has only just begun to elaborate this enormous and most complex topic and is still very far from definitive conclusions in almost all research areas. Nevertheless, on the basis of the results already gathered it can be considered established that the mechanism of conditional reflexes allows us to explain extremely complex and diverse forms of behavior. Thus, conditional reflexes can, evidently, be established and formed not only by combining an unconditional stimulus of a hereditary reaction and an indifferent one, but also by combining a new stimulus with a conditional reflex established previously. Thus, when in a dog a salivary reflex to a blue light has already been formed and we combine the influence of the light with a new stimulus (a bell, ticking), then after several trials we get a reflex to the ticking or bell alone as well. This is a conditional reflex of the second order. In all likelihood, superreflexes of an extremely high order are possible, i.e., we can establish connections between the organism and different parts of the environment that are infinitely remote from the primary, inborn reaction. It has been further established that the influence of any sufficiently strong extraneous stimulus during the course of the reaction inhibits the latter and stops it. A new stimulation, now added to the first two, may already exert a delaying, inhibiting influence on the inhibition itself, inhibit the inhibition or disinhibit the reaction. Very complex cases of different combinations of several stimuli are possible, which elicit extremely diverse and complex reactions. It has also been experimentally established that in animals under certain conditions it is possible to create so-called trace reflexes (in which the response reaction follows only when the stimulus stops its action) and remote (delayed) reflexes (in which the response part of the reaction is delayed in time compared to the beginning of the stimulation). Furthermore, there have been discovered extremely complex laws of the interregulation of reflexes, their mutual inhibition or strengthening and their struggle for the effector organ.

All these and a multitude of other facts, established with all the unquestionable and indisputable strength of exact scientific knowledge, allow us to presuppose that all animal and human behavior (including the highest forms) in all likelihood consists of conditional reflexes in various combinations. Each behavioral act is built according to the model of the reflex. Some authors (Academician Bekhterev and others) assume that the science of behavior should be called reflexology. The psychologist, however, prefers the term "reaction," as it has, biologically speaking, a

broader meaning. "Reaction" includes human behavior in the circle of general biological concepts. Plants react as well, as do the simplest animal organisms. A reflex
is merely a special case of a reaction—to wit, the reaction of animals that have a
nervous system. It absolutely supposes the concept of the reflex arc, i.e., a nervous
path consisting of the centripetal nerve which stimulates, the nerve cell in the central system which transmits this stimulation to the centrifugal nerve, and the latter,
which carries the excitation to the effector organ. "Reflex" is a narrow physiological
concept. Further, the present state of the theory of the nervous system makes very
likely the existence of reactions that do not develop as a result of nervous stimulation of the sense organs which then give rise to the development of a new process
in the central nervous system. Instead, these are probably caused by "variously located independent centers of excitation in the brain, which are determined by radioactive processes caused by potassium chloride." [5] Following Academician
Lazarev[17] we may assume the existence of reactions of a nonreflector type (for
here we have no reflex arc, no external stimulation), which nevertheless have the
strict character of a full reaction: present are the stimulus (radioactive decompo-
sition), the processes inside the organism, and the reaction. Finally, the term "reaction" has a long tradition in experimental psychology. According to all this, the
psychologist of our days who attempts to create a new psychology is happy, however,
to repeat after Lange [1866/1974, p. 823] that

> we have a traditional name for a big, but far from exactly delimited group of
> phenomena. This name came to us from a time when the present requirements of
> strict science were still unknown. Should we now throw away the name because the
> subject matter of science has changed? That would be impractical pedantry. Let us,
> therefore, without hesitation accept a psychology without a soul! (resp. the psychology
> of behavior, L. V.). Its name is still fitting as long as we have a topic that is the subject
> of no other science.

In addition, it is necessary to remark that reflexology, from the viewpoint of
the psychology of behavior, represents the other extreme, which is as unacceptable
as empirical psychology. Whereas the latter studies mind without behavior in an
isolated, abstract form, disconnected from everything, the former seeks to ignore
mind and to study behavior without mind. Such a one-sided, physiological materialism is as far from dialectical materialism as the idealism of empirical psychology.
It confines the study of human behavior to its biological side, ignoring the social
factor. It merely studies the part of man which belongs to the general world of
animal organisms, his physiology, insofar as he is a mammal. From this viewpoint
his whole historical and social experience and the uniqueness of man's active labor
to adapt nature to himself, in contrast to animals' passive adaptation to the environment, remains unexplained. Furthermore, the reflexologists themselves also accept the reality and indisputable existence of the mind. Academician Bekhterev
[1923/1932, p. 103] cautioned against the view of mental processes as superfluous
secondary processes, epiphenomena,

> for we know that everything superfluous in nature becomes atrophied and obliterated,
> whereas our own experience tells us that the subjective phenomena reach their highest
> development in the most complex processes of correlative activity.

Academician Pavlov [1928/1963, p. 219] calls the mind "a reality of the first order."
Biologically speaking it would be completely absurd to claim the reality of the mind
and at the same time assume its complete uselessness and the possibility of explaining all behavior without the mind. Behavior without mind does not exist in
man and neither does mind without behavior, because mind and behavior are the
same. [6] Only a scientific system which discloses the biological meaning of mind
in behavior will exactly point out what new element mind adds to the organism's

reaction and will explain mind as a behavioral fact. Only such a scientific system can claim the name of scientific psychology.

Such a system has not yet been created. We can say with confidence that it will not arise out of the ruins of empirical psychology or in the laboratories of the reflexologists. It will come as a broad biosocial synthesis of the theory of animal behavior and societal man. This new psychology will be a branch of general biology and at the same time the basis of all sociological sciences. It will be the knot that ties the science of nature and the science of man together. It will therefore, indeed, be most intimately connected with philosophy, but with a strictly scientific philosophy which represents the combined theory of scientific knowledge and not with the speculative philosophy that preceded scientific generalizations.

So far we can only indicate the general landmarks by which the new psychology will be guided and the general critical criteria needed to approach the scientific legacy of the previous psychology. As long as no new terminology has been created and no new classification elaborated, we must and will use the old ones in the years to come, but in doing so we should emphasize the whole conventionality of both the old concepts and the old divisions in every way possible.

After all, in the majority of cases we should regard them, speaking in the words of Professor Lazursky, as the terminology of the "psychology of everyday life," of generally accepted, unscientific, popular language. Not without reason did he himself consider that one of the tasks of his book was to establish a link between the complex experimental investigations and "the data of everyday, ordinary life." Let us therefore look at this whole conventional terminology—will, feeling, representation, etc.—and attach to it the same role as to the terminology of everyday life. We happily apply to the author his own words regarding the terminology of rational psychology.

> At the present time . . . we can no longer accept this subdivision without submitting it to very essential changes. If I mentioned it fully it was, first, in view of its historical importance and, second, because in everyday life we very frequently classify mental processes in almost the same way. In general, faculty psychology (we say "empirical psychology," L. V.) approaches the psychology of everyday life rather closely. It is difficult to say who influenced whom in the given case: philosophers on educated people or everyday observations on philosophers. But the mutual closeness is indisputable. This we should always keep in mind, remembering that everyday worldly psychological terminology frequently conforms not so much to contemporary scientific knowledge about spiritual life as to theories of the previous, "rational" (we add: and empirical, L. V.) "psychology."

To us it is beyond question that all concepts, classifications, terminology—the whole scientific apparatus of empirical psychology—will be reconsidered, reconstructed, and created anew in the new psychology. Undoubtedly many firsts in the older psychology will be last in the new one. The new psychology proceeds from instincts and drives as the basic core of the mind and, probably, will not examine them in the last chapter of a course. It will also avoid that atomistic, scattered examination of separate pieces of mind into which the behavior of man was broken in mosaic psychology. But as long as the new system has not been created, we have no choice but to temporarily critically accept the former apparatus of the science both in research and in teaching, keeping in mind that this is the only method to realize and transfer to the new science those indisputable values of the objective observations and exact experiments that were accumulated in the age-old work of empirical psychology. We must simply always keep in mind the whole conventionality of this terminology, this new twist which has been given to each concept and word, this new content which it has been given. We should not forget for one minute that each word of empirical psychology is an old bottle into which we must pour new wine.

Chapter 3

CONSCIOUSNESS AS A PROBLEM FOR THE PSYCHOLOGY OF BEHAVIOR [*],[1]

> *A spider conducts operations that resemble those of a weaver and a bee puts to shame many an architect in the construction of its cells. But what distinguishes the worst architect from the best of bees is this, that the architect raises his structure in imagination before he erects it in reality. At the end of every labor process we get a result that already existed in an ideal form, that is, in the imagination of the laborer at its commencement. He not only effects a change of form in the materials which he works but he also realizes a purpose of his own that gives the law to his modus operandi, and to which he must subordinate his will* [K. Marx, Das Kapital, Vol. I, Part 3, p. 193].

1

The question of the psychological nature of consciousness is persistently and deliberately avoided in our scientific literature. It is attempted not to notice it as if it does not exist at all for the new psychology. As a result the systems of scientific psychology that develop before our eyes from the very beginning carry a number of organic defects with them. We will mention a few of them—the most fundamental and important ones in our view.

1. By ignoring the problem of consciousness, psychology itself blocks the road to the investigation of slightly more complex problems of human behavior. It is forced to confine itself to the elucidation of the most elementary connections of a living being with the world. One can easily convince oneself that this is really true by taking a look at the table of contents of Academician Bekhterev's (1923) book *General Foundations of the Reflexology of Man*. [1]

The principle of conservation of energy. The principle of continuous change. The principle of rhythm. The principle of adaptation. The principle of reciprocal action. The principle of relativity. In a word, fundamental all-embracing principles that not only concern the behavior of animal and man but the entire world as well. And not a single psychological law of the behavior of man that formulates a con-

*First published as Vygotsky, L. S. (1925). Soznanie kak problema psikhologija povedenija. In K. N. Kornilov (Ed.), *Psikhologija i marksizm* (pp. 175-198). Leningrad: Gosudarstvennoe Izdatel'stvo.

nection or dependency established for phenomena characteristic of the uniqueness of human behavior as distinguished from animal behavior.

At the other end of the spectrum, we have the classical experiment of creating a conditional reflex, one tiny experiment which is in principle exceptionally important but cannot fill the tremendous void between a conditional reflex of the first order and the principle of relativity. The disparity between the roof and the foundation, the absence between them of the building itself, easily demonstrates how early it is to formulate fundamental principles on the basis of reflexological material and how easy it is to take laws from other areas of science and to apply them in psychology. Moreover, the broader and more all-embracing the principle we take, the easier we can stretch it to cover the fact we need. But we should not forget that the extension and content of a concept are always inversely proportional. And because the extension of universal principles rushes toward infinity, their psychological content decreases to zero with the same speed.

And this is not a private defect of Bekhterev's course. One way or another this defect pops up and makes itself felt in every attempt to systematically state a theory of human behavior as bare reflexology.

2. The denial of consciousness and the aspiration to create a psychological system without this concept, as a "psychology without consciousness" in the words of Blonsky[2] [2], brings with it the fact that our methods lack a most necessary means to investigate reactions that are nonmanifest and cannot be observed with the naked eye, such as internal movements, internal speech, somatic reactions, etc. The study of only those reactions that can be observed with the naked eye is utterly powerless and invalid for even the most simple problems of human behavior.

Meanwhile the behavior of man is organized in such a way that precisely the internal movements that are difficult to detect direct and guide his behavior. When we create a conditional reflex in a dog we, as a preliminary, organize his behavior using external means in the well-known way—otherwise the experiment would not succeed. We put the dog on the stand, tie it with straps, etc. In exactly the same well-known way, we, as a preliminary, organize a subject's behavior through certain internal movements—through instruction, clarification, etc. And when these internal movements suddenly change in the course of the experiment the whole picture of the behavior changes abruptly. Thus, we always use inhibited reflexes. We know that they continually take place in the organism and that they exert an influential regulatory role in behavior—insofar as it is conscious. But we lack any means to investigate these internal reactions.

To put it more simply: man always thinks to himself. This will always influence his behavior. A sudden change of thought during the experiment will always have immediate repercussions for the whole of the subject's behavior (suddenly a thought: I will not look into the apparatus). But we have no idea how to take this influence into account.

3. Any boundary of principle between animal behavior and human behavior is erased. Biology devours sociology, physiology-psychology. The behavior of man is studied inasmuch as it is the behavior of a mammal. The fundamentally new that consciousness and mind introduce in human behavior is ignored in the process.

Two laws can serve as an example: the law of extinction or internal inhibition of conditional reflexes established by Academician Pavlov [3] and the law of the dominant formulated by Professor Ukhtomsky[3] [4]

The law of extinction (or internal inhibition) of conditional reflexes states that after a prolonged stimulation with a single conditional stimulus, not reinforced by the unconditional one, the conditional reflex will gradually become weaker and finally extinguish entirely. Let us turn to the behavior of man. We create in a subject a conditional reaction to some stimulus: when you hear the bell, press the key. We repeat the experiment forty, fifty, a hundred times. Will there be extinction? On the contrary, the connection is strengthened—from trial to trial, from day to day. We will have exhaustion, but this is not what the law of extinction is about. It is obvious that here we cannot simply transport a law from the area of animal psychology to the psychology of man. We must formulate some fundamental restriction. But we not only do not know it, we do not even know where and how to search for it.

The law of the dominant states that in the animal's nervous system there are centers of excitation that attract other, subdominant excitations present in the nervous system at the same time. Research demonstrates that sexual excitation in the cat, the acts of swallowing and defecation and the embracing reflex in the frog are all strengthened at the expense of all extraneous stimulation. From this one takes a direct step to the act of attention in man and it is claimed that the physiological foundation of this act is the dominant. But now it turns out that precisely attention lacks the characteristic trait of the dominant—the capacity to become strengthened by all extraneous stimulation. On the contrary, each extraneous stimulus diverts and weakens attention. It is obvious once again that the transition from laws of the dominant established in cats and frogs to laws of human behavior cannot be made without essential corrections.

4. Most importantly, the exclusion of consciousness from the sphere of scientific psychology to a considerable extent preserves the whole dualism and spiritualism of the former subjective psychology. Academician Bekhterev claims that the system of reflexology does not contradict the hypothesis "of the soul." [5] [6] He characterizes subjective or conscious phenomena as phenomena of the second order, as specific internal phenomena that accompany the synthesizing reflexes. [7] Moreover, this dualism is strengthened by the fact that he allows for the possibility of the future emergence of a separate science—subjective reflexology—and even accepts it as inevitable. [8]

Reflexology's basic assumption that it is possible to fully explain all of man's behavior without resorting to subjective phenomena (to build a psychology without a mind) is the dualism of subjective psychology turned inside out. It is the counterpart of subjective psychology's attempt to study the pure, abstract mind. It is the other half of the previous dualism: there mind without behavior, here behavior without mind. Both here and there mind and behavior are not one but two.

Exactly because of this dualism, not a single psychologist, not even an extreme spiritualist and idealist, disclaimed the physiological materialism of reflexology. On the contrary, all forms of idealism always invariably presupposed it.

5. By chasing consciousness from psychology we firmly and forever get locked in a circle of biological absurdities. Even Academician Bekhterev [1932, p. 103] [9] cautions against the big mistake of regarding

> subjective processes as completely superfluous or subsidiary phenomena in nature (epiphenomena), for we know that everything superfluous in nature becomes atrophied and obliterated, whereas our own experience tells us that the subjective phenomena reach their highest development in the most complex processes of correlative activity. [10].

Consequently, what remains is to accept one of two alternatives: either this is really true and then it is impossible to study man's behavior, the complex forms of his correlative activity, independently of his mind; or it is not true and then mind is an epiphenomenon, a secondary phenomenon. As soon as everything can be explained without it we are led to a biological absurdity. There is no third possibility.

6. If we accept such a statement of the problem, we forever deny ourselves access to the investigation of the most important problems—the *structure* of our behavior, the analysis of its composition and form. We are forever deemed to stick to the false conception of behavior as a sum of reflexes. At the same time, "man is not at all a skin sack filled with reflexes and the brain is not a hotel for conditional reflexes that happen to pass by." [11]

"Reflex" is an abstract concept. From the methodological viewpoint it is extremely valuable but it cannot become the fundamental concept of psychology viewed as the concrete science of human behavior. In reality we are [not] a leather bag filled with reflexes and the brain is not a hotel for complex groups, combinations and systems built according to the most diverse types.

The investigation of the dominant in animals and the investigation of the integration of reflexes demonstrated with indisputable cogency that the work of each organ, its reflex, is not something static but that it is just a function of the general state of the organism. [12] "The nervous system works as an integrated whole." [13] This statement by Sherrington[4] should form the basis for a theory of the structure of behavior.

Indeed, the reflex, as it is conceived of in Russia, very much resembles the story of Kannitfershtan whose name a poor foreigner heard each time he asked a question in Holland: who is being buried, whose house is this, who drove by, etc. In his naivete he thought that everything in this country was accomplished by Kannitfershtan whereas this word only meant that the Dutchmen he met did not understand his questions. [14]

The "reflex of purpose" and the "reflex of freedom"[5] are other easy proofs for a lack of understanding of the phenomena under study. It is clear to everyone that these are not reflexes in the usual sense—in the sense of a salivary reflex—but behavioral mechanisms that differ from it in structure. And only if we reduce everything to a common denominator can we refer to everything with the same term: this is a reflex and that is Kannitfershtan. Then the word "reflex" becomes meaningless.

What is a sensation? It is a reflex. What are speech, gestures and mimics? Reflexes as well. And instincts, slips of the tongue and emotions? They are all reflexes as well. All the phenomena that the Würzburg school discovered in higher processes of thought, the interpretation of dreams suggested by Freud.[6] [15] They are all the same reflexes. All this is, of course, perfectly true, but the scientific sterility of such bare ascertainments is quite obvious. Using such a method of study, science cannot shed light and clarity on the phenomena under study. It cannot help to differentiate and delimit the objects, forms and phenomena. On the contrary, it forces us to view everything in a dim twilight where everything is blended together and no clear boundaries between the objects exist. *This* is a reflex and *that* as well. But what distinguishes *this from that*?

* * *

We must not study reflexes but behavior—its mechanisms, its composition and its structure. Each time we conduct an experiment with animals or humans we have the illusion that we are studying a reaction or a reflex. In reality, we are always studying behavior because we invariably organize the behavior of the subject in a certain way in advance in order to guarantee the reaction's or reflex's predominance. Otherwise we would not get anywhere.

Does the dog in Academician Pavlov's experiments really react with a salivary reflex and not with a multitude of the most varied of internal and external motor reactions? And do they really not influence the course of the observed reflex? And does the conditional stimulus in these experiments really not itself elicit similar reactions (the orienting reaction of the ear, eye, etc.)? Why is a conditional connection established between the salivary reflex and the bell and not the other way around, i.e., why does the meat not begin to elicit the orienting reaction of the ears? Does a subject who, after a signal, pushes a key really express his whole reaction in this? And the general relaxation of the body, the leaning back against the back of the chair, the turning away of the head, the sigh, etc., don't they constitute essential parts of the reaction?

All this points to the complexity of each reaction, to its dependency on the structure of the behavioral mechanism of which it forms a part, to the impossibility of studying a reaction in an abstract way. Before drawing very grand and crucial conclusions from the classical experiment with the conditional reflex, we must bear in mind that research is only just beginning, that it has covered quite a restricted field, that we have studied only one or two reflexes—the salivary and the defensive motor reflex—and only conditional reflexes of the first and second order and in a direction that is biologically not advantageous for the animal at that (why would an animal salivate to very distant signals, to conditional reflexes of a high order?). Let us therefore be careful with the direct transference of reflexological laws into psychology. Professor Vagner[7] is right in saying that the reflex is the foundation but that from this foundation we cannot possibly deduce what will be built on it. [16]

It would seem that all these considerations should make us change our view of human behavior as a mechanism that can be entirely disclosed with the key of the conditional reflex. We cannot critically reassess the whole scientific capital in this area, select and screen it, translate it into a new language, elaborate new concepts, and create a new view on the problems without a preliminary working hypothesis about the psychological nature of consciousness.

Scientific psychology must not ignore the facts of consciousness but materialize them, translate them into the objective language of the objectively existing. It must forever unmask and bury fictions, phantasmagorias, etc. Without this all work is utterly impossible—both teaching, critique, and research.

It is not difficult to understand that from the biological, physiological and psychological viewpoint consciousness should not be viewed as *a second series* of phenomena. We must find a place for it and interpret it in one and the same series of phenomena with all the reactions of the organism. This is the first requirement our working hypothesis should meet. Consciousness is the problem of the structure of behavior.

Another requirement is that the hypothesis must provide an uncontrived explanation of the basic problems connected with consciousness: the problem of the conservation of energy [17]; self-consciousness; the psychological possibility of knowing other persons' consciousness; the conscious awareness of the three main spheres of empirical psychology—thinking, feeling, and will; the concept of the unconscious; the evolution of consciousness and its identity and unity.

Here, in this short and cursory essay, we have merely stated the most preliminary, most general and most basic ideas. It seems to us that a future working hypothesis about consciousness in the psychology of behavior will originate at their intersection.

2

Let us approach the question from the outside, not from within psychology.

The main forms of all animal behavior consist of two groups of reactions: inborn or unconditional reflexes and acquired or conditional reflexes. The inborn reactions constitute, as it were, the biological extract of the inherited collective experience of the whole species, and acquired reactions evolve on the basis of this inherited experience by establishing new connections encountered in the personal experience of the individual. Thus, we can provisionally describe all animal behavior as inherited experience plus inherited experience multiplied by personal experience. The origin of inherited experience has on the whole been clarified by Darwin. The mechanism of the multiplication of this experience by personal experience is the mechanism of the conditional reflex established by Academician Pavlov. [18]

With this formula, animal behavior can in general be exhaustively described.

The case is different with man. Here, in order to understand behavior more or less completely, we must introduce new members into the formula. Here we must first of all point to the quite extended inherited experience of man in comparison to animals. Man does not only make use of physically inherited experience. Our whole life, work and behavior is based on the tremendously broad use of the experience of previous generations which is not transmitted from father to son through birth. Let us provisionally call it historical experience.

Next to this we must put social experience, the experience of other people, which forms a very significant component in human behavior. I do not only have available the connections formed in my personal experience between various unconditional reflexes and various elements of the environment, but also a multitude of connections established in the experience of other people. If I know the Sahara and Mars although I have never left my own country and never looked through a telescope, then it is obvious that the origin of this experience is due to the experience of other people who have travelled to the Sahara and who have looked through a telescope. It is equally obvious that animals usually do not have such experience. Let us call this the social component of our behavior.

Finally, what is also essentially new for human behavior is that his adaptation and the behavior connected with it takes new forms in comparison to animals. In animals we have passive adaptation to the environment, in humans active adaptation of the environment to oneself. It is true that in animals as well we encounter rudimentary forms of active adaptation in instinctive behavior (nest building, the building of a dwelling, etc.), but in the animal kingdom these forms first are not of predominant, fundamental importance and, second, still remain passive in their essence and in the mechanism of their realization.

Spiders that spin their web and bees that build cells out of wax do this because of an inherited instinct and in a machine-like manner, always in the same way. They do not display more activity than in all their other adaptive activities. It is different with a weaver or an architect. As Marx said, they first build their creation in their imagination. The result of the labor process existed in an ideal form before the beginning of this work. [19]

This perfectly indisputable explanation by Marx refers to nothing other than the *doubling of experience* that is unavoidable in human labor. In the movements of the hands and the transformations of the material, labor repeats what was first, as it were, done in the worker's imagination with models of these movements and this same material. Such *doubled experience* allows man to develop active forms of adaptation which the animal does not have. Let us provisionally call this new type of behavior doubled experience.

Now the new part of the formula of human behavior looks like this: historical experience, social experience, and doubled experience.

The question remains: how, by what kind of signs, can we interconnect these new members and how can they be linked to the first part of the formula?

The sign of multiplication of inherited experience by personal experience is clear for us; it is embodied in the mechanism of the conditional reflex.

The next sections are dedicated to the search for these missing signs.

3

In the preceding section the biological and social aspects of the problem were outlined. Now let us examine just as briefly its physiological side.

Even the most elementary experiments with isolated reflexes run against the problem of the coordination of reflexes or their transition into behavior. Above, it was mentioned in passing that each of Academician Pavlov's experiments already presupposes that the dog's behavior has been preliminarily organized so as to guarantee that only the necessary connection is formed in the collision of reflexes. Academician Pavlov already came across several cases of more complex reflexes in the dog.

Academician Pavlov frequently points to collisions of two different reflexes which occur in the course of the experiments. In such cases the results are not always the same (cf. articles XXI and XXV—in one case the reinforcement of the food reflex by the simultaneous guarding reflex is related, in another the victory of the food reflex over the guarding reflex). [20] In this connection, Academician Pavlov says that "the two reflexes are literally like weights on the two sides of a scale." [21] He does not close his eyes before the unusual complexity of the development of a reflex. He says that

> when one considers that any given reflex, as a response to a certain external stimulus, is not only governed and regulated by other simultaneous reflex actions, but also by a multitude of internal reflexes as well as by the presence of many internal stimuli, viz., chemical, thermal, etc., operating in different regions of the central nervous system or even directly in the executive tissue elements (motor or secretory), then such a conception would grasp the entire complexity of all responsive phenomena. [22]

The basic principle of the coordination of reflexes, as is clarified in the investigations of Sherrington [23], lies in the struggle of different groups of receptors for the common motor path. The point is that there are many more afferent neurons in the nervous system than efferent ones, and therefore each motor neuron has a reflex connection with not just one receptor but with many, probably with all. Thus, in the organism there will always emerge a struggle between the different receptors for the common motor path, for the possession of one effector organ. The outcome of this struggle depends on many very complex and diverse factors. Thus, it turns out that each realized reaction, each victorious reflex, emerges after a struggle, after a conflict at "the point of collision." [24]

Behavior is the system of *victorious* reactions. Sherrington says that

> Under normal conditions, leaving aside the question of consciousness, the animal's whole behavior consists of successive transitions of the final path now to one group of reflexes, now to another. [25]

In other words, all behavior is a struggle that does not abate for a minute. There is every reason to suppose that one of the most important functions of the brain is precisely to establish the coordination between reflexes that come from remote points "owing to which the nervous system is integrated into an integral individual."

According to Sherrington [1904, p. 466], the coordinating mechanism of the common motor path lies at "the very root of the great psychical process of attention."

> The singleness of action from moment to moment thus assured is a keystone in the construction of the individual whose unity it is the specific office of the nervous system to perfect [ibid., p. 466].

"The reflex is an integrative reaction of the organism." Each muscle, each effector organ we must consider as "a check to bearer which any group of receptors may take possession of." The general idea of the nervous system is splendidly clarified by the following comparison.

> The receptor system bears therefore to the efferent paths a relation like the wide ingress of a funnel to its narrow egress. But each receptor stands in connexion not with one efferent only but with many—perhaps with all, though the connexion may be of different strength. Continuing our simile to a funnel, we should say therefore that *the whole nervous system is a funnel of which the base is five times wider than the egress; within this funnel the conducting paths of each receptor may be represented as a funnel inverted so that its wider end is more or less co-extensive with the whole plane of emergence of the final common paths* [Sherrington, 1904, p. 465; 1906, p. 148; Vygotsky's emphasis]. [26]

Academician Pavlov compares the cerebral hemispheres of the brain to a telephone station where new, temporary connections between elements of the environment and different reactions are formed. [27] But much more than a telephone station our nervous systems resemble the narrow doors of some big building through which a crowd of many thousands of people wishes to enter in panic. Only a few people can enter through the doors. Those who enter successfully are but a few of the thousands who were shoved aside and who perished. This better conveys the catastrophic character of that struggle, that dynamic and dialectic process between the world and man and within man which is called behavior.

Two theses necessary for a correct statement of the problem of consciousness as a mechanism of behavior follow naturally.

1. The world is, as it were, poured into the wide ingress of a funnel with thousands of stimuli, inclinations and summons. Inside the funnel there is a continual struggle or collision. All excitation flows out of the narrow egress in the form of the organism's response reactions and is strongly reduced in quantity. Realized behavior is an insignificant part of all possible behavior. Man is every minute full of unrealized possibilities. These unrealized possibilities of our behavior and this difference between the broad and narrow openings of the funnel are a perfect reality. They are just as real as the triumphant reactions, because all three necessary parts of a reaction are present.

If the structure of the final common path is somewhat complex or if the reflexes are complex this unrealized behavior can take very diverse forms.

> In complex reflexes the reflex arcs sometimes ally with respect to one part of the path and struggle with each other with respect to another part [cf. Sherrington, 1906, p. 121]. [28]

Thus, a reaction can remain half realized or unrealized in some of its (always indeterminate) parts.

2. Owing to the extremely complex balance which the complex struggle of reflexes creates in the nervous system, the quite insignificant force of a new stimulus often suffices to decide the outcome of the struggle. In the complex system of strug-

gling forces, a tiny new force can thus also determine the result and the direction of the resultant forces. In a big war, a small state which sides with one of the parties may determine victory or loss. As one easily imagines, this means that reactions which are in themselves negligible, even hardly noticeable, may prove to be leading, depending on the conjuncture in that "point of collision" in which they enter.

4

The most elementary and basic universal law of the connection of reflexes can be formulated as follows. Reflexes are connected according to the laws of conditional reflexes. The response part of one (motor or secretory) reflex can, under suitable conditions, become a conditional stimulus (or inhibition) for another reflex and connect along the sensory pathway the peripheral stimuli connected with it in the reflex arc with a new reflex. Quite a number of such connections are possibly inherited and belong to the unconditional reflexes. The rest of these connections are created in the process of experience—and must be created continually in the organism.

Academician Pavlov calls this mechanism a chain reflex and uses it to explain instinct. [29] In Doctor Zelenyj's experiments,[8] the same mechanism was discovered in research into rhythmic muscle movements, which also turned out to be a chain reflex. [30] Thus, this mechanism explains the unconscious, automatic combination of reflexes best of all.

However, if we do not look at one and the same system of reflexes but at various ones and at the possibility of transfer from one system into another, the same mechanism essentially is the mechanism of consciousness itself in its objective meaning. The capacity of our body to be a stimulus (through its own acts) for itself (for new acts) is the basis of consciousness.

Already we can say without doubt that different systems of reflexes interact and that some systems influence others. A dog reacts to hydrochloric acid by salivating (a reflex), but the saliva itself is a new stimulus for the reflex of swallowing or rejecting it. In free association I pronounce "daffodil" to the word-stimulus "rose"; this is a reflex, but it also forms a stimulus for the next word "gilly-flower." This is all within a single system or in related, cooperating systems. The howling of the wolf as a stimulus causes me to react with somatic and mimic reflexes of fear. The altered respiration, heart beat, trembling and dry throat compel me to say or think: I am afraid. Here we see transmission from one system to another.

We must evidently conceive of awareness itself or the possibility of becoming conscious of our acts and mental states first of all as a system of transmission mechanisms from some reflexes to others, which functions properly in each conscious moment. The more correctly each internal reflex, as a stimulus, elicits a whole series of other reflexes from other systems and is transmitted to other systems, the better we are capable of accounting for ourselves and others for what is experienced, the more consciously it is experienced (felt, fixed in words, etc.).

To account for means to translate some reflexes into others. The psychological unconscious stands for reflexes that are not transmitted to other systems. There can be endlessly varied degrees of awareness, i.e., of cooperation between the systems included in the mechanism of the acting reflex. To be conscious of one's experiences is nothing other than to have them as object (stimulus) for other experiences. Consciousness is the experience of experiences just like experiences are simply experiences of objects. But precisely this capacity of the reflex (the experience of an object) to be a stimulus (the object of an experience) for a new reflex (a new experience)—this mechanism of conscious awareness—is the mechanism of the transmission of reflexes from one system to another. It is approximately the same as what Academician Bekhterev [1932, pp. 44; 421-422] calls the accountable and nonaccountable reflexes.

Psychology must state and solve the problem of consciousness by saying that it is interaction, the mutual influence and stimulation of various systems of reflexes. Conscious is what is transmitted in the form of a stimulus to other systems and elicits a response in them. Consciousness is always an echo, a response apparatus. I will give three references to the literature.

1. Here it is appropriate to mention that in the psychological literature it was frequently pointed out that a circular reaction is a mechanism that feeds its own reflex back into the organism by means of the centripetal currents that originate in the process and that this mechanism lies at the basis of consciousness. [31] The biological importance of this circular reaction was often emphasized. The new stimulus, caused by the reflex, elicits a new, secondary reaction, which either strengthens and repeats or weakens and suppresses the first reaction. This depends on the general state of the organism and on the way that the organism, as it were, evaluates its own reflex. Thus, a circular reaction is not a simple combination of two reflexes but a combination in which one reaction is steered and regulated by another one. A new aspect of the mechanism of consciousness takes shape: its regulatory role with respect to behavior.

2. Sherrington distinguishes between the exteroceptive field as the field of the external surface of the body and the interoceptive field as the internal surface of certain organs to which "a certain part of the external environment is led." Elsewhere he talks about the proprioceptive field that is stimulated by the organism itself, by changes that take place in the muscles, tendons, joints, blood vessels, etc.

> The excitation of the receptors of the proprioceptive field, in contradistinction from those of the exteroceptive, is related only secondarily to the agencies of the environment. The proprioceptive receive their stimulation by some action, e.g., a muscular contraction, which was itself a primary reaction to excitation of a surface receptor by the environment. Reflexes arising from proprioceptive organs come to be habitually attached to reflexes excited by exteroceptive organs [cf. Sherrington, 1906, pp. 132-133]. [32]

Moreover, the combination of these secondary reflexes with the primary reactions, this "secondary connection," can combine, as research demonstrates, reflexes of both the allied and the antagonistic type. In other words, the secondary reaction can both strengthen and terminate the primary one. And this is the mechanism of consciousness.

3. Finally, Academician Pavlov says in one place that

> the reproduction of the nervous processes in the subjective world is unique, and is, as it were, a many times refracted image, so that the entire psychological idea of the nervous activity is extremely conventional and only approximate. [33]

Here Academician Pavlov hardly had in mind more than a simple comparison, but we are prepared to understand his words in a literal and precise sense and claim that consciousness is indeed the "multiple refraction" of reflexes.

5

In this way we have solved the problem of the mind without expense of energy. Consciousness is fully and completely reduced to transmitting mechanisms of reflexes that work according to general laws, i.e., no processes other than reactions can be accepted to exist in the organism.

The solution of the problem of self-consciousness and self-observation now becomes possible as well. Inner perception or introspection is only possible owing to the existence of the proprioceptive field and the secondary reflexes connected to it. It is always, as it were, the echo of a reaction.

This exhaustively explains self-consciousness as the "perception of what goes on in man's own soul," in Locke's expression. Moreover, it becomes clear why this experience is only accessible to one person—the one who is experiencing this experience. Only I and I alone can observe and perceive my own secondary reactions, because only for me do my reflexes serve as new stimuli for the proprioceptive field.

This being so, one can easily explain the split nature of experience: the mental is unlike anything else precisely because it is dealing with stimuli *sui generis* which are met *nowhere else but in my own body*. The movement of my hand perceived by the eye can be a stimulation for my eye as well as for someone else's eye. But the conscious awareness of this movement, the proprioceptive excitation which emerges in that process and which elicits secondary reactions exist only for myself. They have nothing in common with the first stimulation of the eye. Here we have completely different nervous paths, different mechanisms, and different stimuli.

An intricate problem of the psychological method is intimately connected with this: the problem of the value of self-observation. The previous psychology considered it to be the basic and most important source of psychological knowledge. Reflexology either fully rejects it or brings it under the control of objective data, as a source of supplementary information. [34]

The conception of the problem presented here leads us to a very rough and global understanding of the (objective) meaning which the verbal report of the subject may have for scientific investigation. Nonmanifest reflexes (tacit speech), internal reflexes which are not accessible to direct observation by the observer, can often be exposed indirectly, in a mediated way, *via* the reflexes that are accessible to observation and for which they form the stimuli. Through the presence of a full reflex (a word) we judge the presence of a corresponding stimulus, which in this case plays a *double* role: the role of stimulus for the full reflex and of reflex to a preceding stimulus.

Taking into account the enormous and primary role that the mind, i.e., the nonmanifest group of reflexes, plays in the system of behavior, it would be suicidal to refrain from its exposure through the indirect path of its reflection on other systems of reflexes. After all, we are studying reflexes to stimuli that are internal and hidden from us. The logic is the same here, as is the line of thought and the proof.

In this conception, the report of the subject is not at all an act of self-observation that, as it were, puts a spoke in the wheels of objective scientific investigation. *No self-observation whatsoever.* The subject is not put in the position of an observer and does not help the experimenter to observe reflexes hidden to him. The subject *fully* remains, also in his own account, the *object* of the experiment, but through this interrogation some changes, a transformation, are introduced in the experiment itself. A new stimulus (the new interrogation), a new reflex is introduced that allows us to judge the unclarified parts of the foregoing. In this respect the whole experiment is, as it were, filtered through a double objective.

We must introduce such a filtering of experience through the secondary reactions of consciousness in the methods of psychological research. The behavior of man and the formation of new conditional reactions in man are not only determined by the manifest, complete, fully exposed reactions, but also by reactions which do not manifest their external part and are invisible to the naked eye. Why can we study complete speech reflexes and can't we take account of the thought reflexes, "interrupted after two-thirds" [35], although there can be no doubt that the latter, too, are reactions that really and indisputably exist?

When in free association I pronounce aloud, audible for the experimenter, the word "evening," then this word that comes to my mind is taken into account as a verbal reaction, a conditional reflex. But when I pronounce it inaudibly, for myself, when *I think it*, does it really stop being a reflex and change its nature? And where is the boundary between the pronounced and the unpronounced word? When my lips started moving, when I whispered but still inaudibly for the experimenter—what then? Can he ask me to repeat this word aloud or will that be a subjective method that can be practiced only on oneself? If he can (and almost everybody will, probably, agree about this), then why cannot he ask me to pronounce aloud a word that was pronounced *in thought*, i.e., without the movement of the lips and the whispering? After all, it still was and now remains a speech motor reaction, a conditional reaction without which there would be no thought. But this is already an interrogation, an utterance of the subject, his verbal account of reactions that undoubtedly objectively existed but were not manifest and *not perceived by the experimenter's ear* (here we have the sole difference between thoughts and speech). We can convince ourselves by many means that they existed, existed objectively with all the signs of material being. The elaboration of these means is one of the most important tasks of psychological methods. Psychoanalysis[9] is one of these means.

But what is most important is that they themselves will take care to convince us of their existence. They will *express themselves* with such a force and vividness in the further course of the reaction that they *force* the experimenter to take them into account, or to fully refrain from the study of such streams of reactions in which they pop up. And are there many such behavioral processes in which nonmanifest reflexes would not pop up? Thus, either we refrain from the study of human behavior in its most essential forms, or we introduce the obligatory registration of these internal movements in our experiment.

Two examples will clarify this necessity. When I remember something, form a new speech reflex, is it really indifferent what I will think at that moment—whether I will simply repeat to myself the presented word or whether I will establish a logical connection with that word and another? Is it really not clear that in the two cases the results will be essentially different?

In free association I pronounce the word "snake" to the word-stimulus "thunder" but before that I had briefly thought of the word "lightning." Is it really not clear that when we don't take account of this thought that we will wittingly accept the erroneous idea that the reaction to "thunder" was "snake" instead of "lightning"?

Of course, we are not talking about a simple transference of experimental self-observation from traditional psychology into the new psychology. We have in mind, rather, the urgent necessity of elaborating new methods for the investigation of inhibited reflexes. Here we have only defended the fundamental necessity and possibility of such methods.

In order to finish with the problems of method, let us dwell briefly on the instructive metamorphosis that the methods of reflexological investigation currently undergo when applied to man. In one of his articles, Professor Protopopov [36] said about this metamorphosis that

> initially reflexologists applied an electro-cutaneous stimulus on the sole. Then it proved more profitable to select a more perfect apparatus, more suited for orienting reactions. The leg was replaced by the arm. But in for a penny, in for a pound. Man has at his disposal a still much more perfect apparatus by means of which he can establish a broader link with the surrounding world—the speech apparatus. We should turn to verbal reactions. But most curious are "certain facts" upon which the investigators stumbled in their work. The point is that the discrimination of the reflex was reached extremely slowly and difficultly in man and now *it turned out* (my emphasis, L. V.) that by influencing the object with corresponding suitable speech it was possible to create both inhibition and excitation of the conditional reflexes (Protopopov, 1923, p. 16).

In other words, the whole discovery comes down to the fact that with a human being we can verbally agree that after a certain signal he will withdraw his hand and after another he will not withdraw his hand! And the author is forced to make two statements that are important for us here.

1. "Undoubtedly in the future the reflexological investigations of man will primarily have to be carried out by means of secondary conditional reflexes" (Protopopov, 1923, p. 22). This means nothing other than the fact that awareness pops up even in the experiments of reflexologists and essentially changes the picture of behavior. If you chase away consciousness through the door, it will enter through the window.

2. The inclusion of these means of investigation into the reflexological methods merges them completely with the methods for the investigation of reactions, etc. established in experimental psychology a long time ago. This is also observed by Professor Protopopov, but he regards this coincidence as external and accidental. For us it is clear that the purely reflexological methods which have been successfully applied to dogs fail completely for the problems of human behavior.

* * *

It is extremely important to show, albeit in a few words, that, looked at from the viewpoint of the hypothesis presented here, all three spheres of the mind distinguished by empirical psychology—thought, feeling, and will—also display this character of conscious awareness, which is proper to them and can be easily reconciled with both the hypothesis and the methods that follow from it.

1. James' theory of emotions fully reveals the possibility of such an interpretation of the conscious awareness of feelings. The three usual elements—(A) the cause of the feeling, (B) the feeling itself, (C) its bodily manifestations—James rearranges in the following way: A–C–B. [37] I will not reiterate his well-known argumentation. I will just point out that with this argumentation we can fully explain (1) the reflex character of the feeling; the feeling as the system of reflexes A–B; (2) the secondary character of the conscious awareness of the feeling when one's own reaction serves as a stimulus for a new, internal reaction—B–C. What also becomes understandable is the biological importance of the feeling as a quick evaluating reaction of the whole organism to its own behavior, as an act of interest of the whole organism in the reaction, as an internal organizer of all behavior present at a given moment. I can add that Wundt's three-dimensional model of feeling[10]

is also essentially about this evaluative character of the emotion viewed as an echo of the whole organism to its own reaction. Whence the unrepeatability, the unique character of the course of emotions in each particular case.

2. The thought acts of empirical psychology also show their dual nature inasmuch as they take place consciously. Obviously psychology distinguishes two levels: the thought acts and the consciousness of these acts.

Particularly interesting in this area are the results of the exceedingly subtle self-observations of the Würzburg school, this pure "psychology of psychologists." One of the conclusions of these investigations establishes the inobservability of the thought act itself, which escapes perception. Self-observation here exhausts itself. We are at the very bottom of consciousness. The paradoxical conclusion that suggests itself is a certain unawareness of the thought act. The elements that are observed and found by us are surrogates of the thought rather than its essence: they consist of all sorts of scraps, shreds, scum.

Apropos this, Külpe[11] [1922, p. 312] says that

> we have experienced that the 'I' cannot be divided. We cannot completely surrender to our thoughts, immerse in them and observe these thoughts at the same time. [38]

But this means that consciousness cannot be directed at itself and that it is a secondary factor. We cannot think our thought, catch the mechanism of conscious awareness itself because it is not a reflex, i.e., it cannot become an object of experience, a stimulus for a new reflex. It is a transmission mechanism between the systems of reflexes. But as soon as the thought is completed, i.e., as soon as the reflex is formed, it can be consciously observed. "First one thing, then the other," as Külpe [1922, p. 312] says.

In this connection, Professor Krol' says in one of his articles that the new phenomena detected in higher processes of consciousness by the Würzburg investigations resemble Pavlov's conditional reflexes in a surprising way. [39] The spontaneity of thought, the fact that it is found ready-made, the complex feelings of activity and search, etc. speak, of course, in favor of this interpretation. The impossibility of observing thought speaks in favor of the mechanisms outlined here.

3. Finally, it is volition which best and most simply reveals the nature of this conscious awareness. The preliminary presence in consciousness of motor representations (i.e., secondary reactions to movements of the organs) clarifies the point. Each movement must first be carried out unconsciously. Then its kinesthesia (i.e., the secondary reactions) becomes the basis of its conscious awareness.[12] [40] Bair's experiments with ear movements illustrate this. The conscious awareness of the will also gives the illusion of two moments: I thought and I did. And here, in reality, two reactions are present—only in a reversed order: first the secondary, then the basic, primary one. Sometimes the process is more complicated, but the theory of the complex volitional act and its mechanism, complicated by motives, i.e., by the collision of several secondary reactions, is also in complete accordance with the ideas developed above.

But perhaps most important is that in light of these ideas we can clarify the development of consciousness from the moment of its birth, its origin in experience, its *secondary nature* and thus the fact that it is conditioned by the environment. Being determines consciousness—here this law can for the first time, after some elaboration, acquire precise psychological meaning and reveal the very mechanism of this determination.

6

In man, a group of reflexes easily stands out, which we should call the system of reversible reflexes. These are reflexes to stimuli that in turn can be created by man. The word that is heard is a stimulus. The word that is pronounced is a reflex that creates the same stimulus. Here the reflex is reversible, because the stimulus can become a reaction and vice versa. These reversible reflexes create the basis for social behavior and serve the collective coordination of behavior. In the whole multitude of stimuli one group clearly stands out for me, the group of social stimuli coming from people. It stands out because I myself can reconstruct these stimuli, because they very soon become reversible for me and thus determine my behavior *in another way* from all others. They make me comparable to another, identical to myself. The source of social behavior and consciousness also lies in speech in the broad sense of the word.

It is extremely important to state the idea here, albeit in passing, that if this is really so, then the mechanism of social behavior and the mechanism of consciousness are one and the same. Speech is, on the one hand, the system of the "reflexes of social contact" [41] and, on the other hand, the system of the reflexes of consciousness par excellence, i.e., an apparatus for the reflection of other systems.

The key to the problem of another person's Ego, of the knowledge of another person's mind lies here. The mechanism of knowledge of the self (self-consciousness) and knowledge of others is the same. The usual theories about the knowledge of another person's mind either accept that it cannot be known[13] [42], or they try to build a plausible mechanism with the help of various hypotheses. In the theory of *Einfühlung* and in the theory from analogy [43] the essence of such a mechanism is the same: we know others insofar as we know ourselves. When I know another person's anger, I reproduce my own anger. [44]

In reality it would be more correct to put it the other way around. We are conscious of ourselves because we are conscious of others and by the same method as we are conscious of others, because we are the same vis-à-vis ourselves as others are vis-à-vis us. I am conscious of myself only to the extent that I am another to myself, i.e., to the extent that I can again perceive my own reflexes as stimuli. In principle there is no difference in mechanism whatsoever between the fact that I can repeat aloud a word spoken silently and the fact that I can repeat a word spoken by another: both are reversible reflex-stimuli.

That is why the acceptance of the hypothesis proposed will lead directly to the sociologizing of all consciousness, to the acceptance that the social moment in consciousness is primary in time as well as in fact. The individual aspect is constructed as a derived and secondary aspect on the basis of the social aspect and exactly according to its model. [45]

Hence the dual nature of consciousness: the notion of a double is the picture of consciousness that comes closest to reality. It comes close to the differentiation into Ego and Id that Freud disclosed analytically. He says that

> in its relation to the Id the Ego is like a man on horseback, who has to hold in check the superior strength of the horse; with this difference, that the rider tries to do so with his own strength while the Ego uses borrowed forces. The analogy may be carried a little further. Often a rider, if he is not to be parted from his horse, is obliged to guide it where it wants to go; so in the same way the Ego is in the habit of transforming the Id's will into action as if it were its own. [46]

The development of the awareness of speech in deaf-mutes and partly the development of tactile reactions in blind persons beautifully confirms this idea of the identity of the mechanisms of consciousness and social contact and of the fact that consciousness is, as it were, social contact with oneself. In deaf-mutes, speech usually does not develop and gets stuck in the stage of the reflex cry, not because their speech centers are damaged but because the possibility of the reversibility of the speech reflex is paralyzed by the absence of hearing. Speech does not return as a reflex to the speaker himself. That is why it is unconscious and nonsocial. Deaf-mutes usually confine themselves to the conventional language of gestures, which introduces them to the narrow circle of the social experience of other deaf-mutes and develops their conscious awareness because of the fact that these reflexes return to the mute himself via the eye.

From the psychological viewpoint, the education of the deaf-mute lies in the reconstruction of or compensation for the damaged mechanism of the reversibility of reflexes. The mutes are taught to speak by reading the articulatory movements from the lips of the speaker and are taught to speak themselves by using the secondary kinesthetic stimuli which arise in speech-motor reactions. [47]

Here the most remarkable thing is that *conscious awareness of speech and social experience emerge simultaneously and completely in parallel.* Here we have, as it were, a specially arranged experiment of nature which confirms the basic thesis of this article. In a special work, I hope to demonstrate this more clearly and in more detail. The deaf-mute learns to become conscious of himself and his movements to the extent that he learns to become conscious of others. Here the identity of both mechanisms is strikingly clear and almost obvious.

* * *

Now we can bring together the members of the formula of human behavior that were written down in a preceding section. Obviously, historical and social experience do not represent different things from the psychological viewpoint as they cannot be separated in experience and are always given together. Let us combine them with the + sign. Their mechanism is entirely the same, as I tried to prove, as the mechanism of consciousness, because consciousness, too, must be regarded as a particular case of social experience. That is why both of these parts can easily be designated with the same index of doubled experience.

7

It seems extremely important and essential to me to point in the conclusion of this essay to the coincidence in conclusions that exists between the ideas developed here and James' brilliant analysis of consciousness. My ideas, which started from entirely different areas and which went entirely different roads, led to the same view that James presented in his speculative analysis. I am inclined to see this as a partial confirmation of my ideas. Already in *Psychology* he declared that "states of consciousness themselves are not verifiable facts" but rather a deeply rooted prejudice. The data of his brilliant self-observation convinced him of this.

> Whenever I try to become sensible of my thinking activity as such, what I catch is some bodily fact, an impression coming from my brow, or head, or throat, or nose. [48]

And in the article "Does consciousness exist?" he explained that the whole difference between consciousness and the world (between the reflex to a reflex and the reflex to a stimulus) resides merely in the context of the phenomena. In the context of the stimuli it is the world; in the context of my reflexes it is consciousness. Consciousness is merely the reflex of reflexes.

Thus, consciousness as a specific category, as a special type of being, is not found. It proves to be a very complex structure of behavior, in particular, the doubling of behavior, just as this is said of labor in the words used as the epigraph. James says that

> I am as confident as I am of anything that, in myself, the stream of thinking . . . is only a careless name for what, when scrutinized, reveals itself to consist chiefly of the stream of my breathing. The 'I think' which Kant said must be able to accompany all my objects, is the 'I breath' which actually does accompany them . . . thoughts in the concrete are made of the same stuff as things are. [49]

* * *

In this essay I have merely outlined, in a superficial and hurried manner, some very preliminary ideas. However, it seems to me that precisely with this must the work on the study of consciousness begin. Our science is now in such a condition that it is still very far from the concluding formula of a geometrical theorem which crowns the final argument—*what was to be proved*. For us it is still important to have in view *what precisely* we must prove, and then we may turn to the proof. First we have to state the problem and then we can solve it. [50]

The present essay should within its powers serve this statement of the problem.

Chapter 4

APROPOS KOFFKA'S ARTICLE ON
SELF-OBSERVATION
(INSTEAD OF A PREFACE) [*],[1]

The editors decided to include Koffka's article "Introspection and the method of psychology," printed below, in the present volume, reasoning that a correct understanding of contemporary psychological currents is a necessary condition for the building of a system of Marxist psychology. The developments in science have made it impossible to work on its problems in a relatively autonomous and isolated fashion in each different country. There is no bigger error in the understanding of the contemporary crisis in psychology than to limit it to the boundaries and frontiers of Russian scientific thought. This is how the representatives of our empirical psychology picture the situation. If you listen to them, all is stable and quiet in the West, just as in "mineralogy, physics, and chemistry," whereas here the Marxists all of a sudden started reforming our science. We repeat once again, it is impossible to present the real state of affairs in a more false and distorted light.

The orientation toward American militant behaviorism has been marked as the very beginning of the Russian crisis. For a beginning it was correct. It was necessary to conquer objective positions in psychology and to escape from the captivity of spiritualistic and idealistic subjectivism. But already now it is clear to everyone that Marxist psychology can *only to a certain point* follow the path of American behaviorism and Russian reflexology.

Being yesterday's allies in the general war against subjectivism and empiricism, they may turn out to be our enemies of tomorrow—in the struggle for the establishment of the foundations of the social psychology of societal man, for the liberation of the psychology of man from its biological captivity, and for the return of its meaning as an independent science rather than one of the chapters of comparative psychology. In other words, as soon as we turn to the construction of psychology as the science of the behavior of social man, rather than that of a higher mammal, the dividing line with yesterday's allies clearly takes shape.

The struggle is intensified and moves into a new stage. In order to manage it and to calculate each move it is necessary to bear in mind that the struggle does not develop against the background of the idyllic and peaceful landscape of "scientific" empiricism, but under the circumstances of a most intense and acute war in which everything alive in psychology is involved. The present situation of the

*First published as Vygotsky, L. S. (1926). Po povodu stat'i K. Koffka o samonabljudenii (Vmesto predislovija). In K. N. Kornilov (Ed.), *Problemy sovremennoj psikhologii* (pp. 176-178). Leningrad: Gosudarstvennoe Izdatel'stvo.

81

psychological science resembles a pastorale least of all. Everything is quiet at the Shipka [1], but only for those who see nothing. In Western psychology, in particular, such devastating critical work has been carried out that the naive and happy, pre-critical empiricism that we are presented with seems something antediluvian in European science.

Professor Lange (1914, p. 42) summed up the achievements of psychology and ascertained that "the psychologist of our days resembles Priam sitting on the ruins of Troy." He constantly speaks of the crisis of psychology as resembling an earth-quake that "instantly destroyed a seemingly flourishing city" and compares the fall of association psychology with the fall of alchemy. Indeed, the crisis began with the fall of associationism. Since then the firm ground has been pulled from under scientific psychology's feet and the earthquake started. Today we witness an exceed-ingly interesting and instructive *change of direction* of the crisis and the main strug-gling forces. While the beginning of the European crisis was marked by a strengthening of the idealistic and subjectivistic aspect (Husserl,[2] Meinong [2], the Würzburg school), the crisis now takes exactly the opposite direction.

Professor Evergetov [3] says that

> psychology and its method . . . become (and already have become) materialistic in the most precise meaning of that word.

Even if this is not entirely correct it doubtlessly points in the right direction. Psy-chology is becoming materialistic although, perhaps, it will still more than once get stuck in the idealistic swamp. Psychology is obviously divided into two currents. One obviously rests on Bergsonism and emphasizes and straightens the line of spiri-tualism in psychology, the other obviously fights its way to a monistic and materi-alistic construction of a biological psychology.

It is necessary to understand this scientific struggle which is now taking place in Western psychology correctly. We plan to publish the most important fundamen-tal works characteristic of each current in the Russian language and to present an overview of contemporary psychological currents in the West in one of the next volumes. [4] We begin with the most influential and interesting of all currents, so-called *Gestalt-psychologie*, of which Kurt Koffka, the author of the article published below, is one of the most prominent representatives. We do not intend to explain and evaluate this theory in this note and confine ourselves to some brief remarks.

Gestaltpsychologie (the theory of form, the psychology of form, structural psy-chology, as it is usually translated into other languages) has emerged over the course of the last 10 years. It has long since transcended the boundaries of the experi-mental investigation of the perception of form, with which it began and which to the present day forms its main psychological content. It aspires to become a general psychological theory as Koffka says in another article. It extends its conclusions to comparative psychology and child psychology, to social psychology and to all "re-lated sciences" and attempts to re-create their foundations. In its quality of a new psychological theory the new theory opposes empirical traditional (associationist and Würzburg) psychology on the one hand and *behaviorism* on the other hand. It is precisely as a new current that this theory has been attracting attention in all countries: you will find articles about it in French, English, American, and Spanish journals, not to mention the German ones. The sheer fact that *Gestaltpsychologie* opposes empiricism and naive behaviorism and attempts to find synthetic methods already makes this current an extremely valuable ally in *quite a number of issues*. This does not mean that this alliance will be long-lasting or stable or that it is a bloc of principle. Even now we can point to a number of clear points of divergence between this theory and ours. In Koffka's article, the reader will find a presentation of the most important critical and positive views of this school. We will mention its points of agreement with Marxist psychology and leave a detailed critique and assessment for another time.

1. *The monistic materialism of the new system.* Mind and behavior, "the internal and the external" in Köhler's terminology, the phenomenal and bodily reactions [Koffka, 1924, p. 153] do not represent two different heterogeneous areas. "What is internal is external as well" (Köhler). [5] The new theory assumes the fundamental identity of the laws that form the "wholes" (*Gestalten*) in physics, physiology, and the mind. Accepting the dialectical principle of the transition of quality into quantity, the new theory applies it to the explanation of the qualitative diversity of experience (of phenomena). Conscious processes are no longer declared to be the only subject matter of investigation; they themselves are understood as parts of larger psychophysiological integral processes. Here the "psychical phenomena" of empirical psychology definitely lose their unique and isolated meaning. Mind is regarded as the "phenomenal side of behavior," as its constituent part.

2. *The synthetic and functional methods of investigation.* Accepting the unity, but not the identity of the "internal" and "external" in behavior, the psychologists of the new school harshly reject both analyzing self-observation, which in itself cannot be a method of psychology and never forms its main method, and Watson's extreme form of naive objectivism. While they fully accept the whole series of accusations against introspection advanced by behaviorism, they consider it a mistake to disregard the "internal side of behavior" (Koffka) completely. The new methodological approach attempts to ground a functional, subjective–objective method which covers both the descriptive[3] (descriptive–introspective) and the functional (objective–reactological) viewpoint.

3. *Points of divergence.* Although *Gestaltpsychologie* and we doubtlessly show considerable overlap in what regards the elaboration of the subject matter and method of our science, we cannot close our eyes to the points of divergence that exist between both systems and that will grow as both currents develop. But for us this does not depreciate the new current for one bit. We do not at all expect to find a finished system of Marxist psychology in Western science. It would be almost a miracle if it emerged there. But these points of divergence only serve to wet the edge of the new science. We have learned a lot in the struggle with empiricism. We come to a much clearer understanding if we dispense with naive "behaviorism." We shall, probably, sharpen more than one thesis of Marxist psychology in the debate with *Gestalttheorie* and by criticizing it. The critique, evidently, will have to deal with such issues as the attempt of the new theory to avoid vitalism and mechanism; with the excessive tendency to obliterate the difference between the problems of the mind and the theoretical constructions and data of the newest physics; with the absence of a social viewpoint; with the "intuitive" theory of consciousness—and so forth and so on. But let us not forget that the fact itself of the emergence of such a current as *Gestaltpsychologie* in the West doubtlessly points to the fact *that the objective immanent driving forces of the development of psychological science act in the same direction as the Marxist reform of psychology.* To see this we just have to stop looking at the developing crisis in psychology through the narrow window of our debate with the empiricists and view it on the scale of international science.

Chapter 5

THE INSTRUMENTAL METHOD IN PSYCHOLOGY[*,1]

1. In the behavior of man we encounter quite a number of artificial devices for mastering his own mental processes. By analogy with technical devices these devices can justifiably and conventionally be called psychological tools or instruments (internal technique in Claparède's terminology,[2] modus operandi according to Thurnwald). [1]

2. This analogy, like any analogy, cannot be carried through to the very end until all features of both concepts coincide. Therefore, we cannot expect beforehand that we will find each and every feature of a labor tool in these devices. The analogy may be justified if it is correct in the main, central, most essential feature of the two concepts that are being compared. Such a decisive feature is the role these devices play in behavior, which is analogous to the role of a tool in labor.

3. Psychological tools are artificial formations. By their nature they are social and not organic or individual devices. They are directed toward the mastery of [mental] processes—one's own or someone else's—just as technical devices are directed toward the mastery of processes of nature.

4. The following may serve as examples of psychological tools and their complex systems: language, different forms of numeration and counting, mnemotechnic techniques, algebraic symbolism, works of art, writing, schemes, diagrams, maps, blueprints, all sorts of conventional signs, etc.

5. By being included in the process of behavior, the psychological tool modifies the entire course and structure of mental functions by determining the structure of the new instrumental act, just as the technical tool modifies the process of natural adaptation by determining the form of labor operations.

6. In addition to natural acts and processes of behavior we must distinguish artificial, or instrumental, functions and forms of behavior. The former emerged and developed into special mechanisms in the process of evolutionary development and are shared by man and higher animals. The latter represent later acquisitions of mankind. They are the product of historical development and form a specifically human form of behavior. In this sense, Ribot [1888] called involuntary attention natural and voluntary attention artificial. He viewed voluntary attention as the product of historical development (cf. Blonsky's view).

7. We should not conceive of artificial (instrumental) acts as supernatural or meta-natural acts constructed in accordance with some new, special laws. Artificial acts are natural as well. They can, without remainder, to the very end, be decom-

---

*Not published during Vygotsky's life. Based on a manuscript found in his private archives.

posed and reduced to natural ones, just like any machine (or technical tool) can, without remainder, be decomposed into a system of natural forces and processes.

What is artificial is the combination (construction) and direction, the substitution and utilization of these natural processes. The relation between instrumental and natural processes can be clarified with the following scheme—a triangle.

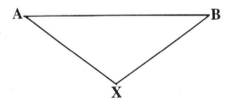

In natural memory a direct associative (conditional reflex) connection A–B is established between two stimuli A and B. In artificial, mnemotechnic memory of the same impression, by means of a psychological tool X (a knot in a handkerchief, a mnemonic scheme) instead of the direct connection A–B, two new ones are established: A–X and X–B. Just like the connection A–B, each of them is a natural conditional reflex process, determined by the properties of the brain tissue. What is new, artificial, and instrumental is the fact of the replacement of one connection A–B by two connections: A–X and X–B. They lead to the same result, but by a different path. What is new is the artificial direction which the instrument gives to the natural process of establishing a conditional connection, i.e., the active utilization of the natural properties of brain tissue.

8. This scheme explains the essence of the instrumental method and the distinctive nature of the viewpoint on behavior and its development that it provides. This method does not negate a single natural scientific method for the study of behavior and nowhere intersects with it. From one viewpoint, we can look at the behavior of man as a complex system of natural processes and try to comprehend the laws governing them, just as we can examine the action of any machine as a system of physical and chemical processes. We can also look at the behavior of man from the viewpoint of his use of his natural mental processes and the methods of this use and try to comprehend how man utilizes the natural properties of his brain tissue and masters the processes that take place in it.

9. The instrumental method proposes a new viewpoint on the relation between a behavioral act and an external phenomenon. Within the general relationship stimulus–response (stimulus–reflex), proposed by natural scientific methods in psychology, the instrumental method distinguishes a twofold relation between behavior and an external phenomenon. An external phenomenon (a stimulus) in one case can play the role of the object toward which the act of behavior is directed. This act strives to solve some problem facing the person (to memorize, compare, choose, assess, consider something, etc.). In another case, the external phenomenon can play the role of a means by means of which we direct and realize the psychological operations (memorizing, comparing, selecting, etc.) necessary for the solution of the problem. In these two cases the psychological nature of the relation between the behavioral act and the external stimulus is essentially and fundamentally different and the stimulus determines, causes and organizes the behavior completely differently, in a completely distinctive way. In the first case it would be correct to call the stimulus the object, but in the second case it is the psychological tool of the instrumental act.

10. At the basis of the instrumental method lies a certain discovery. What makes the instrumental act particularly unique is the simultaneous presence of stim-

uli of both kinds, i.e., of object and tool at the same time, each of which plays a qualitatively and functionally distinct role. [2] Thus, in the instrumental act a new middle term is inserted between the object and the mental operation directed at it: the psychological tool, which becomes the structural center or focus, i.e., the aspect that functionally determines all the processes that form the instrumental act. Any behavioral act then becomes an intellectual operation.

11. The inclusion of a tool in the behavioral process, first, sets to work a number of new functions connected with the use and control of the given tool; second, abolishes and makes unnecessary a number of natural processes, whose work is [now] done by the tool; third, modifies the course and the various aspects (intensity, duration, order, etc.) of all mental processes included in the instrumental act, replacing some functions with others, i.e., it recreates, reconstructs the whole structure of behavior just like a technical tool recreates the entire system of labor operations. Mental processes, taken as a whole, form a complex structural and functional unity. They are directed toward the solution of a problem posed by the object, and the tool dictates their coordination and course. They form a new whole—the instrumental act.

12. From the viewpoint of natural scientific psychology, the whole instrumental act can be reduced without remainder to a system of stimulus–response connections. The nature of the instrumental act as a whole is determined by its unique internal structure, the most important aspects of which have been enumerated above (the stimulus–object and the stimulus–tool, the recreation and combination of responses by means of a tool). For natural scientific psychology the instrumental act is a formation with a complex structure (a system of reactions), a synthetic whole. At the same time, from the viewpoint of the instrumental method, it is the simplest piece of behavior with which research is dealing: an elementary unit of behavior.

13. The most essential feature distinguishing the psychological tool from the technical one is that it is meant to act upon mind and behavior, whereas the technical tool, which is also inserted as a middle term between the activity of man and the external object, is meant to cause changes in the object itself. The psychological tool changes nothing in the object. It is a means of influencing one's own mind or behavior or another's. It is not a means of influencing the object. Therefore, in the instrumental act we see activity toward oneself, and not toward the object.

14. There is nothing in the unique direction of the psychological tool that contradicts the nature itself of this concept, since in the process of activity and labor man "himself confronts the material provided by nature as a force of nature" [Marx, 1890/1981, p. 192]. In this process, by acting on external nature and changing it, he at the same time also changes his own nature and acts upon it. [3] He subordinates the workings of his own natural forces. The subordination to oneself of this "force of nature," i.e., of one's own behavior, is a necessary condition of labor. In the instrumental act man masters himself from the outside—via psychological tools.

15. It goes without saying that one stimulus or another does not become a psychological tool by virtue of the physical properties used in a technical tool (the hardness of steel, etc.). In the instrumental act, the psychological properties of the external phenomenon are used. The stimulus becomes a psychological tool by virtue of its use as a means of influencing the mind and behavior. Therefore, any tool is without fail a stimulus: if it were not a stimulus, i.e., did not have the capacity to influence behavior, it could not be a tool. But not every stimulus is a tool.

16. The application of psychological tools enhances and immensely extends the possibilities of behavior by making the results of the work of geniuses available to everyone (cf. the history of mathematics and other sciences).

17. By its very essence the instrumental method is a historical-genetic method. It introduces a historical viewpoint in the investigation of behavior: behavior can be understood only as the history of behavior (Blonsky). The main areas of investigation in which the instrumental method can be successfully applied are (a) the area of social-historical and ethnic psychology, which studies the historical development of behavior, its various stages and forms; (b) the area of investigation of the higher, historically developed mental functions—higher forms of memory (cf. investigations of mnemotechnics), attention, verbal or mathematical thinking, etc.; (c) child and educational psychology. The instrumental method has nothing in common (other than its name) with the theory of instrumental logic of Dewey[3] and other pragmatists. [4]

18. The instrumental method studies the child not only as a developing, but also as an educable being. It sees in this the essential distinguishing feature of the history of the human young. Education may be defined as the artificial development of the child. Education is the artificial mastery of natural processes of development. Education not only influences certain processes of development, but restructures all functions of behavior in a most essential manner.

19. Whereas the theory of natural endowment (Binet) seeks to understand the process of the natural development of the child, regardless of school experience and the influence of education [5] (i.e., studies the child independently of the fact that he is a schoolboy in a certain grade), the theory of school fitness or giftedness seeks to understand only the process of school development (i.e., studies the schoolboy of the given grade independently of what kind of child he is). The instrumental method studies the process of natural development and education as a unified alloy and aims to reveal how all the natural functions of the given child are restructured at the given level of education. The instrumental method seeks to present the history of how the child in the process of education accomplishes what mankind accomplished in the course of the long history of labor, i.e., how he "changes his own nature . . . develops the forces slumbering in it and subordinates the play of forces to his own power" [Marx, 1890/1981, p. 192]. If the first method studies the child independently of the schoolboy and the second studies the schoolboy independently of his other properties as a child, then the third studies the given child as a schoolboy.

The development of many natural mental functions during childhood (memory, attention) either does not appear to any noticeable extent at all or takes place on such an insignificant scale that it cannot possibly account for the whole, vast difference between the activity of the child and the adult. [6] In the process of development the child arms and re-arms himself with widely varying tools. The child of the highest grade differs from the child of the lowest grade also in the level and character of his armament, his instrumentarium, i.e., in the degree of mastery of his own behavior. The main periods of development are the nonverbal and verbal periods.

20. Differences in children's types of development (giftedness, defectiveness) appear to a great extent connected with the type and character of instrumental development. The inability to utilize one's own natural functions and the mastery of psychological tools fundamentally determine the whole pattern of child development.

21. Investigation of the condition and structure of the child's behavior requires exposing his instrumental acts and taking account of the reform of the natural functions that enter into a given act. The instrumental method is a means of investigating behavior and its development which discloses the psychological tools in behavior and the structure of the instrumental acts created by them.

22. The mastery of a psychological tool and, through it, of one's own natural mental function, always lifts the given function to a higher level, enhances and broadens its activity, recreates its structure and mechanism. Furthermore, the natural mental processes are not eliminated. They join the instrumental act, but they turn out to be functionally dependent in their structure on the instrument being used.

23. The instrumental method provides the principle and method for the psychological study of the child. This method can make use of any methodology, i.e., technical methods of investigation: the experiment, observation, etc.

24. The investigations of memory, counting, and concept formation in schoolchildren, carried out by the author and on his initiative, may serve as examples of the application of the instrumental method. [7]

Chapter 6

ON PSYCHOLOGICAL SYSTEMS[*,1]

What I plan to report here grew out of our joint experimental work and represents a certain, not yet completed, attempt to theoretically interpret what was determined in quite a number of investigations. [1] The main goal of these investigations was to draw together two lines of investigation—the genetic and the pathological one. Thus, this attempt (not formally, but according to its essence) can be regarded as an attempt to point out the new problems that emerge here. These emerge because we now compare a number of psychological problems which have thus far been investigated in the plane of the development of functions with the same problems stated in the plane of the loss of these functions and select what may have practical value for the investigations of our laboratory.

As what I plan to report surpasses in complexity the system of concepts with which we have operated thus far, I first want to repeat an explanation with which the majority of us are acquainted. When we were accused of complicating some extremely simple problems we always replied that we should rather be accused of the opposite, namely that we explained a problem of tremendous complexity in an extremely simplified manner. And now I will deal with a number of phenomena that we interpret as more or less understandable or primitive and try to make you understand that their complexity is greater than it seemed before.

I would like to remind you that this movement toward a more and more complex conception of the problems we study is not accidental, but follows from the specific viewpoint of our research. As you know, our basic viewpoint on the higher functions is that we place these functions in a different relation to the personality than the primitive psychological functions. When we say that man masters his behavior, directs it, then we are using more complex phenomena, such as personality, to explain simple things (voluntary attention or logical memory). We were accused of failing to take account of the concept of personality, which is present in every explanation of the psychological functions with which we are dealing. This is indeed true. And this is the way absolutely all scientific investigations are conducted. According to Goethe's[2] beautiful expression [2], we turn the problem into a postulate, i.e., we first formulate a hypothesis, which is then tested and verified in the process of experimental investigation.

I would like you to bear in mind that however primitive and simple we may have interpreted the higher psychological functions, we nevertheless resorted to some more complex, more integral concept of the personality. We attempted to explain such relatively simple functions as voluntary attention or logical memory

*Not published before. Based on a manuscript found in Vygotsky's private archives.

from their relation to this integral personality. Hence it is understandable that as the work moved forward we had to fill that gap, to justify the hypothesis and gradually transform it into experimentally verified knowledge. We had to select elements from our investigations that would fill the gap between the genetically postulated personality that stands in a special relation to these functions and the relatively simple mechanism offered in our explanation.

In earlier investigations we already stumbled across the theme about which I plan to speak. When I called my talk "On psychological systems," I was thinking of the complex connections that develop between different functions in the process of development and that dissolve or undergo pathological change in the process of dissolution.

When we studied thinking and speech in childhood we saw that the process of development of these functions does not amount to a change within each function. What is changed is chiefly the original link between these functions, the link which is characteristic of phylogenesis in the zoological plane and of child development in the earliest stage. This link and this relation do not remain the same in the further development of the child. Therefore, one of the fundamental ideas in the area of the development of thinking and speech is that there can be no fixed formula which determines the relationship between thinking and speech and which is suitable for all stages of development and forms of loss. In each stage of development and in each form of loss we see a unique and changing set of relations. My report is dedicated to this very theme. Its main (and extremely simple) idea is that in the process of development, and in the historical development of behavior in particular, it is not so much the functions which change (these we mistakenly studied before). Their structure and the system of their development remain the same. What is changed and modified are rather the relationships, the links between the functions. New constellations emerge which were unknown in the preceding stage. That is why intra-functional change is often not essential in the transition from one stage to another. It is inter-functional changes, the changes of inter-functional connections and the inter-functional structure which matter.

The development of such new flexible relationships between functions we will call *a psychological system*, giving it all the content that is usually attached to this, unfortunately, too broad concept.

A few words about the arrangement of my material. That the course of an investigation and the course of its exposition are often in opposition is well known. It would be easier for me to discuss all the material theoretically and not to speak about the investigations carried out in the laboratory. But I cannot do this as I do not yet have a general theoretical view that encompasses all the material and I would consider it a mistake to theorize prematurely. I will simply present a certain ladder of facts in a systematic manner, proceeding from below upwards. I confess beforehand that I am still unable to encompass the whole ladder of facts with a real theoretical conception and cannot yet logically arrange the facts and the links between them. By going from below upwards I only wish to show the tremendous material that has been gathered, material that is often encountered in other authors, and show its connection to the problems for the solution of which this material plays a primary role. I will, in particular, draw on the problems of aphasia and schizophrenia in pathology and the problem of adolescence in genetic psychology. Theoretical considerations I will allow myself to state in passing. It seems to me that at the present time we can do no more than that.

1

Allow me to begin with the most elementary functions—with the relationships between sensory and motor processes. In contemporary psychology the problem of these relationships is stated in a completely new way. Whereas for the older psychology the problem was what kind of associations develop between them, for contemporary psychology the problem is the reverse: how does the division [3] between them develop. Both theoretical considerations and experiments show that the sensorimotor system is an integral psychophysiological whole. This view is defended in particular by the Gestalt psychologists (Goldstein[3] from the neurological viewpoint, Köhler, Koffka and others from the viewpoint of psychology). I cannot mention all considerations that are given in favor of this view. I will just say that, indeed, when we carefully study the experimental investigations dedicated to this problem, we see to what extent the motor and sensory processes represent an integral whole. Thus, the ape's motor solution of a problem is nothing other than a dynamic continuation of the same processes, of the same structure formed in the sensory field. You know the convincing attempt by Köhler and others to prove, in contrast to Bühler's opinion, that apes solve a task not in the intellectual, but in the sensory field. This is confirmed in Jaensch's[4] [1923] experiments, which proved that in eidetics the movement of a tool towards the goal is accomplished in the sensory field. Therefore, the sensory field is not fixed and a problem can be fully solved in the sensory field.

When you pay attention to this process you will see that the idea of a sensorimotor unity is fully confirmed as long as we restrict ourselves to zoological material, or when we are dealing with a very young child or adults in whom these processes are closest to the affective ones. But when we proceed further a striking change sets in. The unity of the sensorimotor processes, the link which makes the motor process a dynamic continuation of a structure established in the sensory field, is destroyed: the motor system becomes relatively independent of the sensory processes and the sensory processes become disconnected from the direct motor impulses. Between them more complex relations develop. These considerations throw new light on Luria's [1928a, b] experiments with the combined motor method. Most interesting is that the direct link between the motor and sensory impulses is restored as soon as the process returns to an affective form. When a person does not realize what he is doing and acts under the influence of an affective reaction, you may again infer his internal state and the character of his perception from his motor behavior. You can observe the return to a structure characteristic of early stages of development.

When an experimenter who conducts an experiment with an ape stands with his back toward some situation and facing the ape and does not see what the ape sees but merely sees its actions, he is able to infer what the experimental animal sees. This is exactly what Luria calls the combined motor method. By the character of the movements we may, as it were, infer the curve of the internal reactions. This is characteristic of early stages of development. In the child the direct connection of motor and sensory processes very often dissolves. For the time being (and disregarding what follows) we may conclude that the motor and sensory processes acquire a relative (psychological) independence from each other (relative in the sense that this unity, this direct connection which characterizes the first stage of development, ceased to exist). The results of the investigations of lower and higher forms of the motor system in twins (concerning the separation of hereditary factors and factors of cultural development) lead to the conclusion that, also from the viewpoint of differential psychology, the motor behavior of adults is, evidently, not characterized by its orginal constitution, but by those new connections, those new relationships which develop between the motor system and the other areas of the personality, the other functions.

Continuing this idea, I now come to perception. In the child perception acquires a certain independence. The child can, in contrast to the animal, contemplate a situation for some time and, knowing what has to be done, not act immediately. We will not discuss *how* this happens, but follow *what* happens with perception. We have seen that perception develops in the same way as do thinking and voluntary attention. What is happening here? As we said, some process of "ingrowing" of methods takes place by means of which the child who perceives an object compares it with another object, etc. This investigation led us into a blind alley and other investigations have shown with full clarity that perception develops further by entering into a complex synthesis with other functions, particularly speech. This synthesis is so complex that in none of us, except in pathological cases, can all primary regularities of perception be distinguished. I will give a very simple example. When we investigate the perception of a picture, as did Stern [1927],[5] we see that in relating the content of the picture the child mentions isolated objects. But when he acts out what is shown in the picture he renders the whole of the integral picture and does not touch upon the isolated parts. In Kohs' [4] experiments, where perception is investigated in more or less pure form, the child, and the deaf-mute in particular, constructs figures fully according to their structure, reproduces the corresponding drawing or a colored blot. But as soon as speech interferes in the designation of these cubes we first get a disorganized compound without structure: the child puts the cubes next to each other but does not order them into a structural whole.

In order to evoke pure perception in us, we must be put in certain artificial conditions, and this is the most difficult methodological task in experiments with adults. If it is necessary in an experiment to present the subject a meaningless figure and you do not just offer him an object but a geometrical figure as well, then to perception is added knowledge (for example, that it is a triangle). And in order to present not a thing but "material for vision," as Köhler says, we must be shown a complex, confusing, and meaningless combination of things or an object with such maximal speed that only a visual impression is left of it. Under other conditions we cannot return to such immediate perception.

In aphasia, in serious forms of loss of intellectual functions and especially perception (observed, in particular, by Pötzl [1928]), we see that perception becomes to some extent again separated from that complex in which it proceeds in us. I cannot put this more simply and briefly other than by pointing out that the per ception of contemporary man became essentially part of visual thinking, because when I perceive I at the same time see which object I perceive. The knowledge of the object comes simultaneously with perception and you know what efforts are necessary to separate the one from the other in the laboratory! Having separated itself from the motor system, perception continues to develop in a nonintrafunctional way: development takes place mainly because perception acquires new relationships with other functions, enters into complex combinations with new functions, and begins to act with them as some new united system which is rather difficult to subdivide and whose dissolution we can only observe in pathology.

When we proceed somewhat further, we will see that the original link which characterizes the relation between the functions dissolves and a new link develops. This is a general phenomenon which we encounter constantly and which we do not notice because we do not pay attention to it. It is observed in our simplest experimental practice. I shall give two examples.

The first one regards absolutely every mediated process, for example, the memorization of words by means of pictures. Already here we stumble upon the shift of functions. The child who memorizes a series of words by means of pictures does not only rely on memory, but also on imagination and the ability to detect similarities and differences. The process of memorization, thus, does not depend on natural factors of memory, but on a number of new functions which take the place of immediate memorization. Both in the work of Leont'ev[6] (1931) and in the work of Zankov[7] [1935] it was shown that the development of the general factors of memorization proceeds along different curves. We observe a reform of the natural functions, their substitution and the appearance of a complex alloy of thinking and memory which in empirical praxis received the name of logical memory.

Zankov's experiments drew my attention to the following remarkable fact. It turned out that in mediated memorization it is thinking which is most important and that, viewed from the perspective of genetic and differential psychology, people do not differ according to the properties of their memory but according to the properties of their logical memory. This thinking is greatly different from thinking in the actual sense of the word. When you suggest to an adult that he memorize 50 words by means of cards, he will try to establish mental relations between the sign (the card) and that which he memorizes. This thinking does not at all correspond to the actual thinking of the person. It is absurd, the person is not interested in whether what he memorizes is correct or incorrect, plausible or not. When we memorize none of us ever thinks as he would while solving a problem. All basic criteria, factors, links, characteristic of thinking as such are completely distorted in thinking aimed at memorization. Theoretically, such a change of all functions of thinking in memorizing would be expected in advance. It would be absurd if here we would stick to all the links and structures of thinking necessary for the solution of practical or theoretical problems. I repeat, not only memory changes when it marries, so to speak, thinking but thinking itself changes its functions and is no more the thinking we know from the study of logical operations. All structural connections, all relationships become changed, and this process of substitution of functions is the formation of a new system which I mentioned earlier.

When we go up one step and pay attention to the results of other investigations, we see still another regularity in the formation of new psychological systems. It brings us au courant and sheds light on the central question of my talk of today—the relationship of these new systems to the brain, to their physiological substrate.

When we studied the processes of the higher functions in children we came to the following staggering conclusion: each higher form of behavior enters the scene twice in its development—first as a collective form of behavior, as an interpsychological function, then as an intra-psychological function, as a certain way of behaving. We do not notice this fact, because it is too commonplace and we are therefore blind to it. The most striking example is speech. Speech is at first a means of contact between the child and the surrounding people, but when the child begins to speak to himself, this can be regarded as the transference of a collective form of behavior into the practice of personal behavior.

According to the beautiful formula of one psychologist [5], speech is not only a means to understand others, but also a means to understand oneself.

Turning to contemporary experimental studies, we can establish that Piaget[8] [1923, pp. 20/74-75] was the first to state and confirm the thesis that thinking in preschool children does not appear before the debate appears in their collective. [6] Children do not think at all until they can argue and adduce arguments. Leaving aside a number of factors, I will mention one conclusion which these authors give and which I change somewhat after my own fashion. Thinking, especially in the preschool age, appears as a transference of the situation of a debate inward, as a discussion with oneself. In the investigation of children's play by Groos[9] (1906) it was shown that the function of the children's collective in the control of behavior and its submission to the rules of games influences the development of attention as well.

But the following is for us of singular interest: each higher function was thus originally shared between two persons. It was a reciprocal psychological process. One process took place in my brain, the other in the brain of the one with whom I have an argument: "That is my place"—"No, mine"—"I occupied it first." The system of thinking is divided here between two children. The same in a dialogue: I speak—you understand me. Only later I begin to speak to myself. The child of preschool age fills hours on end with speech to himself. He develops new links, new relationships between functions, relationships that were not present in the original links between his functions.

This is of special, central significance for the mastery of one's own behavior. The study of the genesis of these processes shows that each volitional process is originally a social, collective, inter-psychological process. This is connected with the fact that the child masters the attention of others or, the other way round, begins to apply to himself those means and forms of behavior that originally were collective. The mother draws the child's attention to something. The child follows the instructions and pays attention to what she points out. Here we always have two separate functions. Then the child himself begins to direct his attention, himself plays the role of the mother vis-à-vis himself. He develops a complex system of functions that were originally shared. One person orders, the other carries out. Man orders and obeys himself. [7]

Experimentally I have been able to establish analogous phenomena in a girl whom I am observing. From everyday observations they are known to anyone. The child begins to command herself: "One, two, three, go!"—just as the adults commanded her before, and then she carries out her own command. A union of those functions that were originally shared by two persons thus emerges in the process of psychological development. The social origin of higher mental functions is a very important fact.

It is also remarkable that signs, whose significance seems to us to be so great in the history of cultural development (as is demonstrated by the history of their development), originally form means of contact, means to act upon others. When we regard its real origin, each sign is a means of contact, and we might say more broadly that it is a means of contact between certain mental functions of a social character. Transferred to the self, it is also a means of combining functions in oneself, and we will be able to demonstrate that without the sign the brain and the original connections cannot form such complex relations as they can due to speech.

The means of social contact are thus also basic means for the formation of the complex psychological links that emerge when these functions become individual functions and grow into a personal style of behavior.

If we go up another step, we see yet another interesting case of the formation of such links. We usually observe them in the child, most of all in play (the experiments of Morozova[10]) [8], when the child changes the meaning of an object. I will try to elucidate this with a phylogenetic example.

When you take a book on primitive man, you stumble across examples of the following type. The unique nature of primitive man's thinking often resides not in the fact that the functions that we have are not sufficiently developed, or that some function is not present, but these functions are, from our viewpoint, arranged in another way. One of the striking examples is the observation by Lévy-Bruhl[11] [1922, p. 184] concerning the Kaffir to whom the missionary suggests that he send his son to the missionary school. The situation is very complex and difficult for the Kaffir and as he does not wish to dismiss this suggestion openly, he says: "I will dream about it." Quite rightly, Lévy-Bruhl remarks that here we have a situation in which each of us would reply: "I will think it over." The Kaffir says: "I will dream about it." For him the dream fulfills the same function as thinking does for us. It is worthwhile dwelling on this example, because the laws of dreaming are in themselves, evidently, the same for the Kaffir and for us.

We have no reason to assume that the human brain underwent an essential biological evolution in the course of human history. We have no reason to assume that the brain of primitive man differed from our brain, was an inferior brain, or had a biological structure different from ours. All biological investigations lead us to assume that biologically speaking the most primitive man we know deserves the full title of man. The biological evolution of man was finished before the beginning of his historical development. [9] And it would be a flagrant mixing up of the concepts of biological evolution and historical development to try to explain the difference between our thinking and the thinking of primitive man by claiming that primitive man stands on another level of biological development. The laws of dreaming are the same everywhere, but the role which the dream fulfills is completely different and we will see that such a difference not only exists between, let us say, the Kaffir and us. The Roman believed in dreams as well, although he would not say in a difficult situation "I will dream about it,"—because he stood on another level of human development and would solve the matter, in the words of Tacitus,[12] "with arms and reason and not like a woman through a dream." The dream was a sign for him, an omen. The Roman did not begin something when he had had a bad dream about it. In the Roman, the dream had another structural connection with other functions.

Even if you turn to the Freudian neurotic, you again get a new relation to dreams. Extremely interesting is the remark of one of Freud's critics that Freud's discovery of the relation between the dream and sexual wishes, characteristic of the neurotic, is characteristic of the neurotic exactly "here and now." [10] For the neurotic the dream serves his sexual wishes, but this is no general law. It is a problem that is open to further investigation.

When you carry this still further, you see that dreams enter into completely new relations with a number of functions. This can also be observed with respect to quite a number of other processes. We see that thinking is at first, in the words of Spinoza [1677/1955, p. 187], the servant of the passions, but that man who has reason is the master of his passions.

The example of the dream of the Kaffir is much more than just a case of a dream. It is applicable to the formation of integral complex psychological systems.

I would like to draw your attention to one fundamental conclusion. It is remarkable that in the Kaffir the new system of behavior develops from certain ideological representations, from what Lévy-Bruhl and other French sociologists and psychologists call collective representations [11] about the dream. It was not the Kaffir himself who, in giving this answer, created such a system. This representation of the dream is part of the ideology of the tribe to which the Kaffir belongs. Such a relation toward dreams is characteristic of them. That is the way they solve complex questions of war, peace, etc. Here we have a psychological mechanism which directly developed from a certain ideological system, from a certain ideological meaning attached to some function. In quite a number of interesting American investigations, dedicated to half-primitive peoples, we see that as they begin to join in the European civilization and receive objects of European general use, they begin to take interest in them and to value the possibilities they bring with them. These investigations show that primitive people initially have a negative opinion about the reading of books. After they have received several very simple agricultural tools and have seen the connection between the reading of books and practice, they began to evaluate the white men's work differently.

The reappraisal of thinking and dreaming has no individual, but a social source. Now this interests us from yet another viewpoint. What we see here is that a new idea about dreaming emerges which was drawn by the person from the social environment in which he lives. We see how a new form of intra-individual behavior is created in such a system as the dream of the Kaffir.

We must note two points which we can use in our further argumentation. On the one hand, several new systems are not just linked with social signs but also with ideology and the meaning which some function acquires in the consciousness of people. On the other hand, new forms of behavior develop from the new content picked up by the person from the ideology of the surrounding environment.

2

When we go up yet another step in the study of those complex systems and relationships that are unknown in the early stages of development and develop relatively late, we arrive at a very complex system of changes of connections and the development of new ones. These changes take place on the path toward the development and formation of a new person in adolescence. Until now the shortcoming of our investigations was that we confined ourselves to early childhood and took little interest in adolescents. When I was faced with the necessity of studying the psychology of adolescence from the viewpoint of our investigations I was surprised at the extent to which this stage contrasts with childhood . . . [12] Here the essence of psychological development is not that the connections increase in number, but that they change.

The tremendous difficulty connected with the psychology of adolescence was caused by the investigation of the adolescent's thinking. Indeed, there is little in the speech of the 14- to 16-year-old adolescent that changes in the sense of the appearance of fundamentally new forms compared to what a child of 12 years old has at his disposal. We do not notice anything that might explain what goes on in the adolescent's thinking. Thus, memory and attention in adolescence hardly show anything new compared to school age. But when you take, in particular, the material worked upon by Leont'ev (1931), then you will see that characteristic of the adolescent age is the transition of these functions inward. What is external in the area of logical memory, voluntary attention, and thinking in the school child becomes internal in the adolescent. Research confirms that here a new aspect emerges. We see that the transition inward takes place because these external operations enter into a complex alloy and synthesis with a number of internal processes. Because of its internal logic the process cannot remain external. Its relation to all other functions becomes different, a new system is formed, strengthened and becomes internal.

I will give a very simple example. Memory and thinking in adolescence. We can notice (I simplify somewhat) the following interesting rearrangement here. You know what a colossal role memory plays in the thinking of the child before adolescence. For him to think means to a significant degree to rely on memory.

C. Bühler,[13] the German investigator, especially studied children's thinking when they solve some task and demonstrated that for children whose memory has fully developed to think means to remember concrete events. You remember Binet's classic immortal example [1890, p. 602] from his study of two girls. When he asked what is an omnibus he got the answer: "It is for many ladies. There are soft seats. You have three horses, they run; you hear 'din'" etc.

Now take adolescence. You will see that for the adolescent to remember means to think. Whereas the thinking of the pre-adolescent child rested on memory and to think meant to remember, for the adolescent memory rests mainly on thinking: to remember is first of all to search for what is needed in a certain logical order. This rearrangement of functions, the change of their relationships, the leading role of thinking in absolutely all functions as a result of which thinking turns out to be not just one function among a number of others, but a function which restructures and changes other psychological processes, we observe in adolescence.

3

Preserving the same order of exposition and proceeding from lower psychological systems to the formation of systems of an ever higher order, we arrive at the systems which form the key to all processes of development and loss: concept formation, a function which fully ripens and takes shape first in adolescence.

We cannot now present a complete theory of the psychological development of the concept, and I will just say that in psychological investigation the concept is (and this is the final result of our research) a psychological system of the same type as those of which I have been speaking.

Until now empirical psychology attempted to found the function of concept formation on some particular function—abstraction, attention, the isolation of features of memory, or the elaboration of certain images—and proceeded from the logical notion that each higher function has its analogue, its representation on a lower plane: memory and logical memory, direct and voluntary attention. The concept was regarded as a modified, elaborated image that was liberated from all superfluous parts, as a sort of polished representation. Galton[14] compared the mechanism of concepts with a collective photograph when a number of people are photographed on one plate—the common traits are emphasized, the accidental ones extinguish each other.

For formal logic the concept is the totality of features that have been selected and accentuated in their common aspects. For example, if we take the simplest concepts—Napoleon, Frenchman, European, man, animal, being, etc.—we get a series of more and more general concepts that are more and more impoverished in terms of the number of concrete features. The concept "Napoleon" is infinitely rich in concrete content. The concept "Frenchman" is already much poorer: not everything that applies to Napoleon applies to a Frenchman. The concept "man" is poorer still, etc. Formal logic considered the concept as the sum-total of features of the object taken from a group, as the totality of common features. The concept thus developed by impoverishing our knowledge of the object. Dialectical logic demonstrated that the concept is not such a formal schema. It is not the totality of features abstracted from the object. It yields much richer and more complete knowledge of the object.

Quite a number of psychological investigations, ours in particular, lead to a completely new statement of the problem of concept formation in psychology. The question as to how the concept, becoming ever more general, i.e., being applicable to an ever larger quantity of objects, becomes richer in content, and not poorer as formal logic thinks—this question receives an unexpected answer in the investigations. It is confirmed in the analysis of the development of concepts from the genetic viewpoint as compared to more primitive forms of our thinking. Research showed that when the subject solves a problem in which new concepts must be formed, the essence of the process that takes place resides in the establishment of connections. When the subject tries to find a number of other objects similar to a given object, he looks for connections between this object and the others. He does not, as in the collective photograph, move a number of features to the background. On the contrary, each attempt to solve the task consists of the formation of connections, and our knowledge of the object is enriched by the fact that we study it in connection with other objects.

I will give an example. Let us compare the direct image of a nine, for example, the figures on playing cards, and the number 9. The group of nine on playing cards is richer and more concrete than our concept "9," but the concept "9" involves a number of judgments which are not in the nine on the playing card; "9" is not divisible by even numbers, is divisible by 3, is 3^2, and the square root of 81; we connect "9" with the series of whole numbers, etc. Hence it is clear that psychologically speaking the process of concept formation resides in the discovery of the connections of the given object with a number of others, in finding the real whole. That is why a mature concept involves the whole totality of its relations, its place in the world, so to speak. "9" is a specific point in the whole theory of numbers with the possibility of infinite development and infinite combination which are always subject to a general law. Two aspects draw our attention: first, the concept is not a collective photograph. It does not develop by rubbing out individual traits of the object. It is the knowledge of the object in its relations, in its connections. Second, the object in the concept is not a modified image but, as contemporary psychological investigations demonstrate, a predisposition for quite a number of judgments. "When a person says 'mammal,' asks one of the psychologists [13], what does it mean psychologically speaking?" It means that the person can develop an idea and in the final analysis that he has a world view, for to determine the place of a mammal in the animal world and the place of the animal world in nature means to have an integral world view.

We see that the concept is a system of judgments brought into a certain lawful connection: the whole essence is that when we operate with each separate concept, we are operating with the system as a whole.

Piaget [1924] gave 12- to 13-year-old children problems in which they had to combine two features simultaneously—an animal having long ears and a short tail or short ears and a short tail. [14] The child solves the problems having only one feature in the field of his attention. He cannot operate with the concept as a system. He masters all features that make up the concept, but all of them separately; he does not master the synthesis in which the concept acts as a unified system. [15] In this sense, Lenin's [1929/1978, p. 160] remark on Hegel[15] is interesting. He says that even the simplest fact of generalization implies a confidence in the lawfulness of the external world of which the subject has not yet become consciously aware. When we make a very simple generalization, we know the things not as existing in themselves, but in a lawful connection and subordinated to a certain law. It is impossible to explain the problem of concept formation now, a problem that is infinitely fascinating and of central importance for contemporary psychology.

Only in adolescence does this function finally take shape. The child turns to thinking in concepts from another system of thinking, from the complex-like connections. [16] We may ask ourselves: what distinguishes the child's complex? First of all, the system of a complex is a system of ordered concrete connections and relationships to the object that rest mainly on memory. A concept is a system of judgments which involves a relation to the entire, broader system. Adolescence is the age when world view and personality take shape, when self-consciousness and coherent notions of the world develop. Thinking in concepts is at its basis. For us the whole experience of contemporary civilized mankind, the external world, the external reality and our internal reality are represented in a certain system of concepts. In concepts we find that unity of form and content which I mentioned above.

To think in concepts means to possess a certain ready-made system, a certain form of thinking which in no way predetermines the further content at which we arrive. Both Bergson[16] and the materialist think in concepts, both use the same form of thinking, although they reach diametrically opposed conclusions.

It is exactly in adolescence that the formation of all the systems is finished. This will become more clear when we turn to what for the psychologist is in a certain sense the key to adolescence: the psychology of schizophrenia.

Busemann introduced a very interesting distinction in the psychology of adolescence. It concerns three types of connections that exist between psychological functions. The primary connections are hereditary. Nobody will deny that directly modifiable connections between certain functions exist. An example is, say, the constitutional system of relations between emotional and intellectual mechanisms. Another system of connections is formed. These are connections established in the process of the meeting of external and internal factors, those connections that are imposed by the environment. We know how we can foster impudence and brutality or sentimentality in the child. These are secondary connections. And, finally, we have the tertiary connections, which develop in adolescence and which really characterize the personality from the genetic and differential perspective. These connections develop on the basis of self-consciousness. The already mentioned mechanism of the "dream of the Kaffir" belongs to them. When we consciously connect this function with other functions so that they form a unified system of behavior, this is because we become conscious of our dream and our relation to it.

Busemann views a radical difference between the psychology of the child and the adolescent in the following: what characterizes the child is a limitation to the psychological plane of direct action. Characteristic of the adolescent is self-consciousness, the ability to view oneself from the outside, reflection, the capacity not only to think but also to consciously grasp the grounds for this thinking.

The problems of schizophrenia and adolescence were connected more than once: the term "dementia praecox" testifies to this tendency. [17] And although in clinical terminology it lost its original meaning, even the most modern authors, like Kretschmer[17] in Germany and Blonsky here, defend the idea that adolescence and schizophrenia form the key to each other. They do this on the basis of external similarity, for all the traits that characterize adolescence are observed in schizophrenia as well.

What is vaguely present in adolescence is carried to an extreme in pathology. Kretschmer (1924) says even more boldly that from the psychological perspective a tempestuous process of sexual maturation cannot be distinguished from a mild form of schizophrenia. Seen from the outside there is some truth to this, but it seems to me that the very statement of the problem and the conclusions that the authors arrive at are false. When we study the psychology of schizophrenia these conclusions are not vindicated.

In actual fact schizophrenia and adolescence are inversely related. In schizophrenia we observe the dissolution of those functions which are formed in adolescence, and when they meet at a certain station [18] their movement is in completely opposite directions. Psychologically speaking, schizophrenia presents an enigmatic picture and even in the works of the best contemporary clinicians we do not find the explanation of the mechanism of symptom formation. It is impossible to demonstrate how these symptoms develop. The debates between the clinicians are about what is dominating—the affective dullness or the diaschisis proposed by Bleuler[18] (which gave rise to the name schizophrenia). However, the core of the matter is not so much in the changes of the intellectual and affective functions, but in the disturbance of the connections that exist.

Schizophrenia yields an enormous wealth of material for the theme about which I am speaking. I will try to present the most important material and show that all the diverse forms of schizophrenia spring from one source and have a certain internal process at their basis which may explain the mechanism of schizophrenia. The first thing that is lost in the schizophrenic is the function of concept formation. It is only later on that the oddities begin. The schizophrenic is characterized by affective dullness. In schizophrenics the relationship to their beloved wife, parents and children is changed. Classic is the description of dullness combined with irritability, the absence of any impulse combined with, as Bleuler [1911] correctly remarks, an unusually intensified affective life. When schizophrenia is accompanied by some other process, such as arteriosclerosis, the clinical picture changes acutely. The sclerosis does not enrich the emotions of the schizophrenic but only changes its main manifestations.

Together with the affective dullness and the impoverishment of emotional life we see that the schizophrenic's thinking begins to be merely determined by his affects (as Storch [1922] notes). It is one and the same disturbance—a change in the relationships between intellectual and affective life. Blondel[19] [1914] developed the clearest and most brilliant theory on the pathological changes of affective life. The essence of this theory is approximately as follows. In the diseased psychological process which comes to the fore (especially when there is no feeble-mindedness), we first see a dissolution of the complex systems that were acquired as the result of collective life, the dissolution of the systems that developed last of all. Ideas, feelings—they all remain the same but lose the functions they fulfilled in the complex system. Thus, if for the Kaffir the dream acquires new relations with other behaviors, then the original system will dissolve and the result will be disorder and unusual forms of behavior. In other words, the first thing we notice about psychological loss in the psychiatric clinic is the dissolution of those systems which, on the one hand, developed last and, on the other hand, were systems of a social origin.

This is particularly evident in schizophrenia, which is enigmatic in the sense that formally speaking the psychological functions are preserved: memory, orientation, perception, and attention do not show changes. Here orientation is preserved and when you cunningly question a patient who is hallucinating and claims that he is in a castle, then you will see that he very well knows where he really is. Characteristic of schizophrenia is that the formal functions as such are preserved but that the system dissolves. From this viewpoint, Blondel speaks of the schizophrenic's affective disorder.

The thinking that the surrounding environment imposes together with a system of concepts also involves our feelings. We do not simply feel—a feeling is consciously grasped as jealousy, anger, an offense, or an insult. When we say that we despise a certain person, this expression changes these feelings, because they enter into some connection with our thinking. Something happens with us that is similar to what happens in memory when it becomes an internal part of the process of thinking and begins to be called logical memory. Just as it is impossible for us to decide where perception of a surface ends and understanding that it is a certain object begins (in perception the structural particularities of the perceptual field and understanding are synthesized and fused), exactly in the same way do we not experience pure jealousy in our affects. We are always consciously aware of the connections expressed in the concepts.

The basis of Spinoza's[20] theory is as follows. He was a determinist and, in contrast to the stoics, claimed that man has power over his affects, that the intellect may change the order and connections of the passions and bring them into accord with the order and connections that are given in the intellect. Spinoza expressed a correct genetic relationship. In the process of ontogenetic development the human emotions get connected with general sets both in what regards the individual's self-consciousness and in what regards his knowledge of reality. My contempt for another person forms part of my appreciation of this person, of my understanding of him. And this is the complex synthesis in which our life proceeds. The historical development of affects or emotions resides mainly in the fact that the original connections become changed and that a new order and new connections develop.

We have said that, as Spinoza [1677/1955, p. 258] correctly said, the knowledge of our affect changes it and modifies it from a passive state to an active one. That I think about objects that exist outside myself does not change anything in them, but that I think about my affects, that I place them in other relationships to my intellect and other processes, changes much in my mental life. To put it more simply, our affects act in a complex system with our concepts and he who does not know that the jealousy of a man who is bound up by the Islamic concepts about women's fidelity and of a man who is bound up by a system of opposite conceptions about women's fidelity is different, does not understand that this feeling is historical, that it changes its essence in different ideological and psychological environments, although there undoubtedly remains a certain basic biological component on the basis of which this emotion develops.

Thus, complex emotions emerge only historically. They are combinations of relationships that develop under the conditions of historical life. In the process of development the emotions become fused. This conception we place at the basis of a theory that explains what goes on in the pathological dissolution of consciousness. Here these systems dissolve, which explains the schizophrenic's affective dullness. When the schizophrenic says "Aren't you ashamed, only a scoundrel acts that way," he remains completely cold. For him this is not the greatest insult. His affects have become detached and act separately from the system. Characteristic of the schizophrenic is also the opposite relation: the affects begin to change his thinking. His thinking is a thinking that serves emotional interests and needs.

To finish with schizophrenia, I want to say that in schizophrenia the functions that developed and formed a synthesis in adolescence dissolve. Here the complex systems dissolve, the affects return to their initial primitive state, lose their connection with thinking, and you will not be able to understand these affects by means of concepts. To a certain degree we return to a condition that exists in early stages of development when it is very difficult to elicit certain affects. To insult a young child is very easy, but to insult him by saying that decent people do not act like that is very difficult. Here the path is entirely different from ours. The same holds true for schizophrenia.

To summarize all this, I would like to say the following. The study of systems and their fate turns out to be instructive not just for the development and formation of mental processes, but also for the processes of loss. This study explains the extremely interesting processes of dissolution which we observe in the psychiatric clinic and which ensue without the gross loss of some functions, such as the function of speech in aphasics. It explains why mild brain damage can cause gross disorders. It explains the paradox of psychology that tabes and organic changes of the whole brain result in insignificant psychological changes whereas schizophrenia and reactive psychosis result in a full disarray of the behavior of the adult person. The key to understanding lies in a conception of psychological systems which do not directly develop from the connections of functions caused by brain development, but from those systems of which we have been speaking. Such psychological symptoms of schizophrenia as affective dullness, intellectual dissolution, and irritability here find their only explanation, their structural coherence.

I would like to end with the following. One of the three cardinal characteristics of schizophrenia is the characterological change which resides in the isolation from the social environment. The schizophrenic becomes more and more isolated and in extreme cases autistic. All the systems we mentioned are systems of social origin. As we said above, they reside in the social relation to oneself. They are characterized by the transfer of collective relationships into the personality. The schizophrenic who loses social relations vis-à-vis the surrounding persons, loses social relations vis-à-vis himself. As one of the clinicians very aptly said without elevating it onto a theoretical level, the schizophrenic not only stops understanding others and talking to them, he stops communicating with himself through speech. The dissolution of the person's socially acquired systems is another aspect of the loss of his external, inter-psychological relationships.

4

I will dwell on just two more issues.

The first is about the (for us) extremely important conclusion to be drawn from all that has been said about psychological systems and the brain. I have to reject the idea developed by Goldstein and Gelb that each higher psychological function has a direct physiological correlate in a function whose physiological structure is similar to its psychological structure. But first I will expound their idea. Goldstein and Gelb say that in the aphasic the function of thinking in concepts is disturbed, which corresponds to a basic physiological function. Already here Goldstein and Gelb contradict themselves, since they earlier in the same book [19] claim that the aphasic returns to a system of thinking characteristic of primitive man. If one of the aphasic's basic physiological functions is damaged and he regresses to that stage of thinking on which stands primitive man, then we must conclude that primitive man does not have that basic physiological function that we possess. That is, a new and basic function develops without a morphological change of the structure of the brain, a function which does not exist in primitive stages of development. What is the basis for the assumption that such a radical reform of the human brain took place in the course of a few thousand years? Already here Goldstein's and Gelb's theory stumbles upon an insurmountable difficulty. But there is also some truth to it. All complex psychological systems—both the dream of the Kaffir, the concept and the person's self-consciousness—ultimately are products of a certain brain structure. Nothing can be isolated from the brain. The whole question is *what* it is in the brain which physiologically corresponds to thinking in concepts.

In order to explain its development in the brain it suffices to assume that the brain contains the conditions and possibilities for a combination of functions, a new synthesis, new systems which do not at all have to be structurally engraved beforehand. I think that all of contemporary neurology leads us to this assumption. More and more we see the infinite diversity and incompleteness of brain functions. It is much more correct to assume that the brain contains enormous possibilities for the development of new systems. This is the fundamental premise. It solves a question that is related to Lévy-Bruhl's work. In the latest discussion of the French philosophical society, Lévy-Bruhl said that primitive man thinks in another way than we do. Does this mean that he has a different brain than we do? Or must we assume that in connection with the new function the brain changed biologically? Or that the spirit merely uses the brain as a tool, consequently, one tool–many uses, and thus it is the spirit which develops and not the brain?

In actual fact, it seems to me that by introducing the concept of psychological system in the form we discussed, we get a splendid possibility of conceiving the real connections, the real complex relationships that exist.

To a certain degree this also holds true for one of the most difficult problems—the localization of higher psychological systems. So far they have been localized in two ways. The first viewpoint considered the brain as a homogeneous mass and rejected the idea that the different parts are not equivalent and play different roles in the formation of psychological functions. This viewpoint is manifestly untenable. Therefore, henceforth it was tried to deduce the functions from different brain parts, distinguishing, for example, a practical area, etc. The areas are mutually connected, and what we observe in mental processes is the joint activity of separate areas. This conception is undoubtedly more correct. What we have is a complex collaboration of a number of separate zones. The brain substrate of the mental processes are not isolated parts but complex systems of the whole brain apparatus. But the problem is the following: if this system is given in the very structure of the brain in advance, i.e., if it is fully determined by connections that exist in the brain between its various parts, then we must assume that those connections from which the concept develops are given beforehand in the structure of the brain. But if we assume that it is possible to have more complex systems which are not given in advance, a new perspective on this problem results.

Allow me to clarify this with an admittedly very rough schema. [20] Forms of behavior that earlier were shared by two persons are now combined in the person: the order and its execution. Before they took place in two brains. One brain acted upon the other with, say, a word. When they are combined in one brain we get the following picture: point A in the brain cannot reach point B through a direct combination. It has no natural connection with it. The possible connections between different parts of the brain are established through the peripheral nervous system, from outside.

Proceeding from such ideas, we can understand a number of facts of pathology. These include, first of all, patients with a lesion of the brain systems who are not capable of doing something directly, but can carry it out when they tell themselves to do so. Such a clinically clear picture is observed in Parkinsonian patients. The Parkinsonian patient cannot take a step. But if you tell him to take a step or if you put a piece of paper on the floor, he will take this step. Everybody knows how well Parkinsonian patients walk on stairs and how badly on the level floor. In order to lead the patient to the laboratory, one has to spread out a number of pieces of paper on the floor. The patient wants to walk, but he cannot influence his motor system, this system is disturbed. Why can the Parkinsonian patient walk when pieces of paper are spread out on the floor? Here there are two explanations. One was given by Sapir[21]: the Parkinsonian patient wants to raise his arm when you tell him to do so, but this impulse alone is insufficient. If you link this request with another (visual) impulse he will raise it. The supplementary impulse acts together with the main one. We can also imagine another picture. The system that allows him to raise his arm is now disturbed. But he can connect one point of his brain with another one via an external sign.

It seems to me that the second hypothesis about the locomotion of Parkinsonian patients is the correct one. The Parkinsonian patient establishes a connection between different points of his brain through a sign, influencing himself from the periphery. That this is so is confirmed by experiments on the exhaustibility of Parkinsonian patients. If it would be simply a matter of fully exhausting the Parkinsonian patient, then the effect of a supplementary stimulus would increase, or at any rate be proportional to a rest, a recovery, and play the role of an external stimulus. One of the Russian authors [21] who first described Parkinsonian patients pointed out that most important for the patient are loud stimuli (a drum, music), but further investigations demonstrated that this is incorrect. I do not want to say that in Parkinsonian patients things proceed exactly like this. It suffices to conclude that it is in principle possible. That such a system is actually possible we can constantly observe in processes of dissolution.

Each of the systems I mentioned goes through three stages. First, an interpsychological stage—I order, you execute. Then an extra-psychological stage—I begin to speak to myself. Then an intra-psychological stage—two points of the brain which are excited from outside have the tendency to work in a unified system and turn into an intracortical point.

Allow me to dwell briefly on the further destinies of these systems. I would like to point out that from the viewpoint of differential psychology I do not differ from you and you do not differ from me because I have somewhat better concentration than you. The essential and practically important characterological difference in the social life of people resides in the structures, relations and connections that exist in us between different points. What I want to say is that most important is not memory or attention per se, but the extent to which the person utilizes this memory, the role it fulfills. We have seen that for the Kaffir the dream may fulfill a central role. For us the dream is a parasite in psychological life which plays no essential role whatsoever. The same is true for thinking. How many idling fruitless minds, how many minds who think but are not at all involved in action! We all remember a situation in which we knew how to act, but acted differently. I want to point out that here we have three extremely important planes. The first plane is the social plane and the plane of social class psychology. We wish to compare the worker and the bourgeois. The point is not, as was thought by Sombart[22] [1913], that for the bourgeois the main thing is greediness, that a biological selection of greedy people takes place for whom miserliness and accumulation are most important. I assume that many workers are more stingy than a bourgeois. Essential is not that the social role can be deduced from the character, but that the social role creates a number of characterological connections. The social and social class type of the person are formed from the systems that are brought into the person from the outside. They are systems of social relationships between people, transferred into the personality. Professiographic [22] investigations of labor processes are based on this. Each profession requires a certain system of these connections. For the tram-driver, for example, it is indeed not so important to be more attentive than the ordinary person, but to utilize this attention correctly. It is important that his attention has a position which it may not have in, say, a writer, etc.

Finally, from a differential and characterological perspective we must make a fundamental distinction between primary characterological connections which yield certain proportions, for example, a schizoid or cycloid constitution, and connections that develop completely differently and which distinguish the honest person from the dishonest, the honest from the deceitful, the dreamer from the business person. These do not reside in the fact that I am less tidy than you, or more deceitful than you, but in the development of a system of relations between the different functions that develop in ontogenesis. Lewin[23] correctly says that the formation of psychological systems coincides with the development of personality. In the highest cases of ethically very perfect human personalities with a very beautiful spiritual life we are dealing with the development of a system in which everything is connected to a single goal. In Spinoza you will find a theory (I am changing it somewhat) which says that the soul can achieve that all manifestations, all conditions relate to a single goal. A system with a single center may develop with a maximal integrity of human behavior. For Spinoza this single idea is the idea of god or nature. Psychologically this is not at all necessary. But a person can indeed not only bring separate functions into a system, but also create a single center for the whole system. Spinoza demonstrated this system in the philosophical plane. There are people whose life is a model of the subordination to a single goal and who proved in practice that this is possible. Psychology has the task of demonstrating that the development of such a unified system is scientifically possible.

I would like to end by pointing out once more that I have presented a ladder of facts which, although it is still incoherent, nevertheless goes from below upwards. I skipped almost all theoretical considerations. It seems to me that this viewpoint sheds light on our investigations and gives them their proper place. I do not have enough theoretical strength to combine all this. I presented a very big ladder, but as the idea that comprehends all this I proposed a general idea. Today I wanted to elucidate whether this main idea, which I nourished during a number of years but hesitated to express fully, is confirmed by the facts. And our next task is to clarify this in the most businesslike and detailed manner. Relying on the above-mentioned facts, I would like to express my fundamental conviction that the entire issue resides not just in the changes within the functions, but in the changes in the connections and in the infinitely diverse forms of development that develop from this. It resides in the development of new syntheses in a certain stage of development, new central functions and new forms of connections between them. We must take interest in systems and their fate. Systems and their fate—it seems to me that for us the alpha and omega of our next work must reside in these four words.

Chapter 7

MIND, CONSCIOUSNESS, THE UNCONSCIOUS[*,1]

The three words given in the title of our essay—mind, consciousness, the unconscious— not only stand for three central and fundamental psychological issues.
They are to a much greater extent methodological issues, i.e., issues about principles
of the formation of psychological science itself. This was superbly expressed by
Lipps[2] [1897, p. 146] in his well-known definition of the problem of the subconscious
which says that the subconscious is not so much *a* psychological problem but *the*
problem of psychology. [1]

Høffding [1892, p. 160] had the same thing in mind when he equated the importance of the introduction of the concept of the unconscious in psychology with
[that of the introduction of] the concept of potential physical energy in physics. It
is only with the introduction of this concept that psychology becomes possible as
an independent science which can combine and coordinate the facts of experience
into a certain system which is subject to special regularities. Münsterberg discusses
the same question and gives an analogy between the problem of the unconscious
in psychology and the problem of the presence of consciousness in animals. He
says that

> The decision whether one mode of explanation or another is to be applied cannot
> itself be deduced from the observed facts, but must precede the study of the facts; in
> other words: the question whether animals have consciousness or not cannot be
> answered by observation but belongs to epistemological arguments. In the same way
> here, no fact of abnormal experience can by itself prove that a psychological and not
> a physiological explanation is needed; it is a philosophical problem which must be
> settled by principle before the explanation of the special facts begins [Münsterberg *et
> al.*, 1910, p. 22].

We see that entire systems and psychological currents undergo a completely
unique development depending on the way they explain the three words in the title
of this essay. It suffices to bear in mind the example of psychoanalysis, which is
built on the concept of the unconscious, and to compare it with traditional empirical
psychology, which exclusively studies conscious phenomena.

It suffices, further, to bear in mind Pavlov's objective psychology and the
American behaviorists, who totally exclude mental phenomena from the range of
their research, and to compare them with the adherents of so-called understanding,
or descriptive psychology[3] whose sole task it is to analyze, classify, and describe the
phenomena of mental life without any appeal to questions of physiology and behavior. One only has to bear all this in mind to become convinced that the problem

*First published as Vygotsky, L. S. (1930). In *Elementy obshchej psikhologii* (pp. 48-61). Moscow:
Izdatelstvo BZO pri Pedfake 2-go MGU.

of mind, consciousness, and the unconscious is of decisive methodological importance for each psychological system. This problem is fundamental for our science, and its very fate depends on the way it is solved.

For some, psychology completely ceases to exist and is replaced by a genuine physiology of the brain or by reflexology. For others it is transformed into eidetic psychology[4] or into a pure phenomenology of the spirit. Finally, still others seek ways to realize a synthetic psychology. We shall not approach this problem historically or critically. We shall not examine the most important types of understanding of all these problems in their entirety. From the very beginning we confine our task to the examination of the meaning of all three motives in the system of objective scientific psychology.

Until very recently the possibility of psychology as an independent science was made dependent on the recognition of the mind as an independent sphere of being. To this day it is widely thought that the content and subject of psychological science is formed by mental phenomena or processes and that, consequently, psychology as an independent science is only possible on the basis of the idealistic philosophical assumption of the independence and primordial nature of the spirit on an equal footing with matter.

That is the way the majority of the idealistic systems proceed which strive to emancipate psychology from its natural tendency to grow together with natural science, from the "refined materialism" (in the words of Dilthey[5]) which penetrates it from physiology. [2] Recently Spranger[6] [1925, p. 130], one of the most important contemporary representatives of understanding psychology, or the psychology as a science of the spirit, proposed a requirement which practically implies that psychology must be developed with exclusively psychological methods. [3] For him it is entirely evident that the elaboration of psychology by means of a psychological method necessarily implies the rejection of all sorts of physiological explanations in psychology and the transition to the explanation of mental phenomena by mental ones.

The same idea is at times expressed by physiologists. Thus, in the investigation of mental salivation, Pavlov at first reached the conclusion that a mental act, an ardent desire for food, indisputably formed the stimulation for the salivary nerves. As is well known, henceforth he rejected this view and came to the conclusion that in the study of animal behavior and of mental salivation in particular we must not refer to all sorts of mental acts. Such expressions as "an ardent desire for food," "the dog remembered," and "the dog guessed" were strictly banned from his laboratory and a special fine was introduced for those collaborators who during their work resorted to such psychological expressions to explain a certain act of the animal.

According to Pavlov, by referring to mental acts we automatically enter the path of noncausal indeterministic thinking and leave the strict path of natural science. That is why in his opinion the true road toward the solution of the problem of behavior and toward the mastery of behavior lies in a genuine physiology of the brain which can investigate the nervous associations and the associations of reflexes corresponding to them and the other units of behavior exactly as if they were not at all accompanied by any mental phenomena.

Pavlov demonstrated, and in this resides his enormous merit, that one can interpret behavior physiologically without making any attempt to penetrate the inner world of the animal and that this behavior can be explained with scientific exactness, subjected to certain regularities and even be predicted, without any attempt to draw oneself even a vague and remote picture of the animal's experiences. In other words, Pavlov demonstrated that an objective physiological study of behavior which ignores mental life is in any case possible for the animal, but in principle for people as well.

At the same time Pavlov, subject to the same logic as Spranger, renders to god the things that are god's and to Caesar the things that are Caesar's by leaving for physiology the objective and for psychology the subjective approach of behavior. And for Pavlov the psychological and the mental fully coincide. As the entire history of our science demonstrated, this problem is totally insoluble on the philosophical basis on which psychology stood until now. A situation evolved which we may summarize as the result of the entire long historical development of our science.

On the one hand, we see that the possibility of studying the mind is totally denied and ignored, because its study makes us enter the path of noncausal thinking. Indeed, mental life is characterized by breaks, by the absence of a continuous and uninterrupted connection between its elements, by the disappearance and reappearance of these elements. Therefore it is impossible to establish causal relationships between the various elements and as a result it is necessary to refrain from psychology as a natural scientific discipline. Münsterberg says that

> In short, even the full conscious mental facts do not really hang together when viewed from a psychological point of view and are thus unfit to explain any results through their causal interplay . . . . Therefore there is no direct causal connection of the psychologized inner life; therefore there is only an indirect causal explanation of psychical phenomena possible insofar as they can be conceived as accompaniments of physiological processes [Münsterberg *et al.*, 1910, pp. 28/27].

One path thus leads to the total denial of the mind and, consequently, of psychology. There remain two other paths, no less interesting and no less evidently testifying to the blind alley into which our science was led by its historical development.

The first of them is that descriptive psychology that we have already mentioned. It takes the mind for a totally isolated realm of reality in which no material laws are active and which is a pure kingdom of the spirit. In this purely spiritual area no causal relations whatsoever are possible. Here we need to aim at understanding, the clarification of meanings and the establishment of values. Here we may describe, differentiate, classify, and establish structures. Under the name of descriptive psychology, this psychology opposes explanatory psychology and in so doing chases the task of explanation from the area of science.

As a science of the spirit, descriptive psychology is opposed by natural scientific psychology. Thus, here too, psychology is divided into two parts that are mutually disconnected. Totally different methods of knowledge dominate descriptive psychology. Here in establishing empirical laws there can be no question of induction and other methods. Here dominates the analytical, or phenomenological method, the method of the contemplation of essences [*Wesensschauung*], or intuition which allows us to analyze the direct data of consciousness.

Husserl [1911/1965, p. 35] says that "in the area of consciousness, the difference between phenomenon and being is obliterated." Here everything apparent is real. Therefore a psychology of this kind reminds us much more of geometry than of a natural science such as physics. It must turn into the mathematics of the spirit of which Dilthey dreamed. Naturally, here the mental is fully equated with the conscious, as intuition presupposes the immediate consciousness of one's experiences. But there is still another method in psychology which, as Spranger [1925, p. 130] notices, also follows the principle proposed by him—the psychological psychologically—but in the opposite direction. For this current the mental and the conscious are not synonyms. The central concept of this psychology is the unconscious, which permits us to fill the missing gaps of mental life, to establish the absent causal links, to theoretically continue the description of mental phenomena in the same terms, considering that the cause should equal the effect or, in any case, that they must be in one and the same series.

In this way the possibility of psychology as a special science is preserved. But this attempt is highly ambiguous as it involves two essentially heterogeneous tendencies. Spranger [1925, p. 130] is fully justified in saying that

> Freud, the main representative of this theory, tacitly proceeds from the same principle as does understanding psychology: in the area of psychology we must proceed purely psychologically, to the extent that this is possible. Premature or accidental excursions into the area of anatomy and physiology may, to be sure, reveal psychophysical connections as facts, but do not contribute to our understanding.

Freud's attempt resides in the tendency to extend the meaningful connections and dependences of mental phenomena to the area of the unconscious. He assumes that behind the conscious phenomena are unconscious ones that determine them and that may be reconstructed by analyzing their traces and interpreting their manifestations. But the same Spranger [1925, p. 133] reproaches Freud severely and points to a curious theoretical error in his theory. He says that whereas Freud has overcome physiological materialism, a psychological materialism continues to exist: the tacit metaphysical presupposition that the presence of sexual drives is self-evident, whereas all others must be understood on their basis.

And indeed the attempt to create a psychology by means of the concept of the unconscious is an ambiguous attempt. On the one hand, it is related with idealist psychology insofar as it fulfills the ordinance to explain mental phenomena by mental ones. On the other hand, inasmuch as he introduces the idea of the strictest determinism of all mental manifestations and reduces their basis to an organic, biological drive, namely the reproductive instinct, Freud remains on materialistic grounds.

Such are the three paths: the refusal to study the mind (reflexology), the "study" of the mind through the mental (descriptive psychology), and the knowledge of mind through the unconscious (Freud). As you see, we get three entirely different systems of psychology dependent on the way each of them solves the fundamental question about the conception of mind. We have already said that the historical development of our science led this problem into a hopeless blind alley from which there is no way out other than a rejection of the older psychology's philosophical foundation.

Only a dialectical approach to this problem reveals that an error was made in the very statement of absolutely all problems connected with mind, consciousness, and the unconscious. These problems were always stated falsely and therefore they were insoluble. What is completely insurmountable for metaphysical thinking, namely the deep difference between mental processes and physiological ones and the nonreducibility of the one to the other, is no stumbling block for dialectical thought which is used to consider processes of development as processes which, on the one hand, are uninterrupted and, on the other hand, are accompanied by leaps or the development of new qualities.

Dialectical psychology proceeds first of all from the unity of mental and physiological processes. Because for dialectical psychology mind is not, in the words of Spinoza [1677/1955, p. 128], something that is situated outside nature or as a kingdom within a kingdom, it is a part of nature itself, directly linked to the functions of the higher organized matter of our brain. As all other nature, it was not created but evolved in a process of development. Its rudimentary forms are present everywhere where the living cell has the capacity to change under the influence of external influences and to react to them.

Somewhere, in some specific stage of animal development, a qualitative change in the development of brain processes took place which, on the one hand, was prepared by the whole preceding course of development but, on the other hand, was a leap in the process of development as it marked the development of a new quality that could not be mechanically reduced to more simple phenomena. When we accept this natural history of mind a second idea also becomes intelligible. This idea is that we must not view mind as [consisting of] special processes which supplementarily exist on top of and alongside the brain processes, somewhere above or between them, but as the subjective expression of the same processes, as a special side, a special qualitative characteristic of the higher functions of the brain.

Through abstraction the mental process is artificially separated or torn from the integral psychophysiological process within which it only acquires its meaning and sense. The insolubility of the mental problem for the older psychology resided to a large extent in the fact that because of its idealistic approach the mental was torn from the integral process of which it forms a part. It was ascribed the role of an independent process existing alongside and apart from the physiological processes.

The recognition of the unity of this psychophysiological process, on the contrary, leads us of necessity to a completely new methodological requirement. We must not study separate mental and physiological processes outside their unity, because then they become completely unintelligible. We must study the integral process which is characterized by both a subjective and an objective side at the same time.

However, the acceptance of the unity of the mental and the physical which is expressed, first, in the assumption that mind appeared at a certain stage of development of organic matter and, second, that mental processes form an inseparable part of more complex wholes outside of which they do not exist and thus cannot be studied either, should not lead us to identify the mental and the physical.

Two basic forms of such an identification exist. One of them is characteristic of that current of idealist philosophy which was reflected in the works of Mach[7] and the other is characteristic of mechanistic materialism and the French materialists of the 18th century. In the latter view the mental process is identified with the physiological nervous process and reduced to the latter. As a result, the problem of the mind is totally obliterated, the difference between higher mental behavior and pre-mental forms of adaptation is erased. The indisputable testimony of immediate experience is obliterated and we inevitably end up with an irreconcilable contradiction with absolutely all data of mental experience.

In the other identification, characteristic of Machism, a mental experience, for example a sensation, is identified with the objective object that corresponds with it. As is well known, in Mach's philosophy this identification leads to the acceptance of the existence of elements in which the objective cannot be distinguished from the subjective.

Dialectical psychology dismisses both the one and the other identification. It does not mix up the mental and physiological processes. It accepts the nonreducible qualitatively unique nature of the mind. But it does claim that psychological processes are one. We thus arrive at the recognition of unique psycho-physiological unitary processes. These represent the higher forms of human behavior, which we suggest calling psychological processes, in contradistinction to mental processes and in analogy with what are called physiological processes. [4]

The question may easily arise: why not refer to the processes that are psychophysiological by nature, as has already been said, by this double name? It seems to us that the main reason is that by calling these processes psychological we proceed from a purely methodological definition. We refer to processes that are studied by psychology and in this way we emphasize the possibility and necessity of a unitary and integral subject of psychology as a science. Next to it and not coinciding with it can exist the psychophysiological study—psychological physiology or physiological psychology—whose special task it is to establish the links and dependences which exist between the one and the other kind of phenomena.

However, in Russian psychology a fundamental mistake is frequently made. This dialectical formula of the unity but not identity of mental and physiological processes is often understood erroneously. It leads researchers to contrast the mental with the physiological as a result of which the idea arises that dialectical psychology should consist of the purely physiological study of conditional reflexes plus introspective analysis, which are mechanically combined with each other. One cannot imagine anything more anti-dialectical.

Dialectical psychology's whole uniqueness precisely resides in the attempt to define the subject matter of its study in a completely novel way. This subject matter is the integral process of behavior which is characterized by the fact that it has its mental and its physiological side. [Dialectical] psychology studies it as a unitary and integral process and only in this way tries to find a way out of the blind alley that was created. We remind you here of the warning that Lenin [1909/1984, p. 143] gave in his book "*Materialism and empiriocriticism*" against the incorrect understanding of this formula. He said that contrasting the mental with the physical is absolutely necessary within the strict confines of the statement of our epistemological goals, but that beyond these confines such a contrast would be a gross mistake.

It is indeed a methodological difficulty of psychology that its viewpoint is a genuinely scientific, ontological one and that here this contrast would be a mistake. Whereas in epistemological analysis we must strictly oppose sensation and object, we must not oppose the mental and physiological processes in psychological analysis.

Let us now from this viewpoint examine the way out of the blind alley that takes shape if we accept these claims. As is well known, to this day two basic problems have been left unsolved by the older psychology: the problem of the biological meaning of the mind and the clarification of the conditions under which brain activity begins to be accompanied by psychological phenomena. Such antipodes as the objectivist Bekhterev and the subjectivist Bühler[8] equally acknowledge that we know nothing of the biological function of mind, but that we cannot assume that nature creates superfluous adaptations and that since mind evolved in the process of evolution it must fulfill some, still for us totally unintelligible, function.

We think that these problems were insoluble because they were stated falsely. It is absurd to first isolate a certain quality from the integral process and then raise the question of the function of this quality as if it existed in itself, fully independently of that integral process of which it forms a quality. It is absurd, for example, to separate the heat from the sun, to ascribe it independent meaning and to ask what meaning this heat may have and what action it can perform.

But until now psychology proceeded in exactly this way. It revealed the mental side of phenomena and then attempted to demonstrate that the mental side of phenomena is entirely unnecessary, that in itself it cannot cause any changes in the activity of the brain. Already in the very statement of this question resides the false presupposition that mental phenomena may act upon brain phenomena. It is absurd to ask whether a given quality can act upon the object of which it forms a quality.

The very presupposition that there can be an interrelation between mental and brain processes presupposes in advance a conception of the mind as a special mechanistic force which according to some can act upon brain processes and according to others may only proceed in parallel with them. Both the theory of parallelism and interaction theory make this false presupposition. Only a monistic view of mind allows us to state the question of the biological meaning of the mind in a completely different way.

We repeat once more: we cannot isolate mind from the processes of which it forms an inalienable part and then ask what is its use, what role does it fulfill in the general process of life. In reality the mental process exists within a complex whole, within the unitary process of behavior, and when we wish to understand the biological function of the mind we must ask about this process as a whole: what function do these forms of behavior fulfill in adaptation? In other words, we must not ask about the biological meaning of mental processes but about the biological meaning of psychological processes, and then the insoluble problem of the mind—which on the one hand cannot be an epiphenomenon, a superfluous appendage, and on the other hand cannot move any brain atom for one bit—appears soluble.

As Koffka [1924, p. 160] says, the mental processes point forward and beyond themselves to the complex psychophysiological wholes of which they form a part. This monistic integral viewpoint is to consider the integral phenomenon as a whole and its parts as the organic parts of this whole. Thus, the detection of the significant connection between the parts and the whole, the ability to view the mental process as an organic connection of a more complex integral process—this is dialectical psychology's basic task.

In this sense, the fundamental debate about the question as to whether mental processes may act upon bodily ones had already been decided by Plekhanov[9] (1956, p. 75). In all cases where there is talk of the influence of mental processes, such as fright, strong grief, painful experiences, etc. on bodily processes, the facts are mostly related correctly, but their interpretation is incorrect. Of course, in all these cases, it is not the experience itself, the mental act itself (the ardent desire for food as Pavlov said) which acts upon the nerves, but the physiological process that corresponds to this experience and that forms a single whole with it, that leads to the result of which we speak.

In the same sense Severcov[10] [1922] talks about mind as the highest form of animal adaptation, essentially having in mind not the mental but the psychological processes in the sense clarified above.

Thus, what is false in the old viewpoint is the idea of a mechanistic action of the mind upon the brain. The older psychologists conceive of it as a second force that exists alongside the brain processes. This brings us to the central point of our whole problem.

As we have already pointed out above, Husserl takes as his point of departure the thesis that in mind the difference between phenomenon and being is obliterated. As soon as we accept this we arrive with logical inevitability at phenomenology, for then it turns out that in the mind there is no difference between what seems and what is. That which seems—the phenomenon—is the real essence. What remains is to establish this essence, to examine it, to subdivide and systematize it, but science in the empirical sense of the word has nothing to do here.

Regarding an analogous problem, Marx [1890/1981b, p. 825] said: " . . . if the form of the manifestation and the essence of things directly coincided all science would be superfluous." Indeed, if things were directly what they seem no scientific investigation whatsoever would be necessary. We would have to register and count these things but not investigate them. A similar situation is created in psychology when we reject the difference between phenomenon and being. Where being and phenomenon directly coincide science has no place, only phenomenology.

In the old conception of mind it was totally impossible to find a way out of this cul-de-sac. It was absurd to state the question as to whether in mind we also ought to differentiate between phenomenon and being. But when we change the basic viewpoint, when mental processes are replaced by psychological processes, the application of Feuerbach's[11] [1971, p. 127] viewpoint in psychology becomes possible. He said that in thinking itself the difference between phenomenon and being is not obliterated. In thinking as well we must distinguish thinking and the thinking of thinking.

When we take into consideration that the subject of psychology is the integral psychophysiological process of behavior it becomes fully intelligible that it cannot find full and adequate expression in just the mental part and be interpreted by a special self-perception on top of that. Self-observation gives us practically always the data of self-consciousness which can and inevitably will distort the data of consciousness. The latter, in turn, never fully and directly reveal the properties and tendencies of the whole integral process, of which they form a part. The relations between the data of self-consciousness and consciousness, between the data of consciousness and the process, [5] are identical with the relations between phenomenon and being.

The new psychology firmly claims that neither in the world of mind do phenomenon and being coincide. It may seem to us that we do something for a certain reason, but in actual fact the reason will be another one. Relying on the sense of obvious truth that immediate experience gives us, we may assume that we are provided with free will but here we may severely deceive ourselves. We now come to another central problem of psychology.

The older psychology identified mind and consciousness. Everything mental was perforce also conscious. The psychologists Brentano,[12] Bain,[13] and others, for example, claimed that the very question as to the existence of unconscious mental phenomena was self-contradictory by definition. The first and direct property of the mental is that it is consciously realized by us, that it is experienced, that it is given to us in immediate inner experience and therefore the very expression "the unconscious mind" seemed to the older authors to be as absurd as the expression "a round square" or "dry water."

Other authors, on the contrary, have for a long time paid attention to three basic points which forced them to introduce the concept of the unconscious in psychology.

The first point was that the awareness of phenomena itself knows several degrees: we experience one thing more consciously and clearly than another. There are things that find themselves almost on the very border of consciousness and that now enter, now leave the field of consciousness. There are dimly felt things, there are experiences that are more or less narrowly connected with the real system of experiences, the dream, for example. That is why they claimed that a phenomenon does not become less mental from the fact that it becomes less conscious. Hence they drew the conclusion that we may allow for unconscious mental phenomena as well.

The second point is that within mental life itself there is a certain competition between different elements, a struggle for entry into the field of consciousness, the suppression of some elements by others, the tendency to resume actions, sometimes to reproduce them in an obsessional way, etc. Herbart,[14] who reduced all mental life to a complex mechanism of ideas, also distinguished inhibited or unconscious ideas which appeared as a result of their suppression from the field of clear consciousness and continued to exist below the threshold of consciousness as a tendency toward representation. Here we already have, on the one hand, an embryonic form of Freud's theory, according to which the unconscious develops from suppression, and, on the other hand, the theory of Høffding for whom the unconscious corresponds with potential energy in physics.

The third point is the following. Mental life, as has already been said, consists of a series of phenomena that are too fragmentary and thus naturally require the assumption that they continue to exist when we are no longer conscious of them. I saw something, then after some time I remember it and the question is: what happened to the idea of the object before I remembered it? That the brain preserves some dynamic trace of this impression psychologists have never doubted. But does this trace correspond to a potential phenomenon? Many thought it did.

In this connection arises the very complex and grand problem that, until now, the conditions under which the brain processes begin being accompanied by consciousness are unknown to us. As with the biological meaning of the mind, the difficulty of the problem resides in its being falsely stated. We should not ask under which conditions does the nervous process start being accompanied by the mental process, because the nervous processes are not at all accompanied by the mental ones. The mental ones form part of a more complex integral process in which the nervous process participates as its organic part.

Bekhterev (1926), for example, assumed that only when the nervous current that spreads out over the brain stumbles upon an obstacle, encounters a difficulty, will consciousness become operative. In actual fact, we have to state the question otherwise, namely: under what conditions do the complex processes arise that are characterized by the presence of a mental side? We must, then, look for specific conditions for the development of psychological integral processes in the nervous system and behavior as a whole, but not for the development of mental processes within the given nervous processes.

Pavlov [1928/1963, pp. 221-222] comes close to this idea when he compares consciousness to a bright spot which moves over the surface of the cerebral hemisphere according to the optimal nervous excitation.

In the older psychology the problem of the unconscious was stated as follows: the basic question was to accept the unconscious as either mental or physiological. Such authors as Münsterberg, Ribot and others, who saw no possibility of explaining mental phenomena other than physiologically, openly pleaded to view the unconscious as physiological.

Thus, Münsterberg [Münsterberg et al., 1910] claims that there is not a single feature ascribed to subconscious phenomena which forces us to count them as mental. In his opinion, even when subconscious processes show an apparent goal-orientedness, we have no grounds to ascribe a mental nature to these processes. He says

> not only that the physiological cerebration is well able to produce the "intellectual" result, but the physiological side alone is fit for it, the psychological is utterly unfit [ibid., p. 26].

That is why Münsterberg comes to the general conclusion that the unconscious is a physiological process, that this explanation

> gives small foothold for that mystical expansion of the theory which seemed so easily reached from the subconscious mental life. But it is not the least merit of the scientific physiological explanation that it obstructs the path of such pseudophilosophy [ibid., p. 31].

Münsterberg [ibid., p. 32] assumes, however, that we may use the terminology of psychology in the investigation of the unconscious provided "that the psychological word is taken as a short label for the very complex neural physiological processes." Münsterberg says, in particular, that if he had to write the history of a woman with a dissociated consciousness [Miss Beauchamp] he should conceive all subconscious processes in physiological conceptions, but [he] should describe them, for clearness and convenience sake ... in the terms of psychological language [ibid., p. 32].

Münsterberg is undoubtedly right about one thing. Such a physiological explanation of the subconscious shuts the doors to mystical theories, while the recognition that the unconscious is mental, on the contrary, often leads, as in the case of Hartmann[15] [1869], to a mystical theory which allows for the existence of a second ego—alongside the conscious personality—which is built according to the same model and which, in essence, forms the resurrection of the old idea of the soul in a new and more confused version.

To make our overview complete and the evaluation of the new solution of the problem sufficiently clear, we have to bear in mind that in the older psychology there is also a third path to explain the problem of the unconscious, namely the path chosen by Freud. We have already pointed out the ambiguity of this path. Freud does not solve the basic and essentially unsolvable question as to whether the unconscious is mental or not. He says that while studying the behavior and experiences of nervous patients he stumbled upon certain gaps, omitted links, forgetfulness which he reconstructed through analysis.

Freud [1917/1973, pp. 277-278] mentions a patient who carried out obsessional actions whose sense eluded her. The analysis revealed the pre-conditions from which these unconscious actions sprang. In the words of Freud, she behaved in precisely the same way as the hypnotized subject to whom Bernheim[16] had suggested opening an umbrella in the hospital ward five minutes after he woke up, and who carried out this suggestion in the waking condition without being able to explain the motive of his act. In such a state of affairs Freud speaks of the existence of unconscious mental processes. Freud is only prepared to renounce his hypothesis about their existence when someone describes these facts in a more concrete scientific way, and until that time he holds fast to this hypothesis and in surprise shrugs his shoulders, dismissing what is said as unintelligible, when someone objects to him that here the unconscious is nothing real in a scientific sense.

It is unclear how something unreal at the same time produces effects of such tangible reality as an obsessional action. We have to look into that, as Freud's theory belongs to the most complex of all conceptions of the unconscious. As we see, on the one hand, for Freud the unconscious is something real which actually causes the obsessional action and is not just a label or a way of speaking. With this he, as it were, directly objects to Münsterberg's claim. On the other hand, however, Freud does not clarify the nature of this unconscious.

It seems to us that here Freud creates a certain concept which is difficult to imagine visually but which often exists in theories of physics. An unconscious idea, he says, is "a phenomenal impossibility just as a weightless, frictionless ether is a physical phenomenal impossibility. It is no more and no less unthinkable than the mathematical conception $\sqrt{-1}$." [6] In the opinion of the author, it is permissible to use such concepts. We just must clearly understand that we speak of abstract concepts and not of facts.

But this is exactly the weak side of psychoanalysis pointed out by Spranger. On the one hand, the unconscious for Freud is a way to describe certain facts, i.e., a system of conventional concepts; on the other hand, he insists that the unconscious is a fact which exerts such a manifest influence as an obsessional action does. In another book, Freud [1920/1973, p. 60] himself says that he would be happy to replace all these psychological terms by physiological ones, but that contemporary physiology does not provide him with such concepts.

It seems to us that Dale, without mentioning Freud, consistently expresses the same viewpoint when he says that mental connections and acts or phenomena must be explained from mental connections and causes, even if this would mean that in order to do so we sometimes must entertain more or less broad hypotheses. For this reason physiological interpretations and analogies can have no more than auxiliary or provisional heuristic meaning for the actual explanatory tasks and hypotheses of psychology. Psychological constructions and hypotheses are no more than the hypothetical continuation of the description of homogeneous phenomena in one and the same independent system of reality. Thus, the goals of psychology as an independent science and theoretical-epistemological demands require us to fight physiology's usurpationist attempts and not to get confused by real or apparent gaps and interruptions in the picture of our conscious mental life. These are filled in by the branches or modifications of the mental which are not the object of full, immediate and continuous consciousness, i.e., by the elements of what is called the subconscious, dimly conscious, or unconscious.

In dialectical psychology the problem of the unconscious is stated very differently. When the mental was viewed as torn and isolated from the physiological processes, the natural question as to absolutely all phenomena was: is it mental or physiological? In the first case, the problem of the unconscious was solved in Pavlov's manner, in the second in the manner of understanding psychology. [7] Hartmann and Münsterberg stand to the problem of the unconscious as Husserl and Pavlov do to the problem of psychology in general.

For us it is important to pose the question as follows: is the unconscious psychological, can it be viewed with similar phenomena as a certain element in the processes of behavior alongside the integral psychological processes that we mentioned above? We have already answered this question beforehand in our examination of the mind. We agreed to view the mind as a compound complex process which is not at all covered by its conscious part, and therefore it seems to us that in psychology it is entirely legitimate to speak about the psychologically conscious or the psychologically unconscious: the unconscious is the potentially conscious.

We would just like to point out how this viewpoint differs from Freud's viewpoint. As we have already said, for him the concept of the unconscious is, on the one hand, a way to describe the facts and, on the other hand, something real that leads to direct actions. But this is the whole problem. We can state the ultimate question as follows: let us assume that the unconscious is mental and has all the properties of the mental except for the fact that it is not a conscious experience. But is it really true that a conscious mental phenomenon can directly cause an action? For, as we have said above, in all cases where mental phenomena were held responsible for an action, we were dealing with actions that were carried out by the whole psychophysiological integral process and not only by its mental side. Thus, the very character of the unconscious, that it exerts influence on conscious processes and behavior, requires that it be recognized as a psychophysiological phenomenon.

Another thing is that for the description of facts we have to use concepts that correspond to the nature of these facts, and the advantage of the dialectical viewpoint on this question is that it claims that the unconscious is neither mental nor physiological, but psychophysiological, or to be more exact, psychological. The present definition corresponds to the real nature and real properties of the subject itself, as all phenomena of behavior are examined by us in the plane of the integral processes.

Further, we would like to point out that more than once attempts were made to get out of the blind alley in which the older psychology wound up by its inability to solve the fundamental problems connected with mind and consciousness. Stern [1927, p. 28], for example, attempts to overcome this blind alley by introducing the concept of psychophysical neutral functions and processes, i.e., processes that are neither physical nor mental but lie beyond this distinction.

But, of course, only mental and physical processes really exist and only a conventional construction can be neutral. It is perfectly clear that such a conventional construction will always lead us away from the real subject matter, because this really exists. Only dialectical psychology, by claiming that the subject matter of psychology is not what is psychophysically neutral but the psycho-physiological unitary integral phenomenon that we provisionally call the psychological phenomenon, is capable of indicating the way out.

All attempts similar to Stern's attempt are significant in the sense that they want to demolish the opinion created by the older psychology that we can draw a sign of equality between the mental and the psychological. They show that the subject matter of psychology is not mental phenomena but something more complex and integral, of which the mental only forms an organic part and which we might call psychological. It is only in the disclosure of the content of this concept that dialectical psychology diverges sharply from all other attempts.

In conclusion, I would like to point out that all positive achievements of both subjective and objective psychology find their genuine realization in this new statement of the problem provided by dialectical psychology.

Let me first point out one aspect: already subjective psychology has detected quite a number of properties of mental phenomena which can only receive their real explanation, their real evaluation, with this new statement of the problem. Thus, the older psychology listed as special distinguishing characteristics of mental phenomena their immediateness, the unique way of knowing them (self-observation), or the more or less intimate link with the person, the "ego," etc. Brentano proposed the intentional relation to the object as the main feature of mental phenomena. They find themselves in a unique relation with the object which is only characteristic of mental phenomena, i.e., they relate to or represent this object in a unique way.

Leaving aside the feature of immediateness as a purely negative feature, we see that in the new statement of the problem all such properties as the unique representation of the object in the mental phenomenon, the special link of mental phenomena with the person, and the fact that they can be observed or experienced only by the subject are functional characteristics of no small importance of these special psychological processes viewed from their mental side. All these aspects, which for the older psychology were simply dogmas, are vivified and become the subject of investigation in the new psychology.

Let us take another element, from the opposite end of psychology, but demonstrating the same thing with no less clarity. Objective psychology in the person of Watson [1924/1970] attempted to approach the problem of the unconscious. This author distinguishes verbalized and unverbalized behavior, pointing out that part of the processes of behavior are accompanied by words from the very beginning. They can be caused or replaced by verbal processes. They are accountable, as Bekhterev [1932, pp. 44; 421-422] said. The other part is nonverbal, not connected with words and therefore not accountable. In his time Freud as well proposed the feature of the connection with words and pointed out that the unconscious is formed by precisely those ideas that are disconnected from words.

Several of Freud's critics who are inclined to equate the unconscious with the unsocial and the unsocial with the nonverbal also pointed to the intimate link between verbalization and the conscious awareness of processes. Watson [1924/1970, pp. 261-264], too, sees in verbalization the main distinguishing characteristic of the conscious. He openly states that everything which Freud called unconscious is actually nonverbal. From this statement Watson draws two conclusions that are highly interesting. According to the first one, we cannot remember the earliest childhood events, because they took place when our behavior was not yet verbalized and therefore the earliest part of our life will remain unconscious forever. The second conclusion points to a weak point of psychoanalysis, which is that the physician attempts to influence the unconscious, i.e., unverbalized processes, by means of a conversation, i.e., by means of verbal reactions.

We do not wish to say now that these statements by Watson are absolutely correct or that they should become the point of departure for the analysis of the unconscious. We merely wish to say that the correct core which this link between the unconscious and the unverbalized contains (it has been noticed by other authors as well) can receive its genuine realization and development only on the basis of dialectical psychology.

Chapter 8

PREFACE TO LEONT'EV[*][1]

Contemporary scientific psychology suffers from a very deep crisis in its methodological foundations. It arose from the whole course of the historical development of this science and seized the whole area of psychological research with such completeness and force that it will indisputably mark the beginning of a new era in psychology. The crisis makes it impossible to develop further along the old paths. Whatever the future psychology will be, it certainly cannot be a direct continuation of the old psychology.

That is why the crisis signifies a turning point in the history of psychology's development. The great complexity of this crisis resides in the fact that the characteristics of the former and the future psychology have been interwoven in such a fantastically complex pattern that the task to disentangle it at times presents the greatest difficulties and requires special historical, methodological, and critical investigations dedicated to this question.

As has already been said, this crisis has such an all-embracing character that there is not a single significant problem of psychology that is not involved in it. Of course, each chapter of scientific psychology experiences the crisis in its own way. In each problem the crisis finds its own unique expression and refraction, depending on the character of the problem itself and on the historical path of its development. But the methodological nature of this crisis remains essentially the same in all the diversity of its expressions, in all the wealth of its refractions through the prism of different concrete problems. That is why not only the attempt to outline the foundations and the system of psychological knowledge but also each concrete investigation dedicated to some specific psychological problem can come to a methodological understanding of its starting points, its method, its statement of the problem only in the light of the crisis in which the problem as a whole is involved.

The problem of memory, to which Leont'ev's investigation for which these lines serve as an introduction is dedicated, forms no exception in this respect. More than that, memory is the psychological problem in which the basic characteristics of the crisis are most distinct and clear.

As is well known, the basic content of the psychological crisis is formed by the struggle between two irreconcilable and fundamentally different tendencies which in different mixtures underlay psychological science during the entire course of its development. Presently these tendencies are sufficiently understood by the most far-sighted of psychology's representatives. The majority of them have also under-

*First published as Vygotsky, L. S. (1931). Predislovie. In A. N. Leont'ev, *Razvitie Pamjati. Eksperimental'noe Issledovanie Vysshikh Psikhologicheskikh Funkcij* (pp. 6-13). Moscow–Leningrad: Uchpedgiz.

stood the idea that no reconciliation between these two tendencies is possible, and a few of the bravest of these thinkers begin to understand that psychology's development is in for a cardinal turning-point caused by the radical repudiation of these two tendencies which until this time directed its development and determined its content.

This crisis found its expression in the false idea of two psychologies as two autonomous and mutually completely independent theoretical disciplines: natural scientific, causal, or explanatory psychology and teleological, descriptive, or understanding psychology.

This struggle of two mutually irreconcilable tendencies basically determined the fate of memory research in psychology as well. According to Münsterberg's [1920, p. 13] proper remark, teleological psychology seldom appears in a really pure and consistent form.

> Often it is somehow superficially connected with elements of causal psychology. In such a case, for example, memory processes are pictured as causal and the processes of feeling and thought as intentional—a mixture that can easily arise under the influence of the naive conception of everyday life.

And, indeed, in psychology memory processes were usually viewed from the viewpoint of natural scientific, causal psychology. Hering[2] expressed the great idea that memory is a general property of organized matter. This idea inspired a whole series of investigations which formed a spontaneously materialistic stream in the study of memory within the general, dual, mixed river-bed of empirical psychology. It is not surprising, therefore, that the extreme physiological viewpoint in psychology, which found its highest expression in the associationist current in psychology and which led to the development of the psychology of behavior [1] and reflexology, made the problem of memory its favorite and central theme.

But, as often happens in the history of science, the very presence of this viewpoint inevitably led to the fact that completely contradictory ideas about the nature of memory gathered on the other pole. Special psychological regularities of memory, specifically human forms and ways of functioning, could not, of course, be satisfactorily explained in this throughly analytical statement of the problem. In this view, the ultimate research goal was to reduce higher forms of memory to lower, primary and rudimentary ones, to their general organic basis and to dissolve the whole problem in the general, indeterminate, vague and almost metaphysical concept of the *mneme* as a general universal property of matter.

Metaphysical materialism, consistently following its path, became thus inevitably transformed into the other pole, into idealistic metaphysics.

This idealistic conception of memory found its highest expression in Henri Bergson's well-known work *Matter and Memory* in which this mutual determination of mechanistic and idealistic viewpoints comes out with most clarity. Bergson analyzes motor memory, the memory which lies at the basis of habit formation, and assumes that it is impossible to subject the activity of human memory as a whole to the regularities of this memory. We cannot deduce and explain the function of remembering from the laws of habit: that is the hidden but central nerve of the whole theory, its basic assumption, its single real foundation on which it rests and together with which it will fall. Hence his theory of two memories—the memory of the brain and the memory of the spirit.

In this theory, of which one of the most important arguments is the consistently mechanistic view of organic memory, the dualism characteristic of psychology as a whole and of the psychology of memory in particular acquires its metaphysical basis. The brain is, for Bergson, as it is for the consistent behaviorist, simply an apparatus for the connection of external impulses with body movements. He says that

> in our opinion, the brain is nothing other than a sort of telephone station, its role is
> to transmit a message or to delay it [Bergson, 1896, p. 26]. [2]

All brain development resides in the fact that the points of space which it connects with motor mechanisms become more numerous, remote and complex.

But the fundamental role of the nervous system remains the same in the whole course of its development. It does not acquire fundamentally new functions and the brain, this basic organ of thinking of man, according to Bergson, is in principle not different from the spinal cord.

> Between the so-called perceptual faculties of the brain and the reflex functions of the
> spinal cord there is only a difference of degree, not of kind [Bergson, 1896, p. 253].

Hence Bergson's natural distinction between two theories of memory. For one—memory is no more than a function of the brain and between perception and memory there is only a difference in intensity. For the other—memory is something other than a function of the brain and perception and memory differ not in degree but in kind. Bergson himself sides with the second theory. For him memory is "something other than a function of the brain" [Bergson, 1896, pp. 266/268]. It is something "absolutely independent of matter" [Bergson, 1896, p. 76]. "With memory we truly are in the domain of the spirit," as he formulates his basic idea [Bergson, 1896, p. 271]. The brain is simply a tool that allows this purely spiritual activity to manifest itself. From his viewpoint

> all facts and all analogies speak in favor of a theory which views the brain only as an
> intermediary between sensations and movements [Bergson, 1896, p. 198].

We thus see that the dualistic approach that holds sway in all psychology found a striking expression in the theory of two memories. Further, we see that this dualism inevitably leads—whether from above or from below, it does not matter—to an idealistic conception of memory, to Bergson's theory of spiritual memory as being absolutely independent of matter or to the theory of the primordial and universal memory of matter, the theory of Semon [1920].

When you study the psychological investigations of memory belonging to this orientation it begins to seem as if these works belong to an era of scientific research long since passed when the historical method was foreign to all sciences and when Comte[3] saw the privilege of sociology in the application of this method. The historical method of thinking and investigating penetrates psychology later than it does all other sciences.

The situation has radically changed since the times of Comte. Not only biology but also astronomy, geology, and in general all other natural sciences have mastered this method of thinking, with psychology the only exception. In his time Hegel considered history the privilege of the spirit and denied nature this privilege. He says that "only spirit has history, but in nature all forms are simultaneous." Now the situation changed into its reverse. Long ago the natural sciences assimilated the truth that all forms in nature are not simultaneous but can only be understood in their historical development. Only psychology makes an exception by assuming that psychology deals with eternal and immutable phenomena, whether these eternal and immutable properties are deduced from matter or from spirit. In one case or the other, the metaphysical approach of psychological phenomena remains in equal force.

This anti-historic idea found its highest expression in the well-known thesis of associationist ethnic psychology, which says that the laws of the human spirit are always and everywhere the same. Strange as it may seem, the idea of development has not been assimilated by psychology to the present day, despite the fact that whole branches of psychology are dedicated to nothing other than the study of the problem of development. This internal contradiction leads these psychologists to state the problem of development itself in metaphysical terms.

It is well known that the problem of memory development in childhood presents the psychology of memory with enormous problems. Some psychologists, who based themselves on indisputable facts, have claimed that memory develops in childhood, just as all other functions do. Others, leaning on equally indisputable facts, claimed that memory is weakened and reduced as the child develops. Finally, still others attempted to reconcile both claims by stating that memory develops in the first half of childhood and is reduced in the second half.

Such a situation is characteristic not only of child psychology. It is just as characteristic of pathopsychology which also could not grasp the regularities of the changes of memory in disintegration. The same can be said of zoological psychology. For all these sciences the development of memory was nothing other than the purely quantitative growth of inherently immutable functions.

We may summarize all these difficulties by saying that for the psychology of memory it was most difficult to study memory in its development and to catch the various forms of this development. It goes without saying that in such a situation psychological research is confronted with insurmountable problems.

Presently it is customary to complain about the imperfect and poor state of psychology. Many think that psychology as a science has not yet begun and will only begin in the more or less remote future. Prefaces to psychological books are written in minor key. In the happy expression of Lange (1914, p. 42), who found no better comparison for contemporary psychology: Priam on the ruins of Troy is on every page of our psychological books.

Very serious thinkers like, for example, Academician Pavlov, are ready to accept as fatal difficulties for the science itself the difficulties which some German professor has in compiling a program for a university course in psychology. He says that

> before the war (1913), in Germany arose a discussion as to the separation of psychology from philosophy, that is, the founding of separate chairs of philosophy and psychology. Wundt opposed this separation on the grounds that it was impossible to fix a common examination schedule in psychology, since every professor had his own special ideas as to what psychology really was. Does not this clearly show that psychology cannot yet claim the status of an exact science? [Pavlov, 1926/1960, p. 3].

By means of such facile arguments about a program, the problem of the science, the problem of the previous and future centuries, is solved in two lines.

But to the chagrin of the mourners psychology did not even think of dying. It attempts to realize its own plan of investigation, to create its own methodology and while some, for example Möbius [3], declare "the hopelessness of all psychology" to be the main argument in favor of metaphysics, others attempt to overcome metaphysics by means of scientific psychology.

The first starting point of such investigations is the idea of development: to explain the development of memory not from its properties but to deduce its properties from its development—that is the basic aim of the new investigations to which also Leont'ev's work belongs.

The wish to lay the historical approach of memory at the basis of his work leads the author to a combination of research methods which hitherto were metaphysically separated. He is interested in the development and loss of memory, in genetic and pathological analysis. He is interested in prodigious memory as well as in the memory of the half-idiot. And this combination is not accidental. It follows with logical necessity from the basic starting point of the whole investigation, from the wish to study memory in its historical development.

The empirical distinction of higher memory functions is not new. We owe it to experimental psychology, which empirically managed to establish such functions as voluntary attention and logical memory but which gave them a metaphysical explanation. In the present investigation an attempt is made to base the investigation of the higher functions of attention and memory—in all their uniqueness as compared to the elementary ones and in their unity and connections with the latter ones—on the uniqueness of this developmental process to which they owe their development. To experimentally show the *becoming* of so-called logical memory and so-called voluntary attention, to reveal their *psychogenesis*, to trace their further *destiny*, to understand the basic phenomena of memory and attention in *the perspective of development*—this is the aim of this investigation.

In this sense Leont'ev's work is methodologically determined by our central idea, the idea of the historical development of the behavior of man that forms the cornerstone of our theory, the historical theory of the higher psychological functions. From the viewpoint of this theory the historical origin and development of the higher psychological functions of man, and the higher functions of memory in particular, provide the key to the understanding of their nature, composition, structure, form of activity, and at the same time the key to the whole problem of the psychology of man. The theory attempts to adequately lay bare the truly human content of this psychology.

With the introduction into psychology of the historical viewpoint, the specifically psychological treatment of the phenomena under study and their regularities are also brought to the forefront. This investigation starts from the conviction that specifically psychological regularities, connections, relations and dependences of phenomena exist and have to be studied as such, i.e., psychologically.

We might repeat the thesis put forward by one of the eminent representatives of contemporary idealistic psychology—*psychologica psychologice*—giving it however a fundamentally different content. [4] For idealistic psychology the demand to study what is psychological psychologically means first of all the demand to study the mind in isolation, as an independent kingdom of the spirit without any relation to the material basis of human existence. For this author this thesis essentially means that the mental is absolutely independent. But from a formal viewpoint this principle which demands the study of psychological regularities from a psychological viewpoint is profoundly true. Leont'ev changed the fundamental content of this demand and then attempted to consistently carry through the psychological viewpoint on the object of study.

In this connection, the work proposes quite a number of theses that have direct practical meaning. Not without reason has the question of the educability of memory always been the other side of the question of the development of memory, and we must say openly that the metaphysical statement of the question in the psychology of memory led to a situation in which the education of memory remained without a psychological basis. It is only the new viewpoint that attempts to lay bare the psychological nature of memory from the viewpoint of its development, which can lead us for the first time to a really scientifically sound pedagogics of memory, to the psychological underpinning of its education.

In all these respects Leont'ev's work forms the first step toward the investigation of memory from the new viewpoint and, like all first attempts, it naturally cannot comprehend the whole question in its entirety and cannot pretend to serve as its more or less complete solution. But the first step has been taken in an entirely new and extremely important direction of which the final aim can be determined in a few simple words, which even now are unfortunately still foreign to the majority of the psychological investigations in this field. These words are: the memory of *man*.

Chapter 9

THE PROBLEM OF CONSCIOUSNESS[*],[1]

1. INTRODUCTION

Psychology has defined itself as the science of consciousness, but about consciousness psychology hardly knew anything.

The statement of the problem in the older psychology. Lipps, for example: "unconsciousness is _the_ problem of psychology." [1] _The problem of consciousness was stated outside, before psychology._

In descriptive psychology: in contrast to the subject of natural sciences, phenomenon and being coincide. That is why psychology is a speculative science. But since in the experience of consciousness only fragments of consciousness are given, the study of consciousness as a whole is impossible for the investigator.

We know a number of formal laws for consciousness: the uninterrupted nature of consciousness, the relative clarity of consciousness, the unity of consciousness, the identity of consciousness, the stream of consciousness.

The theory of consciousness in classic psychology. Two basic ideas about consciousness.

The first idea. Consciousness is regarded as something _nonspatial_ in comparison to the mental functions, as some mental space (for example, Jaspers: consciousness as the stage on which a drama is being performed; in psychopathology we correspondingly also distinguish two basic cases: either the action is disturbed, or the stage itself). According to this idea, _consciousness (as every other space) thus has no qualitative characteristics._ That is why the science of consciousness is presented as the science of ideal relations (Husserl's geometry [2], Dilthey's "geometry of the spirit").

The second idea. Consciousness is some intrinsic _general quality_ of all psychological processes. This quality can therefore be discounted, not taken into account. In this idea as well, consciousness is presented as _something which is nonqualitative, nonspatial, immutable, not developing._

"Psychology's sterility was caused by the fact that the problem of consciousness was not yet worked out."

The most important problem. [Consciousness was now considered as a system of functions, now as a system of phenomena (Stumpf).]

<The problem of orientation points [in the history of psychology].

[Two basic viewpoints existed about the question of consciousness' relation to the psychological functions]:

---

*Not published during Vygotsky's life. Based on material found in A. N. Leont'ev's private archives.

1. Functional systems. The prototype was faculty psychology. The idea of a mental organism possessing activities.

2. The psychology of emotional experience which studied the mirror image without studying the mirror (particularly obvious in association psychology, paradoxically Gestalt). The second (the psychology of emotional experience) (a) was never and could not be consistent, (b) always transferred the laws of one function to all others, etc.

[Questions that arise in this connection]:

1. The relation between activity and emotional experience (the problem of meaning).

2. The relation between functions. Can one function explain all others? (the system problem).

3. The relation between function and phenomenon (the problem of intentionality)>.

How did psychology understand the relation between the different activities of consciousness? (This problem was of minor importance; for us it is of paramount importance). Psychology answered this question with three postulates:

1. All activities of consciousness work together.

2. The link between the activities of consciousness does not essentially change these activities, for they are *not necessarily* connected, but only because they belong to one personality ("they have one boss"; James in a letter to Stumpf). [3]

3. This link is accepted as a postulate but not as a problem <the connection between the functions is immutable>.

2. OUR MAIN HYPOTHESIS PRESENTED FROM OUTSIDE

Our problem. The connection between the activities of consciousness is not constant. It is essential for each different activity. We must make this connection the problem of our research.

A remark. Our position is a position opposite to Gestaltpsychologie. Gestaltpsychologie "made a postulate out of the problem"—assumed in advance that each activity is structural; [for us the opposite is characteristic: we make a problem out of the postulate].

The connection between the activities—this is the central point in the study of each system.

A clarification. From the very beginning the problem of the connection must be opposed to the atomistic problem. *Consciousness is primordially something unitary*—this we postulate. *Consciousness determines the fate of the system, just like the organism determines the fate of the functions.* Each interfunctional change must be explained by a change of consciousness as a whole.

3. THE HYPOTHESIS "FROM WITHIN" (FROM THE VIEWPOINT OF OUR WORKS)

(Introduction: the importance of the sign; its social meaning). In older works we ignored that the sign has meaning. <But there is "a time to cast away stones, and a time to gather stones together" (*Ecclesiastes*).> [4] We proceeded from the principle of the constancy of meaning, we discounted meaning. But the problem of meaning was already present in the older investigations. Whereas before our task was to demonstrate what "the knot" [5] and logical memory have in <u>common</u>, now our task is to demonstrate the difference that exists between them.

From our works it follows that *the sign changes the interfunctional relationships.*

4. THE HYPOTHESIS "FROM BELOW"

The psychology of animals.

After Köhler began a new era in zoopsychology . . . .

Vagner's conception: (1) development along pure and mixed lines; (2) . . . . (p. 38); (3) along pure lines—mutationist development; (4) along mixed lines—adaptive development; (5) . . . . (pp. 69-70). [6]

Is the behavior of anthropoid apes human-like? Are Köhler's criteria for intelligence correct? The closed integral action in accordance with the structure of the field and the swallow . . . [7] The limited nature of the ape's action is due to the fact that its actions are bound. *For the ape things have no constant meaning.* For the ape the stick does not become a tool, *it does not have the meaning of a tool.* The ape only "completes" the triangle, and that's it. The same is true for Gibier's dogs.

Conclusions that follow from this. Three levels. Conditional reflex activity is activity that elicits the instinct. The ape's activity is instinctive as well, it is no more than an *intellectual variation of the instinct*, i.e., a <u>new mechanism of the same activity.</u> The ape's intellect is the result of development along pure lines: the intellect has not yet restructured its consciousness.

(Köhler's apologia in Selz.[2] In the new edition, Köhler remarks that Selz "is the only one who interpreted my experiments correctly" [pp. 675-677].) [8]

In Koffka: "The deep similarity" of the ape's behavior to human intellect; but a restriction as well: *in the ape the action is <u>elicited</u> by the instinct and only the method used is rational.* These actions are *not voluntary.* For will implies freedom from the situation (the sportsman stops competing when he sees that he has no chance of winning the competition).

Man wants the stick, the ape wants the fruit. <The ape does not want the tool. It does not prepare it for the future. For the ape it is a means to satisfy an instinctive wish.>

The tool. *The tool requires abstraction from the situation. Tool use requires another type of stimulation and motivation. The tool is connected with meaning (of the object).*

(**Köhler**) (Köhler wrote his work in a polemic with Thorndike).

Conclusions

1. In the animal world the appearance of new functions is connected with a change of the brain (according to Edinger's formula) [9]; this is not the case in man. <The parallelism between psychological and morphological development in the animal world, in any case when it proceeds along pure lines.>

2. In the animal world—development along pure lines. Adaptive development already proceeds according to the system principle <Man cannot be distinguished by a single feature (intellect, will), but in principle by his relation to reality.>

3. The intellect of Köhler's apes is in the realm of the instinct. Two aspects that distinguish it: (a) the intellect does not restructure the system of behavior, (b)

there is no tool, the tool has no meaning, no objective [10] meaning either. The stimulation remains instinctive ("A tool requires abstraction.").

Buytendijk [11]: The animal does not detach itself from the situation, is not consciously aware of it.

The animal differs from man because its consciousness is organized in another way. "Man differs from the animal by his consciousness."

James [12]:	In animals	In man
	isolate	abstract
	construct	
	recept	concept
	influent	

(Gestalt psychology) [Our difference from structural psychology: structural psychology is a naturalistic psychology, just like reflexology. Meaning and structure are often identified in this psychology.]

5. "INSIDE"

1. A Sign-Based [Semicheskyj] Analysis in the Strict Sense

Each word has meaning; what is the meaning of a word?

—*Meaning does not coincide with logical meaning* (nonsense has meaning). *What are the characteristics of our statement of the problem*?

—Speech has been considered as the clothing of thought (the Würzburg school) or a habit (behaviorism). When meaning was studied, it was studied either (a) from the associationist viewpoint, i.e., meaning was the reminder of the thing, or (b) from the viewpoint of what goes on inside us (phenomenologically) in the perception of word meanings (Watt[3]).

[Speech is not essential for thinking—Würzburg; speech is equal to thinking—the behaviorists.]

The constant claim in all authors: the meaning of all words is fixed, meaning does not develop.

The change of words has been examined:

in linguistics—as the development of the word; the common character is the abstract character, this is the linguistic meaning, not the psychological one;

in psychology (Paulhan) [13]; meaning remains frozen; it is the sense that changes. The sense of the word is equal to all the psychological processes elicited by the given word. Neither here do we see development or movement, for the principle of sense formation remains the same. Paulhan broadens the concept of "sense";

in psychological linguistics and in psychology the change of meaning by the context was examined (metaphorical meaning, ironic meaning, etc.).

In all these theories (+ W. Stern) the development of meaning is given as the starting point which terminates the process as well.

(Stern: the child discovers the nominative function. This remains the constant principle of the relation between sign and meaning. Development in Stern is reduced to the broadening of vocabulary, to the development of grammar and syntax,

to the broadening or tightening of meaning. *But the principle remains the same.*)
[14]

"At the basis of the analysis was always the claim that meaning is constant, i.e., that *the relation of the thought to the word remains constant.*"

"Meaning is the path from the thought to the word." <Meaning is not the sum of all the psychological operations which stand behind the word. Meaning is something more specific—it is the internal structure of the sign operation. It is what is lying between the thought and the word. Meaning is not equal to the word, not equal to the thought. This disparity is revealed by the fact that their lines of development do not coincide.>

2. From External Speech to Inner Speech

a. External Speech

What does it mean to discover meaning?

In speech we may distinguish the semiotic [semicheskyj] and the phasic sides; they are connected by a relation of unity but not identity. The word is not simply the substitute for the thing. For example, Ingenieros' experiments with "meanings which are present." [15]

The proof. The first word is phasically a word but semiotically [semicheskyj] it is a sentence.

Development proceeds: *phasically* from the isolated word to the sentence, to the subordinate clause, *semiotically* [semicheskyj] from the sentence to the name. i.e., "*the development of the semiotic [semicheskyj] side of speech does not go in parallel with (does not coincide with) the development of its phasic side.*" [The development of the phasic side of speech runs ahead of the development of its semiotic [semicheskyj] side.]

"Logic and grammar do not coincide." Neither in thought nor in speech do the psychological predicate and subject and the grammatical predicate and subject coincide. <"The mind's grammar." It was thought that the phasic aspect was the stamp of the mind on speech.> There are two syntaxes—*the semantic one and the phasic one.*

Gelb: the grammar of thinking and the grammar of speech.

"*The grammar of speech does not coincide with the grammar of thought.*"

[What kind of changes are provided by the psychopathological material? (a) a person may speak awkwardly . . . ; (b) the speaker himself doesn't know what he wants to say; (c) the limits of language are hindering (a conscious, realized divergence); (d) grammatical competition.]

[The example from Dostoyevsky ("Diary of a writer").] [16]

Thus: *the semiotic [semicheskyj] and phasic sides of speech do not coincide.*

Notes of Vygotsky's Speech on the Occasion of Luria's Talk

[The shortcoming of Lévy-Bruhl is that he takes speech for something constant. This leads him to paradoxes. [17] If only we accept that the meanings and their combinations (syntax) are different from ours, then all absurdities disappear. The same with the investigations into aphasia—phoneme and meaning are not distinguished.]

<Earlier we carried out our analysis in the plane of behavior and not in the plane of consciousness—hence the abstract nature of our conclusions. (Now) most important for us is the development of meanings. For example, the similarity between the external structure of the sign operations in aphasics, schizophrenics, idiots, and primitives. But the semiotic analysis reveals that their inner structure, their meanings are different (the problem of semiotic aphasia).>

Meaning is not the same as thought expressed in a word.

In speech the semiotic [semicheskyj] and phasic sides do not coincide: thus, phasically the development of speech proceeds from the word to the phrase, but semiotically [semicheskyj] the child begins with the phrase [cf. the merging of words in the phrases of illiterates].

Neither do the logical and syntactical coincide. An example: "The clock fell"—syntactically here "clock" is the subject, "fell" the predicate. But when it is said in reply to the question "What happened?"; "What fell?", then logically *"fell"* is the subject and *"clock"* is the subject (i.e., what is new). Another example: "My brother has read this book"—the logical emphasis can be on each word.

[Speech without judgment in cases of microcephaly, etc.]

The thought which the person wants to express neither coincides with the phasical nor with the semiotical [semicheskyj] side of speech. An example: the thought "I couldn't help it" can be expressed in the meanings: "I wanted to dust it"; "I did not touch it"; "The clock fell of itself," etc. Neither does "I couldn't help it" itself absolutely express a thought (is not identical with it?); this phrase itself has its semiotic syntax.

The thought is a cloud from which speech is shed in drops.

The thought has another structure besides its verbal expression. The thought cannot be directly expressed in the word.

(Stanislavsky: behind the text lies a hidden meaning.) *All speech has an ulterior motive. All speech is allegory.* [In what does this ulterior motive consist? Uspensky's peasant petitioner says: "Our sort does not have language".] [18]

But a thought is not something ready-made which must be expressed. The thought strives, fulfills some function and work. This work of the thought is the transition from the feeling of the task—via the formation of meaning—to the unfolding of the thought itself.

[Semiotically [semicheskyj] "the clock has fallen" stands to the corresponding thought as the semantic connection in mediated memorization stands to what needs to be memorized.]

The thought is completed in the word and not just expressed in it.

A thought is an internally mediated process. <It is the path from a vague wish to the mediated expression through meaning, more correctly, not to its expression but to the perfection of the thought in the word.>

Inner speech exists already primordially (?).

There is no sign without meaning. The formation of meaning is the main function of the sign. Meaning is everywhere where there is a sign. This is the internal aspect of the sign. But in consciousness there is also something which does not mean anything.

[The] Würzburg approach consisted in the attempt to fight one's way to the thought. The task of psychology is to study not only these clots, but also their mediation, i.e., to study how these clots act, how the thought is completed in the word. <It is incorrect to think (as did the Würzburgians) that the task of psychology is to investigate these clouds which did not shed their water.> [19]

b. Inner Speech

In inner speech the noncoincidence of the semantic and phasic sides is still more acute.

What is inner speech?

(1) Speech minus the sign (i.e., everything that precedes phonation). <We must distinguish between unspoken speech and inner speech (Here Jackson and Head were mistaken).> [20]

(2) The pronunciation of words in thought (verbal memory—Charcot). Here the theory of types of inner speech coincides with types of ideas (of memory). It is, as it were, the preparation of external speech.

(3) *The modern* (our) *conception of inner speech.*

Inner speech has an entirely different structure than external speech. It has another relation between the phasic and the semiotic [semicheskyj] aspects.

Inner speech is abstract in two respects: (a) it is abstract in relation to <u>all vocal speech</u>, i.e., it reproduces only its semasiologized phonetic characteristics (for example: three r's in the word *rrrevolution* . . .), and (b) it is a-grammatical; each of its words is predicative. It has a different grammar from the grammar of semiotic external speech: in inner speech the meanings are interconnected in a different way than in external speech; the merging in inner speech proceeds along the lines of agglutination.

[The agglutination of words is possible due to the inner agglutination.] <Idioms are most widely spread in inner speech.>

The influence of sense: the word in a context becomes both restricted and enriched; the word <u>absorbs</u> the sense of the contexts = agglutination. The next word contains its predecessor.

"Inner speech is built predicatively."

[The difficulty of translation depends on the complex path of the transitions from one plane to another: thought → meanings → phasic external speech.

<u>Written speech.</u> [The difficulties of written speech: there is no intonation, no interlocutor. It represents the symbolization of symbols; motivation is more difficult.

Written speech stands in another relation to inner speech, it develops later than inner speech, it is the most grammatical. But it stands closer to inner speech than external speech; it is associated with meanings and passes by external speech.]

Summary: in inner speech we meet with a <u>new</u> form of speech where everything is different.

c. Thought

The thought also has independent existence; it does not coincide with the meanings.

We have to find a certain construction of the meanings in order to be able to express a thought [text and ulterior motive].

Clarification. This can be clarified with the example of amnesia. One can forget:

(a) the motive, intention;
(b) what exactly? (the thought?);
(c) the meanings through which one wished to express something;
(d) the words.

"The thought is completed in the word." [21] The difficulties of the completion. <The impossibility of expressing a thought directly. The levels of amnesia—the levels of mediation (transition) from the thought to the word—are levels of mediation of the word by meaning.>

Understanding. Real understanding lies in the penetration into the motives of the interlocutor.

The sense of the words is changed by the motive. Therefore, the ultimate explanation lies in motivation; this is especially obvious in infancy <The investigation by Katz of children's utterances. The work of Stolz (psychologist—linguist—mail censor in war time); the analysis of the letters of prisoners of war about hunger.>

Conclusions from this part. Word meaning is not a simple thing given once and for all (against Paulhan).

Word meaning is always a generalization; behind the word is always a process of generalization—meaning develops with generalization. The development of meaning = the development of generalization!

The principles of generalization may change. *"The structure of generalization is changed in development"* (develops, becomes stratified, the process is realized differently).

[The process of the realization of the thought in meaning is a complex phenomenon which proceeds inward "from motives to speaking" (?).]

In meaning it is always a generalized reality that is given (L. S.).

6. IN BREADTH AND AFAR

[The basic questions]: (1) word meaning germinates in consciousness; what does this mean for consciousness itself?; (2) as a result of what and how does meaning change?

[First answers]: (1) the word that germinates in consciousness changes all relationships and processes; (2) word meaning itself develops depending on changes in consciousness.

The Role of Meaning in the Life of Consciousness

"To speak = to present a theory."

"The world of objects develops with the world of names" (L. S.–J. S. Mill). [22]

"The constancy and categorical objectivity [23] of the object is the meaning of the object" [Lenin about distinguishing oneself from the world]. <This meaning, this objectivity is already given in perception.>

"All our perception has meaning." All meaningless things we perceive (as meaningful), attaching meaning to it.

The meaning of the object is not the meaning of the word. "The object has meaning"—this means that it enters into communication.

To know the meaning is to know the singular as the universal.

"The processes of human consciousness have their meaning due to the fact that they are given a name, i.e., are being generalized" (not in the sense as with the word.— L. S.).

Meaning is inherent in the sign.

Sense is what enters into meaning (the result of the meaning) but is not consolidated behind the sign.

The formation of sense is the *result, the product of meaning.* Sense is broader than meaning.

Consciousness is (1) knowledge in connection; (2) consciousness (social).

[The first questions of children are never questions about names; they are questions about the sense of the object.] <The meaningful is not simply the structural (against Gestalt theory).>

Consciousness as a whole has a semantic structure. *We judge consciousness by its semantic structure, for sense, the structure of consciousness, is the relation to the external world.*

New semantic connections develop in consciousness (shame, pride—hierarchy . . . the dream of the Kaffir, Masha Bolkonskaya prays when another would think . . .). [24]

The sense-creating activity of meanings leads to a certain semantic structure of consciousness itself.

Speech was thus incorrectly considered only in its relation to thinking. *Speech produces changes in consciousness.* "Speech is a correlate of consciousness, not of thinking"

"Thinking is no gateway through which speech enters into consciousness" (L. S.). Speech is a sign for the communication between consciousnesses. The relation between speech and consciousness is a psychophysical problem <And at the same time transgresses the boundaries of consciousness.>

The first communications of the child, just like early praxis, are not intellectual <Nobody tried to prove that the first communication is intellectual.> It is not at all true that the child is only speaking when he thinks.

"By its appearance speech fundamentally changes consciousness." What moves the meanings, what determines their development? "The cooperation of consciousnesses." The process of alienation of consciousness.

Consciousness is prone to splintering. Consciousness is prone to merging. <They are essential for consciousness.>

How does generalization develop? How does the structure of consciousness change?

Either: man has resort to the sign; the sign gives birth to meaning; meaning sprouts in consciousness. It is *not* like that.

Meaning is determined by the interfunctional relationships = by consciousness, by the activity of consciousness. "The structure of meaning is determined by the systemic structure of consciousness." Consciousness has a systemic structure. The systems are stable and characterize consciousness.

CONCLUSION

"Semiotic analysis is the only adequate method for the study of the systemic and semantic structure of consciousness." Just like the structural method is an adequate method for the investigation of animal consciousness.

Our word in psychology: away from superficial psychology—in consciousness, being and phenomenon are not equal. But we also oppose depth psychology. Our psychology is a peak psychology (does not determine the "depths" of the personality but its "peaks").

The path toward internal hidden developments as a tendency in modern science (chemistry toward the structure of the atom, the physiology of digestion toward vitamins, etc.). In psychology we first attempted to understand logical memory as the tying of a knot, now as semantic memorization. Depth psychology claims that things are what they always have been. The unconscious does not develop—this is a great discovery. The dream shines with reflected light, just like the moon.

This is clear from the way we understand development. As a transformation of what was given initially? As a novel form? In that case most important is what developed last!

"In the beginning was the thing (and not: the thing was in the beginning), in the end came the word, and this is the most important" (L. S.). What is the meaning of what has been said? "For me this knowledge is enough," i.e., now it is enough that the problem has been stated. [25]

APPENDIX

(From the preparatory work for the theses for the debate in the years 1933-1934. Record of Vygotsky's speeches on the 5th and 9th of December, 1933).

The central fact of our psychology is the fact of mediation.

Communication and generalization. The internal side of mediation is revealed in the double function of the sign: (1) communication, (2) generalization. For: all communication requires generalization.

Communication is also possible directly, but mediated communication is communication in signs, here generalization is necessary. ("Each word (speech) already generalizes.") [26]

A fact: for the child communication and generalization do not coincide: that is why communication is direct here.

Intermediate is the pointing gesture. The gesture is a sign that can mean anything.

A law: the form of generalization corresponds to the form of communication. "Communication and generalization are internally connected."

People communicate with meanings insofar as these meanings develop.

The schema here is: not person–thing (Stern), not person–person (Piaget). But: person–thing–person.

Generalization. What is generalization?

Generalization is the exclusion from visual structures and the inclusion in thought structures, in semantic structures.

Meaning and the system of functions are internally connected.

Meaning does not belong to thinking but to consciousness as a whole.

Chapter 10

PSYCHOLOGY AND THE THEORY OF THE LOCALIZATION OF MENTAL FUNCTIONS[*,1]

It is legitimate and fruitful to approach the problem of localization from the psychological viewpoint because the dominant psychological views of various periods have always greatly influenced the ideas about the localization of mental functions (association psychology and the atomistic theory of localization; structural psychology and the tendency of modern scholars toward an integral conception of localization). The problem of localization ultimately is a problem of the relation between structural and functional units in brain activity. That is why the conception about what is being localized cannot be irrelevant for the solution of the problem of the character of the localization.

The most progressive modern theories of localization managed to overcome the main shortcomings of the classical theory. But they could not satisfactorily solve the problem of the localization of mental functions mainly because of the inadequacy of the structural psychological analysis of localized functions they applied. Although the theory of localization has advanced vigorously due to the successes of histology, the cytoarchitectonics of the brain and the clinic, it still cannot fully realize its potential because it lacks a system of psychological analysis of corresponding complexity and adequate strength. This makes itself most acutely felt in the problem of the localization of specifically human areas of the brain. That the delocalization theory and the formula "the brain as a whole" are inadequate is acknowledged by the majority of modern investigators. However, the functional analysis they habitually use, based on the principles of structural psychology, appeared as powerless to lead the theory of localization beyond the boundaries of this formula as it was productive and valuable in the solution of the first, critical part of the task these new theories faced (to overcome atomistic theory).

Structural psychology, on which the newest theories are based, by its very essence does not allow us to attribute more than two functions to each brain center: a specific one connected with a specific type of activity of consciousness and a nonspecific one connected with any other activity of consciousness (Goldstein's figure–ground theory, Lashley's[2] theory of the specific and nonspecific functions of the visual cortex). This theory essentially combines the old classical theory of the strict correspondence between structural and functional units and the specialization of different areas for specific limited functions (the theory of the specific function of centers) with the new delocalized view which denies such a correspondence and

*First published as Vygotsky, L. S. (1934). Psikhologija i uchenie o lokalizacii psikhicheskikh funkcij. In *Pervyj vseukrainskij s'ezd nevropatologov i psikhiatrov* (pp. 34-41). Kharkov.

such a functional specialization of separate areas and proceeds from the formula "the brain as a whole" (the theory of the nonspecific functions of centers for which all centers are equivalent).

These theories thus constitute no improvement to both extremes in the theory of localization but combine them mechanically. They have all the shortcomings of the old (strictly localizationist) and the new (anti-localizationist) theories. This is particularly telling in the problem of the localization of higher mental functions connected with specifically human areas of the brain (the frontal and parietal lobes). Here the investigators were forced by the facts to transcend the boundaries of the concepts of structural psychology and to introduce new psychological concepts (Goldstein's theory of categorical thinking, Head's[3] theory of symbolic functions, Pötzl's theory of the categorization of perception, etc.). [1]

However, these psychological concepts are by the same investigators again reduced to basic and elementary structural functions ("the basic function of the brain" in Goldstein, structuralization in Pötzl) or they turn into primordial metaphysical entities (Head). Orbiting in the vicious circle of structural psychology, the theory of the localization of specifically human functions thus wavers between the poles of extreme naturalism and extreme spiritualism.

In our view, a system of psychological analysis that is adequate from the viewpoint of the theory of localization must be based on a historical theory of the higher mental functions. At the basis of such a theory lies a theory of the systemic and semantic structure of human consciousness. This theory proceeds from the paramount importance of (a) the mutability of the interfunctional connections and relations; (b) the formation of complex dynamic systems which integrate quite a number of elementary functions; (c) the generalized reflection of activity in consciousness. From the viewpoint of the theory defended by us these three aspects represent the most essential, fundamental, and united properties of human consciousness. They form the expression of the law according to which not only the transition from inanimate matter to sensation, but also the transition from sensation to thinking, forms a dialectical leap. In the course of several years we have applied this theory as a working hypothesis, and in the investigation of a number of problems of clinical psychology it has led us to three basic claims about the problem of localization. In turn, they can be regarded as working hypotheses which adequately explain the most important clinical facts about the problem of localization known to us and allow us to conduct experimental investigations.

The *first* of our conclusions concerns the problem of the function of the whole and the part in brain activity. The analysis of aphasic, agnostic, and apraxic disorders compels us to accept that the solution of the problem of the functions of the whole and the part which we find in the theories of Goldstein and Lashley is of no use. The positing of a double (specific and nonspecific) function for each center cannot adequately explain the whole complexity of the experimentally gathered facts with the disorders mentioned above. Research compels us to proceed to a solution of the problem that is in a certain sense its opposite. It demonstrates, first, that no specific function is ever connected with the activity of one single brain center. It is always the product of the integral activity of strictly differentiated, hierarchically interconnected centers. Research demonstrates, secondly, that neither does the function of the brain as a whole, which serves as the formation of the ground, consist of the undifferentiated and functionally uniform combined activity of all other brain centers. It is the product of the integral activity of dispersed, differentiated and also hierarchically interconnected functions of different brain areas which do not directly participate in the formation of the figure. Neither the function of the whole nor the function of the part in brain activity thus represent a simple, uniform and undifferentiated function which in one case is fulfilled by the functionally homogeneous brain as a whole and in the other by an equally homogeneous and specialized center. We find differentiation and unity, integral activity of the centers and their functional differentiation both in the function of the whole and in the function of the part. Differentiation and integration not only do not exclude but rather presuppose each other and in a certain sense proceed in parallel. Moreover, most essential appears to be the circumstance that for various functions we must posit a different structure for the relations between centers. At any rate, it can be considered an established fact that the relations between the functions of the whole and the functions of the part are essentially different depending on whether the figure in brain activity is represented by higher mental functions and the ground by lower ones, or whether, the reverse, the figure is represented by the lower functions and the ground by the higher ones. Such phenomena as the automatic or nonautomatic course of some process or the realization of one and the same function on a different level can be hypothetically explained from the viewpoint of the properties of the structure of the relations between centers, which we have just described, in different forms of the activity of consciousness.

The experimental investigations that served as the factual material for the generalizations formulated above lead us to the following two statements [2]:

1. In case of a focal lesion (aphasia, agnosia, apraxia), all other functions not directly connected with the damaged part will suffer in a specific way and will never show the uniform loss one would expect according to the theory of the equivalence of all areas of the brain with respect to their nonspecific function.

2. One and the same function which is not connected with the damaged area will suffer in a completely unique, completely specific way depending on the localization of the lesion and will, with a different localization of the focus, not show equal loss or disturbance as one would expect according to the theory of the equivalence of the different brain areas which participate in the formation of the ground.

These two statements compel us to conclude that the function of the whole is organized and formed as an integral activity at the basis of which are intercentral relations which are highly differentiated, hierarchically combined and dynamic.

Another series of experimental investigations enabled us to make the following claims:

1. Each complex function (e.g., speech) will suffer as a whole, in all of its parts, although unevenly, when an area is damaged which is connected with one particular aspect of this function (the sensory, motor, or mnemic aspect). This points to the fact that the normal functioning of such a complex psychological system is not provided for by the sum total of the functions of the specialized areas, but by the united system of the centers which takes part in the formation of each of the particular aspects of the given function.

2. Each complex function not directly connected with the damaged area will suffer in a completely specific way, not only because of the loss of the ground, but also because the lesion may be in an area which is functionally closely connected with it. This again points to the fact that the normal functioning of each complex system is provided for by the integral activity of a certain system of centers which includes not just centers directly connected with some aspect of the given psychological system.

The two claims compel us to conclude that both the function of the part and the function of the whole are built as an integrative activity based on complex intercentral relationships.

While structural localizationist analysis made great progress in isolating and studying these complex hierarchical intercentral relations, the leading investigators have until now confined functional analysis to the application of the same hierarchically undifferentiated functional concepts to the activity of both the higher and the lower centers. These investigators interpret the disturbance of functionally higher centers (e.g., Pötzl's broader visual sphere) from the viewpoint of the psychology of the functions of the lower centers (the narrow visual sphere). Structural psychology, on which these authors rely, is by the very essence of its principles incapable of adequately reflecting the whole complexity and hierarchical nature of these intercentral relations. As a result, the investigators do not transcend the boundaries of purely descriptive analysis (more primitive–more complex, shorter–longer). They are forced to reduce the specific functions of higher centers with respect to lower ones to inhibition and excitation and ignore that the function of each of these higher centers introduces something new into the brain's activity. From this viewpoint, higher centers can inhibit and sensitize the activity of lower ones but cannot create anything principally new and add it to the brain's activity. Our investigations, on the contrary, lead us to the opposite assumption. We think that the specific function of each special intercentral system is first of all to provide for a completely new, productive form of conscious activity and not just one that inhibits or stimulates the activity of lower centers. Most important in the specific function of each higher center is the new *modus operandi* of consciousness.

The *second* of the general theoretical conclusions that we reached as the result of our experimental investigations concerns the question of the interrelationship of functional and structural units in disturbances of child development caused by some brain defect and the disintegration of psychological systems following an analogous (with respect to the localization) damage of the mature brain. The comparative study of the symptoms of disturbances in mental development after some brain defect and the pathological changes and disturbances that develop after an analogous lesion in the adult brain lead us to the conclusion that in child and adult different lesions can lead to a similar symptomatic picture. And, the other way around, that lesions located at the same place may lead to a completely different symptomatic picture in child and adult.

From the positive side, these deep differences in the consequences of similar lesions in development and loss can be covered by the following general law: in disturbances of development caused by some cerebral defect, other conditions being equal, what functionally suffers most is the next higher center relative to the damaged area and what suffers relatively less is the next lower center. In disintegration the opposite dependency can be observed: what suffers most in the case of a lesion of a center, other conditions being equal, is the center that is next lower to the damaged area and that is dependent on it and what suffers relatively less is the next higher center on which the damaged center is itself functionally dependent.

The factual confirmation of this law we find in all cases of inborn or early childhood aphasia and apraxia, in cases of disturbances observed in children and adults as a result of epidemic encephalitis, and in cases of oligophrenia with various localizations of the defect.

The explanation of this regularity resides in the fact that the complex relationships between different cerebral systems evolve as a product of development and that, consequently, we should observe a different interdependency of centers during brain development and in the functioning of the mature brain: lower centers—which in the history of the brain serve as the prerequisite for the development of the functions of higher centers which are consequently dependent in their development on these lower centers—are themselves dependent and subordinate levels which depend in their activity on the higher centers as a result of the law of the transition of functions upward. Development proceeds from below upwards but disintegration from the top downward.

Additional factual confirmations of this claim are the observations of the compensatory, alternative paths and detours of development in the presence of a defect. These observations show that in the mature brain it is often the higher centers which take care of the compensatory function in the case of some defect, whereas in the developing brain this is done by centers which are lower with respect to the damaged area. Due to this law, the comparative study of development and loss is in our opinion one of the most fruitful methods in the investigation of the problems of localization and in particular of the problems of chronogenic localization.

The last of the three general theoretical claims mentioned above, which was proposed by us on the basis of experimental investigations, concerns some details of the localization of functions in the specifically human areas of the brain. The investigation of aphasia, agnosia, and apraxia leads us to the conclusion that in the localization of these disorders an essential role is played by the disturbance of extracerebral connections in the activity of the system of centers which in the normal brain ensure correct functioning of the higher forms of speech, cognition, and action. Observations of the history of development of the higher forms of activity of consciousness may serve as factual confirmation of such a conclusion. This history demonstrates that initially all these functions function in intimate connection with external activity and only later on, as it were, disappear inward and change into inner activity. Research into the compensatory functions which develop in these disorders also shows that the objectification of a disturbed function, i.e., bringing it outside and changing it into external activity, is one of the basic roads in the compensation of disorders.

The system of psychological analysis that we defend and that we apply to the investigation of the problem of localization presupposes a radical change in the method of the psychological experiment. This change comes down to two basic points:

(1) analysis which decomposes the complex psychological whole into its composite elements and which as a result loses the properties proper to the whole as a whole which need to be explained, must be replaced by analysis which decomposes the complex whole into units which are not further decomposable and which retain in most simple form the properties proper to the whole as a certain unity;

(2) structural and functional analysis which is incapable of comprehending activity as a whole must be replaced by interfunctional or systemic analysis which for each given form of activity finds the interfunctional connections and relations that determine it.

When applied in clinical-psychological investigation, this method enables us to (a) explain the plus and minus symptoms observed in a certain disorder using a single principle; (b) reduce all symptoms, even those which are most remote from each other, to a unity, to a lawfully built structure; and (c) outline the path leading from focal disorders of a certain kind to a specific alteration of the whole personality and his way of life.

Theoretically there is every reason to suppose that the solution of the problem of localization is different in animals and man. The direct transfer of data from animal experiments (e.g., extirpation of different parts of the brain) to the area of the clinical elaboration of the problem of localization (Lashley) can thus lead to nothing other than gross mistakes. The theory of the evolution of mental capacities in the animal world according to pure and mixed lines [3], which is gaining a stronger and stronger foothold, compels us to think that the relations of structural and functional units specific to man can hardly exist in the animal world and that the human brain possesses a localization principle which, compared to that of the animal, is new and due to which it became the brain of man, the organ of human consciousness.

PART 2

DEVELOPMENTAL PATHS OF PSYCHOLOGICAL KNOWLEDGE

Chapter 11

PREFACE TO THORNDIKE[*][1]

1

The general revolution in the views and fundamental opinions about the essence, subject, and methods of psychological science, which now in Russia has taken especially acute and vivid forms, cannot pass by, of course, without leaving a trace in the whole field of applied psychology and pedagogical psychology in particular. When a radical breaking from old concepts and ideas, a fundamental reform of ideas and methods, takes place in the realm of theoretical knowledge, then the same painful and fruitful processes of destruction and reconstruction of the whole scientific system are also inevitable in the applied disciplines which form offshoots of the general trunk. They may lag behind but cannot escape such a reform.

There is no doubt that the critical revision of the whole scientific legacy of pedagogical psychology will also take place with such an inevitable delay—a legacy that is indissolubly connected with classical and new, empirical and experimental psychology. As long as this revision has not been carried out, it is all the more important to find suitable books that don't lead us astray. Such books might be used in this transitional revolutionary period when the old and previous concepts are hopelessly compromised and not fit for further use, and adequate new concepts that can replace them have not yet been created. A fruitful and beneficial revolution and crisis in science implies almost always a painful and excruciating crisis in the teaching and study of this science. However, to refrain from teaching psychology in the system of pedagogical education would mean to refrain from any possible scientific foundation and clarification of the educational process itself, from the practice itself of the teacher's labor. Incidentally, it would mean that we build the whole theory of social education and the labor school upon bare ideology. It would mean that we refrain from the foundation in the structure of the education of teachers and from the center that ties the motley heap of methodological and pedagogical disciplines together. To express it more simply and briefly: to refrain from psychology means to refrain from scientific pedagogics. Here we must choose the line of most resistance.

All this, while being perfectly correct in itself, acquires even more meaning and force when we take into account that the reform of psychological ideas which is taking place at the moment directly leads to a radical revolution in the scientific views on the very essence of the pedagogical process. It may be said that here

*First published as Vygotsky, L. S. (1926). Predislovie. In E. L. Thorndike, *Principy Obuchenija, osnovannye na psikhologii* (pp. 5-23). Moscow: Rabotnik Prosveshchenija.

147

education is for the first time revealed in its genuine essence for science. Here for the first time the pedagogue finds grounds to speak about the precise meaning and the scientific laws of the educational process and not about conjectures and metaphors.

As will be clarified below, the pedagogical problem stands at the very center of the new viewpoint on the mind of man so that the new psychology, to a much greater degree than the former one, forms the foundation for pedagogics. Below this will be made perfectly clear. The new system does not have to draw pedagogical conclusions from its laws or adjust its theses to practical application in the school, because the solution of the pedagogical problem and education—its first word—is contained in the very basis of this system. The relation itself between psychology and pedagogics is thus essentially altered—and in the direction of a tremendous increase and growth in the mutual meaning, connection, and support of both sciences.

Thorndike's book [1], for which these pages serve as a preface, meets the demands of the school and the ordinary teacher for a handbook on pedagogical psychology which serves the needs and tasks of our time of transition. It may easily happen that after some years this book will be replaced by a more perfect work in the Russian language and lose its exclusive significance. But it can be said with confidence that for the next few years the book will have all the qualities to become the main textbook and guide on the pedagogical psychology of our teacher, a book for the period of transition. It can claim this right, first, because of the general theoretical position in psychology that the author defends when he deals with all the general and particular problems of the course. This viewpoint can be defined most accurately and aptly as a perfectly consistent objective view on the mind and behavior of man which is always combined with an equally objective method to study and expound the subject.

Thorndike is one of the most prominent experimental psychologists of our time. He is in all likelihood the founder of the psychology of behavior, the so-called American behaviorism, and of objective psychology in general. It is interesting that his name is mentioned by Academician Pavlov [1928/1963, p. 40] in his preface to "Twenty years of objective study of the higher nervous activity (behavior) of animals" as the first one who created the new psychology. There it is said that

> I must acknowledge that the honor of having taken the first steps along this path belongs to Edward L. Thorndike ("Animal intelligence: An experimental study of the associative processes in animals," 1898), who anticipated our experiments by two or three years and whose book must be considered a classic, both for its bold outlook on an immense task and for the accuracy of its results.

This alone indicates with transparent clarity that Thorndike's theoretical position coincides completely with the starting points of the new psychological systems that are developing before our eyes. And one only has to leaf through Thorndike's book for a few seconds to become convinced that he fully shares the basic idea of the new psychology—the view on human mind and behavior as a system of reactions of the organism to external stimuli, coming from the environment, and internal stimuli, arising in the organism itself. For Thorndike, behavior is a system of reactions. In his conception the mind consists of no more than special and complex forms of behavior, i.e., in the final analysis it consists of the same reactions.

This viewpoint treats absolutely all aspects of the child's mind as behavioral reactions to certain stimuli and reduces the whole educational process to the modification of innate reactions and the elaboration of reactions that have been acquired in experience. Naturally, this viewpoint determined in advance that each chapter is based on the exceptionally indisputable and scientifically reliable material of experimental psychology and totally excludes all speculative analysis of subjective mental experiences according to scholastic classificatory schemes.

When we add to this what perhaps is the most important feature of Thorndike's book—its practical orientation, which is evident from the structure of each sentence and line of thought—then the value of the book is seen beyond any doubt. It is wholly geared to practice, wholly created to meet the needs of the school and the teacher. The rich practical material which the book contains for exercises, discussions, lessons, critique, etc. allows for the possibility of working through the content of each chapter not only theoretically. In the process of mastering the material of the course it can be independently checked in a most convincing way. When he explains the principles of pedagogics based on psychology in his book, Thorndike himself acts as a vivid example and embodiment of this psychological current in pedagogics. He takes all of his own rules about teaching a subject into account and pulls out all the stops of the psychology of the reader in order to make him master the subject. He demands of the reader the same activity, the same test of the book against the personal experience of the student which is the central theme of his book.

Judging by all these qualities, the book, in our view, is destined to become the main textbook for each pedagogue and ordinary teacher for the period to come. It will be the basic book that provides needed clarification both in the study of pedagogical work and intensifying the study of the foundations of the educational process. When we take the highly unsatisfactory nature of almost all Russian textbooks on this subject into account, the value of this book becomes especially convincing and tangible.

Indeed, the courses on pedagogical psychology for institutes and the textbooks that defend the traditional viewpoint are of very little help for the elaboration of a scientific conception of education. Leaving a detailed discussion of other things aside, we point out that they do not explain the central problem—the psychological nature itself of the development, growth, and formation of the child's mind and personality; the mechanisms that propel this evolution and the essence of educational influence remain unclarified and obscure in traditional psychology. They are passed by in silence or mentioned in opaque words which explain nothing and throw no light on them.

And this is not a defect particular to Russian textbooks but an organic and inevitable flaw of the very psychological system which underlies the ordinary course. Traditional school psychology considers the mind statically and not dynamically. It considers the frozen, stiffened forms and not the processes of the coming into being, growth, and ascent of new forms. Even the idea of evolution is almost always conspicuously absent in the most popular courses. The ready-made consciousness with all its attributes and parts is described and analyzed, dissected and classified as if it existed from time immemorial in the form in which it is revealed to us in introspection.

Moreover, the child's mind is usually construed by the rather elementary operation of subtracting all those manifestations and particularities from adult consciousness which can't be found in the child at the given age level. What is left as the result of such operations is construed as the child's mind of this or that age. Science in its previous form lacked in principle the resources to avoid this path which is obviously and clearly false. It had no other paths available as its core and the source of its validity was the self-observation of adult man. What remained was to follow the levels of childhood in reverse order, to apply subtraction—and to determine and describe the child's mind constantly by its minus points, by what it lacks, always in negative concepts and terms.

This is an exaggerated but not distorted statement of the older psychology. Incidentally, below we will have occasion to contrast these viewpoints briefly but sharply. Let us just say that traditional psychology could not possibly take the only right course—to proceed from the child to the adult in the study of mind. By its very essence it was confined to a fruitless statement of some odd aspects of the child's mind. It knew neither the secret of the generalizing scientific idea of the development of the mind nor the essence of education. The course of the new psychology—it is also Thorndike's course—is the opposite. Consequently, it lacks these shortcomings of the academic course of the usual type and leads us from a descriptive and fragmentary psychology to a scientific, explanatory and generalizing system of knowledge about the behavior of man, the mechanisms of his development, and the educational guidance of the processes of his development, formation and growth.

Despite all this the book has its shortcomings—and they are of no small importance. The most important one is the obvious theoretical discordance between the pedagogical and the psychological parts of the book. At times the author does not draw the fundamentally important pedagogical conclusions that are inexorably dictated by his own psychological arguments. It is as if the new view of the mind does not commit him to a new word on education. He is, if I am allowed to say so, a bolshevik in psychology but remains a cadet in his theory of education. [2] His extreme radicalism is easily reconciled and goes along with his liberalism in the adjacent and scientifically dependent area.

In the book, the psychological foundation is placed under a pedagogical practice that is foreign to our school system. For the author the school remains primarily a tool to develop the intellect. His critique of training is very moderate. He introduces the labor principle (manual labor, handicraft, etc.) as an auxiliary method to an insignificant extent. The divergence of the two lines is particularly telling in the chapters where the author deals with moral education. He claims [1906, p. 180] that the school is virtually powerless in this domain. "The mind must be supplied with noble ideas through the right examples at home, in school," etc.. This is what his sober and exact scientific style turns into when he gets to morals. Here psychology is fitted and tailored to the school of practical training of the American mold and not to the labor school.

Connected with this is the almost complete neglect of the social factor in education. The teacher remains the highest authority, the prime mover of the pedagogical mechanism, the source of light and sermon. Education is addressed from the teacher to the pupil, remains deeply individualistic all the time and—in the words of one author—reminds us of a pedagogical duet between the teacher and the pupil. Meanwhile it is precisely Thorndike's psychological theory that harbors enormous possibilities for the development of social pedagogics and allows us to develop it on a scale that would have been completely impossible previously.

But insofar as they found a (very modest) place in the book, the goals of education and the school, the ideology of the school, are explained and described by Thorndike in flat contradiction to the currently developing pedagogics. It all clearly diverges from our pedagogics and bears the obvious traces of the official American system. "The ideals of efficiency, honor, duty, love and service"—these are the ideals of this system in the words of Thorndike [1906, p. 4].

The book is called *The Principles of Teaching Based on Psychology*. This aptly expresses and describes the different angle of Thorndike's book in comparison to our pedagogics, which was briefly sketched above. It is indeed a school system primarily based on teaching and learning, and as a result all questions of pedagogics, as might be expected from this title alone, will be narrowed down and belittled unevenly. The problems are often reduced to a miniature. The fundamental tasks of education are distorted and presented in a false light.

Another discomforting feature of the book which makes us become pensive is the absence of any generalizing biological and social psychological theory of behavior composed of innate and acquired reactions. The precious and correct ideas are always applied to details and are never taken together and made fully explicit. This explains the obvious incoherent and fragmentary nature of the different remarks about reactions, the laws of their development and growth. It explains why he is so vague about the fundamental grounds for the classification, the terminology and the other methods used to present a scientific explanation of the material.

The second shortcoming of the book is not organic. On the contrary, here the parts and different statements are in complete internal harmony. They are all united by one generalizing psychological theory. Each chapter has its basis in common with the others. This generalizing fundamental theory is present, so to speak, on each page of the book, but invisibly, vaguely, and imperceptibly. Even the attentive reader may fail to notice it. It must be disclosed.

The book is written in such a way that each chapter presupposes the knowledge of some theoretical foundations. In the original, the author refers before each chapter to the corresponding paragraph of his book *The Elements of Psychology*, which is indispensable for the theoretical preparation. And in the preface he writes [1906, p. v] that the book

> demands of students knowledge of the elements of psychology, particularly of dynamic psychology. The references entitled 'Preparatory' (or their equivalent) will fulfill this prerequisite. These references are to the author's *Elements of Psychology*, which is in a sense an introduction to the present volume, but any standard course in psychology which gives due emphasis to the laws of mental connections will supply the preparation needed.

Here it is clearly said that *The Principles of Teaching* is written with this theoretical introduction in mind and that its study is a necessary requirement for the study of the book. It [*The Elements of Psychology*] is thus purposely made into a separate course.

Leaving aside some minor details and uneven parts, the two remarks given above exhaust the critical evaluation of the book. It is obvious that both of the book's shortcomings are as momentous as its merits. The purpose of this preface is to attempt, if not to eliminate them completely, in any case to take away their sharp edges and to deprive them of their capital importance by introducing two critical corrections to the text of the book—one concerning our pedagogics and one concerning psychological theory. This gives the book a social-pedagogical and biopsychological foundation. It seems to us that these two necessary corrections can most easily and best be made in the form of a critical preface to the book and two short introductory essays. These then form the content of the following chapters and explain in the most concise and summary way the basic psychological and pedagogical schemes and formulas necessary for a critical assimilation of the book. We have refrained from a polemic with the author in the form of editorial notes both because these would have to be added so frequently as to become very tiresome and because the very purpose of the book excludes the possibility of such a polemic. The same is true for additions. To intrude in the author's text, to rewrite it in the process of translation, to subject whole passages in the book to a fundamental reworking would mean to deprive it of all integrity and scientific style. This might easily lead to a change for the worse rather than to an improvement of the matter.

On these grounds, we settled on introductory essays which critically guide the perception of the reader in the pedagogical part and provide him with a generalizing viewpoint in the psychological part. Both essays exclusively serve this auxiliary goal. If one has no suitable literature at hand, these essays may be successfully used, in our opinion, as introductory chapters to the book.

We once more make the proviso that while in the pedagogical part and in the essays a critical view of the author is defended (which, however, directly follows from his own theory), in the psychological part the scientific assumptions formulated below, compiled mainly on the basis of the Russian literature, are far from being something extraneous, some mechanical appendage to the system of ideas developed in the book. They merely reveal the system of ideas lying at the basis of the book and formulate it, although perhaps in words and terms that are not quite close to the style of the author, in scientific concepts and principles which fully coincide with his view. Academician Pavlov's remark mentioned above may serve as the best evidence for this.

2

In the popular ordinary views of man, mind is usually regarded as a very special category of phenomena. It is regarded as something that is absolutely dissimilar from the rest of the world, as something nonphysical that stands above matter. When we speak about memory, will and thoughts, we think of something which is totally different from all the rest that takes place in the world. We think of something which is fundamentally different, of phenomena of a special kind which cannot be compared to anything else.

In this respect, the popular view and terminology fully coincide with the scientific claims of traditional psychology which views the radical border between the mental and the physical as its basic assumption. Naturally, in such a view the most basic questions about the mind of man, its origin, purpose and development were left unanswered.

Such a view of soul and body, which proceeds from the duality of human nature, the heterogeneous nature of its parts, the impossibility of reducing them to a single principle, the separate, independent existence of spiritual beings and phenomena, we call dualism and spiritualism. Such a theory necessarily implies the inexplicability of the fundamental particularities of the mind. To study something in complete isolation from the rest of the world, separated from the general connection of the phenomena, implies that one is doomed in advance to conclude that the subject of study itself is inexplicable. To explain something means no more than to show the link with other phenomena, to include the new into the chain and system of what is already known. This directly opposes the traditional viewpoint. Hence the obvious sterility of psychological science, its helplessness—both theoretical and practical—concerning the basic problems. Such a viewpoint may be sufficient to explain details and tie them together, but the key to general concepts is forever lost in such a conception.

Apart from its purely methodological barrenness, traditional psychology suffers from another flaw. The point is that reality, as is obvious to anyone, does not at all justify such a view of mind. On the contrary, every fact and event loudly testifies to another and directly opposite state of affairs: the mind with all its subtle and complex mechanisms forms part of the general system of human behavior. It is in every point nourished and permeated by these interdependences. Not for a single millisecond, used by psychology to measure the exact duration of mental processes, is it isolated and separated from the rest of the world and the other organic processes. Who claims and studies the opposite, studies the unreal constructions of his own mind, chimeras instead of facts, scholastic, verbal constructions instead of genuine reality.

That is why an observer of great authority concluded that traditional psychology has no "generally accepted system." This investigator (Lange, 1914, p. 42) says that "The psychologist of our days resembles Priam sitting on the ruins of Troy." He also calls the crisis that is now taking place in empirical psychology a crisis in the very foundations of the science and compares it to an earthquake. He says that it suffices to bear in mind the fall of alchemy, despite a great number of precise experiments by the old alchemists, or similar radical revolutions in the history of medicine. It is extremely important to note that this crisis manifested itself very clearly long before the debate between the adherents of objective and subjective psychology now taking place in Russia. James already called traditional psychology a string of raw facts and characterized it as follows. What is psychology at the present moment?

> A string of raw facts, a little gossip and wrangle about opinions; a little classification and generalization on the mere descriptive level; a strong prejudice that we *have* states of mind, and that our brain conditions them: but not a single law in the sense in which physics shows us laws, not a single proposition from which any consequence can causally be deduced [see p. 401 of Burkhardt, 1984].

It goes without saying that the general helplessness of the psychological science manifested itself more prominently and vividly in the application to pedagogics. Above we pointed out that by its very nature this psychology could not appreciate and handle the problems of dynamics, development, increasing changes and education. Moreover, its practical conclusions always suffered from being approximate and crudely empirical. They were generalizations of the most primary raw experience. Psychology regarded the child's personality and the whole educational process as a mechanical process consisting of a number of psychological functions (capacities, phenomena) fenced off from each other by a Chinese wall and surrounded by impassable entrenchments from all other vital processes in the child's organism. And this psychological mosaic, this scrappy and fragmentary theory of development was in great harmony with an equally mosaic-like pedagogics. A pedagogics which tore the integral organism of the growing child to tatters, to subjects and capacities.

The new psychology takes as its point of departure the idea of mind's indissoluble link with all other vital processes of the organism and seeks the sense, meaning and laws of development of this mind precisely in the integral inclusion of the mind in the series of the organism's vital functions. The biological expediency of mind here serves as the basic explanatory principle. Mind is understood as one of the functions of the organism similar in its most important and essential aspect to all other functions, i.e., like all other functions of the organism it is a biologically useful vital adaptation to the environment. The general biological meaning of mind and its place amid a number of other forms of adaptation can easily be determined by means of the classificatory schema of the basic forms of adaptation which we borrow from Academician Severcov's (1922) book *Evolution and Mind*.

All adaptations of organisms to the environment can quite easily be divided, first, into inherited ones and noninherited ones which arise in the process of individual experience; second, both can consist of changes in the animal's structure (changes in the organs, etc.) or may manifest themselves in a change in the behavior of the animals without altering their organization. [3] That the structure of virtually all animal organs (the structure of the organs of birds, fish, rodents, etc.) became adapted to the biologically important conditions of life as a result of evolution is obvious to anyone. The mechanism of these hereditary adaptations, called natural selection and explained by Darwin, consolidates biologically useful adaptive features through hereditary transmission.

But the hereditary change of organs is an extremely slow process, because it responds to the slow changes of the environment. Organisms possess another much faster and more flexible adaptation to changes in the environment—the functional change of an organ which takes place as a result of the personal experience of the individual. These are cases of rapid adaptation by means of insignificant changes of organs as a result of intensified exercise. This second group of adaptations consists of changes in animals' behavior which are not accompanied by a change in their organization.

Reflexes (cough reflex, defense reflexes—closing of the eyelid, jerking back, etc.) and instincts form the first group of hereditary adaptations. They are the biological capital of the experience gathered by the whole species and entirely belong to the first group of hereditary changes in the structure of the organism. They are just as expedient (the building instincts of ants, birds, bees, etc.), just as adapted to the environmental conditions and change just as slowly and by the same evolutionary path through natural selection or mutation.

The second group of adaptations through a change in behavior without a change in organization consists of so-called behavior of the intelligent type. It consists of the domain of mind in the proper sense of the word, and these adaptations originate in the process of individual experience. This domain covers the whole gamut of personal movements, deeds and acts of the animal which serve the same goal of adaptation to the environment and have the same biological purpose. The general schema of the four most important forms of biological adaptation thus looks like this:

1. Hereditary adaptations to very slow changes in the environment:
    (a) hereditary changes of the animals' structure;
    (b) hereditary changes in behavior without changes in the structure (reflexes and instincts).
2. Nonhereditary adaptations to relatively rapid changes in the environment:
    (a) functional changes in the animals' structure;
    (b) changes in the behavior of animals of the intelligent (mental) type.

This schema allows us to comfortably clarify the place and nature of mind amid other forms of biological adaptation. Behavior represents a most flexible, diverse and complex mechanism which adds tremendous variety and unprecedented subtlety to the adaptive reactions. Man owes his dominion of nature, the higher forms of active adaptation of nature to his needs in contrast to animals' passive adaptation to the environment, to behavior.

The behavior of animal and man consists of reactions. The reaction is the basic mechanism. All behavior is built according to its model, from the most elementary forms of reactions of the infusoria to the most complex acts and deeds of man. Reaction is a broad concept, a general biological one. We may speak about the reactions of plants when they turn to the light; about the reactions of animals when the moth flies into the flame of a candle or when the dog salivates at the sight of meat; about the reactions of man when, having listened to the conditions of a problem, he carries out a number of calculations to solve it. In all these cases the three basic components of each reaction clearly manifest themselves. A reaction is a response of the organism, its adaptive action to some element of the environment that influences it.

That is why each reaction must absolutely include as its first component the organism's perception of this environmental influence, this stimulation which either reaches the organism from outside or originates inside the organism itself. In our example, the light for the plant, the flame for the moth, the sight of meat for the dog, and the conditions of the problem for man are such stimuli, such starting points and elicitors of a reaction. Then the second component of the reaction inevitably follows—some internal processes in the organism called forth by the received stimulation which give rise to the organism's response. This is, so to speak, the processing of the stimulation within the organism. In our example, this would be the chemical processes that originate in the plant under the influence of light and in the organism of the moth under the influence of the flame of the candle, the memory of food in the dog, thought in man. Finally, the internal processes are completed by the third component of the reaction—the response act of the organism itself, the adaptive movement, the secretion, etc. This is the bending of the stem of the plant, the flight of the moth, the salivation of the dog, the calculations on paper by man.

All three components are without fail present in each reaction. But at times one of these components or even all three of them may take such complex and subtle forms that all three of them cannot be observed by the naked eye. But an exact scientific analysis will always absolutely reveal the presence of all three of them. Sometimes the stimulation consists of such a complex compound of the most diverse elements of environment and organism that it is difficult to distinguish and indicate its action. Sometimes the response act takes such convoluted, abbreviated, and elusive forms that it seems totally absent at first sight. In these cases it takes special methods in order to establish and observe it. This happens, for example, in internal speech, so-called tacit thinking, when the vocal motor reactions are inhibited, not manifest, and proceed in the form of hardly perceptible internal movements, or in changes in the pulse, respiration, and other somatic reactions that form the basis of emotion.

Finally, the least studied internal processes, which we termed the second component of the reaction, often acquire special complexity. Stimulation and response are sometimes so widely separate in time that it can be difficult to correlate them without a very complex and special analysis. Even more common is such a complex interaction of the internal processes simultaneously elicited by a multitude of the most heterogeneous stimuli, such a struggle or collision of now allied, now hostile stimulations, that the process of the reaction acquires a tremendously complex and not always predictable character. But man's behavior, however complex it may be, has, always and everywhere, the form of a reaction.

This mechanism can explain hereditary and acquired forms of behavior equally well. The group of hereditary reactions consists of reflexes, which are usually defined as reactions of the function of different organs, and of instincts, which are more complex forms of reaction of the behavior of the whole organism. Both are hereditary, uniform, extremely inflexible, and as a whole expedient. Their biological meaning and origin are totally similar to the hereditary changes of the organism's structure and they also originated through natural selection.

The question of the origin of nonhereditary forms of behavior was long thought to be much more complex. It can be said that it only obtained its final scientific solution in the last decades in connection with the experimental work of the Russian physiological school (the experiments by Pavlov and Bekhterev) and the investigations of the American psychology of behavior (Thorndike and others). The essence of this discovery, which is directly linked to Darwin's idea and explains the origin of individual experience, comes down to the following.

It was unshakably established in experiments that the innate reactions of animal and man are not immutable, constant, and indissoluble. The link established in each of these reactions between some element of the environment and the organism's response act may under certain conditions be changed: a new link between the same act of the organism and a new element of the environment may develop.

For example, when we give meat to a dog it will start salivating. This is an elementary, or unconditional reflex, an innate reaction. When we simultaneously with the meat (or somewhat earlier) influence the dog with another stimulus, for example a bell, after several of these joint presentations of both stimuli the dog will start salivating to the sound of the bell, although it has not been given or shown any meat at all. A new link was formed in the dog—between the previous act and a new element of the environment (the bell)—which was not given in the hereditary experience of the animal. The dog learned to react to the bell as it would normally never have reacted to it. This new reaction (salivation as a response to the bell) may be called a conditional reflex as it arose in the individual experience of the animal and was formed under a special condition, namely under the condition that the new and the old stimulus are simultaneously operative.

Through such experiments one was able to clarify that new conditional links may be formed between any element of the environment and any reaction of the organism. In other words, any phenomenon, any object, may under certain conditions become the stimulus for any reaction, any movement or act. Here unfolds the whole grandiose biological importance of this type of new reactions between the organism and the environment—the conditional reflexes. The development of such links implies an infinite diversity of the organism's responses to the different combinations of elements of the environment, a grandiose complexity of the possible links between the organism and the environment, a tremendous flexibility of the organism's adaptive movements.

This importance increases even more when we add to this another property of conditional reflexes. The fact is that new links may be established not only by combining an unconditional reflex with an indifferent stimulus but also by combining a conditional reflex with a new stimulus. In other words, new links may be formed and develop not only on the basis of innate, but also on the basis of conditional reflexes. When we have established a conditional salivary reflex to a bell in a dog, it suffices to combine the bell with some new stimulus, let us say the scratching of the dog, to form some new conditional reflex in the dog after some time has elapsed. It will now start salivating to the scratching. This is a conditional reflex of the second degree, or second order, as it was itself created on the basis of a conditional reflex.

Superreflexes of a still higher order are possible—a conditional reflex of the third degree, formed on the basis of the second, etc. We have every reason to believe that the limit of these superreflexes, if it exists at all, lies tremendously far away and that tremendously high degrees of conditional reflexes are thus possible, that is, tremendously remote from the original basis and the innate link between the organism and the environment. This circumstance allowed higher animals to develop preventive reactions, to adapt to remote signals and precursors of future stimuli, to the extent that behavior of this type began playing an enormous role in the preservation of the individual. These superreflexes allowed man in particular to develop all complex forms of mental activity and labor reactions.

Experimental research has shown that neither is the character of the link strictly uniform. So-called trace reflexes are possible, in which the response act appears after the conditional stimulus has stopped, or delayed reflexes, in which the response is, as it were, delayed, comes later than the stimulus, and appears some time after the stimulus became operative. It further proved possible to establish a very fine differentiation of the stimuli according to their strength, quality, and rate. Before the organism reacts it carries out a most complex analysis. It, as it were, decomposes reality into very fine elements and is capable of tuning its reactions to various elements of the environment with tremendous subtlety.

Finally, the cooperation of several reflexes and stimuli introduces enormous complexity in the behavior of the animal. When, during a conditional reflex, some other stimulus of sufficient strength becomes operative, it will inhibit the course of the reaction, suspend its action. When we now add to the action of this inhibitory stimulus another new and third stimulation, it will exert an inhibitory influence on the second one, inhibit the inhibition, and a disinhibition of the reaction will take place. Tremendously complex relations of complete and partial inhibition and different interrelations between groups of simultaneously acting reflexes are possible.

All these and many more data, established with unquestionable scientific reliability, allow us to conceive of the process of the development of man in the following way. All behavior should be regarded as a sum-total of reactions of the widest variety and complexity. At the basis of behavior are the innate reactions (reflexes, instincts, and emotional reactions). This is, as it were, the hereditary capital of biologically useful adaptations which have been acquired in the extremely long experience of the whole species. Upon the basis of innate reactions a new floor of personal experience is built: the conditional reflexes which are essentially the same innate reactions, but differentiated, combined and in new and diverse links with the surrounding world. "Conditional reflex" is thus the name for the mechanism which adapts the hereditary biological experience of the species to the individual conditions of the individual's life and transforms it into personal experience.

The behavior of man thus manifests itself not just as a static system of elaborated reactions, but as a process of the development of new links, the establishment of new dependences, the elaboration of new superreflexes and simultaneously the disconnection and destruction of old links, the dying off of previous reactions. This process does not halt for a single minute. But most importantly, it is a struggle between man and the world which does not stop for a second and requires instantaneous combinations, exceedingly complex strategies of the organism and a struggle of the multitude of diverse reactions within the organism for predominance, for the predominance of the executive effector organs. In short, man's behavior is revealed in all its real complexity, in its grandiose meaning, as the dynamic and dialectic process of a struggle between man and the world and within man. This is the first basic idea of the new psychology.

3

The socially determined character of human reactions has already become very clear in the concise and cursory sketch of the composition of our behavior given above. [4] Indeed, we have seen that experimental natural science established the mechanism of the formation of individual experience and personal behavior. It turned out that personal behavior (as a system of conditional reactions) inevitably originates on the basis of innate or unconditional reactions under certain conditions which completely regulate and determine the process of their formation.

What are these conditions? It is not difficult to see that they lie in the organization of the environment: personal experience is formed and organized as a copy of the organization of the various elements in the environment. Actually, all Pavlov's experiments came down to a certain experimental organization of the environment in which the dog was placed, and his main efforts were meant to organize this environment as perfectly as possible, with maximal purity of the different combinations of elements realized.

Neither is it difficult to see that the environment, as the source of all stimulation that reaches the organism, plays the same role with respect to each of us as the Pavlovian laboratory does with respect to his experimental dogs. In the one case, the artificial combination of certain elements (meat, bell) leads to the connection of new links and the development of a conditional reflex. In the other case, the presence and coincidence of elements leads in exactly the same way, only through infinitely more complex influences, to the formation of new conditional reflexes. In the final analysis, the environment (for man, the social environment in particular, because for contemporary man the natural environment is only part of the social environment since no relationship and no connections whatever can exist outside the social ones) has in its organization those conditions that form all our experience.

The whole process of the adaptation of hereditary experience to individual conditions is thus fully determined by the social environment. But, after all, hereditary experience as well is ultimately conditioned and determined by earlier influences of the environment. After all, in the final analysis it owes its origin and structure to the same environment. All of man's behavior consists of unconditional reactions given in hereditary experience multiplied by those new conditional links that appear in personal experience. Man's behavior is, as it were, environment multiplied by environment or squared sociality.

A first and extremely important conclusion follows from this. The whole process of education acquires an exact psychological explanation. We can no longer imagine the newborn child to be a *tabula rasa*, a white sheet of paper upon which the educator can write whatever he likes. And we will not speak vaguely about the influence of hereditary and educational influences as of some mechanical combination of two groups of reactions. We think that it is approximately as follows.

Already at the minute of its birth the newborn child has all the functioning effector organs and is the heir of the species' enormous capital of adaptive, unconditional reactions. No movement ever made by man, whether when Shakespeare's books were written, Napoleon's campaigns were made, or America was discovered by Columbus, contains something that was not already given in the infant's cradle. The whole difference is in the degree of organization and coordination.

How does the organized and rational behavior of man develop from the chaos of uncoordinated movements of the child? As far as we can judge by today's scientific data, it develops from the planned, systematic, and autocratic influence of the environment in which the child happens to be. His conditional reactions are organized and formed under the predetermining influence of elements of the environment.

Of course, we must not close our eyes to the role which the child's organism plays in the elaboration and formation of personal experience. But first, in a broad sense the organism itself forms part of the environment (it acts upon itself). The organism plays the role of environment in relation to itself. Secondly, the biological organization of the organism is, in the final analysis, conditioned and determined by preceding influences of the environment. Finally, such basic biological functions of the organism as its growth, the formation of body parts and organs, their physiological function, etc. (as is shown, for example, by the theory of internal secretion) are intimately connected to other functions of the organism and to behavior, this mechanism of the most intimate contact with the environment. All this gives us the right to speak of the organism in interaction with the environment.

But when we theoretically contrast the processes within the organism with the processes outside it and try to determine what accounts for what, we see that the very character of this interdependency is determined by the environment. That is why the psychologist can easily define education as the process of gathering and elaborating conditional reactions, a process of adaptation of hereditary forms of behavior to environmental conditions, a process of establishing new links between organism and environment, i.e., a process conditioned at every point of its path.

And such a character education has always had, in all epochs, whatever it was called and whatever was its ideology. All education was always a function of the social structure. All education was essentially always social in the sense that in the end the decisive factor in the formation of new reactions in the child were conditions whose roots lay in the environment or—more broadly—in the interrelations of the organism with the environment.

In the old gymnasium, seminary, or institute for girls of nobility, it was in the end not the teacher, not the form monitors and form-master who educated, but the social environment established in each of these institutions. This is why the traditional view of the teacher as the most important and almost sole mover of the educational process cannot be upheld. The child is no longer an empty vessel into which the teacher pours the wine or water of his sermons. The teacher is no longer a pump who pumps his pupils with knowledge. The teacher is even completely bereft of any direct influence, any direct educational influence upon the pupil as long as he himself forms no part of their environment.

And the enormously large, exaggerated importance which the teacher had in the school was determined by the fact that the main motor, the main part of the educational environment was the teacher. And because of this he forgot his direct duties. From the scientific viewpoint the teacher is merely the organizer of the social educational environment, the regulator and inspector of its interaction with each pupil. This must be clarified.

The point is that the labor of a teacher, like any other human labor, has a dual character. This can most easily be shown with an example. Let us compare the Japanese rickshaw puller, who himself is harnessed to the carriage and conducts passengers through the streets of the city, with the tram-driver. The rickshaw puller fulfills a double role. On the one hand, he simply replaces the horse or the tractive force of steam or electricity, he is simply a source of a certain physical energy which he applies to his simple cart, he is part of the whole simple machine for transportation. On the other hand, he fulfills, albeit to a small degree, a totally different role—the role of the organizer of this simple uncomplicated workshop, the role of the commander of this contrivance, its manager. He fulfills a part of the work that can only be done by man: he starts and stops the cart, avoids obstacles, lets down the shaft, etc. The same duality is preserved in the labor of the tram-driver: he too is a source of physical energy, a simple part of the machine, when he moves the handle of the brakes or the power lever, moves them by physical force. But much more noticeable is his other role of organizer and director of this machine, of master of the electric current, the wheels, and the car.

However, these two elements, which are necessarily present in all human labor, have changed places. Physical labor dominates in the rickshaw. When he tires it is because of the fact that he replaces a horse. Nevertheless, man can manage without a horse but a horse can never manage without man, i.e., although the rickshaw puller's role as organizer and director of the machine is close to zero, it still is of some significance. We see an inverse relation with the tram-driver. Here the expenditure of physical energy has almost been reduced to zero, but the second aspect has become more complicated—the driving of the machine.

This comparison shows very vividly in which direction the development of technology is heading. Human labor goes from the rickshaw puller to the tram-driver as culture grows and continues far beyond the most extreme point of our example. And, in parallel with this, human labor acquires higher and higher forms. The serfdom by the machine, the role of slave of the machine, its appendage, or its tiny screw, will disappear into the historical past. [5] And, in parallel with this, man's power over nature and the productivity of his labor will grow. The comparison of the rickshaw puller with the tram-driver demonstrates this convincingly.

The teacher's labor, although it is not subject to the technical perfection which moves and pushes it from the rickshaw to the tram-driver, has nevertheless the same two aspects. It was always the environment that educated. The teacher was sometimes invited as a supplementary part of this environment (tutors, private teachers). That is the way it was in all schools. The teacher had the duty of organizing the environment. Sometimes people especially assigned for this purpose did it for him. The teacher then played only a minimal part in the organization of the environment. That is the way it sometimes was in the Russian classical gymnasium, where the teacher appeared in the lessons, explained, narrated and asked questions. He played the role of part of the environment. He might have been replaced (and nowadays he has been successfully replaced) by books, pictures, excursions, etc.

And with some exaggeration it may be said that the whole reform of contemporary pedagogics revolves around this theme: how to reduce the role of teacher as closely as possible to zero when he, just like the rickshaw-puller, plays the role of the engine and part of his own pedagogical machine, and how to base everything on his other role—the role of organizer of the social environment? The Dalton plan, the labor method, the action school, etc., etc. hit this target. In complete harmony with this viewpoint, Thorndike reduces the teacher's role to the regulation of stimuli for the pupils' reactions. But, contrary to the viewpoint presented here, he on the whole still reduces the educational process to the teacher. From a perfectly correct psychological statement of the question, namely, that our educators are our movements, that the pupil educates himself, i.e., himself consolidates his reactions, he does not draw the inevitable pedagogical conclusion about the need for a radical reform of school and the teacher's labor.

Instruction is the word for the role of the teacher that brings him closer to the rickshaw-puller than to the tram-driver. And everywhere in Thorndike the teacher is still an instructor, i.e., a perfect rickshaw-puller who drags the educational process instead of keeping to his duty to organize and guide it.

Directly dependent upon this is the fact that the basic goals of education play a much greater role for us than for Thorndike. The teacher must know these goals very well and not limit himself to the vague formulas which the author presents.

> To increase the sum of human energy and happiness and decrease the sum of discomfort of the human beings that are or will be [Thorndike, 1906, p. 3].

Such a formula cannot satisfy the teacher. He needs to know exactly how this can be done and to direct all education toward this goal. But these words, like the "ideals of efficiency, honor, duty, love, and service," are, of course, the half-hypocritical, half-candid ideals of a bourgeois society. These cannot be used, of course, to equip the teacher.

Thorndike himself said of instincts and other innate reactions of the child that while it is impossible to make the Niagara river return to Lake Erie and keep it there, it is possible, by building discharge channels, to make it set in motion the wheels of factories in the service of man. This is an apt formulation of education. And to this end the teacher must know very concretely and exactly into which channels the child's natural drives must be led, which wheels of which factories they can be made to make turn.

Thorndike is very right when he speaks about the one-sidedness of a school which teaches only one capacity—the ability to operate with ideas. In his opinion the teacher himself, a man of this type of thinking, is far from being enough for the school. He knows that the pupil educates himself. In the end the pupils are educated by what they themselves do and not by what the teacher does. It is not what we give but what we receive that is important. It is only by being independent that the pupils change. But, in spite of all this, he does not develop this idea to the end.

The role of the teacher as an organizer of the social environment is especially underestimated by Thorndike when we take the extraordinary complexity of human behavior into account. We must imagine the educational process, as has already been said above, as a most complex process of struggle within the organism. Several laws and mechanisms of this struggle have already been discovered.

Quite a number of stimulations perish in this struggle. What is realized is realized after a struggle, after the victory. The task of organizing the social environment thus acquires very subtle and complex forms. We cannot say

> Give me absolutely all innate reactions of the infant, absolutely all of the environment's influences upon him and I will predict his behavior with mathematical exactitude. [6]

We must correct for the complicating factor of the internal struggle of the reflexes. And to organize and guide this struggle is the teacher's work. To ensure the victory of necessary reactions is his task.

That is why we must agree with the author when he says [1906, p. 2] that the questions dealt with in the book are not the questions that are usually treated under the heading "Principles of education."

> The question as to how best to achieve those changes which education strives for is discussed under the headings: "Principles of teaching," or "Methods of teaching," or "Theory and practice of teaching," or "Educational psychology." This book will try to answer the latter question—to give a scientific basis for the art of actual teaching rather than for the selection of aims for the schools as a whole or of the subjects to be taught or of the general results to be gained from any subject. Not the "What" or the "Why" but the "How" is its topic.

We must accept the "*how*" of this book and completely change its "*why*" and "*what*." This "how" we must understand very practically. Thorndike [1906, p. 1] is right in saying that the nature of education resides in change. This change can be directed in various directions. We can set ourselves various educational goals.

> But the problem is always fundamentally the same: given these children to be changed and this change to be made, how shall I proceed? [1906, p. 6].

Let it be clear that we nowhere changed the author's text.

Chapter 12

PREFACE TO BÜHLER[*],[1]

1

Bühler's book *Outline of the Mental Development of the Child* [1], which we bring to the attention of the reader in Russian translation, combines two merits that one seldom finds together in a single book: a genuine scientific approach and an account that is truly simple and concise. This makes it easily understood and equally interesting for pedagogues, students of child psychology, and expert psychologists. Its completeness, the systematic inclusion of all aspects of the psychological development of the child, the wealth of factual material and the theoretical constructions and hypotheses distinguish this book, which is rich in content and laconic in form. In general, it is obviously the best of all modern books on child psychology, books that are meant for the broad public and primarily for educators and parents. This was the reason we undertook the translation of this interesting *Outline*.

Bühler is one of the greatest contemporary German psychologists, an investigator and a thinker. Not only his big works, but also the *Outline*, are based on a very broad theoretical foundation. The most important aspects that determine the theoretical basis of the whole *Outline* are the attempt to rest child psychology on a biological foundation and thus to create a general theory of psychological development, the tendency to bring the integral understanding of psychological processes—so characteristic of all new psychology—to the fore, and a strict, consistent use of the idea of development as the fundamental explanatory principle.

Together with all new psychology, Bühler's theoretical and fundamental views in the last two decades went through a very serious, complex and deep evolution, and in themselves they can only be appreciated and properly understood in light of the recent development of psychological science. Bühler began his scientific activity as an active participant in Külpe's so-called Würzburg school,[2] which had declared that intensive self-observation is the only source of psychological knowledge. Now, in the book *The Mental Development of the Child* [2], with which the present *Outline* links up, and especially in the book *The Crisis in Psychology*,[3] Bühler acts as the representative of a broad synthesis of all fundamental aspects of modern psychological investigation, a synthesis which organically includes subjective and objective psychology, the psychology of experiencing and the psychology of behavior, the psychology of the unconscious and structural psychology, natural scientific psy-

*First published as Vygotsky, L. S. (1930). Predislovie. In K. Bühler, *Ocherk dukhovnogo razvitija rebenka* (pp. 5-26). Moscow: Rabotnik Prosveshchenija.

chology and psychology as a science of the spirit. Bühler sees this synthesis as the confirmation of the unity of psychology as a science and the historical fate of psychology as a whole. To a certain extent, Bühler's synthesis rests upon a teleological foundation that has not been overcome by this investigator. The tendency to synthesize widely differing and often irreconcilable currents of psychological thought and the teleological way of examining a number of problems lead the author at times to an eclectic combination of very diverse theories and theoretical views. It makes him distort the facts and squeeze them into general schemes. It is true, in the *Outline* this tendency is hardly present. The other negative feature of the book shows through all the more acutely: the biological and social factors in the child's psychological development are not distinguished.

It comes as no surprise that the development of speech and drawing, the formation of concepts and thinking are regarded as processes that are, in principle, not different from the development of the rudiments of intellectual activity in the animal world. Not without reason, Bühler [1929, p. 48] was carried away by the abstract similarity between the primitive tool use of anthropoid apes (the chimpanzee) and [that of] the human child and called the period of appearance of the first forms of thinking in the child the chimpanzee age. This fact alone vividly reveals Bühler's basic tendency—to reduce the facts of biological and sociocultural development to a common denominator and to ignore the fundamental, unique nature of human child development.

Whereas Köhler [1921b] in his well-known investigation, on which the present *Outline* relies in many respects, attempted to lay bare the intellectual actions of the chimpanzee, to reveal their human-like nature, Bühler in his investigation of the development of the child's intellect follows the opposite tendency: he attempts to reveal the chimpanzee-like nature of the young child's behavior. For him the course of development of the human child is simply a missing intermediate rung of the biological ladder. For him the whole path of development from ape to adult cultural man is accomplished by ascending a single biological ladder. Bühler does not know the fundamental transition in psychological development from the biological to the historical type of evolution or, at any rate, does not regard it as a fundamental turning point. Neither does he distinguish between the line of biological development and the sociocultural formation of the child's personality in ontogenesis—for him both lines are merged together.

Hence the overestimation of the internal regularities of development to the detriment of the formative influence of the social environment. In the *Outline,* environment as the main factor of development of the higher intellectual functions constantly remains in the background. The history of the development of higher forms of child behavior is, in principle, not distinguished from the general history of the development of elementary biological processes. The history of the formation of concepts is, in principle, not different from the history of some elementary function directly connected to the organic evolution of the child.

Nature does not make leaps, development always proceeds gradually—that is how Bühler himself formulates this anti-dialectical viewpoint. The attempt to smooth over the leaps in the name of the gradual nature of development leaves him blind to the real leap from biology to history in the development of man—in that process which Bühler himself calls the genesis of man.

This tendency to consider the development of higher forms of behavior which appear in the plane of phylogenesis as the product of the historical evolution of mankind and which have a special history and path in ontogenesis in the same plane as the development of elementary functions leads to two unfortunate consequences. First, what is relative and proper to a child of a certain era and a certain social environment is passed off as something absolute, universal, as an essential part of development. In addition to the chimpanzee age, Bühler distinguishes as special periods in child development the age of fairy tales (and even more exact and detailed—the age of *Struwwelpeter*) and the Robinson age. [3] Bühler views the child and his fairy tale through the looking glass of psychological analysis and transforms the age of fairy tales into something of a natural category, into some biological stage of development. He elevates a regularity which developed historically and is determined by social class to the level of an eternal law of nature.

Second, due to the same fundamental tendency a general and deep distortion of the whole age perspective in child psychology develops. Not only in the sense of a fundamental mixing up of biological and social criteria in the determination of stages and periods in child development but also with respect to the objective distribution of the whole process of child development over the different age periods.

It is no accident that Bühler comes to the conclusion that child psychology's main interest must always be focused on the first years of the child's life. In the eyes of this investigator, child psychology is the psychology of early childhood when the basic and elementary psychological functions mature. According to the author of the *Outline*, children take big steps in their development shortly after birth, and it is just these first steps (the only ones accessible to that contemporary child psychology to which Bühler belongs) which the psychologist must study, just as the study of the development of the body is restricted to the investigation of embryos.

This analogy, phrased by Bühler [1918, p. 10] in his big book on the mental development of the child, reflects the real state of affairs in the psychology of the child in a surprisingly correct way. All considerations about the central importance of the first steps of psychological development and the fundamental claim that child psychology essentially is the psychology of infancy and early childhood are in perfect agreement with what we said above. The contemporary trends in child psychology to which Bühler belongs can essentially only understand the embryonic development of the higher functions, only the embryology of the human mind to which they thus consciously refer when they render an account of their own methodological boundaries. Contemporary child psychology, too, actually studies nothing but embryos.

But, apart from being correct, the comparison with embryology is treacherous. It points to the weak spot of child psychology, gives away its Achilles' heel and exposes that forced abstinence and self-restraint of which psychology wishes to make a virtue.

In the *Outline*, too, we actually see nothing but an "embryology of the human mind." All age periods are moved to infancy and early childhood. Each function is investigated in its infancy. Infancy itself is moved to the biologically contiguous area which lies between the thinking of the chimpanzee and man. This is the strength and weakness of Bühler's whole psychological conception. This is where we find the strength and weakness of the *Outline*.

We find it necessary to preface the Russian translation of Bühler's book with all these remarks for the sole reason that we wish to provide the thoughtful reader with a firm basis from which to master all the valuable material that is contained in *Outline of the Mental Development of the Child* and to think through its theoretical claims and grounds.

2

In comparison to the big book dedicated to the same problem, what is new in *Outline of the Mental Development of the Child* is the attempt to present the biological foundations of child psychology more clearly and to develop a corresponding general theory of child development, as Bühler [1929, p. 3] himself explains in his foreword to the *Outline*. It would probably not be easy to find another example of such an outline which presents the basic content of the great capital work on child psychology in a most accessible way to the broad circles of lay readers and at the same time forms an attempt to build a general theory of child development.

This combination of fine theoretical and fundamental research with a simple and clear exposition of the most elementary foundations of child psychology, realized in the form of an outline, forms a rare exception in the scientific literature. Usually both aspects are not encountered in a single book. The construction of general theories is rarely combined with a presentation of the basic elements of the same scientific area. Usually both tasks are divided between different authors. Their combination in one author and one book gives the whole *Outline* a deeply original and essentially ambivalent stamp.

On the one hand, due to such a combination, the presentation of elementary information from psychology is raised to an unusual height. Before the eyes of the reader takes place the enlivening of elements of theoretical thought, their test, critique, and their introduction into a new system; the latter fact gives a new appearance to many truisms which were learned long ago and sheds, as it were, new light on them. Removed from its ordinary spot and included in another system, each truism becomes a problem.

The whole book, which is actually fully dedicated to those scientific truths that we are wont to call truisms, is filled with rich theoretical content. It attempts to think through the old truths in a new plane and to present them in a new light. That is why it requires not just assimilation by the reader but keen and critical thinking as well. It does not simply give information but waves a tissue of conclusions into a theoretical system before the reader's eyes and requires him to examine, criticize, and follow the whole process of reasoning.

Here we have the other aspect of the matter which gives the whole book not only its original but also its ambivalent appearance. By enlivening the elementary truths by means of theoretical thought, by removing them from their old familiar spots, by turning them into grand problems, the book at the same time introduces a good deal of questionable, contradictory, very problematic and at times downright incorrect information into the factual material. This factual material is in itself unquestionable but is often presented in the wavering and false light of theoretical thought which has not fully freed itself from pre-scientific—metaphysical or idealistic—elements.

This circumstance engendered the need to preface *Outline of the Mental Development of the Child* with a cursory critical analysis of several of the basic theoretical notions from which Bühler proceeds. The sole task of this analysis is to introduce some improvements to the theoretical construction which underlies *Outline* and to provide the reader's critical thinking with basic guidelines to overcome what needs to be overcome in the book, what must not be assimilated but indeed overcome.

What in Bühler's book must be critically overcome in this way? Above, in Sec. 1, we have attempted in a very general way, illustrated with a number of concrete examples, to give a very general sketch of the fundamental part of the book against which our critique has to be directed in the first place. We have seen that the merits and shortcomings, the pluses and minuses of the whole *Outline*, find their origin in one general methodological root. That is why we cannot separate and isolate them mechanically by removing one part of the book or another. We must look into the whole complex fabric.

In common with all contemporary child psychology, Bühler proceeds from the rejection of the atomistic approach in child development and searches for an integral conception of child psychology. He says [1929, p. 3] that

> It seems to me that at this moment most important is to attempt once again, as did Pestalozzi one hundred years ago, to understand the significance of the whole. When we succeed in understanding the biological functions of the mind and the internal rhythm of its development, then Pestalozzi's work will know a revival in our time.

That's all there is to it. One cannot express the very essence of Bühler's fundamental idea in a more exhaustive, concise, rich and laconic way: the investigator must understand the psychological development of the child as a whole, and this whole is revealed as the biological functions of the mind and the internal rhythm of its development. Once again: the biological functions of the mind and the internal rhythm of development connected with it are passed off as the whole of child psychology. Such a simple solution of the problem of the whole in child psychology is reached at the expense of a complete and absolute neglect of the social functions of the mind and the socially determined rhythm of its development.

These objections are not roused, of course, by the attempt itself to isolate the biological bases of child psychology more clearly, but by the attempt to pass these biological foundations off as the whole whose meaning is uncovered in the child's mental development. In itself, Bühler's attempt to rest child psychology upon a biological foundation testifies to the enormous theoretical step forward which the author made (together with all of child psychology) from the metaphysical, subjective idealistic conception of the mind which reigned in the works of the Würzburg school to a natural scientific, biological and, consequently, spontaneously materialistic conception. Scientific child psychology must, of course, be built on a firm biological foundation.

Three ideas are most valuable in Bühler's construction: the idea of development that runs through the book from the first to the last page, the author's general attempt to find the causes of the big and typical successes in the mental life of the normal child in the structural development of the cerebral cortex, and, connected with this, the tendency to consider the psychological development of the child in the general perspective of his biological development. All of these ideas follow directly from the biological foundations of child psychology which Bühler regards as most important.

But the attempt to reduce the whole content of child psychology to the biological functions of the mind, to reduce the whole psychological development of the child to these functions, means for psychology nothing other than to be taken prisoner by biology. Such an attempt inevitably leads to the dissemination of the biological viewpoint in psychology beyond its legitimate methodological boundaries and gives rise to quite a number of theoretical errors, the most important of which have already been mentioned above in Sec. 1.

3

When we try to reduce these errors to a common denominator, by uniting them and extracting what they have in common, we will find two basic lines of theoretical thinking as their general roots. They are equally false and internally connected, although they go in opposite directions. The first line is that of psychologizing biology, the second that of biologizing psychology. Both are to an equal extent entirely legitimate conclusions from the deeply false premises which equate the two parts of Bühler's basic methodological equation: "the meaning of the whole" of all child psychology and the "biological functions of the mind."

Let us first consider the first line of thinking. However strange and paradoxical it may seem at first sight, in practice the attempt to completely biologize psychology leads inevitably to its opposite: the psychologizing of biology. For in practice—to turn to a concrete example—to consider concept formation in the light of the biological functions of the mind means not just to distort the psychological nature of the process of concept formation and to equate it in principle with "practical inventions" or other forms of intellectual activity of the chimpanzee. It also deeply distorts the nature of the biological functions and ascribes something to them which they do not have. It elevates them to the highest rank and assumes—let it be only assuming!—that they contain something more than the simply organic, vital processes.

In turn, this means opening the door to vitalism and presupposing an affirmative answer to vitalism's question: don't the biological functions to which all of human psychology belongs already contain a psychological—or psychoid, i.e., mental-like—beginning? Otherwise, how does one explain that thinking in concepts develops in the biological realm of functions and processes?

Bühler—despite the rigor and caution that distinguish his biological thinking and of which he gives proof at every moment in *Outline* when he examines such questions as the conscious nature of instincts, the processes of consciousness in infants, the development of the brain and thinking (none of which he, by the way, solves in the spirit of vitalism)—is theoretically forced to accept the vitalistic conception of Driesch,[4] the spiritual leader of contemporary vitalism, as possible. Bühler [1929, pp. 10-11] refers to Driesch in entertaining the possibility that the most general phenomena of organic life (growth, reproduction, regeneration) require the presence of a mind-like natural factor in all living beings. [4]

One cannot prove more clearly and convincingly that the attempt to reduce the child's whole mental development to biological, innate and elementary factors leads in practice to the vitalistic assumption of the soul as an elementary natural factor. This is how the work by Driesch is conceived to which Bühler refers.

The other side of this same line of thought is what we above have called the second line and which we termed the biologizing of psychology.

It is no accident that Bühler develops the idea of the direct transfer of variants of the zoopsychological experiment into child psychology and considers this method to be the principal form of experimental investigation in the first years of the child's life. He fails to mention all the technical changes that must be carried out in such a case and does not point to a single fundamental difference in the study of the behavior of children and animals in one and the same experimental situation.

It is no accident, further, that Bühler agrees with Rickert,[5] Dilthey, and others that presently personality cannot—and, who knows, perhaps never will—be understood as the calculable product of the influences that took part in its formation. Bühler [1929, p. 36] actually accepts a metaphysical conception of personality and at the same time—in the plane of the scientific investigation of personality development—he in principle finds nothing new with respect to the three levels of psychological development which we already find in the animal world. [5]

It is remarkable that an investigator claims that personality cannot be known and at the same time finds nothing in that same personality which transcends the boundaries of the basic forms of animal behavior. It is a fact central to Bühler's whole system that the fundamental theory of the three levels in the development of behavior is equally applicable to all human and animal behavior. Is this really not tantamount to accepting that in human development and in the human child nothing fundamentally new developed? No new level of behavior distinctive of and specific to man? That this development falls entirely within the framework of the biological evolution of behavior?

As has already been said, it is only natural that the elementary, basic and biologically primary is moved to the forefront in child development to the detriment of the higher, specifically human, historical and social in the psychology of man. Doesn't it sound great when Bühler claims that the nursery, the asylums for idiots, and the auxiliary schools form the best places to study the structure of the human mind and the basic lines of its development?

One and the same tendency shows through everywhere: the tendency to deduce the plentitude of psychological functions and forms from the biological roots; to make absolute what is primitive, primary and basic; to attach universal importance to the embryonic stages of development. It is the tendency which we have already mentioned in Sec. 1 of our introductory sketch.

4

But now we are faced with a task of dissection and analysis. What is wrong, one might think, in taking the primary for the basic? For the primary indeed is the basic. The foundation is formed by the lower, elementary and primitive functions, and the higher ones are something derivative, secondary or even tertiary.

This is all true. And to the extent that Bühler's idea resides in this, he is indisputably right. But analysis reveals something else behind this truth. He, who does not stop here, but attempts to reduce all development to this primary basis and thereby attaches absolute meaning to primary forms, ignores the objective dialectic of development in which new formations that are not reducible to it are superimposed on this primary foundation. He ignores the dialectical method of the scientific acquisition of knowledge as the sole adequate way of revealing the objective dialectic of development.

The anti-dialectical approach—as has already been said—is the main flaw of Bühler's whole system. This is the root of all his errors.

"Nature does not make leaps, development always proceeds gradually"—this is the anti-dialectical rule which Bühler [1929, p. 22] formulates in connection with the problem of animal and human behavior. Leaps from biology to history do not exist for him, and thus no leap exists from the biological to the historical development of behavior, the basic leap in the transition from zoopsychology to the psychology of man. Just like all European child psychology, Bühler's theory attempts to avoid the social in the problem of man. The central idea, the focus of all his theoretical lines, is the anti-dialectical understanding of psychological development.

Both in the conception of phylogenesis and in the conception of ontogenesis this disposition leads to errors. The most important one is that all sorts and types of development are merged together and mechanically identified: first of all, phylogenesis and ontogenesis, the development of mankind and the development of the child.

Bühler is convinced that the history of primitive mankind can be no other than the history of the mental development of our children. But, further, the history of primitive mankind—via the development of the child—is equated with biological evolution which led to the origin of man. Bühler [1929, p. 23] says that

> We know of no intermediary rungs on the biological ladder between the mentality of the chimpanzee and that of man, but we can follow the course of development of the human child. This must show how the transition takes place.

In principle, the author views neither the line of biological evolution of behavior and its historical development in phylogenesis nor the two lines in ontogenesis as two different types of development. He further places phylogenesis and child development on the same level and declares that in child development certain basic laws of mental progress manifest themselves which are completely independent of external influences, i.e., they are equally operative in the development of man in pre-historical times and in childhood.

Of course, if we disregard external influences, i.e., the environment, then the laws operative in human development cannot be differentiated into lower and higher forms of behavior and thinking. Then neither can we distinguish between biological and social factors of development, nor between regularities that are relative, particular and specific to the child of a given time period and a given social class and universal biological regularities of development. Then the whole task of the investigator—as he himself admits—is to find in a pure form the laws of development that are eternal, fundamental and independent of outside influences, to abstract them from everything that is concrete and historical and to discern the characteristic features of the universal child in the vague outlines of the concrete image.

Quite a number of problems are inadequately treated as a result of this basic conception. We have already mentioned the problem of the higher intellectual functions, which the author places in the same biological plane. It is typical in attempts of this kind that the direct cause of such mental achievements of the normal child as concept formation is sought in the structural development of the cerebral cortex.

Instead of assuming that what develops are necessary connections in the structural development of the cerebral cortex, that what is created is a potential, that what is formed are the biological prerequisites for the development of the function of concept formation—a higher, historically evolved and socially determined form of thinking—it is claimed that the history of all higher forms of behavior is caused by structural changes of the cortex.

We might further point to the purely naturalistic theory of child play which Bühler adopts from Groos. He says that here we have a further development of capacities already present in animal play. And this basically determines his view of the link between child play and animal play: it is a further development of the same capacity and that is all there is to it.

We will not further enumerate all the concrete problems which one way or another show the methodological flaws of Bühler's whole system. In conclusion, we will only dwell on one other problem which is characteristic of the whole book: the problem of the heredity of mental properties as explained by Bühler.

5

In the analysis of the problem of the heredity of mental properties, Bühler [1929, p. 28] refers to the results of his own investigation of one hundred genealogies of criminals. These results demonstrate, from the viewpoint of the author, that there are people who from childhood have the ineradicable tendency to roam around and steal and who, in later life, belong to the regular inhabitants of prisons and houses of correction. They have inherited a fatal inclination which is just as lawfully passed on from generation to generation as some kind of physical property and which is recessive with respect to normal inclinations. But it must be taken into account that these inclinations only lead men to prisons and houses of correction in the frequency to be expected according to the Mendelian rules. [6]

According to Bühler, criminality is thus based on hereditary inclinations and passed on from fathers to sons as some kind of simple physical property with the exactness required by Mendel's laws. However monstrous this claim may be, however obvious it may be that the author, in following the old and false theory of "inborn criminality," reduces the presence of parents and children in prison to "fatal heredity" and ignores the socioeconomical factors of criminality, we must dwell on this example and analyze how such conclusions become possible, more than that, how they become inevitable with certain theoretical premises.

Here we have a striking example which shows that certain facts can in themselves be correct, but still lead to absolutely false conclusions if their interpretation is guided by a false theoretical conception.

The facts established in Bühler's investigation are in themselves correct. What are the facts? That there is quite a high correlation between the prison stay of parents and children. Bühler, for example, investigated the fate of children both of whose parents had spent a long time in prison. Of the 30 children of this group, 28 also ended up in prison. Such are the facts. There is a link—these facts say—between the presence in prison of father and son. And that's all. Not a word more.

What follows is the interpretation and the explanation of the facts. What kind of link is it? Bühler claims that it is a hereditary link, that criminal inclinations are inherited according to Mendel's laws just like some simple physical property. In the present case, he acts just like Galton in his famous investigation of the heredity of genius and like many others. That is, he repeats a very naive and well-known error in the theory of heredity which has already become a cliché.

Bühler's investigations, just like many other investigations of this type, lead to totally false results. The reason is that the similarity in features between parents and children is taken—without further analysis—as the basis for judgments about heredity. Pearson[6] as well defines heredity as the correlation between the degree of kinship and the degree of similarity. This definition lies at the basis of Bühler's investigation as a tacit assumption.

In our scientific literature, Blonsky has given a critique of this widespread error. Pearson's definition, from which all who time and again repeat this error proceed as from a tacit assumption, inevitably leads to what is called a *circulos vitiosus* in logic: the investigator traces a vicious circle by proceeding from what actually has to be proved. Bühler, for example, assumes in advance that if a link exists between the prison stay of parents and children, then this link is hereditary. And meanwhile this was exactly what was to be proved.

Indeed, does every resemblance in features between parents and children point with certainty to the transfer of these features from parents to children through heredity? Pearson's definition is too broad and therefore false. It includes not only biological heredity but also what Blonsky calls the social heredity of the social conditions of life and existence, which does not follow Mendel's rules but the laws of societal life.

Heredity, says Blonsky (1925), is no simple biological phenomenon. We must distinguish chromatin heredity [7] from the social heredity of the conditions of life and social position. It is on the basis of this social, class-based heredity that dynasties are built. In a highly productive, rich class society with high material security and high fecundity of these dynasties, their chances to produce a great quantity of talents are enhanced. On the other hand, continual heavy work, physical labor, and poverty give the hereditary genius of the working masses no chance whatsoever to manifest itself.

What Blonsky says of the "heredity of genius" on the occasion of Galton's research can be word for word applied to the heredity of prison inclinations according to Bühler's theory and to Peters' investigation of the heredity of mental capacities to which Bühler [1929, pp. 28-29] refers. [8] Peters compared the school marks of children, parents and grandparents and came to the conclusion that mental capacities as revealed in school marks are hereditarily transmitted. He ignored the fact that school success is the result of many factors and of social factors in the first place. Peters regards the talent for good school performance as a dominating quality which is transmitted according to the laws of Mendel.

It is easy to see that all these investigations mix up heredity in the strict sense of the word with social heredity, the heredity of the conditions of life. For the similarity between parents and children, the similarity between their fates can be explained, of course, not only by the direct transmission of hereditary qualities, but also by the transmission of living conditions.

The child both of whose parents are subjected to a protracted prison term has, of course, very many chances to repeat their fate—not only because the parents' crime often serves as an edifying example for the children and not only because the fact itself that both parents are in prison condemns the normal child to be unattended. Most important is that the same social reasons that led one's parents to commit a crime usually remain operative in the second generation as well and determine the fate of the children as they first determined the fate of the parents. Do not poverty, unemployment, being unattended, etc. and other well-studied factors of criminality act upon the children with the same irresistibility as they did upon their parents?

In exactly the same way those social conditions (material security, the cultural conditions of domestic life, leisure, etc., etc.) which at the time guaranteed the grandparents and parents good marks in their school education will on average guarantee the children of these parents the same good marks.

The scientific misunderstandings mentioned above, such as Bühler's statements about "prison inclinations," Peters' statements about the heredity of good school marks, and Galton's statements about the heredity of the talent for functioning as a minister, judge, and in the academic professions, only became possible on the basis of a gross mixing up of biological and social heredity. Rather than analyzing the socioeconomic factors that determine criminality, this purely social phenomenon—a product of social inequality and exploitation—is passed off as a hereditary biological feature, transmitted from forebears to offspring with the same lawfulness as eye color.

We did not dwell in such detail upon Bühler's analysis of the problem of heredity because it occupies a central place in the system of his considerations so much as because it is characteristic of his methodological flaws and demonstrates how false basic presuppositions lead to false theoretical conclusions. After all, Bühler did not set himself the task of analyzing the methodological foundations of the problem of heredity in psychology, to determine what in general is inherited in forms of behavior, how hereditary inclinations hang together with the development of intricate complex and higher psychological functions and forms of behavior. But, imperceptible to the author himself, without such an analysis his fundamental biological conception begins to determine the whole course of his considerations. And once more—in this problem just in all other problems—the social is turned into the biological. The biological is given a universal and absolute significance in the whole drama of the mental development of the child, as Bühler expresses it. No other *dramatis personae* besides the biological factors are recognized.

Here we can end our critical sketch. We began by pointing out that the fact that social and biological factors in the psychological development of the child are not being distinguished is the fundamental methodological flaw of Bühler's whole theory. In the end—as the result of our whole examination of his book—we arrived at the same conclusion. Obviously, this is the alpha and the omega of his whole *Outline*.

Chapter 13

PREFACE TO KÖHLER[*][,1]

1

The development of scientific ideas and views proceeds dialectically. Opposite ideas concerning one and the same subject replace each other in the process of development of scientific knowledge and a new theory is often not a direct continuation of the preceding one but its negation, a dialectical negation, however. It includes all the positive achievements of its predecessor which have stood the test of time, but it itself strives in its constructions and conclusions to transcend its predecessor's boundaries and to conquer new and deeper layers of phenomena.

The development of the scientific views on the intellect of animals proceeded just as dialectically. We can clearly distinguish and follow three stages in the *recent* development of this doctrine.

The first stage was formed by those anthropomorphic theories of animal behavior which, deceived by the external similarity of animal and human behavior in certain cases, ascribed to animals the views, thoughts, and intentions of man. They transferred the human mode of action to animals and assumed that in similar situations the animal reaches the same results as does man and by means of the same psychological processes and operations. At that time one ascribed to the animal human thinking in its most complex forms.

The reaction against this viewpoint was formed by the objective scientific investigation of animal behavior which through careful observations and experiments succeeded in establishing that a considerable part of those operations which the previous theory was inclined to consider as intelligent acts belonged simply to the number of instinctive, innate activity modes and that the appearance of another part—the *seemingly* intellectual modes of behavior—was due to the method of trial and error.

Thorndike—this father of objective psychology—in his investigation of the intellect of animals succeeded in demonstrating experimentally that animals that acted according to the method of trial and error developed complex forms of behavior which *seemingly* were similar to the same forms in man, but *in essence* were deeply different from them. These animals in Thorndike's experiments opened relatively complex bolts and latches and managed with mechanisms of various complexity, but all this took place exclusively through self-training, without the slightest understanding of the situation or mechanism itself. These experiments started a new era

*First published as Vygotsky, L. S. (1930). Predislovie. In W. Köhler, *Issledovanie intellekta chelovekopodobnykh obez'jan* (pp. v-xxi). Moscow: Rabotnik Prosveshchenija.

in animal psychology. Thorndike himself beautifully described this new current in the study of animal intellect and its contrast with the old viewpoint.

Thorndike [1911, p. 22] says that

> Formerly everybody was very happy to speak about animal intelligence, never about animal stupidity. The main goal of the new current has become to demonstrate that animals, when placed in a situation in which man usually "thinks," display precisely "stupidity," *unintelligent behavior*, which has essentially nothing in common with the behavior of thinking man, and therefore there is no need at all to ascribe intellect to animals in order to explain this behavior.

Such was the most important result of these investigations which created, as has already been said, a whole era in our science.

Apropos this, Köhler [1921a, p. 87] correctly says that until very recently the theory of intellect was dominated by those negativistic tendencies which investigators used to prove the nonrational, the "nonhumanlike," and the mechanical nature of animal behavior.

Köhler's investigations mark, as do a number of other investigations in this field, a new, *third* stage in the development of this problem. Köhler asks *the same question* as Thorndike did and wishes to investigate whether higher animals, anthropoid apes, have intellect in the real sense of the word, i.e., that type of behavior which from time immemorial has been considered the defining characteristic of man. But Köhler attempts to solve this question in another way. He makes use of other means and sets himself other theoretical goals than Thorndike did.

Thorndike's indisputable historical merit lies in the fact that he once and for all succeeded in doing away with the anthropomorphic tendencies in the science of animal behavior and introduced objective natural scientific methods in zoopsychology. Mechanistic natural science celebrated its greatest triumph in these investigations.

However, after this task had been solved and the mechanism of habit formation had been revealed, the development of science itself confronted the investigators with a new task which had in essence already been suggested by Thorndike's investigations. These investigations created a very sharp gap between animal and human behavior. It was impossible, as demonstrated in these investigations, to detect the slightest trace of intellect in animal behavior and—*precisely from the natural scientific viewpoint*—it remained incomprehensible how human intellect evolved and through what genetic threads it was connected with animal behavior. The intelligent behavior of man and animals' nonintelligent behavior seemed divided by an abyss, and this gap itself pointed not only to the mechanistic viewpoint's incapacity to explain the origin of the higher forms of behavior of man but also to an essential fundamental conflict in genetic psychology.

Indeed, at this point psychology stood before a junction: *either* to move away from evolutionary theory with respect to this question and fully refrain from the attempt to examine thinking genetically, i.e., to accept a metaphysical viewpoint in the theory of intellect, *or to avoid* the problem of thinking instead of *solving* it, to dismiss the very question and to attempt to show that human behavior as well—including his thinking—can be fully reduced to the processes of mechanical habit formation which in essence do not differ at all from similar processes in chickens, cats, and dogs. The first path leads to an idealistic conception of thinking (the Würzburg school), the second to naive behaviorism.

Köhler correctly remarks that even in his first investigations Thorndike tacitly assumed the existence of intelligent behavior, however narrowly we define its characteristics and whatever criteria we may propose to distinguish it from other forms of behavior.

Just like Thorndike's psychology, association psychology starts from the thesis that processes which to the naive observer seem intelligent can be reduced to the action of a simple association mechanism. Köhler [1921b, p. 2] says that in Thorndike, the radical representative of this current, we find the following thesis as the main result of his investigations with dogs and cats: nothing whatsoever in the behavior of these animals is intelligent. He who formulates his conclusions in this way, continues Köhler [ibid., p. 2], has to accept that other behavior is intelligent. From immediate observation of, say, man, he already knows its counterpart, although he attempts to deny it in theory.

It goes without saying that one animal species is of extraordinary importance for the question at issue. The anthropoid apes, which are our closest relatives on the evolutionary ladder, occupy a unique place among the other animals. It is here that investigations must shed light on the origin of human intelligence.

As Köhler [ibid., p. 1] points out, it is precisely this closeness to man which is the main motive which elicits our naive interest in the investigation of the anthropoid apes' intellect. Previous investigations demonstrated that anthropoid apes, in the chemistry of their body, inasmuch as it is reflected in the blood and in the structure of their brain, are closer to man than to other types of apes. The question naturally arises whether in a special investigation it is possible to demonstrate the kinship of man and apes in the area of behavior as well.

The fundamental and most important meaning of Köhler's work, the main conclusion he was able to draw, lies in the scientific justification of this naive expectation. The anthropoid ape stands closer to man than to the lower types of apes not only in what regards certain morphological and physiological characteristics but also psychologically.

Köhler's investigations thus for the first time lead to the factual foundation of Darwinism in psychology in its most critical, important, and difficult point. They add the data of comparative psychology to those of comparative anatomy and physiology and thereby fill in the missing link of the evolutionary chain. It can be said without any exaggeration that through these investigations evolutionary theory for the first time found its factual substantiation and confirmation in the area of higher human behavior. In addition, these investigations bridged the gap between human and animal behavior that had been created in the theory by Thorndike's works. They bridged the abyss which divided intelligent and nonintelligent behavior. They demonstrated the—from the viewpoint of Darwinism—indisputable truth that the beginnings of the intelligent activity of man are already present in the animal world.

Granted, there is absolutely no reason to expect that the anthropoid ape will display the same traits of behavior as man.

As Vagner [1927, p. 54] correctly points out

> Lately, the idea of the descent of man from the anthropoid apes has been called into doubt. There is reason to suppose that his ancestor was some extinct animal from which man developed in a direct evolutionary line.

Kloach [2] argues in a whole series of extremely convincing considerations that the anthropoid apes represent no more than a branch that branched off from the forefather of man. Adjusting to particular conditions of life, they had to "sacrifice" in the struggle for existence those parts of their organization that opened the road for the central forms of progressive evolution and led to man. Kloach says that

> The reduction of the thumb alone cut these collateral branches off from the way upwards. From this viewpoint, the anthropoid apes represent the blind alley of the mainstream of progressive evolution [in Vagner, 1928, p. 54].

It would thus be an enormous mistake to consider the anthropoid ape as our direct ancestor and to expect that we find in it the germs of all forms of behavior which are proper to man. In all likelihood, the common ancestor of man and the anthropoid apes has disappeared and, as Kloach correctly points out, the anthropoid ape is merely a collateral branch of this original species.

It is therefore to be expected in advance that we will not find a *direct* genetic continuity between the chimpanzee and man, that much will be reduced in the chimpanzee—even in comparison with our common ancestor—that much will have diverged from the main line of development. That is why nothing can be decided in advance and only experimental investigation can give a valid answer to this problem.

Köhler approaches this question with all the accuracy of a scientific experiment. He transformed a theoretical probability into an experimentally established fact. After all, even if we accept Kloach's remarks as completely correct, we still must see the enormous theoretical likelihood that—in view of the considerable closeness of the chimpanzee to man in what regards the chemistry of the blood as well as the structure of the brain—we may expect to find in the chimpanzee the germs of the specifically human forms of activity. We thus see that not only the naive interest in the anthropoid ape but also the much more important problems of evolutionary theory were touched upon by these investigations.

Köhler managed to demonstrate that anthropoid apes display intellectual behavior of the *same type and sort* that is the distinguishing characteristic of man. To wit, he succeeded in demonstrating that the higher apes are capable of inventing and using tools. Tool use, which forms the basis of human labor, determines, as is well known, the fundamental uniqueness of man's adaptation to nature and distinguishes him from other animals.

It is well known that, according to the theory of historical materialism, the use of tools forms the starting point which determines the uniqueness of man's historical development in contrast to the zoological development of his ancestors. However, Köhler's discovery that anthropoid apes are capable of inventing and using tools comes as not at all unexpected for historical materialism and was theoretically anticipated and expected in advance.

In this connection Marx [1890/1981, p. 194] says that

> The use and creation of labor means, although in embryonic form typical of certain animal species, characterize the specifically human labor process and Franklin therefore defines man as 'a tool-making animal,' an animal that manufactures tools.

Already in this statement, we see that it is pointed out that tools do not only form a turning point in human development but also that the germs of tool use can already be found in certain animals.

Plekhanov [1922, p. 138] says that

> When man becomes an animal producing tools he enters a new stage of his development: his *zoological development* ends and his *historical* life path commences . . .. It is quite clear that the use of tools, however imperfect they may be, presupposes an enormous development of the mental capacities. A lot of water flowed under the bridge before our ape-human ancestors reached such a degree of development of the 'spirit.' How did they reach it? This we should not ask history but zoology . . . . Be it as it may but zoology hands down to history *homo* (man) who already has the capacity to invent and use the most primitive tools.

We thus see with all clarity that the capacity to invent and use tools forms the *presupposition* for the historical development of man and originates already in the zoological period of development of our ancestors. In this respect it is extremely important to remark that when he speaks about the tool use of our ancestors Plekhanov is not referring to the *instinctive* use of tools in several lower animals (for example, the construction of nests by birds or the construction of dams by beavers), but to *the invention of tools,* which presupposes *an enormous development of the mental capacities.*

Köhler's experimental investigations do not form a *direct* factual confirmation of these theoretical assumptions. That is why here as well we must add a correction when we turn from theoretical considerations to the experimental investigation of apes—the correction about which we spoke above. We should not forget for one minute that the anthropoid apes which Köhler investigated and our ape-human ancestors about whom Plekhanov speaks are *not identical.* However, even having made this correction, we may not relinquish the thought that between the one and the other indisputably exists *the closest genetic kinship.*

Köhler observed in experiments and in the free play of the animals ample tool use which is undoubtedly genetically related to that prerequisite of the historical development of man about which Plekhanov speaks.

Köhler gives descriptions of the most diverse ways of using sticks, boxes and other objects as tools by means of which the chimpanzees "act upon" the things that surround them and he also provides examples of primitive tool manufacture. For example: a chimpanzee combines two or three sticks, by putting the end of one stick into the opening of another one, in order to have a longer tool, or it breaks off a branch in order to use it as a stick, or it dismantles an apparatus for the cleaning of boots which stood in the anthropoid station in order to remove iron bars from it, or it digs a half-buried stone out of the ground, etc.

But, as Köhler [1921b, pp. 50-60] showed, it was only the stick, which was for the apes a favorite and universal instrument, which they applied in most diverse ways. Historians of culture and psychology will easily view in this stick a universal tool, the prototype of our most diverse tools. The chimpanzee uses the stick as a jumping pole, the stick is used as a fishing rod or spoon to fish out the ants gathered on it and to lick it afterwards. The stick is for the chimpanzee a lever by means of which it opens the lid of a reservoir. With the stick as a shovel it digs the ground. With the stick as a weapon they threaten each other. By means of a stick the lizard or mouse is wiped from their body, with a stick they touch the electric wire, etc.

In all these different ways of tool use we have the indisputable beginnings, the embryonic traces, the psychological prerequisites from which man's labor activity developed. Engels [1925/1978, p. 444] ascribed a decisive role to labor in the process of humanizing the ape and said that "labor created man himself." With great thoroughness Engels therefore attempts to trace the *prerequisites* which might lead to the beginning of labor activity. He points to the division in function between arm and leg. He says [Engels, ibid., p. 444] that "thereby the decisive step was made for the transition from ape to man."

In complete agreement with Darwin [1871/1981, p. 141], who also claimed that "man could not have attained his present dominant position in the world without the use of his hands which are so admirably adapted to act in obedience to his will," Engels views the decisive step in the liberation of the hand from the function of locomotion. Equally well in agreement with Darwin, Engels [1925/1978, p. 444] assumes that our ancestors were "an extremely highly developed genus of the anthropoid ape."

In Köhler's experiments we have experimental proof that the transition to tool use as well was in fact already prepared in the zoological period of development of our ancestors.

It may seem that there is some internal contradiction in what we have just said. Indeed, is there no contradiction between the data established by Köhler and what we would have expected according to the theory of historical materialism? In fact, we just said that Marx views the defining characteristic of human labor in the use of tools, that he considers it possible to disregard in this definition the germs of tool use in animals. Does not the fact about which we spoke above, i.e., the fact that we meet in apes a relatively widespread tool use of a type that stands close to that of man, contradict the thesis that tool use is a specific property of man?

As is well known, Darwin [1871/1981, p. 51] objected to the opinion according to which only man is capable of tool use. He points out that many mammals display this same capacity in rudimentary form. Thus, a chimpanzee uses a stone to crack a fruit with a hard shell. Elephants tear off twigs of trees and use them to keep off the flies.

Plekhanov says about Darwin's opinion that

> He is, of course, perfectly right from his viewpoint, i.e., in the sense that in the notorious 'nature of man' there is not a single trait that will not be met in one or another animal species and that there is therefore no reason whatsoever to consider man as some special creature, to assign him a special 'kingdom.' But we should not forget that *quantitative differences turn into qualitative ones*. That which exists *in embryonic form* in one animal species may become the *distinguishing characteristic* of another animal species. This must be said in particular of tool use. The elephant tears off branches and uses them to keep off the flies. This is interesting and instructive. But in the history of the species 'elephant' the use of branches in the fight against flies probably played a far from essential role: elephants did not become elephants because their more or less elephant-like ancestors fanned themselves with branches. With man it is different. The Australian savage's whole existence depends on his boomerang just like the whole existence of contemporary England depends on its machines. Take away the Australian's boomerang, make him into a farmer, and he will be forced to change his whole way of life, all his customs, his whole way of thinking, his whole 'nature.'

We already pointed out that the tool use in the chimpanzees studied and observed by Köhler is encountered in the latter not in that instinctive form about which Plekhanov is speaking here. Plekhanov himself says that at the border between the animal and human world stands *tool use of another type*, which he calls the *invention* of tools and which requires highly developed mental capacities and presupposes their presence.

Engels [1925/1978, p. 449] also points out that "labor begins with the manufacture of tools." We may thus expect in advance that the use of tools must reach a relatively high degree of development in the animal world in order to make the transition to the labor activity of man possible. But what Plekhanov said about the qualitative difference between the tool use of man and animals *remains fully applicable to Köhler's apes*.

We will provide a simple example which shows in the best possible way that tools still play an *insignificant* role in the biological adaptation of the higher apes. Above we have already said that the apes use a stick as a tool. But they mostly utilize this tool only in "war games." The ape takes a stick, menacingly approaches another one, stabs it. The opponent also arms itself with a stick and before us develops the "war game" of the chimpanzees. But when, says Köhler [1921b, p. 60], a misunderstanding takes place and the play turns into a serious fight, the tool is immediately thrown to the ground and the apes attack each other using their hands, legs, and teeth. The speed allows us to distinguish play from a serious fight. When the ape slowly and clumsily swings the stick it is playing. When things get serious the chimpanzee throws itself at lightning speed on its adversary and the latter is left no time to grab a stick. [3]

From this, Vagner [1927, pp. 49/51] draws a general conclusion which does not seem fully justified to us. He says that we must be very careful not to attribute to intellectual capacities what can to a considerable extent be attributed to instincts: the use of a door, the use of a rope to reach a basket hanging from the ceiling, etc. . . . To suppose that such an animal can build syllogisms is as unfounded as to suppose that it can use a stick or tool when the facts demonstrate that a chimpanzee which has a stick in its hands and thus has a tool, rather than using it, throws it away in conflicts and uses its hands, legs and teeth.

It seems to us that these facts, as described by Köhler, are indeed of fundamental importance for the correct assessment of tool use in apes. They show that this use has not yet become a distinguishing characteristic of the chimpanzees and does not yet play a role of any importance in the adaptation of the animal. The use of tools in the fights of chimpanzees is practically nonexistent. But it seems to us that from the fact that in moments of emotional excitement, as during a fight, the chimpanzee throws away its tool, we may not draw a conclusion regarding its incapability of using the stick as a tool. The *uniqueness* of the stage of development reached by the chimpanzee is rather that it already *has* the capacity for inventing and intelligently using tools but that this capacity has not yet become the basis of its biological adaptation.

It is therefore fully justified that Köhler [1921b, p. 192] not only points to the aspects that condition the similarity between chimpanzees and man but also to the great difference between ape and man, to the boundary that separates the most highly developed ape from the most primitive man. According to Köhler [ibid., p. 192], the absence of speech, this most important auxiliary means of thinking, and the fundamentally limited nature of the chimpanzee's most important material for the intellect, the so-called "representations," are the reasons for the fact that the chimpanzee somehow does not even have the slightest beginnings of cultural development. The life of a chimpanzee proceeds within very narrow boundaries in what concerns past and future. The time in which it lives is in this respect very limited, and all its behavior, it appears, is almost fully dependent on the momentarily given situation.

Köhler [1922, p. 3] asks to what extent can the chimpanzee's behavior be oriented toward the future. The solution of this problem seems important to him for the following reasons. A great number of very different observations of anthropoids reveal a phenomenon usually only seen in beings that have some, albeit primitive, culture. Since the chimpanzees have nothing that deserves to be called culture, the question arises as to what is the reason for their limitedness in this respect.

Even the most primitive man prepares a stick for digging despite the fact that he does not leave right away to dig and despite the fact that the external conditions for the use of the tool are absent. And the fact itself of preparing a tool for the future, according to Köhler [ibid., p. 3], is connected with the origin of culture. However, he only states the question but makes no attempt to solve it.

It seems to us that the absence of culture, which *from the psychological side* indeed forms a very important aspect which separates chimpanzees from man, is determined by the absence in the chimpanzees' behavior of anything comparable to, albeit remotely, human speech and, speaking more broadly, to all *sign* use.

Köhler [ibid., p. 27] says that observing the chimpanzees, it is possible to establish that they have speech which *in some respects* is highly similar to human speech. To wit, their "speech" has a considerable number of phonetic elements which come close to the sounds of human speech. And that is why Köhler [ibid., p. 27] assumes that the absence of speech in higher apes cannot be explained by *peripheral causes*, by deficiencies or shortcomings of the vocal and articulatory apparatus.

But the chimpanzees' sounds always only express their emotional state. They invariably have just subjective meaning and never signify something objective, are never used as signs that signify something external to the animal. Köhler's [1921b, p. 70] observations of the chimpanzees' play also showed that although chimpanzees do "draw" with colored clay, one can never observe anything even remotely resembling a sign.

Other investigators as well, such as Yerkes [1929, p. 306], had the opportunity to establish the absence of "speech in the human sense" in these animals. Meanwhile, the psychology of primitive man demonstrates that the whole cultural development of the *human mind* is connected with the use of signs. And, evidently, cultural development became possible for our apelike ancestors only from the moment when articulate speech developed *on the basis of the development of labor.* Precisely the absence of this latter factor "explains" the absence of the rudiments of cultural development in chimpanzees.

Regarding the second aspect about which Köhler speaks, the limitedness in operating with nonvisual situations or with representations, it seems to us that it is also intimately connected with the absence of speech or some sign in general, for speech indeed forms the most important means through which man begins to operate with nonvisual situations.

But neither the absence of speech nor the limitedness of "life in time" [4] *explain* anything of the question which Köhler raises, for *they themselves need to be explained.* The absence of speech cannot be considered the *cause* for the absence of cultural development in anthropoid apes because it *forms part* of this general phenomenon itself. The *cause* in the present sense is the difference in the type of adaptation. Labor, as Engels demonstrated, played a decisive role in the process of the transformation of ape into man. "Labor created man himself"—and *human* speech, and *human* culture, and *human* thinking, and *human* "life in time."

2

While Köhler solves the task he set himself in a purely experimental way, for us the problem of intellect itself, as a particular type of behavior which we can follow in chimpanzees in its purest and most clearly expressed form, becomes very important. Indeed, under suitable conditions the chimpanzee's behavior in this respect is a highly profitable object, for it allows us to investigate the "pure culture" of the intellect. Here we can see reactions, which in the human adult have already become stereotyped and automatic, in their primitive form, in the process of development.

When we recall that the investigator's task is to demonstrate that the chimpanzee is not only capable of the instinctive use but also of the primitive manufacture of tools and their intelligent application, then we immediately see what important fundamental meaning for the whole investigation of the intellect this principle of tool use acquires.

Köhler [1921b, p. 2] says that before asking the question whether intelligent behavior exists in anthropoids we have to agree on how it is at all possible to distinguish between intelligent reactions and reactions of another type. Köhler [ibid., p. 2] takes this difference for common knowledge from the everyday observation of man. As has already been said, he points out that the tacit assumption of such a difference lies at the basis of association theory and at the basis of Thorndike's theory.

Already the sheer fact that Thorndike and his followers *contest* the existence of intellectual behavior in animals and that the associationists attempt to *reduce* intellectual action to associations speaks *in favor of the fact* that both parties *proceed from the same assumption* as Köhler did, i.e., they assume an immediate, naive distinction between actions based on blind, mechanical trial and error and intelligent actions based on an understanding of the situation.

That is why Köhler [ibid., p. 2] says that he starts and ends his theoretical investigation without taking a positive or negative position concerning association psychology. The starting point of his investigation is the *same* as Thorndike's. His goal is not to investigate in the anthropoids "something fully determined in advance" [ibid., p. 2]. First we need to solve the general question as to whether the behavior of higher apes rises to the type that we *very approximately* know from experience and that we call intelligent. In doing so we proceed according to the logic of scientific knowledge itself, because clear and exact definitions are impossible at the beginning of empirical sciences. Only after a long development and successful investigations can such precise definitions be given [ibid, p. 2].

In his book, Köhler thus does not develop any theory of intelligent behavior. He touches on theoretical questions *only from the negative side* and attempts to demonstrate that the factual data he gathered *cannot* be interpreted from the viewpoint of the theory of chance and that according to their *type* the chimpanzee's actions are *fundamentally* different from trial and error. Köhler does not even give a hypothetical answer to the question about the psychophysiological mechanism of these intelligent reactions, about the changes in the reflex arc which take place in the animal. He consciously confines his task to the establishment of the existence of reactions of a certain type and to a very careful search for objective criteria for a reaction of this type.

We just said that Köhler at the beginning of his work does not start from a precise definition of intelligent behavior. Let us try to sketch what Köhler *does* have in mind when he speaks of intelligent behavior. This *type* of intelligent behavior is not fully *undefined*. Experience shows, says Köhler [ibid., p. 3], that we do not speak of intelligent behavior when man or animal reach goals directly, in an unproblematic way.

But the impression of intelligence arises when the circumstances prevent such a direct route to the goal and leave open an *indirect* mode of action, and when man or animal develops a *detour* that corresponds to the situation. Precisely such an understanding, he says [ibid., p. 3], lies at the basis of almost all investigations of animal behavior which ask the same question—no matter whether they solve it positively or negatively.

Köhler states his research principle in very general terms as follows. In the experiment a situation is created in which the direct path toward a goal is blocked but in which there remains an indirect path. The animal is placed in this situation, which should be as graphic and surveyable as possible. The experiment must show to what extent the animal has the capacity to make use of a detour.

A further complication of the same principle is the introduction into the experimental situation of tools. The detour toward the goal is not made by movements of the animal's own body but by means of other objects, which in the given case take the role of tools. It must be said that from this viewpoint the inclusion of tools in the process of behavior itself radically and fundamentally changes the whole character of behavior and gives it the character of a "*detour*."

Köhler [ibid., p. 137] himself points out that the most important *objective criterion* which allows us to distinguish intelligent tool use from instinctive activity and trial and error is the objective structure of the operation of tool use itself in accordance with the structure of the objective situation. He is further fully justified in pointing out that the instinct exists for the animal's body, for the innervation of its members but not for the stick which it holds in its hand [ibid., p. 150]. We may therefore consider the animal's actual instinctive movements toward the goal to be instinctive but not its complex movements conducted with a tool. When the movements of the organs are replaced by the movements of tools and become "mediated," what we see is an intellectual operation of the animal. This gives us a second very important criterion of intellectual behavior, namely tool use. This goal-directed use of tools according to the structure of the situation forms an objective index for intellectual reactions in animals, for the use of tools presupposes an understanding of the objective properties of things. And finally, for Köhler the third and last criterion is the structural (integral, form) character of the whole operation which is carried out by the animal.

By structure, the new psychology means integral processes that have a whole series of properties which cannot be deduced from the simple addition of the properties of its parts and which—in their quality of wholes—are distinguished by a whole series of regularities. The sharpest factual contrast between the intelligent operations of the chimpanzee and the operations that develop in self-training through the method of trial and error is that the operations of the chimpanzee do not develop from isolated elements. They do not develop from a chaos of isolated parts which are given in advance amid a multitude of others which are not connected to the solution of the problem. They do not develop because successful reactions are selected from the animal's movements and then—after frequent repetition—united into a general chain reaction. Characteristic of the intellectual reaction (operation) is precisely that it does not develop as an aggregate of separate parts but right away as a whole which determines the properties and functional meaning of its separate parts.

Köhler gave a brilliant experimental proof of the integral character of the chimpanzee's intellectual reactions. He demonstrated that an isolated, singular, partial action which is included in the whole operation of the animal, considered in itself, is meaningless and at times may lead away from the goal. But in combination with the others and *only* in connection with them do they acquire their sense.

Köhler [ibid., p. 165] says that the integral act is the only possible way of finding the solution in the present case. And Köhler advances this characteristic as the criterion for any real "detour," i.e., any intellectual operation. The animal is placed in a situation such that in order to seize a fruit that lies in front of it it must perform a detour. For example, it must not first pull the fruit toward itself but push it away—in order to roll it to a spot from where it can be reached with the arm when the animal has walked around the box. It is perfectly obvious that in this case the whole contains parts which in a certain sense form its opposites. Such a dialectical unity of the parts of an integral process forms the real criterion for an intellectual reaction.

But this reaction as a whole is a direct result of the influence of the structure of the situation on the animal, and its intelligence is verified by the extent to which the operation of the animal corresponds to the objective structure of this situation.

Köhler thus chooses the path of a purely objective investigation of intellect. He [ibid., p. 73] openly says that when we point to these integral operations of the animal we do not yet say anything about the animal's consciousness and that he will for the time being exclusively speak about its behavior. In his words, the difference between meaningful and nonmeaningful operations fully belongs to the elementary phenomenology of the chimpanzees' behavior.

Köhler thus fights the mechanistic tendencies in natural scientific psychology and attempts to demonstrate that in the transition to a higher type of behavior we may entirely *objectively* establish that the new stage in the development of animal behavior is qualitatively different from pure self-training.

Köhler's investigations gave rise to an extended literature in which both the basic claims of the author and his interpretation of various aspects of his investigation were critically analyzed.

Not one of the critics denies the factual side of Köhler's communications, but many differ with him as to the interpretation of the experiments. We will dwell only on the most typical and fundamental critical viewpoints which will help us to find a correct assessment and understanding of the theses put forward by Köhler.

Köhler first of all met with criticism from the side of objective psychologists. Thus, Lindworsky [1919, pp. 288/391] [5] assumes that the ape cannot display intelligent behavior on two grounds: first, because the ape, in contrast to man, displays a standstill in its mental development over the course of millennia, and second, because for this author intellect is equivalent to the understanding of relations, and the operations of apes *cannot* be based on understanding of such a kind.

Highly characteristic of this critique is that in its interpretation of the chimpanzee's behavior it advances a *methodological principle that differs completely* from Köhler's. It rests on the old subjectivistic and mechanistic viewpoint for which objective and structural criteria are not convincing. For Köhler the criterion of intellect is the handling of things according to their structural properties, but Lindworsky assumes that from the viewpoint of this criterion we would have to count instinctive actions as belonging to intellect as well.

In discussing this opinion, Koffka [1925a, p. 163], another eminent representative of structural psychology, correctly points out that in purely instinctive actions, as has been shown in numerous observations and experiments (by Volkelt and others), we can observe highly non-goal-directed behavior with respect to fundamentally important structural properties each time the situation differs from the normal type.

But the most important and fundamental aspect of Lindworsky's critique is that he *breaks down* the intelligent operations of chimpanzees into different parts and then asks the question *where* in this operation does intelligence come in. The question itself radically contradicts Köhler's statement of the problem, because for Köhler intellect does not "come in" at a certain moment of the given operation. The operation *as a whole*, its structure, corresponds to the external structure of the situation and *consequently* is intelligent. Köhler himself demonstrated that the separate parts of an operation are as such meaningless and acquire their relative meaning only in the structure of the whole action.

If we would accept the criteria of subjective empirical psychology put forward in this critique, then we would thereby be compelled in advance, independently of the outcome of any investigation, to ascribe intellect to only those properties that introspective analysis detects in man's thinking. Thus, Bühler [1918, pp. 278-279] agrees that judging by all *objective characteristics* the behavior of the apes in Köhler's experiments rises above instinct and training, but he still refuses to see intelligent activity in these operations. He sees in these operations the accidental, "blind, i.e., nonintelligent action of the association mechanism."

For Bühler, as for the other subjective psychologists, intellect is without fail connected with judgments, with the feeling of confidence. He [Bühler, 1918, p. 281] says that "one should prove that the chimpanzees form judgments." At the same time he fully accepts Köhler's objective interpretation.

> In his theory Köhler will prove, as he already indicates, that the behavior of the apes
> is determined by relations between things. I think this can surely be proved and I find
> it an important beginning of thinking [ibid., p. 281].

The debate, then, concerns the conception of intellect and not the interpretation of the experiments.

To explain the behavior of apes, Bühler advances quite a number of hypotheses whose basis comes down to the following. He [ibid., pp. 281-282] assumes that

> the principle of detours and the principle of getting hold of a fruit through the bending
> of a branch or tearing off and subsequent grabbing of a branch is given to the animals
> by nature: given like other instinctive mechanisms which we cannot explain in detail
> but have to acknowledge as facts.

In this way, attributing, not without sufficient grounds, part of the chimpanzee's success to instinct and self-training in the course of its preceding life, Bühler further assumes, and this time entirely arbitrarily, that the animal can get a feeling of the ultimate situation and act on its basis. He is ready to explain the behavior of chimpanzees by the *play of representations*. He says [Bühler, 1919, p. 17] that

> The inhabitant of trees must be well acquainted with the connection between branches
> and fruits. When the animal in the experimental room sits in front of the bars and
> outside lies a fruit without a branch and inside a branch without fruit, then from the
> psychological viewpoint the principal accomplishment is to bring both together *in
> perception or representation*. The rest is self-evident. The same is true for the boxes.
> When in the forest an ape detects a fruit high in a tree, nothing is more natural than
> to look for a stem which can be used to climb up and seize the fruit; in the experimental
> room there is no tree but a box in the perceptual field, and the mental accomplishment
> is to place it at the right spot in imagery; to wish it and to do it then amounts to the
> same thing, since the captive chimpanzee is carrying around the boxes all the time
> during play.

We see that Bühler, in contrast to Köhler, is inclined to reduce the mechanism of the chimpanzees' actions to the automatic play of representations. It seems to us that this whole interpretation is not at all based on the actual facts gathered by Köhler, because *nothing* in his investigation indicates that the ape really first solves the task in imagery. But most important is that Bühler attributes to the chimpanzees, as Koffka says [1925a, p. 160], an exceedingly complex representational activity which, judging by Köhler's experiments, is highly unlikely. Indeed, where are the objective grounds for attributing to the animal, as Bühler does, the capacity to represent the ultimate situation and to operate on the basis of this goal?

Köhler, on the contrary, demonstrated, as we have already pointed out above, that *precisely* the extremely limited nature of the life of "representations" is a characteristic trait of the chimpanzee's intellect and that these animals as a rule already turn to a blind mode of action when the visual situation becomes just a little bit unclear or optically confused. It is exactly the chimpanzee's *incapacity* to determine his actions by "representations," i.e., nonvisual or "trace" stimuli, which distinguishes the whole chimpanzee's behavior. Köhler succeeded in experimentally demonstrating that the slightest complication or confusion in the external situation leads to the chimpanzee's failure to solve a task which in itself it can solve without any effort.

But the decisive proof that the chimpanzee's actions do not simply form a play of representations is seen in Köhler's experiment. Indeed, if the ape, as Bühler assumes, only uses the stick as a tool because it imagines a branch from which a fruit is hanging, then a real branch growing on a tree should be made into a tool *more easily and faster*. The experiment, however, shows the opposite: for the ape it is an extremely difficult task to tear a real branch from a tree and to make it into a tool—much more difficult than using a ready-made stick.

We thus see that the experiment does not speak in favor of Bühler's assumption, and with Koffka we assume that the chimpanzee's operation—the "combination" of the stick and the fruit—does not take place in the field of representations or a similar psychophysiological process but in the visual field. This operation does not constitute a reproduction of previous "experience" but the establishment of a new structural connection.

The analogous experiments by Jaensch on eidetic children are serious experimental evidence for this claim. These experiments demonstrated that

> the approximation of tool and goal, the establishment of a purely optical connection between them, proceeds in the eidetic's visual field itself [Jaensch, 1927, p. 194].

But there are statements in Bühler's critique which seem to us to be quite correct and important. They not only do not "refute" Köhler's theses but corroborate them and shed new light on them.

Bühler [1918, pp. 277-278] acknowledges that the chimpanzees' actions have the character of objectively meaningful actions, but he says that

> it appears that in perfection and methodical purity this natural performance lags behind many others: one need only compare the rickety structures of boxes of the apes with the honeycombs of bees or with the web of spiders, etc.! The speed and confidence as well with which the spiders and bees work to reach their goal as soon as the eliciting circumstances are there stands high above the often insecure and hesitant behavior of the apes.

But we, on the contrary, see this characteristic as *evidence* in favor of the fact that here we really do not have an instinctive but a newly formed action of the ape or, as Bühler [ibid., p. 278] says, "a discovery in the technical sense of this word."

But the most valuable idea of Bühler's whole critique is the idea that we should *not only* emphasize what distinguishes the chimpanzee's behavior from instinctive actions and habits but also point out what unites them.

That is why it seems to us that Bühler is quite right in noting the enormous part the apes' previous experience plays in their behavior in new situations, the remarkable similarity between the situation encountered in natural forest life and the situation created by the experimenter, even if it may prove impossible to reduce the chimpanzee's behavior to direct "recall" from natural life, to a habit formed previously.

Bühler [ibid., pp. 271-277] demonstrates in great detail, and in our opinion fully convincingly, that both what the chimpanzee is capable of during the experiment and what it cannot do can be explained from the conditions of the apes' natural life in the forest. Thus, the prototype of the use of sticks he sees in the tearing off of fruit by means of a branch, climbing by means of boxes he connects with the climbing of trees, and the animals' inability to remove obstacles he reduces to the fact that

> The climbing animal will avoid *obstacles* that block the way. *There is hardly ever reason* to remove them. All problems with obstacles are therefore quite difficult for the chimpanzees. To remove a box which stands close to the bars and occupies the spot from which a fruit can be reached is most obvious to us human beings while some chimpanzees labored for hours with other means before it occurred to them.

That is why Bühler [1919, p. 23] is justified in saying that in the chimpanzees' actions

> we are not struck by a gap with the past. Some slight progress in the life of representations, a little more free play of associations—that is, perhaps, all in which the chimpanzee is higher than the dog. The only thing was to correctly utilize what was available. In this resided the whole novelty.

We cannot deny that Bühler's thought is correct in that there is no gap between the chimpanzee's intellect and the preceding activity and that the intellectual operation itself, as we can also establish with respect to human thinking, is certainly built on the system of previous habits and serves their new combination. But in this highest form of behavior the habits which participate in an intellectual operation and form part of its structure have already become a "superseded category." Bühler makes the fundamental error of assuming that nature makes no leaps in development and proceeds gradually. He does not accept a basic principle of dialectics which says that nature and development do make leaps, that the quantitative changes about which he speaks when comparing dog and chimpanzee turn into qualitative ones and that one type of behavior is replaced by another one. The overcoming of the errors of mechanistic natural science lies in the acknowledgment of this dialectical principle of the transition of quantity into quality.

But the critique against Köhler "from below," from the side of zoopsychology, is marred by the same error.

Vagner [1927, pp. 49-50], in assessing the chimpanzee's behavior in Köhler's experiments, comes to the conclusion that

> goal-understanding seems to be present when we consider the first and last moments. But when we consider the details of the actions between these moments provided by Köhler himself, then the capacity for goal-understanding becomes more doubtful. The attempts the apes make, the mistakes they make, their inability to place one box on top of the other, etc.—all this speaks against the intelligence of their actions.

Just like Bühler, Vagner believes that it is possible to reduce the chimpanzee's actions to instincts,

> because in their eyes all these objects are not at all different from the ones they use in freedom: a door and a stub, a rope and a twig, a liana and a string are things that differ in our eyes but they are completely identical in the eyes of the ape as means of solving the task.

As soon as we accept this we will with natural inevitability come to the conclusion that Thorndike was right in detecting nothing but actions of the association mechanism in the (lower!) apes. This author admits that in mental capacity the apes occupy the highest place, but nevertheless they are nothing compared to man, because they show a complete incapacity for even the most elementary thinking.

Considering the experiment with the *manufacture* of tools, Vagner says

> Is this true? The fact is, of course, related truthfully but its genuine meaning is undoubtedly hidden behind the deletions of those hundreds, maybe thousands, of nonsensical, meaningless actions which the apes carried out in their attempts to reach the fruits.

Pointing to the apes' use of *unsuitable* tools, he says that

> we can hardly agree with Köhler when he says that the chimpanzee displays intellectual capabilities of a kind fully akin to those proper of man. This scholar is much closer to the truth when he says that the absence of *representations* of objects and phenomena and the absence of the ability to speak create a sharp boundary between the anthropoid apes and the lowest human races.

It seems to us that Vagner makes two mistakes here. First, as Köhler *demonstrated*, the apes' errors themselves often speak in favor of attributing to them intelligent capacities ("good errors") and not against it. Second, the fact that *besides* meaningful actions we also encounter, and in far greater number, nonmeaningful ones, *as we do in man*, does not at all speak against the fact that we should, in general, distinguish two types of behaviors.

But most important, most fundamental is that Vagner ignores the basic criterion advanced by Köhler, namely the structural character of the operation itself
and its correspondence to the external structure of the situation. Neither of them
is refuted by Vagner, nor does he show that these aspects can be deduced from
instinctive actions.

In exactly the same way, Borovsky [1927, p. 184] sees no grounds whatsoever
for fully classifying the chimpanzee's actions into a special type of behavior and
attributing intellect to these animals. He is inclined to think that there is no difference *in principle* between the behavior of apes and the behavior of rats. He says
that if the ape

> does not carry out any visible tests (does not stretch out its arms), then it 'contrives'
> with some muscles; carries out uncompleted attempts just like the rat; assesses the
> distance on the basis of previous experience; somehow 'experiments' and after this
> appears 'the sudden solution' and to the extent that we do not know exactly how
> precisely it appeared, do not know its history and mechanism, we do not have the
> possibility of deciphering various forms of 'Einsicht' or 'ideation.' For us these labels
> can only serve as signals for a problem that is still open, if it is not a pseudo-problem.

Like the other authors, Borovsky runs ahead of Köhler and attempts to demonstrate that the ape solves the task via internal tests and contrivances. To this we
may reply that Köhler himself leaves entirely open the question as to whether the
operation of the chimpanzee is reducible to the action of the associative mechanism.
In another place he is even clearer about this.

The rejection of the principle of chance in the explanation of the chimpanzee's
behavior does not yet mean that we occupy one or the other position as to associationism in general. Associationists accept the empirically established difference
between meaningful and nonmeaningful behavior. The whole question is whether
they succeed, on the basis of the association principle, in explaining the structure
of the chimpanzee's operations and their correspondence to the structure of the
situation. We should deduce from the association principle, Köhler [1921b, p. 159]
continues, how the understanding of an essential internal relation between two
things develops or—more generally—the understanding of the structure of the situation. How *the connection between actions* develops *on the basis of the properties of
the things themselves* and not from the accidental combination of instinctive reactions.

As to whether the actions of the chimpanzee can thus be reduced to the association of movements, i.e., to habit formation—*this question is left open*. Furthermore, Köhler himself and other psychologists of the same current always point to
the fact that we must accept structural, i.e., integral actions in animal instincts and
in their habits as well.

Köhler [ibid., p. 141] himself showed that apes, like other animals, form structural actions in *training* and that even in Thorndike's experiments not all of the
animals' behavior is fully meaningless. On the contrary, the animals display a sharp
difference between cases where their solution is not meaningfully connected with
the situation and other cases where this connection is present.

Thus, Köhler seems to abolish the sharp gap between intellect and other, lower
types of activity. Koffka [1925a, p. 173] is fully justified in pointing out, in contrast
to Bühler, that structural psychology regards the instinct, habits, and intellect not
as different apparatuses or completely different mechanisms but as structural formations that are internally connected and fused. The psychologists of this current
are inclined to erase the sharp boundary between different stages in the development of behavior and assume that *already* in habit formation and in the activity of

instincts we have the beginnings of an activity that is not blind, not mechanical but structural.

The principle of structure fulfills a double methodological role in the works of these psychologists and in this lies its real dialectical meaning. On the one hand, this principle *unites* all the stages in the development of behavior, abolishes the gap about which Bühler speaks, points to the continuity in the development of the higher from the lower, points out that structural properties are already present in instincts and habits. On the other hand, the same principle also allows us to establish the whole deep, fundamental, qualitative difference between the one and the other stage, all the new things which each stage introduces into the development of behavior and which distinguishes it from its predecessor.

Koffka [1925a, p. 173] says that

> in our understanding intellect, training and instinct are based upon structural functions that are formed differently, determined differently, and proceed differently but not upon different *apparatuses* that may be switched on "when the need arises" as Bühler assumes.

3

Within the limits of our essay, we cannot possibly provide a detailed examination and critique of structural psychology and *Gestalttheorie* to which Köhler's investigation belongs. It seems to us, however, that for a correct assessment and even for a correct understanding of Köhler's investigation it is essential to dwell very briefly on the underlying philosophical principle of this investigation.

Not only because ideas reveal their true face only when they are carried to their logical extreme, when they have received their philosophical expression, but mainly because the problem raised by Köhler itself—the problem of intellect—is always both historically and, according to its essence, inevitably and intimately linked with philosophical problems. We can positively affirm, without fear of committing a mistake or exaggeration, that not a single psychological problem is as critical and as central in what regards its methodological meaning for the whole system of psychology as is the problem of intellect. [6]

Not long ago Külpe [1922, p. 329], summarizing the results of experimental investigation in the area of the processes of thinking, established that "we again find ourselves on the road toward ideas." In reality, the attempt of the Würzburg school to fight its way forward from associationism, the attempt to prove the uniqueness of thought processes and the fact of their not being reducible to associations turned out to be a road leading backward—to Plato. This is one side. The other side is that the associationism of Ebbinghaus and Ribot or Watson's behaviorism usually led to the dismissal of the problem of intellect itself, to the dissolution of thinking in processes of a more elementary order. In the most recent years, this psychology replied to Külpe's statement with the words of Watson [1926, p. 295] that thinking is not essentially different from playing tennis or swimming.

With regard to this question, Köhler's book occupies a completely *new* position, which is deeply different from both the position of the Würzburg school and naive behaviorism. Köhler fights on two fronts and contrasts his investigations on the one hand with the attempts to erase the boundary between thinking and ordinary motor habit. On the other hand, he contrasts them with the attempts to picture thinking as a purely mental action, an *actus purus* which has nothing in common with more elementary forms of behavior and which takes us back to Platonic ideas. In this struggle on two fronts lies the whole novelty of Köhler's philosophical approach to the problem of intellect.

It might easily seem, judging by external characteristics, that we now apparently contradict what was pointed out above.

Above we said that there is no theory of intellect in Köhler's book but only a factual description and analysis of experimentally gathered data. From this it is easy to conclude that Köhler's investigation gives rise to no philosophical generalizations at all and that the attempt to examine and critically assess the philosophical basis of this investigation is deemed to fail from the very start inasmuch as we thereby attempt to jump over a missing psychological theory of thinking. But this is not so. The *system of facts* which Köhler communicates is at the same time a *system of ideas* by means of which these facts were unearthed and in light of which they were interpreted and explained. And *precisely* the absence of any developed theory of thinking in Köhler forces us to dwell on the philosophical foundations of his work. If the ideas and philosophical assumptions that lie at the basis of an investigation are given in an *implicit form*, then for a correct understanding and assessment of this book it is even more important to try to make them explicit.

It is, of course, out of the question to run ahead, to attempt to anticipate, albeit in rough outlines, Köhler's still undeveloped theory of thinking. But for a correct understanding of the *facts* communicated by Köhler it is necessary to examine the philosophical viewpoints which lay at the basis of the collection, investigation, and systematization of these facts.

Above, we have already said that Köhler's concept of intellect radically differs from the one which Külpe and his collaborators reached as a result of their investigations. They investigated the intellect *from above*—in the most developed, highest and most complex forms of human abstract thinking.

Köhler attempts to investigate the intellect *from below*—from its roots, from its first beginnings as they appear in anthropoid apes. Not only does he approach the investigation from the other end, but Köhler's conception of intellect itself is essentially opposite to the one which formed the basis of the previous experimental investigations of intellect.

Külpe [1922, pp. 329-330] says that

> Ancient wisdom has found the distinguishing characteristic of the human being in the ability to think. The church father Augustine and after him Descartes viewed in thinking the only firm ground for the existence of the person who is tormented by doubts. We however do not only say: I think, therefore I am, but also: the world is as we establish and determine it in thought.

The distinguishing property of human nature and, moreover, the property that determines and establishes the existence of the world—that is what human thinking represents for these psychologists. For Köhler [1921b, p. 191] the question of primary and fundamental importance is first of all the evidence he found that the chimpanzee displays intelligent behavior *of the same type* as man, that the *type* of human intelligent thinking can indisputably be established in anthropoid apes, that thinking in its biological development *is not* the distinguishing characteristic of "human nature," but developed, like all human nature, from the more primitive forms we meet in animals. Human nature converges with animal nature—via the anthropoids—not only according to its morphological and physiological characteristics but also according to that form of behavior which is considered to be specifically human. Above, we have seen that tool use, which has always been considered the distinguishing characteristic of human activity, was experimentally established in apes by Köhler.

But at the same time Köhler not only places the development of the intellect in the same plane as the development of other properties and functions of animals and man. He also proposes a criterion of intellectual activity which is completely opposite to the previous one. For him intelligent behavior, as expressed in tool use, is first of all a particular way of acting upon the surrounding world which is fully determined by the objective properties of the objects upon which we act and by the tools we use. For Köhler, intellect is not thought which determines and establishes the existence of the world. Thought itself is guided by the important objective properties of things, reveals the structural properties of the external situation and allows us to act according to this objective structure of things.

Remember that from the practical side the intellectual activity of the ape, as is described in Köhler's book, is fully covered by the use of tools. From the theoretical side Köhler proposes an objective criterion for intellectual activity. He says [ibid., p. 137] that only that behavior of animals seems necessarily intelligent to us which corresponds—as a closed integral process—with the structure of the external situation, with the general structural field. That is why, he says, we can accept the following characteristic as a criterion for intellect: *the coming into being of the solution as a whole, in accordance with the structure of the field.*

We thus see that instead of idealistic claims concerning the dependency of existence on thinking—which were explicitly present in Külpe's conclusions—Köhler proposes the opposite viewpoint, which rests upon the dependency of thinking on objective things that exist outside of us and act upon us.

At the same time, for Köhler thinking does not lose its uniqueness and it is only to thinking that he ascribes the capacity to detect and distinguish the objective structural relations of things and to influence things making use of these relations. The thought operation of the chimpanzee, about which Köhler [ibid., p. 159] himself says that it very roughly resembles what Selz managed to establish with respect to man's thinking activity, is in the end nothing other than a structural action whose intelligence resides in its correspondence with the structure of the objective situation. It is *exactly this* which delimits the intellectual operations of the chimpanzee from the method of trial and error by means of which animals establish more or less complex habits.

Köhler fights against the attempts of Thorndike and other Americans to reduce all animal behavior exclusively to the method of trial and error. He demonstrates with experimental precision in which objective aspects a genuine solution of the task differs from its accidental solution. We will not repeat Köhler's conclusions here, let alone add something to them. We only wish to emphasize that while Köhler does not provide the beginnings of a positive theory explaining the intellectual behavior of apes, he nevertheless provides an exhaustive "negative" analysis of the facts and points out that the behavior of the apes he observed fundamentally differs from trial and error.

In the preceding section, we dwelled in great detail on the evaluation and the weighing of these conclusions by Köhler and his critics. Now we are interested in the philosophical side of this same "negative" thesis which Köhler understands very clearly. He says [ibid., p. 151] that by rejecting the theory of chance in the development of the solutions of the apes, he comes into apparent conflict with natural science. However, in his opinion, this conflict is *only apparent and external* because the theory of chance, which gives a detailed scientific explanation of the facts in other cases, appears untenable in the given case *exactly from the natural scientific viewpoint.* That is why Köhler sharply delimits his construction and views from the views developed previously which were similar to the ones developed by him in *the negative respect.*

He says [ibid., pp. 152-153] that the rejection of the theory of chance can already be found in Von Hartmann

> who considers it impossible that a bird builds its nest by chance and concludes that the foreman is 'the unconsciousness'; Bergson regards an accidental combination of the elements of the eye as far too improbable and has the 'élan vital' accomplish the miracle; neither are the neo-vitalists and psycho-vitalists satisfied by Darwinian chance, and everywhere in living matter they find 'goal-directed forces' of the same type as in human thinking but without the property of being consciously experienced. With the above-mentioned currents of thinking my book only has in common that both they and we reject the theory of chance.

Although many think that the rejection of this theory will inevitably lead to the acceptance of one of the theories of this type, Köhler [ibid., p. 153] states that "the alternative is surely not either chance or supernatural agents." This alternative is based on the fundamental error of assuming that *all* processes in inorganic nature are subject to the laws of chance. Precisely from the viewpoint of physics, Köhler considers the "either–or" untenable, because in reality other possibilities exist as well.

With this, Köhler touches upon a very important theoretical point of structural psychology, namely its attempt to *overcome* the two fundamental blind alleys of contemporary natural science—the mechanistic and the vitalistic conception. Wertheimer was the first to point out that these conceptions are untenable from the viewpoint of structural theory.

Wertheimer [1912] wished to present the nervous processes which take place in the brain in the light of the new theory and came to the conclusion that these processes in the nervous system have to be considered not as sums of different excitations but as integral structures. He says that theoretically there is no need to assume, as do vitalists, that beyond and above the different excitations there exist special, specific central processes. We should rather assume that each physiological process in the brain represents a single whole which is not a simple sum of the excitations of separate centers but has all the properties of a structure about which we spoke above.

The concept of structure, i.e., a whole that has its own properties which cannot be reduced to the properties of the separate parts, thus helps the new psychology to overcome mechanistic and vitalistic theory. In contrast to Ehrenfels and other psychologists, who considered structure as a property of higher mental processes, as something introduced by consciousness into the elements from which the perception of the whole is constructed, the new psychology proceeds from the assumption that these wholes we call structures are not only not the privilege of higher conscious processes but not even an exclusive property of mind.

Koffka [1924, pp. 159-160] says that

> If we begin to look for them we find them everywhere in nature. Consequently we are forced to assume such wholes in the nervous system, to consider psychophysical processes as such wholes, whenever we have reasons that suggest such a view. There are many such reasons . . . .. We must assume that conscious processes are part-processes of larger wholes and that, by pointing to other parts of the same whole, they give us evidence that the physiological process is just as whole as the mental one.

We thus see that structural psychology arrives at a monistic solution of the psychophysical problem and that it in principle assumes that both mental processes and physiological processes in the brain are structurally formed. Koffka [1925a, p. 77] says that nervous processes which correspond to such phenomena as rhythm, melody, and the perception of figures must have the essential properties of these phenomena, i.e., above all their structure.

In order to answer the question as to whether structures exist in the realm of nonmental processes, Köhler investigated whether what we call structure is possible in the world of physical phenomena. In a special investigation dedicated to this question, Köhler [1920] attempts to demonstrate that in the area of physical phenomena exist integral processes that we are fully entitled to call structural in the sense in which we use this word in psychology. The characteristic particularities and properties of these wholes cannot be deduced by adding the properties and characteristics of their parts.

At first glance, it may seem that any chemical compound is a model of such a nonpsychological structure; such a compound as PCN, for example, has properties that are not proper to one of the elements that make up its composition: potassium, carbon, and nitrogen. But such a *too simple* proof is, strictly speaking, not convincing, because when we use this analogy, Köhler [1920, pp. xi-xii] says, we, on the one hand, cannot reveal many very important properties of psychological structures in chemical compounds (the functional dependency of the parts on the whole) and, on the other hand, we may expect that with further successes of physical chemistry these properties will be reduced to certain primary physical properties. That is why in order to attain the fundamental possibility of examining the processes of the central nervous system as structural processes, Köhler set himself the task of investigating whether structure is at all possible in the world of *physical* phenomena. Köhler gives a positive answer to this question.

For Köhler, the whole traditional statement of the psychophysical problem is radically changed in connection with this investigation. As soon as we accept with the new psychology that the physiological processes in the brain have the same structure as mental processes, then the gap which existed during psychology's whole history between the mental and the physical will disappear completely and a monistic understanding of the psychophysical processes will take its place. Köhler [ibid., p. 193] says that

> Usually it is said that even with the most exact physical observation and knowledge of the brain processes we nevertheless would not learn anything from them about the corresponding experiences. I must claim the opposite. *In principle* it is fully conceivable that observation of the brain reveals processes that are structurally, and consequently in their essential properties, similar to what is experienced phenomenally by the subject. *In practice* it is almost inconceivable, not only for technical reasons in the usual sense of this word, but above all because of another difficulty, because of the difference between the anatomical-geometrical and the functional brain space.

Köhler further says that one of the main recurring arguments against the assumption of a physical correlate of thinking (and higher mental processes in general) is the remark that "units with a specific composition" do not exist and cannot exist as a physical reality. Because the latter presupposition can be dismissed when we accept "physical structures," it is easy to understand, says Köhler [ibid., p. 192], what significance structural psychology will acquire in the future for the psychology of higher processes and, particularly, the psychology of thinking.

Bühler [1927/1978, p. 119], in a book dedicated to the crisis in contemporary psychology, points to the kinship of structural psychology "with the old Spinozism." This remark is perfectly justified. Indeed, structural psychology rejects the traditional dualism of empirical psychology, which—in Spinoza's [1677/1955, p. 128] words—regarded mental processes as "matters outside nature rather than natural phenomena following nature's general laws." We easily discover that at the basis of this monistic view lies a philosophical understanding of the mental and the physical that comes quite close to Spinoza's doctrine and that in any case is connected with it through its roots.

Chapter 14

PREFACE TO KOFFKA[*],[1]

The Problem of Development in Structural Psychology.
A Critical Investigation

1

In the present study [1], we wish to investigate the problem of development in structural psychology. The aim of this investigation is to separate what is genuine from what is false in this theory. We will approach this goal following a path that has been tested repeatedly. We will rely in our investigation upon what is true in this theory, and with its help we will lay bare the false premises that obscure it, for according to Spinoza's [1677/1955, p. 115] great idea the truth displays both itself and falsity. [2]

We dedicate our study of the problem of development to the version expressed in Koffka's book, for whose edition in the Russian language this study should serve as a critical introduction.

To critically investigate a book such as Koffka's, which represents a whole era in the development of scientific knowledge in the present field and which contains an enormous amount of facts, generalizations, and laws, means to penetrate into the inner complex of the ideas that shape it, into the very essence of its conception. *To critically investigate such a work means to correlate theory and the reality reflected in it*. This investigation can be nothing other than a critique via reality.

A critique of this kind is possible when we have an—albeit most general—idea of the nature of those phenomena of reality which are reflected in the theory under consideration. The culmination point of such an investigation is the critical experiment which transposes the critique into the domain of facts and which submits the crucial disputed aspects separating two theoretical systems to their verdict. Unfortunately, it is not our task here to present critical experiments. We can only refer to them in passing in connection with the theoretical analysis of the problem. The most important factual material on which we must rely and which represents the reality reflected in the theory will have to be the factual material contained in the book itself.

*First published as Vygotsky, L. S. (1934). Predislovie. In K. Koffka, *Osnovy psikhicheskogo razvitija* (pp. ix-lvi). Moscow–Leningrad: Gosudarstvennoe Social'no-Ekonomicheskoe Izdatel'stvo.

Actually, to critically investigate Koffka's book would mean to write another book on the same theme, and studies like the present one are no more than a synopsis of such unwritten books.

Koffka's book is one of the few books on child psychology written from the viewpoint of a single theoretical principle. At its basis is the principle of structure, or form (*Gestalt*), which originally developed in general psychology. The present book is nothing other than an attempt to examine all basic facts of child psychology from the viewpoint of this principle.

The book's main theoretical goal is the ideological struggle with two fundamental deadlocks of scientific thought in which the development of many contemporary scientific theories resulted. There is no doubt, says Koffka, that faced with the alternative between mechanistic and psychovitalistic explanations we find ourselves between the Scylla of vitalism which forces us to renounce our scientific principles and the Charybdis of mechanism's spiritless nature.

To surmount mechanism and vitalism is the main goal leading to the origin and development of structural psychology. But neither structural psychology in general nor the present book in particular were equal to this task. In this sense, the book is the culmination point of European psychology which we must dispense with (that is, on which we must rely while at the same time rejecting it) in order to discover the starting points for the development of our own conception of child psychology. Our critical investigation must therefore on the whole follow the same road as did the author of the present book. Our aim is to verify to what extent the new explanatory principle which Koffka introduced into child psychology *really* permits us to overcome the mechanistic and vitalistic theory of development in child psychology.

We will not, of course, examine this book chapter by chapter but will single out *two fundamental principles*, which we will subject to a critical investigation. Koffka [1925a, p. iii] himself says that it seemed to him that there was only one way to the solution of the task of his work. He wanted to try to critically present the principles of mental development and to examine the different facts from this viewpoint. We must do essentially the same. We must examine the basic principles that lie at the basis of this work from the viewpoint of their correspondence with the facts they must explain.

The two basic principles that must be the immediate subject of our examination are the *principle of structure* and the *principle of development*. We will consider these concepts in three basic aspects. First of all, we will turn to the analysis of the concept of structure, i.e., the basic principle of the whole book, on the basis of its own facts, i.e., from the viewpoint of the correspondence of this principle with the factual material on the basis of which it was first formulated and proved. Next, we will examine the application of this principle to the facts from the area of child psychology—from the viewpoint of their correspondence with the latter. After we have thus shed light upon this principle—from the viewpoint of its connection to reality—from two different sides, we will gather everything necessary to critically weigh the theory of the psychological development of the child as a whole as it was developed from this explanatory principle.

2

Thus, we will begin with the examination of the basic principle of structural psychology in the light of its own facts. Koffka [1925a, p. 2] himself says that child psychology did not create its own explanatory principle and is forced to use analogous principles which arose in general and comparative psychology. He says that there is no psychological principle of development which we owe to child psychology. Before these principles were used by child psychology they developed in general or animal psychology.

Following the author, this compels us to begin with the examination of a psychological principle that has a broader and more general meaning than the sphere of child psychology. The basis of Koffka's whole work is nothing other than the application of *this general principle, which developed in general and comparative psychology, to the facts of the psychological development of the child.*

That is why we must begin with the facts for which the given theory was originally created, when we wish, as has already been said, *the comparison of facts and principles, the examination of facts in the light of the principles, and the verification of principles by the facts, to be the main method of our critical investigation.* Here we may hope to reveal the facts' inner resistance against the universal principles proposed to explain them, a resistance which is hidden and repressed by the orderly and consistent application of a fixed system. In a most general sense, then, the critical examination of some theory almost always implies a certain kind of ideological struggle between different fundamental views.

In this sense the present book facilitates the task of critical investigation, as the book itself, unlike many systematic expositions of child psychology, is founded upon a theoretical investigation. The characteristic of a scientific exposition, says Koffka [1925a, pp. iv-v], is not the simple communication of knowledge. It must show the direct dependency of this knowledge upon the science, it must show its dynamics, the ongoing investigation. We must, therefore, also throw light on principles that ultimately prove to be false and sterile. It must be clear to the reader why these principles turn out to be untenable, what their weak spot is and how we must improve the explanation. Owing to the numerous discussions of different views the reader will be able to understand the growth process of psychological science. Every science grows in a vivid struggle for its basic principles, and this book wants to join in this struggle. [3]

Reading the book, the reader will indeed easily become persuaded that it is permeated with the struggle with opposite theories. It does not violate the character of the book, therefore, to perceive and master it from a critical viewpoint. On the contrary, this clearly fits its intrinsic nature. However, the struggle of theories in some concrete scientific area can only be fruitful when this struggle is based on facts. That is why in our investigation we first of all attempt to rely on the facts which the author himself uses in the present book.

We proceed from the assumption that to unravel the theoretical question of the applicability of the structural principle to the formation of child psychology means to unravel one of the most complex and central issues of contemporary theoretical psychology while at the same time preserving everything that is true and fruitful in this principle.

The meaning of this basic principle can be best understood when we pay attention to the history of its development. The principle of structure originally arose as a reaction against the atomistic and mechanistic tendencies that dominated the older psychology. According to these conceptions, psychological processes were considered as the sum-total of separate and mutually independent elements of mental life that were linked by association. The main difficulty which theories of this kind stumbled upon was that it was impossible to explain adequately how the accidental associative linking of heterogeneous independent elements can give rise to the development in our mental life of meaningful [4] integral experiences, to the rational and goal-directed behavioral processes that are so characteristic of our consciousness.

As one of its critics remarked, the new theory began by turning, in the words of Goethe, the problem into a postulate. [5] It took the idea that mental processes are *originally closed*, organized, integral formations which have an intrinsic sense and determine the meaning and proportions of their composite parts, and made it into its basic assumption. In the new psychology these integral processes received the name of structures, or forms (*Gestalten*), and from the very beginning they were contrasted with accidental conglomerates of mental atoms combined by mere summation.

We will not dwell on the development of the concept of structure in general psychology. What interests us now is the interpretation of this principle from the viewpoint of the problem of development. As has already been said, originally this principle was not applied to the problem of development in the domain of child psychology but in the domain of animal psychology.

The first issue that we are confronted with when we state the problem of development is the issue of the formation of new forms of behavior. It seems to us that Koffka is fully justified in moving this problem to the center, as development indeed means in the first place the unfolding of something new. Every theory will solve the problem of development from one viewpoint or another, depending on how it solves the question of the formation of new forms.

We first stumble upon this question of the formation of new forms of behavior in connection with the theory of animal learning. Here we encounter in its most simple and primitive form the fact of the appearance of new forms in the process of the individual life of the animal. Here we see these forms constantly appear in a form that is most accessible to the experiment. And this is why from time immemorial the fundamental questions connected with this problem have been decided in the theory of animal learning. Koffka consequently begins his examination of the problem of development with the theory of the formation of new forms of behavior in animal learning.

But here, in connection with the change in the basic psychological research principle, structural psychology states this question in another way than was usual. Usually the problem of learning was stated from the viewpoint of pure and consistent empiricism as a problem of learning, training, or memorization, in short, as a memory problem. What is new in Koffka's statement of the problem is that he focuses on the problem of learning itself. He shifts the essence of the whole problem from memory to the development of so-called *first novel actions*.

He says that the problem of learning cannot be stated as the question as to how later actions depend on earlier ones. This actually is the problem of memory. The problem of learning resides first of all in the question as to how these first novel forms of activity are formed. [6]

Thus, the question of the origin of the first novel actions, independent of the question of their memorization, consolidation, and reproduction, is posed at the very beginning of the investigation. In examining this question Koffka develops his own theory, contrasting it with two others we encounter when discussing this problem in psychology: first, the theory of trial and error, which found its highest expression in the works of Thorndike; second, the three-level theory developed by Bühler. In his struggle with these theories, Koffka relies chiefly on the factual material procured by Köhler in his zoopsychological experiments with anthropoid apes. Koffka, however, includes other material as well. He, in particular, submits the factual material of Thorndike himself to a critical investigation.

A correct understanding of the problem of development in structural psychology is impossible without a clarification of the whole theoretical situation in which it only acquires its full sense. Therefore, we will turn to a short exposition of the two theories which the new psychology rejects.

According to the theory of trial and error, each new action develops according to the principle of fortuitous actions. A certain combination of movements which corresponds to the successful solution of the task is selected from them and then consolidated. But this principle, says Koffka [1925a, p. 116], does not untie the knot but cuts it. According to this principle, behavior which is not innate does not exist at all. Consequently, there can be no first action in the sense of a novel action.

And, indeed, from the viewpoint of this theory only innate forms of activity exist. The novel ones which develop in the individual development of the action are nothing other than an accidental combination of innate reactions which was selected according to the principle of trial and error.

Step by step, Koffka examines the concrete facts which led to the development of this questionable principle, and he comes to the fully convincing conclusion that the theory of trial and error is untenable. He demonstrates that the animal in Thorndike's own experiments does not only experience a certain general situation but that, due to learning, this situation from the very beginning is structured in a new way. [7] A new focus is formed with respect to which the other elements of the situation acquire a subordinate meaning.

The whole situation doesn't seem completely blind and meaningless to the animal. Koffka [1925a, p. 130] says that the situation basically means the following for the animal: it is a circumstance from which I must escape in order to reach the food lying outside. The animal somehow connects his actions with the food outside. Thus, the theory of fully meaningless learning is untenable.

When we carefully and step by step examine the course of the whole experiment presented by Thorndike, as does Koffka, we must agree that in the process of the activity (escaping from the box) various elements of the situation acquire a specific meaning for the animal and that we obtain something completely new in our analysis. Generally speaking, says Koffka [1925a, p. 131], the learning in Thorndike's experiments led to *novel forms* [8] in the sensory area. The animal solves well-known tasks and, consequently, its activity cannot be a chain of trials and errors.

Koffka refers to the experiments of Adams, who comes to the conclusion that learning cannot be conceived of as the gradual removal of useless movements. He refers to Tolman, who summarizes his rich experience with animal learning in the following words: "Each learning process is a process of problem solving." [9]

Thus, Koffka comes to the conclusion that in Thorndike's experiments as well the facts are in sharp contradiction to the theoretical explanation adduced for their interpretation. The facts tell us that the animals act sensibly, solve the specific task, structure the perceived situation and connect their movements with the goal that exists outside the box. The theory explains their actions as the sum-total of meaningless and blind reactions which are purely mechanically consolidated or discarded due to their external success or failure. This leads to the development of an aggregative combination of a series of reactions which are not only mutually disconnected but have nothing in common with the situation in which they developed.

We may learn about Koffka's high opinion of the animals' actions in Thorndike's experiments from a fact which, as we will see below, has principal significance for his whole theory and which is that Koffka is inclined to view Thorndike's experiments in the light of Ruger's comparative experiments with persons. [10]

Ruger also placed persons in a situation that was incomprehensible to them. The results of his investigations, as presented by Koffka, lead to a single general conclusion. In these cases, the behavior by means of which these persons reached the solution was very often similar to the behavior of the animals in Thorndike's experiments. Thus, Koffka's first argument against the theory of trial and error is that it does not correspond with the facts on the basis of which it originally developed.

But for Koffka the main argument against this theory is the famous investigations with anthropoid apes by Köhler, who, as is well known, indisputably established that anthropoid apes are capable of sensible intellectual actions in the form of tool use to reach a goal or in the form of detours toward the goal. We will not present the experiments so brilliantly described in Koffka's book. We will only remark that for Koffka they are the *central and basic argument* in favor of the rejection of the theory of trial and error.

We may formulate this new principle with the statement that animals genuinely solve the new tasks presented to them. We consider that the essence of this solution is not that movements each of which already existed enter into a new combination, but that the whole field is structured anew. [11] According to Köhler's experiments, the essence of the latter principle is that the animals develop a closed [12], goal-directed action in accordance with the structure of the perceived field.

Such an action is diametrically opposed to the accidental combination of reactions which develops from blind trial and error. Koffka, thus, arrives at a view on learning which is totally different from the one that follows from Thorndike's theory. Learning, he says, can never be completely specific. When the organism masters some task it not only masters how to solve the same task again, but it will become more capable of solving tasks which it couldn't manage before, because in some cases the new processes will make other similar processes easier; in other cases new conditions are created which make new processes possible. [13]

Thus, learning is really development and not the simple mechanical acquisition of isolated forms of behavior. For the author [1925a, p. 157], only that theory is tenable which can explain

> why from the innumerable quantity of relations in every situation the most important ones are observed and determine the behavior. We say: a meaningful [*sinnvoll*] field structure develops in relation to the goal. The solution is nothing other than the formation of such a structure. Therefore, for us this problem does not arise, because the other "relations" do not yield a meaningful structure. But when we exclude meaning, when we regard an idea as the blind working of the association mechanism, then we must explain why only meaningful relations are observed and meaningless ones are not.

Koffka, thus, comes to the conclusion that *the essence of the development of the first actions resides in the formation of new structures.* Remarkable in his conception is that he doesn't only apply the principle of structure to the intellectual actions of anthropoid apes, but to the actions of the lower animals in Thorndike's experiments as well. Thus, *Koffka views some primary, primordial and essentially primitive principle of the organization of behavior in these structures.* It would be a mistake to think that this principle is only characteristic of higher or intellectual forms of activity. It is present in the most elementary and early forms of development as well. These considerations, says the author [1925a, pp. 101-106], confirmed our conception of the primitive nature of the structural functions [*Strukturfunktionen*]. When the structural functions are really that primitive, then they must appear in the primitive behavior which we call instinct as well. We see that the rejection of the theory of trial and error leads Koffka to the conclusion that *the*

principle of structure is applicable to an equal extent to both the higher intellectual
actions of the anthropoid apes and the training of the lower mammals in Thorndike's
experiments, and, finally, to the instinctive reactions of spiders and bees.

Thus, Koffka finds in the principle of structure the general tenet which enables him to understand from a single viewpoint both the most primitive (instinctive) and the new reactions of the animal arising in the process of training and intellectual activity. As we see, the basis of this principle is still the same opposition of the meaningful, closed, goal-directed process to the accidental combination of different elements-reactions.

But the full meaning of this principle only becomes clear to us when we can show its divergence with another theory of an opposite character. This is the three-level theory according to which the development of behavior passes through three basic levels.

Koffka [1925a, p. 172] presents this theory and says that the highest level of intellect or the ability to make discoveries is followed by the level of training, purely associative memory, and after that by instinct as the lowest level. Instinct and training have their advantages and shortcomings. The advantage of instinct is the confidence and perfection with which it immediately operates the very first time. The advantage of training is the ability to adjust to different circumstances of life. In contrast with this are the negative sides: the rigidity of the instinct and the inertia of training, i.e., the fact that learning through training takes considerable time. In intellect the advantages of both lower levels are combined.

Whereas Thorndike's theory aimed to prove the meaningless and accidental nature of the development of novel actions in animals, Bühler's theory requires too much of intellectual activity, separates it too much from the lower levels and ascribes only to the highest level a meaningful and structurally closed character. Bühler proceeds from the assumption that intellect presupposes judgment which is accompanied by a feeling of confidence which the chimpanzee lacks.

Thus, whereas the theory of trial and error attempts to explain the development of novel actions in animals from the viewpoint of the mechanistic principle of the accidental combination of heterogeneous elementary reactions, the three-level theory attempts to examine development as a series of mutually disconnected levels which cannot be understood with a single principle. "What is the relation between these three forms of behavior?" Koffka [1925a, p. 172] asks. We can assume they are all totally different. In that case, development would be no more than the incomprehensible addition of one level to another.

Koffka's [1925a, p. 157] critique of this theory is, firstly, aimed at Bühler's claim that intellect absolutely presupposes judgment. Even if this restriction were applicable to actions that we call intelligent in adult man, this wouldn't necessarily imply that this characteristic is present in the simplest forms of intelligent behavior as well. Secondly, Koffka attempts to erase the strict boundaries between the different levels in the development of animal activity. For him, instinct imperceptibly turns into training. The theory of associative learning [training] and the theory of instinct are very intimately connected. In the same way he attempts to erase the strict boundaries, as we have seen above, between training and intellect.

He does not assume three totally heterogeneous forms but attempts to find a certain relationship between them. He says [1925a, p. 173] that

> the attentive reader will have noticed that for us as well the principal role is played by a certain principle which is equally applicable to the explanation of instinct, training and intellect: our principle of structure. We attempt to use the phenomenon [*das Geschehen*] itself, its closed nature and its direction [*Richtungsbestimmtheit*] as the main principle of all explanation . . . .. The principle of structure is most conspicuously

present in intellectual achievements. We utilize, consequently, a principle capable of explaining higher behavior to explain lower forms of behavior, whereas formerly, in contrast, a principle of which it was thought that it could explain primitive behavior was transposed to the highest levels.

According to Koffka, intellect, training, and instinct are based upon structural functions that are formed differently, determined differently, and proceed differently but not upon different apparatuses that may be switched on "when the need arises" as Bühler assumes. [14]

We thus arrive at the extremely important conclusion that the principle of structure is equally applicable to the whole variety of psychological phenomena in the animal world, beginning from the very lowest and up to the very highest ones. In a certain sense, Koffka traverses a path opposite to the one followed by previous investigators. Whereas Thorndike attempted to explain apparently intelligent forms of animal activity by reducing them to lower, inborn reactions, Koffka attempts to follow the opposite path—from the top downwards—by applying the principle of structure found in the intellectual actions of higher animals to explain the outwardly meaningless actions of animals in training and even in instincts.

The result is a sweeping generalization of enormous scope which covers all forms of mental activity—from the very lowest to the very highest. This generalization is not confined, however, to the area of learning. It is also transposed to the physiological phenomena which lie at the basis of all forms of mental activity. Koffka refers to Wertheimer's hypothesis concerning the structural nature of physiological phenomena and to the work of Lashley, who proposed a dynamic theory of physiological processes which also function as structural phenomena.

Koffka [1925a, p. 177] views in this attempt to transfer the principle of structure to the physiological processes that lie at the basis of mental activity a means of saving us from psychovitalism. He attempts to find the explanation of the psychological structures in the physiological structures of the nervous system.

From this viewpoint he says [1925a, p. 177] that instinct, training, and intellect are not three completely distinct principles but that in each of them we find the same principle in varying degrees. Because of this, the transition from one level to another becomes fluctuating and vague and it proves impossible to determine where intellectual behavior in the strict sense of the word begins. We cannot say, he says, that intellect begins where instinct ends, because it would be one-sided to exaggerate the rigidity of instinctive actions. He further says that our intellectual criteria could even be applied to the instinctive behavior of insects in the same way they are applied to human behavior.

To complete [our overview of] this viewpoint, it must be said that in the new psychology the principle of structure is not only transposed to the physiological phenomena that lie at the basis of mental activity but to all biological processes and phenomena as well and even to physical structures. Koffka [1925a, p. 177] refers to Köhler's [1920] well-known theoretical investigation in which he set himself the goal of proving that in the world of physical phenomena we see physical systems that have the distinguishing features of structures and that are closed integral processes of which each separate part is determined by the whole to which it belongs.

To complete the presentation of Koffka's theory, it only remains for us to give his own considerations regarding the place his theory occupies with respect to the two other theories it opposes. If we, he says, compare the mechanistic theory of mental development with Bühler's three-level theory we may call the one unitary and the other pluralistic. But how to describe our own theory? It is pluralistic because it assumes an innumerable quantity of existing structures and a multitude of forms of structural change. But it is not pluralistic in the sense that it claims that there is a limited number of fixed capacities, such as reflexes and instincts, the capacity for training and intellect. Koffka concludes that it is unitary not in the sense that it attributes each process to the mechanism of nervous combinations or associations, but because it searches for the ultimate explanation of development in the most general structural laws.

We can now proceed to the critical examination of the theory just presented. Let us say from the very beginning that this critique is in essence already completely present in the facts and generalizations communicated by Koffka himself. With these we will commence.

3

The central question in our critical investigation of this problem must be the question of the fundamental assessment and clarification of the genuine importance, the genuine psychological nature of the facts on which the present theory rests.

It seems to us that these facts fully confirm the negative part of Koffka's theory. They completely convincingly defeat the mechanistic theory of trial and error and the semi-vitalistic three-level theory. They indeed reveal the untenability of both the one and the other. But on close scrutiny, when we compare them with the wider sphere of phenomena in light of which they acquire their genuine meaning, it becomes clear at the same time that their explanation by the author contains both a true and a false core.

Actually, the inner core of Koffka's whole construction discussed above is the fundamental conclusion at which Köhler arrived as a result of his investigations. Köhler formulates this conclusion in the form of a general claim which says that we find in the chimpanzee intelligent behavior of the same kind as we find in man. The intelligent actions of the chimpanzee do not always have the same external form as the actions of man, but intelligent behavior itself can be reliably established under suitably chosen experimental conditions.

This anthropoid stands out in the animal kingdom and approaches man not only for its morphological and physiological traits in the strict sense of the word, but it also displays a form of behavior which is specifically human. [15] So far we know very little of its neighbors which stand lower on the evolutionary ladder, but the little we know and the data of this book do not exclude the possibility that in the area of our investigation the anthropoid stands closer to man than to many lower species of apes with respect to insight as well, according to Köhler [1921b, p. 191].

Koffka's whole theory stands or falls with this claim.

That is why the first question we must answer is the question as to what extent this claim has essentially proved tenable in the light of the investigations carried out after Köhler, to what extent *the behavior of the ape is human-like in the fundamental sense of this word and to what degree the intellect of the chimpanzee stands closer to man than to the lower species of apes.*

As has already been said, in his entire construction Koffka proceeds from this claim. As we will see below, Koffka tries to extend this principle, which was found in these investigations and which found its clearest expression in the intellectual actions of the chimpanzee, on the one hand downward, to explain the training and instinct of animals, and on the other hand upward, to explain the whole psychological development of the child. Is such an extension of this principle legitimate?

This solely depends on the degree to which the facts on which this principle is based are by their psychological nature similar or akin to the facts to which one tries to extend it.

It might be said that the most eminent representatives of psychology have hardly realized that a new era in contemporary psychology is developing before our eyes, which might be coined the "post-Köhler" era. It stands in the same relation to Köhler's works as his investigations stand to Thorndike's works, i.e., it is the dialectical negation of Köhler's theory that preserves his claim "in superseded form."

This era develops before our eyes from two historical tendencies which directly sprang from Köhler's works and which in some embryonic form had already been observed by him. For him, however, they didn't change the essence of the matter and were collateral or secondary aspects rather than the central core of the whole problem. For him neither of these tendencies, about which we will have more to say below, could shake the basic thesis according to which the chimpanzee's intellect is identical in type and kind to human intellect and displays actions specific for man.

The first of these tendencies is the attempt to extend the positive results of Köhler's works downward. The second attempts to extend them upward.

The direct goal of Köhler's thesis that—contrary to Thorndike's assumption—animals do not act mechanically but in a sensible, structural, human-like manner was to fill the abyss between man and animals that had been dug out by Thorndike.

The extension of this thesis was basically accomplished along two paths. On the one hand, the investigators began extending Köhler's claims downward to lower animals and found in principle the same intelligent structural action in them. A number of such works showed that the criterion which Köhler proposed for intellectual actions and which he found in purest form in the intellectual actions of the ape is actually not specific for the intellect.

As we have already said, Koffka considers it possible to apply this criterion to instinctive actions as well, assuming that instinct, training, and intellect are not three entirely distinct principles, but that we find the same principle to a different extent in all of them. This is actually fatal for the principle found by Köhler. We may take the development of the solution as a whole, in accordance with the structure of the field, as the criterion of insight, says Köhler [1921b, p. 137]. By applying this criterion to training, as did Koffka, or to the instinctive actions of animals, as did other investigators, Köhler's followers did him a disservice. By further developing his idea, *as it seemed from the outside*, they showed that the instinctive and trained actions of animals are subject to the same criterion as are intellectual actions. Consequently, in itself the chosen criterion is not specific for the intellect. All behavior of animals turned out to be *equally* intelligent and structured.

In its extreme forms this movement led to the resurrection of the theory of thinking animals and to the attempt to prove that a dog has the capacity to master human speech.

Thus as it spread downward unrestrictedly, the idea of the universal intelligent and structural nature of animal actions led to the fact that these characteristics no longer clearly distinguished intelligent behavior as such. All girls appeared fair in the dark of this universal structural principle: the instinctive actions of bees as much as the intellectual actions of the chimpanzee. Behind one and the other was the same principle, only to a different degree. While it correctly observed the link between the three stages of development of the mind, the theory was powerless to reveal their difference. It is not hard to see that in its extreme form this tendency led exactly to what Koffka attempted to avoid—to a hidden psychovitalism, as it led us back to the theory of thinking and understanding animals.

The second tendency was accomplished along other paths by other investigators who more and more humanized the higher animals, lifting the ape to the human level, as did, for example, Yerkes, who argued in approximately the following way: since the ape is capable of tool use, why would it be impossible to teach it human speech?

Thus, the further development of Köhler's thesis of the human-like nature of the chimpanzee's actions gave rise to a tendency, on the one hand, to prove the human-like nature of the most primitive instinctive animal actions, subjecting them to the same principle as intellect and, on the other hand, to the tendency to completely erase the boundaries that separate the higher anthropoids from man.

The significance of these tendencies, which grew directly from Köhler's works, is that they carried Köhler's principle of the intelligent and structured nature of animal behavior to the very end, to its logical limit. One began finding this principle in trivialities, in details, and all that is meaningless and blind was chased from the field of zoopsychology and the situationally structured and intelligent character of each behavioral action was uncovered.

The result of both tendencies—and it is important to remark that from the very beginning they only attempted to defend, strengthen, and deepen Köhler's idea and had no idea whatsoever that they would lead to the opposite result—was in fact, as has already been said, that they refuted the theory that gave rise to them. The seemingly straightforward logical continuation of this theory led to a historical zigzag analogous to the zigzag which we also observed (and traced elsewhere) in the transition from the anthropomorphic thinkers to Thorndike and from Thorndike to Köhler.

The remarkable fact is that the consistent further application of the genuine phenomenon found by Köhler revealed it in its entirety and demonstrated that behind the apparent similarity between the operations of the chimpanzee and human tool use is their fundamental difference and that *the ape's intellect, which is outwardly similar to the corresponding human actions, is not identical in type and kind with the human intellect.*

Without suspecting this himself, the main argumentation in favor of this thesis is given by Koffka in his work, although, as has already been said, he builds his whole theory exactly upon this claim. But, as can easily be proved, the course of his argumentation cuts the branch upon which his whole construction rests. Most important in his argumentation, the crux of the matter, the main conclusion of the whole chain of his arguments is that also the instinctive action is goal-directed, meaningful and closed in its structure and that, consequently, the criterion of intellect proposed by Köhler is fully suited to instinctive actions as well. The development of the solution of the task as a whole, in accordance with the structure of the field, turns out to be a criterion that does not so much correspond to the specifically human intelligent action, but rather to the most primitive, instinctive animal action.

Thus, the criterion of intellect proposed by Köhler turns out to be patently false. A structured action is not necessarily an intellectual one. It may be instinctive as Koffka demonstrated. Consequently, this characteristic will not do to clarify the distinct nature of intellect as such. This criterion is fully applicable to whatever instinctive action, like the nest building of swallows. In this case as well, as Koffka [1925a, pp. 64-66] correctly shows, the solution of the instinctive task develops as a whole, in accordance with the structure of the field.

If this is true, then the suspicion arises, consequently, that actually neither do the actions of the anthropoid apes in Köhler's experiments rise above the level of instinctive actions and that their psychological nature comes much closer to the instinctive actions of animals than to the intelligent actions of man, although, we repeat, in appearance they remind us very much of tool use in the proper sense of the word.

In another work, Koffka himself states this problem and in agreement with everything that is presented in the present book solves it in exactly the same spirit as we do, i.e., contrary to Köhler's main conclusion. He doesn't suspect, however, that he at the same time saps the roots of his own theory. He analyzes the intellectual actions of the chimpanzee and asks: how do these intellectual actions originate?

> In Köhler's experiments it was always the case that the animal faced a piece of fruit located at an inaccessible spot and strived to get this fruit. In our terms: the chimpanzee is here, the visible fruit there, this is not a situation in balance. The mobile system, the animal, is motivated to restore a balance. But the circumstance that the fruit motivates the animal to act does not make it an intellectual action. Above we have seen that it is a feature of instinct that a complex of specific circumstances disturbs the organism's balance. We will, consequently, say that the action is instinctively evoked. If the fruit would be directly accessible, then the whole process following it we would also call instinctive. Consequently, the difference between instinctive and intellectual actions does not necessarily reside in the way actions are evoked, in the disturbance of the balance, but in the way it is restored. This leads us to the other pole which is contrasted with the instinctive action—the *volitional action*. Is each noninstinctive (and not quasi-instinctive, automatic) action a volitional action? Does it make sense to call the actions of a chimpanzee volitional actions? I raise this question first of all to show how cautious we must be in using ordinary words in psychological theories. What does the animal want? The fruit, of course, but not on the basis of a volitional decision, but on an instinctive basis. It surely does not want the stick—it would be an intellectualistic re-interpretation to say here that the animal must want the stick as a means when it wants the fruit as a goal—but the stick brings the satisfaction of its wish. After all, it cannot want the stick before it has understood the stick's use. Thus, there are actions which are neither instinctive nor volitional, but are typical intellectual actions.

4

Actually, what Koffka [1925b, pp. 594-595] says in these lines is more than enough to see the enormous fundamental gap that separates the purely instinctive actions of the ape from the intellectual and volitional process of tool use. As we have seen above, Koffka attempts to cover instinctive and intellectual processes with a single principle. Because of this, the fundamental difference between the one and the other is wiped out. The ape's instinctive action, which is outwardly extremely similar to tool use, as Koffka demonstrates himself, but which in fact has nothing in common with it, is passed off as intelligent behavior of the same type and kind as human insight.

Nobody has expressed the difference between the activity of animals and man better than Köhler himself. In one of his later works he dwells on the question why tool use in apes is not connected with even the smallest beginnings of culture. The answer to this question he sees partially in the circumstance that even the most primitive of men prepares a stick for digging even when he does not intend to dig immediately, even when the objective conditions for tool use are fully absent. In Köhler's [1922, p. 3] opinion, this circumstance is undoubtedly linked to the beginning of culture.

Obviously, the structural principle in itself proves insufficient when we wish to reduce to its common denominator all the most fundamentally distinct processes that can be found in the psychological processes of animals and man. The fact that the action of the most primitive man in tool use is independent of the presence of an instinctive motive to act, and is independent of the actual optical situation, is diametrically opposed to the most essential characteristic of the chimpanzee's operations.

For man a tool remains a tool no matter whether it is at that moment in a situation which requires its use or not. For the animal the object loses its functional meaning outside the situation. A stick that is not in one visual field with the goal stops being perceived by the animal as a tool. A box (Koffka himself dwells on this in great detail) on which another ape is seated thereby stops serving as a tool to reach the goal and begins to be perceived by the animal in the new situation as a box to lie on.

Thus, for the animal a tool doesn't stand out in the visual situation. It is dependent on the more general structure and changes its meaning conforming to the situation of which it forms a part. Because of this, things which have an external visual similarity with a stick, such as, for example, a straw, can easily serve the ape as an illusory tool. It suffices to think of all the facts so carefully analyzed by Koffka in the present book to see to what extent the instinctive actions of the ape and the most primitive tool use by man are diametrically opposed.

In general, all subsequent investigations broadened the meaning of the aspects that Köhler himself proposed as restricting the identity of the behavior of man and chimpanzee to such an extent that they changed the sense of his fundamental claim. Already Köhler [1921b, p. 192] remarks that the ape doesn't understand mechanical connections; that their behavior in a situation is fully determined by the visible field; that what is only thought, only imagined cannot serve to determine their actions; that they do not live in even the nearest future. [16]

Further investigations demonstrated that here we are not dealing with differences of degree between the two processes but with fundamental and basic characteristics which change the quantitative difference pointed out by Köhler into a fundamental qualitative difference of kind. Comparative investigations of the intellectual operations of the chimpanzee with the simpler processes in lower animals, to which the tendency to extend Köhler's principle downward gave rise, led to the claim that this principle is valid for lower actions and thereby undermined the faith in the claim that this principle might serve as the actual criterion for intellect. Koffka himself showed that this principle is applicable to the training of animal behavior in Thorndike's experiments.

As we have seen above, Koffka views the fact that the structural principle is equally applicable to instinctive and intellectual actions as the main argument against the three-level theory which sharply separates instinct from intellect. This leads the author to reject a precise distinction and digress from a fundamental demarcation of the intellectual structures and the instinctive ones. Köhler's principle thus dissolves altogether in the structural actions.

This merging of instinctive and intellectual reactions under the common roof of the structural principle finds a clear expression in the words of Koffka given above, in which he unambiguously establishes that the chimpanzee's action cannot be counted as volitional actions and that judging by the nature of their development they do not at all rise above the level of instinctive actions. The acting animal's principal relation to the situation turns out to be the same as the one we observe in the swallow building its nest. A tool, however, requires a fundamentally different relation to the situation.

As we have seen in Köhler's example given above, a tool requires *a relation to a future situation*. It requires a certain independence of the tool's meaning from the situation, i.e., from the actually perceived structure. It requires a generalization. To this category belong only tools that are applicable to a number of optically different situations. It requires, finally, that man subordinate his operations to a plan projected in advance.

It is outside our scope to give a detailed overview of the psychology of tool use. But what was mentioned above is sufficient to see to what extent the psychological structure of this operation differs radically and essentially from the chimpanzee's operation.

As has already been said above, the other tendency—to raise the ape to [the level of] man—also led to negative results, because it was shown in a number of experiments that the presence of human-like intellect in the chimpanzee is completely insufficient to teach these animals human-like speech and in general to elicit human-like activity in them.

Thus, in both its positive and negative results, this tendency led to the dialectical negation of Köhler's claim about the identity of the intellect of ape and man.

This tendency, consisting in the extension of Köhler's principle to its logical extreme, showed that what was taken by these investigators to be the strength of the ape's intellect, i.e., its fully developed structural intelligence, the presence of situational meaning in its operations, appeared to be its weakness. According to an expression used by Köhler [1929] in another work, the animals are the slaves of their visual field. According to Lewin's apt remark, it is free intention—an absolutely essential element of genuine tool use—which distinguishes man from animal.

As Köhler observed many times, neither were his apes capable of changing the given sensory organization by will. *They are to a much greater degree than man slaves of their sensory field.* Indeed, the whole behavior of the ape as it is presented in Koffka's book shows that animals' actions are *slavishly dependent* upon the structure of the visual field. They only develop such intentions as are caused by structural aspects of the situation itself.

As Lewin says, it is remarkable in itself that man possesses an extraordinary freedom to create intentions with regard to arbitrary and even meaningless actions. This freedom is characteristic of cultural man. In children and primates it is much less present and it distinguishes man much more, apparently, from the animals that stand closest to him than his higher intellect does.

Actually, one easily sees that all of the above-mentioned authors—Köhler, who says that animals are the slaves of the visual field; Koffka, who points to the non-volitional but instinctive nature of the chimpanzee's operations; Lewin, who singles out the freedom to form intentions as the most striking distinguishing trait between man and animals—have in mind one and the same fact which these authors noted well, *but which they insufficiently evaluated on principle*, as it did not lead them to what would seem an obvious conclusion: that it is impossible to understand both man and animals using a single principle when there is such a fundamental difference between their operations.

Later investigations, for example those of Meyerson and Guillaume [1930; 1931], showed that if it is at all possible to speak of human-like operations in the chimpanzee, then it is not with respect to the healthy, normal person but with respect to a person with a sick brain, who suffers from aphasia, i.e., who has lost his speech and all the specific particularities of the human intellect connected with it. In characterizing these people, Gelb draws attention to the fact that together with speech they very often lose the free relation to the situation specific of man, the possibility of forming a free intention, and that they are as much *slaves of their sensory field* as were the chimpanzees in Köhler's investigations.

It is only man who, in Gelb's brilliant expression, can do something meaningless, i.e., something that does not directly spring from the perceived situation and is meaningless from the viewpoint of the given actual situation, for example, to prepare a stick for digging when the objective conditions for its use and the subjective conditions in the form of hunger are absent. But the investigations showed the opposite for animals: the chimpanzee doesn't isolate a tool from the given situation as a whole. The tool lacks all the properties of an object [17] and in actual tool use the intelligence of the chimpanzee's behavior has thus *nothing but the word in common* with the intelligent behavior of the most primitive man.

It is only this which makes us understand a remarkable fact to which Köhler himself pays attention, namely that *the human-like intellect, after it became the chimpanzee's property, did not change a thing in the system of the ape's consciousness* and was, in the words of zoopsychology, a product of evolution according to a pure and not a mixed line. [18] This implies that it is indisputably a novel form, but not one reconstructing the whole system of consciousness and the relationships with reality proper to the animal. In other words, what we see in Köhler's experiments are *intellectual operations in the system of instinctive consciousness.*

As the most important and basic conclusion, the crux of the matter, we might say that if we confine ourselves to the structural principle as such and do not introduce supplementary criteria that allow us to distinguish the higher from the lower, then the essence of the intellectual operation of the chimpanzee, which Koffka advances as the factual foundation of his single explanatory principle for child psychology as a whole, is in principle indistinguishable from any instinctive reaction.

In this sense we may use their own weapon against the structuralists. [19] Relying on the principle of the dependency of the part upon the whole, which they proposed, we might say that the nature of intellect belonging to another structure of consciousness must be fundamentally different from the nature of the intellect we encounter in the totally new whole which is the consciousness of man.

Such an isolated analysis of one narrow field of activity regardless of the whole actually fundamentally contradicts the structural principle on which Koffka himself relies. Indeed, the instinctive action is goal-directed and structurally meaningful *within its situation, but meaningless beyond its boundaries. The ape as well*—and this we must accept as entirely proven—*acts sensibly exclusively within the boundaries of the field and its structures.* Outside of it it acts blind. Thus, *the factual basis of the structural principle lies entirely in the realm of the instinct.*

Not without purpose, Koffka is fully justified in advancing this as the main argument against Bühler's three-level theory. It would, however, be incorrect to think that by arguing against this principle we return to Bühler's three-level theory. Koffka is perfectly right when he argues that this theory is the product of a serious mistake. In essence, all three levels are given within a single level, namely *within the [level of] instinct.* After all, the conditional reflex, the typical specimen of Bühler's second level, is the *same instinct, but then individualized, adapted to the special circumstances.* The character of the activity itself remains as much determined by instinct as in the case of the unconditional reflex. The same is valid for the ape's behavior, which represents, as we have seen, just like the conditional reflex, something new with respect to the executive mechanism and the conditions of its appearance, but still lies fully in the plane of instinctive consciousness.

Bühler's very attempt to cover the whole development of animals and man with his three-level theory is as unconvincing as is the attempt by the structuralists to erase the fundamental border between instinct and intellect. [20]

We thus see that *the highest product of animal development,* i.e., the intellect of the chimpanzee, *is not identical in kind and type with the human intellect.* This is a conclusion of no little importance. It is sufficient to make us radically reconsider the legitimacy of Koffka's application of the structural principle to explain the psychological development of the child. If the highest product of animal development is not human-like, we must conclude that the development which led to its formation is fundamentally different from what is at the basis of the perfection of the human intellect.

This alone suffices to see that *all naturalistic psychology, which considers human consciousness as the product of just nature and not history,* by attempting to understand the structure of all animal and human psychology with a single principle will always prove untenable when faced with the facts. It will necessarily be metaphysical and not dialectical.

As is well known, Köhler's work is polemically aimed at Thorndike's mechanistic views which dominated before him. This part of his work preserves its fundamental importance. He showed that chimpanzees are not automatons, that they act sensibly, that intelligent operations develop in animals not by chance, through trial and error, not as a mechanical conglomerate of separate elements. This is the solid and unshakable achievement of theoretical psychology which we must not relinquish in solving any problem of development.

Therefore, when we consider his claims from this side, i.e., from below, in comparison with the blind and meaningless actions of animals, they retain their full strength. But when we look at them from the other side, from above, when we compare them with genuine tool use in man, when we ask ourselves the question whether the chimpanzee stands closer to man than to the lower apes, then we must give an answer to that question which flatly opposes the one found in Köhler.

The difference between the ape's actions in Köhler's experiments and the behavior of the animals in Thorndike's experiments, i.e., the difference between intelligent and blind animal actions, is in principle less important than the difference between the operations of the chimpanzee and genuine tool use. The chimpanzee's operations are more fundamentally distinct from tool use in man in the genuine sense than from the instinctive and conditional reflex activity of animals. That is why Koffka is right when, in contradistinction to the three-level theory, he points to the inner kinship that permeates all three levels of the animal mind.

The chimpanzee's intellect is thus the highest product of behavior in the animal kingdom rather than the lowest in the kingdom of human thinking. It is the latest and final link of animal evolution rather than the vaguest beginning of the history of human consciousness.

As has already been said, we may observe in man in a number of cortical diseases, especially of the specifically human areas, behavior that is to some extent similar to the behavior of the ape. We are prepared to insist that it is only here that the parallels between the behavior of the chimpanzee and man are legitimate and allowed, that it is only here (*and only in particular aspects*) that we find a real and not imaginary analogy, a real identity of the two intellectual processes.

When we learn of such a patient that he is capable of pouring water from a decanter into a glass when he wants to drink, but is unable to perform the same operation voluntarily in another situation, we actually learn about behavior that is really analogous to what we encounter in the ape when it stops recognizing in the box upon which another animal is lying the same thing, the same tool which it used in another situation in what on the surface seemed a human-like manner.

We think, as has already been said, that the chimpanzee's operations in so-called tool use are intrinsically much closer and akin to the nest-building of the swallow than to the most primitive tool use in man.

We dwell upon the critique of Koffka's main principle in such detail because only the critique of the fundamental principle of his whole construction can be a fundamental critique of his whole theory of child psychology.

5

In these pages we have touched upon the most important, most essential borders, beyond which the specifically human problems of psychology and the psychological development of the child begin—we have talked about what distinguishes man from the animal as a whole, in the whole structure of his consciousness and his relationships to reality, and not about the similarity of some partial function.

We have thus clarified the main thesis of our critical investigation. The main flaw of Koffka's whole work is that he attempts to reduce the basic phenomena of the psychological development of the child to a principle which dominates in the psychology of animals. He attempts to place the psychological development of the animal and child development on the same level. He wants to understand animal and man by means of a single principle.

In doing so he naturally stumbled upon fierce resistance of the facts. We will just examine two basic examples in which the facts resist the attempt to bring them together under one roof with a number of facts gathered in the experimental investigation of animals.

Let us begin with practical intelligence. It is remarkable, in our view, that the intellectual operations in animals found by Köhler are in themselves not capable of development, as research demonstrates. As Koffka says, Köhler judges the possibility of development here to be very small.

Elsewhere, in comparing the behavior of children and animals in operations that require practical intellect, Koffka is even clearer. He dwells upon the data of Allport, which showed that in children these capacities develop rapidly in the first years of life, whereas apes, despite frequent exercise, hardly make progress in this direction.

We encounter analogous statements when we examine the problem of imitation. Again Koffka [1925a, pp. 230-240] proceeds from the analogy between imitation in animals and imitation in the child. Both are subject to structural laws. He regards the difference between lower and higher forms of imitation as inessential and says that for him the problem of imitation turned into a general structural problem similar to the problem as to how the structure of movement develops from the structure of perception.

However, when we examine the role of imitation in development we again stumble upon the same difference mentioned above. Köhler [1921b, p. 161] writes that unfortunately even in the chimpanzee we very rarely observe imitation, and this always only when both the given situation and the solution lie almost within the boundaries of spontaneously accomplished actions.

Thus, even the most intelligent animal can only imitate what stands more or less close to its own possibilities. In contrast to this, for the child imitation mainly forms a path to master those activities that completely transcend the limits of his own possibilities. It is a means to master such functions as speech and all higher psychological functions. In this sense, says Koffka [1925a, p. 240], imitation is a mighty factor of development.

Even when we confine ourselves to the two examples given above, we can clearly formulate a basic question whose answer we will seek in vain in Koffka's work. If it is correct that the child's practical intellect and his imitation can in principle be understood by referring to the same laws that determine the activity of these two functions in the chimpanzee, then how do we explain the fact that these functions play a fundamentally different role in child development than they do in the behavior of the ape? From the viewpoint of development, the difference appears more essential than the similarity. Consequently, in our eyes the structural principle is insufficient to explain what is the central core of the whole problem, namely development.

We will not dwell upon further examples which are richly spread throughout the book and which testify to what we already expressed in general terms above. The reader will easily find not a few places which show him more vividly than we can do in this cursory preface that the actions of the chimpanzee are indissolubly connected with instinctive motivation and affect, to what extent they are inseparable from the immediate action, to what extent in perception itself the animals lack an objective [see note 17] relation to the tool and are slavishly dependent upon the visible situation.

In light of what has been said above, the reader cannot without astonishment follow Koffka's basic leit-motif, which all the time sketches the outlines of a single idea—the idea of identity, the fundamental identity of the behavior of animal and man. It suffices to look at the aspects that characterize the extent to which the chimpanzee's operations are tied to the visual situation to find another multitude of proofs in favor of our idea that it is illegitimate to extend the structural principle to the whole area of psychological development of the child.

In order to express our idea in its final form, it remains for us to formulate the following. As we have already indicated above, the gist of all structural psychology is the idea of the intelligent nature of psychological processes, which is contrasted with the mechanical, blind, and meaningless nature attributed to them in older theories. But after what was said above there can be hardly any doubt that the new psychology regards this intelligent nature as being fundamentally identical in animals and man. Everything we said above compels us to acknowledge that this is a radical flaw in the structural principle.

Now it remains for us to demonstrate that the intelligence about which Koffka speaks on occasion of the animals' actions and the intelligence present in the psychological development of the child are, to be sure, both structural phenomena, but they form two distinct categories of intelligence according to their psychological nature.

No one will dispute the basic idea that the investigation of psychological development must reveal the origin of the meaningful relationship to reality, the experience of insight. *But the crux of the matter is whether the intelligence characteristic of animal and human consciousness is identical or different.*

Koffka says that he regards the development of an intelligent perception of the situation as an essential characteristic of the operations which he considers to be the factual basis of the structural principle. He says that an action has an intelligent character when the meaning of the situation is consciously perceived. In exactly the same way the transfer, i.e., the successful application of a method acquired under certain conditions to new ones, to changed conditions, is always an intelligent transfer that presupposes understanding. As soon as a meaning has been mastered, it extends to all other subjects which have properties in common with the given one. Thus, he says [1925a, p. 145], transfer is the intelligent [*singemässe*] application of a structural principle.

This idea of intelligence dominates to such an extent in all of Koffka's descriptions and analyses that it indisputably takes precedence in his construction. However, the fact that the situation itself is meaningful to both animal and child means fundamentally different things in these two cases.

We will allow ourselves to illustrate this with a single example. Koffka describes experiments with unsuccessful problem solving in children. These experiments may serve as an example that is of more general importance than the author ascribes to it. Thus, in one of the experiments the child turns out to be incapable of solving a task that requires the use of a stick. This is easily explained. The child had a stick which he utilized as a horse until he was told that this was strictly forbidden. Because of this, the stick that was present in the situation, which was similar to the one with which the child had played before, acquired the character of something forbidden and therefore couldn't be used for the solution.

An analogous phenomenon was observed by Tudor-Hart in experiments with boxes which stood in a room in front of a number of chairs. Without exception, almost every child failed to solve this task. The reason was that they were not allowed to stand on the chairs. When these experiments with boxes were repeated in the playground the results were positive.

This example clearly demonstrates what we have in mind. Obviously, the stick that had acquired the meaning of something forbidden and the action—standing on a chair—which was also forbidden, fundamentally differ from the box in which the chimpanzee no longer recognizes a support to get a piece of fruit because another animal is lying on it. Obviously, in these experiments with children the things acquired *a meaning that transcended the boundaries of the optical field.*

The difficulty of using a chair as a support or a stick as a tool is not that the child has lost the perception of these objects in the situation from the viewpoint of their suitability for reaching the goal. The reason is that for the child the things indeed have acquired some meaning, namely the meaning of a chair or stick with which the child was not allowed to play, in other words, for the child social rules become involved in the problem-solving process. It seems to us that in these examples we encounter an aspect which is by no means an exception to the general rule in child behavior in analogous situations.

We more than once came across such a state of affairs in our experiments. The child begins to solve the task and amazingly enough does not utilize things that are obviously in his visual field. It is as if he tacitly assumes that he should act in the situation according to certain rules. Only the permission to use the stick or chair leads to the immediate solution of the problem. These experiments demonstrate to what extent for the child the visible situation is part of a more complex semantic field, if we may say so, within which things may only enter into certain relations with each other. [21]

In these cases we see striking examples of what is also clearly manifest in all other experiments with the child. The main finding is that in solving the task for the child it is *the laws of the semantic field* that come to the fore, i.e., in some way the child interprets the situation and his relation to it. [22] Here we have what will be the subject of examination in one of the following sections, namely the problem of speech and thinking.

As Koffka says, the majority of problems are probably connected with this issue, because it is most difficult to answer the question as to how man through thinking liberates himself from immediate perception and thereby masters the world. This liberation from immediate perception through thinking—on the basis of practice—is the most important result to which the study of the experiments with children leads us. As our experiments have shown, *a most essential role in this issue is played by the word,* about which Koffka himself says that at a certain stage of child development it stops being connected to wishes and affects and gets connected to things.

As the experiments show, the word liberates the child from that slavish dependency which Köhler observed in animals. It liberates the child's actions. It fills the visible elements of the situation with meaning and generalizes them and leads to the development of the *objective nature* of the tool, which remains the same independent of the structure into which this object enters.

The fact that the child during problem solving usually speaks to himself is not new. Many investigators have observed this before us. Almost all protocols of analogous experiments thus far published have confirmed this fact. But the enormous majority of investigators ignore this fact, do not understand its fundamental importance, do not see that the word and the meaning connected with it put the child into fundamentally new relationships to the situation, radically change the simple act of his perception, create that possibility for free intention of which Lewin speaks as the most essential trait distinguishing man from the animal. [23]

Here we will not dwell in detail upon these experiments to which we already referred elsewhere. We will just say that the attempt to consider the speech that goes with the child's practical action as a simple accompaniment of his activity contradicts the structural principle proposed by Koffka himself. To consider that the inclusion of speech, and with it the semantic field, into the activity of the child in a certain situation leaves the structure of his operations unchanged is to defend an anti-structural viewpoint and sharply contradicts what the author himself is relying upon.

Thus, proceeding from his own ideas, he should acknowledge that the practical operations of the child are fundamentally different from the superficially analogous operations of the animal.

6

We may now conclude our examination of the first principle that lies at the basis of Koffka's book and sum up the results that we arrived at. After what has been said above there can hardly remain any doubt that Koffka's theory is an exceptionally brave and grandiose attempt to reduce the higher forms of activity of the human child to the lower ones observed in animals.

It is not hard to see that such a reduction of all higher forms of the intelligence of human action and perception to the intelligence of the lower instinctive actions of animals is actually the very high price the author must pay in order to overcome vitalism. He essentially overcomes vitalism by making concessions to mechanism, for not only those theories that reduce the behavior of man to the activity of a machine are mechanistic but also those which reduce the behavior of man to the activity of animals. Here we have the basic difference between Koffka's and our understanding of mechanism.

As one easily sees from Koffka's speech [24] dedicated to this problem, he views the main danger of mechanism in the reduction of what is alive and conscious to what is dead, automatic and inorganic. He understands mechanism in the literal sense of the word as the reduction to a mechanism. That is why he thinks [1925a, p. 82] that if only we understand dead nature not from the viewpoint of mechanism but from the viewpoint of physical systems, as did Köhler in his investigations, i.e., if we allow for the presence of structural-integral processes in inorganic nature itself which determine the role and meaning of their composite parts, then such a reduction becomes, in principle, possible.

But to overcome vitalism by attempting to reduce the behavior of man to regularities observed in the behavior of animals in reality means to stop halfway. It is, of course, better than Thorndike's attempt to interpret the activity connected with higher processes in a purely automatic fashion, but it is nevertheless pure mechanism in the proper sense of the word.

While the attempt to understand the behavior of animals and man with a single structural principle thus leads Koffka to the overcoming of vitalism at the cost of concessions to mechanism and compels him to stop halfway, it also leads to the opposite result, namely to the overcoming of mechanism through concessions to vitalism, i.e., it again forces him to stop halfway between mechanism and vitalism. This position—halfway between the dead ends of contemporary scientific thought—is most characteristic of contemporary structural psychology and of Koffka's book in particular.

These psychologists who have solidly entrenched themselves in an intermediate position view themselves at equal distance from both mechanism and vitalism. But in reality they exclusively move along a path determined by these two points and inadvertently include something into their constructions of both extremes that they want to dismiss. Koffka's attempt to apply the structural principle with its idea of intelligence to instinctive activity actually inevitably leads to the intellectualization of instincts, i.e., what is most important from his viewpoint does not arise in development but is given from the very beginning.

Structure turns out to be a primordial phenomenon which stands at the beginning of all development. The rest follows through logical deduction, through the further multiplication of structures. It is no accident that in his analysis of instincts Koffka leaves aside another problem—the fact that instincts are totally unintelligent, entirely blind, without any insight. And by accepting intelligence as a primordial phenomenon *which existed before the very process of development* he at the same time considerably lightens his task, the most difficult one that research psychologists ever faced—*the task of explaining the origin and development of intelligence.*

Indeed, if everything is meaningful [see note 4], then the border between meaningful and meaningless is lost in exactly the same way as when everything is meaningless. As in Thorndike, everything is reduced to a single category—more or less. Here it is more or less meaningless, there it is more or less meaningful. Child development and animal development are not distinguished. In the words of Koffka [1925, p. iv] himself, he attempts to merge two problems, i.e., the central problem of comparative psychology and the central problem of child psychology.

He says [ibid., p. iv] that in order to supply a broad foundation for the explanation he proposes for the psychological development of the child it is essential to include other areas of comparative psychology into account as well. Both goals are intimately tied together. He attempted to merge them, to create a uniform "Gestalt" and not a fragmentary presentation of parallel problems. But this is also the Achilles' heel of this work. The attempt to merge child development and animal development, to create a unified, undifferentiated structure into which both enter as dependent parts means to create (in Koffka's own words) the most primitive "Gestalt" characteristic of the early, initial levels of the development of scientific knowledge, as he brilliantly showed in the book under consideration.

Theoretically speaking, what Koffka [1925, pp. 96-108] says in characterizing the first structures of infant consciousness can be fully reconciled with his own unified structure of animal and child development. He emphasizes that he is dealing with the very simple situations and structures which we see as primary and most simply construed: some quality against a uniform background. [25] With literally the same words we might also concisely express our impression of the structure presented in Koffka's theory: *some quality against a uniform background.* This quality is the structure or not yet differentiated intelligence.

We thus have a consistent naturalistic theory of the psychological development of the child which consciously merges animal and human aspects and ignores the historical nature of the development of human consciousness. Specifically human problems are only present as factual material but in principle do not lie at the basis of the theory itself. Small wonder, then, that these specifically human problems of the psychological development of the child, when they speak the language of facts, offer fierce resistance to the naturalistic attempt to interpret them and attempt to tear the cover of this single undifferentiated Gestalt to pieces.

That is why Koffka is essentially adducing an argument against himself when he reminds us of Köhler's remarkable expression that in itself intelligent behavior and intellectual capacities resist intellectualistic explanations, that intellectualism is nowhere as little tenable as in the area of the problem of the intellect. For it is exactly he himself who attempts to explain the basic principle of development intellectualistically, i.e., proceeding from the nature of the intellectual operation of the chimpanzee. But what does intellectualism mean other than the attempt to understand development as the analogue of the intellectual operation?

Admittedly, as we have seen, Koffka tries to take the sting out of this claim by dissolving the intellectual processes in instinctive activity. But thereby he gets a result that is even worse, i.e., in practice he explains the most primitive forms of behavior from this viewpoint as well.

On the whole, Koffka's theory violates the key principle he chose as his basis. As is well known, this principle resides in the acknowledgment of the primacy of the whole over the parts. If we wish to be faithful to this principle we must admit that, as the whole structure, the whole system of consciousness of man is different from the structure of animal consciousness, it becomes impossible to equate any particular element (the intellectual operation) of these systems, for the meaning of this element becomes clear only in light of the whole of which it forms a part.

Thus, the very principle of structure indicates the fundamental error of Koffka's whole theoretical construction. *The truth of his theory displays its falsity.* [26]

The conclusion we arrive at on the basis of the preceding examination of Koffka's theory unexpectedly leads us to paradoxical results. We remember that Koffka himself characterized the path of his whole investigation as a path *from the top downward,* as distinct from the usual path *from the bottom upward.* Its essence Koffka views in the fact that whereas usually the principles found in lower forms of activity were applied in the explanation of higher ones, he attempts to apply the principles found in the higher forms of activity in the explanation of lower ones.

But Koffka's path nevertheless turns out to be a path *from below upward* as well. From below, with a principle found in the behavior of animals he attempts to shed light on the psychological development of the child.

Koffka's situation of the application of the structural principle to the explanation of the *whole* rich content of child psychology is very reminiscent of an analogous situation which was wittily described by James when he first stated his famous principle of the restricted nature of emotions. The principle seemed to him to be so important, so decisive for the whole problem, such a key to all locks, that for him the actual analysis of the phenomena for the explanation of which this principle was created was moved to the background.

James says of his principle that having the goose that lays the golden eggs, the description of each egg already laid is a minor matter. [27] It is no surprise therefore that for him the analysis of the various emotions receded to the background. Meanwhile it was exactly the system of the facts against which his theory was later tested which showed the faultiness of his initial assumptions.

In a certain sense this applies to the structural principle as well. It too is regarded as a goose laying golden eggs, as a result of which the description and analysis of each different egg is considered to be a minor matter. It is no surprise, therefore, that the explanations of the most diverse facts of child psychology turn out to be as surprisingly similar as two eggs laid by the same goose.

Koffka ascertains that already the starting point of the child's psychological development is structural. Already the infant has meaningful perceptions. The world as it is perceived by the youngest child is already to some extent structured. Thus, structure is at the very beginning of child development.

The question naturally arises as to how the world is structured differently in earlier and later periods. The *factual description* of these more complex structures that arise in the process of child development we find in detail in the present book. But with the best will in the world we do not find the answer to the question about the fundamental, *and not just the factual*, difference between the structures that arise in the process of child development and those given from the very beginning. On the contrary, one gets the impression that such a fundamental difference does not exist for the author, that the difference is only factual. The goose that is laying golden eggs from the very beginning remains the same during the whole course of child development. *This is the crux of the whole debate.* When we take this view we must agree with the claim that *in the process of child development nothing fundamentally new develops,* nothing that wasn't already comprised in the psychology of the chimpanzee or in the consciousness of the infant.

Meanwhile, the resistance by the facts about which we are constantly speaking makes itself particularly felt when we turn from the area of zoopsychological facts to the area of the factual content of child psychology.

7

In the present section, we wish to subject the structural principle to a critical investigation from the viewpoint of its correspondence with the facts of child psychology and to establish *what* in the application of this principle is based on simple analogy and *what* is proven, and most importantly—what is the explanatory value of these analogies and these proofs. The problem that Koffka calls "the child and his world" is the main theme of the present chapter. The problems of ideational learning, thinking and speech, and play must now become the subject of our examination.

We begin with a particular aspect that, in our view, is of more general significance and may therefore serve as the introduction to the whole subsequent analysis. Moreover, it is directly connected with the issue that concluded the preceding chapter. In discussing the problem of the development of children's memory, Koffka [1925a, p. 183], among other things, says that the child initially relates passively to his memories and only gradually begins to master them and begins to return voluntarily to specific events. Elsewhere, speaking about the relation of structure to intellect, he remarks that the formation of ever more perfect and comprehensive structures is the function of the intellect, that structures develop, consequently, not where meaningful structures develop. They are to be found mostly in other centers.

In these two examples resides a problem of enormous theoretical importance. In claiming this, we have in mind that what is *most essential in the history of children's memory is exactly the transition from passive recollection of memories to their voluntary evocation and use.* Obviously, this transition is not determined by a particular, accidental or secondary aspect. *Everything that is specifically human in the development of the child's memory is concentrated or focused in the problem of this transition from passive to active memory.* For this transition implies a change in the very principle of organization of this function, this activity connected with the reconstruction of the past in consciousness.

One may ask to what extent the structural principle of universal intelligence is sufficient and suitable to explain this development of voluntary behavior in the child's mental life.

Likewise, when we learn that structures do not develop when *meaningful* structures develop the question naturally arises: *what, then, distinguishes these meaningful structures from nonmeaningful ones?* We ask: does the development of *meaningful structures* really not bring with it something fundamentally new in comparison with the development and perfection of *nonmeaningful structures*? Or, in other words, we ask *how tenable and suitable the principle of structure is, not just to explain the problems of voluntary behavior but also the problem of intellect in the mental life of the child.* [28]

That we are not dealing here with accidental examples but with something fundamentally important can be seen from a randomly chosen third illustration which shows that we stumble upon the same questions whatever section of the psychological development of the child we may choose. Koffka [1925a, p. 251] discusses the development of the concept of number in the child, having in mind that "number is the most perfect product of our thinking."

It would seem that *in the analysis of the most perfect product of our thinking* those specific traits that distinguish thinking as such should be the focus of the investigator's attention. It is characteristic of our thinking, says Koffka [1925a, p. 251], that we may carry out our thought operations arbitrarily upon any material, regardless of the natural relations between the objects. On other levels of development this is different: the things themselves determine the thought operations that can be carried out with them. And the whole chapter is further dedicated to these "other levels of development." [29]

Thus, this chapter as well turns out not to be dedicated to what makes number the most perfect product of our thinking. Number in the early stages of development is negatively presented as something lacking the most essential features of human thinking.

8

It seems to us that on the basis of the three examples given above we may demonstrate a common feature that dominates our whole problem of interest. The structural principle proves to be tenable wherever it must explain the initial, starting points of development. It shows what number was before it became the most perfect product of thinking. But how it was transformed from a primitive structure into an abstract concept that is the prototype of all abstract concepts—this the structural principle leaves unexplained. Here principal explanation makes room for factual description of a certain sequence or the establishment of facts.

In the same way, the structural principle superbly explains the origins of the development of memory. But *how* these primitive structures of memory turn into the active handling of reminiscences—this the structural principle does not explain, as it again merely states that passive memorization is replaced by active memorization.

The same takes place in relation to nonmeaningful and meaningful structures. From the viewpoint of this principle, the *transformation of the one into the other* remains an unsolvable enigma.

Because of this, a very curious relation is created between the explanatory principle and the factual material to which it is applied. The clarification from the *bottom upward* inevitably leads the author to shed light on the early, initial, pre-historical stages of child development in an adequate and convincing way. But the course of development itself, i.e., the process of negation of these initial stages and their transformation into the stages of mature thinking, remains unexplained.

This is no accident. All these facts taken together rest upon a single point which we cannot leave unclarified if we wish to make any progress. *This point lies in the area of the problem of meaning.*

As we have already seen, structural psychology begins the historical path with the problem of intelligence. But behind this problem it only views a primitive, primordial intelligence which is equally present in instinctive and intellectual, lower and higher, animal and human, historical and pre-historical forms of psychological life. The processes of the development of speech and thinking in the child are explained by means of a principle found in the semi-instinctive behavior of the ape.

Touching upon the question of the origin of speech, Koffka [1925a, p. 241] reproduces Stern's well-known claim: at the beginning of the development of intelligent speech is a great discovery which the child makes and which is that each thing has a name. He accepts Bühler's [1929, p. 58] analogy between this "great discovery in the child's life" and the tool use by apes. Following Bühler, he says [Koffka, 1925a, p. 243] that the word enters into the structure of the thing as for the chimpanzee the stick enters into the situation of "wishing to have some fruit."

In exactly the same way, Koffka explains the child's first generalization, which is clear from the fact that the child applies a word once mastered to other and still other objects. "How should we understand these transfers [*Uebertragungen*]," he asks [Koffka, 1925a, p.246]. Bühler is fully justified in comparing the transfer that we observe in the period of naming to the transfer in a chimpanzee when it, for example, uses the brim of a hat as a stick. This determines the direction in which we have to search for the solution. [30]

If this analogy between the mastering of speech and the use of a stick by the ape were legitimate, nothing could be said against Koffka's whole further construction. However, on closer inspection it appears to be radically false, and all the problems linked with it are presented in a false light. The error of this analogy is that what is most essential for a word is ignored—the psychological feature that determines its psychological nature. What is ignored is that without which the word stops being a word, namely *word meaning.*

Admittedly, in applying the structural principle to the explanation of the origin of speech in childhood, Koffka points to the intelligent character of these first speech operations of the child. But he puts a sign of equality between the meaning which the stick acquires in the visual situation of the ape and word meaning. *To us this seems illegitimate in principle.*

For we owe to word meaning the fact that abstract thinking in concepts becomes possible for the first time. A specifically human activity becomes possible which is impossible in the ape and whose essence resides in the fact that man begins to be determined in his behavior not by what he visually perceives, the structure of the visual field, but by mere thoughts.

Here Koffka overlooks the dialectical leap which development makes in the transition from sensation to thinking. Not for nothing has the whole problem of thinking been least developed in structural psychology and built almost everywhere upon the formal analogy with visual structures. We cannot but agree with the opinion which has lately been particularly energetically defended by Brunswik[2] and which is that the most difficult problems for structural psychology are the problems of meaning. This psychology dissolves the problem of specific word meaning in the general problem of the nonspecific intelligence of all behavior. That is why such a clear difference as that existing between the restricted behavior of the ape and the free behavior of thinking man remains, in principle, disregarded.

We repeat once more that the whole paradoxical nature of the situation resides in the fact that Koffka does not overlook the facts. He sees the whole variety of phenomena that do not fit the framework of structural explanation. But he is nowhere inclined to attach fundamental importance to this factual state of affairs, and, because of this, the facts themselves are not explained in principle and the analysis of development is reduced to a simple factual description of the state of affairs.

Michotte's [1927] experiments proved that in itself structural perception is impoverished in comparison to the intelligent perception of some graphic whole. Sander's [1927] experiments demonstrated that the parts of some optical image, when they gradually increase in size, suddenly reach a minimal level of meaning and begin to be perceived as parts of a whole that has a certain meaning. Ch. Bühler's [1928] experiments showed that structure and meaning in the child's perception develop from two totally different roots.

It is true that Koffka considers these experiments not convincing enough. The facts are, however, as says Bühler [1928/1967, p. 108], that all children who were capable of understanding the meaning of a drawing were without exception children who had mastered the nominative function of speech, and only one of all the children who understood speech did not yet point to the drawing. Hence it follows, says the author, that *meaning and structure develop from two totally different roots*. The recent experiments by Hetzer and Wiehemeyer [1929, pp. 277-284] also demonstrated that the child only develops meaningful perception of a drawing when it has mastered the significative function of speech.

We cannot but agree with Brunswik that meanings can to a large extent determine the structural processes and are so intimately enlaced with them that they ultimately turn into organic parts of unified meaningful perception. He says with full justification that here the explanatory possibility of structural theory obviously finds its outer limit.

It is remarkable that in one of his recent works Köhler himself also strictly distinguishes the goal from the meaning. The latter he considers as developing empirically, and for the time being he leaves the question open as to whether the functional principles of structural theory play a role in this process of meaning development and how they would be operative. This most cautious statement of the question leaves the basic question of the history of the development of concepts, abstract thinking, or abstraction essentially unsolved, i.e., processes that are at the center of the whole psychological development of the child. But at the same time such a statement of the question seems more cautious to us than a simple play with analogies which, in principle, views in the processes of abstract thinking nothing other than the same structures we know from the area of visual thinking. With the latter we are left with a far from satisfactory explanation of the circumstance that structural processes in ape and man which are, in principle, identical lead in practice to fundamentally different forms of the relationship to reality, which Köhler himself indicates and which are so important that the very possibility of cultural, i.e., specifically human, development of the mind is directly connected with them.

We will briefly dwell upon the problem of meaning, inasmuch as it *is the key to all further problems.*

As we have seen already, Koffka dissolves the problem of meaning in the general structural and intelligent nature of each mental process. It [meaning] is practically a special element of structure; in principle it cannot be separated from the general mass of structurally shaped processes.

In his latest systematic work, Köhler [1933, p. 45] was directly confronted with this problem. He proceeds from the correct assumption that in immediate experience we are always dealing with intelligent perception. As he correctly says, when we claim that we *see* a book before us, one might object that nobody *can see a book* and therefore he suggests distinguishing strictly between sensation and perception. In his words, we cannot *see* a book, inasmuch as this word involves knowledge of a certain class of objects to which the given book belongs. Köhler views it as the task of psychologists to isolate these meanings from the visible material as such. Speaking in general, sensory processes as such can never represent any objects for us. Objects cannot arise before the sensory experience has become fused with meanings.

It seems to us that in the whole elaboration of this problem, an elaboration which proceeds along idealistic lines, Köhler is unconditionally right in only one point—and this has to be mentioned right away. He is right in objecting to the theory that attempts to present meaning as something primary in relation to the sensory organization of the perceived structures. He fully convincingly argues that meanings are no such primary aspects, that they emerge much later in the process of individual development, that structural perception is primary, independent and more primitive than meaning, education. Here Köhler is indisputably right.

However, it is not difficult to point out what are his most essential mistakes. Even if we didn't have the meanings of the perceived objects, he claims [1933, p. 95], they still would continue to be perceived by us as certain organized and isolated units. When I see a green object I can immediately mention its color. Afterwards I may learn that this color is used as a railway signal and as a symbol of hope. But I do not think that the green color as such could be explained by these meanings. Initially it exists independently and only afterwards does it acquire certain secondary properties which are attached to it. All organized sensory units exist prior to meanings. It is exactly this conception that structural psychology defends.

But we only have to remember Köhler's own experiments, given by Koffka, with the training of animals on the perception of shades of a gray color in order to see that perception as such is, of course, not absolutely independent of meaning. Apparently, it is only with the development of meaning that the child begins to perceive the absolute quality of a color, independent of the color that is next to it. Thus, the merging of meaning with sensory structures, of which Köhler speaks, cannot but change the sensory organization of the perceived objects themselves.

For Köhler it is obvious that our knowledge of the practical experience with things does not determine their existence as isolated wholes. But we only have to recall his own experiments with the ape that stops recognizing a box in another situation to see that such an isolated existence of things is impossible without the specific objective meaning of these things. It is exactly because a meaningful structure develops that object constancy develops which in a most essential way distinguishes the relationship to reality of animal and man.

Taking this viewpoint, Köhler himself is forced into a sharp contradiction with the structural principle when he points out that the isolated existence of sensory structures is independent of meaning. Just as in physics a molecule can be isolated as a functional unit, he says [1933, p. 96], in the same way specific wholes are dynamically isolated in the sensory field.

As is well known, structural psychology began by attempting to demolish atomistic theory in psychology. Obviously, it has only done so to replace the atom by the molecule, for if we take Köhler's view we must admit that the perceived reality consists of a number of isolated molecules that do not depend on their semantic meaning.

Elsewhere, Köhler [1933, p. 96] openly says that if the forms exist primordially they may easily acquire meaning. The whole with all its formal properties is given in advance and then meaning, as it were, enters into it. Consequently, there is nothing new in meaning. It does not yield anything that was not already present in the primordially given form. After this it comes as no surprise that Köhler basically considers the origin of meanings as a process of reproduction, i.e., a process that is essentially associative.

It is a remarkable fact that *structural psychology began with a critique of the experiments with nonsense syllables and arrived at a theory of meaningless perception.* It began with a struggle against associationism and ends with the triumph of this principle, as it attempts to explain everything that is specifically human in mental life with the principle of association. After all, Köhler himself acknowledges that it is the presence of meanings which distinguishes the perception of man from the perception of animals. When it [meaning] owes its origin to associative processes these processes, consequently, lie at the basis of all specifically human forms of activity. Meaning is simply recalled, reproduced, and associatively reproduced.

Here Köhler himself changes the structural principle and wholly returns to the theory of meanings against which he at first was struggling. Köhler claims that this is the way the matter stands when we examine the question in principle. But in reality our perceptions and meanings appear inseparably merged. Thus, principle and reality diverge. Structural psychology acquires an analytically abstract character and carries us far away from the immediate, vivid, naive and meaningful experience that we actually have in immediate experience.

Meanwhile, Köhler himself knows that in normal adult man nothing can be free from such a merging with meaning. He also knows what is true of von Kries'[3] idealistic formula—a strikingly idealistic formula—which says that meanings *turn sensations into things* and that consequently the origin of objective consciousness is directly connected with meanings. He also knows that meaning, inasmuch as it is tied to a visual situation, seems localized in the visual field. And at the same time he defends the same position as does Koffka, i.e., in arguing that structures are primary, primordial and primitive in comparison with meanings, he assumes that he is claiming their supremacy, their dominant importance.

But the reverse is true. Exactly because structure is something primitive and primordial, it cannot be the key factor in the explanation of specifically human forms of activity. When Köhler says that any visual perception is organized in a specific structure he is completely right. He [1933, p. 97] gives the structure of constellations as an example. But it seems to us that this example speaks against him. Cassiopeia can, of course, serve as an example of such a structure. But heaven for an astronomer who connects what is immediately perceived with meanings and heaven for a person not knowing astronomy are, of course, structures of a totally different order.

As we here touch upon a question of central importance, we must give our general view on the history of child perception in order to contrast it with Koffka's viewpoint. It seems to us that this view can be best expressed using a simple comparison. Let us compare how a chessboard with pieces is perceived by different persons: a person who cannot play chess, a person who has only just begun to play, and an average and an outstanding player. We can say with confidence that all four persons will see the chessboard totally differently. The person who cannot play chess will perceive the structure of pieces from the viewpoint of their external features. The meaning of the pieces, their arrangement and interrelation fall outside his field of vision. The same board has a totally different structure for a person who knows the meaning of the pieces and their moves. For him some parts of the board become the ground and others the figure. The average and outstanding chess players will see the whole in yet another way.

Something similar happens in the process of development of the child's perception. Meaning leads to the development of a meaningful picture of the world. And just as one of the chess players examined by Binet [1894, p. 303] [31] told him that he perceived the rook as a straight force and the bishop as an oblique force, the child begins to perceive the things with meaning and introduces elements of thinking into his immediate perceptions.

When we compare this with what we read in Koffka's book about perception we cannot but see how vehemently Koffka tries to defend the opposite purely naturalistic view on the history of the development of child perception. As a result, for him the whole history of perception is a single series beginning with the perception of colors and ending with the categories according to which we perceive and interpret reality.

We will only consider these two extremes in order to give us an understanding of the path that Koffka takes here and why this path is incorrect.

Koffka [1925a, pp. 206-212] objects to Peters' experiments on the determining role that the development of the color concept plays in the structure of the perception of colors. In the latest edition, however, he has to return to this question and reconsider it. [32] On the basis of his experiments, Peters is unquestionably right in his statement of the problem. He shows that the development of color perception in older children is not simply a process of evolution of innate sensory functions or their morphological substrate. In his words, they are based upon the formation in the plane of the senses of so-called higher intellectual processes of understanding, reproduction, and thinking. [33] Perception is [not] solely determined by the sensation. The knowledge of the color name may turn out to be stronger than the sensory components. Equal names force the child to count the color as belonging to the same category.

As has already been said, Koffka at first strongly objected to this theory of the verbal-perceptory development of color perception. He says [1925a, p. 211] that Peters indeed proved the influence of names on the perception and comparison of colors but that we should not conceive of perception and comparison as processes of a higher order which are added to lower immutable sensory processes. They are structural processes which themselves determine the quality of their parts, the sensations.

But after the appearance of the works of Gelb and Goldstein [1925] on amnesia for color names, Koffka regards this interpretation of Peters' experiments as incomplete. According to Gelb and Goldstein, speech specifically influences perception which they call categorial behavior. In categorial behavior, for instance, a color may be liberated from the graphically given compound and be perceived as the representative of only a specific color category, for example, the color red, yellow, blue, etc. [34] Here we are not dealing with a simple combination of color and name.

It is only in occasional places in his book—like the one just mentioned—that Koffka makes a concession by acknowledging the specific influence of speech on perception. He actually defends a nonstructural view when he assumes that speech develops as a special type of structure alongside other structures which does not change a thing in the processes of perception itself. Thus, he is inclined—following Bühler—to assume that the structural constancy of perception forms a parallel to our concepts. Consequently, he defends the viewpoint that object constancy, which animals lack, as we have seen, and form constancy, which animals possess, can in principle be equated.

Discussing the categories that develop in perception and thinking (substance, action, quality), Koffka [1925a, pp. 223-226] comes to the conclusion that they arise as simple structures that are, in principle, not at all different from primitive structures. Our experiments, however, have shown that these stages in the perception of a drawing by the child change considerably, depending on whether he conveys the content of the drawing through speech or whether he expresses it dramatically. [35]

Whereas in the first case he displays clear symptoms of the substance stage, i.e., he lists the separate objects drawn on the picture, in the second case he conveys the content as a whole, i.e., reveals the event expressed in the picture. It seems to us that we must view this as the direct proof of the specific influence of speech upon perception, which obviously also finds its expression in the history of children's drawings to which Koffka himself refers.

Indeed, while Ch. Bühler demonstrated that the child perceives a structure and a meaningful drawing differently, Volkelt [1924][4] managed to show that the child himself draws a meaningless form fundamentally differently from a meaningful object. A meaningful object the child draws schematically, translating words into a drawing. The word with its specific meaning of the object is pushed in between the pictured object and the picture itself. In the communication of a directly felt or perceived meaningless form, the child follows a totally different route and conveys the immediate sensation of this form.

Taken together it would seem that all this is no accident. It shows, in the words of Gelb, that whereas for the animal only the surroundings (*Umwelt*) exist, for man a concept of the world (*Welt*) develops. The history of the development of this concept of the world has its beginnings in human praxis and in the meanings and concepts that arise in it, which are free from the immediate perception of the object.

That is why the correct solution of the problem of meaning determines everything that follows. As contemporary zoopsychology argues, for the animal the world really does not exist. The stimulation from the surrounding environment creates a solid wall that separates the animal from the world and locks it, as it were, in the stone walls of its own house, hiding from it the rest of the world that is foreign to it. In the case of the child we see something which is different in principle.

Koffka [1925a, p. 244] says that, as a rule, already the very first name is for the child a property of the thing mentioned. But the development of this new property of the thing can hardly leave unchanged the very structure of the thing as it existed before the development of this new property. The very first name already includes a new process, namely the process of generalization, and, as is well known, the simplest generalization involves a zigzag-like process of abstraction, a departure from reality, "a piece of phantasy." [36]

James is right in saying that one of the psychological differences between animal and man is the lack of imagination. James says about animals that their thinking hardly transcends the concrete facts.

"They are forever enslaved to routine. If the most prosaic of human beings could be transported into his dog's soul, he would be appalled at the utter absence of fancy which there reigns. Thoughts would not be found to well up their similars, but only their habitual successors. Sunset would not suggest heroes' deaths, but supper-time. This is why man is the only metaphysical animal. To wonder why the universe should be as it is presupposes the notion of its being different, and a brute, who never reduces the actual to fluidity by breaking up its literal sequences in his imagination, can never form such a notion. He takes the world simply for granted, and never wonders at it at all [see p. 320 of Burkhardt, 1984].

The thought experiment that James suggests carrying out by moving into the soul of a dog is essentially performed by Koffka when he applies the principle found in the behavior of the ape to the whole development of the child. No wonder, therefore, that the very essence of ideational learning, which in Koffka's [1925a, p. 240] words rests upon our liberation from the direct power of reality, and gives us power over this reality, contradicts the basic principle of Koffka himself.

9

In the present case, to overcome the one-sidedness of the structural viewpoint does not imply to return to the structureless, atomistic and chaotic accumulation of different elements. The structural principle remains a great, unshakable achievement of theoretical thought, and in criticizing its application to the explanation of child development we do not wish to say that the opposite principle, rejected by Koffka, is correct. We must not return to a prestructural principle, but move forward from the structural principle while relying on it.

The structural principle is not so much incorrect in its application to the facts of child development as incomplete, provisional and limited. For it only reveals in child development what is not specific for man but is common to man and animal. And that is why the main methodological mistake in the application of this principle to child psychology is not that it is incorrect, but that it is too universal and therefore insufficient for revealing the distinct and specific properties of human development as such.

As we tried to show repeatedly, the author's mistakes always contradict the consistent application of his own principle. The very essence of the structural principle compels us to assume that the novel structures which arise in the process of child development are not floating on the surface, isolated from the primitive, primordial structures that existed before the beginning of development and not merging with them.

The most essential difference of opinion taking shape in the application of this principle boils down to *seeking the new principle not outside structure, but within structure.* For if the perception of a chicken and the actions of a mathematician, which represent the most perfect model of human thinking, *are equally structured,* then it is obvious that the principle itself which does not allow us to make this distinction is insufficiently differentiated, insufficiently dynamic to bring out the novel phenomena that arise in the course and process of development itself.

The structural principle, as we have already said, is retained in superseded form during the whole course of child development. The task of our critical investigation is not to reject this principle or to replace it by its opposite, but to reject its universal and undifferentiated application. It is nonspecific and anti-historic exactly because it is equally applicable to instinct and mathematical thinking. We must seek what lifts the psychological development of the child above the structural principle. We must proceed to the higher, specifically human, historical foundations of psychological development.

Here the truth of the structural principle must again help us to overcome its falsity.

10

Now it only remains for us to bring together the remarks that were made earlier and to generalize them somewhat. It remains for us to examine the general definitions of the problem of development that we meet in Koffka. As is already apparent from what was said before, the main methodological shortcoming in the solution of this problem is that the basic question with which we began our critical examination is not satisfactorily answered by Koffka's structural principle.

We recall that he began with the question as to how novel forms are possible in the course of psychological development. This is indeed a touchstone for each theory that attempts to explain development. And the most essential result of our investigation is the claim that it is exactly novel forms that turn out to be impossible from the viewpoint applied by Koffka. We tried to show—and now there is no need to repeat this in any elaborate form—that the application of the structural principle implies reducing child and animal psychology to a common denominator, erasing the borders between the historical and the biological and, consequently, rejecting the possibility of novel forms.

If structure is given primordially in infant consciousness, if everything that arises in the further course of development is no more than just new factual variations on this primordially structural theme, then this implies that in the course of development nothing fundamentally new evolves. It means that from the very beginning the given principle gives rise to the simple multiplication of structures which according to their psychological nature are different in practice, but identical in principle.

How does Koffka state the problem of development?

As the reader will easily see, Koffka distinguishes two main forms of development. He breaks up this process, distinguishing development as maturation and development as learning. Admittedly, he more than once dwells upon their mutual influence and mutual dependency. However, this mutual dependency of maturation and learning is always raised by Koffka when he is describing a factual state of affairs, and nowhere do we find a fundamental solution of the question as to how we should conceive of both these aspects of the unitary process of development in the course of child development.

Actually, the unitary process of development is split into two processes, and in Koffka we in principle meet with a dualistic approach to child development. Nothing appears to be dominating and commanding, leading and determining in this mutual influence of maturation and learning. Both processes participate on equal terms, with equal rights in the history of the origin of child consciousness. Admittedly, here too Koffka remarks more than once that in practice the structures which develop in learning are always more important. But again this factual state of affairs is not used to shed a fundamental light on the facts.

That the principle of maturation in itself is the basis of the naturalistic theory of child development hardly needs special proof. Let us therefore examine the second aspect of the matter, namely, the problem of learning. It is a remarkable fact that Koffka, while dedicating his book to teachers, nevertheless examines learning only in the early stages of child development, i.e., in the forms in which it is met before school. He frequently says that we can determine the meaning of learning in its pure form when we examine it in the most primitive phenomena. But this attempt to explain the higher from the primitive implies the path *from below upward* of which we said above that it is one of the central shortcomings of Koffka's whole theory.

In his own words, in Koffka's book [1925a, p. iv]

> we essentially deal with the pre-school child. This might not seem overly interesting to the teacher. But I wanted to show that the problems of development that the teacher meets in school develop in the human mind from the very beginning and wished to emphasize the beginnings of this development. If I have succeeded, to use the most important example, in scientifically explaining what the 'learning' of the very young child means, the teacher will have a better understanding of the performances of his pupils and be in a better position to support them. However, to understand the essence of learning is in many respects much easier when one turns to the most primitive forms, when one investigates the very first forms of learning.

The fact that Koffka sets himself the task of investigating the *beginning of development* in its most primitive forms is no accident. We have seen that according to the very methodological nature of his explanatory principle *only the beginning of development,* only its starting points can be adequately represented in light of his basic idea. It is therefore not for nothing that until now structural psychology has not elaborated (and hardly can elaborate without radically changing its basic set) a theory of thinking. Neither is it accidental that the best chapter of Koffka's whole book is the chapter on infant consciousness. It is only here that the structural principle gains its highest victories, here it celebrates its highest theoretical triumphs.

Far be it from us to deny the importance of the initial stages of development. On the contrary, we are inclined to view the paramount significance of Koffka's work in the fact that he erases the sharp boundary between school learning and learning that takes place in the pre-school period. Further, we cannot but see that Koffka's conception regarding the link between learning and development states the theory of development itself in a new and revolutionary way.

Indeed, earlier we mentioned the struggle of the ideas of structural psychology with Thorndike's ideas in the area of animal psychology. For a correct understanding of the meaning of Koffka's work and its shortcomings it is necessary to bring this struggle to the plane of pedagogical psychology in order to see all the novel things that structural psychology introduced.

As is well known, Thorndike logically developed the idea that lies at the basis of his zoological experiments and arrived at a completely specific theory of learning which Koffka resolutely overthrows, thereby freeing us from the power of false and prejudiced ideas. The decisive question here is the old question of the "formal discipline." Thorndike [1906, pp. 235-236] says that

> the problem of how far the particular responses made day by day by pupils improve their mental powers in general is called the problem of the disciplinary value or disciplinary effect of studies, or, more briefly, the problem of formal discipline. How far, for instance, does learning to be accurate with numbers make one more accurate in keeping his accounts, in weighing and measuring, in telling anecdotes, in judging the characters of his friends? How far does learning to reason out rather than guess at or learn by heart a problem in geometry make one more thoughtful and logical in following political arguments or in choosing a religious creed or in deciding whether it is best for him to get married?

The anecdotal form in which the question is phrased already clearly points to the negative solution of the problem that Thorndike gives. Whereas the common answer is to acknowledge that each special mental acquisition, each special form of training, improves directly and equally the general ability, Thorndike gives a directly opposite answer. He points out that mental capacities only develop insofar as they are subjected to special training with specific material. Referring to a number of experiments carried out on the most elementary and primitive functions, Thorndike shows that the specialization of abilities is greater than it seems on superficial inspection. He assumes that special training has specific effects and can exert influence on general development only inasmuch as the learning process includes identical elements, identical substance, an identical character of the operation itself.

However, he refuses to believe that the topics to be learned may themselves in some enigmatic way lead to knowledge of the whole. He says [ibid., pp. 247-248] that

> Each separate task adds its mite to the general store. Intellect and character are strengthened, not by any subtle and easy metamorphosis, but by the establishment of certain particular ideas and acts under the law of habit. There is no way of becoming self-controlled except by today, tomorrow and all the days in each little conflict controlling oneself . . . . No one becomes honest save by telling the truth, or trustworthy save by fulfilling each obligation he accepts . . . .. The price of a disciplined intellect and will is eternal vigilance in the formation of habits.

According to Thorndike's idea we are ruled by habit. To develop consciousness is to develop a multitude of particular, mutually independent capacities, to form a multitude of particular habits, for the activity of each capacity depends upon the material with which this capacity operates. The improvement of one function of consciousness or one side of its activity can influence the development of another one only insofar as there exist elements that are common to both functions or activities.

Koffka's theory liberates us from this mechanistic viewpoint on the processes of learning. He shows that learning is never specific, that the formation of a structure in some area inevitably leads to the facilitation of development of structural functions in other areas. However, Koffka fully preserves Thorndike's claim that learning is equal to development. The whole difference is merely that Thorndike reduces learning to habit formation and Koffka to the formation of a structure.

But the idea that the processes of learning stand in another and far more complex relation to the processes of development—that development has an inner character, that it is a unitary process in which the influence of maturation and learning are merged together, that this process has its inner laws of self-development—this idea remains equally foreign to both theories.

It is not surprising, therefore, that Koffka in his treatment of learning avoids all questions connected with the development of specifically human properties of consciousness. The liberation from reality, he says, in the way it is possible and accessible for our thinking, is a specific achievement of our culture.

However, the whole structural principle is not intended to show this path to liberation from the immediate perception of reality, but to show the path that enables us to view the dependency of each of our steps upon the visual structures in which we perceive reality.

11

There are two problems that may serve as the touchstone for the correct evaluation of Koffka's position. The first is the problem of play and the second, connected with it, is the problem of the particular world in which the child lives.

Play is a touchstone for structural theory because characteristic of play is exactly the beginning of ideational behavior. The play activity of the child proceeds outside real perception—in an imaginary situation. In this sense Koffka is entirely right when he demands the revision of Groos' theory about the meaning of play and points out that both the animal and the very young child lack play in the proper sense of the word. Here his psychological intuition helps him to view the facts and the real boundaries between them properly. But again Koffka does not reject Groos' theory on principal grounds. He does not reject the theory because of its naturalistic character, and attempts to replace it by another, equally naturalistic, theory.

It comes as no surprise, then, that Koffka ultimately arrives at strange and unexpected results which contradict, it would seem, his own starting positions. He himself is fully justified in rejecting Piaget's opinion regarding the *mystical* character of children's explanations and points to the child's tendency toward naturalistic explanation which is directly linked with the child's realism. He further correctly points out that the child's egocentrism has a functional and not a phenomenal character. But at the same time—and in sharp contradiction with this—he ascertains [1925a, p. 258] that Lévy-Bruhl's statement about the mystical character of primitive perception can be applied to the perception of the child as well. He is inclined to claim that religious experiences as well are intrinsically close to the structure of the child's world.

There is an area, he says [1925a, p. 266], that children learn from adults and that is very close to the child's world. He means religion.

As is well known, Koffka's basic idea is that for the child there exist two worlds—the world of adults and the child's own world. What the child borrows from the world of adults must be intrinsically akin to his own world. Religion and the experiences connected with it are such elements of the world of adults which the child accepts in its inner world.

Koffka tries to apply this theory to child play and explains the way a child handles a toy. The fact that the child may play with a piece of wood and deal with it as if it were a living thing and after some time, if we distract him from this activity, may break it or throw it into the fire, is explained by assuming that this piece of wood enters into two different structures [Koffka, 1925a, pp. 255-264]. In the inner world of the child this piece of wood is an animated object, in the world of adults it is simply a piece of wood. The two distinct ways of dealing with the same object develop because it enters into two different structures.

It is difficult to imagine a greater distortion of the facts than such a type of theory of child play. After all, the very essence of child play is the creation of an imaginary situation, i.e., a certain semantic field which transforms the child's whole behavior and forces him to be governed in his actions and deeds solely by these imaginary situations and not by the visual situation. The content of these imaginary situations always indicates that they develop in the world of the adults.

We already once had occasion to dwell in detail on this theory of the two worlds—the world of the child and the world of adults—and the theory of the two spirits that coexist simultaneously in the child's consciousness which follows from it. Now we will only point out what this theory implies for the general conception of development presented by Koffka.

It seems to us that due to such a conception the very development of the child is pictured by Koffka as the mechanical suppression of the child's world by the world of adults. Such a conception inevitably leads to the conclusion that the child grows into a world of adults which is hostile to him, that the child develops in his own world, that the structures from the world of adults simply supplant the child's structures and take their place. Development is turned into the process of suppression and substitution that is so well known to us from Piaget's theory.

12

In connection with this, the whole character of child development acquires exceedingly strange features on which we must dwell in conclusion.

Initially, for the child exist structures of very limited size. Koffka [1925a, p. 261] thinks that we will best psychologically understand play when we consider to which larger structures the actions of the child belong for the child himself. Then we will find an initial period in which the child is completely incapable of creating larger time structures that would transcend the actions just performed.

It is consequently here, Koffka claims, that all different action complexes are mutually independent, enjoy equal rights and are of equal value. But gradually the child begins to create time structures as well and now it is characteristic that these different structures remain side by side without exerting much influence on each other. The relative mutual independence of the different structures is not only extended to these two large groups of the world of the child and the adult world, but also exists for different dependences within each of them.

It suffices to give this description to see to what degree Koffka pictures the process of child development as something without structure. Initially we have separate molecules-structures that are mutually independent and exist side by side. Development consists in the fact that the dimensions or size of these structures change. Thus, at the beginning of development is again a chaos of disorganized molecules which are subsequently combined and lead to the development of an integrated relationship to reality.

It is amazing. Above we have seen how Köhler, having smashed atomism, replaced the atom by the independent and isolated molecule. Here we see the same. The fragmentary nature of the initial structures and the growth of the size of these structures—these are the two decisive factors which depict the process of child development in Koffka's conception. But this amounts to saying that the different elementary actions which Thorndike dealt with are replaced by more complex experiences or structures, i.e., the unit is changed, it is enlarged, the atom is replaced by the molecule, but the course of development remains the same.

Again we see that Koffka contradicts the structural principle and changes it. In his account the processes of development essentially look as if they have no structure. It is correct, it has been indisputably proved that everything develops and grows from structures. But *how* does it grow? Apparently, through the augmentation of the dimensions of these structures and by overcoming the fragmentary nature which exists from the very beginning. The starting point of development is, as has already been said, the highest triumph of structural psychology. The beginning of development dominates its whole further course. The highest forms of development remain a closed book to this psychology.

That is why we shouldn't be surprised by the conclusion which forms the main result of our investigation.

We have seen that Koffka overcomes mechanicism by introducing the intellectualistic principle. Koffka overcomes mechanicism by making concessions to vitalism (he accepts that structures are primordial), and he overcomes vitalism by making concessions to mechanicism. For, as we have seen, mechanicism not only means reducing man to a machine but also man to an animal. In the name of Beelzebub he chases the devil and in the name of the devil, Beelzebub.

In his investigation development is not self-development but replacement and suppression. Development is not a unitary process but a dual process consisting of maturation and learning. Learning itself which leads to development is explained purely intellectualistically. Whereas for the empiricists learning was memorization and habit formation, for Koffka, as he doesn't grow tired of repeating, learning is the solution of problems, an intellectual action. The intellectual action of the chimpanzee is for him the key to all learning and the development of the human child. Development is pictured as the solution of a number of tasks, as a number of thought operations, i.e., we are dealing with pure intellectualism, which Koffka tries to de-intellectualize by finding the same principle in pre-intellectual, primitive and instinctive reactions as well.

But when we unravel, as we have tried to do above, this hidden intellectualism, which leads to the fact that instinct is illuminated by the light of intellect and intellect is discovered as the key to instinct, then there can hardly remain any doubt that we are faced with a construction which is psychovitalistic and mechanistic at the same time.

As we have already said above, knowing that the two theories are untenable, Koffka occupies a middle position halfway between both of them and thinks that he can escape from both. But the fragmentary nature of the structures ultimately contradicts the final chord of his book which says that the essence of psychological development is presented in this book not as the combination of different elements but as the formation and perfection of structures [Koffka, 1925a, p. 270].

As we have seen, in the beginning of development exists the fragmentary nature of the structures and these structures-molecules are combined into a general structure. This conception of development amounts to a conception of development as the modification, realization, and combination of innate structures. The structure is primordial and its development Koffka explains as the growth of precision, duration, and differentiation of the structures, i.e., he places development in the category of "more and less."

That is why our investigation leads us to the conclusion that the question as to whether structure is suitable as a general principle of psychological development can only be answered in the negative. Relying on the structural principle, we must overcome its narrowness. We must show that inasmuch as it really proves something, this proof covers only what is nonspecific, what has receded to the background in the course of development, what is pre-historic in the human child. When Koffka attempts to shed light on the factual course of child development with the structural principle, he takes recourse to formal analogy and reduces everything to the common denominator of structure and essentially, as he confesses himself, sheds light on *just the beginning of development.*

That is why we must search for the origin and development of higher specifically human properties of consciousness and in the first place for the intelligent character of human consciousness which arises with the word and the concept, through the word and through the concept. In other words, *we must search for a historical conception of child psychology.*

It is not hard to see that on our path we will not be able to avoid structural psychology, although development as such is absent in it. For the whole description of child development in Koffka's book shows us that—as in the French proverb—the more it changes, the more it remains the same [37], i.e., it remains the same structure which existed primordially. Historically the structural principle is, nevertheless, more progressive than the concepts it replaced in the course of the development of our science. That is why on the path toward a historical conception of child psychology we must negate the structural principle dialectically, which means to preserve and to overcome it at the same time.

We must try to solve the problem of the meaningful nature of human consciousness *in a new fashion*. This meaningful nature has only its name in common with the concept with which structural psychology begins and ends. In Spinoza's [1677/1955, p. 61] words, there is as much correspondence between the two as there is between the Dog, the heavenly constellation, and a dog, an animal that barks.

Chapter 15
THE HISTORICAL MEANING OF THE CRISIS IN PSYCHOLOGY:
A METHODOLOGICAL INVESTIGATION*,1

> *The stone which the builders rejected*
> *is become the head stone of the corner* [1]

1

Lately more and more voices are heard proclaiming that the problem of general psychology is a problem of the first order. What is most remarkable is that this opinion does not come from philosophers who have made generalization their professional habit, nor even from theoretical psychologists, but from the psychological practitioners who elaborate the special areas of applied psychology: psychiatrists and industrial psychologists [2], the representatives of the most exact and concrete part of our science. The various psychological disciplines have obviously reached a turning point in the development of their investigations, the gathering of factual material, the systematization of knowledge, and the statement of basic positions and laws. Further advance along a straight line, the simple continuation of the same work, the gradual accumulation of material, are proving fruitless or even impossible. In order to go further we must choose a path.

Out of such a methodological crisis, from the conscious need for guidance in different disciplines, from the necessity—on a certain level of knowledge—to critically coordinate heterogeneous data, to order uncoordinated laws into a system, to interpret and verify the results, to cleanse the methods and basic concepts, to create the fundamental principles, in a word, to pull the beginnings and ends of our knowledge together, out of all this, a general science is born.

This is why the concept of a general psychology does not coincide with the concept of the basic theoretical psychology that is central to a number of different special disciplines. The latter, in essence the psychology of the adult normal person, should be considered one of the special disciplines along with zoopsychology and psychopathology. That it has so far played and in some measure still plays the role of a generalizing factor, which to a certain extent forms the structure and system of the special disciplines, furnishes their main concepts, and brings them into line with their own structure, is explained by the historical development of the science, rather than by logical necessity. This is the way things have been and to some extent

*Not previously published. Based on a manuscript found in Vygotsky's private archives.

233

still are, but they should not and will not remain this way since this situation does not follow from the very nature of the science, but is determined by external, extraneous circumstances. As soon as these conditions change, the psychology of the normal person will lose its leading role. To an extent we are already beginning to see this happen. In the psychological systems that cultivate the concept of the unconscious, the role of such a leading discipline, the basic concepts of which serve as the starting points for the related sciences, is played by psychopathology. These are, for example, the systems of Freud, Adler,[2] and Kretschmer.

In the latter, this leading role of psychopathology is no longer connected with the central concept of the unconscious, as in Freud and Adler, i.e., not with the actual priority of the given discipline in the elaboration of the basic idea, but with a fundamental methodological view according to which the essence and nature of the phenomena studied by psychology can be revealed in their purest form in the extreme, pathological forms. We should, consequently, proceed from pathology to the norm and explain and understand the normal person from pathology, and not the other way around, as has been done until now. The key to psychology is in pathology, not only because it discovered and studied the root of the mind earlier than other branches, but because this is the internal nature of things, and the nature of the scientific knowledge of these things is conditioned by it. Whereas for traditional psychology every psychopath as a subject for study is more or less—to a different degree—a normal person and must be defined in relation to the latter, for the new systems each normal person is more or less insane and must be psychologically understood precisely as a variant of some pathological type. To put it in more straightforward terms, in certain systems the normal person is considered as a type and the pathological personality as a variety or variant of this main type; in others, on the contrary, the pathological phenomenon is taken as a type and the normal as one of its varieties. And who can predict how the future general psychology will decide this debate?

On the basis of such dual motives (based half on facts, half on principle) still other systems assign the leading role to zoopsychology. Of this kind are, for example, the majority of the American courses in the psychology of behavior and the Russian courses in reflexology, which develop their whole system from the concept of the conditional reflex and organize all their material around it. A number of authors propose that animal psychology, apart from being given the actual priority in the elaboration of the basic concepts of behavior, should become the general discipline with which the other disciplines should be correlated. As the logical beginning of a science of behavior, the starting point for every genetic examination and explanation of the mind, and a purely biological science, it is precisely this science which is expected to elaborate the fundamental concepts of the science and to supply them to kindred disciplines.

This, for example, is the view of Pavlov. What psychologists do can in his opinion have no influence upon animal psychology, but what zoopsychologists do determines the work of psychologists in a very essential way. The latter build the superstructure, but the former lay the foundation [Pavlov, 1928/1963, p. 113]. And indeed, the source from which we derive all our basic categories for the investigation and description of behavior, the standard we use to verify our results, the model according to which we align our methods, is zoopsychology.

Here again the matter has taken a course opposed to that of traditional psychology. There the starting point was man; one proceeded from man in order to get an idea of the mind of the animal. One interpreted the manifestations of its soul by analogy with ourselves. In so doing, the matter was by no means always reduced to a crude anthropomorphism. Serious methodological grounds often dictated such a course of research: with subjective psychology it could not be otherwise. It regarded man as the key to the psychology of animals; always the highest forms as the key to the lower ones. For, the investigator need not always follow the same path that nature took; often the reverse path is more advantageous.

Marx [1978, p. 636] referred to this methodological principle of the "reverse" method when he stated that "the anatomy of man is the key to the anatomy of the ape."

> The allusions to a higher principle in lower species of animals can only be understood when this higher principle itself is already known. Thus, bourgeois economy gives us the key to antique economy etc., but not at all in the sense understood by the economists who slur over all historical differences and see bourgeois forms in all forms of societies. We can understand the quitrent, the tithe, etc., when we are acquainted with the ground rent, but we must not equate them with the latter.

To understand the quitrent on the basis of the ground rent, the feudal form on the basis of the bourgeois form—this is the same methodological device used to comprehend and define thinking and the rudiments of speech in animals on the basis of the mature thinking and speech of man. A certain stage of development and the process itself can only be fully understood when we know the endpoint of the process, the result, the direction it took, and the form into which the given process developed. We are, of course, speaking only of the methodological transference of basic categories and concepts from the higher to the lower, not of the transference of factual observations and generalizations. The concepts of the social category of class and class struggle, for instance, are revealed in their purest form in the analysis of the capitalist system, but these same concepts are the key to all pre-capitalist societal formations, although in every case we meet with different classes there, a different form of struggle, a particular developmental stage of this category. But those details which distinguish the historical uniqueness of different epochs from capitalist forms not only are not lost, but, on the contrary, can only be studied when we approach them with the categories and concepts acquired in the analysis of the other, higher formation.

Marx [1978, p. 636] explains that

> bourgeois society is the most developed and diverse historical organization of production. The categories which express its relationships and an understanding of its composition yield therefore at the same time an insight into the composition and the productive relations of all societal forms which have disappeared. Bourgeois society was built with the rubbish and elements of these societies, parts of which have not been fully overcome and still drag on and the mere indications of which have developed into full-fledged meanings.

Having arrived at the end of the path we can more easily understand the whole path in its entirety as well as the meaning of its different stages.

This is a possible methodology; it has been sufficiently vindicated in a whole number of disciplines. But can it be applied to psychology? It is precisely on methodological grounds that Pavlov rejects the route from man to animal. He defends the reverse of the "reverse," i.e., the direct path of investigation, repeating the route taken by nature. This is not because of any factual difference in the phenomena, but rather because of the inapplicability and epistemic barrenness of psychological categories and concepts. In his words,

> it is impossible by means of psychological concepts, which are essentially nonspatial, to penetrate into the mechanism of animal behavior, into the mechanism of these relations [Pavlov, 1928/1963, p. 192].

Thus it is not a matter of facts but of concepts, that is, the way one conceives of these facts. He [ibid., p. 113] says that

> Our facts are conceived of in terms of time and space; they are purely scientific facts;
> but psychological facts are thought of only in terms of time.

The issue is about different concepts, not different phenomena. Pavlov wishes not only to win independence for his area of investigation, but to extend its influence and guidance to all spheres of psychological knowledge. This is clear from his explicit references to the fact that the debate is not only about the emancipation from the power of psychological concepts, but also about the elaboration of a psychology by means of new spatial concepts.

In his opinion, science, "guided by the similarity or identity of the external manifestations" [ibid., p. 59], will sooner or later apply to the mind of man the objective data obtained. His path is from the simple to the complex, from animal to man. He says [ibid., p. 113] that

> The simple, the elementary is always conceivable without the complex, whereas the
> complex cannot be conceived of without the elementary.

These data will become "the basis for psychological knowledge." And in the preface to the book in which he presents his twenty years of experience with the study of animal behavior, Pavlov [ibid., p. 41] declares that he

> is deeply and irrevocably convinced that along this path [we will manage] to find the
> knowledge of the mechanisms and laws of human nature [ibid., p. 41].

Here we have a new controversy between the study of animals and the psychology of man. The situation is, in essence, very similar to the controversy between psychopathology and the psychology of normal man. Which discipline should lead, unify, and elaborate the basic concepts, principles, and methods, verify and systematize the data of all other areas? Whereas previously traditional psychology has considered the animal as a more or less remote ancestor of man, reflexology is now inclined to consider man, with Plato, as a "featherless biped." [3] Formerly the animal mind was defined and described in concepts and terms acquired in the study of man. Nowadays the behavior of animals gives "the key to the understanding of the behavior of man," and what we call "human" behavior is understood as the product of an animal which, because it walks and stands erect, has a developed thumb and can speak.

And again we may ask: which discipline other than general psychology can decide this controversy between animal and man in psychology; for, on this decision will rest nothing more and nothing less than the whole future fate of this science.

2

From the analysis of the three types of psychological systems we have considered above, it is already obvious how pressing is the need for a general psychology with the boundaries and approximate content partially outlined here. The path of our investigation will at all times be as follows: we will proceed from an analysis of the facts, albeit facts of a highly general and abstract nature, such as a particular psychological system and its type, the tendencies and fate of different theories, various epistemological methods, scientific classifications and schemes, etc. We will examine these facts not from the abstract-logical, purely philosophical side, but as particular facts in the history of science, as concrete, vivid historical events in their tendency, struggle, in their concrete context, of course, and in their epistemological-theoretical essence, i.e., from the viewpoint of their correspondence to the reality they are meant to cognize. We wish to obtain a clear idea of the essence of individual and social psychology as two aspects of a single science, and of their historical fate, not through abstract considerations, but by means of an analysis of scientific reality. From this we will deduce, as a politician does from the analysis of events, the rules for action and the organization of scientific research. The methodological investigation utilizes the historical examination of the concrete forms of the sciences and the theoretical analysis of these forms in order to obtain generalized, verified principles that are suitable for guidance. This is, in our opinion, the core of this general psychology whose concept we will attempt to clarify in this chapter.

The first thing we obtain from the analysis is the demarcation between general psychology and the theoretical psychology of the normal person. We have seen that the latter is not necessarily a general psychology, that in quite a number of systems theoretical psychology itself turns into one of the special disciplines, defined by another field; that both psychopathology and the theory of animal behavior can and do take the role of general psychology. Vvedensky (1917, p. 5) assumed that general psychology

> might much more correctly be called basic psychology, because this part lies at the basis of all psychology.

Høffding [1908, p. 37], who assumed that psychology "can be practiced in many modes and ways," that "there is not *one*, but *many* psychologies," and who saw no need for unity, was nevertheless inclined to view subjective psychology "as the basis and the *center*, around which the contributions of the other approaches should be gathered." In the present case it would indeed be more appropriate to talk about a basic, or central, psychology than about a general one; but to overlook the fact that systems may arise from a completely different basis and center, and that what the professors considered to be the basis in those systems, by the very nature of things, drifts to the periphery, would be more than a little dogmatic, and naively complacent. Subjective psychology was basic or central in quite a number of systems, and we must understand why. Now it loses its importance, and again we must understand why. In the present case it would be terminologically most correct to speak of theoretical psychology, as opposed to applied psychology, as Münsterberg [1920] does. Applied to the adult normal person it would be a special branch alongside child psychology, zoopsychology, and psychopathology.

Theoretical psychology, Binswanger[3] [1922, p. 5] notes, is not general psychology, nor a part of it, but is itself the object or subject matter of general psychology. The latter deals with the questions whether theoretical psychology is in principle possible and what are the structure and suitability of its concepts. Theoretical psychology cannot be equated with general psychology, if only for the reason that precisely the matter of building theories in psychology is a fundamental question of general psychology.

There is a second thing that we may reliably infer from our analysis. The very fact that theoretical psychology, and later other disciplines, have performed the role of a general psychology, is conditioned by, on the one hand, the absence of a general psychology, and on the other hand, the strong need for it to fulfill its function temporarily in order to make scientific research possible. Psychology is pregnant with a general discipline but has not yet delivered it.

The third thing we may gather from our analysis is the distinction between two phases in the development of any general science, any general discipline, as is shown by the history of science and methodology. In the first phase of development the general discipline is only quantitatively distinct from the special one. Such a distinction, as Binswanger [1922, p. 3] rightly says, is characteristic of the majority of sciences. Thus, we distinguish general and special botany, zoology, biology, physiology, pathology, psychiatry, etc. The general discipline studies what is common to all subjects of the given science. The special discipline studies what is characteristic of the various groups or even specimens from the same kind of objects. It is in this sense that the discipline we now call differential psychology was called special. In the same sense this area was called individual psychology. The general part of botany or zoology studies what is common to all plants or animals, the general part of psychology what is common to all people. In order to do this the concept of some trait common to most or all of them was abstracted from the real diversity and in this form, abstracted from the real diversity of concrete traits, it became the subject matter studied by the general discipline. Therefore, the characteristic and task of such a discipline was seen to be the scientific study of the facts common to the greatest number of the particular phenomena of the given area [Binswanger, 1922, p. 3].

This stage of searching and of trying to apply an abstract concept common to all psychological disciplines, which forms the subject matter of all of them and determines what should be isolated from the chaos of the various phenomena and what in the phenomena has epistemic value for psychology—this stage we see vividly expressed in our analysis. And we may judge what significance these searches and the concept of the subject matter of psychology looked for and the desired answer to the question what psychology studies may have for our science in the present historical moment of its development.

Any concrete phenomenon is completely inexhaustible and infinite in its separate features. We must always search in the phenomenon what makes it a scientific fact. Exactly this distinguishes the observation of a solar eclipse by the astronomer from the observation of the same phenomenon by a person who is simply curious. The former discerns in the phenomenon what makes it an astronomic fact. The latter observes the accidental features which happen to catch his attention.

What is most common to all phenomena studied by psychology, what makes the most diverse phenomena into psychological facts—from salivation in a dog to the enjoyment of a tragedy, what do the ravings of a madman and the rigorous computations of the mathematician share? Traditional psychology answers: what they have in common is that they are all psychological phenomena which are nonspatial and can only be perceived by the experiencing subject himself. Reflexology answers: what they share is that all these phenomena are facts of behavior, correlative activity, reflexes, response actions of the organism. Psychoanalysts answer: common to all these facts, the most basic factor which unites them is the unconscious which is their basis. For general psychology the three answers mean, respectively, that it is a science of (1) the mental and its properties; or (2) behavior; or (3) the unconscious.

From this it is obvious that such a general concept is important for the whole future fate of the science. Any fact which is expressed in each of these three systems will, in turn, acquire three completely different forms. To be more precise, there will be three different forms of a single fact. To be even more precise, there will be three different facts. And as the science moves forward and gathers facts, we will successively get three different generalizations, three different laws, three different classifications, three different systems—three individual sciences which, the more successfully they develop, the more remote they will be from each other and from the common fact that unites them. Shortly after beginning they will already be forced to select different facts, and this very choice of facts will already determine the fate of the science as it continues. Koffka [1924, p. 149] was the first to express the idea that introspective psychology and the psychology of behavior will develop into two sciences if things continue as they are going. The paths of the two sciences lie so far apart that "it is by no means certain whether they will eventually lead to the same end."

Pavlov and Bekhterev share essentially the same opinion. They accept the existence of two parallel sciences—psychology and reflexology—which study the same object, but from different sides. In this connection Pavlov [1928/1963, p. 329] said that "certainly psychology, insofar as it concerns the subjective state of man, has a natural right to existence." For Bekhterev, reflexology neither contradicts nor excludes subjective psychology but delineates a special area of investigation, i.e., creates a new parallel science. He talks about [Bekhterev, 1932, p. 380] the intimate interrelation of both scientific disciplines and even about subjective reflexology as an inevitable future development. Incidentally, we must say that in reality both Pavlov and Bekhterev reject psychology and hope to understand the whole area of knowledge about man by exclusively objective means, i.e., they only envision the possibility of one single science, although by word of mouth they acknowledge two sciences. In this way the general concept predetermines the content of the science.

At present psychoanalysis, behaviorism, and subjective psychology are already operating not only with different concepts, but with different facts as well. Facts such as the Oedipus complex, indisputable and real for psychoanalysts, simply do not exist for other psychologists; for many it is wildest phantasy. For Stern [1913, p. 73], who in general relates favorably to psychoanalysis, the psychoanalytic interpretations so commonplace in Freud's school and as far beyond doubt as the measurement of one's temperature in the hospital, and consequently the facts whose existence they presuppose, resemble the chiromancy and astrology of the 16th century. For Pavlov as well, it is pure phantasy to claim that a dog remembers the food on hearing the bell. Likewise, the fact of muscular movements during the act of thinking, posited by the behaviorist, does not exist for the introspectionist.

But the fundamental concept, the primary abstraction, so to speak, that lies at the basis of a science, determines not only the content, but also predetermines the character of the unity of the different disciplines, and through this, the way to explain the facts, i.e., the main explanatory principle of the science.

We see that a general science, as well as the tendency of various disciplines to develop into a general science and to spread their influence to adjacent branches of knowledge, arise out of the need to unify heterogeneous branches of knowledge. When similar disciplines have gathered sufficient material in areas that are relatively remote from each other, the need arises to unify the heterogeneous material, to establish and define the relation between the different areas and between each area and the whole of scientific knowledge. How to connect the material from pathology, animal psychology, and social psychology? We have seen that the substrate of the unity is first of all the primary abstraction. But the heterogeneous material is not united merely by adding one kind of material to another, nor via the conjunction "and," as the Gestalt psychologists say, nor through simply joining or adding parts so that each part preserves its balance and independence while being included into the new whole. Unity is reached by subordination, dominion, through the fact that different disciplines renounce their sovereignty in favor of one single general science. The various disciplines do not simply co-exist within the new whole, but form a hierarchical system, which has primary and secondary centers, like the solar system. Thus, this unity determines the role, sense, meaning of each separate area, i.e., not only determines the content, but also the way to explain things, the most important generalization, which in the course of the development of the science becomes its explanatory principle.

To take the mind, the unconscious, or behavior as the primary concept implies not only to gather three different categories of facts, but also to offer three different ways of explaining these facts.

We see that the tendency to generalize and unite knowledge turns or grows into a tendency to explain this knowledge. The unity of the generalizing concept grows into the unity of the explanatory principle, because to explain means to establish a connection between one fact or a group of facts and another group, to refer to another series of phenomena. For science to explain means to explain causally. As long as the unification is carried out within a single discipline, such an explanation is established by the causal linkage of the phenomena that lie within a single area. But as soon as we proceed to the generalization across different disciplines, the unification of different areas of facts, the generalization of the second order, we immediately must search for an explanation of a higher order as well, i.e., we must search for the link of all areas of the given knowledge with the facts that lie outside of them. In this way the search for an explanatory principle leads us beyond the boundaries of the given science and compels us to find the place of the given area of phenomena amidst the wider circle of phenomena.

This second tendency, which is the basis of the isolation of a general science, is the tendency toward a unified explanatory principle and toward transcending the borders of the given science in the search for the place of the given category of being within the general system of being and the given science within the general system of knowledge. This tendency can already be observed in the competition of the separate disciplines for supremacy. Since the tendency of becoming an explanatory principle is already present in every generalizing concept, and since the struggle between the disciplines is a struggle for the generalizing concept, this second tendency must inevitably appear as well. And in fact, reflexology advances not only the concept of behavior, but the principle of the conditional reflex as well, i.e., an explanation of behavior on the basis of the external experience of the animal. And it is difficult to say which of these two ideas is more essential for the current in question. Throw away the principle and you will be left with behavior, that is, a system of external movements and actions, to be explained from consciousness, i.e., a conception that has existed within subjective psychology for a long time. Throw away the concept of behavior and retain the principle, and you will get sensationalist associative psychology. About both of these we will come to speak below. Here it is important to establish that the generalization of the concept and the explanatory principle determine a general science only together, as a unified pair. In exactly the same way, psychopathology does not simply advance the generalizing concept of the unconscious, but also interprets this concept causally, through the principle of sexuality. For psychoanalysis to generalize the psychological disciplines and to unite them on the basis of the concept of the unconscious means to explain the whole world, as studied by psychology, through sexuality.

But here the two tendencies—towards unification and generalization—are still merged and often difficult to distinguish. The second tendency is not sufficiently clear-cut, and may even be completely absent at times. That it coincides with the first tendency must again be explained historically rather than by logical necessity. In the struggle for supremacy among the different disciplines, this tendency usually shows up; we found it in our analysis. But it may also fail to appear and, most importantly, it may also appear in a pure form, unmixed and separate from the first tendency, in a different set of facts. In both cases we have each tendency in its pure form.

Thus, in traditional psychology the concept of the mental may be explained in many ways, although admittedly not just any explanation is possible: associationism, the actualistic conception,[4] faculty theory,[5] etc. Thus the link between generalization and unification is intimate, but not unambiguous. A single concept can be reconciled with a number of explanations and the other way around. Further, in the systems of the psychology of the unconscious this basic concept is not necessarily interpreted as sexuality. Adler and Jung[6] use other principles as the basis of their explanation. Thus in the struggle between the disciplines, the first tendency of knowledge—the tendency towards unification—is logically necessary, while the second tendency is not logically necessary but historically determined, and will be present to a varying degree. That is why the second tendency can be most easily and comfortably observed in its pure form—in the struggle between the principles and schools within one and the same discipline.

3

It can be said of any important discovery in any area, when it transcends the boundaries of that particular realm, that it has the tendency to turn into an explanatory principle for all psychological phenomena and lead psychology beyond its proper boundaries into broader realms of knowledge. In the last several decades this tendency has manifested itself with such amazing strictness and consistency, with such regular uniformity in the most diverse areas, that it becomes absolutely possible to predict the course of development of this or that concept, discovery, or idea. At the same time this regular repetition in the development of widely varying ideas evidently—and with a clarity that is seldom observed by the historian of science and methodologist—points to an objective necessity underlying the development of the science, to a necessity which we may observe when we approach the facts of science from an equally scientific point of view. It points to the possibility of a scientific methodology built on a historical foundation.

The regularity in the replacement and development of ideas, the development and downfall of concepts, even the replacement of classifications etc.—all this can be scientifically explained by the links of the science in question with (1) the general socio-cultural context of the era; (2) the general conditions and laws of scientific knowledge; (3) the objective demands upon the scientific knowledge that follow from the nature of the phenomena studied in a given stage of investigation (in the final analysis, the requirements of the objective reality that is studied by the given science). After all, scientific knowledge must adapt and conform to the particularities of the studied facts, must be built in accordance with their demands. And that is why we can always show how the objective facts studied by a certain science are involved in the change of a scientific fact. In our investigation we will try to take account of all three viewpoints.

We can sketch the general fate and lines of development of such explanatory ideas. In the beginning there is some factual discovery of more or less great significance which reforms the ordinary conception of the whole area of phenomena to which it refers, and even transcends the boundaries of the given group of phenomena within which it was first observed and formulated.

Next comes a stage during which the influence of these ideas spreads to adjacent areas. The idea is stretched out, so to speak, to material that is broader than what it originally covered. The idea itself (or its application) is changed in the process, it becomes formulated in a more abstract way. The link with the material that engendered it is more or less weakened, and it only continues to nourish the cogency of the new idea, because this idea accomplishes its campaign of conquest as a scientifically verified, reliable discovery. This is very important.

In the third stage of development the idea controls more or less the whole discipline in which it originally arose. It has partly changed the structure and size of the discipline and has itself been to some extent changed by them. It has become separated from the facts that engendered it, exists in the form of a more or less abstractly formulated principle, and becomes involved in the struggle between disciplines for supremacy, i.e., in the sphere of action of the tendency toward unification. Usually this happens because the idea, as an explanatory principle, managed to take possession of the whole discipline, i.e., it in part adapted itself, in part adjusted to itself the concept on which the discipline is based, and now acts in concert with it. In our analysis, we have found such a mixed stage in the existence of an idea, where both tendencies help each other. While it continues expanding due to the tendency toward unification, the idea is easily transferred to adjacent disciplines. Not only is it continually transformed, swelling from ever new material, but it also transforms the areas it penetrates. In this stage the fate of the idea is completely tied to the fate of the discipline it represents and which is fighting for supremacy.

In the fourth stage the idea again breaks away from the basic concept, as the very fact of the conquest—at least in the form of a project defended by a single school, the whole domain of psychological knowledge, or all disciplines—this very fact pushes the idea to develop further. The idea remains the explanatory principle until the time that it transcends the boundaries of the basic concept. For to explain, as we have seen, means to transcend one's proper boundaries in search of an external cause. As soon as it fully coincides with the basic concept, it stops explaining anything. But the basic concept cannot develop any further on logical grounds without contradicting itself. For its function is to define an area of psychological knowledge. By its very essence it cannot transcend its boundaries. Concept and explanation must, consequently, separate again. Moreover, unification logically presupposes, as was shown above, that we establish a link with a broader domain of knowledge, transcend the proper boundaries. This is accomplished by the idea that separates itself from the concept. Now it links psychology with the broad areas that lie outside of it, with biology, physics, chemistry, mechanics, while the basic concept separates it from these areas. The functions of these temporarily co-operating allies have again changed. The idea is now openly included in some philosophical system, spreads to the most remote domains of being, to the whole world—while transforming and being transformed—and is formulated as a universal principle or even as a whole world view.

This discovery, inflated into a world view like a frog that has swollen to the size of an ox, a philistine amidst the gentry, now enters the fifth and most dangerous stage of development: it may easily burst like a soap-bubble. In any case it enters a stage of struggle and negation which it now meets from all sides. Admittedly, there had been a struggle against the idea in the previous stages as well. But that was the normal opposition to the expansion of an idea, the resistance of each different area against its aggressive tendencies. The initial strength of the discovery that engendered it protected it from a genuine struggle for life just like a mother protects her young. It is only now, when the idea has entirely separated itself from the facts that engendered it, developed to its logical extremes, carried to its ultimate conclusions, generalized as far as possible, that it finally displays what it is in reality, shows its real face. However strange it may seem, it is actually only now, reduced to a philosophical form, apparently obscured by many later developments and very remote from its direct roots and the social causes that engendered it, that the idea reveals what it wants, what it is, from which social tendencies it arose, which class interests it serves. Only having developed into a world view or having become attached to it, does the particular idea change from a scientific fact into a fact of social life again, i.e., it returns to the bosom from which it came. Only having become part of social life again, does it reveal its social nature, which of course was present all the time, but was hidden under the mask of the neutral scientific fact it impersonated.

And in this stage of the struggle against the idea, its fate is approximately as follows. Just like a new nobleman, the new idea is shown in light of its philistine, i.e., its real, origin. It is confined to the areas from which it sprang. It is forced to go through its development backwards. It is accepted as a particular discovery but rejected as a world view. And now new ways are being proposed to interpret this particular discovery and the related facts. In other words, other world views which represent other social tendencies and forces even reconquer the idea's original area, develop their own view of it—and then the idea either withers away or continues to exist more or less tightly integrated in some world view amidst a number of other world views, sharing their fate and fulfilling their functions. But as an idea which revolutionizes the science it ceases to exist. It is an idea that has retired and has received the rank of general from its department.

Why does the idea as such cease to exist? Because operating in the domain of world views is a law discovered by Engels, a law that says that ideas gather around two poles—those of idealism and materialism, which correspond to the two poles of social life, the two basic classes that fight each other. The idea reveals its social nature much more readily as a philosophical fact than as a scientific fact. And this is where its role ends—it is unmasked as a hidden, ideological agent dressed up as a scientific fact and begins to participate in the general, open struggle of ideas. But exactly here, as a small item within an enormous sum, it vanishes like a drop of rain in the ocean and ceases to exist independently.

4

Every discovery in psychology that has the tendency to turn into an explanatory principle follows this course. The ascent of such ideas itself may be explained by the presence of an objective scientific need, rooted in the final analysis in the nature of the studied phenomena, as it is revealed in the given stage of knowledge. It can be explained, in other words, by the nature of the science and thus, in the final analysis by the nature of the psychological reality studied by this science. However, the history of the science can only explain why, in a given stage of its development, the need for the ideas developed, why this was impossible a hundred years before. It cannot explain more. Exactly which ideas turn into world views and which not; which ideas are advanced, which path they cover; what is their fate—this all depends upon factors that lie outside the history of the science and determine this very history.

We may compare this with Plekhanov's (1922) theory of art. Nature has provided man with an aesthetic need, it enables him to have aesthetic ideas, tastes, and feelings. But precisely which tastes, ideas, and feelings a given person in the society of a given historical period will have cannot be deduced from man's nature;

only a materialistic conception of history can give the answer. Actually, this argument is not even a comparison, nor is it a metaphor. It literally falls under the same general law which Plekhanov specifically applied to matters of art. Indeed, the scientific acquisition of knowledge is one type of activity of societal man amongst a number of other activities. Consequently, scientific knowledge acquisition, viewed as the acquisition of knowledge about nature and not as ideology, is a certain type of labor. And as with any labor, it is first of all a process between man and nature, in which man himself confronts nature as a natural force. This process is determined in the first place by the properties of the nature which is being transformed and the properties of the natural force which is transforming, i.e., in the present case, by the nature of the psychological phenomena and the epistemic conditions of man. [4] But precisely because they are natural, i.e., immutable, these properties cannot explain the development, movement, and change in the history of a science. This is generally known. Nevertheless, in each stage of the development of a science we may distinguish, differentiate, or abstract the demands put forward by the very nature of the phenomena under investigation as they are known in the given stage, a stage determined, of course, not by the nature of the phenomena, but by the history of man. Precisely because the natural properties of mental phenomena at a certain level of knowledge are a purely historical category—for the properties change in the process of knowledge acquisition—and because the sum total of known properties is a purely historical quantity, they can be considered as the cause or one of the causes of the historical development of the science.

To illustrate the model for the development of general ideas in psychology just described, we will examine the fate of four ideas which have been influential in the last few decades. In doing so our sole interest will be the fact that made the development of these ideas possible, rather than the ideas in themselves, i.e., a fact rooted in the history of the science, not outside of it. We will not investigate why it is precisely these ideas and their history that is important as a symptom or indication of the stage that the history of the science is going through. At the moment we are interested not in a historical but a methodological question: to what extent are the psychological facts elicited and known at the moment, and what changes in the structure of the science do they require in order to make possible the further acquisition of knowledge on the basis of what is already known? The fate of the four ideas must bear witness to the need of the science at the present moment, to the content and dimensions of this need. The history of the science is important for us insofar as it determines the degree to which psychological facts are cognized.

These four ideas are: psychoanalysis, reflexology, Gestalt psychology, and personalism.[7]

The idea of psychoanalysis sprang from particular discoveries in the area of neuroses. The unconscious determination of a number of mental phenomena and the hidden sexuality of a number of activities and forms, until then not included in the field of erotic phenomena, were established beyond doubt. Gradually this discovery, corroborated by the success of therapeutic measures based on this conception, i.e., sanctioned by practice, was transferred to a number of adjacent areas—the psychopathology of everyday life and child psychology—and it conquered the whole field of the theory of neuroses. In the struggle between the disciplines this idea brought the most remote branches of psychology under its sway. It has been shown that on the basis of this idea a psychology of art and an ethnic psychology can be developed. [5] But psychoanalysis at the same time transcended the boundaries of psychology: sexuality became a metaphysical principle amidst all other metaphysical ideas, psychoanalysis became a world view, psychology a metapsychology. Psychoanalysis has its own theory of knowledge and its own metaphysics, its own sociology and mathematics. Communism and totem,[8] the church and Dostoyevsky's creative work, occultism and advertising, myth and Leonardo da Vinci's[9] inventions—it is all disguised and masked sex and sexuality, and that is all there is to it.

The idea of the conditional reflex followed a similar course. Everybody knows that it originated in the study of mental salivation in dogs. But then it was extended to a number of other phenomena as well. It conquered animal psychology. In Bekhterev's system it is applied and used in all domains of psychology and reigns over them. Everything—sleep, thought, work, and creativity—turns out to be a reflex. It ended up dominating all psychological disciplines: the collective psychology of art, industrial psychology and pedology, psychopathology, even subjective psychology. And at the moment reflexology only rubs shoulders with universal principles, universal laws, first principles of mechanics. Just as psychoanalysis grew into a metapsychology via biology, reflexology via biology grows into a world view based on energy. The table of contents of a textbook in reflexology is a universal catalogue of global laws. And again, just as with psychoanalysis, it turned out that everything in the world is a reflex. Anna Karenina and kleptomania, the class struggle and a landscape, language and dream are all reflexes (Bekhterev, 1921; 1923).

Gestalt psychology also originally arose in the concrete psychological investigation of the processes of form perception. There it received its practical christening; it passed the truth test. But, as it was born at the same time as psychoanalysis and reflexology, it covered the same path with amazing uniformity. It conquered animal psychology, and it turned out that the thinking of apes is also a Gestalt process. It conquered the psychology of art and ethnic psychology, and it turned out that the primitive conception of the world and the creation of art are Gestalten as well. It conquered child psychology and psychopathology and both child development and mental disease were covered by the Gestalt. Finally, having turned into a world view, Gestalt psychology discovered the Gestalt in physics and chemistry, in physiology and biology, and the Gestalt, withered to a logical formula, appeared to be the basis of the world. When God created the world he said: let there be Gestalt—and there was Gestalt everywhere (Koffka, 1925; Köhler, 1917, 1920; Wertheimer, 1925).

Finally, personalism originally arose in differential psychological research.[10] Being an exceptionally valuable principle of personality in the theory of psychometrics and in the theory of occupational choice, etc., it migrated first to psychology in its entirety and then crossed its boundaries. In the form of critical personalism it extended the concept of personality not only to man, but to animals and plants as well. One more step, well known to us from the history of psychoanalysis and reflexology, and everything in the world is personality. The philosophy which began by contrasting the personality with the thing, by rescuing the personality from the power of things, ended up by accepting all things as personalities. The things disappeared altogether. A thing is only a part of the personality: it does not matter whether we are dealing with the leg of a person or the leg of a table. But as this part again consists of parts etc. and so on to infinity, it—the leg of a person or a table—again turns out to be a personality in relation to its parts and a part only in relation to the whole. The solar system and the ant, the tram-driver and Hindenburg, a table and a panther—they are all personalities (stern, 1924).

These fates, similar as four drops of the same rain, drag the ideas along one and the same path. The extension of the concept grows and reaches for infinity and according to the well-known logical law, its content falls just as impetuously to zero. Each of these four ideas is extremely rich, full of meaning and sense, full of value and fruitful in its own place. But elevated to the rank of universal laws, they are worthy of each other, they are absolutely equal to each other, like round and empty zeros. Stern's personality is a complex of reflexes according to Bekhterev, a Gestalt according to Wertheimer, sexuality according to Freud.

And in the fifth stage of development these ideas meet with exactly the same criticism, which can be reduced to a single formula. To psychoanalysis it is said: the principle of unconscious sexuality is indispensable for the explanation of hysterical neuroses, but it can explain neither the composition of the world nor the course of history. To reflexology it is said: we must not make a logical mistake, the reflex is only one single chapter of psychology, but not psychology as a whole and even less, of course, the world in its entirety (Vagner, 1923; Vygotsky, 1925a). To Gestalt psychology it is said: you have found a very valuable principle in your own area. But if thinking consists of no more than the aspects of unity and the integrated whole, i.e., of no more than the Gestalt formula, and this same formula expresses the essence of each organic and even physical process, then the picture of the world becomes, of course, amazingly complete and simple—electricity, gravity, and human thinking are reduced to a common denominator. We must not throw both thinking and relation into one single pot of structures: let it first be shown that it belongs in the same pot as structural functions [*Strukturfunktionen*]. The new factor guides a broad though limited area. But as a universal principle it does not stand up to critique. Let the thinking of bold theoreticians in their attempts to explain be characterized by the motto "it's all or nothing." But as a sound counterpoise the cautious investigator should take account of the stubborn opposition of the facts. After all, to try and explain everything means to explain nothing.

Doesn't this tendency of each new idea in psychology to turn into a universal law show that psychology really should rest upon universal laws, that all these ideas wait for a master-idea which comes and puts each different, particular idea in its place and indicates its importance? The regularity of the path covered with amazing constancy by the most diverse ideas testifies, of course, to the fact that this path is predetermined by the objective need for an explanatory principle and it is precisely because such a principle is needed and not available that various special principles occupy its place. Psychology, realizing that it is a matter of life or death to find a general explanatory principle, grabs for any idea, albeit an unreliable one.

Spinoza [1677/1955, p. 5] in his "Treatise on the improvement of the understanding" describes a similar state of knowledge:

> A sick man struggling with a deadly disease, when he sees that death will surely be upon him unless a remedy is found, is compelled to seek such a remedy with all his strength, inasmuch as his whole hope lies therein.

5

We have traced a distinct tendency towards explanation—which already took shape in the struggle between disciplines for supremacy—in the development of particular discoveries into general principles. But in so doing we already proceeded to the second phase of development of a general science which we have mentioned in passing above. In the first phase, which is determined by the tendency towards generalization, the general science is at bottom quantitatively different from the special ones. In the second phase—the phase in which the tendency towards explanation predominates—the internal structure of the general science is already qualitatively distinct from the special disciplines. Not all sciences, as we will see, go through both phases in their development. The majority knows only a general science in its first phase. The reason for this will become clear as soon as we carefully state the qualitative difference of the second phase.

We have seen that the explanatory principle carries us beyond the boundaries of a given science and must interpret the whole unified area of knowledge as a special category or stage of being amidst a number of other categories, i.e., at stake are highly generalized, ultimate, essentially philosophical principles. In this sense the general science is the philosophy of the special disciplines.

In this sense Binswanger [1922, p. 3] says that a general science such as, for example, general biology elaborates the foundations and problems of a whole area of being. Interestingly, the first book that lay the foundation of general biology was called "The philosophy of zoology" (Lamarck[11]). The further a general investigation penetrates, continues Binswanger, the larger the area it covers, the more abstract and more remote from directly perceived reality the subject matter of such an investigation will become. Instead of living plants, animals, persons, the subject matter of science becomes the manifestations of life and, finally, life itself, just as in physics force and matter replaced bodies and their changes. Sooner or later for each science the moment comes when it must accept itself as a whole, reflect upon its methods and shift the attention from the facts and phenomena to the concepts it utilizes. But from this moment on the general science is distinct from the special one not because it is broader in scope, but because it is organized in a qualitatively different way. No longer does it study the same objects as the special science; rather, it investigates the concepts of this science. It becomes a critical study in the sense Kant used this expression. No longer being a biological or physical investigation, the critical investigation is concerned with the concepts of biology or physics. Consequently, general psychology is defined by Binswanger as a critical reflection upon the basic concepts of psychology, in short, as "a critique of psychology." It is a branch of general methodology, i.e., of the part of logic that studies the different applications of logical forms and norms in the various sciences in accordance with the formal and material reality of the nature of their objects, their procedures, and their problems. [6]

This argumentation, based on formal logical premises, is only half true. It is correct that the general science is a theory of ultimate foundations, of the general principles and problems of a given area of knowledge, and that consequently its subject matter, methods of investigation, criteria and tasks are different from those in the special disciplines. But it is incorrect to view it as merely a part of logic, as merely a logical discipline, as if general biology is no longer a biological discipline but a logical one, as if general psychology stops being psychology but becomes logic. It is incorrect to view it as merely critique in the Kantian sense, to assume that it only studies concepts. It is first of all incorrect historically, but also according to the essence of the matter and the inner nature of scientific knowledge.

It is incorrect historically, i.e., it does not correspond with the actual state of affairs in any science. There does not exist a single general science in the form described by Binswanger. Not even general biology in the form in which it actually exists, the biology whose foundations were laid by the works of Lamarck and Darwin, the biology which is until now the canon of genuine knowledge of living matter, is, of course, part of logic, but a natural science, albeit of the highest level. Of course, it does not deal with living, concrete objects such as plants and animals, but with abstractions such as organism, evolution of species, natural selection and life, but in the final analysis it nevertheless studies by means of these abstractions the same reality as zoology and botany. It would be as much a mistake to say that it studies concepts and not the reality reflected in these concepts, as it would to say of an engineer who is studying a blueprint of a machine that he is studying a blueprint and not a machine, or of an anatomist studying an atlas that he studies a drawing and not the human skeleton. For concepts as well are no more than blueprints, snapshots, schemas of reality and in studying them we study models of reality, just as we study a foreign country or city on the plan or geographical map.

When it comes to such well-developed sciences as physics and chemistry, Binswanger [1922, p. 4] himself is compelled to admit that a broad field of investigations developed in between the critical and empirical poles and that this area is called theoretical, or general, physics, chemistry, etc. He remarks that natural-scientific theoretical psychology, which in principle wishes to be like physics, acts likewise. However abstractly theoretical physics may formulate its subject of study, for example as "the theory of causal dependencies between natural phenomena," it nevertheless studies real facts. General physics studies the concept of the physical phenomenon itself, of the physical causal link, but not the various laws and theories on the basis of which the real phenomena may be explained as physically causal. The subject matter of investigation of general physics is rather the physical explanation itself.

As we see, Binswanger himself admits that his conception of the general science diverges in one point from the actual conception as it is realized in a number of sciences. They are not differentiated by a greater or lesser degree of abstraction of the concepts—what can be further from the real, empirical things than causal dependency as the subject matter of a whole science?—but by their ultimate focus: general physics, in the end, focuses on real facts which it wishes to explain by means of abstract concepts. The general science is in principle not focused on real facts, but on the concepts themselves and has nothing to do with the real facts.

Admittedly, when a debate between theory and history arises, when there is a discrepancy between the idea and the fact, as in the present case, the debate is always solved in favor of history or fact. The argument from the facts may itself not always be appropriate in the area of fundamental research. Then to the reproach that the ideas and facts do not correspond we are fully justified to answer: so much the worse for the facts. In the present case, so much the worse for the sciences when they find themselves in a phase of development in which they have not yet attained the stage of a general science. When a general science in this sense does not yet exist, it does not follow that it will never exist, that it should not exist, that we cannot and must not lay its foundations. We must therefore examine the essence, the logical basis of the problem, and then it will also become possible to clarify the meaning of the historical deviation of the general science from its abstract idea.

It is important to make two points.

1. Every natural-scientific concept, however high the degree of its abstraction from the empirical fact, always contains a clot, a sediment of the concrete, real and scientifically known reality, albeit in a very weak solution, i.e., to every ultimate concept, even to the most abstract, corresponds some aspect of reality which the concept represents in an abstract, isolated form. Even purely fictitious, not natural-scientific but mathematical concepts ultimately contain some echo, some reflection of the real relations between things and the real processes, although they did not develop from empirical, actual knowledge, but purely a priori, via the deductive path of speculative logical operations. As Engels demonstrated, even such an abstract concept as the series of numbers, or even such an obvious fiction as zero, i.e., the idea of the absence of any magnitude, is full of properties that are qualitative, i.e., in the end they correspond in a very remote and dissolved form to real, actual relations. Reality exists even in the imaginary abstractions of mathematics.

> 16 is not only the addition of 16 unities, it is also the square of 4 and the biquadrate of 2 . . . . Only even numbers can be divided by two . . . . For division by 3 we have the rule of the sum of the figures . . . . For 7 there is a special law . . . . Zero destroys any other number by which it is multiplied; when it is made divisor or dividend with regard to some other number, this number will in the first case become infinitely large, in the second case infinitely small [Engels, 1925/1978, pp. 522/524].

About both concepts of mathematics one might say what Engels, in the words of Hegel, says about zero: "The non-existence of something is a *specific* non-existence" [ibid., p. 525], i.e., in the end it is a real non-existence. [7] But maybe these qualities, properties, the *specificity* of concepts as such, have no relation whatsoever to reality?

Engels [ibid., p. 530] clearly rejects the view that in mathematics we are dealing with purely free creations and imaginations of the human mind to which nothing in the objective world corresponds. Just the opposite is the case. We meet the prototypes of each of these imaginary quantities in nature. The molecule possesses exactly the same properties in relation to its corresponding mass as the mathematical differential in relation to its variable.

> Nature operates with these differentials, the molecules, in exactly the same way and according to the same laws as mathematics with its abstract differentials [ibid., p. 531].

In mathematics we forget all these analogies and that is why its abstractions turn into something enigmatic. We can always find

> the real relations from which the mathematical relation . . . was taken . . . and even the natural analogues of the mathematical way to make these relations manifest [ibid., p. 534].

The prototypes of mathematical infinity and other concepts lie in the real world.

> The mathematical infinite is taken, albeit unconsciously, from reality, and that is why it can only be explained on the basis of reality, and not on the basis of itself, the mathematical abstraction (ibid., p. 534).

If this is true with respect to the highest possible, i.e., mathematical abstraction, then how much more obvious it is for the abstractions of the real natural sciences. They must, of course, be explained only on the basis of the reality from which they stem and not on the basis of themselves, the abstraction.

2. The second point that we need to make in order to present a fundamental analysis of the problem of the general science is the opposite of the first. Whereas the first claimed that the highest scientific abstraction contains an element of reality, the second is the opposite theorem: even the most immediate, empirical, raw, singular natural scientific fact already contains a first abstraction. The real and the scientific fact are distinct in that the scientific fact is a real fact included into a certain system of knowledge, i.e., an abstraction of several features from the inexhaustible sum of features of the natural fact. The material of science is not raw, but logically elaborated, natural material which has been selected according to a certain feature. Physical body, movement, matter—these are all abstractions. The fact itself of naming a fact by a word means to frame this fact in a concept, to single out one of its aspects; it is an act toward understanding this fact by including it into a category of phenomena which have been empirically studied before. Each word already is a theory, as linguists have noted for quite some time and as Potebnya [1913/1993] has brilliantly demonstrated. [8]

Everything described as a fact is already a theory. These are the words of Goethe to which Münsterberg refers in arguing the need for a methodology. [9] When we meet what is called a cow and say: "This is a cow," we add the act of thinking to the act of perception, bringing the given perception under a general concept. A child who first calls things by their names is making genuine discoveries. I do not see that this is a cow, for this cannot be seen. I see something big, black, moving, lowing, etc., and understand that this is a cow. And this act is an act of classification, of assigning a singular phenomenon to the class of similar phenomena, of systematizing the experience, etc. Thus, language itself contains the basis and possibilities for the scientific knowledge of a fact. The word is the germ of science and in this sense we can say that in the beginning of science was the word.

Who has seen, who has perceived such empirical facts as the heat itself in steam-generation? It cannot be perceived in a single real process, but we can infer this fact with confidence and to infer means to operate with concepts.

In Engels we find a good example of the presence of abstractions and the participation of thought in every scientific fact. Ants have other eyes than we have. They see chemical beams that are invisible to us. [10] This is a fact. How was it established? How can we know that "ants see things that are invisible to us"? Naturally, this is based on the perceptions of our eye, but in addition to that we have not only the other senses but the activity of our thinking as well. Thus, establishing a scientific fact is already a matter of thinking, that is, of concepts.

> To be sure, we will never know *how* these chemical beams look to the ants. Who deplores this is beyond help [Engels, 1925/1978, p. 507]. [11]

This is the best example of the non-coincidence of the real and the scientific fact. Here this non-coincidence is presented in an especially vivid way, but it exists to a certain degree in each fact. We never saw these chemical beams and did not perceive the sensations of ants, i.e., that ants see certain chemical beams is not a real fact of immediate experience for us, but for the collective experience of mankind it is a scientific fact. But what to say, then, about the fact that the earth turns around the sun? For here in the thinking of man the real fact, in order to become a scientific fact, had to turn into its opposite, although the earth's rotation around the sun was established by observations of the sun's rotations around the earth.

By now we are equipped with all we need to solve this problem and we can go straight for the goal. If at the root of every scientific concept lies a fact and, vice versa, at the basis of every scientific fact lies a concept, then from this it inevitably follows that the difference between general and empirical sciences as regards the object of investigation is purely quantitative and not fundamental. It is a difference of degree and not a difference of the nature of the phenomenon. The general sciences do not deal with real objects, but with abstractions. They do not study plants and animals, but life. Their subject matter is scientific concepts. But life as well is part of reality and these concepts have their prototypes in reality. The special sciences have the actual facts of reality as their subject matter, they do not study life as such, but actual classes and groups of plants and animals. But both the plant and the animal, and even the birch tree and the tiger, and even *this* birch tree and *this* tiger are already concepts. And scientific facts as well, even the most primitive ones, are already concepts. Fact and concept form the subject matter of all disciplines, but to a different degree, in different proportion. Consequently, general physics does not cease being a physical discipline and does not become part of logic because it deals with the most abstract physical concepts. Ultimately, even these serve to know some part of reality.

But perhaps the nature of the objects of the general and the special disciplines is really the same, maybe they differ only in the proportion of concept and fact, and the fundamental difference which allows us to count the one as logic and the other as physics lies in the direction, the goal, the point of view of both investigations, so to speak, in the different role played by the same elements in both cases?

Could we perhaps put it like this: both concept and fact participate in the development of the subject matter of any science, but in one case—the case of empirical science—we utilize concepts to acquire knowledge about facts, and in the second— general science—we utilize facts to acquire knowledge about concepts? In the first case the concepts are not the subject matter, the goal, the objective of knowledge, but its tools, means, auxiliary devices. The goal, the subject matter of knowledge are the facts. As a result of the growth of knowledge the number of known facts is enhanced, but not the number of concepts. Like any tool of labor the concepts, in contrast, suffer wear and tear in their use, become worn down, in need of revision and often of replacement. In the second case it is the other way around; we study the concepts themselves as such, their correspondence with the facts is only a means, a way, a method, a verification of their suitability. As a result we do not learn of new facts, but acquire either new concepts or new knowledge about the concepts. After all, we can look twice at a drop of water under the microscope and this will be two completely distinct processes, although both the drop and the microscope will be the same both times: the first time we study the composition of the drop of water by means of the microscope; the second time we verify the suitability of the microscope itself by looking at a drop of water—isn't it like that?

But the whole difficulty of the problem is exactly that it is not like that. It is true that in a special science we utilize concepts as tools to acquire knowledge of facts. But using tools means at the same time to test them, to study and master them, to throw away the ones that are unfit, to improve them, to create new ones. Already in the very first stage of the scientific processing of empirical material the use of a concept is a critique of the concept by the facts, the comparison of concepts, their modification. Let us take as an example the two scientific facts mentioned above, which definitely do not belong to general science: the earth's rotation around the sun and the vision of ants. How much critical work on our perceptions and, thus, on the concepts linked with them, how much direct study of these concepts—visibility, invisibility, apparent movement—how much creation of new concepts, of new links between concepts, how much modification of the very concepts of vision, light, movement etc. was needed to establish these facts! And, finally, does not the very selection of the concepts needed to know these facts require an analysis of the concepts in addition to the analysis of the facts? After all, if concepts, as tools, were set aside for particular facts of experience in advance, all science would be superfluous: then a thousand administrator-registrators or statistician-counters could note down the universe on cards, graphs, columns. Scientific knowledge differs from the registration of a fact in that it selects the concept needed, i.e., it analyzes both fact and concept.

Any word is a theory. To name an object is to apply a concept to it. Admittedly, by means of the word we wish to comprehend the object. But each name, each application of the word, this embryo of science, is a critique of the word, a blurring of its form, an extension of its meaning. Linguists have clearly enough demonstrated how words change from being used. After all, language otherwise would never be renewed, words would not die, be born, or become obsolete.

Finally, each discovery in science, each step forward in empirical science is always at the same time an act of criticizing the concept. Pavlov discovered the fact of conditional reflexes. But didn't he really create a new concept at the same time? Did we really call a trained, well-learned movement a reflex before? And it cannot be otherwise: if science would only discover facts without extending the boundaries of its concepts, it would not discover anything new. It would make no headway in finding more and more new specimens of the same concepts. Each tiny new fact is already an extension of the concept. Each newly discovered relation between two facts immediately requires a critique of the two corresponding concepts and the establishment of a new relation between them. The conditional reflex is a discovery of a new fact by means of an old concept. We learned that mental salivation develops directly from the reflex, more correctly, that it is the same reflex, but operating under other conditions. But at the same time it is a discovery of a new concept by means of an old fact: by means of the fact "salivation occurs at the sight of food," which is well known to all of us, we acquired a completely new concept of the reflex, our idea of it diametrically changed. Whereas before, the reflex was a synonym for a pre-mental, unconscious, immutable fact, nowadays the whole mind is reduced to reflexes, the reflex has turned out to be a most flexible mechanism, etc. How would this have been possible if Pavlov had only studied the fact of salivation and not the concept of the reflex? This is essentially the same thing expressed in two ways, for in each scientific discovery knowledge of the fact is to the same extent knowledge of the concept. The scientific investigation of facts differs from registration in that it is the accumulation of concepts, the circulation of concepts and facts with a conceptual return.

Finally, the special sciences create all the concepts that the general science studies. For the natural sciences do not spring from logic, it is not logic that provides them with ready-made concepts. Can we really assume that the creation of ever more abstract concepts proceeds completely unconsciously? How can theories, laws, conflicting hypotheses exist without the critique of concepts? How can we create a theory or advance a hypothesis, i.e., something which transcends the boundaries of the facts, without working on the concepts?

But perhaps the study of concepts in the special sciences proceeds in passing, accidentally as the facts are being studied, whereas the general science studies only concepts? This would not be correct either. We have seen that the abstract concepts with which the general science operates possess a kernel of reality. The question arises what science does with this kernel—is it ignored, forgotten, covered in the inaccessible stronghold of abstractions like pure mathematics? Does one never in the process of investigation, nor after it, turn to this kernel, as if it did not exist at all? One only has to examine the method of investigation in the general science and its ultimate result to see that this is not true. Are concepts really studied by pure deduction, by finding logical relations between concepts, and not by new induction, by new analysis, the establishing of new relations, in a word—by work on the real contents of these concepts? After all, we do not develop our ideas from specific premises, as in mathematics, but we proceed by induction—we generalize enormous groups of facts, compare them, analyze and create new abstractions. This is the way general biology and general physics proceed. And not a single general science can proceed otherwise, since the logical formula "A is B" has been replaced by a definition, i.e., by the real A and B: by mass, movement, body, and organism. And the result of an investigation in a general science is not new forms of inter-relations of concepts, as in logic, but new facts: we learn of evolution, heredity, inertia. How do we learn of this, how do we reach the concept of evolution? We compare such facts as the data of comparative anatomy and physiology, botany and zoology, embryology and photo- and zootechnics etc., i.e., we proceed as we proceed with the individual facts in a special science. And on the basis of a new study of the facts elaborated by the various sciences we establish new facts, i.e., in the process of investigation and in its result we are constantly operating with facts.

Thus, the difference between the general and the special science as concerns their goal, orientation, and the elaboration of concepts and facts, again appears to be only quantitative. It is a difference of degree of one and the same phenomenon and not of the nature of two sciences. It is not absolute or fundamental.

Finally, let us proceed to a positive definition of the general science. It might seem that if the difference between general and special science as to their subject matter, method, and goal of study is merely relative and not absolute, quantitative and not fundamental, we lose any ground to distinguish them theoretically. It might seem that there is no general science at all as distinct from the special sciences. But this is not true, of course. Quantity turns into quality here and provides the basis for a qualitatively distinct science. However the latter is not torn away from the given family of sciences and transferred to logic. The fact that at the root of every scientific concept lies a fact does not mean that the fact is represented in every scientific concept in the same way. In the mathematical concept of infinity reality is represented in a way completely different from the way it is represented in the concept of the conditional reflex. In the concepts of a higher order with which the general science is dealing, reality is represented in another way than in the concepts of an empirical science. And the way, character, and form in which reality is represented in the various sciences in every case determines the structure of every discipline.

But this difference in the way of representing reality, i.e., in the structure of the concepts, should not be understood as something absolute either. There are many transitional levels between an empirical science and a general one. Binswanger [1922, p. 4] says that not a single science that deserves the name can "leave it at the simple accumulation of concepts, it strives rather to systematically develop concepts into rules, rules into laws, laws into theories." The elaboration of concepts, methods, and theories takes place within the science itself during the whole course of scientific knowledge acquisition, i.e., the transition from one pole to the other, from fact to concept, is accomplished without pausing for a single minute. And thereby the logical abyss, the impassable line between general and special science is erased, whereas the factual independence and necessity of a general science is created. Just like the special science itself internally takes care of all the work of funneling facts via rules into laws and laws via theories into hypotheses, general science carries out the same work, by the same method, with the same goals, but for a number of the various special sciences.

This is entirely similar to Spinoza's argumentation about method. A theory of method is, of course, the production of means of production, to take a comparison from the field of industry. But in industry the production of means of production is no special, primordial production, but forms part of the general process of production and itself depends upon the same methods and tools of production as all other production.

Spinoza [1677/1955, pp. 11-12] argues that

> We must first take care not to commit ourselves to a search going back to infinity, that is, in order to discover the best method for finding the truth, there is no need of another method to discover such method; nor of a third method for discovering the second, and so on to infinity. By such proceedings, we should never arrive at the knowledge of the truth, or, indeed, at any knowledge at all. The matter stands on the same footing as the making of material tools, which might be argued about in a similar way. For, in order to work iron, a hammer is needed, and the hammer cannot be forthcoming unless it has been made; but in order to make it, there was need of another hammer and other tools, and so on to infinity. We might thus vainly endeavor to prove that men have no power of working iron. But as men at first made use of the instruments supplied by nature to accomplish very easy pieces of workmanship, laboriously and imperfectly, and then, when these were finished, wrought other things more difficult with less labor and greater perfection; and so gradually mounted from the simplest operations to the making of tools, and from the making of tools to the making of more complex tools, and fresh feats of workmanship, till they arrived at making, with small expenditure of labor, the vast number of complicated mechanisms

which they now possess. So, in like manner, the intellect, by its native strength, makes
for itself intellectual instruments, whereby it acquires strength for performing other
intellectual operations, and from these operations gets again fresh instruments, or the
power of pushing its investigations further, and thus gradually proceeds till it reaches
the summit of wisdom.

The methodological current to which Binswanger belongs also admits that the
production of tools and that of creative work are, in principle, not two separate
processes in science, but two sides of the same process which go hand in hand.
Following Rickert, he defines each science as the processing [Bearbeitung] of material, and therefore for him two problems arise in every science—one with respect
to the material and the other concerning its processing. One cannot, however, draw
such a sharp dividing line, since the concept of the object of the empirical science
already contains a good deal of processing. And he (Binswanger, 1922, pp. 7-8)
distinguishes between the raw material, the real object [wirklichen Gegenstand] and
the scientific object [wissenschaftlichen Gegenstand]. The latter is created by science
from the real object via concepts. When we raise a third cluster of problems—about
the relation between the material and its processing, i.e., between the object and
the method of science—the debate must again focus on what is determined by what:
the object by the method, or vice versa. Some, like Stumpf, suppose that all differences in method are rooted in differences between the objects. Others, like Rickert, are of the opinion that various objects, both physical and mental, require one
and the same method. [12] But, as we see, we do not find grounds for a demarcation
of the general from the special science here either.

All this only indicates that we can give no absolute definition of the concept
of a general science and that it can only be defined relative to the special science.
From the latter it is distinguished not by its object, nor by the method, goal, or
result of the investigation. But for a number of special sciences which study related
realms of reality from a single viewpoint it accomplishes the same work and by the
same method and with the same goal as each of these sciences accomplish for their
own material. We have seen that no science confines itself to the simple accumulation of material, but rather that it subjects this material to diverse and prolonged
processing, that it groups and generalizes the material, creates a theory and hypotheses which help to get a wider perspective on reality than the one which follows
from the various uncoordinated facts. The general science continues the work of
the special sciences. When the material is carried to the highest degree of generalization possible in that science, further generalization is possible only beyond the
boundaries of the given science and by comparing it with the material of a number
of adjacent sciences. This is what the general science does. Its single difference
from the special sciences is that it carries out its work with respect to a number
of sciences. If it carried out the same work with respect to a single science it would
never come to the fore as an independent science, but would remain a part of that
single science. The general science can therefore be defined as a science that receives its material from a number of special sciences and carries out the further
processing and generalization of the material which is impossible within each of
the various disciplines.

The general science therefore stands to the special one as the theory of this
special science to the number of its special laws, i.e., according to the degree of
generalization of the phenomena studied. The general science develops out of the
need to continue the work of the special sciences where these end. The general
science stands to the theories, laws, hypotheses and methods of the special sciences
as the special science stands to the facts of the reality it studies. Biology receives
material from various sciences and processes it in the way each special science does

with its own material. The whole difference is that [general] biology begins where embryology, zoology, anatomy etc. stop, that it unites the material of the various sciences, just as a [special] science unites various materials within its own field.

This viewpoint can fully explain both the logical structure of the general science and the factual, historical role of the general science. If we accept the opposite opinion that the general science is part of logic, it becomes completely inexplicable why it is the highly developed sciences, which already managed to create and elaborate very refined methods, basic concepts and theories, which produce a general science. It would seem that new, young, beginning disciplines are more in need of borrowing concepts and methods from another science. Secondly, why does only a group of adjacent disciplines lead to a general science and not each science on its own—why do botany, zoology and anthropology lead to biology? Couldn't we create a logic of just zoology and just botany, like the logic of algebra? And indeed such separate disciplines can exist and do exist, but this does not make them general sciences, just as the methodology of botany does not become biology.

Like the whole current, Binswanger proceeds from an idealistic conception of scientific knowledge, i.e., from idealistic epistemic premises and a formal logical construction of the system of sciences. For Binswanger, concepts and real objects are separated by an unbridgeable gap. Knowledge has its own laws, its own nature, its *a priori*, which it projects unto the reality that is known. That is why for Binswanger these *a priori*, these laws, this knowledge, can be studied separately, in isolation from what is cognized by them. For him a critique of scientific reason in biology, psychology, and physics is possible, just like the critique of pure reason was possible for Kant. Binswanger is prepared to admit that the method of knowing determines reality, just as in Kant reason dictated the laws of nature. For him the relations between sciences are not determined by the historical development of these sciences and not even by the demands of scientific experience, i.e., in the final analysis they are not determined by the demands of the reality studied by this science, but by the formal logical structure of the concepts.

In another philosophical system such a conception would be unthinkable, i.e., when we reject these epistemological and formal logical premises, the whole conception of the general science falls immediately. As soon as we accept the realistic, objective, i.e., the materialistic viewpoint in epistemology and the dialectical viewpoint in logic and in the theory of scientific knowledge, such a theory becomes impossible. With that new viewpoint we must immediately accept that reality determines our experience, the object of science and its method and that it is entirely impossible to study the concepts of any science independent of the realities it represents.

Engels [1925/1978, p. 514] has pointed out many times that for dialectical logic the methodology of science is a reflection of the methodology of reality. He says that

> The classification of sciences of which each analyzes a different form of movement, or a number of movements that are connected and merge into each other, is at the same time a classification, an ordering according to the inherent order of these forms of movement themselves and in this resides their importance.

Can it be said more clearly? In classifying the sciences we establish the hierarchy of reality itself.

> The so-called *objective* dialectic reigns in all nature, and the so-called subjective dialectic, dialectical thinking, is only a reflection of the movement by opposition, that reigns in all nature [ibid., p. 481].

Here the demand to take account of the objective dialectic in studying the subjective dialectic, i.e., dialectical thinking in some science, is clearly expressed. Of course, by no means does this imply that we close our eyes to the subjective conditions of this thinking. The same Engels who established a correspondence between being and thinking in mathematics says that "all laws of number are dependent upon and determined by the system that is used. In the binary and ternary system 2×2 does not $= 4$, but $= 100$ or $= 11$" [ibid., p. 523]. Extending this, we might say that subjective assumptions which follow from knowledge will always influence the way of expressing the laws of nature and the relation between the different concepts. We must take them into account, but always as a reflection of the objective dialectic.

We must, therefore, contrast epistemological critique and formal logic as the foundations of a general science with a dialectic "which is conceived of as the science of the most general laws of *all* movement. This implies that its laws must be valid for both movement in nature and human history and movement in thinking" [ibid., p. 530]. This means that the dialectic of psychology—this is what we may now call the general psychology in opposition to Binswanger's definition of a "critique of psychology"—is the science of the most general forms of movement (in the form of behavior and knowledge of this movement), i.e., the dialectic of psychology is at the same time the dialectic of man as the object of psychology, just as the dialectic of the natural sciences is at the same time the dialectic of nature.

Engels does not even consider the purely logical classification of judgments in Hegel to be based merely on thinking, but on the laws of nature. This he regards as a distinguishing characteristic of dialectical logic.

> What in Hegel seems a development of the judgment as a category of thinking as such, now appears to be a development of our knowledge of the nature of movement based on *empirical* grounds. And this proves that the laws of thinking and the laws of nature correspond necessarily with each other as soon as they are known properly [ibid., p. 493].

The key to general psychology as a part of dialectics lies in these words: this correspondence between thinking and being in science is at the same time object, highest criterion, and even method, i.e., general principle of the general psychology.

6

General psychology stands to the special disciplines as algebra to arithmetic. Arithmetic operates with specific, concrete quantities; algebra studies all kinds of general forms of relations between qualities. Every arithmetical operation can, consequently, be considered as a special case of an algebraic formula. From this it obviously follows that for each special discipline and for each of its laws the question as to which general formula they form a special case of is not at all indifferent. The general science's fundamentally guiding and supreme role, so to speak, does not follow from the fact that it stands above the sciences, it does not come from above, from logic, i.e., from the ultimate foundations of scientific knowledge, but from below, from the sciences themselves which delegate the authorization of truth to the general science. The general science, consequently, develops from the special position it occupies with regard to the special ones: it integrates their sovereignties, forms their representative. If we graphically represent the system of knowledge which covers all psychological disciplines as a circle, general science will correspond to the center of the circumference.

Now let us suppose that we have various centers as in the case of a debate between separate disciplines that aspire to become the center, or in the case of different ideas claiming to be the central explanatory principle. It is obvious that to these will correspond different circumferences and each new center will at the same time be a peripheral point on the former circumference. Consequently, we get several circumferences that intersect with each other. In our example this new position of each circumference graphically represents the special area of knowledge that is covered by psychology depending on the center, i.e., the general discipline.

Whoever takes the viewpoint of the general discipline, i.e., deals with the facts of the special disciplines not on a footing of equality, but as the material of a science, just as these disciplines themselves deals with the facts of reality, will immediately change the viewpoint of critique for the viewpoint of investigation. Criticism is on the same level as what is being criticized; it proceeds fully within the given discipline; its goal is exclusively critical and not positive; it wishes to know only whether and to what extent some theory is correct; it evaluates and judges, but does not investigate. A criticizes B, but both occupy the same position as to the facts. Things change when A begins to deal with B as B does with the facts, i.e., when he does not criticize B, but investigates him. The investigation already belongs to general science, its tasks are not critical, but positive. It does not wish to evaluate some theory, but to learn something new about the facts themselves which are represented in the theory. While science uses critique as a means, the course [of the investigation, Russian eds.] and the result of this process nevertheless differ fundamentally from a critical examination. Critique, in the final analysis, formulates an opinion about an opinion, albeit a very solid and well-founded opinion. A general investigation establishes, ultimately, objective laws and facts.

Only he who elevates his analysis from the level of the critical discussion of some system of views to the level of a fundamental investigation by means of the general science will understand the objective meaning of the crisis that is taking place in psychology. He will see the lawfulness of the clash of ideas and opinions that is taking place, which is determined by the development of the science itself and by the nature of the reality it studies at a given level of knowledge. Instead of a chaos of heterogeneous opinions, a motley discordance of subjective utterances, he will see an orderly blueprint of the fundamental opinions concerning the development of the science, a system of the objective tendencies which are inherent in the historical tasks brought forward by the development of the science and which act behind the backs of the various investigators and theorists with the force of a steel spring. Instead of critically discussing and evaluating some author, instead of establishing that this author is guilty of inconsistency and contradictions, he will devote a positive investigation to the question what the objective tendencies in science require. And as a result, instead of opinions about an opinion he will get an outline of the skeleton of the general science as a system of defining laws, principles and facts.

Only such an investigator realizes the real and correct meaning of the catastrophe that is taking place and has a clear idea of the role, place, and meaning of each different theory or school. Rather than by the impressionism and subjectivism inevitable in each criticism, he will be led by scientific reliability and veracity. For him (and this will be the first result of the new viewpoint) the individual differences will vanish—he will understand the role of personality in history. He will understand that to explain reflexology's claims to be a universal science from the personal mistakes, opinions, particularities, and ignorance of its founders is as impossible as to explain the French revolution from the corruption of the king or court. He will see what and how much in the development of science depends upon the good and bad intention of its practitioners, what can be explained from their intentions and what from this intention itself should, on the contrary, be explained on the basis of the objective tendencies operative behind the backs of these practitioners. Of course, the particularities of his personal creativity and the entire weight of his scientific experience determined the specific form of universalism which the idea of reflexology acquired in the hands of Bekhterev. But in Pavlov [1928/1963, p. 41] as well, whose personal contribution and scientific experience are entirely different, reflexology is the "ultimate science," "an omnipotent method," which brings "full, true and permanent human happiness." And in their own way behaviorism and Gestalt theory cover the same route. Obviously, rather than the mosaic of good and evil intentions among the investigators we should study the unity in the processes of regeneration of scientific tissue in psychology, which determines the intention of all the investigators.

7

Precisely what the dependency of each psychological operation upon the general formula means can be illustrated with any problem that transcends the boundaries of the special discipline that raised it.

When Lipps [1897, p. 146] says about the unconscious that it is less a psychological problem than *the* problem for psychology, he has in mind that the unconscious is a problem of general psychology. By this he wished to say, of course, no more than that this question will be answered not as a result of this or that particular investigation, but as a result of a fundamental investigation by means of the general science, i.e., by comparing the widely varying data of the most heterogeneous areas of science; by correlating the given problem with several of the basic premises of scientific knowledge, on the one hand, and with several of the most general results of all sciences, on the other; by finding a place for this concept in the system of the basic concepts of psychology; by a fundamental dialectical analysis of the nature of this concept and the features of being that it corresponds to and reflects. This investigation logically precedes any concrete investigation of particular questions of subconscious life and determines the very formulation of the problem in such investigations.

As Münsterberg [1920, p. v], defending the need for such an investigation for another set of problems, splendidly put it: "In the end it is better to get an approximately exact preliminary answer to a question that is stated correctly than to answer with a precision to the last decimal point a question that is stated inaccurately." A correct statement of a question is no less a matter of scientific creativity and investigation than a correct answer—and it is much more crucial. The vast majority of contemporary psychological investigations write out the last decimal point with great care and precision in answer to a question that is stated fundamentally incorrectly.

Whether we accept with Münsterberg [1920, pp. 158-163] that the subconscious is simply physiological and not psychological; or whether we agree with others that the subconscious consists of phenomena that temporarily are absent from consciousness, like the whole mass of potentially conscious reminiscences, knowledge and habits; whether we call those phenomena subconscious that do not reach the threshold of consciousness, or those of which we are minimally conscious, which are peripheral in the field of consciousness, automatic and unnoted; whether we find a suppression of the sexual drive to be the basis of the subconscious, like Freud, or our second *ego*, a special personality; finally, whether we call these phenomena un-, sub-, or superconscious, or like Stern accept all of these terms—it all fundamentally changes the character, quantity, composition, nature, and properties of the material which we will study. The question partially predetermines the answer.

It is this feeling of a system, the sense of a [common] style, the understanding that each particular statement is linked with and dependent upon the central idea of the whole system of which it forms a part, which is absent in the essentially eclectic attempts at combining the parts of two or more systems that are heterogeneous and diverse in scientific origin and composition. Such are, for instance, the synthesis of behaviorism and Freudian theory in the American literature; Freudian theory without Freud in the systems of Adler and Jung; the reflexological Freudian theory of Bekhterev and Zalkind; finally, the attempts to combine Freudian theory and Marxism (Luria, 1925; Fridman, 1925). So many examples from the area of the problem of the subconscious alone! In all these attempts the tail of one system is taken and placed against the head of another and the space between them is filled with the trunk of a third. It isn't that they are incorrect, these monstrous combinations, they are correct to the last decimal point, but the question they wish to answer is stated incorrectly. We can multiply the number of citizens of Paraguay with the number of kilometers from the earth to the sun and divide the product by the average life span of the elephant and carry out the whole operation irreproachably, without a mistake in any number, and nevertheless the final outcome might mislead someone who is interested in the national income of this country. What the eclectics do, is to reply to a question raised by Marxist philosophy with an answer prompted by Freudian metapsychology.

In order to show the methodological illegitimacy of such attempts, we will first dwell upon three types of combining incompatible questions and answers, without thinking for one moment that these three types exhaust the variety of such attempts.

The first way in which any school assimilates the scientific products of another area consists of the direct transposition of all laws, facts, theories, ideas etc., the usurpation of a more or less broad area occupied by other investigators, the annexation of foreign territory. Such a politics of direct usurpation is common for each new scientific system which spreads its influence to adjacent disciplines and lays claim to the leading role of a general science. Its own material is insufficient and after just a little critical work such a system absorbs foreign bodies, submits them, filling the emptiness of its inflated boundaries. Usually one gets a conglomerate of scientific theories, facts, etc. which have been squeezed into the framework of the unifying idea with horrible arbitrariness.

Such is the system of Bekhterev's reflexology. He can use anything: even Vvedensky's theory about the unknowability of the external ego, i.e., an extreme expression of solipsism and idealism in psychology, provided that this theory clearly confirms his particular claim about the need for an objective method. [13] That it breaches the general sense of the whole system, that it undermines the foundations of the realistic approach to personality does not matter to this author (we observe that Vvedensky, too, fortifies himself and his theory with a reference to the work of . . . Pavlov, without understanding that by turning for help to a system of objective psychology he extends a hand to his grave-digger). But for the methodologist it is highly significant that such antipodes as Vvedensky-Pavlov and Bekhterev–Vvedensky do not merely contradict each other, but necessarily presuppose each other's existence and view the coincidence of their conclusions as evidence for "the reliability of these conclusions." For this third person [the methodologist, Russian eds.] it is clear that we are not dealing here with a coincidence of conclusions which were reached fully independently by representatives of different specialties, for example the philosopher Vvedensky and the physiologist Pavlov, but with a coincidence of the basic assumptions, starting-points and philosophical premises of dualistic idealism. This "coincidence" is presupposed from the very start: Bekhterev presupposes Vvedensky—when the one is right, the other is right as well.

Einstein's principle of relativity and the principles of Newtonian mechanics, incompatible in themselves, get on perfectly well in this eclectic system. In Bekhterev's "Collective reflexology" he absolutely gathered a catalogue of universal laws. Characteristic of the methodology of the system is the way imagination is given free reign, the fundamental inertia of the idea which by direct communication, omitting all intermediate steps, leads us from the law of the proportional correlation of the speed of movement with the moving force, established in mechanics, to the fact of the USA's involvement in the great European war, and back again—from the experiment of a certain Dr. Schwarzmann on the frequency limits of electro-cutaneous irritation leading to an association reflex to the "universal law of relativity which obtains everywhere and which, as a result of Einstein's brilliant investigations, has been finally demonstrated in regard to heavenly bodies." [14]

Needless to say, the annexation of psychological areas is carried out no less categorically and no less boldly. The investigations of the higher thought processes by the Würzburg school, like the results of the investigations of other representatives of subjective psychology, "may be harmonized with the scheme of cerebral or association reflexes." [15] Never mind that this very phrase strikes out all the fundamental premises of his own system: for if we can harmonize everything with the reflex schema and everything "is in perfect accord" with reflexology—even what has been discovered by subjective psychology—why take up arms against it? The discoveries made in Würzburg were made with a method which, according to Bekhterev, cannot lead to the truth. However, they are in complete harmony with the objective truth. How is that?

The territory of psychoanalysis is annexed just as carelessly. For this it suffices to declare that "in Jung's doctrine of complexes we find complete agreement with the data of reflexology." [16] But one passage higher it was said that this doctrine was based on subjective analysis, which Bekhterev rejects. No problem: we live in the world of pre-established harmony, of the miraculous correspondence, of the amazing coincidence of theories based on false analyses and the data of the exact sciences. To be more precise, we live in the world—according to Blonsky (1925a, p. 226)—of "terminological revolutions."

Our whole eclectic epoch is filled with such coincidences. Zalkind, for example, annexes the same areas of psychoanalysis and the theory of complexes in the name of the dominant. It turns out that the psychoanalytic school developed the same concepts about the dominant completely independently from the reflexological school, but "in our terms and by another method." The "complex orientation" of the psychoanalysts, the "strategical set" of the Adlerians, these are dominants as well, not in general physiological but clinical, general therapeutic formulations. The annexation—the mechanical transposition of bits of a foreign system into one's own—in this case, as always, seems almost miraculous and testifies to its truth. Such an "almost miraculous" theoretical and factual coincidence of two doctrines, which work with totally different material and by entirely different methods, forms a convincing confirmation of the correctness of the principal path that contemporary reflexology is following. [17] We remember that Vvedensky too saw in his coincidence with Pavlov a testimony of the truth of his statements. And more: this coincidence testifies, as Bekhterev more than once showed, to the fact that we may arrive at the same truth by entirely different methods. Actually, this coincidence testifies only to the methodological unscrupulousness and eclecticism of the system within which such a coincidence is observed. "He that toucheth pitch shall be defiled," as the saying goes. He who borrows from the psychoanalysts—Jung's doctrine of complexes, Freud's catharsis, Adler's strategical set—gets his share of the "pitch" of these systems, i.e., the philosophical spirit of the authors.

Whereas the first method of transposition of foreign ideas from one school into another resembles the annexation of foreign territory, the second method of comparing foreign ideas is similar to a treaty between two allied countries in which both retain their independence, but agree to act together proceeding from their common interests. This method is usually applied in the merger of Marxism and Freudian theory. In so doing the author uses a method that by analogy with geometry might be called the method of the logical superposition of concepts. The system of Marxism is defined as being monistic, materialistic, dialectic etc. Then the monism, materialism etc. of Freud's system is established; the superimposed concepts coincide and the systems are declared to have fused. Very flagrant, sharp contradictions which strike the eye are removed in a very elementary way: they are simply excluded from the system, are declared to be exaggerations, etc. Thus, Freudian theory is de-sexualized as pan-sexualism obviously does not square with Marx's philosophy. No problem, we are told—we will accept Freudian theory without the doctrine of sexuality. But this doctrine forms the very nerve, soul, center of the whole system. Can we accept a system without its center? After all, Freudian theory without the doctrine of the sexual nature of the unconscious is like Christianity without Christ or Buddhism with Allah.

It would be a historical miracle, of course, if a full-grown system of Marxist psychology were to originate and develop in the West, from completely different roots and in a totally different cultural situation. That would imply that philosophy does not at all determine the development of science. As we can see, they started from Schopenhauer and created a Marxist psychology! But this would imply the total fruitlessness of the attempt itself to merge Freudian theory with Marxism, just as the success of Bekhterev's coincidence would imply the bankruptcy of the objective method: after all, if the data of subjective analysis fully coincide with the data of objective analysis, one may ask in what sense subjective analysis is inferior. If Freud, without knowing it himself, thinking about other philosophical systems and consciously siding with them, nevertheless created a Marxist doctrine of the mind, then in the name of what, may one ask, is it necessary to disturb this most fruitful delusion: after all, according to these authors, we need not change anything in Freud. Why, then, merge psychoanalysis with Marxism? In addition, the following interesting question arises: how is it possible that this system which entirely coincides with Marxism logically led to making the idea of sexuality, which is obviously irreconcilable with Marxism, into its cornerstone? Is not the method to a large extent responsible for the conclusions arrived at with its help? And how could a true method which creates a true system, based on true premises, lead its authors to a false theory, to a false central idea? One has to dispose of a good deal of methodological carelessness not to see these problems which inevitably arise in each mechanical attempt to move the center of any scientific system—in the given case, from Schopenhauer's doctrine of the will as the basis of the world to Marx's doctrine about the dialectical development of matter.

But the worst is still to come. In such attempts one often simply must close one's eyes to the contradictory facts, pay no attention to vast areas and main principles, and introduce monstrous distortions in both of the systems to be merged. In so doing, one uses transformations like those with which algebra operates, in order to prove the identity of two expressions. But the transformation of the systems to be merged operates with unities that are absolutely different from the algebraic ones. In practice, it always leads to the distortion of the essence of these systems.

In the article by Luria [1925, p. 55], for example, psychoanalysis is presented as "a system of monistic psychology," whose methodology "coincides with the methodology" of Marxism. In order to prove this a number of most naive transformations of both systems are carried out as a result of which they "coincide." Let us briefly look at these transformations. First of all, Marxism is situated in the general methodology of the epoch, alongside Darwin, Comte, Pavlov, and Einstein,[12] who together create the general methodological foundations of the epoch [ibid., p. 47]. The role and importance of each of these authors is, of course, deeply and fundamentally different, and by its very nature the role of dialectical materialism is totally different from all of them. Not to see this means to deduce methodology from the sum total of "great scientific achievements" [ibid., p. 47]. As soon as one reduces all these names and Marxism to a common denominator it is not difficult to unite Marxism with any "great scientific achievement," because this was presupposed: the "coincidence" looked for is in the presupposition and not in the conclusion. The "fundamental methodology of the epoch" consists of the sum total of the discoveries made by Pavlov, Einstein, etc. Marxism is one of these discoveries, which belong to the "group of principles indispensable for quite a number of closely-related sciences" [ibid., p. 47]. Here, on the first page, that is, the argumentation might have ended: after Einstein one would only have to mention Freud, for he is also a "great scientific achievement" and, thus, a participant in the "general methodological foundations of the epoch." But one must have much uncritical trust in scientific reputation to deduce the methodology of an epoch from the sum total of famous names!

There is no unitary basic methodology of the epoch. What we have is a system of fighting, deeply hostile, mutually exclusive, methodological principles and each theory—whether by Pavlov or Einstein—has its own methodological merit. To distill a general methodology of the epoch and to dissolve Marxism in it means to transform not only the appearance, but also the essence of Marxism.

But also Freudian theory is inescapably subjected to the same type of transformations. Freud himself would be amazed to learn that psychoanalysis is a system of monistic psychology and that "methodologically he carries on... historical materialism" [Fridman, 1925, p. 159]. Not a single psychoanalytic journal would, of course, print the papers by Luria and Fridman. That is highly important. For a very peculiar situation has evolved: Freud and his school have never declared themselves to be monists, materialists, dialecticians, or followers of historical materialism. But they are told: you are both the first, and the second, and the third. You yourselves don't know who you are. Of course, one can imagine such a situation, it is entirely possible. But then it is necessary to give an exact explanation of the methodological foundations of this doctrine, as conceived of and developed by its authors, and then a proof of the refutation of these foundations and to explain by what miracle and on what foundations psychoanalysis developed a system of methodology which is foreign to its authors. Instead of this, the identity of the two systems is declared by a simple formal-logical superposition of the characteristics—without a single analysis of Freud's basic concepts, without critically weighing and elucidating his assumptions and starting-points, without a critical examination of the genesis of his ideas, even without simply inquiring how he himself conceives of the philosophical foundations of his system.

But, maybe, this formal-logical characterization of the two systems is correct? We have already seen how one distills Marxism's share in the general methodology of the epoch, in which everything is roughly and naively reduced to a common denominator: if both Einstein and Pavlov and Marx belong to science, then they must have a common foundation. But Freudian theory suffers even more distortions in this process. I will not even mention how Zalkind (1924) mechanically deprives it of its central idea. In his article it is passed over in silence, which is also noteworthy. But take the monism of psychoanalysis—Freud would contest it. The article mentions that he turned to philosophical monism, but where, in which words, in connection with what? Is finding empirical unity in some group of facts really always monism? On the contrary, Freud always accepted the mental, the unconscious as a special force which cannot be reduced to something else. Further, why is this monism materialistic in the philosophical sense? After all, medical materialism which acknowledges the influence of different organs etc. upon mental structures is still very far from philosophical materialism. In the philosophy of Marxism this concept has a specific, primarily epistemological sense and it is precisely in his epistemology that Freud stands on idealist philosophical grounds. For it is a fact, which is not refuted and not even considered by the authors of the "coincidences," that Freud's doctrine of the primary role of blind drives, of the unconscious as being reflected in consciousness in a distorted fashion, goes back directly to Schopenhauer's[13] idealistic metaphysics of the will and the idea. Freud [1920/1973, pp. 49-50] himself remarks that in his extreme conclusions he is in the harbor of Schopenhauer. [18] But his basic assumptions as well as the main lines of his system are connected with the philosophy of the great pessimist, as even the simplest analysis can demonstrate.

In its more "concrete" works as well, psychoanalysis displays not dynamic, but highly static, conservative, anti-dialectic and anti-historical tendencies. It directly reduces the higher mental processes—both personal and collective ones—to primitive, primordial, essentially prehistorical, prehuman roots, leaving no room for history. The same key unlocks the creativity of a Dostoyevsky and the totem and taboo of primordial tribes; the Christian church, communism, the primitive horde—in psychoanalysis everything is reduced to the same source. That such tendencies are present in psychoanalysis is apparent from all the works of this school which deal with problems of culture, sociology and history. We can see that here it does not continue, but contradicts, the methodology of Marxism. But about this one keeps silent as well.

Finally, the third point. Freud's whole psychological system of fundamental concepts goes back to Lipps [1903]: the concepts of the unconscious, of the mental energy connected with certain ideas, of drives as the basis of the mind, of the struggle between drives and repression, of the affective nature of consciousness, etc. In other words, Freud's psychological roots lead back to the spiritualistic strata of Lipps' psychology. How is it possible to disregard this when speaking about Freud's methodology?

Thus, we see where Freud and his system have come from and where they are heading for: from Schopenhauer and Lipps to Kolnay and mass psychology.[14] But to apply the system of psychoanalysis while saying nothing about metapsychology, social psychology [19] and Freud's theory of sexuality is to give it a quite arbitrary interpretation. As a result, a person not knowing Freud would get an utterly false idea of him from such an exposition of his system. Freud himself would protest against the word "system" first of all. In his opinion, one of the greatest merits of psychoanalysis and its author is that it consciously avoids becoming a system. [20] Freud himself rejects the "monism" of psychoanalysis [21]: he does not demand that the factors he discovered be accepted as exclusive or primary. He does not at all attempt to "give an exhaustive theory of the mental life of man," but demands only that his statements be used to complete and correct the knowledge which we have acquired through whatever other way. [22] In another place he says that psychoanalysis is characterized by its technique and not by its subject matter [23], in a third that psychological theory has a temporary nature and will be replaced by an organic theory. [24]

All this may easily delude us: it might seem that psychoanalysis really has no system and that its data can serve to correct and complete any system of knowledge, acquired in whatever way. But this is utterly false. Psychoanalysis has no *a priori*, conscious theory-system. Like Pavlov, Freud discovered too much to create an abstract system. But like Molière's hero [25] who, without suspecting it, spoke prose all his life, Freud, the investigator, created a system: introducing a new word, harmonizing one term with another, describing a new fact, drawing a new conclusion, he created, in passing and step by step, a new system. This implies that the structure of his system is unique, obscure, complex and very difficult to grasp. It is much easier to find one's way in methodological systems which are deliberate, clear, and free from contradictions, which acknowledge their teachers and are unified and logically structured. It is much more difficult to correctly evaluate and reveal the true nature of unconscious methodologies which evolved spontaneously, in a contradictory way, under various influences. But it is precisely to the latter that psychoanalysis belongs. For this reason psychoanalysis requires a very careful and critical methodological analysis and not a naive superposition of the features of two different systems.

Ivanovsky (1923, p. 249) says that "For a person who is not experienced in matters of scientific methodology all sciences seem to share the same method." Psychology suffered most of all from such a misunderstanding. It was always counted as either biology or sociology and rarely were psychological laws, theories, etc., judged by the criterion of psychological methodology, i.e., with an interest in the thought of psychological science as such, its theory, its methodology, its sources, forms and foundations. That is why in our critique of foreign systems, in the evaluation of their truth, we lack what is most important: after all, it is only from an understanding of its methodological basis that we can correctly assess the extent to which knowledge has been corroborated and established beyond doubt (Ivanovsky, 1923). And the rule that one must doubt everything, take nothing on trust, ask each claim what it rests on and what is its source, is, therefore, the first rule and methodology of science. It safeguards us against an even grosser mistake— not only to consider the methods of all sciences to be equal, but to imagine that the structure of each science is uniform.

> The inexperienced mind imagines each separate science, so to speak, in one plane: given that science is reliable, indisputable knowledge, everything in it must be reliable. Its whole content must be obtained and proven by one and the same method which yields reliable knowledge. In reality this is not true at all: each science has its different facts (and groups of analogous facts) which have been established beyond doubt, its irrefutably established general claims and laws, but it also has pre-suppositions, hypotheses which sometimes have a temporary, provisional character and sometimes indicate the ultimate boundaries of our knowledge (at least for the given epoch); there are conclusions which follow more or less indisputably from firmly established theses; there are constructions which sometimes broaden the boundaries of our knowledge, sometimes form deliberately introduced 'fictions'; there are analogies, approximate generalizations etc., etc. Science has no homogeneous structure and the understanding of this fact is of the greatest significance for a person's understanding of science. Each different scientific thesis has its own individual degree of reliability depending upon the way and degree of its methodological foundation, and science, viewed methodologically, does not represent a single solid uniform surface, but a mosaic of theses of different degrees of reliability" (ibid., p. 250).

That is why (1) merging the method of all sciences (Einstein, Pavlov, Comte, Marx) and (2) reducing the entire heterogeneous structure of the scientific system to one plane, to a "single solid uniform surface," comprise the main mistakes of the second way of fusing two systems. To reduce personality to money; cleanliness, stubbornness and a thousand other, heterogeneous things to anal erotics (Luria, 1925), is not yet monism. And with regard to its nature and degree of reliability it is a fundamental error to mix up this thesis with the principles of materialism. The principle that follows from this thesis, the general idea behind it, its methodological meaning, the method of investigation prescribed by it, are deeply conservative: like the convict to his wheelbarrow, the character in psychoanalysis is chained to child-hood erotics. Human life is in its inner essence predetermined by childhood con-flicts. It is all the overcoming of the Oedipal conflict, etc. Culture and the life of mankind are again brought close to primitive life. [But] it is a first indispensable condition for analysis to be able to distinguish the first apparent meaning of a fact from its real meaning. By no means do I want to say that everything in psycho-analysis contradicts Marxism. I only want to say that I am in principle not dealing with this question at all. I am only pointing out how we should (methodologically) and should not (uncritically) fuse two systems of ideas.

With an uncritical approach, everybody sees what he wants to see and not what is: the Marxist finds monism, materialism, and dialectics in psychoanalysis, which is not there; the physiologist, like Lenz (1922, p. 69), holds that "psycho-analysis is a system which is psychological in name only; in reality it is objective, physiological." And the methodologist Binswanger remarks in his work dedicated to Freud, as the only one amongst the psychoanalysts it seems, that precisely the psychological in his conception, i.e., the anti-physiological, constitutes Freud's merit in psychiatry. But he adds [1922, p. v] that "this knowledge does not know itself yet, i.e., it has no insight into its own conceptual foundations, its logos."

That is why it is especially difficult to study knowledge that has not yet become aware of itself and its own logos. This does by no means imply, of course, that Marxists should not study the unconscious because Freud's basic concepts contradict dialectical materialism. On the contrary, precisely because the area elaborated by psychoanalysis is elaborated with inadequate means it must be conquered for Marx-ism. It must be elaborated with the means of a genuine methodology, for otherwise, if everything in psychoanalysis would coincide with Marxism, psychologists might develop it in their quality as psychoanalysts and not as Marxists. And for this elabo-ration one must first take account of the methodological nature of each idea, each thesis. And under this condition the most metapsychological ideas can be interesting and instructive, for example, Freud's doctrine of the death drive.

In the preface which I wrote for the translation of Freud's book on this theme, I attempted to show that the fictitious construct of a death drive—despite the whole speculative nature of this thesis, the not very convincing nature of the factual con-firmations (traumatic neurosis and the repetition of unpleasant experiences in chil-dren's play), its giddy paradoxical nature and the contradiction of generally accepted biological ideas, its conclusions which obviously coincide with the philosophy of the Nirvana, despite all this and despite the whole artificial nature of the concept—satisfies the need of modern biology to master the idea of death, just like mathe-matics in its time needed the concept of the negative number. I adduced the thesis that the concept of life has been carried to great clarity in biology, science has mastered it, it knows how to work with it, how to investigate and understand living matter. But it cannot yet cope with the concept of death. Instead of this concept we have a gaping hole, an empty spot. Death is merely seen as the contradictory opposite of life, as not-life, in short, as non-being. But death is a fact that has its positive sense as well, it is a special type of being and not merely non-being. It is a specific something and not absolutely nothing. [26] And biology does not know this positive sense of death. Indeed, death is a universal law for living matter. One cannot imagine that this phenomenon would in no way be represented in the organism, i.e., in the processes of life. It is hard to believe that death would have no sense or just a negative sense. [27]

Engels [1925/1978, p. 554] expresses a similar opinion. He refers to Hegel's opinion that only that philosophy can count as scientific that considers death to be an essential aspect of life and understands that the negation of life is essentially contained in life itself, so that life can be understood in relation to its inevitable result which is continually present in embryonic form: death. The dialectical understanding of life entails no more than that. "To live means to die."

It was precisely this idea that I defended in the mentioned preface to Freud's book: the need for biology to master the concept of death from a fundamental viewpoint and to designate this still unknown entity which no doubt exists—let it be with the algebraic "x" or the paradoxical "death drive"—and which represents the tendency towards death in the processes of the organism. Despite this I did not declare Freud's solution to this equation to be a highway in science or a road for all of us, but an Alpine mountain track above the precipice for those free of vertigo. I stated that science needs such books as well: they do not reveal the truth, but teach us the search for truth, although they have not yet found it. I also resolutely said that the importance of this book does not depend upon the factual confirmation of its reliability: in principle it asks the right question. And for the statement of such questions, I said, one needs sometimes more creativity than for the umpteenth standard observation in whatever science [see pp. 13-15 of Van der Veer and Valsiner, 1994].

And the judgment of one of the reviewers of this book showed a complete lack of understanding of the methodological problem, a full trust in the external features of ideas, a naive and uncritical fear of the physiology of pessimism. He decided on the spot that if it is Schopenhauer, it must be pessimism. He did not understand that there are problems that one cannot approach flying, but that one must approach on foot, limping, and that in such cases it is no shame to limp, as Freud [1920/1973, p. 64] openly says. But he, who only sees lameness here, is methodologically blind. For it would not be difficult to show that Hegel is an idealist, it is proclaimed from the housetops. But it needed genius to see in this system an idealism that stood materialism on its head, i.e., to distinguish the methodological truth (dialectics) from the factual falsehood, to see that Hegel went limping towards the truth. [28]

This is but a single example of the path towards the mastery of scientific ideas: one must rise above their factual content and test their fundamental nature. But for this one needs to have a buttress outside these ideas. Standing upon these ideas with both feet, operating with concepts gathered by means of them, it is impossible to situate oneself outside of them. In order to critically regard a foreign system, one must first of all have one's own psychological system of principles. To judge Freud by means of principles obtained from Freud himself implies a vindication in advance. And such an attempt to appropriate foreign ideas forms the third type of combining ideas to which we will now turn.

Again it is easiest to disclose and demonstrate the character of the new methodological approach with a single example. In Pavlov's laboratory it was attempted to experimentally solve the problem of the transformation of trace-conditional stimuli and trace-conditional inhibitors into actual conditional stimuli. For this one must "banish the inhibition" established through the trace reflex. How to do this? In order to reach this goal, Frolov resorted to an analogy with some of the methods of Freud's school. [29] Trying to destroy the stable inhibitory complexes, he exactly recreated the situation in which these complexes were originally established. And the experiment succeeded. I consider the methodological technique at the basis of this experiment to be an example of the right approach to Freud's theme and to claims by others in general. Let us try to describe this technique. First of all, the problem was raised in the course of Pavlov's own investigations of the nature of internal inhibition. The task was framed, formulated, and understood in the light of his principles. The theoretical theme of the experimental work and its significance were conceived of in the concepts of Pavlov's school. We know what a trace reflex is and we also know what an actual reflex is. To transform the one into the other means to banish inhibition etc., i.e., the whole mechanism of the process we understand in entirely specific and homogeneous categories. The value of the analogy with catharsis was merely heuristic: it shortened the path of Pavlov's experiments and led to the goal in the shortest way possible. But it was only accepted as an assumption that was immediately verified experimentally. And after the solution of his own task the author came to the third and final conclusion that the phenomena described by Freud can be experimentally tested upon animals and should be analyzed in more detail via the method of conditional salivary reflexes.

To verify Freud via Pavlov's ideas is totally different from verifying them via his own ideas; and this possibility as well was established not through analysis, but through the experiment. What is most important is that the author, when confronted with phenomena analogous to those described by Freud's school, did not for one moment step onto foreign territory, did not rely on other people's data, but used them to carry through his own investigation. Pavlov's discovery has its significance, value, place and meaning in his own system, not in Freud's. The two circles touch at the point of intersection of both systems, the point where they meet, and this one point belongs to both at the same time. But its place, sense and value is determined by its position in the first system. A new discovery was made in this investigation, a new fact was found, a new trait was studied—but it was all in the [framework of the] theory of conditional reflexes and not in psychoanalysis. In this way each "almost miraculous" coincidence disappeared!

One has only to compare this with the purely verbal way Bekhterev [1932, p. 413] comes to a similar evaluation of the idea of catharsis for the system of reflexology, to see the deep difference between these two procedures. Here the interrelation of the two systems is also first of all based on catharsis, i.e.,

> discharge of a 'strangulated' affect or an inhibited mimetic-somatic impulse. Is not this the discharge of a reflex which, when inhibited, oppresses the personality, shackles and diseases it, while, when there is discharge of the reflex (catharsis), naturally the pathological condition disappears? Is not the weeping out of a sorrow the discharge of an impeded reflex?

Here every word is a pearl. A mimetic-somatic impulse—what can be more clear or precise? Avoiding the language of subjective psychology, Bekhterev is not squeamish about philistine language, which hardly makes Freud's term any clearer. How did this inhibited reflex "oppress" the personality, shackle it? Why is the wept-out sorrow the discharge of an *inhibited* reflex? What if a person weeps in the very moment of sorrow? Finally, elsewhere it is claimed that thought is an inhibited reflex, that concentration is connected with the inhibition of a nervous current and is accompanied by conscious phenomena. Oh salutary inhibition! It explains conscious phenomena in one chapter and unconscious ones in the next!

All this clearly indicates the theme with which we started this section: in the problem of the unconscious one must distinguish between a methodological and an empirical problem, i.e., between a psychological problem and *the* problem for psychology. [30] The uncritical combination of both problems leads to a gross distortion of the whole matter. The symposium on the unconscious showed that a fundamental solution of this matter transcends the boundaries of empirical psychology and is directly tied to general philosophical convictions. Whether we accept with Brentano that the unconscious does not exist, or with Münsterberg that it is simply physiology, or with Schubert–Soldern that it is an epistemologically indispensable category, or with Freud that it is sexual—in all these cases our argumentation and conclusions transcend the boundaries of empirical psychology. [31]

Among the Russian authors it is Dale who emphasizes the epistemological motives which led to the formation of the concept of the unconscious. In his opinion it is precisely the attempt to defend the independence of psychology as an explanatory science against the usurpation of physiological methods and principles that is the basis of this concept. The demand to explain the mental from the mental, and not from the physical, that psychology in the analysis and description of the facts should stay itself, within its own boundaries, even if this implied that one had to enter the path of broad hypotheses—this is what gave rise to the concept of the unconscious. Dale observes that psychological constructions or *hypotheses* are no more than the theoretical continuation of the description of *homogeneous* phenomena in one and the same independent system of reality. [32] The tasks of psychology and theoretical-epistemological demands require that it fight the usurpationist attempts of physiology by means of the unconscious. Mental life proceeds with interruptions, it is full of gaps. What happens with consciousness during sleep, with reminiscences that we do not now recollect, with ideas of which we are not consciously aware at the moment? In order to explain the mental from the mental, in order not to turn to another domain of phenomena—physiology—to fill the pauses, gaps and blanks in mental life, we must assume that they continue to exist in a special form: as the unconscious *mental*. Stern [1919, pp. 241-243] as well develops such a conception of the unconscious as both an essential assumption and a hypothetical continuation and complement to mental experience.

Dale distinguishes two aspects of the problem: the factual and the hypothetical or methodological, which determines the epistemological or methodological value of the category of the unconscious for psychology. Its task is to clarify the meaning of this concept, the domain of phenomena it covers, and its role for psychology as an explanatory science. Following Jerusalem [33], for the author it is first of all a category or a way of thinking which is indispensable in the explanation of mental life. Apart from that, it is also a specific area of phenomena. He is completely right in saying that the unconscious is a concept created on the basis of indisputable mental experience and its necessary hypothetical completion. Hence the very complex nature of each statement operating with this concept: in *each* statement one must distinguish what comes from the data of indisputable mental experience, what comes from the hypothetical completion, and what is the degree of reliability of both. In the critical works examined above, the two things, both sides of the problem, have been mixed up: hypothesis and fact, principle and empirical observation, fiction and law, construction and generalization—it is all lumped together.

Most important of all is the fact that the main question was left out of consideration. Lenz and Luria assure Freud that psychoanalysis is a physiological system. But Freud himself belongs to the opponents of a physiological conception of the unconscious. Dale is completely right in saying that this question of the psychological or physiological nature of the unconscious is the *primary*, most important phase of the whole problem. Before we describe and classify the phenomena of the unconscious for psychological purposes, we must know whether we are operating with something physiological or with something mental. We must prove that the unconscious in fact is a mental reality. In other words, before we turn to the solution of the problem of the unconscious as a psychological problem, we must first solve it as *the* problem for psychology.

8

The need for a fundamental elaboration of the concepts of the general science—this algebra of the particular sciences—and its role for the particular sciences is even more obvious when we borrow from the area of *other* sciences. Here, on the one hand, it would seem that we have the best conditions for transferring results from one science into the system of another one, because the reliability, clarity and the degree to which the borrowed thesis or law have been fundamentally elaborated are usually much higher than in the cases we have described. We may, for example, introduce into the system of psychological explanation a law established in physiology or embryology, a biological principle, an anatomical hypothesis, an ethnological example, a historical classification etc. The theses and constructions of these highly developed, firmly grounded sciences are, of course, methodologically elaborated in an infinitely more precise way than the theses of a psychological school which by means of newly created and not yet systematized concepts is developing completely new areas (for example, Freud's school, which does not yet know itself). In this case we borrow a more elaborated product, we operate with better-defined, exact, and clear unities; the danger of error has diminished, the likelihood of success has increased.

On the other hand, as the borrowing here comes from other sciences, the material turns out to be more foreign, methodologically heterogeneous, and the conditions for appropriating it become more difficult. This fact, that the conditions are both easier and more difficult compared with what we examined above, provides us with an essential method of variation in theoretical analysis which takes the place of real variation in the experiment.

Let us dwell upon a fact which at first sight seems highly paradoxical and which is therefore very suitable for analysis. Reflexology, which in all areas finds such wonderful coincidences of its data with the data of subjective analysis and which wishes to build its system on the foundation of the exact natural sciences, is, very surprisingly, forced to protest precisely against the transfer of natural scientific laws into psychology.

After studying the method of genetic reflexology, Shchelovanov[15]—with an indisputable thoroughness quite unexpected for his school—rejected the imitation of the natural sciences in the form of a transfer of its basic methods into subjective psychology. Their application in the natural sciences has produced tremendous results, but they are of little value for the elaboration of the problems of subjective psychology.* Herbart and Fechner[16] mechanically transferred mathematical analysis and Wundt the physiological experiment into psychology. Preyer[17] raised the problem of psychogenesis by analogy with biology and then Hall and others borrowed the Müller-Haeckel principle from biology and applied it in an uncontrolled way not only as a methodological principle, but also as a principle for the explanation of the "mental development" of the child. It would seem, says the author, that we cannot object to the application of well-tried and fruitful methods. But their use is only possible when the problem is correctly stated and the method corresponds to the nature of the object under study. Otherwise one only gets the illusion of

*Similar ideas were developed in great detail in Shchelovanov (1929) [Russian Eds.].

science (the characteristic example is Russian reflexology). The veil of natural science which was, according to Petzoldt,[18] thrown over the most backward metaphysics, saved neither Herbart nor Wundt: neither the mathematical formulas nor the precision equipment saved an imprecisely stated problem from failure.

We are reminded of Münsterberg and his remark about the last decimal point given in the answer to an incorrectly stated question. In biology, clarifies the author, the biogenetic law is a theoretical generalization of masses of facts, but its application in psychology is the result of superficial speculation, exclusively based upon an analogy between different domains of facts (Does not reflexology do the same? Without investigation of its own it borrows, using similar speculations, the ready-made models for its own constructions from the living and the dead—from Einstein and from Freud). And then, to crown this pyramid of mistakes, the principle is not applied as a working hypothesis, but as an established theory, as if it were scientifically established as an explanatory principle for the given area of facts.

We will not deal with this matter, as does the author of this opinion, in great detail. There is abundant, including Russian, literature on it. We will examine it to illustrate the fact that many questions which have been incorrectly stated by psychology acquire the outward appearance of science due to borrowings from the natural sciences. As a result of his methodological analysis, Shchelovanov comes to the conclusion that the genetic method is in principle impossible in empirical psychology and that because of this the relations between psychology and biology become changed. But why was the problem of development stated incorrectly in child psychology, which led to a tremendous and useless expenditure of effort? In Shchelovanov's opinion, child psychology can yield nothing other than what is already contained in general psychology. But general psychology as a unified system does not exist, and these theoretical contradictions make a child psychology impossible. In a very disguised form, imperceptible to the investigator himself, the theoretical presuppositions fully determine the whole method of processing the empirical data. And the facts gathered in observation, too, are interpreted in accordance with the theory which this or that author holds. Here is the best refutation of the sham natural-science empiricism. Thanks to this, it is impossible to transfer facts from one theory to another. It would seem that a fact is always a fact, that one and the same subject matter—the child—and one and the same method—objective observation—albeit combined with different objectives and starting points, allow us to transfer facts from psychology to reflexology. The author is mistaken in only two respects.

His first mistake resides in the assumption that child psychology got its positive results only by applying general biological, but not psychological principles, as in the theory of play developed by Groos [1899]. In reality, this is one of the best examples not of borrowing, but of a purely psychological, comparative-objective study. It is methodologically impeccable and transparent, internally consistent from the first collection and description of the facts to the final theoretical generalizations. Groos gave biology a theory of play created with a psychological method. He did not take it from biology; he did not solve his problem in the light of biology, i.e., he did not set himself general psychological goals as well. Thus, exactly the opposite is correct: child psychology obtained valuable theoretical results precisely when it did not borrow, but went its own way. The author himself is constantly arguing against borrowing. Hall, who borrowed from Haeckel, gave psychology a number of curious topics and far-fetched senseless analogies, but Groos, who went his own way, gave much to biology—not less than Haeckel's law. Let me also remind you of Stern's theory of language, Bühler's and Koffka's theory of children's thinking, Bühler's theory of developmental levels, Thorndike's theory of training: these are all psychological theories of the purest water. Hence the mistaken conclusion: the role of child psychology cannot be reduced, of course, to the gathering of factual data and their preliminary classification, i.e., to the preparatory work. But the role of the logical principles developed by Shchelovanov and Bekhterev can and must precisely be reduced to this. After all, the new discipline has no idea of childhood, no conception of development, no research goal, i.e., it does not state the problem of child behavior and personality, but only disposes of the principle of objective observation, i.e., a good technical rule. However, using this weapon nobody has drawn out any great truths.

The author's second mistake is connected with this. The lack of understanding of the positive value of psychology and the underestimation of its role results from the most important and methodologically childish idea that one can study only what is given in immediate experience. His whole "methodological" theory is built upon a single syllogism: (1) psychology studies consciousness; (2) given in immediate experience is the consciousness of the adult; "the empirical study of the phylogenetic and ontogenetic development of consciousness is impossible"; (3) therefore, child psychology is impossible.

But it is a gross mistake to suppose that science can only study what is given in immediate experience. How does the psychologist study the unconscious; the historian and the geologist, the past; the physicist-optician, invisible beams, and the philologist—ancient languages? The study of traces, influences, the method of interpretation and reconstruction, the method of critique and the finding of meaning have been no less fruitful than the method of direct "empirical" observation. Ivanovsky used precisely the example of psychology to explain this for the methodology of science. Even in the experimental sciences the role of immediate experience becomes smaller and smaller. Planck[19] says that the unification of the whole system of theoretical physics is reached due to the liberation from anthropomorphic elements, in particular from specific sense perceptions. Planck [1919/1970, p. 118] remarks that in the theory of light and in the theory of radiant energy in general, physics works with such methods that

> the human eye is totally excluded, it plays the role of an accidental, admittedly highly sensitive but very limited reagent; for it only perceives the light beams within a small area of the spectrum which hardly attains the breadth of one octave. For the rest of the spectrum the place of the eye is taken by other perceiving and measuring instruments, such as, for example, the wave detector, the thermo-element, the bolometer, the radiometer, the photographic plate, the ionization chamber. The separation of the basic physical concept from the specific sensory sensation was accomplished, therefore, in exactly the same way as in mechanics where the concept of force has long since lost its original link with muscular sensations.

Thus, physics studies precisely what cannot be seen with the eye. For if we, like the author, agree with Stern [1914, p. 7] that childhood is for us "a paradise lost forever," that for us adults it is impossible to "fully penetrate in the special properties and structure of the child's mind" as it is not given in direct experience, we must admit that the light beams which cannot be directly perceived by the eye are a paradise lost forever as well, the Spanish inquisition a hell lost forever, etc., etc. But the whole point is that scientific knowledge and immediate perception do not coincide at all. We can neither experience the child's impressions, nor witness the French revolution, but the child who experiences his paradise with all directness and the contemporary who saw the major episodes of the revolution with his own eyes are, despite that, farther from the scientific knowledge of these facts than we are. Not only the humanities, but the natural sciences as well, build their concepts in principle independently from immediate experience. We are reminded of Engels' words about the ants and the limitations of our eye.

How do the sciences proceed in the study of what is not immediately given? Generally speaking, they reconstruct it, they re-create the subject of study through the method of interpreting its traces or influences, i.e., indirectly. Thus, the historian interprets traces—documents, memoirs, newspapers, etc.—and nevertheless history is a science about the past, reconstructed by its traces, and not a science about the traces of the past, it is about the revolution and not about documents of the revolution. The same is true for child psychology. Is childhood, the child's mind, really inaccessible for us, does it not leave any traces, does it not manifest or reveal itself? It is just a matter of how to interpret these traces, by what method. Can they be interpreted by analogy with the traces of the adult? It is, therefore, a matter of finding the right interpretation and not of completely refraining from any interpretation. After all, historians too are familiar with more than one erroneous construct based upon genuine documents which were falsely interpreted. What conclusion follows from this? Is it really that history is "a paradise forever lost"? But the same logic that calls child psychology a paradise lost would compel us to say this about history as well. And if the historian, or the geologist, or the physicist were to argue like the reflexologist, they would say: as we cannot immediately experience the past of mankind and the earth (the child's mind) and can only immediately experience the present (the adult's consciousness)—which is why many falsely interpret the past by analogy with the present or as a small present (the child as a small adult)— history and geology are subjective, impossible. The only thing possible is a history of the present (the psychology of the adult person). The history of the past can only be studied as the science of the traces of the past, of the documents etc. as such, and not of the past as such (through the methods of studying reflexes without any attempt at interpreting them).

This dogma—of immediate experience as the single source and natural boundary of scientific knowledge—in principle makes or breaks the whole theory of subjective and objective methods. Vvedensky and Bekhterev grow from a single root: both hold that science can only study what is given in self-observation, i.e., in the immediate perception of the psychological. Some rely on the mental eye and build a whole science in conformity with its properties and the boundaries of its action. Others do not rely on it and only wish to study what can be seen with the real eye. This is why I say that reflexology, methodologically speaking, is built entirely according to the principle that history should be defined as the science of the documents of the past. Due to the many fruitful principles of the natural sciences, reflexology proved to be a highly progressive current in psychology, but as a theory of method it is deeply reactionary, because it leads us back to the naive sensualistic prejudice that we can only study what can be perceived and to the extent we perceive it.

Just as physics is liberating itself from anthropomorphic elements, i.e., from specific sensory sensations and is proceeding with the eye fully excluded, so psychology must work with the concept of the mental: direct self-observation must be excluded like muscular sensation in mechanics and visual sensation in optics. The subjectivists believe that they refuted the objective method when they showed that genetically speaking the concepts of behavior contain a grain of self-observation—cf. Chelpanov (1925),[20] Kravkov (1922),[21] Portugalov (1925).[22] But the genetic origin of a concept says nothing about its logical nature: genetically, the concept of force in mechanics also goes back to muscular sensation.

The problem of self-observation is a problem of technique and not of principle. It is an instrument amidst a number of other instruments, as the eye is for physicists.

We must use it to the extent that it is useful, but there is no need to pronounce judgments of principle about it—e.g., about the limitations of the knowledge obtained with it, its reliability, or the nature of the knowledge determined by it. Engels demonstrated how little the natural construction of the eye determines the boundaries of our knowledge of the phenomena of light. Planck says the same on behalf of contemporary physics. To separate the fundamental psychological concept from the specific sensory perception is psychology's next task. This sensation itself, self-observation itself, must be explained (like the eye) from the postulates, methods, and universal principles of psychology. It must become one of psychology's particular problems.

When we accept this, the question of the nature of interpretation, i.e., the indirect method, arises. Usually it is said that history interprets the traces of the past, whereas physics observes the invisible as directly as the eye does by means of its instruments. The instruments are the extended organs of the researcher. After all, the microscope, telescope, telephone etc. make the invisible visible and the subject of immediate experience. Physics does not interpret, but sees.

But this opinion is false. The methodology of the scientific instrument has long since clarified a new role for the instrument which is not always obvious. Even the thermometer may serve as an example of the introduction of a fundamentally new principle into the method of science through the use of an instrument. On the thermometer we read the temperature. It does not strengthen or extend the sensation of heat as the microscope extends the eye; rather, it totally liberates us from sensation when studying heat. One who is unable to sense heat or cold may still use the thermometer, whereas a blind person cannot use a microscope. The use of a thermometer is a perfect model of the indirect method. After all, we do not study what we see (as with the microscope)—the rising of the mercury, the expansion of the alcohol—but we study heat and its changes, which are indicated by the mercury or alcohol. We interpret the indications of the thermometer, we reconstruct the phenomenon under study by its traces, by its influence upon the expansion of a substance. All the instruments Planck speaks of as means to study the invisible are constructed in this way. To interpret, consequently, means to re-create a phenomenon from its traces and influences relying upon regularities established before (in the present case—the law of the extension of solids, liquids, and gases during heating). There is no fundamental difference whatsoever between the use of a thermometer on the one hand and interpretation in history, psychology, etc. on the other. The same holds true for any science: it is not dependent upon sensory perception.

Stumpf mentions the blind mathematician Saunderson who wrote a textbook of geometry; Shcherbina (1908)[23] relates that his blindness did not prevent him from explaining optics to sighted people. And, indeed, all instruments mentioned by Planck can be adapted for the blind, just like the watches, thermometers, and books for the blind that already exist, so that a blind person might occupy himself with optics as well. It is a matter of technique, not of principle.

Kornilov (1922)[24] beautifully demonstrated that (1) disagreement about the procedural aspect of the design of experiments makes for conflicts which lead to the formation of different currents in psychology, just as the different philosophies about the chronoscope—which resulted from the question as to in which room this apparatus should be placed during the experiments—determined the question of the whole method and system of psychology and divided Wundt's school from Külpe's; and (2) the experimental method introduced nothing new into psychology. For Wundt it is a correction of self-observation. For Ach[25] the data of self-observation can only be checked against other data of self-observation, as if the sensation of heat can be checked only against other sensations. For Deichler the quantitative estimations give a measure for the correctness of introspection. In sum, experiment does not extend our knowledge, it checks it. Psychology does not yet have a methodology of its equipment and has not yet raised the question of an apparatus which would—like the thermometer—liberate us from introspection rather than check or amplify it. The philosophy of the chronoscope is a more difficult matter than its technique. But about the indirect method in psychology we will come to speak more than once.

Zelenyj (1923) is right in pointing out that in Russia the word "method" means two different things: (1) the research methods, the technology of the experiment; and (2) the epistemological method, or methodology, which determines the research goal, the place of the science, and its nature. In psychology the epistemological method is subjective, although the research methods may be partially objective. In physiology the epistemological method is objective, although the research methods may be partially subjective as in the physiology of the sense organs. Let us add that the experiment reformed the research methods, but not the epistemological method. For this reason, he says that the psychological method can only have the value of a diagnostic device in the natural sciences.

This question is crucial for all methodological and concrete problems of psychology. For psychology the need to fundamentally transcend the boundaries of immediate experience is a matter of life and death. The demarcation, separation of the scientific concept from the specific perception, can take place only on the basis of the indirect method. The reply that the indirect method is inferior to the direct one is in scientific terms utterly false. Precisely because it does not shed light upon the plentitude of experience, but only on one aspect, it accomplishes scientific work: it isolates, analyzes, separates, abstracts a single feature. After all, in immediate experience as well we isolate the part that is the subject of our observation. Anyone who deplores the fact that we do not share the ant's immediate experience of chemical beams is beyond help, says Engels, for on the other hand we know the nature of these beams better than ants do. The task of science is not to reduce everything to experience. If that were the case it would suffice to replace science with the registration of our perceptions. Psychology's real problem resides also in the fact that our immediate experience is limited, because the whole mind is built like an instrument which selects and isolates certain aspects of phenomena. An eye that would see everything, would for this very reason see nothing. A consciousness that was aware of everything would be aware of nothing, and knowledge of the self, were it aware of everything, would be aware of nothing. Our knowledge is confined between two thresholds, we see but a tiny part of the world. Our senses give us the world in the excerpts, extracts that are important for us. And in between the thresholds it is again not the whole variety of changes which is registered, and new thresholds exist. Consciousness follows nature in a saltatory fashion as it were, with blanks and gaps. The mind selects the stable points of reality amidst the universal movement. It provides islands of safety in the Heraclitean stream. It is an organ of selection, a sieve filtering the world and changing it so that it becomes possible to act. In this resides its positive role—not in reflection (the non-mental reflects as well; the thermometer is more precise than sensation), but in the fact that it does not always reflect correctly, i.e., subjectively distorts reality to the advantage of the organism.

If we were to see everything (i.e., if there were no absolute thresholds) including all changes that constantly take place (i.e., if no relative thresholds existed), we would be confronted with chaos (remember how many objects a microscope reveals in a drop of water). What would be a glass of water? And what a river? A pond reflects everything; a stone reacts in principle to everything. But these reactions equal the stimulation: *causa aequat effectum*. [34] The reaction of the organism is "richer": it is not like an effect, it expends potential forces, it selects stimuli. Red, blue, loud, sour—it is a world cut into portions. Psychology's task is to clarify the advantage of the fact that the eye does not perceive many of the things known to optics. From the lower forms of reactions to the higher ones there leads, as it were, the narrowing opening of a funnel.

It would be a mistake to think that we do not see what is for us biologically useless. Would it really be useless to see microbes? The sense organs show clear traces of the fact that they are in the first place organs of selection. Taste is obviously a selection organ for digestion, smell is part of the respiratory process. Like the customs checkpoints at the border, they test the stimuli coming from outside. Each organ takes the world *cum grano salis* [35]—with a coefficient of specification, as Hegel says, [and] with an indication of the relation, where the quality of one object determines the intensity and character of the quantitative influence of another quality. For this reason there is a complete analogy between the selection of the eye and the further selection of the instrument: both are organs of selection (accomplish what we accomplish in the experiment). So that the fact that scientific knowledge transcends the boundaries of perception is rooted in the psychological essence of knowledge itself.

From this it follows that as methods for judging scientific truth, direct evidence and analogy are in principle completely identical. Both must be subjected to critical examination; both can deceive and tell the truth. The direct evidence that the sun turns around the earth deceives us; the analogy upon which spectral analysis is built, leads to the truth. On these grounds some have rightly defended the legitimacy of analogy as a basic method of zoopsychology. This is fully acceptable, one must only point out the conditions under which the analogy will be correct. So far the analogy in zoopsychology has led to anecdotes and curious incidents, because it was observed where it actually cannot exist. It can, however, also lead to spectral analysis. That is why methodologically speaking the situation in physics and psychology is in principle the same. The difference is one of degree.

The mental sequence we experience is a fragment: where do all the elements of mental life disappear and where do they come from? We are compelled to continue the known sequence with a hypothetical one. It was precisely in this sense that Høffding [1908, p. 92/114] introduced this concept which corresponds with the concept of potential energy in physics. This is why Leibnitz[26] introduced the infinitely small elements of consciousness [cf. Høffding, 1908, p. 108].

> We are forced to continue the life of consciousness into the unconscious in order not to fall into absurdities [ibid., p. 286].

However, for Høffding (ibid., p. 117) "the unconscious is a boundary concept in science" and at this boundary we may "weigh the possibilities" through a hypothesis, but

> a real extension of our factual knowledge is impossible . . . . Compared to the physical world, we experience the mental world as a fragment; only through a hypothesis can we supplement it.

But even this respect for the boundary of science seems to other authors insufficient. About the unconscious it is only allowed to say that it exists. By its very definition it is not an object for experimental verification. To argue its existence by means of observations, as Høffding attempts, is illegitimate. This word has two meanings, there are two types of unconscious which we must not mix up—the debate is about a twofold subject: about the hypothesis and about the facts that can be observed.

One more step in this direction, and we return to where we started: to the difficulty that compelled us to hypothesize an unconscious.

We can see that psychology finds itself here in a tragicomic situation: I want to, but I cannot. It is forced to accept the unconscious so as not to fall into absurdities. But accepting it, it falls into even greater absurdities and runs back in horror. It is like a man who, running from a wild animal and into an even greater danger, runs back to the wild animal, the lesser danger—but does it really make any difference from what he dies? Wundt views in this theory an echo of the mystical philosophy of nature [*Naturphilosophie*] of the early 19th century. With him Lange (1914, p. 251) accepts that the unconscious mind is an intrinsically contradictory concept. The unconscious must be explained physically and chemically and not psychologically, else we allow "mystical agents," "arbitrary constructions that can never be verified," to enter science.

Thus, we are back to Høffding: there is a physico-chemical sequence, which in some fragmentary points is suddenly *ex nihilo* accompanied by a mental sequence. Please, be good enough to understand and scientifically interpret the "fragment." What does this debate mean for the methodologist? We must psychologically transcend the boundary of immediately perceived consciousness and continue it, but in such a way as to separate the concept from sensation. Psychology as the science of consciousness is in principle impossible. As the science of the unconscious mind it is doubly impossible. It would seem that there is no way out, no solution for this quadrature of the circle. But physics finds itself in exactly the same position. Admittedly, the physical sequence extends further than the mental one, but this sequence is not infinite and without gaps either. It was science that made it in principle continuous and infinite and not immediate experience. It extended this experience by excluding the eye. This is also psychology's task.

Hence, interpretation is not only a bitter necessity for psychology, but also a liberating and essentially most fruitful method of knowledge, a *salto vitale*, which for bad jumpers turns into a *salto mortale*. Psychology must develop its philosophy of equipment, just as physics has its philosophy of the thermometer. In practice both parties in psychology have recourse to interpretation: the subjectivist has in the end the words of the subject, i.e., his behavior and mind are interpreted behavior. The objectivist will inevitably interpret as well. The very concept of reaction implies the necessity of interpretation, of sense, connection, relation. Indeed, *actio* and *reactio* are concepts that are originally mechanistic—one must observe both and deduce a law. But in psychology and physiology the reaction is not equal to the stimulus. It has a sense, a goal, i.e., it fulfills a certain function in the larger whole. It is qualitatively connected with its stimulus. And this sense of the reaction as a function of the whole, this quality of the interrelation, is not given in experience, but found by inference. To put it more easily and generally: when we study behavior as a system of reactions, we do not study the behavioral acts in themselves (by the organs), but in their relation to other acts—to stimuli. But the relation and the quality of the relation, its sense, are never the subject of immediate perception, let alone the relation between two heterogeneous sequences—between stimuli and reactions. The following is extremely important: the reaction is an answer. An answer can only be studied according to the quality of its relation with the question, for this is the sense of answer which is not found in perception but in interpretation.

This is the way everybody proceeds.

Bekhterev distinguishes the creative reflex. A problem is the stimulus, and creativity is the response reaction or a symbolic reflex. But the concepts of creativity and symbol are semantic concepts, not experiential ones: a reflex is creative when it stands in such a relation to a stimulus that it creates something new; it is symbolic when it replaces another reflex. But we cannot see the symbolic or creative nature of a reflex.

Pavlov distinguishes the reflexes of freedom and purpose, the food reflex and the defense reflex. But neither freedom nor purpose can be seen, nor do they have an organ like, for example, the organs for nutrition; nor are they functions. They consist of the same movements as the other ones. Defense, freedom, and purpose— they are the meanings of these reflexes.

Kornilov distinguishes emotional reactions, selective, associative reactions, the reaction of recognition, etc. It is again a classification according to their meaning, i.e., on the basis of the interpretation of the relation between stimulus and response.

Watson, accepting similar distinctions based on meaning, openly says that nowadays the psychologist of behavior arrives by sheer logic at the conclusion that there is a hidden process of thinking. By this he is becoming conscious of his method and brilliantly refutes Titchener, who defended the thesis that the psychologist of behavior, exactly because of being a psychologist of behavior, cannot accept the existence of a process of thinking when he is not in the situation to observe it immediately and must use introspection to reveal thinking. Watson demonstrated that he in principle isolates the concept of thinking from its perception in intro-spection, just like the thermometer emancipates us from sensation when we develop the concept of heat. That is why he [1926, p. 301] emphasizes:

> If we ever succeed in scientifically studying the intimate nature of thought . . .then we will owe this to a considerable extent to the scientific apparatus.

However even now the psychologist

> is not in such a deplorable situation: physiologists as well are often satisfied with the observation of the end results and utilize logic . . . . The adherent of the psychology of behavior feels that with respect to thinking he must keep to exactly the same position [ibid., p. 302].

Meaning as well is for Watson an experimental problem. We find it in what is given to us through thinking.

Thorndike (1925) distinguishes the reactions of feeling, conclusion, mood, and cunning. Again [we are dealing with] interpretation.

The whole matter is simply *how* to interpret—by analogy with one's introspec-tion, biological functions, etc. That is why Koffka [1925, pp. 10/13] is right when he states: There is no objective criterion for consciousness, we do not know whether an action has consciousness or not, but this does not make us unhappy at all. How-ever, behavior is such that the consciousness belonging to it, if it exists at all, must have such and such a structure. Therefore behavior must be explained in the same way as consciousness. Or in other words, put paradoxically: if everybody had only those reactions which can be observed by all others, nobody could observe anything, i.e., scientific observation is based upon transcending the boundaries of the visible and upon a search for its meaning which cannot be observed. He is right. He was right [Koffka, 1924, pp. 152/160] when he claimed that behaviorism is bound to be fruitless when it will study only the observable, when its ideal is to know the di-rection and speed of the movements of each limb, the secretion of each gland, resulting from a fixed stimulation. Its area would then be restricted to the physiology of the muscles and the glands. The description "this animal is running away from some danger," however insufficient it may be, is yet a thousand times more char-acteristic for the animal's behavior than a formula giving us the movements of all its legs with their varying speeds, the curves of breath, pulse, and so forth.

Köhler (1917) demonstrated in practice how we may prove the presence of thinking in apes without any introspection and even study the course and structure of this process through the method of the interpretation of objective reactions. Kornilov (1922) demonstrated how we may measure the energetic budget of different thought operations using the indirect method: the dynamoscope is used by him as a thermometer. Wundt's mistake resided in the *mechanical* application of equipment and the mathematical method to check and correct. He did not use them to extend introspection, to liberate himself from it, but to tie himself to it. In most of Wundt's investigations introspection was essentially superfluous. It was only necessary to single out the unsuccessful experiments. In principle it is totally unnecessary in Kornilov's theory. But psychology must still create its thermometer. Kornilov's research indicates the path.

We may summarize the conclusions from our investigation of the narrow sensualist dogma by again referring to Engels' words about the activity of the eye which in combination with thinking helps us to discover that ants see what is invisible to us.

Psychology has too long striven for experience instead of knowledge. In the present example it preferred to share with the ants their visual experience of the sensation of chemical beams rather than to understand their vision scientifically.

As to the methodological spine that is supporting them there are two scientific systems. Methodology is always like the backbone, the skeleton in the animal's organism. Very primitive animals, like the snail and the tortoise, carry their skeleton on the outside and they can, like an oyster, be separated from their skeleton. What is left is a poorly differentiated fleshy part. Higher animals carry their skeleton inside and make it into the internal support, the bone of each of their movements. In psychology as well we must distinguish lower and higher types of methodological organization.

This is the best refutation of the sham empirism of the natural sciences. It turns out that nothing can be transposed from one theory to another. It would seem that a fact is always a fact. Despite the different points of departure and the different aims one and the same object (a child) and one and the same method (objective observation) should make it possible to transpose the facts of psychology to reflexology. The difference would only be in the interpretation of the same facts. In the end the systems of Ptolemy[27] and Copernicus[28] rested upon the same facts as well. [But] It turns out that facts obtained by means of different principles of knowledge are *different* facts.

Thus, the debate about the application of the biogenetic principle in psychology is not a debate about facts. The facts are indisputable and there are two groups of them: the recapitulation of the stages the organism goes through in the development of its structure as established by natural science and the indisputable traits of similarity between the phylo- and ontogenesis of the mind. It is particularly important that neither is there any debate about the latter group. Koffka [1925, pp. 32], who contests this theory and subjects it to a methodological analysis, resolutely declares that the analogies, from which this false theory proceeds, exist beyond any doubt. The debate concerns the *meaning* of these analogies and it turns out that it cannot be decided without analyzing the principles of child psychology, without having a general idea of childhood, a conception of the meaning and the biological sense of childhood, a certain theory of child development. It is quite easy to find analogies. The question is *how* to search for them. Similar analogies may be found in the behavior of adults as well.

Two typical mistakes are possible here: one is made by Hall.[29] Thorndike and Groos have brilliantly exposed it in critical analyses. The latter [Groos, 1904/1921,

p. 7] justly claims that the purpose of any comparison and the task of comparative science is not only to distinguish similar traits, but even more to search for the differences within the similarity. Comparative psychology, consequently, must not merely understand man as an animal, but much more as a non-animal.

The straightforward application of the principle led to a ubiquitous search for similarity. A correct method and reliably established facts led to monstrously strained interpretations and distorted facts when applied uncritically. Children's games have indeed traditionally preserved many echoes of the remote past (the play with bows, round dances). For Hall this is the repetition and expression in innocent form of the animal and pre-historic stages of development. Groos considers this to show a remarkable lack of critical judgment. The fear of cats and dogs would be a remnant of the time when these animals were still wild. Water would attract children because we developed from aquatic animals. The automatic movements of the infant's arms would be a remnant of the movements of our ancestors who swam in the water, etc.

The mistake resides, consequently, in the interpretation of the child's whole behavior as a recapitulation and in the absence of any principle to verify the analogy and to select the facts which must and must not be interpreted. It is precisely the play of animals which cannot be explained in this way. "Can Hall's theory explain the play of the young tiger with its victim?"—asks Groos [1904/1921, p. 73]. It is clear that this play cannot be understood as a recapitulation of past phylogenetic development. It foreshadows the future activity of the tiger and not a repetition of his past development. It must be explained and understood in relation to the tiger's future, in the light of which it gets its meaning, and not in the light of the past of his species. The past of the species comes out in a *totally* different sense: through the individual's *future* which it predetermines, but not directly and not in the sense of a repetition.

What are the facts? This quasi-biological theory appears to be untenable precisely in *biological* terms, precisely in comparison with the nearest homogeneous analogue in the *series of homogeneous phenomena* in other stages of evolution. When we compare the play of a child with the play of a tiger, i.e., a higher mammal, and consider not only the similarity, but the *difference* as well, we will lay bare *their common* biological essence which resides exactly in their *difference* (the tiger plays the chase of tigers; the child that he is a grown-up; both practice necessary functions for their life to come—Groos' theory). But despite all the seeming similarity in the comparison of *heterogeneous* phenomena (play with water—aquatic life of the amphibian—man) the theory is biologically meaningless.

Thorndike [1906] adds to this devastating argument a remark about the different order of the *same biological principles* in onto- and phylogenesis. Thus, consciousness appears very early in ontogenesis and very late in phylogenesis. The sexual drive, on the other hand, appears very early in phylogenesis and very late in ontogenesis. Stern [1927, pp. 266-267], using similar considerations, criticizes the same theory in its application to play.

Blonsky (1921) makes another kind of mistake. He defends—and very convincingly—this law for embryonic development from the viewpoint of biomechanics and shows that it would be miraculous if it did not exist. The author points out the hypothetical nature of the considerations ("not very conclusive") leading to this contention ("it may be like this"), i.e., he gives arguments for the methodological possibility of a working hypothesis, but then, instead of proceeding to the investigation and verification of the hypothesis, follows in Hall's footsteps and begins to *explain* the child's behavior on the basis of very intelligible analogies: he does not view the climbing of trees by children as a recapitulation of the life of apes, but of primitive people who lived amidst rocks and ice; the tearing off of wallpaper is an atavism of the tearing off of the bark of trees etc. What is most remarkable of all is that the error leads Blonsky to the same conclusion as Hall: to the *negation of play*. Groos and Stern have shown that exactly where it is easiest to find analogies between onto- and phylogenesis is this theory untenable. And neither does Blonsky, as if illustrating the irresistible force of the methodological laws of scientific knowledge, search for new terms. He sees no need to attach a "new term" (play) to the child's activity. This means that on his methodological path he first lost its *meaning* and then—with creditable consistency—refrained from the term that expresses this meaning. Indeed, if the activity, the child's behavior, is an atavism, then the term "play" is out of place. This activity has nothing in common with the play of the tiger as Groos demonstrated. And we must translate Blonsky's declaration "I don't like this term" in methodological terms as "I lost the understanding and meaning of this concept."

Only in this way, by following each principle to its ultimate conclusions, by taking each concept in the extreme form toward which it strives, by investigating each line of thinking to the very end, at times completing it for the author, can we determine the methodological nature of the phenomenon under investigation. That is why a concept that is used deliberately, not blindly, in the science for which it was created, where it originated, developed, and was carried to its ultimate expression, *is blind*, leads nowhere when transposed to another science. Such *blind* transpositions of the biogenetic principle, the experiment, the mathematical method from the natural sciences, created the appearance of science in psychology which in reality concealed a total impotence in the face of the studied facts.

But to complete the sketch of the circle described by the meaning of a principle introduced into a science in this way, we will follow its further fate. The matter does not end with the detection of the fruitlessness of the principle, its critique, the pointing out of curious and strained interpretations at which schoolboys poke their finger. In other words, the history of the principle does not end with its simple expulsion from the area that does not belong to it, with its simple rejection. After all, we remember that the foreign principle penetrated into our science via a *bridge of facts*, via really existing analogues. Nobody has denied this. While this principle became strengthened and reigned, the number of facts upon which its false power rested increased. They were partially false and partially correct. In its turn the critique of these facts, the critique of the principle itself, draws still other new facts into the scope of the science. The matter is not confined to the facts: the critique must provide an explanation for the colliding facts. The theories assimilate each other and on this basis the *regeneration* of a new principle takes place.

Under the pressure of the facts and foreign theories, the newcomer changes its face. The same happened with the biogenetic principle. It was reborn and in psychology it figures in two forms (a sign that the process of regeneration is not yet finished): (1) as a theory of utility, defended by neo-Darwinism and the school of Thorndike, which finds that individual and species are subject to the same laws—hence a number of coincidences, but also a number of non-coincidences. Not everything that is useful for the species in its early stage is useful for the individual as well; (2) as a theory of synchronization, defended in psychology by Koffka and the school of Dewey, in the philosophy of history by Spengler.[30] It is a theory which says that all developmental processes have some general stages, some successive forms, in common—from elementary to more complex and from lower to higher levels.

Far be it from us to consider any of these conclusions the right one. We are in general still far from a fundamental examination of the question. For us it is important to follow the dynamics of the spontaneous, blind reaction of a scientific body to a foreign, inserted object. It is important for us to trace the forms of scientific inflammation relative to the kind of infection in order to proceed from pathology to the norm and to clarify the normal functions of the different composite parts—the organs of science. This is the purpose and meaning of our analyses, which seemingly sidetrack us, but although we make no mention of it we continually hold to the comparison (prompted by Spinoza) of the psychology of our days to a severely diseased person. If we wish to formulate the aim of our last digression from this viewpoint, the positive conclusion which we have reached, the result of the analysis, we must determine it as follows: previously—on the basis of the analysis of the unconscious—we studied the nature, the action, the manner of the spreading of the infection, the penetration of the foreign idea after the facts, its lording over the organism, the disturbance of the organism's functions; now—on the basis of the analysis of the biogenesis—we were able to study the counter-action of the organism, its struggle with the infection, the dynamic tendency to resolve, throw out, neutralize, assimilate, degenerate the foreign body, to mobilize forces against the contagion. We studied—to stick to medical terms—the elaboration of antibodies and the development of immunity. What remains is the third and final step: to distinguish the phenomena of the disease from the reactions, the healthy from the diseased, the processes of the infection from the recovery. This we will do in the analysis of scientific terminology in the third and final digression. After that we will directly proceed to the statement of a diagnosis and prognosis for our patient— to the nature, meaning and outcome of the present crisis.

9

If one would like to get an objective and clear idea of the contemporary state of psychology and the dimensions of its crisis, it would suffice to study the psychological *language*, i.e., the nomenclature and terminology, the dictionary and syntax of the psychologist. Language, scientific language in particular, is a tool of thought, an instrument of analysis, and it suffices to examine which instruments a science utilizes to understand the character of its operations. The highly developed and exact language of contemporary physics, chemistry, and physiology, not to speak of mathematics where it plays an extraordinary role, was developed and perfected during the development of science and far from spontaneously, but deliberately under the influence of tradition, critique, and the direct terminological creativity of scientific societies and congresses. The psychological language of contemporaneity is first of all terminologically insufficient: this means that psychology does not yet have its *own* language. In its dictionary you will find a conglomerate of words of three kinds: (1) the words of everyday language, which are vague, ambiguous, and adapted to practical life (Lazursky levelled this criticism against faculty psychology; I succeeded in showing that it is more true of the language of empirical psychology and of Lazursky himself in particular; see Preface to Lazursky in this volume). Suffice it to remember the touchstone of all translators—the visual *sense* (i.e., sensation) to realize the whole metaphorical nature and inexactness of the practical language of daily life; (2) the words of philosophical language. They too pollute the language of psychologists, as they have lost the link with their previous meaning, are ambiguous as a result of the struggle between the various philosophical schools, and are abstract to a maximal degree. Lalande (1923) views this as the main source of the vagueness and lack of clarity in psychology. The tropes of this language favor vagueness of thought. These metaphors are valuable as illustrations, but dangerous as formulas. It also leads to personifications through the ending -ism, of mental facts, functions, systems and theories, between which small mythological dramas are invented; (3) finally, the words and ways of speaking taken from the natural sciences which are used in a figurative sense bluntly serve deception. When the psychologist discusses energy, force, and even intensity, or when he speaks of excitation etc., he always covers a non-scientific concept with a scientific word and thereby either deceives, or once again underlines the whole indeterminate nature of the concept indicated by the exact foreign term.

Lalande [1923, p. 52] correctly remarks that the obscurity of language depends as much upon its syntax as upon its dictionary. In the construction of the psychological phrase we meet no fewer mythological dramas than in the lexicon. I want to add that the *style*, the manner of expression of a science is no less important. In a word, all elements, all functions of a language show the traces of the age of the science that makes use of them, and determine the character of its workings.

It would be mistaken to think that psychologists have not noticed the mixed character, the inaccuracy, and the mythological nature of their language. There is hardly any author who in one way or another has not dwelt upon the problem of terminology. Indeed, psychologists have pretended to describe, analyze and study very subtle things, full of nuances, they have attempted to convey the unique mental experience, the facts *sui generis* which occur only once, when science wished to convey the experience itself, i.e., when the task of its language was equal to that of the word of the artist. For this reason psychologists recommended that psychology be learned from the great novelists, spoke in the language of the impressionistic fine literature themselves, and even the best, most brilliant stylists among the psychologists were unable to create an exact language and wrote in a figurative-expressive way. They suggested, sketched, described, but did not record. This was the case for James, Lipps, and Binet.

The 6th International Congress of psychologists in Geneva (1909) put this question on its agenda and published two reports—by Baldwin and Claparède—on this topic, but did no more than establishing rules for linguistical possibilities, although Claparède tried to give a definition of 40 laboratory terms. Baldwin's dictionary in England and the technical and critical dictionary of philosophy in France have accomplished much, but despite this the situation becomes worse every year and to read a new book with the help of the above-mentioned dictionaries is impossible. The encyclopedia from which I take this information views it as one of its tasks to introduce solidity and stability into the terminology, but gives occasion to new instability as it introduces a new system of terms [Dumas, 1923].[31] [36]

The language reveals as it were the molecular changes that the science goes through. It reflects the internal processes that take shape—the tendencies of development, reform, and growth. We may assume, therefore, that the troubled condition of the language reflects a troubled condition of the science. We will not deal any further with the essence of this relation. We will take it as our point of departure for the analysis of the contemporary molecular terminological changes in psychology. Perhaps, we will be able to read in them the present and future fate of the science. Let us first of all begin with those who are tempted to deny any fundamental importance to the language of science and view such debates as scholastic logomachy. Thus, Chelpanov (1925) considers the attempt to replace the subjective terminology by an objective one as a ridiculous pretension, utter nonsense. The zoopsychologists (Beer, Bethe, Von Uexküll) have used "photoreceptor" instead of "eye", "stiboreceptor" instead of "nose," "receptor" instead of "sense organ" etc. (Chelpanov, 1925). [37]

Chelpanov is tempted to reduce the whole reform carried out by behaviorism to a play of words. He assumes that in Watson's writings the word "sensation" or "idea" is replaced by the word "reaction." In order to show the reader the difference between ordinary psychology and the psychology of the behaviorist, Chelpanov (1925) gives examples of the new way of expressing things:

> In ordinary psychology it is said: 'When someone's optical nerve is stimulated by a mixture of complementary light waves, he will become *conscious* of the white color.' According to Watson in this case we must say: 'He *reacts* to it as if it were a white color.'

The triumphant conclusion of the author is that the matter is not changed by the words used. The whole difference is in the words. Is this really true? *For a psychologist of Chelpanov's kind it is definitively true.* Who does not investigate nor discover anything new cannot understand why researchers introduce new terms for new phenomena. Who has no view of his own about the phenomena and accepts indifferently both Spinoza, Husserl, Marx, and Plato,[32] for such a person a fundamental change of words is an empty pretension. Who eclectically—in the order of appearance—assimilates all Western European schools, currents and directions, is in need of a vague, undefined, levelling, everyday language—"as is spoken in ordinary psychology." For a person who conceives of psychology only in the form of a textbook it is a matter of life and death to preserve everyday language, and as lots of empiricist psychologists belong to this type, they speak in this mixed and motley jargon, in which the *consciousness of the white color* is simply a fact which is in no need of any further critique.

For Chelpanov it is a caprice, an eccentricity. But why is this eccentricity *so regular*? Doesn't it contain something essential? Watson, Pavlov, Bekhterev, Kornilov, Bethe and Von Uexküll (Chelpanov's list may be continued *ad libitum* from any area of science), Köhler, Koffka and others and still others demonstrated this eccentricity. This means that there is some objective necessity in the tendency to introduce new terminology.

We can say in advance that *the word that refers to a fact at the same time provides a philosophy of that fact*, its theory, its system. When I say: "the consciousness of the color" I have scientific associations of a *certain* kind, the fact is included in a *certain* series of phenomena, I attach a *certain* meaning to the fact. When I say: "the reaction to white" everything is wholly *different*. But Chelpanov is only pretending that it is a matter of words. For him the thesis "*a reform of terminology is not needed*" forms the conclusion from the thesis "*a reform of psychology is not needed.*" Never mind that Chelpanov gets caught in contradictions: on the one hand Watson is only changing words; on the other hand behaviorism is *distorting* psychology. It is one of two things: either Watson is playing with words—then behaviorism is a most innocent thing, an amusing joke, as Chelpanov likes to put it when he reassures himself; or behind the change of words is concealed a change of the matter—then the change of words is not all that funny. A revolution always tears off the old names of things—both in politics and in science.

But let us proceed to other authors who do understand the importance of new words. It is clear to them that new facts and a new viewpoint necessitate new words. Such psychologists fall into two groups. Some are pure eclectics, who happily mix the old and new words and view this procedure as some eternal law. Others speak in a mixed language out of necessity. They do not coincide with any of the debating parties and strive for a unified language, for the creation of their own language.

We have seen that such outspoken eclectics as Thorndike equally apply the term "reaction" to temper, dexterity, action, to the objective and the subjective. As he is not capable of solving the question of the nature of the studied facts and the principles of their investigation, he simply deprives both the subjective and the sub-jective terms of their meaning. "Stimulus-reaction" is for him simply a convenient way to describe the phenomena. Others, such as Pillsbury [1917, pp. 4-14], make eclecticism their principle: the debates about a general method and viewpoint are of interest for the technically-minded psychologist. Sensation and perception he ex-plains in the terms of the structuralists, actions of all kinds in those of the behav-iorists. He himself is inclined towards functionalism. The different terms lead to discrepancies, but he prefers the use of the terms of many schools to those of a single specific school. In complete accordance with this he explains the subject mat-ter of psychology with illustrations from everyday life, in vague words, instead of giving formal definitions. Having given the three definitions of psychology as the science of mind, consciousness, or behavior, he concludes that they may very well be neglected in the description of the mental life. It is only natural that terminology leaves our author indifferent as well.

Koffka (1925) and others try to realize a fundamental synthesis of the old and the new terminology. They understand very well that the word is a theory of the fact it designates and, therefore, they view behind two systems of terms two systems of concepts. Behavior has two aspects—one that must be studied by natural scien-tific observation and one that must be experienced and to these correspond func-tional and descriptive concepts. The functional objective concepts and terms belong to the category of natural scientific ones, the phenomenal descriptive ones are ab-solutely foreign to it (to behavior). This fact is often obscured by the language which does not always have separate words for this or that kind of concept, as everyday language is not scientific language.

The merit of the Americans is that they have fought against subjective anec-dotes in animal psychology. But we will not fear the use of descriptive concepts when describing animal behavior. The Americans have gone too far, they are too objective. What is again highly remarkable: Gestalt theory, which is internally deeply dualistic, reflecting and uniting two contradictory tendencies which, as will be shown below, currently determine the whole crisis and its fate, wishes in principle to pre-serve this *dual* language forever, for it proceeds from the *dual* nature of behavior. However, sciences do not study what is closely related in nature, but what is con-ceptually homogeneous and similar. How can there be *one* science about *two* ab-solutely different kinds of phenomena, which evidently require *two* different methods, *two* different explanatory principles, etc.? After all, the unity of a science is guaranteed by unity of the viewpoint on the subject. How then can we build a science with *two* viewpoints? Once again a contradiction in terms corresponds to a contradiction in principles.

Matters are slightly different with another group of mainly Russian psycholo-gists, who use various terms but view this as the attribute of a period of transition. This "demi-saison," as one psychologist calls it, requires clothes that combine the properties of a fur coat and a summer dress, warm and light at the same time. Thus, Blonsky holds that it is not important how we designate the phenomena under study but how we understand them. We utilize the ordinary vocabulary for our speech but to these ordinary words we attach a content that corresponds to the science of the 20th century. It is not important to avoid the expression "The dog is angry." What is important is that this phrase is not the explanation, but the prob-lem (Blonsky, 1925). Strictly speaking, this implies a complete condemnation of the old terminology: for there this phrase was the explanation. But this phrase must be formulated in an appropriate way and not with the ordinary vocabulary. This is the main thing required to make it a scientific problem. And those whom Blonsky calls the pedants of terminology appreciate much better than he does that the phrase conceals a content given by the history of science. However, like Blonsky many utilize two languages and do not consider this a question of principle. This is the way Kornilov proceeds, this is what I do, repeating after Pavlov: what does it matter whether I call them mental or higher nervous [processes]?

But already these examples show the *limits* of such a bilingualism. The limits themselves show again most clearly what our whole analysis of the eclectics showed: bilingualism is the external sign of dual thinking. You may speak in two languages as long as you convey dual things or things in a dual light. Then it really does not matter what you call them.

So, let us summarize. For empiricists it is necessary to have a language that is colloquial, indeterminate, confused, ambiguous, vague, in order that what is said can be reconciled with whatever you like—today with the church fathers, tomorrow with Marx. They need a word that neither provides a clear philosophical qualification of the nature of the phenomenon, nor simply its clear description, because the empiricists have no clear understanding and conception of their subject. The eclectics, both those that are so by principle and those that adhere to eclecticism only for the time being, are in need of two languages as long as they defend an eclectic point of view. But as soon as they leave this viewpoint and attempt to designate and describe a newly discovered fact or explain their own viewpoint on a subject, they lose their indifference to the language or the word.

Kornilov (1922), who made a new discovery, is prepared to turn the *whole* area to which he assigns this phenomenon from a chapter of psychology into an independent science—reactology. Elsewhere he contrasts the reflex with the reaction and views a fundamental difference between the two terms. They are based on wholly different philosophies and methodologies. Reaction is for him a biological concept and reflex a strictly physiological one. A reflex is only objective, a reaction is subjective objective. This explains why a phenomenon acquires one meaning when we call it a reflex and another when we call it a reaction.

Obviously, it makes a difference how we refer to the phenomena and there is a reason for pedantry when it is backed by an investigation or a philosophy. A wrong word implies a wrong understanding. It is not for nothing that Blonsky notices that his work and the outline of psychology by Jameson (1925)—this typical specimen of philistinism and eclecticism in science—overlap. To view the phrase "the dog is angry" as the problem is wrong if only because, as Shchelovanov (1929) justly pointed out, the finding of the term is the end point and not the starting point of the investigation. As soon as one or the other complex of reactions is referred to with some psychological term all further attempts at analysis are finished. If Blonsky would leave his eclectic stand, like Kornilov, and acknowledge the value of investigation or principle, he would find this out. There is not a single psychologist with whom this would not happen. And such an ironic observer of the "terminological revolutions" as Chelpanov suddenly turns out to be an astonishing pedant: he objects to the name "reactology." With the pedantry of one of Chekhov's gymnasium teachers he preaches that this term causes misunderstanding, first etymologically and second theoretically. The author declares with aplomb that etymologically speaking the word is entirely incorrect—we should say "reactiology" [reaktsiologija]. This is of course the summit of linguistic illiteracy and a flagrant violation of all the terminological principles of the 6th Congress on the international (Latin–Greek) basis of terms. Obviously, Kornilov did not form his term from the home-bred "reaktsija," but from *reactio* and he was perfectly right in doing so. One wonders how Chelpanov would translate "reactiology" into French, German, etc. But this is not what it is all about. It is about something else: Chelpanov declares that this term is inappropriate in Kornilov's system of psychological views. But let us speak to the point. The important thing is that *the meaning of a term is accepted in a system of views*. It turns out that even reflexology *conceived of in a certain way* has its raison d'être.

Let people not think that these trifles have no importance, because they are too obviously confused, contradictory, incorrect, etc. Here there is a difference between the scientific and the practical points of view. Münsterberg explained that the gardener loves his tulips and hates the weeds, but the botanist who describes and explains loves or hates nothing and, from his point of view, cannot love or hate. For the science of man, he says, stupidity is of no less interest than wisdom. It is all indifferent material that merely claims to exist as a link in the chain of phenomena. As a link in the chain of causal phenomena, this fact—that terminology suddenly becomes an urgent question for the eclectic psychologist who does not care about terminology unless it touches his position—is a valuable methodological fact. It is as valuable as the fact that other eclectics *following the same path* come to the same conclusion as Kornilov: neither the conditional nor the correlative reflexes appear sufficiently clear and understandable. Reactions are the basis of the new psychology, and the whole psychology developed by Pavlov, Bekhterev and Watson is called neither reflexology nor behaviorism, but 'psychologie de reaction,' i.e., reactology. Let the eclectics come to opposite conclusions about a specific thing. They are still related by the method, the process by which they arrive at their conclusions.

We find the same regularity in all reflexologists—both investigators and theoreticians. Watson [1914, p. 9] is convinced that we can write a course in psychology without using the words "consciousness," "content," "introspectively verified," "imagery" etc. And for him this is not a terminological matter, but one of principle: just as the chemist cannot use the language of alchemy nor the astronomer that of the horoscope. He explains this brilliantly with the help of one specific case: he regards the difference between a visual reaction and a visual image as extremely important because behind it lies the difference between a consistent monism and a consistent dualism [1914, pp. 16-20]. A word is for him the tentacle by which philosophy comprehends a fact. Whatever is the value of the countless volumes written in the terms of consciousness, it can only be determined and expressed by translating them into objective language. For according to Watson consciousness and so on are no more than undefined expressions. And the new textbook breaks with the popular theories and terminology. Watson condemns "half-hearted psychology of behavior" (which brings harm to the whole current) claiming that when the theses of the new psychology will not preserve their clarity its framework will be distorted, obscured, and it will lose its genuine meaning. Functional psychology perished from such half-heartedness. If behaviorism has a future then it must break completely with the concept of consciousness. However, thus far it has not been decided whether behaviorism will become the dominating *system* of psychology or simply remain a methodological approach. And therefore Watson (1926) too often takes the methodology of common sense as the basis of his investigations. In the attempt to liberate himself from philosophy he slips into the viewpoint of the "common man," understanding by this latter not the basic feature of human practice but the common sense of the average American businessman. In his opinion the common man must welcome behaviorism. Ordinary life has taught him to act that way. Consequently, when dealing with the science of behavior he will not feel a change of method or some change of the subject (ibid.). This [viewpoint] implies the verdict on all behaviorism. Scientific study absolutely requires a *change* of the subject (i.e., its treatment in concepts) and the *method*. But behavior itself is understood by these psychologists in its everyday sense and in their arguments and descriptions there is much of the philistine way of judgment. Therefore, neither radical nor half-hearted behaviorism will ever find—either in style and language, or in principle and method—the *boundary* between everyday and philistine understanding. Having liberated themselves from the "alchemy" in language, the behaviorists have polluted it with everyday, non-terminological speech. This makes them akin to Chelpanov: the whole difference can be attributed to the life style of the American or Russian philistine. The reproach that the new psychology is a philistine psychology is therefore partially justified.

This vagueness of language in the Americans, which Blonsky considers a lack of pedantry, is viewed by Pavlov [1928/1963, pp. 213-214] as a failing. He views it as a

> gross defect which prevents the success of the work, but which, I have no doubt, will sooner or later be removed. I refer to the application of psychological concepts and classifications in this essentially objective study of the behavior of animals. Herein lies the cause of the fortuitous and conditional character of their complicated methods, and the fragmentary and unsystematic character of their results, which have no well planned basis to rest on.

One could not express the role and function of language in scientific investigation more clearly. And Pavlov's entire success is first of all due to the enormous consistency in his language. His investigations led to a theory of higher nervous activity and animal behavior, rather than a chapter on the functioning of the salivary glands, exclusively because he lifted the study of salivary secretion to an enormously high theoretical level and created a transparent system of concepts that lies at the basis of the science. One must marvel at Pavlov's principled stand in methodological matters. His book introduces us into the laboratory of his investigations and teaches us how to create a scientific language. At first, what does it matter what we call the phenomenon? But gradually each step is strengthened by a new word, each new principle requires a term. He clarifies the sense and meaning of the use of new terms. The selection of terms and concepts predetermines the outcome of an investigation:

> I cannot understand how the non-spatial concepts of contemporary psychology can be fitted into the material structure of the brain [ibid., p. 224].

When Thorndike speaks of a mood reaction and studies it, he creates concepts and laws that lead us away from the brain. To have recourse to such a method Pavlov calls cowardice. Partly out of habit, partly from a "certain anxiety," he resorted to psychological explanations.

> But soon I understood that they were bad servants. For me there arose difficulties when I could see no natural relations between the phenomena. The succor of psychology was only in words (the animal has 'remembered,' the animal 'wished,' the animal 'thought'), i.e., *it was only a method of indeterminate thinking, without a basis in fact* (italics mine, L. V.) [ibid., p. 237].

He regards the manner in which psychologists express themselves as an insult against serious thinking.

And when Pavlov introduced in his laboratories a penalty for the use of psychological terms this was no less important and revealing for the history of the theory of the science than the debate about the symbol of faith for the history of religion. Only Chelpanov can laugh about this: the scientist does not fine for [the use of] an incorrect term in a textbook or in the exposition of a subject, *but in the laboratory—in the process of the investigation*. Obviously, such a fine was imposed for the non-causal, non-spatial, indeterminate, mythological thinking that came with that word and that threatened to blow up the whole cause and to introduce—as in the case of the Americans—a fragmentary, unsystematic character and to take away the foundations.

Chelpanov (1925) does not suspect at all that new words may be needed in the laboratory, in an investigation, that the sense [and] meaning of an investigation are determined by the words used. He criticizes Pavlov, stating that "inhibition" is a vague, hypothetical expression and that the same must be said of the term "disinhibition." Admittedly, we don't know what goes on in the brain during inhibition, but nevertheless it is a brilliant, transparent concept. First of all, it is well defined, i.e., exactly determined in its meaning and boundaries. Secondly, it is honest, i.e., it says no more than is known. Presently the *processes* of inhibition in the brain are not wholly clear to us, but the *word* and the *concept* "inhibition" are wholly clear. Thirdly, it is principled and scientific, i.e., it includes a fact into a system, underpins it with a foundation, explains it hypothetically, but causally. Of course, we have a clearer image of an eye than of an analyzer. Exactly because of this the word "eye" doesn't mean anything in science. The term "visual analyzer" says both less and more than the word "eye." Pavlov revealed a new function of the eye, compared it with the function of other organs, connected the whole sensory path from the eye to the cortex, indicated its place in the system of behavior—and all this is expressed by the new term. It is true that we must think of visual sensations when we hear these words, but the genetic origin of a word and its terminological meaning are two absolutely different things. The word contains *nothing* of sensations; it can be adequately used by a blind person. Those who, following Chelpanov, catch Pavlov making a slip of the tongue, using fragments of a psychological language, and find him guilty of inconsistency, do not understand the heart of the matter. When Pavlov uses [words such as] happiness, attention, idiot (about a dog), this only means that the mechanism of happiness, attention etc. *has not yet been studied*, that these are the as yet obscure spots of the system; it does not imply a fundamental concession or contradiction.

But all this may seem incorrect as long as we do not take the opposite aspect into account. Of course, terminological consistency may become pedantry, "verbalism," commonplace (Bekhterev's school). When does that occur? When the word is like a label stuck on a finished article and is not born in the research process. Then it does not define, delimit, but introduces vagueness and shambles in the system of concepts.

Such a work implies the pinning on of new labels which explain absolutely nothing, for it is not difficult, of course, to invent a whole catalogue of names: the reflex of purpose, the reflex of God, the reflex of right, the reflex of freedom, etc. [38] A reflex can be found for everything. The problem is only that we gain nothing but trifles. This does not refute the general rule, but indirectly confirms it: new words keep pace with new investigations.

Let us summarize. We have seen everywhere that the word, like the sun in a drop of water, *fully* reflects the processes and tendencies in the development of a science. A certain fundamental unity of knowledge in science comes to light which goes from the highest principles to the selection of a word. What guarantees this *unity* of the whole scientific system? The fundamental methodological skeleton. The investigator, insofar as he is not a technician, a registrar, an executor, is always a philosopher who during the investigation and description is *thinking* about the phenomena, and his way of thinking is revealed in the words he uses. A tremendous discipline of thought lies behind Pavlov's penalty. A discipline of mind similar to the monastic system which forms the core of the religious world view is at the core of the scientific conception of the world. He who enters the laboratory with his own word is deemed to repeat Pavlov's example. The word is a philosophy of the fact; it can be its mythology and its scientific theory. When Lichtenberg[33] said: "Es denkt, sollte man sagen, so wie man sagt: es blitzt," he was fighting mythology in language. [39] To say "cogito" is saying too much when it is translated as "I think." Would the physiologist really agree to say "I conduct the excitation along my nerve"? To say *"I think"* or *"It comes to my mind"* implies two opposite theories of thinking. Binet's whole theory of the mental poses requires the first expression, Freud's theory the second and Külpe's theory now the one, now the other. Høffding [1908, p. 106, footnote 2] sympathetically cites the physiologist Foster who says that the impressions of an animal deprived of [one of] its cerebral hemispheres we must "either call sensations, or we must *invent an entirely new word for them*," for we have stumbled upon a *new* category of facts and must choose a way to think about it—whether in connection with the old category or in a new fashion.

Among the Russian authors it was Lange (1914, p. 43) who understood the importance of terminology. Pointing out that there is no shared system in psychology, that the crisis shattered the whole science, he remarks that

> Without fear of exaggeration it can be said that the description of any psychological process becomes different whether we describe and study it in the categories of the psychological system of Ebbinghaus or Wundt, Stumpf or Avenarius, Meinong or Binet, James or G. E. Müller. Of course, the purely factual aspect must remain the same. However, in science, at least in psychology, to separate the described fact from its theory, i.e., from those scientific categories by means of which this description is made, is often very difficult and even impossible, for in psychology (as, by the way, in physics, according to Duhem[34]) each description is always already a certain theory . . . . Factual investigations, in particular those of an experimental character, seem to the superficial observer to be free from those fundamental disagreements about basic scientific categories which divide the different psychological schools.

But the very statement of the questions, the use of one or the other psychological term, always implies a certain way of understanding them which corresponds to some theory, and consequently the whole factual result of the investigation stands or falls with the correctness or falsity of the psychological system. Seemingly very exact investigations, observations, or measurements may, therefore, prove false, or in any case lose their meaning when the meaning of the basic psychological theories is changed. Such crises, which destroy or depreciate whole series of facts, have occurred more than once in science. Lange compares them to an earthquake that arises due to deep deformations in the depths of the earth. Such was [the case with] the fall of alchemy. The dabbling that is now so widespread in science, i.e., the isolation of the technical executive function of the investigation—chiefly the maintenance of the equipment according to a well-known routine—from scientific thinking, is noticeable first of all in the breakdown of scientific language. In principle, all thoughtful psychologists know this perfectly well: in methodological investigations the terminological problem which requires a most complex analysis instead of a simple note takes the lion's share. Rickert regards the creation of unequivocal terminology as the most important task of psychology which precedes any investigation, for already in primitive description we must select word meanings which "by generalizing simplify" the immense diversity and plurality of the mental phenomena [Binswanger, 1922, p. 26]. Engels [1925/1978, p. 553] essentially expressed the same idea in his example from chemistry:

> In organic chemistry the meaning of some body and, consequently, its name are no longer simply dependent upon its composition, but rather upon its place in the *series* to which it belongs. That is why its old name becomes an obstacle for understanding when we find that a body belongs to such a series and must be replaced by *a name that refers to this series* (paraffin, etc.).

What has been carried to the rigor of a chemical rule here exists as a general principle in the whole area of scientific language.

Lange (1914, p. 96) says that

> Parallelism is a word which seems innocent at first sight. It conceals, however, a terrible idea—the idea of the secondary and accidental nature of technique in the world of physical phenomena.

This innocent word has an instructive history. Introduced by Leibniz it was applied to the solution of the psychophysical problem which goes back to Spinoza, changing its name many times in the process. Høffding [1908, p. 91, footnote 1] calls it the identity hypothesis and considers that it is the

> only precise and opportune name . . . . The frequently used term 'monism' is etymologically correct but inconvenient, because it has often been used . . .by a more vague and inconsistent conception. Names such as 'parallelism' and 'dualism' are inadequate, because they . . .smuggle in the idea that we must conceive of the mental and the bodily as two completely separate series of developments (almost as a pair of rails) which is exactly what the hypothesis does *not* assume.

It is Wolff's[35] hypothesis which must be called dualistic, not Spinoza's.

Thus, a *single* hypothesis is now called (1) monism, now (2) dualism, now (3) parallelism, and now (4) identity. We may add that the circle of Marxists who have revived this hypothesis (as will be shown below)—Plekhanov, and after him Sarab'janov,[36] Frankfurt and others—view it precisely as a *theory of the unity, but not identity* of the mental and the physical. How could this happen? Obviously, the hypothesis itself can be developed on the basis of different more general views and may acquire different meanings depending on them: some emphasize its dualism, others its monism etc. Høffding [1908, p. 96] remarks that it does not exclude a deeper metaphysical hypothesis, in particular idealism. In order to become a philosophical world view, hypotheses must be elaborated anew and this new elaboration resides in the emphasis on now this and now that aspect. Very important is Lange's (1914, p. 76) reference:

> We find psychophysical parallelism in the representatives of the most diverse philosophical currents—the dualists (the followers of Descartes[37]), the monists (Spinoza), Leibnitz (metaphysical idealism), the positivists-agnostics (Bain, Spencer[38]), Wundt and Paulsen[39](voluntaristic metaphysics).

Høffding [1908, p. 117] says that the unconscious follows from the hypothesis of identity:

> In this case we act like the philologist who via conjectural critique [*Konjekturalkritik*] supplements a fragment of an ancient writer. Compared to the physical world the mental world is for us a fragment; only by means of a hypothesis can we supplement it.

This conclusion follows inevitably from [his] parallelism.

That is why Chelpanov is not all that wrong when he says that before 1922 he called this theory parallelism and after 1922 materialism. He would be entirely right if his philosophy had not been adapted to the season in a slightly mechanical fashion. The same goes for the word "function" (I mean function in the mathematical sense). The formula "consciousness is a function of the brain" points to the theory of parallelism; "physiological sense" leads to materialism. When Kornilov (1925) introduced the concept and the term of a functional relation between the mind and the body, he regarded parallelism as a dualistic hypothesis, but despite this fact and *without noticing it himself, he introduced this theory*, for although he rejected the concept of function in the physiological sense, its second sense remained.

Thus, we see that, beginning with the broadest hypotheses and ending with the tiniest details in the description of the experiment, the word reflects the general disease of the science. The specifically new result which we get from our analysis of the word is an idea of the molecular character of the processes in science. Each cell of the scientific organism shows the processes of infection and struggle. This gives us a better idea of the character of scientific knowledge. It emerges as a deeply unitary process. Finally, we get an idea of what is healthy or sick in the processes of science. What is true of the word is true of the theory. The word can bring science further, as long as it (1) occupies the territory that was conquered by the investigation, i.e., as long as it corresponds to the objective state of affairs; and (2) is in keeping with the right basic principles, i.e., the most general formulas of this objective world.

We see, therefore, that scientific research is at the same time a study of the fact and of the methods used to know this fact. In other words, methodological work is done in science itself insofar as this science moves forward and reflects upon its results. The choice of a word is already a methodological process. That methodology and experiment are worked out simultaneously can be seen with particular ease in the case of Pavlov. Thus, science is philosophical down to its ultimate elements, to its words. It is permeated, so to speak, by methodology. This coincides with the Marxist view of philosophy as "the science of sciences," a synthesis that penetrates science. In this sense Engels [1925/1978, p. 480] remarked that

> Natural scientists may say what they want, but they are ruled by philosophy . . . . Not until natural science and the science of history have absorbed dialectics will all the philosophical fuss . . .become superfluous and disappear in the positive science.

The experimenters in the natural sciences imagine that they free themselves from philosophy when they ignore it, but they turn out to be slaves of the worst philosophy, which consists of a medley of fragmentary and unsystematic views, since investigators cannot move a single step forwards without thinking, and thinking requires logical definitions. [40] The question of how to deal with methodological problems—"separately from the sciences themselves" or by introducing the methodological investigation in the science itself (in a curriculum or an investigation)—is a matter of pedagogical expediency. Frank[40] (1917/1964, p. 37) is right when he says that in the prefaces and concluding chapters of all books on psychology one is dealing with problems of philosophical psychology. It is one thing, however, to explain a methodology—"to establish an understanding of the methodology"—this is, we repeat, a matter of pedagogical technique. It is another thing to carry out a methodological investigation. This requires special consideration.

Ultimately the scientific word aspires to become a mathematical sign, i.e., a pure term. After all, the mathematical formula is also a series of words, but words which have been very well defined and which are therefore conventional in the highest degree. This is why all knowledge is scientific insofar as it is mathematical (Kant). But the language of empirical psychology is the direct antipode of mathematical language. As has been shown by Locke, Leibnitz and all linguistics, *all words* of psychology are metaphors taken from the spatial world.

10

We proceed to the positive formulations. From the fragmentary analyses of the separate elements of a science we have learned to view it as a complex whole which develops dynamically and lawfully. In which stage of development is our science at this moment, what is the meaning and nature of the crisis it experiences and what will be its outcome? Let us proceed to the answer to these questions. When one is somewhat acquainted with the methodology (and history) of the sciences, science loses its image of a dead, finished, immobile whole consisting of ready-made statements and becomes a living system which constantly develops and moves forward, and which consists of proven facts, laws, suppositions, structures, and conclusions which are continually being supplemented, criticized, verified, partially rejected, interpreted and organized anew, etc. Science commences to be understood *dialectically* in its movement, i.e., from the perspective of its dynamics, growth, development, evolution. It is from this point of view that we must evaluate and interpret each stage of development. Thus, the first thing from which we proceed is the acknowledgement of a *crisis*. What this crisis signifies is the subject of different interpretations. What follows are the most important kinds of interpretation of its meaning.

First of all, there are psychologists who totally deny the existence of a crisis. Chelpanov belongs among them, as do most of the Russian psychologists of the old school in general (only Lange and Frank have seen what is being done in science). In the opinion of such psychologists everything is all right in our science, just as in mineralogy. The crisis came from outside. Some persons ventured to reform our science; the official ideology required its revision. But for neither was there any objective basis in the science itself. It is true, in the debate one had to admit that a scientific reform was undertaken in America as well, but for the reader it was carefully—and perhaps sincerely—concealed that not a single *psychologist* who left his trace in science managed to avoid the crisis. This first conception is so blind that it is of no further interest to us. It can be fully explained by the fact that psychologists of this type are essentially eclectics and popularizers of other persons' ideas. Not only have they never engaged in the research and philosophy of their science, they have not even critically assessed each new school. They have accepted everything: the Würzburg school and Husserl's phenomenology, Wundt's and Titchener's[41] experimentalism and Marxism, Spencer and Plato. When we deal with the great revolutions that take place in science, such persons are outside of it not only theoretically. In a practical sense as well they play no role whatever. The empiricists betrayed empirical psychology while defending it. The eclectics assimilated all they could from ideas that were hostile to them. The popularizers can be enemies to no one, they will popularize the psychology that wins. Now Chelpanov is publishing much about Marxism. Soon he will be studying reflexology, and the first textbook of the victorious behaviorism will be compiled by him or a student of his. On the whole they are professors and examiners, organizers and "Kulturträger," but not a single investigation of any importance has emerged from their school.

Others see the crisis, but evaluate it very subjectively. The crisis has divided psychology into two camps. For them the borderline lies always between the author of a specific view and the rest of the world. But, according to Lotze,[42] even a worm that is half crushed sets off its reflection against the whole world. This is the official viewpoint of militant behaviorism. Watson (1926) thinks that there are two psychologies: a correct one—his own—and an incorrect one. The old one will die of its halfheartedness. The biggest detail he sees is the existence of halfhearted psychologists. The medieval traditions with which Wundt did not want to break ruined the psychology without a soul. As you see, everything is simplified to an extreme. There is no particular problem in turning psychology into a natural science. For Watson this coincides with the point of view of the ordinary person, i.e., the methodology of common sense. Bekhterev, on the whole, evaluates the epochs in psychology in the same way: everything before Bekhterev was a mistake, everything after Bekhterev is the truth. Many psychologists assess the crisis likewise. Since it is subjective, it is the easiest initial naive viewpoint. The psychologists whom we examined in the chapter on the unconscious [41] also reason this way: there is empirical psychology, which is permeated by metaphysical idealism—this is a remnant; and there is a genuine methodology of the era, which coincides with Marxism. Everything which is not the first must be the second, as no third possibility is given.

Psychoanalysis is in many respects the opposite of empirical psychology. This already suffices to declare it to be a Marxist system! For these psychologists the crisis coincides with the struggle they are fighting. There are allies and enemies, other distinctions do not exist.

The objective-empirical diagnoses of the crisis are no better: the severity of the crisis is measured by the number of schools that can be counted. Allport, in counting the currents of American psychology, defended this point of view (counting schools): the school of James and the school of Titchener, behaviorism and psychoanalysis. The units involved in the elaboration of the science are enumerated *side by side*, but not a single attempt is made to penetrate into the objective meaning of what each school is defending and the dynamic relations between the schools.

The error becomes more serious when one begins to view this situation as a fundamental characteristic of a crisis. Then the boundary between *this* crisis and any other, between the crisis in *psychology* and any *other science*, between every particular disagreement or debate and a crisis, is erased. In a word, one uses an anti-historical and anti-methodological approach which usually leads to *absurd results*.

Portugalov (1925, p. 12) wishes to argue the incomplete and relative nature of reflexology and not only slips into agnosticism and relativism of the purest order, but ends up with obvious nonsense. "In the chemistry, mechanics, electrophysics and electrophysiology of the brain everything is changing dramatically and nothing has yet been clearly and definitely demonstrated." Credulous persons believe in natural science, but "when we stay in the realm of medicine, do we really believe, with the hand on our heart, in the unshakable and stable force of natural science . . .and does natural science itself . . .believe in its unshakable, stable, and genuine character?"

There follows an enumeration of the theoretical changes in the natural sciences which are, moreover, lumped together. A sign of equality is put between the lack of solidity or stability of a particular theory and the whole of natural science, and what constitutes the foundation of the truth of natural science—the change of its theories and views—is passed off as the proof of its impotence. That this is agnosticism is perfectly clear, but two aspects deserve to be mentioned in connection with what follows: (1) in the whole chaos of views that serve to picture the natural sciences as lacking a single firm point, it is only . . . subjective child psychology based upon introspection which turns out to be unshakable; (2) amidst all the sciences which demonstrate the unreliability of the natural sciences, geometry is listed alongside optics and bacteriology. It so happens that

> Euclid[43] said that the sum of the angles of a triangle equals two right angles; Lobachevsky[44] dethroned Euclid and demonstrated that the sum of the angles of a triangle is less than two right angles, and Riemann[45] dethroned Lobachevsky and demonstrated that the sum of the angles of a triangle is more than two right angles (ibid., p. 13).

We will still have more than one occasion to meet the analogy between geometry and psychology, and therefore it is worthwhile to memorize this model of a-methodological thinking: (1) geometry is a natural science; (2) Linné,[46] Cuvier,[47] and Darwin "dethroned" each other in the same way as Euclid, Lobachevsky, and Riemann did; finally (3) Lobachevsky *dethroned* Euclid and demonstrated that . . . [42]. But even people with only elementary knowledge of the subject know that here we are not dealing with the knowledge of *real* triangles, but with *ideal* forms in mathematical, *deductive* systems, that these *three* theses follow from *three* different assumptions and do not contradict each other, just like other arithmetical counting systems do not contradict the decimal system. They *co-exist* and this determines their whole meaning and methodological nature. But what can be the value for the diagnosis of the crisis in an inductive science of a viewpoint which regards each two consecutive names as a crisis and each new opinion as a refutation of the truth?

Kornilov's (1925) diagnosis is closer to the truth. He views a struggle between two currents—reflexology and empirical psychology and their synthesis—Marxist psychology.

Already Frankfurt (1926) had advanced the opinion that reflexology cannot be viewed as a united whole, that it consists of contradictory tendencies and directions. This is even more true of empirical psychology. A unitary empirical psychology does not exist at all. In general, this simplified schema was created more as a program for operations, critical understanding, and demarcation than for an analysis of the crisis. For the latter it lacks reference to the causes, tendency, dynamics, and prognosis of the crisis. It is a logical classification of viewpoints present in the USSR and no more than that.

Thus, there has been no *theory of the crisis* in anything so far discussed, but only subjective communiqués compiled by the staffs of the quarreling parties. Here what is important is to beat the enemy; nobody will waste his time studying him.

Still closer to a theory of the crisis comes Lange (1914, p. 43), who already presents an embryonic description of it. But he has more feeling for than understanding of the crisis. Not even his historical information is to be trusted. For him the crisis commenced with the fall of associationism, i.e., he takes an accidental circumstance for the cause. Having established that "presently some general crisis is taking place" in psychology, he continues: "It consists of the replacement of the previous associationism by a new psychological theory." This is incorrect if only because associationism never was a generally accepted psychological system which formed the core of our science, but *to the present day remains* one of the fighting currents which has become much stronger lately and has been revived in reflexology and behaviorism. The psychology of Mill, Bain, and Spencer was never more than what it is now. It has fought faculty psychology (Herbart) like it is doing now. To see the root of the crisis in associationism is to give a very subjective assessment. Lange himself views it as the root of the rejection of the sensualistic doctrine. But today as well Gestalt theory views associationism as the main flaw of *all* psychology, including the newest.

In reality, it is not the adherents and opponents of this principle who are divided by some basic trait, but groups that evolved upon much more fundamental grounds. Furthermore, it is not entirely correct to reduce it to a struggle between the views of individual psychologists: it is important to lay bare what is shared and what is contradictory behind these various opinions. Lange's false understanding of the crisis ruined his own work. In defending the principle of a realistic, biological psychology, he fights Ribot and relies upon Husserl and other *extreme* idealists, who reject the possibility of psychology as a natural science. But some things, and not the least important ones, he established correctly. These are his correct propositions:

(1) There is no generally accepted system of our science. Each of the expositions of psychology by eminent authors is based upon an entirely different system.

All basic concepts and categories are interpreted in various ways. The crisis touches upon the very foundations of the science.

(2) The crisis is destructive, but wholesome. It reveals the growth of the science, its enrichment, its force, not its impotence or bankruptcy. The serious nature of the crisis is caused by the fact that the territory of psychology lies between sociology and biology, between which Kant wanted to divide it.

(3) Not a single psychological work is possible without first establishing the basic principles of this science. One should lay the foundations before starting to build.

(4) Finally, the common goal is to elaborate a new theory—a "renewed system of the science." However, Lange's understanding of this goal is entirely incorrect. For him it is "the critical evaluation of all contemporary currents and the attempt to reconcile them" (Lange, 1914, p. 43). And he tried to reconcile what cannot be reconciled: Husserl and biological psychology; together with James he attacked Spencer and with Dilthey he renounced biology. For him the idea of a possible reconciliation followed from the idea that "a revolution took place" "*against associationism* and physiological psychology" (ibid., p. 47) and that all new currents are connected by a common starting point and goal. That is why he gives a global characteristic of the crisis as an earthquake, a swampy area, etc. For him "a period of chaos has commenced" and the task is reduced to the "critique and logical elaboration" of the various opinions engendered by a common cause. This is a picture of the crisis as it was sketched by the participants in the struggle of the 1870s. Lange's personal attempt is the best evidence for the struggle between the real operative forces which determine the crisis. He regards the combination of subjective and objective psychology as a necessary *postulate of psychology*, rather than as a topic of discussion and a *problem*. As a result he introduces this dualism into his *whole* system. By contrasting his realistic or biological understanding of the mind with Natorp's[48] [1904] idealistic conception, he in fact accepts the existence of two psychologies, as we will see below.

But the most curious thing is that Ebbinghaus, whom Lange considers to be an associationist, i.e., a pre-critical psychologist, defines the crisis more correctly. In his opinion the relative imperfection of psychology is evident from the fact that the debates concerning almost all of the most general of its questions have never come to a halt. In other sciences there is unanimity about all the ultimate principles or the basic views which must be at the basis of investigation, and if a change takes place it does not have the character of a crisis. Agreement is soon reestablished. In psychology things are entirely different, in Ebbinghaus' [1902, p. 9] opinion. Here these basic views are constantly subjected to vivid doubt, are constantly being contested.

Ebbinghaus considers the disagreement to be a chronic phenomenon. Psychology lacks clear, reliable foundations. And in 1874 the same Brentano, with whose name Lange would have the crisis start, demanded that instead of the many psychologies, one psychology should be created. Obviously, already at that time there existed not only many currents instead of a single system, but *many psychologies*. Today as well this is a most accurate diagnosis of the crisis. Now, too, methodologists claim that we are at the same point as Brentano was [Binswanger, 1922, p. 6]. This means that what takes place in psychology is not a struggle of views which may be reconciled and which are united by a common enemy and purpose. It is not even a struggle between currents or directions within a single science, but a *struggle between different sciences*. There are many psychologies—this means that it is different, mutually exclusive and really existing types of science that are fighting. Psychoanalysis, intentional psychology,[49] reflexology—all these are *different types of science*, separate disciplines which tend to turn into a *general psychology*, i.e., to the subordination and exclusion of the other disciplines. We have seen both the meaning and the objective features of this tendency toward a general science. There can be no bigger mistake than to take this struggle for a struggle of views. Binswanger (1922, p. 6) begins by mentioning Brentano's demand and Windelband's[50] remark that with each representative psychology begins anew. The cause of this he sees neither in a lack of factual material, which has been gathered in abundance, nor in the absence of philosophical-methodological principles, of which we also have enough, but in the lack of *cooperation* between philosophers and empiricists in psychology: "There is hardly a single science where theorists and practitioners took such diverse paths." Psychology lacks a methodology—this is the author's conclusion, and the main thing is that we *cannot* create a methodology now. We cannot say that general psychology has already fulfilled its duties as a branch of methodology. On the contrary, wherever you look, imperfection, uncertainty, doubt, contradiction reign. We can only talk of the *problems* of general psychology and not even of that, but of an introduction to the problems of general psychology [ibid., p. 5]. Binswanger sees in psychologists a "courage and will toward (the creation of a new) psychology." In order to accomplish this they must break with the prejudices of centuries, and this shows one thing: that to this day, the general psychology has not been created. We must not ask, with Bergson, what would have happened if Kepler, Galileo,[51] and Newton had been psychologists, but what can still happen *despite* the fact that they were mathematicians [ibid., p. 21].

Thus, it may seem that the chaos in psychology is entirely natural and that the meaning of the crisis which psychology became aware of is as follows: *there exist many psychologies which have the tendency to create a single psychology by developing a general psychology*. For the latter purpose it is not enough to have a Galileo, i.e., a genius who would create the foundations of the science. This is the general opinion of European methodology as it had evolved toward the end of the nineteenth century. Some, mainly French, authors hold this opinion even today. In Russia, Vagner (1923)—almost the only psychologist who has dealt with methodological questions—has always defended it. He expresses the same opinion on the occasion of his analysis of the *Annés Psychologiques*, i.e., a synopsis of the international literature. This is his conclusion: *thus, we have quite a number of psychological schools, but not a unified psychology as an independent area of psychology* [sic]. From the fact that it doesn't exist does not follow that it cannot exist (ibid.). The answer to the question where and how it may be found can only be given by the history of science.

This is how biology developed. In the seventeenth century two naturalists lay the foundation for two areas of zoology: Buffon[52] for the description of animals and their way of life, and Linné for their classification. Gradually, both sections engendered a number of new problems, morphology appeared, anatomy, etc. The investigations were isolated from each other and represented as it were different sciences, which were in no way connected but for the fact that they both studied animals. The different sciences were at enmity, attempted to occupy the prevailing position as the mutual contacts increased and they *could not* remain apart. The brilliant Lamarck succeeded in integrating the uncoordinated pieces of knowledge into one book, which he called "Philosophy of Zoology." [43] He united his investigations with those of others, Buffon and Linné included, summarized the results, harmonized them with each other, and created the area of science which Treviranus called general biology. A single and abstract science was created from the uncoordinated disciplines, which, since the works of Darwin, could stand on its own feet. It is the opinion of Vagner that what was done with the disciplines of biology before their combination into a general biology or abstract zoology at the beginning of the nineteenth century is now taking place in the field of psychology at the beginning of the twentieth century. This belated synthesis in the form of a *general psychology* must repeat Lamarck's synthesis, i.e., it must be based on an analogous principle. Vagner sees more than a simple analogy in this. For him psychology must traverse *not a similar, but the same path*. Biopsychology is *part* of biology. It is an abstraction of the concrete schools or their synthesis, the *achievements of all of these schools* form its content. It cannot have, and neither has general biology, its own special method of investigation. Each time it makes use of the method of a science that is its composite part. It takes account of the achievements, *verifying them from the point of view of evolutionary theory and indicating their corresponding places in the general system* (Vagner, 1923). This is the expression of a more or less general opinion.

Some details in Vagner call forth doubt. In his understanding, general psychology (1) now forms a *part* of biology, is based upon the theory of evolution (its basis) etc. Consequently, it is in no need of its *own* Lamarck and Darwin, or their discoveries, and can realize its synthesis on the basis of already present principles; (2) now still must develop in the same way general biology developed, which is not included in biology as its part, but exists side by side with it. Only in this way can we understand the *analogy*, which is possible between two similar independent wholes, but not between the fate of a *whole* (biology) and its *part* (psychology).

Vagner's (ibid., p. 53) statement that biopsychology provides "exactly what Marx requires from psychology" causes another embarrassment. In general it can be said that Vagner's *formal* analysis is, evidently, as irreproachably correct as his attempt to solve the essence of the problem, and to outline the *content* of general psychology is methodologically untenable, even simply underdeveloped (part of biology, Marx). But the latter does not interest us now. Let us turn to the formal analysis. Is it correct that the psychology of our days is going through the same crisis as biology before Lamarck and is heading for the same fate?

To put it this way is to keep silent about the *most important and decisive aspect* of the crisis and to present the whole picture in a false light. Whether psychology is heading for agreement or rupture, whether a general psychology will develop from the combination or separation of the psychological disciplines, depends on what these disciplines bring with them—parts of the future whole, like systematics, morphology and anatomy, or mutually exclusive principles of knowledge. It also depends on what is the nature of the *hostility* between the disciplines—whether the contradictions which divide psychology are soluble, or whether they are irreconcilable. And it is precisely this analysis of the specific conditions under which psychology proceeds to the creation of a general science that we do not find in Vagner, Lange and the others. Meanwhile, European methodology has already reached a much higher degree of understanding of the crisis and has shown *which* and *how many* psychologies exist and *what* are the possible outcomes. But before we turn to this point we must first quit radically with the misunderstanding that psychology is following the path biology already took and in the end will simply be attached to it as its part. To think about it in this way is to fail to see that sociology edged its way between the biology of man and animals and tore psychology into two parts (which led Kant to divide it over two areas). We must develop the theory of the crisis in such a way as to be able to answer *this question*.

11

There is one fact that prevents all investigators from seeing the genuine state of affairs in psychology. This is the empirical character of its constructions. It must be torn off from psychology's constructions like a pellicle, like the skin of a fruit, in order to see them as they really are. Usually empirism is taken on trust, without further analysis. Psychology with all its diversity is treated as some fundamental scientific unity with a common basis. All disagreements are viewed as secondary phenomena which take place within this unity. But this is a false idea, an illusion. In reality, empirical psychology as a science of general principle—even *one* general principle—does not exist, and the attempts to create it have led to the defeat and bankruptcy of the very idea of creating an empirical psychology. The same persons who lump together many psychologies according to some common feature which contrasts with their own, e.g., psychoanalysis, reflexology, behaviorism (consciousness—the unconscious, subjectivism—objectivism, spiritualism–materialism), do not see that *within such an* empirical psychology *the same* processes take place which take place between it and a branch that breaks away. They do not see that the development of *these branches themselves* is subject to more *general tendencies* which are being operative in and can, in consequence, only be properly understood on the basis of the whole field of science. It is the *whole of psychology* which should be lumped together. What does the *empiricism* of contemporary psychology mean? First of all, it is a *purely negative* concept both according to its historical origin and its methodological meaning, and this is not a sufficient basis to unite something. Empirical means first of all "psychology without a soul" (Lange), psychology without any metaphysics (Vvedensky), psychology based on experience (Høffding). It is hardly necessary to explain that these are *essentially* negative definitions as well. They do not say a word about *what psychology is dealing with*, what is its positive meaning.

However, the objective meaning of this negative definition is now completely different from what it used to be. Once it concealed nothing—the task of the science was to liberate itself *from something*, the term was a slogan for that. Now it *conceals* the positive definitions (which each author introduces in his science) and the genuine processes taking place in the science. It was a temporary slogan and could not be anything else in principle. Now the term "empirical" attached to psychology designates the *refusal* to select a certain philosophical principle, the refusal to clarify one's ultimate premises, to become aware of one's own scientific nature. As such this refusal has its historical meaning and cause—we will dwell upon it below—but about the nature of the science it says essentially nothing, it conceals it. The Kantian thinker Vvedensky (1917, p. 3) expressed this most clearly, but *all* empiricists subscribe to his formula. Høffding, in particular, says the same. All more or less lean towards one side—Vvedensky provides the ideal balance: *"Psychology must formulate all its conclusions in such a way that they will be equally acceptable and equally binding for both materialism, spiritualism, and psychophysical monism."*

From this formula alone it is evident that empiricism formulates its tasks in such a way as to reveal their *impossibility*. Indeed, on the basis of empiricism, i.e., completely discarding basic premises, no scientific knowledge whatever is logically and historically possible. Natural science, which psychology wishes to liken through this definition, was by its nature, its undistorted essence, always *spontaneously materialistic*. All psychologists agree that natural science, like, of course, all human praxis, does not solve the problem of the essence of matter and mind, but starts from a certain solution to it, namely the assumption of an objective reality which exists outside of us, in conformity with certain laws, and which can be known. And this is, as Lenin has frequently pointed out, the very *essence* of materialism. The existence of natural science *qua* science is due to the ability to distinguish in our experience between what exists objectively and independently and what exists subjectively. This is not at variance with the different philosophical interpretations or whole schools in natural science which think idealistically. Natural science *qua* science is in itself, and independently from its proponents, materialistic. Psychology proceeded as spontaneously, despite the different ideas of its proponents, from an idealistic conception.

In reality, *there is not a single* empirical system of psychology. All transcend the boundaries of empiricism and this we can understand as follows: from a purely negative idea one can deduce nothing. Nothing can be born from "abstinence," as Vvedensky has it. In reality, all the systems were rooted in metaphysics and their conclusions were overstated. First Vvedensky himself with his theory of solipsism, i.e., an extreme manifestation of idealism.

Whereas psychoanalysis openly speaks about metapsychology, each psychology without a soul concealed its soul, the psychology without any metaphysics—its metaphysics. The psychology based on experience included what was not based on experience. In short, each psychology had its metapsychology. It might not consciously realize it, but this made no difference. Chelpanov (1924), who more than anyone else in the current debate seeks shelter under the word "empirical" and wants to demarcate his science from the field of philosophy, finds, however, that it must have its philosophical "superstructure" and "substructure." It turns out that there are philosophical concepts which must be examined *before one turns to the study of psychology* and a study which prepares psychology he calls the substructure. This does not prevent him from claiming on the next page that psychology must be freed from all philosophy. However, in the conclusion he once more acknowledges that it is precisely the *methodological problems which are the most acute problems of psychology.*

It would be wrong to think that from the concept of empirical psychology we can learn nothing but negative characteristics. It also points to positive processes which take place in our science and which are concealed by this name. With the word "empirical" psychology wants to join the natural sciences. Here all agree. But it is a very specific concept and we must examine what it designates when applied to psychology. In his preface to the encyclopedia, Ribot [1923, p. ix] says (heroically trying to accomplish the agreement and unity of which Lange and Vagner spoke and in so doing showing its impossibility) that psychology forms part of biology, that it is neither materialistic nor spiritualistic, else it would lose all right to be called a science. In what, then, does it differ from other parts of biology? *Only* in that it deals with phenomena which are '*spirituels*' and not physical.

What a trifle! Psychology wanted to be a natural science, but one that would deal with things of a very different nature from those natural science is dealing with. But doesn't the nature of the phenomena studied determine the character of the science? Are history, logic, geometry, and history of the theater really possible as natural sciences? And Chelpanov, who insists that psychology should be as empirical as physics, mineralogy etc., naturally does not join Pavlov but immediately starts to vociferate when the attempt is made to realize psychology as a genuine natural science. What is he hushing up in his comparison? He wants psychology to be a natural science about (1) phenomena which are completely different from physical phenomena, and (2) which are conceived in a way that is completely different from the way the objects of the natural sciences are investigated. One may ask what the natural sciences and psychology can have in common if the subject matter and the method of acquiring knowledge are different. And Vvedensky (1917,

p. 3) says, after he has explained the meaning of the empirical character of psychology: "Therefore, contemporary psychology often characterizes itself as a *natural science about mental phenomena or a natural history of mental phenomena.*" But this means that psychology wants to be a natural science about unnatural phenomena. It is connected with the natural sciences by a purely *negative* feature—the rejection of metaphysics—and not by a single *positive* one.

James explained the matter brilliantly. Psychology is to be treated as a natural science—that was his main thesis. But no one did as much as James to prove that the mental is "not natural scientific." He explains that all the natural sciences accept some assumptions on faith—natural science proceeds from the materialistic assumption, in spite of the fact that further reflection leads to idealism. Psychology does the same—it accepts other assumptions. Consequently, it is similar to natural science only in that it uncritically accepts some assumptions; the assumptions themselves are contrary [see pp. 9–10 of Burkhardt, 1984].

According to Ribot, this tendency is the main trait of the psychology of the 19th century. Apart from this he mentions the attempts to give psychology its own principle and method (which it was denied by Comte) and to put it in the same relation to biology as biology occupies with respect to physics. But in fact the author acknowledges that what is called psychology consists of several categories of investigations which differ according to their goal and method. And when the authors, in spite of this, attempted to beget* a system of psychology and included Pavlov and Bergson, they demonstrated that this task cannot be realized. And in his conclusion Dumas [1924, p. 1121] formulates that the unity of the 25 authors consisted in the *rejection* of ontological speculation.

It is easy to guess what such a viewpoint leads to: the rejection of ontological speculations, empirism, *when it is consistent*, leads to the rejection of *methodologically constructive principles* in the creation of a system, to eclecticism; insofar as *it is inconsistent*, it leads to a hidden, uncritical, vague methodology. Both possibilities have been brilliantly demonstrated by the French authors. For them Pavlov's psychology of reactions is just as acceptable as introspective psychology if only they are in different chapters of the book. In their manner of describing the facts and stating the problems, even in their vocabulary, the authors of the book show tendencies of associationism, rationalism, Bergsonism, and synthesism. It is further explained that Bergson's conception is applied in some chapters, the language of associationism and atomism in others, behaviorism in still others, etc. The "Traité" wants to be impartial, objective, and complete. If it has not always been successful, Dumas [1924, p. 1156] concludes, at least the difference of opinion testifies to intellectual activity and ultimately in that sense it represents its time and country. We couldn't agree more.

This disagreement—we have seen how far it goes—only convinces us of the fact that an impartial psychology is impossible today, leaving aside the fatal dualism of the "Traité de psychologie" for which psychology is now part of biology, now stands to it as biology itself stands to physics.

Thus, the concept of empirical psychology contains an insoluble methodological contradiction. It is a natural science about unnatural things, a tendency to develop with the methods of natural science, i.e., proceeding from totally opposite premises, a system of knowledge which is contrary to them. This had a fatal influence upon the methodological construction of empirical psychology and broke its back.

Two psychologies exist—a natural scientific, materialistic one and a spiritualistic one. This thesis expresses the meaning of the crisis more correctly than the thesis

---

*As in the manuscript [Russian eds.].

about the existence of *many* psychologies. For *psychologies* we have *two*, i.e., two different, irreconcilable types of science, two fundamentally different constructions of systems of knowledge. All the rest is a difference in views, schools, hypotheses: individual, very complex, confused, mixed, blind, chaotic combinations which are at times very difficult to understand. But the real struggle only takes place between two tendencies which lie and operate behind all the struggling currents.

That this is so, that two psychologies, and not many psychologies, make up the meaning of the crisis, that all the rest is a struggle *within* each of these two psychologies, a struggle which has quite another meaning and operational field, that the creation of a general psychology is not a matter of agreement, but of a rupture—all this methodology realized long ago and *nobody contests it*. (The difference of this thesis from Kornilov's three directions resides *in the whole range of the meaning of the crisis*: (1) the concepts of materialistic psychology and reflexology do not coincide (as he says); (2) the concepts of empirical and idealistic psychology do not coincide (as he says), (3) our evaluation of the role of Marxist psychology differs.) Finally, here we are dealing with two tendencies which show up in the struggle between the multitude of concrete currents and within them. Nobody contests that the general psychology will not be a third psychology added to the two struggling parties, but one of them.

That the concept of empiricism contains a methodological conflict which a self-reflective theory must solve in order to make investigation possible—this idea was made well known by Münsterberg [1920]. In his capital methodological work he declared that this book does not conceal the fact that it wants to be a militant book, it defends idealism against naturalism. It wants to guarantee an unlimited right for idealism in psychology. He lays the theoretical epistemological foundations of empirical psychology and declares that this is the most important thing the psychology of our day needs. Its main concepts have been gathered haphazardly, its logical means of acquiring knowledge have been left to the instinct. Münsterberg's theme is the synthesis of Fichte's ethical idealism with the physiological psychology of our day, for the victory of idealism does not reside in its dissociating itself from empirical investigation, but in finding a place for it in its own area. Münsterberg showed that naturalism and idealism are irreconcilable, that is why he talks about a book of militant idealism, says of general psychology that it is bravery and a risk—and not about agreement and unification. And Münsterberg [ibid., p. 10] openly advanced the idea of the existence of two sciences, arguing that psychology finds itself in the strange position that we know incomparably more about psychological facts than we ever did, but much less about the question as to what psychology actually is.

The unity of external methods cannot conceal from us that the different psychologists are talking about a totally different psychology. This internal disturbance can only be understood and overcome in the following way.

> The psychology of our day is struggling with the prejudice that only one type of psychology exists . . . . The concept of psychology involves two totally different scientific tasks, which must be distinguished in principle and for which we can best use special designations since, in reality, there are two kinds of psychology [ibid., p. 10].

In contemporary science all sorts of forms and types of mixing two sciences into a seeming unity are represented. What these sciences have in common is their object, but this does not say anything about these sciences themselves. Geology, geography, and agronomics all study the earth, but their construction, their principle of scientific knowledge differs. We may through description change the mind into a chain of causes and actions and may picture it as a combination of elements—objectively and subjectively. If we carry both conceptions to the extreme and give them a sci-

entific form we will get two "fundamentally different theoretical disciplines . . . .
One is causal, the other is teleological and intentional psychology" [ibid., pp. 12-13].

The existence of two psychologies is so obvious that it is accepted by all. The
disagreement is only about the precise definition of each science. Some emphasize
some nuances, others emphasize others. It would be very interesting to follow all
these oscillations, because each of them testifies to some objective tendency, to a
striving toward one or the other pole, and the scope, the range of contradictions
shows that both types of science, like two butterflies in one cocoon, still exist in
the form of as yet undifferentiated tendencies.

But now we are not interested in the contradictions, but in the common factor
that lies behind them.

We are confronted with two questions: what is the common nature of both
sciences and what are the causes which have led to the *bifurcation of empiricism
into naturalism and idealism*?

All agree that precisely these two elements lie at the basis of the two sciences,
that, consequently, one is natural scientific psychology, and the other is idealistic
psychology, whatever the different authors may call them. Following Münsterberg
all view the difference not in the material or subject matter, but in the way of
acquiring knowledge, in the principle. The question is whether to understand the
phenomena in terms of causality, in connection with and having fundamentally the
same meaning as all other phenomena, or intentionally, as spiritual activity, which
is oriented towards a goal and exempt from all material connections. Dilthey
[1894/1977, pp. 37-41], who calls these sciences explanatory and descriptive psychology, traces the bifurcation to Wolff, who divided psychology into rational and
empirical psychology, i.e., to the very origin of empirical psychology. He shows that
the division has always been present during the whole course of development of
the science and again became explicit in the school of Herbart (1849) and in the
works of Waitz. The method of explanatory psychology is identical to that of natural
science. Its postulate—there is not a single mental phenomenon without a physical
one—leads to its bankruptcy as an independent science and its affairs are transferred into the hands of physiology (ibid.). Descriptive and explanatory psychology
do not have the same meaning as systematics and explanation—its two basic parts
according to Binswanger (1922) as well—have in the natural sciences.

Contemporary psychology—this doctrine of a soul without a soul—is intrinsically contradictory, is divided into two parts. Descriptive psychology does not seek
explanation, but description and understanding. What the poets, Shakespeare in particular, presented in images, it makes the subject of analysis in concepts. Explanatory,
natural scientific psychology cannot lie at the basis of a science about the mind, it
develops a deterministic criminal law, does not leave any room for freedom, cannot
be reconciled with the problem of culture. In contrast, descriptive psychology

> will become the foundation of the human studies, as mathematics is that of the natural
> sciences [Dilthey, 1894/1977, p. 74].

Stout[53] [1909, pp. 2-6] openly refuses to call analytic psychology a physical science. It is a positive science in the sense that it investigates matter of fact, reality,
what is and is not a norm, not what ought to be. It stands next to mathematics,
the natural sciences, theory of knowledge. But it is not a physical science. Between
the mental and the physical there is such a gulf that there is no means of tracing
their connections. No science of matter stands to psychology in a relation analogous
to that in which chemistry and physics stand to biology, i.e., in a relation of more
general to more special, but in principle homogeneous, principles.

Binswanger [1922, p. 22] divides *all* problems of methodology into those due to a natural scientific and those due to a non-natural scientific concept of the mind. He openly and clearly explains that there are two radically different psychologies. Referring to Sigwart he calls the struggle against natural psychology the source of the split. This leads us to the phenomenology of experiencing, the basis of Husserl's pure logic and empirical, but non-natural scientific psychology (Pfänder,[54] Jaspers[55]).

Bleuler defends the opposite position. He rejects Wundt's opinion that psychology is not a natural science and, following Rickert, he calls it a generalizing psychology, although he has in mind what Dilthey called explanatory or constructive psychology.

We will not thoroughly examine the question as to *how* psychology as a natural science is possible and the concepts by means of which it is constructed—all this belongs to the debate *within one* psychology and it forms the subject of the positive exposition in the next part of our work. What is more, we also leave open another question—whether psychology really is a natural science in the exact sense of the word. Following the European authors we use this word to designate the materialistic nature of this kind of knowledge as clearly as possible. Insofar as Western European psychology did not know or hardly knew the problems of social psychology, this kind of knowledge was thought to coincide with natural science. But to demonstrate that psychology is possible as a materialistic science is still a special and very deep problem, which does not, however, belong to the problem of the meaning of the crisis as a whole.

Almost all Russian authors who have written anything of importance about psychology accept the division—from hearsay, of course—which shows the extent to which these ideas are generally accepted in European psychology. Lange (1914), who mentions the disagreement between Windelband and Rickert on the one hand (who regard psychology as a natural science) and Wundt and Dilthey on the other, is inclined with the latter authors to distinguish two sciences. It is remarkable that he criticizes Natorp as an exponent of the idealistic conception of psychology and contrasts him with a realistic or biological understanding. However, according to Münsterberg, Natorp has from the very beginning demanded the same thing he did, i.e., a subjectivating and an objectivating science of the mind, i.e., two sciences.

Lange merged both viewpoints into a single postulate and expounded both irreconcilable tendencies in his book, considering that the meaning of the crisis resides in the struggle with associationism. He explains Dilthey and Münsterberg with real sympathy and states that "two different psychologies resulted." Like Janus, psychology showed two different faces: one turned to physiology and natural science, the other to the sciences of the spirit, history, sociology; one science about causal effects, the other about values (ibid., p. 63). It would seem that what remains is to opt for *one of the two*, but Lange unites them.

Chelpanov proceeded in the same way. In his current polemics he implores us to believe him that psychology is a materialistic science, refers to James as his witness and does not with a single word mention that in the Russian literature the idea of two sciences belongs to *him*. This deserves further reflection.

Following Dilthey, Stout, Meinong, and Husserl he explains the idea of the analytic method. Whereas the inductive method is distinctive of natural scientific psychology, descriptive psychology is characterized by the analytic method which leads to the knowledge of *a priori* ideas. Analytic psychology is the *basic* psychology. It must precede the development of child psychology, zoopsychology, and objective experimental psychology and provide the foundation for all types of psychological investigation. This does not look like the relation of mineralogy to physics, or like the complete separation of psychology from philosophy and idealism.

To show *what kind* of jump Chelpanov made in his psychological views since 1922, one must not dwell upon his general philosophical statements and accidental phrases, but upon his theory of the analytic method. Chelpanov protests against mixing the tasks of explanatory psychology with those of descriptive psychology and explains that they are absolutely contradictory. In order not to leave any doubt about the question as to which psychology he regards as of primary importance, he connects it with Husserl's phenomenology, with his theory of ideal essences, and explains that Husserl's *eidos* or essence is basically equivalent to Plato's ideas. For Husserl, phenomenology stands to descriptive psychology as mathematics does to physics. Phenomenology and mathematics are, like geometry, sciences about essences, about ideal possibilities; descriptive psychology and physics are about facts. Phenomenology makes explanatory and descriptive psychology possible.

Despite Husserl's opinion, for Chelpanov phenomenology and analytic psychology partially overlap and the phenomenological method is completely identical with the analytic method. Chelpanov explains Husserl's refusal to regard eidetic psychology and phenomenology as being identical in the following way. By contemporary psychology he understands only empirical, i.e., inductive psychology, despite the fact that it also contains phenomenological truths. Thus, there is no need to separate phenomenology from psychology. The phenomenological method must be laid at the basis of the objective experimental methods, which Chelpanov timidly defends against Husserl. This is the way it was, this is the way it will be, the author concludes.

How can we square this with his claim that psychology is only empirical, excludes idealism by its very nature and is independent from philosophy?

We can summarize. Whatever the division in question is called, whatever shades of meaning in each term are emphasized, the basic essence of the question remains the same and it can be reduced to two propositions.

1. In psychology empiricism indeed proceeded just as spontaneously from idealistic premises as natural science did from materialistic ones, i.e., empirical psychology was idealistic in its foundation.

2. For certain reasons (to be considered below), in the era of the crisis empiricism split into idealistic and materialistic psychology. Münsterberg (1920, p. 14), too, interprets the difference in terminology as unity of meaning. We can speak of causal and intentional psychology, or about the psychology of the spirit and the psychology of consciousness, or about understanding and explanatory psychology. But the only thing of principal importance is that we recognize the dual nature of psychology. Elsewhere Münsterberg [1920, pp. vii-viii] contrasts the psychology of the contents of consciousness with the psychology of the spirit, the psychology of contents with the psychology of acts, and the psychology of sensations with intentional psychology.

We have basically reached an opinion which established itself in our science long ago: psychology has a deeply dualistic nature which pervades its whole development. We have, thus, arrived at an indisputably historic situation. The history of the science does not belong to our tasks and we may leave aside the question as to the historical roots of dualism and confine ourselves to pointing out this fact and explaining the proximate causes which led to the exacerbation and bifurcation of dualism in the crisis. It is, essentially, the fact that psychology is attracted to two poles, this intrinsic presence of a "psychoteleology" and a "psychobiology," which Dessoir [1911, p. 230] called the singing in two voices of contemporary psychology, and which in his opinion will never cease.

12 [44]

Now we must briefly dwell upon the proximate causes or driving forces of the crisis.

Which factors lead us to the crisis, the rupture, and which passively *experience* it as an inevitable evil? Naturally, we will dwell here only upon the driving forces *within* our science, leaving all others aside. We are justified in doing so, because the external—social and ideological—causes and phenomena are, one way or the other, represented in the final analysis by forces within the science, and they act through them. It is our intention, therefore, to analyze the proximate causes lying within the science and to refrain from a deeper analysis.

Let us say right away that *the main driving force of the crisis in its final phase is the development of applied psychology as a whole.*

The attitude of academic psychology toward applied psychology has up until not remained somewhat disdainful as if it had to do with a semi-exact science. Not everything is well in this area of psychology, there is no doubt about that, but nevertheless there can be no doubt for an observer who takes a bird-eye's view, i.e., the methodologist, that the leading role in the development of our science belongs to applied psychology. It represents everything of psychology which is progressive, sound, which contains a germ of the future. It provides the best methodological works. It is only by studying this area that one can come to an understanding of the meaning of what is going on and the possibility of a genuine psychology.

The center has shifted in the history of science: what was at the periphery became the center of the circle. One can say about applied psychology what can be said about philosophy which was rejected by empirical psychology: "the stone which the builders rejected is become the head stone of the corner."

We can elucidate this by referring to three aspects. The first is *practice*. Here psychology was *first* (through industrial psychology, psychiatry, child psychology, and criminal psychology) confronted with a highly developed—industrial, educational, political, or military—practice. This confrontation compels psychology to reform its principles so that they may withstand the highest test of practice. It forces us to accommodate and introduce into our science the supply of practical psychological experiences and skills which has been gathered over thousands of years; for the church, the military, politics, and industry, insofar as they have consciously regulated and organized the mind, base themselves on an experience which is enormous, although not well ordered from the scientific viewpoint (every psychologist experienced the reforming influence of applied science). For the development of psychology, applied psychology plays the same role as medicine did for anatomy and physiology and technique for the physical sciences. The importance of the new practical psychology for the *whole* science cannot be exaggerated. The psychologist might dedicate a hymn to it.

A psychology which is called upon to confirm the truth of its thinking in practice, which attempts not so much to explain the mind but to understand and master it, gives the practical disciplines a fundamentally different place in the whole structure of the science than the former psychology did. There practice was the colony of theory, dependent in all its aspects on the metropolis. Theory was in no way dependent on practice. Practice was the conclusion, the application, an excursion beyond the boundaries of science, an operation which lay outside science and came after science, which began after the scientific operation was considered completed. Success or failure had practically no effect on the fate of the theory. Now the situation is the opposite. Practice pervades the deepest foundations of the scientific operation and reforms it from beginning to end. Practice sets the tasks and serves as the supreme judge of theory, as its truth criterion. It dictates how to construct the concepts and how to formulate the laws.

This leads us directly to the *second aspect, to methodology*. However strange and paradoxical it may seem at first glance, it is precisely practice as the constructive principle of science which requires a philosophy, i.e. a methodology of science. This does not in any way contradict the frivolous, "light-hearted" (in the words of Münsterberg) relation of psychotechnics to its principles. In reality, both the practice and the methodology of psychotechnics are often amazingly helpless, weak, superficial, and at times ludicrous. Psychotechnic diagnoses are vacuous and remind us of the physicians's reflections about medicine in Molière. [45] The methodology of psychotechnics is invented *ad hoc* each time and lacks critical sense. It is often called picnic psychology [46], i.e., it is something light, temporary, half-serious. All this is true. But it does not for one moment change the fundamental state of affairs, that it is exactly this psychology which will create an iron methodology. As Münsterberg [1920, p. v] says, not only the general part, but also the examination of particular questions will force us time and again to investigate the principles of psychotechnics.

That is why I assert: despite the fact that it has compromised itself more than once, *that its practical meaning is very close to zero and the theory often ludicrous, its methodological meaning is enormous*. The principle and philosophy of practice is—once again—the stone which the builders rejected and which became the head stone of the corner. Here we have the whole meaning of the crisis.

Binswanger [1922, p. 50] says that we do not expect to get the solution to the most general question—the supreme question of all psychology, the problem which includes all problems of psychology, the question of subjectivating and objectivating psychology—from logic, epistemology, or metaphysics, but from methodology, i.e., the theory of scientific method. We would say: from the methodology of psychotechnics, i.e., the *philosophy of practice*. The practical and theoretical value of Binet's measuring scale or other psychotechnic tests may be obviously insignificant, the test bad in itself, but as an idea, a methodological principle, a task, a perspective it is enormous. The most complex contradictions of psychological methodology are transferred to the grounds of practice and only there can they be solved. There the debate stops being fruitless, it comes to an end. "Method" means "way," we view it as a means of knowledge acquisition. But in all its points the way is determined by the goal to which it leads. That is why practice reforms the whole methodology of the science.

The *third aspect* of the reforming role of psychotechnics may be understood from the first two. It is that psychotechnics *is a one-sided* psychology, it instigates a rupture and creates a real psychology. Psychiatry too transcends the boundaries of idealistic psychology. One cannot treat or cure relying on introspection. One can hardly carry this idea to a more absurd consequence than when applying it to psychiatry. Psychotechnics also realized, as was observed by Spiel'rejn, that it cannot separate psychological functions from physiological ones, and it is searching for an integral concept. About psychologists who demand inspiration from teachers, I have written that hardly any one of them would entrust the control of a ship to the captain's inspiration or the management of a factory to the engineer's enthusiasm. Each of them would select a professional sailor and an experienced technician. And these highest possible requirements for the science, this most serious practice, will revive psychology. Industry and the military, education and treatment will revive and reform the science. Husserl's eidetic psychology, which is not interested in the truth of its claims, is not fit for the selection of tram-drivers. Neither is the contemplation of essences fit for that goal, even values are without interest. But all this will not in the least protect it against a catastrophe. The goal of such a psychology is not Shakespeare in concepts, as it was for Dilthey, but *in one word—psychotechnics*, i.e., a scientific theory which would lead to the subordination and mastery of the mind, to the artificial control of behavior.

And it is Münsterberg, this militant idealist, who lays the foundations for psychotechnics, i.e., a materialistic psychology in the highest sense of the word. Stern, no less enthusiastic about idealism, is elaborating a methodology for differential psychology and reveals with fatal precision the untenability of idealistic psychology.

How could it happen that extreme idealists play into the hands of materialism? It shows that the two struggling tendencies are deeply and with objective necessity rooted in the development of psychology; how little they coincide with what the psychologist says about himself, i.e., with his subjective philosophical convictions; how inexpressibly complex the picture of the crisis is; in what mixed forms both tendencies meet; what tortuous, unexpected, paradoxical zigzags the front line in psychology makes, frequently *within* one and the same system, frequently *within* one term. Finally, it shows that *the struggle between the two psychologies does not coincide with the struggle between the many conceptions and psychological schools, but stands behind them and determines them.* It shows how deceptive the external forms of the crisis are and that we need to take account of the genuine meaning behind them.

Let us turn to Münsterberg [1920, p. ix]. The question of causal psychology's legitimacy is of decisive importance for psychotechnics.

> This one-sided causal psychology only now comes into its own . . . explanatory psychology is the answer to an unnatural, artificial question; mental life requires understanding, not explanation. Psychotechnics, however, which can only work with a causal psychology, testifies to the necessity of such an artificial statement of the question and legitimizes it. The genuine meaning of explanatory psychology is only revealed in psychotechnics and, thus, the whole system of the psychological sciences culminates in it.

It is difficult to demonstrate the objective force of this tendency and the non-coincidence of the philosopher's convictions with the objective meaning of his work more clearly: materialistic psychology is unnatural, says the idealist, but *I am forced to work with precisely such a psychology.*

Psychotechnics is oriented toward action, practice—and there we act in a way which is fundamentally different from purely theoretical understanding and explanation. That is why psychotechnics *cannot* hesitate in the selection of the psychology it needs (not even when it is elaborated by consistent idealists). It is dealing exclusively with causal, objective psychology. Non-causal psychology plays no role whatsoever for psychotechnics.

It is precisely this situation that is of decisive importance for all psychotechnical sciences. It is consciously one-sided. It is the only empirical science in the full sense of the word. It is—inevitably—a comparative science. The link with physical processes is for this science so fundamental that it is a physiological psychology. It is an experimental science. And its general formula is

> We proceeded from the assumption that the only psychology relevant for psychotechnics must be a descriptive-explanatory science. We may now add that, on top of that, it must be an empirical, comparative science which takes physiology into account, and which, finally, is experimental [Münsterberg, 1920, p. 18].

This means that psychotechnics introduces a revolution in the development of the science and marks an era in its development. From this viewpoint Münsterberg [ibid., p. 19] says that empirical psychology hardly *originated* before the second half of the 19th century. Even in the schools which rejected metaphysics and studied the facts research was guided by another interest. Application [of the experiment; Soviet eds.] was impossible as long as psychology did not become a natural science. But along with the introduction of the experiment there evolved a paradoxical situation which would be unthinkable in the natural sciences: equipment equivalent to the first steam engine or the telegraph was well known in the laboratories, but not applied in practice. [47] Education and law, trade and industry, social life and medicine were uninfluenced by this movement. To this very day it is considered a profanation of the investigation to connect it with practice and it is advised to wait until psychology has completed its theoretical system. But the experience of the natural sciences tells us another story. Medicine and technique did not wait until anatomy and physics celebrated their ultimate triumphs. It is not only that life needs psychology and practices it in different forms everywhere: we must also expect an upsurge in psychology from this contact with life. [48]

Of course, Münsterberg would not be an idealist if he accepted this situation as it is and did not retain a special area for the unlimited rights of idealism. He merely transfers the debate to another area when he accepts the untenability of idealism in the area of a causal psychology that feeds on practice. He explains this "epistemological tolerance" [ibid., p. 31] and deduces it from an idealistic understanding of the essence of science which does not seek for the distinction "between true and false concepts, but between those suited or not suited for certain ultimate hypothetical [*gedankliche*] goals" [ibid., p. 29]. He believes that a temporary truce between psychologists can be established as soon as they leave the battlefield of psychological theory [ibid., p. 31].

Münsterberg's work is a striking example of the internal discord between a methodology determined by science and a philosophy determined by a world view, precisely because he is a methodologist who is consistent to the very end and a philosopher who is consistent to the very end, i.e., a contradictory thinker to the very end. He understands that in being a materialist in causal psychology and an idealist in teleological psychology he arrives at some sort of double-entry bookkeeping which inevitably must be unscrupulous, because the entries on the one side are different from those on the other side. For in the end only one truth is conceivable. But for him the truth is not life itself, but the logical elaboration of life, and the latter can vary, as it is determined by many viewpoints [ibid., pp. 42-43]. He understands that empirical science does not require the rejection of an epistemological point of view, but a *certain theory*, but in various sciences different epistemological viewpoints are possible. In the interest of practice we express the truth in one language, in another in the interests of the mind [*Geist*].

When natural scientists have differences of opinion these do not touch upon the fundamental assumptions of the science.

> It is no problem at all for a botanist to communicate about his subject with all other plant researchers. No botanist bothers to stop to answer the question what it actually means that plants live in space and time and are ruled by causal laws [ibid., p. 28].

But the nature of psychological material does not allow us to separate the psychological propositions from philosophical theories to the extent that other empirical sciences have managed to do that. The psychologist fundamentally deceives himself when he imagines that his laboratory work can lead him to the solution of the basic questions of his science; they belong to philosophy.

> The psychologist who does not want to join the philosophical debate about fundamental questions must simply tacitly accept one or the other epistemological theory as the basis of his particular investigations [ibid., p. 29].

It was exactly epistemological tolerance and not a rejection of epistemology which led Münsterberg to the idea of two psychologies, one of which contradicts the other, but both of which can be accepted by the philosopher. After all, tolerance does not stand for atheism. In the mosque he is a Mohammedan, but in the cathedral a Christian.

There is only one fundamental misunderstanding that may arise: that the idea of a dualistic psychology leads to the *partial* acceptance of the rights of causal psychology, that the dualism is transferred into psychology itself, which is divided into two phases [49]; that *Münsterberg proclaimed tolerance also within* causal psychology. *But this is absolutely not the case.* This is what he [ibid., p. 15] says:

> The fundamental question as to whether a psychology that thinks along teleological lines may really exist alongside a causal psychology, whether in scientific psychology we can and should deal with apperception, task awareness, affect, will, or thought in a teleological fashion, does not concern the psychotechnician, for he knows that we can always somehow handle these events and mental performances in the language of causal psychology and that psychotechnics can only deal with this causal conception.

Thus, the two psychologies do not overlap, do not supplement each other, but they serve *two* truths, one in the interest of practice, the other in the interest of mind [*Geist*]. Double-entry bookkeeping is practiced in Münsterberg's world view, but not in psychology. The materialist will *fully* accept Münsterberg's conception of causal psychology and will reject dualism in science. The idealist will reject dualism as well and will *fully* accept the conception of a teleological psychology. Münsterberg himself proclaims epistemological tolerance and accepts both sciences, but elaborates one of them as materialist and the other as idealist. Thus, the debate and the dualism exist beyond the boundaries of causal psychology. It is not part of anything and *in itself* does not form part of any science.

This instructive example of the fact that in science idealism is *forced* to find its grounds in materialism is fully confirmed by the example of *any* other thinker.

Stern followed the same path. He was led to objective psychology through the problems of differential investigation, which is likewise one of the main reasons for the new psychology. We do not investigate thinkers, however, but their fate, i.e., the objective processes that stand behind them and control them. And these are not revealed through induction, but through analysis. In the words of Engels [1925/1978, p. 496], one steam engine demonstrates the law of transformation of energy no less convincingly than 100,000 engines. We add as a mere curiosity that in the preface to the translation of Münsterberg the Russian idealistic psychologists list among his merits that he meets the aspiration of the psychology of behavior and the requirements of an integral approach of man without pulverizing man's psychophysical organization into atoms. What the great idealists accomplish as a tragedy, the small ones repeat as a farce. [50]

We can summarize. We view the cause of the crisis as its driving force, which is therefore not only of historical interest, but also of primary—methodological— importance, as it not only led to the development of the crisis, but continues determining its further course and fate. This cause lies in the development of applied psychology, which has led toward the reform of the whole methodology of the science on the basis of the principle of practice, i.e., towards its transformation into a natural science. This principle is pressing psychology heavily and pushing it to split into two sciences. It guarantees the right development of materialistic psychology in the future. Practice and philosophy are becoming the head stone of the corner.

Many psychologists have viewed the introduction of the experiment as a fundamental reform of psychology and have even equated experimental and scientific psychology. They predicted that the future would belong solely to experimental psychology and have viewed this epithet as a most important methodological principle. But in psychology the experiment remained on the level of a technical device, it was not utilized in a fundamental way and it led, in the case of Ach for instance, to its own negation. Nowadays many psychologists see a way out *in methodology*, in the correct formation of principles. They expect salvation from the other end. But their work is fruitless as well. Only a fundamental rejection of the blind empiricism which is trailing behind immediate introspectional experience and which is internally split into two parts; only the emancipation from introspection, its exclusion just like the exclusion of the eye in physics; only a rupture and the selection of a single psychology will provide the way out of the crisis. The dialectic unity of methodology and practice, applied to psychology from two sides, is the fate and destiny of one of the psychologies. A complete severance from practice and the contemplation of ideal essences is the destiny and fate of the other. A complete rupture and separation is their common destiny and fate. This rupture began, continues, and will be completed along the lines of *practice*.

13

However obvious the historical and methodological dogma about the growing gap between the two psychologies as the formula for the dynamics of the crisis may seem after our analysis, it is disputed by many. In itself this is of no concern to us. The tendencies we found seem to us to express the truth, because they exist objectively and do not depend on the views of some author. On the contrary, they themselves determine these views insofar as they become psychological views and are involved in the process of the science's development.

That is why we should not be surprised to find that different views exist on this account. From the very beginning we have not set ourselves the task to investigate views, but what these views are aimed at. It is this that distinguishes a critical investigation of the views of some author from the methodological analysis of the problem itself. But we must nevertheless pay attention to one thing: we are not entirely indifferent as to views; we must be able to *explain* them, to lay bare their objective, their inner logic. To put it more simply, we must be able to present each struggle between views as a complex expression of the struggle between the two psychologies. On the whole, this is a critical task which should be *based* on the present analysis and it should show for the most important psychological currents *what* the dogma found by us can yield toward understanding them. But to show its *possibility*, to establish the fundamental course of the analysis, forms part of our present task.

This can be done most easily by analyzing those systems which openly side with one or the other tendency or even merge them. But it is much more difficult and therefore more attractive to demonstrate it for those systems which in principle place themselves *outside* the struggle, outside these two tendencies, which seek a way out in a third tendency and seemingly reject our dogma about the existence of only two paths for psychology. They say there is a third way: the two struggling tendencies may be merged, or one of them may be subjected to the other, or both may be totally removed and a new one created, or both may be subjected to a third one, etc. For the confirmation of our dogma it is in principle extremely important to show *where* this third way leads, as the dogma stands or falls with it.

Following the method we adopted we will examine how both objective tendencies operate in the conceptual systems of the adherents of a third way. Are they bridled or do they remain masters of the situation? In short, who is leading, the horse or the horseman?

First of all, we will clearly distinguish between conceptions and tendencies. A conception may identify itself with a certain tendency and nevertheless not coincide with it. Thus, behaviorism is right when it asserts that a scientific psychology is only possible as a natural science. This does not mean, however, that it has *realized* psychology as a natural science, that it has not compromised this idea. For each conception the tendency is a *task* and not something given. To realize what the task is does not yet imply the ability to solve it. Different conceptions may exist on the basis of one tendency, and in one conception both tendencies may be represented to different degrees.

With this precise demarcation in mind we may proceed to the systems which advocate a third way. Very many of them exist. However, the majority belong either to blind men who unconsciously mix the two ways up, or to deliberate eclectics who run from path to path. Let us pass them by; we are interested in principles, not in their distortions. There are three of these fundamentally pure systems: Gestalt theory, personalism, and Marxist psychology. Let us examine them from the point of view that fits our goal. All three schools share the conviction that psychology as a science is neither possible on the basis of empirical psychology, nor on the basis of behaviorism and that there is a third way which stands above these two ways and which allows us to realize a scientific psychology which does not reject either of the two approaches but unites them into a single whole. Each system solves this task in its own way and each has its own fate, but together they exhaust *all* logical possibilities of a third way, as if it were a methodological experiment especially designed for this purpose.

Gestalt theory solves this problem by introducing the basic concept of structure (Gestalt), which combines both the functional and the descriptive side of behavior, i.e., it is a *psychophysical* concept. To combine both aspects in the subject matter of one science is only possible if one finds something fundamental which both have *in common* and makes this *common factor* the subject of study. For if we accept mind and body as two different things which are separated by an abyss and do not coincide in a single aspect, then, naturally, a single science about these two absolutely distinct things will be impossible. This is the crux of the whole methodology of the new theory. The Gestalt principle is equally applicable *to the whole of nature*. It is not only a property of the mind; the principle has a psychophysical character. It is applicable to physiology, physics and in general to all real sciences. Mind is only *part* of behavior, conscious processes are part-processes of larger wholes [Koffka, 1924, p. 160]. Wertheimer (1925, p. 7) is even clearer about this. The formula of the whole Gestalt theory can be reduced to the following: *what takes place in a part of some whole is determined by the internal structural laws of this whole.* "This is Gestalt theory, no more and no less." The psychologist Köhler [1920] showed that in principle the same processes take place in physics. *Methodologically* this is a striking fact and for Gestalt theory it is a decisive argument. The investigative principle is identical for the mental, organic, and non-organic. This means that psychology is connected with the natural sciences, that psychological investigation is possible on the basis of physical principles. Gestalt theory does not view the mental and physical as absolutely heterogenous things which are combined in a meaningless way, but instead asserts their connection. They are parts of one whole. Only persons belonging to recent European culture can divide the mental and the physical as we do. A person is dancing. Do we really have a sum-total of muscular movements on the one hand and joy and inspiration on the other? The two sides are structurally similar. Consciousness brings nothing fundamentally new which would require other investigative methods. Where is the boundary between materialism and idealism? There are psychological theories and even many textbooks which, despite the fact that they only talk about the elements of consciousness, are more devoid of mind and sense and are more torpid and materialistic than a growing tree.

What does all this mean? Only that Gestalt theory realizes a materialistic psychology insofar as it fundamentally and methodologically consistently lays down its system. This is *seemingly* in contradiction with Gestalt theory's doctrine about phenomenal reactions, about introspection, but only seemingly, because for these psychologists the mind is the phenomenal *part of behavior*, i.e., in principle they choose *one of the two ways* and not a third one.

Another question is whether this theory advances its view consistently, whether it does not run against contradictions in its conceptions, whether the means to realize this third way have been chosen correctly. But this does not interest us here, only the methodological system of principles. And we can add to this that everything in the conceptions of Gestalt theory which does not coincide with this tendency is a manifestation of the other tendency. When the mind is described in the same concepts as physics we have the way of natural scientific psychology.

It is easy to show that Stern [1919] in his theory of personalism follows the opposite path of development. In his wish to avoid the two ways and to defend a third, he in reality also defends *only one of the two ways:* the way of idealistic psychology. He proceeds from the assumption that we do not have a psychology, but many psychologies. In order to preserve the subject of psychology in the perspective of both tendencies he introduces the concept of psychophysically neutral acts and functions and ends up with the following hypothesis: the mental and the physical go through identical levels of development. The division is secondary, it arises from the fact that the personality may appear before itself and before others. The basic fact is the existence of the psychophysically neutral person and his psychophysically neutral acts. Thus, unity is reached by the introduction of the concept of the psychophysically neutral act.

Let us consider what is in reality hidden behind this formula. It turns out that Stern follows a road opposite to the one known to us from Gestalt theory. For him the organism and even anorganic systems are also psychophysical neutral persons. Plants, the solar system, and man must in principle be understood identically, by extending the teleological principle to the non-mental world. We are faced with a teleological psychology. Once again a third way proved to be *one of the two* well-known ways. Once again we are talking about personalism's methodology; about the question what a psychology created according to these principles would look like. What it is in reality is another question. In reality, Stern is forced, like Münsterberg, to be an adherent of causal psychology in differential psychology. In reality, he provides a materialist conception of consciousness, i.e., within his system that same struggle is still going on which is well known to us and which he, unsuccessfully, wished to overcome.

The third system which attempts to defend a third way is the system of Marxist psychology which is developing before our eyes.[56] It is difficult to analyze, because it does not yet have its own methodology[57] and attempts to find it ready-made in the haphazard psychological statements of the founders of Marxism,[58] not to mention the fact that to find a ready-made formula of the mind in the writings of others would mean to demand "science before science itself." [51] It must be remarked that the heterogeneity of the material, its fragmentary nature, the change of meaning of phrases taken out of context and the polemical character of the majority of the pronouncements—correct in their contradiction of a false idea, but empty and general as a positive definition of the task—do not allow us to expect of this work anything more than a pile of more or less accidental citations and their Talmudic interpretation. But citations, even when they have been well ordered, never yield systems.

Another formal shortcoming of such work is the mixing up of two goals in these investigations. For it is one thing to examine the Marxist doctrine from the historical-philosophical point of view and quite another one to investigate the problems themselves which these thinkers stated. If they are combined, a double disadvantage results: some particular author is used to solve the problem, the problem is stated only on a scale and in a context which fits this author, who is dealing with it *in passing* and for quite another reason. The distorted statement of the question deals with its accidental aspects, does not touch on its core, does not develop it *in a way* which the essence of the question requires.

The fear of verbal contradiction leads to a confusion of epistemological and methodological viewpoints, etc.

But neither can the second goal—the study of the author—be attained via this road, because the author is willy-nilly being modernized, is drawn into the present debate, and, most importantly, is grossly distorted by arbitrarily combining into a system citations found in different places. We might put it as follows: they are looking, firstly, *in the wrong place;* secondly, *for the wrong thing;* thirdly, *in the wrong manner.*

In the wrong place, because neither in Plekhanov nor in any of the other Marxists can one find *what one is looking for,* for not only do they not have an accomplished methodology of psychology, they do not even have the beginnings of one. For them this problem never arose, and their utterances concerning this theme have first of all a nonpsychological character. They do not even have an epistemological theory about the way to know the mental.[59] As if it were really such a simple matter to create so much as a hypothesis about the psychophysical relation! Plekhanov would have inscribed his name in the history of philosophy next to that of Spinoza had he himself created some psychophysical theory. He could not do that, because he himself never dealt with psychophysiology and science could not yet give occasion to the construction of such a hypothesis.

Behind Spinoza's hypothesis was the whole of Galileo's physics. Translated into philosophical language, it expressed the whole fundamentally generalized experience of physics which first discovered the unity and regularity of the world. And what in psychology might have engendered such a theory? Plekhanov and others were always interested in their local goals: polemics, explanation, in general, a goal tied to a specific context, not an independent, generalized idea elevated to the level of a theory.

For the wrong thing, because what is needed is a methodological system of principles by means of which the investigation can be started and what they are looking for is a fundamental answer, the still vague scientific end point of many years of joint research. If we already had the answer, there would be no need to build a Marxist psychology. The external criterion for the formula we seek must be its methodological suitability. Instead, they are looking for a pompous ontological formula which is as empty and cautious as possible and avoids any solution. What we need is a formula which *would serve us* in research. What they are searching for is a formula which we must serve, which we must prove. As a result they stumble upon formulas—such as negative concepts, etc.—which *paralyze* the investigation. They do not show how we can realize a science proceeding from these accidental formulas.

In the wrong manner, because their thinking is fettered by authoritarian principles. They study not methods but dogmas. They do not come any further than stating that two formulas are logically equivalent. They do not approach the matter in a critical, free and investigative way.

But all these three flaws follow from a common cause: a misunderstanding of the historical task of psychology and the meaning of the crisis. The next section is specially dedicated to this matter. Here I state everything necessary to make the boundary between conceptions and a system clearer, to relieve the system from the responsibility for the sins of the conceptions. We will call it a falsely understood system. We are all the more justified in doing this as this understanding itself did not realize where it would lead to.

The new system lays the concept of reaction—as distinct from the reflex and the mental phenomenon—at the basis of the third way in psychology. The integral act of the reaction includes both the subjective and the objective aspect. However, in contrast with Gestalt theory and Stern, the new theory refrains from methodological assumptions which unite both parts of the reaction into one concept. Neither viewing fundamentally the same structures in the mind as in physics, nor finding goals, entelechy and personality in anorganic nature, e.g., neither the way of Gestalt theory, nor the way of Stern, lead to the goal.

Following Plekhanov, the new theory accepts the doctrine of psychophysical parallelism and the complete irreducibility of the mental to the physical. Such a reduction it regards as crude, vulgar materialism. But how can there be one science about *two* categories of being which are fundamentally, qualitatively heterogeneous and irreducible to each other? How can they merge into the integral act of the reaction? We have two answers to these questions. Kornilov, by seeing a functional relation between them, immediately destroys any *unity*: it is two *different* things that can stand in a functional relation to each other. Psychology cannot be studied with the concepts of reaction, for *within* the reaction we find two functionally independent elements which cannot be unified. This is not solving the psychophysical problem, but moving it into each element. Therefore it makes any research impossible, just as it has impeded psychology as a whole. At the time it was the relation of the whole area of the mind to the whole area of physiology which was unclear. Now the same insolubility is entangled in each separate reaction. What does this solution of the problem offer, *methodologically speaking*? Instead of solving it problematically (hypothetically) at the start of the investigation one must solve it experimentally, empirically in each separate case. But this is impossible. And how can there be one science with two fundamentally different methods of knowledge acquisition (not research methods: Kornilov regards introspection as the only adequate way to know the mind and not just as a technical device)? It is clear that methodologically the integral nature of the reaction remains a *pia desiderata* [52] and in reality such a concept leads to two sciences with two methods which study two different aspects of reality.

Frankfurt (1926) provides a different answer. Following Plekhanov, he becomes entangled in a hopeless and insoluble contradiction. He wishes to prove the material nature of the nonmaterial mind and to link two ways of science for psychology which cannot be linked. The outline of his argumentation is as follows: the idealists view matter as another form of existence of the mind; the mechanistic materialists view the mind as another form of being of matter. The dialectical materialist preserves both parts of the antinomy. For him the mind is (1) a special property amidst *many* other properties which is irreducible to movement; (2) an internal state of moving matter; (3) the subjective side of a material process. The contradictory nature and the heterogeneity of these formulas will be revealed in the systematic exposition of the concepts of psychology. There I hope to show how the juxtaposition of ideas plucked from absolutely different contexts distorts their meaning. Here we deal exclusively with the *methodological* aspect of the question: can there be *one* science about *two* fundamentally different kinds of being? They have nothing in common, cannot be unified. But perhaps there is an unequivocal link between them that allows us to combine them? No. Plekhanov (cf. Frankfurt, 1926, p. 51) clearly says that Marxism does not accept "the possibility of explaining or describing one kind of phenomenon by means of ideas or concepts 'developed' to explain or describe another kind." Frankfurt (ibid., pp. 52-53) says that "Mind is a *special* property which we can describe or explain by means of *special* concepts or ideas." Once again the same—*different* concepts. But this means that there are two sciences, one about behavior as a unique form of human movement, the other about the mind as non-movement. Frankfurt also talks about physiology in a narrow and a broad sense—including the mind. But will this be physiology? Is our wish sufficient to make a science appear according to our *fiat*? Let them show us so much as a single example of *one* science about *two* different kinds of being which are being explained and described by means of different concepts, or let them show us the possibility of such a science.

There are two points in this argumentation which categorically show that such a science is *impossible*.

1. Mind is a special quality or property of matter, but a quality is not part of a thing, but a special capacity. But matter has many qualities, mind is *just one of them*. Plekhanov compares the relation between mind and movement with the relations between the properties of growth and combustibility of wood, with the hardness and shine of ice. But why, then, are there only two parts in the antinomy? There should be as many as there are qualities, i.e., many, infinitely many. Obviously, notwithstanding Chernychevsky, all qualities have something in common. There is a *general concept* under which all the qualities of matter can be subsumed: both the shine of ice and its hardness, both the fact that wood is easy to burn and the way it grows. If not, there would be as many sciences as there are qualities: one science about the shine of ice, another about its hardness. What Chernychevsky says is *simply absurd* as a methodological principle. After all, also within the mind we find different qualities: pain resembles lust in the same way as shine resembles hardness—once again a special property.

The whole matter is that Plekhanov is operating with a general concept of the mind under which a multitude of the most heterogeneous qualities are subsumed, and that movement, under which all other qualities are subsumed, is also such a general concept. Obviously, mind stands in principle in another relation to movement than qualities do to each other: both shine and hardness are in the end movement; both pain and lust are in the end mind. Mind is not one of many properties, but one of two. But this means that in the end there are *two* principles and not one or many. Methodologically this means that the dualism of the science is completely preserved. This becomes particularly clear from the second point.

2. The mental does not influence the physical, according to Plekhanov (1922). Frankfurt (1926) clarifies that it influences itself mediately, via physiology, it exerts its influence in a peculiar way. If we combine two right-angled triangles, their forms will combine into a new form—a square. The forms themselves do not exert influence "as a second, 'formal' aspect of the combination of our material triangles." We observe that this is an exact statement of the famous *Schattentheorie*, the theory of shadows: two men shake hands and their shadows do the same. According to Frankfurt the shadows "influence" each other via the body.

But this is not the methodological problem. Does the author understand that, for a materialist, he arrived at a monstrous formulation of the nature of our science? Really, what sort of science about shadows, forms and mirror reflections is this?

The author half understands what he arrived at, but does not see what it implies. Is a natural science about forms as such really possible, a science which uses induction, the concept of causality? It is only in geometry that we study abstract forms. The final word has been said: psychology is possible as geometry. But exactly this is the highest expression of Husserl's eidetic psychology. Dilthey's descriptive psychology as mathematics of the spirit is like that and so are Chelpanov's phenomenology, Stout's, Meinong's, and Schmidt-Kovazhik's analytic psychology. What unites them all with Frankfurt is the whole fundamental structure. They are using the same analogy.

1. The mind must be studied as geometrical forms, *outside causality*. Two triangles do not engender a square, the circle knows nothing of the pyramid. No relation of the real world may be transferred to the ideal world of forms and mental essences: they can only be described, analyzed, classified, but not explained. Dilthey [1894/1977, p. 93] regards it as the main property of the mind that its parts are not linked by the law of causality:

> Representations contain no sufficient ground for going over into feelings; one could imagine a purely representational creature who would be, in the midst of a battle's tumult, an unconcerned spectator indifferent about his own destruction. Feelings contain no sufficient ground for being transformed into volitional processes. One could imagine the same creature whose awareness of the surrounding combat would be accompanied by feelings of fear and terror, yet without movements of defense resulting from these feelings.

Precisely because these concepts are a-deterministic, noncausal and nonspatial, precisely because they have been formed like geometrical abstractions, Pavlov rejects their suitability for science: they are incompatible with the material construction of the brain. Following Pavlov, we say that, precisely because they are geometrical, they are not fit for real science.

But how can there be a science which combines the geometrical method with the scientific-inductive one? Dilthey [ibid., p. 46] understood perfectly well that materialism and *explanatory* psychology presuppose each other. Materialism is "in all its nuances, an explanatory psychology. Every theory which depends on the system of physical processes and merely incorporates mental facts into that system, is a materialism." Exactly the wish to defend the independence of the mind and all the sciences of the mind, the fear of transferring to this world the causality and necessity which reign in nature, leads to the fear of explanatory psychology. "No explanatory psychology . . . is capable of serving as the basis of the human studies" [ibid., p. 73]. This signifies that the sciences of the mind must not be studied materialistically. Oh, if Frankfurt only understood what it really implies to demand a psychology as geometry! To accept a special link—"efficacy"—instead of the physical causality of the mind, to reject explanatory psychology, means no more and no less than *to reject the concept of regularity in the whole field of the mind. This is what the debate is about.* The Russian idealists understand this perfectly well. For them Dilthey's thesis about psychology is a thesis that contrasts with the mechanistic conception of the historical process.

2. The second feature of the psychology at which Frankfurt arrived resides in its method, in the nature of the knowledge of this science. If the mind cannot be linked with natural processes, if it is noncausal, then it cannot be studied inductively, by observing real facts and generalizing them. It must be studied by the method of speculation, through the direct contemplation of the truth in these Platonic ideas or mental essences. There is no place for induction in geometry; what has been proved for one triangle, has been proved for all of them. It does not study real triangles, but ideal abstractions—the different properties which have been ab-

stracted from things are carried to the extreme and studied in their ideally pure form. For Husserl, phenomenology stands to psychology as mathematics to natural science. But according to Frankfurt it would be impossible to realize geometry and psychology as natural sciences. Their method is different. Induction is based on the repeated observation of facts and their empirically-based generalization. The analytical (phenomenological) method is based on a single immediate contemplation of the truth. This deserves reflection. We must know exactly with which science we want to break all ties. This theory about induction and analysis involves an essential misunderstanding which we must lay bare.

Analysis is applied entirely systematically in both causal psychology and the natural sciences. And there we often *deduce a general regularity from a single observation.* The domination of induction and mathematical elaboration and the underdevelopment of analysis substantially damaged the case of Wundt and experimental psychology as a whole.

What is the difference between one analysis and the other, or, not to make a mistake, between the analytical method and the phenomenological one? When we know this we can add to our map the last characteristic distinguishing the two psychologies.

The method of analysis in the natural sciences and in causal psychology consists of the study of a *single* phenomenon, a typical representative of a whole series, and the deduction of a proposition *about the whole series* on the basis of that phenomenon. Chelpanov (1917) clarifies this idea by giving the example of the study of the properties of different gases. Thus, we assert something about the properties of all gases after we conducted an experiment with only one type of gas. When we arrive at such a conclusion we assume that the gas we experimented upon has the same properties as all other gases. According to Chelpanov, in such an inference the inductive and the analytical method are simultaneously present.

Is this really true, i.e., is it really possible to merge the geometrical method with the natural scientific one, or do we have here a simple mixture of terms, with Chelpanov using the word *analysis* in two entirely distinct senses? The question is too important to ignore. We must not only distinguish the two psychologies, we must set apart their methods as deeply and as far as possible as they *cannot have* methods in common. Apart from the fact that we are interested in that part of the method which after the separation falls to the lot of descriptive psychology, because we want to know it exactly—apart from all this, *we do not wish to concede one bit* of the territory that belongs to us in the process of division. As we will see below, the analytical method is in principle too important for the development of the whole of social psychology, to render it without striking a blow.

When our Marxists explain the Hegelian principle in Marxist methodology they rightly claim that each thing can be examined as a microcosm, as a universal measure in which the whole big world is reflected. On this basis they say that to study one single thing, one subject, one phenomenon *until the end*, exhaustively, means to know the world in all its connections. In this sense it can be said that each person is to some degree a measure of the society, or rather class, to which he belongs, for the whole totality of social relationships is reflected in him.

From this alone we see that knowledge gained on the path from the special to the general is the key to all social psychology. We must reconquer the right for psychology to examine what is special, the individual as a social microcosm, as a type, as an expression or measure of the society. But about this we must only speak when we are face to face with causal psychology. Here we must exhaust the theme of the division.

What is undoubtedly correct in Chelpanov's example is that analysis in physics does not contradict induction, since it is precisely due to analysis that a single observation can lead to a general conclusion. Indeed, what justifies us in extending our conclusion about one gas to all others? Obviously, it is only because we elaborated the concept of gas *per se* through previous inductive observations and established the extension and content of this concept. Further, because we study the given particular gas *not as such*, but from a special viewpoint. We study the general *properties of a gas* realized in it. It is exactly this possibility, i.e., this viewpoint that in the particular, the special can be separated from the general, which we owe to analysis.

Thus, analysis is in principle not opposed to induction, but related to it. It is its highest form which contradicts its essence (repetition). It rests on induction and guides it. It states the question. It *lies at the basis of each experiment*. Each *experiment is an analysis in action, as each analysis is an experiment in thought*. That is why it would be correct to call it an *experimental method*. Indeed, when I am experimenting, I am studying A, B, C . . ., i.e., a number of concrete phenomena, and I assign the conclusions to different groups: to all people, to school-aged children, to activity, etc. The analysis suggests to what extent the conclusions may be generalized, i.e., it distinguishes in A, B, C . . . the characteristics that a given group has in common. But even more: in the experiment I always observe just one feature of a phenomenon, and this is again the result of analysis.

Let us now turn to the inductive method in order to clarify the analysis. Let us examine a number of applications of this method.

Pavlov is studying the activity of *the salivary gland in dogs*. What gives him the right to call his experiments the study of the higher nervous activity of *animals*? Perhaps, he should have verified his experiments on horses, crows, etc., on all, or at least the majority of animals, in order to have the right to draw these conclusions? Or, perhaps, he should have called his experiments "a study of salivation in dogs"? But it is precisely the salivation of dogs *per se* which Pavlov did not study and his experiments have not for one bit increased our knowledge of dogs as such and of salivation as such. In the dogs he did not study the dog, but *an animal in general*, and in salivation *a reflex in general*, i.e., in this animal and in this phenomenon he distinguished what they have in common with all homogeneous phenomena. That is why his conclusions do not just concern all animals, but the whole of biology as well. The established fact that Pavlov's dogs salivated to signals given by Pavlov immediately became a general biological principle—the principle of the transformation of inherited experience into personal experience. This proved possible because Pavlov *maximally abstracted* the phenomenon he studied from the specific conditions of the particular phenomenon. He brilliantly *perceived the general in the particular.*

What did the extension of his conclusions rest upon? Naturally, on the following: we extend our conclusions to something which has to do *with the same elements* and we rely upon similarities established in advance (the class of hereditary reflexes in all animals, the nervous system, etc.). Pavlov discovered a *general biological* law while studying *dogs*. But in the dog he studied what forms the basis of any animal.

This is the methodological path of any explanatory principle. In essence, Pavlov did not extend his conclusions, and the degree of their extension was determined in advance. It was implied in the very statement of the problem. The same is true for Ukhtomsky. He studied several preparations of frogs. If he had generalized his conclusions to all frogs this would have been induction. But he talks about the dominant as a principle of psychology applicable to the heroes of "War and Peace," and this he owes to analysis. Sherrington studied the scratching and flexive reflexes of the hind leg in many cats and dogs, but he established the principle of the struggle for the motor path which lies at the basis of the personality. But neither Ukhtomsky nor Sherrington added anything to the study of frogs or cats as such.

It is, of course, a very special task to find *the precise factual boundaries* of a general principle in practice and the *degree* to which it can be applied to different species of the given genus. Perhaps the conditional reflex has its highest boundary in the behavior of the human infant and its lowest in invertebrates and is found in absolutely different forms beyond these extremes. Within these limits it is more applicable to the dog than to a chicken and to what extent it is applicable to each of them can be exactly ascertained. But all this is already induction, the study of the specifically particular in relation to a principle and on the basis of analysis. There is no end to this process. We can study the application of a principle to different breeds, ages, sexes of the dog; further, to an individual dog, still further, to a particular day or hour of the dog's life, etc. The same is true of the dominant and the general motor path.

I have tried to introduce such a method into conscious psychology[60] and to deduce the laws of the psychology of art on the basis of the *analysis* of one fable, one short story, and one tragedy. In doing so I proceeded from the idea that the well-developed forms of art provide the key to the underdeveloped ones, just as the anatomy of man provides the key to the anatomy of the ape. I assumed that Shakespeare's tragedy explains the enigmas of primitive art and not the other way around. Further, *I talk about all art* and do not verify my conclusions on music, painting, etc. What is even more: I do not verify them on *all* or the majority of the *types* of literature. I take *one* short story, *one* tragedy. Why am I entitled to do so? I have not studied the fable, the tragedy, and still less a *given* fable or a *given* tragedy. I have studied in them what makes up the basis of all art—the nature and mechanism of the aesthetic reaction. I relied upon the general elements of form and material which are inherent in any art. For the analysis I selected the most difficult fables, short stories and tragedies, precisely those in which the general laws are particularly evident. I selected the monsters among the tragedies etc. The analysis presupposes that one abstracts from the concrete characteristics of the fable as such, as a specific genre, and concentrates the forces upon the essence of the aesthetic reaction. That is why I say *nothing* about the fable as such. And the subtitle "An analysis of the aesthetic reaction" itself indicates that the goal of the investigation is not a systematic exposition of a psychological theory of art in its entire volume and width of content (all types of art, all problems, etc.) and not even the inductive investigation of a specific number of facts, but precisely *the analysis of the processes in their essence.*

The objective-analytical method, therefore, is similar to the experiment. Its meaning is broader than its field of observation. Naturally, the principle of art as well is dealing with a reaction which in reality *never manifested itself* in a pure form, but always with its "coefficient of specification." [53]

To find the factual boundaries, levels and forms of the applicability of a principle is a matter of factual research. Let history show *which* feelings in *which* eras, via *which* forms have been expressed in art. My task was to show *how* this proceeds in general. And this is the common methodological position of contemporary art theory: it studies the essence of a reaction knowing that it will never manifest itself in exactly that form. But the type, norm or limit will always be part of the concrete reaction and determine its specific character. Thus, a purely aesthetic reaction never occurs in art. In reality it will be combined with the most complex and diverse forms of ideology (morals, politics, etc.). Many even think that the aesthetic aspects are no more essential in art than coquetry in the reproduction of the species. It is a facade, *Vorlust*, a lure, and the meaning of the act lies in something else (Freud and his school). Others assume that historically and psychologically art and aesthetics are two intersecting circles which have a common and a separate surface (Utitz). [54] This is all true, but it does not change the veracity of a principle, because it is *abstracted* from all this. It only says that the *aesthetical reaction is like this*. It is another matter to find the boundaries and sense of the aesthetic reaction itself within art.

Abstraction and analysis does all this. The similarity with the experiment resides in the fact that here, too, we have an artificial combination of phenomena in which the action of a specific law must manifest itself in the purest form. It is like a snare for nature, an analysis in action. In analysis we create a similar artificial combination of phenomena, but then through abstraction in thought. This is particularly clear in its application to art constructions. They are not aimed at scientific, but at practical goals and rely upon the action of some specific psychological or physical law. Examples are a machine, an anecdote, lyrics, mnemonics, a military command. Here we have a practical experiment. The analysis of such cases is an experiment with finished phenomena. Its meaning comes close to that of pathology—this experiment arranged by nature itself—to its own analysis. The only difference is that disease causes the loss or demarcation of superfluous traits, whereas we here have the presence of necessary traits, a selection of them—but the result is the same.

Each lyrical poem is such an experiment. The task of the analysis is to reveal the law that forms the basis of nature's experiment. But also when the analysis does not deal with a machine, i.e., a practical experiment, but with any phenomenon, it is in principle similar to the experiment. It would be possible to prove how infinitely much our equipment complicates and refines our research, how much more intelligent, stronger and more perspicuous it makes us. Analysis does the same.

It may seem that analysis, like experiment, distorts reality by creating artificial conditions for observation. Hence the demand that the experiment should be realistic and natural. If this idea goes further than a technical demand—not to scare off what we are searching for—it leads to absurdity. The strength of analysis is in abstraction, just as the strength of experiment is in its artificiality. Pavlov's experiments are the best specimen: for the dogs it is a *natural* experiment—they are fed etc.; for the scientist it is the summit of artificiality—salivation takes place when a specific area is scratched, which is an unnatural combination. Likewise, we need destruction in the analysis of a machine, mental or real damage to the mechanism, and in the [analysis of the] aesthetic form we need deformation.

If we remember what was said above about the indirect method, then it is easy to observe that analysis and experiment presuppose *indirect* study. From the analysis of the stimuli we infer the mechanism of the reaction, from the command, the movements of the soldiers, and from the form of the fable the reactions to it.

Marx [1867/1981, p. 12] says essentially the same when he compares abstraction with a microscope and chemical reactions in the natural sciences. The whole of *Das Kapital* is written according to this method. Marx analyzes the "cell" of bourgeois society—the form of the commodity value—and shows that a mature body can be more easily studied than a cell. He discerns the structure of the whole social order and all economical formations in this cell. He says that "to the uninitiated its analysis may seem the hair-splitting of details. We are indeed dealing with details, but such details as microscopic anatomy is also dealing with." He who can decipher the meaning of the cell of psychology, the mechanism of one reaction, has found the key to all psychology.

That is why analysis is a most potent tool in methodology. Engels [1925/1978, p. 496] explains to the "all-inductionists" that "no induction whatever might ever explain the *process* of induction. This could only be accomplished by the *analysis* of this process." He further gives mistakes of induction which are frequently encountered. Elsewhere he compares both methods and finds in thermodynamics an example which shows that the pretensions of induction to be the only or most fundamental form of scientific discovery are ill-founded.

> The steam engine formed the convincing proof of the fact that one can use heat to accomplish mechanical movements. One hundred thousand steam engines would not prove this more convincingly than a single engine . . . Sadi Carnot was the first to study it seriously. But not through induction. He studied the steam engine, analyzed it, found that the relevant process does not appear in it in a *pure* form but was concealed by all sorts of incidental processes, removed these inessentials which are indifferent for the essential process, and construed an ideal steam engine . . . which, to be sure, is as imaginary as, for example, a geometrical line or plane, but fulfills the same service as these mathematical abstractions: it represents the process in a pure, independent, and undistorted form [ibid., pp. 496–497].

It would be possible to show how and when such an analysis is possible in the methods of investigation of this applied branch of methodology. But we can also generally say that analysis is the application of methodology to the knowledge of a fact, i.e., it is an evaluation of the method used and of the meaning of the obtained phenomena. In this sense it can be said that analysis is *always* inherent in investigation, otherwise induction would turn into registration.

How does this analysis differ from Chelpanov's analysis? By four characteristics: (1) the analytical method is aimed at the knowledge of realities and strives for the same goal as induction. The phenomenological method does not at all presuppose the existence of the essence it strives to know. Its subject matter can be pure phantasy, deprived of any existence; (2) the analytical method studies facts and leads to knowledge which has the trustworthiness of a fact. The phenomenological method obtains apodictic truths which are absolutely trustworthy and universally valid; (3) the analytical method is a special case of empirical knowledge, i.e., factual knowledge, according to Hume. The phenomenological method is *a priori*, it is not a kind of experience or factual knowledge; (4) via the study of new special facts the analytical method, which relies on facts which have been studied and generalized before, ultimately leads to new relative and factual generalizations which have a boundary, a variable degree of applicability, limitations and even exceptions. The phenomenological method does not lead to knowledge of the general, but of the idea, the essence. The general is known through induction, the essence by intuition. It exists outside time and reality and is not related to any temporal or real thing.

We see that the difference is as big as a difference between two methods can be. One method—let us call it the analytical method—is the method of the real, natural sciences, the other—the phenomenological, *a priori* one—is the method of the mathematical sciences and of the pure science of the mind.

Why does Chelpanov call it the analytical method and assert that it is identical to the phenomenological one? Firstly, it is a plain *mistake* which the author himself tries to sort out several times. Thus, he points out that the analytical method is not identical to normal analysis in psychology. It yields knowledge of another kind than induction—we are reminded of the precise distinctions, all of them established by Chelpanov. Thus, there are *two types of induction* which have nothing in common but their name. This general term is confusing and we must distinguish its two meanings.

Further, it is clear that the analysis in the case of a gas, which the author adduces as a possible counterargument against the theory which says that the main feature of the "analytical" method is that it examines phenomena just once, is a natural scientific and not a phenomenological analysis. The author is simply *mistaken* when he sees a combination of analysis and induction here. It is analysis, but of another kind. Not one of the four points distinguishing both methods leaves any doubt about the fact that: (1) it is aimed at real facts, not at "ideal possibilities"; (2) it has only factual and not apodictic validity; (3) it is *a posteriori*; (4) it leads to generalizations which have boundaries and degrees, not to the contemplation of essences [*Wesensschau*]. In general, it results from experience, from induction and not from intuition.

That we are dealing with a mistake and a mixture of terms is absolutely clear from the absurd attempt to combine the phenomenological and the inductive method in one experiment. This is what Chelpanov does in the case of gases. It is as if we partly tried to prove Pythagoras' theorem and partly completed it with the study of real triangles. It is absurd. But behind the mistake is some dimension: the psychoanalysts have taught us to be sensitive to and suspicious about mistakes. Chelpanov belongs to the harmonizers: he sees the dualism of psychology, but unlike Husserl he does not accept psychology's complete separation from phenomenology. For him psychology is partly phenomenology. Within psychology there are phenomenological truths and they are the fundamental core of the science. But at the same time Chelpanov sympathizes with the experimental psychology which Husserl slighted with contempt. Chelpanov wishes to *combine what cannot be combined* and his story about the gases is the only one where he combines the analytical (phenomenological) method with induction in physics in the study of real gases. And this mixture he conceals with the general term "analytical."

The split of the dual analytical method into a phenomenological and an inductive-analytical one leads us to the ultimate points upon which the bifurcation of the two psychologies rests—their epistemological premises. I attach great importance to this distinction, see it as the crown and center of the whole analysis, and at the same time for me it is now as obvious as a simple scale. [55] Phenomenology (descriptive psychology) proceeds from a radical distinction between physical nature and mental being. In nature we distinguish phenomena in being. "In other words, in the mental sphere there is no distinction between phenomenon [*Erscheinung*] and being [*Sein*], and while nature is existence [*Dasein*] which manifests itself in the phenomena," this cannot be asserted about mental being (Husserl, 1910/1965, p. 35). Here *phenomenon and being coincide*. It is difficult to give a more precise formulation of psychological idealism. And this is the epistemological formula of psychological materialism: "The difference between *thinking* and *being* has not been destroyed in psychology. Even concerning thinking one must distinguish the thinking of thinking and the thinking as such" [Feuerbach, 1971, p. 127]. *The whole debate is in these two formulas.*

We must be able to state the epistemological problem *for the mind* as well and to find the distinction between being and thinking, as materialism teaches us to do in the theory of knowledge of the external world. The acceptance of a radical difference between the mind and physical nature conceals the identification of *phenomenon* and *being*, mind and matter, within *psychology*, the solution of the antinomy by removing one part—matter—in psychological knowledge. This is Husserl's idealism of the purest water. Feuerbach's whole materialism is expressed in the distinction of phenomenon and being within psychology and in the acceptance of being as the real object of study.

I venture to prove for the whole council of philosophers—idealists as well as materialists—that the essence of the divergence of idealism and materialism in psychology lies precisely here, and that only Husserl's and Feuerbach's formulas give a consistent solution of the problem in the two possible variants and that the first is the formula of phenomenology and the second that of materialistic psychology. I venture, proceeding from this comparison, to cut the living tissue of psychology, cutting it as it were into two heterogeneous bodies which grew together by mistake. This is the only thing which corresponds with the objective order of things, and *all* debates, *all* disagreements, *all* confusion merely result from the absence of a clear and correct statement of the epistemological problem.

From this it follows that by only accepting from empirical psychology its *formal* acceptance of the mind, Frankfurt also accepts its whole epistemology and all its conclusions—he is forced to resort to phenomenology. It follows that by demanding a method for the study of the mind which corresponds to its qualitative nature, he is demanding a phenomenological method, although he does not realize it himself. His conception is the materialism of which Høffding [1908, p. 86, footnote 1] is entirely justified in saying that it is "a miniature dualistic spiritualism." Precisely *"miniature,"* i.e., with the attempt to reduce, quantitatively diminish the reality of the nonmaterial mind, to leave 0.001 of influence for it. But the fundamental solution *in no way* depends on a quantitative statement of the question. It is one of two things: either god exists, or he does not; either the spirits of dead people manifest themselves, or they do not; either mental (spiritistic—for Watson) phenomena are nonmaterial, or they are material. Answers which have the form "god exists, but he is very small," or "the spirits of dead people do not manifest themselves, but tiny parts of them very rarely visit spiritists," or "the mind is material, but distinct from all other matter," are humorous. Lenin wrote of the "bogostroiteli" ["God-builders"] that they differ little from the "bogoiskateli" ["God-seekers"] [56]: what is important is to either accept or reject deviltry in general; to assume either a blue or a yellow devil does not make a big difference.

When one mixes up the epistemological problem with the ontological one by introducing into psychology not the whole argumentation but its final results, this leads to the distortion of *both*. In Russia the subjective is identified with the mental and later it is proved that the mental cannot be objective. Epistemological consciousness as part of the antinomy "subject–object" is confused with empirical, psychological consciousness and then it is asserted that consciousness cannot be material, that to assume this would be Machism. [57] And as a result one ends up with neoplatonism, in the sense of infallible essences for which being and phenomenon coincide. They flee for idealism only to plunge into it headlong. They dread the identification of being with consciousness more than anything else and end up in psychology with their perfectly Husserlian identification. We must not mix up the relation between subject and object with the relation between mind and body, as Høffding [1908, p. 298, footnote 1] splendidly explains. The distinction between mind [*Geist*] and matter is a distinction in the content of our knowledge. But the distinction between subject and object manifests itself independently from the content of our knowledge.

> Both mind and body are for us objective, but whereas mental objects [*geistigen Objekte*] are by their nature related to the knowing subject, the body exists *only* as an object for us. The relation between subject and object is an epistemological problem [*Erkenntnisproblem*], the relation between mind and matter is an ontological problem [*Daseinsproblem*].

This is not the place to give both problems a precise demarcation and basis in materialistic psychology, but to indicate the possibility of two solutions, the boundary between idealism and materialism, the existence of a materialistic formula. For distinction, distinction to the very end, is psychology's task today. After all, many "Marxists" are not able to indicate the difference between theirs and an idealistic theory of psychological knowledge, because it does not exist. Following Spinoza, we have compared our science to a mortally ill patient who looks for an unreliable medicine. Now we see that it is only the surgeon's knife which can save the situation. A bloody operation is immanent. Many textbooks we will have to rend in twain, like the veil in the temple [58], many phrases will lose their head or legs, other theories will be slit in the belly. We are only interested in the border, the line of the rupture, the line which will be described by the future knife.

And we assert that this line will lie in between the formulas of Husserl and Feuerbach. The thing is that in Marxism the problem of epistemology with regard to psychology has not been stated at all and the task of distinguishing the *two* problems about which Høffding is talking did not arise. The idealists, on the other hand, elaborated this idea with great clarity. And we claim that the viewpoint of our "Marxists" is *Machism in psychology*: it is the identification of being and consciousness. *It is one of two things:* either the mind is directly given to us in introspection, and then we side with Husserl; or we must distinguish subject and object, being and thinking in it, and then we side with Feuerbach. But what does this imply? It implies that my joy and my introspectional comprehension of this joy are different things.

There is a citation from Feuerbach that is very popular in Russia: "what *for me* [or *subjectively*] is a [purely] mental, nonmaterial, suprasensory act, is *in itself* [or *objectively*] a material, sensory act" [Feuerbach, 1971, p. 125]. It is usually cited in confirmation of subjective psychology. But this speaks *against* it. One may wonder what we must study: this act as such, as it is, or as it appears to me? As with the analogous question about the objective existence of the world, the materialist does not hesitate and says: the objective act *as such*. The idealist will say: my perception. But then one and the same act will turn out to be different depending on whether I am drunk or sober, whether I am a child or an adult, whether it is today or yesterday, whether it regards me or you. What is more, it turns out that in introspection we cannot directly perceive thinking, comparison—these are unconscious acts and our introspectional comprehension of them is not a functional concept, i.e., it is not deduced from objective experience. What must we, what can we study: thinking as such or the thinking of thinking? There can be no doubt whatsoever about the answer to this question. But there is one complication which prevents us from reaching a clear answer. *All* philosophers who have attempted to divide psychology have stumbled upon this complication. Stumpf distinguished mental functions from phenomena and asked who, which science, will study the phenomena rejected by physics and psychology. He assumed that a *special science* would develop which is neither psychology nor physics. Another psychologist (Pfänder, 1904) refused to accept sensations as the subject matter of psychology for the sole reason that physics refuses to accept them. What place is left for them? *Husserl's phenomenology is the answer to this question.*

In Russia it is also asked: if you will study thinking as such and not the thinking of thinking; the act as such and not the act for me; the objective and not the subjective—who, then, will study the subjective itself, the subjective distortion of objects? In physics we try to eliminate the subjective factor from what we perceive as an object. In psychology, when we study perception it is again required to separate perception as such, as it is, from how it seems to me. Who will study what has been eliminated both times, this *appearance*?

But the problem of appearance is an apparent problem. After all, in science we want to learn about the *real* and not the *apparent* cause of appearance. This means that we must take the phenomena as they exist independently from me. The appearance itself is an illusion (in Titchener's [1910/1980, pp. 333-335] basic example: Müller-Lyer's lines are physically equal, psychologically one of them is longer). This is the difference between the viewpoints of physics and psychology. It *does not exist in reality,* but results from two non-coincidences of two really existing processes. If I would know the physical nature of the two lines and the objective laws of the eye, as they are in themselves, I would get the explanation of the appearance, of the illusion as a result. The study of the subjective factor in the knowledge of this illusion is a subject of logic and the historical theory of knowledge: just like being, the subjective is the result of two processes which are objective in themselves. The mind is not always a subject. In introspection it is split into object and subject. The question is whether in introspection phenomenon and being coincide. One has only to *apply* the epistemological formula of materialism, given by Lenin [1975, p. 260] (a similar one can be found in Plekhanov) *for the psychological subject-object,* in order to see what is the matter:

> the only 'property' of matter connected with philosophical materialism is the property of being an objective reality, of existing outside of our consciousness . . . . Epistemologically the concept of matter means *nothing* other than objective reality, existing independently from human consciousness and reflected by it.

Elsewhere Lenin says that this is, essentially, the principle of *realism,* but that he avoids this word, because it has been captured by inconsistent thinkers.

Thus, this formula *seemingly* contradicts our viewpoint: it cannot be true that consciousness exists outside our consciousness. But, as Plekhanov has correctly established, self-consciousness is the consciousness of consciousness. And consciousness *can* exist without self-consciousness: we become convinced of this by the unconscious and the relatively unconscious. I can see not knowing that I see. That is why Pavlov [1928/1963, p. 219] is right when he says that we can live according to subjective states, but that we cannot analyze them.

Not a single science is possible without separating direct experience from knowledge. It is amazing: only the psychologist-introspectionist thinks that experience [59] and knowledge coincide. If the essence of things and the form of their appearance directly coincided, says Marx [1890/1981b, p. 825], all science would be superfluous. If in psychology appearance and being were the same, then *everybody would be a scientist-psychologist* and science would be impossible. Only registration would be possible. But, obviously, it is *one thing* to live, to experience, and *another* to analyze, as Pavlov says.

A most interesting example of this we find in Titchener [1910/1980, pp. 38-39]. This consistent adherent of introspection and parallelism arrives at the conclusion that mental phenomena can only be described, but not explained. He asserts that

> If, however, we attempted to work out a merely descriptive psychology, we should find that there was no hope in it of a true science of the mind. A descriptive psychology would stand to scientific psychology very much . . .as the view of the world which a boy gets from his cabinet of physical experiments stands to the trained physicist's view . . .there would be no unity or coherence in it . . . . In order to make psychology scientific we must not only describe, we must also explain mind. We must answer the question 'why.' But here is a difficulty. It is clear that we cannot regard one mental process as the cause of another mental process . . . . Nor can we, on the other hand, regard nervous processes as the cause of mental processes . . . . The one cannot be the cause of the other.

This is the real situation in which descriptive psychology finds itself. The author finds a way out in a purely *verbal subterfuge:* mental phenomena can only be explained in relation to the body. Titchener [ibid., pp. 39-40] says that

> The nervous system does not cause, but it does explain mind. It explains mind as the map of a country explains the fragmentary glimpses of hills and rivers and towns that

> we catch on our journey through it . . . . Reference to the body does not add one iota
> to the data of psychology . . . . It does furnish us with an explanatory principle for
> psychology.

If we refrain from this, only two ways to overcome the fragmentary nature of
mental life remain: either the purely descriptive way, the rejection of explanation,
or to assume the existence of the unconscious.

> Both courses have been tried. But, if we take the first, we never arrive at a science of
> psychology; and if we take the second, we voluntarily leave the sphere of fact for the
> sphere of fiction. These are scientific alternatives [ibid., p. 40].

This is perfectly clear. [60] But is a science possible with the explanatory principle
which the author has selected? Is it possible to have a science about the *fragmentary
glimpses of hills, rivers, and towns*, with which in Titchener's example the mind is
compared? And further: how, why does the map explain these views, how does the
map of a country help to explain its parts? The map is a copy of the country, it
explains insofar as the country is reflected upon it, i.e., similar things explain each
other. A science based on such a principle is impossible. In reality, the author reduces everything to *causal explanation*, as for him both causal and parallelistic explanation are defined as the indication of "proximate circumstances or conditions
under which the described phenomenon occurs" [ibid., p. 41]. But, after all, this
way will not lead to science either. Good "proximate conditions" are the ice age
in geology, the fission of the atom in physics, the formation of planets in astronomy,
evolution in biology. After all, "proximate conditions" in physics are followed by
other "proximate conditions" and the causal chain is *infinite in principle*, but in
parallelistic explanations the matter is hopelessly limited to merely *proximate* causes.
Not without reason the author [ibid., p. 41] confines himself to comparing his explanation with the explanation of dew in physics. It would be a nice physics which
did not go farther than pointing out the proximate conditions and similar explanations. It would simply cease to exist as a science.

Thus, we see that for psychology as a field of knowledge there are two alternatives: either the way of science, in which case it must be able to explain, or the
knowledge of fragmentary visions, in which case it is impossible as *science*. For the
use of the geometrical analogy deludes us. A geometrical psychology is absolutely
impossible, for it lacks the basic characteristic: being an ideal abstraction it nevertheless refers to real objects. In this respect we are first of all reminded of Spinoza's
attempt to investigate human vices and stupidities by means of the geometrical
method and to examine human actions and drives exactly as if they were lines,
surfaces, and bodies. This method is suitable for descriptive psychology and not for
any other approach. For it takes from geometry only its verbal style and the outward
appearance of irrefutability of its proofs, and all the rest—its core included—is
based upon a nonscientific way of thinking.

Husserl bluntly states the difference between phenomenology and mathematics:
mathematics is an exact science and phenomenology a descriptive one. Neither
more nor less: phenomenology cannot be apodictic for lack of such a trifle as ex-
actitude! Try and imagine inexact mathematics and you will get geometrical psychology.

In the end, the question can be reduced, as has already been said, to the differentiation of the ontological and the epistemological problem. In epistemology
appearance exists, and to assert that it is being is false. In ontology *appearance* does
not exist at all. Either mental phenomena exist, and then they are material and
objective, or they do not exist, and then they do *not* exist and cannot be studied.
No science can be confined to the subjective, to *appearance*, to phantoms, to what

does not exist. What does not exist, *does not exist at all* and it is not half-nonexistent, half-existent. This must be understood. We cannot say: in the world there exist real and *unreal* things—the unreal does not exist. The unreal must be explained as the non-coincidence, generally as the relation of two real things; the subjective as the corollary of two objective processes. The subjective is apparent and therefore it does *not exist*.

Feuerbach [1971, p. 125] comments upon the distinction between the subjective and the objective [factor] in psychology: "In a similar way, for me my body belongs to the category of imponderabilia, it does not have weight, although in itself or for others it is a heavy body."

From this it is clear what kind of reality he ascribed to the subjective. He openly says that "Psychology is full of godsends; only the conclusions are present in our consciousness and feeling, but not the premises, only the results, but not the processes of the organism" [ibid., p. 124]. But can there really be a science about results without premises?

Stern [1924, p. 143] expressed this well when he said, following Fechner, that the mental and the physical are the concave and the convex. [61] A single line can represent now this and now that. But in itself it is neither concave nor convex, but round, and it is precisely as such that we want to know it, independently from how it may appear.

Høffding compares it with the same content expressed in two languages which we do not manage to reduce to a common protolanguage. But we want to know the *content* and not the *language* in which it is expressed. In physics we have freed ourselves from language in order to study the content. We must do the same in psychology.

Let us compare consciousness, as is often done, with a mirror image. Let the object A be reflected in the mirror as *a*. Naturally, it would be false to say that *a* in itself is as real as A. It is real *in another way*. A table and its reflection in the mirror are not equally real, but real in a different way. The reflection as reflection, as an image of the table, as a second table in the mirror is not real, it is a phantom. But the reflection of the table as the refraction of light beams on the mirror surface—isn't that a thing which is equally material and real as the table? Everything else would be a miracle. Then we might say: there exist things (a table) and their phantoms (the reflection). But *only* things exist—(the table) and the reflection of light upon the surface. The phantoms are just *apparent* relations between the things. That is why no science of mirror phantoms is possible. But this does not mean that we will never be able to explain the reflection, the phantom. When we know the *thing* and the *laws of reflection of light*, we can always explain, predict, elicit, and change the phantom. And this is what persons with mirrors do. They study not mirror reflections but the movement of light beams, and explain the reflection. A science about mirror phantoms is impossible, but the theory of light and the things which cast and reflect it fully explain these "phantoms."

It is the same in psychology: the subjective itself, as a phantom, must be understood as a consequence, as a result, as a godsend of *two* objective processes. Like the enigma of the mirror, the enigma of the mind is not solved by studying phantoms, but by studying the two series of objective processes from the cooperation of which the phantoms as apparent reflections of *one thing in the other* arise. In itself the appearance does not exist.

Let us return to the mirror. To identify A and *a*, the table and its mirror reflection, would be idealism: *a* is nonmaterial, it is only A which is material and its material nature is a synonym for its existence independent of *a*. But it would be exactly the same idealism to identify *a* with X—with the processes that take place in the mirror. It would be wrong to say: being and thinking do not coincide *outside* the mirror, in nature (there A is not *a*, there A is a thing and *a* a phantom); being and thinking, however, do coincide inside the mirror (here *a* is X, *a* is a phantom and X is also a phantom). We cannot say: the *reflection* of a table is a table. But neither can we say: the *reflection* of a table is the refraction of light beams and *a* is neither A nor X. Both A and X are real processes and *a* is their apparent, i.e., unreal *result*. The reflection does not exist, but both the table and the light exist. The reflection of a table is identical neither with the real processes of the light in the mirror nor with the table itself.

Not to mention the fact that otherwise we would have to accept the existence in the world of both things and phantoms. Let us remember that the mirror itself is, after all, *part of the same nature as the thing outside the mirror*, and subject to all of its laws. After all, a cornerstone of materialism is the proposition that consciousness and the brain are a product, a part of nature, which reflect the rest of nature. And, therefore, the objective existence of X and A independent of *a* is a dogma of materialistic psychology.

Here we can end our protracted argumentation. We see that the third way of Gestalt psychology and personalism was, essentially, both times one of the two ways already known. Now we see that the third way, the way of so-called "Marxist psychology," is an attempt to combine both ways. This attempt leads to their renewed separation within one and the same scientific system: one who combines them is, like Münsterberg, following two different roads.

Like the two trees in the legend which were tied up in their tops and which tore apart the ancient knight, so any scientific system will be torn apart if it binds itself to two different trunks. Marxist psychology can only be a natural science. Frankfurt's way leads to phenomenology. Admittedly, in one place he himself consciously denies that psychology can be a natural science (Frankfurt, 1926). But, firstly, he mixes up the natural sciences with the biological ones, which is not correct. Psychology can be a natural science without being a biological science. Secondly, he understands the concept "natural" in its proximate, factual meaning, as a reference to the sciences about organic and non-organic nature and not in its fundamental methodological sense.

Such a usage of this term, which had long since been accepted in Western science, has been introduced into the Russian literature by Ivanovsky (1923). He says that mathematics and applied mathematics must be strictly distinguished from the sciences which deal with things, with "real" objects and processes, with what "actually" exists, or *is*. That is why these sciences can be called *real* or *natural* (in the broad sense of this word). In Russia the term "natural sciences" is usually used in a more narrow sense as merely designating the disciplines which study non-organic and organic nature. It does not cover the social and conscious nature which in such a usage of the word frequently appears different from "nature" as something which is "unnatural," or "supernatural," if not "contra-natural." I am convinced that the extension of the term "natural" to everything which really exists is entirely rational.

Whether psychology is possible as a science is, above all, a methodological problem. In no other science are there so many difficulties, insoluble controversies and combinations of incompatible things as in psychology. The subject matter of psychology is the most complicated of all things in the world and least accessible to investigation. Its methods must be full of special contrivances and precautions in order to yield what is expected of them.

All the time I am speaking about precisely this latter thing—the principle of a science about [what is] the real. In this sense Marx [1890/1981a, p. 16] studies, in his own words, the process of the development of economic formations as a *natural-historical process*. [62]

Not a single science represents such a diversity and plentitude of methodological problems, such tightly stretched knots, such insoluble contradictions, as ours. That is why we cannot take a single step without thousands of preparatory calculations and cautions.

Thus, it is acknowledged all the same that the crisis gravitates toward the creation of a methodology, that the struggle is for a general psychology. Anyone who attempts to skip this problem, to jump over methodology in order to build some special psychological science right away, will inevitably jump over his horse while trying to sit on it. This has happened with Gestalt theory and Stern. Starting from universal principles which are equally applicable in physics and psychology but which have not been made concrete in methodology, we cannot proceed to a particular psychological investigation. That is why these psychologists are accused of knowing just one predicate and thinking it equally applicable to the whole world. We cannot, as Stern does, study the psychological differences between people with a concept that covers both the solar system, a tree, and man. For this we need another scale, another measure. The whole problem of the general and the special science, on the one hand, and methodology and philosophy, on the other, is a problem of scale. We cannot measure human height in miles, for this we need a tape-measure. And while we have seen that the special sciences have a tendency to transcend their boundaries towards the struggle for a common measure, a larger scale, philosophy is going through the opposite tendency: in order to approximate science it must narrow, decrease the scale, make its theses more concrete.

Both tendencies—of philosophy and of the special science—lead equally to methodology, to the general science. But this idea of scale, the idea of a general science, is so far foreign to "Marxist psychology" and this is its weak spot. It attempts to find a direct measure for psychological elements—the reaction—in universal principles: the law of the transition of quantity into quality and "the forgetting of the nuances of the gray color" according to Lehmann and the transition from thrift into stinginess; Hegel's triad and Freud's psychoanalysis. Here the absence of a measure, scale, an intermediate link between the two, makes itself clearly felt. That is why the dialectical method will fall with fatal inevitability into the same category as the experiment, the comparative method, and the method of tests and surveys. A feeling for hierarchy, the difference between a technical research method and a method by which to know "the nature of history and thinking," is missing. The direct frontal collision of particular factual truths with universal principles; the attempt to decide the matter-of-fact debate about instinct between Vagner and Pavlov by references to quantity–quality; the step from dialectics to the survey; the criticism of irradiation from the epistemological viewpoint; the use of miles where a tape-measure is needed; the verdicts of Bekhterev and Pavlov from the height of Hegel; these attempts to swat a fly with a sledgehammer, have led to the false idea of a third way.

Binswanger [1922, p. 107] reminds us of Brentano's words about the amazing art of logic which makes *one* step forward with a thousand steps forward in science as a result. This strength of logic they do not want to know in Russia. According to the apt expression, methodology is the linchpin through which philosophy guides science. The attempt to realize such a guidance without methodology, the direct application of force to the point of application without a linchpin—from Hegel to Meumann—makes science impossible.

I advance the thesis that the analysis of the crisis and the structure of psychology indisputably testifies to the fact that no philosophical system can take possession of psychology directly, without the help of methodology, i.e., without the creation of a general science. The only rightful application of Marxism to psychology would be to create a general psychology—its concepts are being formulated in direct dependence upon general dialectics, for it is the dialectics of psychology. Any application of Marxism to psychology via other paths or in other points outside this area, will inevitably lead to scholastic, verbal constructions, to the dissolution of dialectics into surveys and tests, to judgment about things according to their external, accidental, secondary features, to the complete loss of any objective criterion and the attempt to deny all historical tendencies of the development of psychology, to a terminological revolution, in sum to a gross distortion of both Marxism and psychology. This is Chelpanov's way.

Engels' [1925/1978, p. 348] formula—not to foist the dialectical principles on nature, but to find them in it—is changed into its opposite here. The principles of dialectics are introduced into psychology from outside. The way of Marxists should be different. The *direct* application of the theory of *dialectical materialism* to the problems of natural science and in particular to the group of biological sciences or psychology *is impossible*, just as *it is impossible to apply it directly* to history and sociology. In Russia it is thought that the problem of "psychology and Marxism" can be reduced to creating a psychology which is up to Marxism, but in reality it is far more complex. Like history, sociology is in need of the intermediate *special theory* of historical materialism which explains the *concrete* meaning, for the given group of phenomena, of the abstract laws of dialectical materialism. In exactly the same way we are in need of an as yet undeveloped but inevitable theory of biological materialism and psychological materialism as an intermediate science which explains the concrete application of the abstract theses of dialectical materialism to the given field of phenomena.

Dialectics covers nature, thinking, history—it is the most general, maximally universal science. The theory of the psychological materialism or dialectics of psychology is what I call general psychology.

In order to create such intermediate theories—methodologies, general sciences—we must reveal the *essence* of the given area of phenomena, the laws of their change, their qualitative and quantitative characteristics, their causality, we must create categories and concepts appropriate to it, in short, we must create our own *Das Kapital*. It suffices to imagine Marx operating with the general principles and categories of dialectics, like quantity–quality, the triad, the universal connection, the knot [of contradictions], leap etc.—without the abstract and historical categories of value, class, commodity, capital, interest, production forces, basis, superstructure etc.—to see the whole monstrous absurdity of the assumption that it is possible to create any Marxist science while bypassing by *Das Kapital*. Psychology is in need of its own *Das Kapital*—its own concepts of class, basis, value etc.—in which it might express, describe and study its object. And to discover a confirmation of the law of leaps in Lehmann's statistical data of the forgetting of the nuances of the grey color means not to change dialectics or psychology one jot. This idea of the need for an intermediate theory without which the various special facts cannot be examined in the light of Marxism has long since been realized, and it only remains for me to point out that the conclusions of our analysis of psychology match this idea.

Vishnevsky develops the same idea in his debate with Stepanov (it is clear to anyone that historical materialism is not dialectical materialism, but its application to history. Therefore, only the social sciences which have their general basis in the history of materialism can, strictly speaking, be called Marxist; other Marxist sciences do not yet exist). "Just as historical materialism is not identical with dialectical materialism, the latter is not identical with specifically natural scientific theory, which, incidentally, is still in the process of being born" (Vishnevsky, 1925, p. 262). But Stepanov (1924) identifies the dialectical-materialist understanding of nature with the mechanistic one and finds that it is given and can already be found in the mechanistic conception of the natural sciences. As an example the author mentions the debate in psychology about the question of introspection.

Dialectical materialism is a most abstract science. The direct application of dialectical materialism to the biological sciences and psychology, as is common nowadays, does not go beyond the formal logical, scholastic, verbal subsumption of particular phenomena, whose internal sense and relation is unknown, under general, abstract, *universal* categories. At *best* this leads to an accumulation of *examples* and illustrations. But not more than that. Water—steam—ice and natural economy—feudalism—capitalism are one and the same, one and the same process from the viewpoint of *dialectical materialism*. But historical materialism would lose much qualitative wealth in such a generalization!

Marx called his *Das Kapital* a critique of political economy. Such a critique of psychology one wants to skip today. "A *textbook* of psychology, explained from the viewpoint of dialectical materialism," must sound essentially like "a textbook of mineralogy, explained from the viewpoint of formal logic." After all, this goes without saying—to reason logically is not a property of the given textbook or mineralogy as a whole. And dialectics is not logic, it is broader. Or: "a textbook of sociology, from the viewpoint of dialectical materialism" instead of "historical." We must develop a theory of psychological materialism. We cannot yet create textbooks of dialectical psychology.

But we would lose our main criterion in critical judgment as well. The way one now determines, as in the assay office, whether a given theory is in accord with Marxism, can be understood as a method of "logical superposition," i.e., one checks whether the forms, the logical features coincide (monism, etc.). It should be known what can and must be looked for in Marxism. Man is not made for the sabbath, but the sabbath is made for man. [63] We must find a theory which would help us to know the mind, but by no means the solution of the question of the mind, not a formula which would give the ultimate scientific truth. We cannot find it in the citations from Plekhanov for the simple reason that it is not there. Neither Marx, nor Engels, nor Plekhanov possessed such a truth.[61] Hence the fragmentary nature, the brevity of many formulations, their rough character, their meaning which is strictly limited to the context. Such a formula can in principle not be given in advance, before the scientific study of the mind, but develops as the result of the scientific work of centuries. What can be searched for in the teachers of Marxism beforehand is not a solution of the question, not even a working hypothesis (as these are developed on the basis of the given science), but the method to develop it [the hypothesis; Russian eds.]. I do not want to learn what constitutes the mind for free, by picking out a couple of citations, I want to learn from Marx's whole method how to build a science, how to approach the investigation of the mind.

That is why Marxism is not only applied in the wrong place (in textbooks instead of a general psychology), but why one takes the wrong things from it. We do not need fortuitous utterances, but a method; not dialectical materialism, but historical materialism. *Das Kapital* must teach us many things—both because a genuine social psychology begins *after Das Kapital* and because psychology nowadays is a psychology *before Das Kapital*. Struminsky is fully right when he calls the very idea of a Marxist psychology as a synthesis of the thesis "empirism" with the antithesis "reflexology" a scholastic construction. After a real path has been found, one may for clarity's sake signal these three points, but to search for real paths by means of this schema would mean taking the road of speculative combination and dealing with the dialectics of ideas rather than the dialectics of facts or being. Psychology has no independent paths of development; we must find the real historical processes behind them, which condition them. He is only wrong when he asserts that to select the paths of psychology on the basis of the contemporary currents in a Marxist fashion is impossible in principle (Struminsky, 1926).

The idea he develops is right, but it only concerns the historical analysis of the development of science and not the methodological one. Because the methodologist takes no interest in what *really* will take place in the process of development of psychology tomorrow, he also ignores factors outside of psychology. But he is interested in the kind of disease psychology is suffering from, what it lacks in order to become a science, etc. After all, the external factors as well push psychology along the road of its development and can neither abolish the work of centuries nor make it skip a century. The logical structure of knowledge grows organically.

Struminsky is also right when he points out that the new psychology virtually came so far as to frankly accept the position of the older subjective psychology. But the trouble is not that the author fails to take account of the external, real factors of the development of the science he attempts to take account of; the trouble is that he does not take the methodological nature of the crisis into account. The course of development of each science has its *own* strict sequence. External factors can speed up or slow down this course, they may sidetrack it, and finally, they can determine the qualitative character of each stage, but to change the sequence of these stages is impossible. Using the external factors we can explain the idealistic or materialistic, religious or positive, individualistic or social, pessimistic or optimistic character of the stage, but no external factors can establish that a science which finds itself in the stage of gathering raw material can proceed straight to the creation of technical, applied disciplines, or that a science with well-developed theories and hypotheses, with well-developed technique and experimentation will start dealing with the gathering and description of primary material.

Thanks to the crisis, the division into two psychologies through the creation of a methodology has been put on the agenda. How it will turn out depends on external factors. Titchener and Watson in their American and socially different way, Koffka and Stern in a German and again socially different way, Bekhterev and Kornilov in their Russian and again different way—they all *solve one problem*. What this methodology will be and how fast it will be there we do not know, but that psychology does not move any further as long as the methodology has not been created, that the methodology will be the first step forward, is beyond doubt.

The fundamental stones have in principle been laid correctly. The general way, which will take decades, has also been indicated correctly. The goal is also correct, as is the general plan. Even the practical orientation in contemporary currents is correct, though incomplete. But the next path, the next steps, the plan of action, suffer from deficits: they lack an analysis of the crisis and a correct orientation on methodology. The works of Kornilov are the beginning of this methodology, and anyone who wants to develop the idea of psychology and Marxism further will be forced to repeat him and to continue his road. As a road this idea is unequalled in strength in European psychology. If it does not lose itself in criticism and polemics, if it does not turn into a paper war [war with pamphlets] but rises to a methodology, if it does not search for ready-made answers, and if it understands the tasks of contemporary psychology, then it will lead to the creation of a theory of psychological materialism.

14 [64]

We have finished our investigation. Did we find everything we were looking for? In any case, we have come quite close. We have prepared the ground for research in the field of psychology and, in order to justify our argumentation, we must test our conclusions and construct a model of general psychology. But before that we would like to dwell on one more aspect which, admittedly, is of more stylistic than fundamental importance. But the stylistic completion of an idea is not totally irrelevant to its complete articulation.

We have split the tasks and method, the area of investigation and the principle of our science. What remains is to split its name. The processes of division which became evident in the crisis have also influenced the fate of the name of our science. Various systems have half broken with the old name and use their own to designate the whole research area. In this fashion one sometimes speaks of behaviorism as the science of behavior as a synonym for psychology and not for one of its currents. Psychoanalysis and reactology are often mentioned in this way. Other systems break completely with the old name as they see the traces of a mythological origin in it. Reflexology is an example. This latter current emphasizes that it rejects the tradition and builds on a new and vacant spot. It cannot be disputed that such a view has some truth to it, although one must look at science in a very mechanical and unhistorical manner not to understand the role of continuity and tradition at all, even during a revolution. Watson, however, is partly right when he demands a radical rupture with the older psychology, when he points to astrology and alchemy and to the danger of an ambiguous psychology.

Other systems have so far remained without a name—Pavlov's is an example. Sometimes he calls his area physiology, but by terming his work the study of behavior and higher nervous activity he has left the question of the name open. In his early works Bekhterev openly distinguished himself from physiology; for Bekhterev reflexology is not physiology. Pavlov's students set forth his theory under the name "science of behavior." And indeed, two sciences which are so different should have two different names. Münsterberg [1922, p. 13] expressed this idea long ago:

> Whether the intentional understanding of inner life should really be called psychology is, of course, still a question that can be debated. Indeed, much speaks in favor of keeping the name psychology for the *descriptive* and *explanatory* science, excluding the science of the understanding of mental experiences and inner relations from psychology [emphasis by Vygotsky].

However, this knowledge nevertheless exists under the name of psychology; "It is true that it seldom appears in pure and consistent form. It is mostly somehow superficially connected with elements of causal psychology" [ibid., p. 13]. But as we know the author's opinion that the whole confusion in psychology is due to this mixture, the only conclusion is to select another name for intentional psychology. In part this is how it goes. Right before our eyes phenomenology is producing a psychology which is "necessary for certain logical goals" [ibid., p. 13] and instead of a division into two sciences by means of adjectives, which cause enormous confusion . . . [65], it begins to introduce various substantives. Chelpanov observes that "analytical" and "phenomenological" are two names for one and the same method, that phenomenology partially coincides with analytical psychology, that the debate as to whether the phenomenology of psychology exists or not is a terminological matter. If we add to this that the author considers this method and this part of psychology to be basic, then it would be logical to call analytical psychology phenomenology. Husserl himself prefers to confine himself to an adjective in order to preserve the purity of his science and he talks about "eidetic psychology." But Binswanger [1922, p. 135] openly writes: we must distinguish "between pure phenomenology and . . . empirical phenomenology (= descriptive psychology)" and bases this on the adjective "pure" introduced by Husserl himself. The sign of equality is written down in a highly mathematical fashion. If we recall that Lotze called psychology applied mathematics; that Bergson in his definition almost identified empirical metaphysics with psychology; that Husserl wishes to regard pure phenomenology as a metaphysical theory about essences (Binswanger, 1922), then we will understand that idealistic psychology itself has both a tradition and a tendency to abandon a decrepit and compromised name. And Dilthey explains that explanatory psychology goes back to Wolff's rational psychology, and descriptive psychology, to empirical psychology.

It is true, some idealists are against attaching this name to natural scientific psychology. Thus, Frank [1917/1964, pp. 15-16] uses harsh words to point out that two different sciences are living under a single name, writing that

> It is not at all a matter of the more or less scientific nature of two different *methods* of a single science, but of simply *supplanting one science by a totally different one*, which though it has retained some weak traces of kinship with the first, has essentially a totally different subject . . . Present-day psychology declares itself to be a natural science . . . .. This means that contemporary so-called psychology is not at all *psycho-logy*, but *physio-logy* . . . *The excellent term "psychology"*—theory of the soul—was simply illegally stolen and used as a title for a completely different scientific field. It has been stolen so thoroughly that when you now think about the nature of the soul . . .you are doing something which is destined to remain nameless or for which one must invent some new term.

But even the current *distorted* name "psychology" does not correspond to its essence for three quarters of it—it is psychophysics and psychophysiology. And the new science he wants to call philosophical psychology in order to "revive the real meaning of the term 'psychology' and give it back to its legitimate owner after the theft mentioned before, which already cannot be redeemed directly" [ibid., p. 36].

We see the remarkable fact that reflexology, which strives to break with "alchemy," and philosophy, which wishes to contribute to the resurrection of the rights of *psychology* in the old, literal and precise meaning of this word, are both looking for a new term and remain nameless. What is even more remarkable is that their motives are identical. Some fear the traces of its materialistic origin in this name, others fear that it lost its old, literal and precise meaning. Can we find a—stylistically—better manifestation of the dualism of contemporary psychology? However, Frank also agrees that natural scientific psychology has stolen the name irredeemably and thoroughly. And we propose that it is the materialistic branch which must call itself psychology. There are two important considerations which speak in favor of this and against the radicalism of the reflexologists. Firstly, it is exactly the materialistic branch which forms the crown of *all genuinely scientific tendencies, eras, currents, and authors which are represented in the history of our science, i.e., it is indeed psychology according to its very essence*. Secondly, by accepting this name, the new psychology does not at all 'steal' it, does not distort its meaning, nor does it commit itself to the mythological traces which are preserved in it, but, on the contrary, it retains a vivid historical reminder of its whole development from the very starting point.

Let us start with the second consideration.

Psychology as a science of the soul, in Frank's sense, in the precise and old sense of the word, *does not exist*. He himself is forced to ascertain this after he convinced himself with amazement and almost despair that such literature is virtually *nonexistent*. Further, empirical psychology as a complete science *does not exist at all*. And what is going on now is at bottom not a revolution, not even a reform of science and not the completion through synthesis of some foreign reform, but the *realization* of psychology and the *liberation* of what is capable of growing in science from what is not capable of growth. Empirical psychology itself (incidentally, it will soon be 50 years since the name of this science has not been used at all, since each school adds its own adjective) is as dead as a cocoon left by the butterfly, as an egg deserted by the nestling. James says that

> When, then, we talk of 'psychology as a natural science' we must not assume that that means a sort of psychology that stands at last on solid ground. It means just the reverse; it means a psychology particularly fragile, and into which the waters of metaphysical criticism leak at every joint, a psychology all of whose elementary assumptions and data must be reconsidered in wider connections and translated into our terms. It is, in short, a phrase of diffidence, and not of arrogance; and it is indeed strange to hear people talk of 'the New Psychology,' and write 'Histories of Psychology,' when into the real elements and forces which the word covers not the first glimpse of clear insight exists. A string of raw facts; a little gossip and wrangle about opinions; a little classification and generalization on the mere descriptive level; a strong prejudice that we *have* states of mind, and that our brain conditions them: but not a single law in the sense in which physics shows us laws, not a single proposition from which any consequence can causally be deduced. We don't even know the terms between which the elementary laws would obtain if we had them. This is no science, it is only the hope of a science [see pp. 400-401 of Burkhardt, 1984].

James gives a brilliant inventory of what we inherit from psychology, a list of its possessions and fortune. It gives us a string of raw facts and the hope of a science.

How are we connected with mythology through this name? Psychology, like physics before Galileo or chemistry before Lavoisier, is not yet a science which may somehow influence the future science. But have the circumstances perhaps fundamentally changed since James wrote this? At the 8th Congress of Experimental Psychology in 1923, Spearman repeated James' definition and said that psychology was still not a science but the hope for a science. [66] One must have a considerable amount of philistine provincialism to represent the matter as Chelpanov did. As if there exist unshakable truths which are accepted by everybody, which have been corroborated over the centuries and which some wish to destroy for no reason at all.

The other consideration is even more serious. In the final analysis we must openly say that psychology does not have two, but only one heir, and that there can be no serious debate about its name. The second psychology is impossible as a science. And we must say with Pavlov that from the scientific viewpoint we consider the position of this psychology to be hopeless. As a real scientist, Pavlov [1928/1963, p. 77] does not ask whether a mental aspect exists, but how we can study it. He says:

> How must the physiologist treat these psychical phenomena? *It is impossible to neglect them, because they are closely bound up with purely physiological phenomena and determine the work of the whole organ.* If the physiologist decides to study them, he must answer the question, How?

Thus, in this division we *do not yield a single phenomenon* to the other side. We study everything on our path that exists and explain everything that [merely] seems [to exist].

> For how many thousands of years has man elaborated psychical facts . . . . Millions of pages have been written to describe the internal world of the human being, but with what result? Up to the present we have no laws of the psychic life of man [ibid., p. 114].

What is left after the division, will go to the realm of art. Already now Frank [1917/1964, p. 16] calls the writers of novels the teachers of psychology. [67] For Dilthey [1894/1977, p. 36] psychology's task is to catch in the web of its descriptions what is hidden in King Lear, Hamlet, and Macbeth as he saw in them "more psychology than in all the manuals of psychology together." [68] It is true, Stern laughed maliciously at such a psychology procured from novels and said that you cannot milk a painted cow. But in contrast with his idea and in accordance with Dilthey's, descriptive psychology is *really* developing into fiction. The first congress on individual psychology, which regards itself as this second psychology, heard Oppenheim's paper, who seized in the web of his concepts what Shakespeare gave in images—exactly what Dilthey wanted. [69] The second psychology becomes metaphysics whatever it is called. It is precisely the impossibility of such knowledge as *science* which determines our choice.

Thus, there is only one heir for the name of our science. But, perhaps, it should decline the heritage? Not at all. We are dialecticians. We do not at all think that the developmental path of science follows a straight line, and if it has had zigzags, returns, and loops we understand their historical significance and consider them to be necessary links in our chain, inevitable stages of our path, just as capitalism is an inevitable stage on the road toward socialism. We have set store by each step which our science has ever made toward the truth. We do not think that our science started with us. We will not concede to anyone Aristotle's idea of association, nor the theory about the subjective illusions of sensations by him and the skeptics, nor J. Mill's idea of causality, nor J. S. Mill's idea of psychological chemistry, nor the "refined materialism" of Spencer which Dilthey [1924, p. 45] viewed not as a "sure foundation, but a danger." In a word, we will not concede to anyone this whole line of materialism in psychology which the idealists sweep aside so carefully. We know that they are right in one thing: "The hidden materialism of [Spencerian] explanatory psychology has played a disintegrating role in the economic and political sciences and in criminal law" (ibid., p. 45).

Herbart's idea of a dynamic and mathematical psychology, the works of Fechner and Helmholtz, Taine's idea about the motor nature of the mind as well as Binet's theory of the mental pose or internal mimics, Ribot's motor theory, the James–Lange peripheral theory of emotions, even the Würzburg school's theory of thinking and of attention as activity—in one word, every step toward truth in our science, belongs to us. After all, we did not choose one of the two roads because we liked it, but because we consider it to be the right one.

Consequently, this road encompasses absolutely everything which was scientific in psychology. The attempt itself to study the mind *scientifically*, the effort of free thought to master the mind, however it became obscured and paralyzed by mythology, i.e., the very idea of a *scientific* conception of the soul, contains the whole future path of psychology. For science is the path to truth, even if by way of delusion. But this is precisely the road of our science: we struggle, we overcome errors, via incredible complications, in a superhuman fight with age-old prejudices. We do not want to deny our past. We do not suffer from megalomania by thinking that history begins with us. We do not want a brand-new and trivial name from history. We want a name covered by the dust of the centuries. We regard this as our historical right, as an indication of our historical role, our claim to realize psychology as a science. We must view ourselves in connection with and in relation to the past. Even when denying it we rely upon it.

It might be said that in its literal sense this name is not applicable to our science now, as it changes its meaning in every epoch. But be so kind as to mention a single word that has not changed its meaning. Don't we make a logical mistake when we talk of blue ink or a pilot's art? [70] But on the other hand we are loyal to another logic—the logic of language. If the geometer even today calls his science with a name which means "measuring the earth," then the psychologist can refer to his science by a name which once meant "theory of the soul." Whereas the concept of measuring the earth is now too narrow for geometry, it was once a decisive step forward, to which the whole science owes its existence. Whereas the idea of the soul is now reactionary, it once was the first scientific hypothesis of ancient man, an enormous achievement of thought to which we owe the existence of our science now. Animals probably do not have the idea of the soul, nor do they have psychology. We understand that, historically, psychology had to begin with the idea of the soul. We are as little inclined to view this as simply ignorance and error as we consider slavery to be the result of a bad character. We know that science on its path toward the truth inevitably involves delusions, errors and prejudices. Essential for science is not that these exist, but that they, being errors, nevertheless lead to the truth, that they are overcome. That is why we accept the name of our science with all its age-old delusions as a vivid reminder of our victory over these errors, as the fighting scars of wounds, as a vivid testimony of the truth which develops in the incredibly complicated struggle with falsehood.

All sciences essentially proceed this way. Do the builders of the future really start from scratch, aren't they those who complete and follow all that is genuine in human experience? Do they really not have allies and forebears in the past? Let us be shown but a single word, a single scientific name, which can be applied in a literal sense. Or do mathematics, philosophy, dialectics and metaphysics signify what they once signified? Let it not be said that two branches of knowledge about a single object must absolutely carry the same name. Let logic and the psychology of thinking be remembered. Sciences are not classified and named according to their object of study, but according to the principles and goals of the study. Does Marxism really not want to know its ancestors in philosophy? *Only unhistorical and uncreative minds* are inventive with respect to new names and sciences. Such ideas do not become Marxism. Chelpanov comes with the information that during the French revolution the term "psychology" was replaced by the term "ideology," since for that era psychology was the science about the soul. But ideology formed part of zoology and was divided into physiological and rational ideology. This is correct, but what incalculable harm results from such unhistorical word usage can be seen from the difficulty which we now have in deciphering different loci about ideology in Marx's texts, how ambiguous this term sounds. It gives occasion to such "investigators" as Chelpanov to claim that for Marx ideology signified psychology. This terminological reform is *partly* responsible for the fact that the role and meaning of the older psychology is undervalued in the history of our science. And finally, it leads to a clear rupture with its genuine descendants, it severs the vivid line of unity. Chelpanov, who declared (1924, p. 27) that psychology has nothing in common with physiology, now vows for the Great Revolution. Psychology has always been physiological and "contemporary scientific psychology is the child of the psychology of the French revolution." Only *extreme ignorance* or the expectation that *others would be so ignorant* can have dictated these phrases. Whose *contemporary* psychology? Mill's or Spencer's, Bain's or Ribot's? Correct. But that of Dilthey and Husserl, Bergson and James, Münsterberg and Stout, Meinong and Lipps, Frank and *Chelpanov?* Can there be a bigger untruth? After all, all of these builders of the new psychology advanced another system as the *foundation* of science, a system which was hostile to Mill and Spencer, Bain, and Ribot. The same name which Chelpanov uses as a shelter they slighted "like a dead dog." [71] But Chelpanov shelters behind names which are foreign and hostile to him and speculates on the

ambiguity of the term "contemporary psychology." Yes, in contemporary psychology
there is a branch which can regard itself as the child of revolutionary psychology.
But during his entire life (and today) Chelpanov has done nothing but attempt to
chase this branch into a dark corner of science, to separate it from psychology.

But once again: how dangerous is a common name and how unhistorically did
the psychologists of France act who betrayed it!

This name was first introduced into science in 1590 by Goclenius, professor in
Marburg, and accepted by his student Casmann in 1594. It was not introduced by
Christian Wolff around the mid-eighteenth century and is not found for the first
time in Melanchthon, as is usually incorrectly thought. It is mentioned by Ivanovsky
as a name to indicate part of anthropology, which together with somatology formed
one science. That this term is ascribed to Melanchthon is based on the preface of
the publisher to the 13th volume of his writings, in which Melanchthon is incorrectly
indicated as the first author of psychology. [72] This name was quite rightly retained
by Lange, the author of the psychology without a soul. But isn't psychology called
the theory of the soul?, he asks. How can we conceive of a science which doubts
whether it has a subject matter to study at all? However, he found it pedantic and
unpractical to throw away the traditional name once the subject matter of the science had changed, and called for the unwavering acceptance of a psychology without a soul.

The endless fuss about psychology's name started precisely with Lange's reform. This name, taken in itself, ceased to mean anything. Each time one had to
add: "without a soul," "without any metaphysics," "based on experience," "from an
empirical viewpoint," etc. Psychology *per se* ceased to exist. Here resided Lange's
mistake. Having accepted the old name he did not embrace it *fully*, completely, did
not distinguish, separate it from tradition. Once psychology is without a soul, then
with a soul we do not have psychology, but something else. But here, of course,
he did not so much lack good intentions, as strength. The time was not yet ripe
for a division.

We, too, must now face this terminological matter which belongs to the theme
of the division into two sciences.

How will we call natural scientific psychology? It is now often called objective,
new, Marxist, scientific, the science of behavior. Of course, we will reserve the name
psychology for it. But what kind of psychology? How do we distinguish it from
every other system of knowledge which uses the same name? We only have to sum
up a small part of the definitions which are now being applied to psychology in
order to see that there is no logical unity at the basis of these divisions. Sometimes
the epithet designates the school of behaviorism, sometimes Gestalt psychology;
sometimes the method of experimental psychology, psychoanalysis; sometimes the
principle of construction (eidetic, analytical, descriptive, empirical); sometimes the
subject matter of the science (functional, structural, actual, intentional); sometimes
the area of investigation (*Individualpsychologie*); sometimes the world view (personalism, Marxism, spiritualism, materialism); sometimes many things (subjective-ob-
jective, constructive-reconstructive, physiological, biological, associative, dialectical,
etc. etc.). On top of that one talks about historical and understanding, explanatory
and intuitive, scientific (Blonsky) and "scientific" (used by the idealists in the sense
of natural-scientific) psychology.

What does the word "psychology" signify after this? Stout [1909, p. ix] says
that "The time is rapidly approaching when no one will think of writing a book on
Psychology in general, anymore than of writing a book on Mathematics in general."
All terms are unstable, they do not logically exclude each other, are not well-de-
fined, are vague and obscure, ambiguous, accidental, and refer to secondary fea-

tures, which not only does not facilitate the understanding, but hampers it. Wundt called his psychology "physiological," but later he repented and regarded this as an error and reasoned that the same work should be called "experimental." This illustrates best how little all these terms mean. For some, "experimental" is a synonym for "scientific," for others, it is only the designation of a method. We will only point out the epithets which are most widely used in psychology, considered in the light of Marxism.

I consider it inexpedient to call it "objective." Chelpanov correctly pointed out that in foreign psychology this term is used in most diverse senses. In Russia as well it engendered many ambiguities and furthered confusion in the epistemological and methodological problem of mind and matter. The term promoted the confusion of method as a technical procedure and as a method of knowledge. This resulted in the treatment of the dialectical method alongside the survey method as equally objective, and in the conviction that the natural sciences have done away with all use of subjective indicators, subjective (in their genesis) concepts and divisions. The term "objective" is often vulgarized and equated with "truthful," while the term "subjective" is equated with "false" (the influence of the common use of these words). Further, it does not express the crux of the matter at all. It expresses the essence of the reform only in a conditional sense and concerning one aspect. Finally, a psychology which also wishes to be a theory about the subjective or also wishes to explain the subjective on its paths, must not falsely call itself "objective."

It would also be incorrect to call our science "the psychology of behavior." Apart from the fact that this new epithet, like the preceding one, does not distinguish us from quite a number of currents and, therefore, does not reach its goal; apart from the fact that it is false, for the new psychology wants to know the mind as well; it is a philistine, everyday term, which is why it attracted the Americans. When Watson equates "the concept of personality in the science of behavior and in common sense" (1926, p. 355), when he sets himself the task of creating a science so that the "ordinary man" "who takes up the science of behavior would not feel a change of method or some change of the object" (ibid., p. ix); a science which among its problems also has the following one: "Why George Smith left his wife" (ibid., p. 5); a science which begins with the exposition of everyday methods; which cannot formulate the difference between them and scientific methods and views the *whole* difference in the study of those cases which are of no interest for everyday life, which do not interest common sense—then the term "behavior" is the most appropriate one. But if we become convinced, as will be shown below, that it is logically untenable and does not provide a criterion by which we might decide why the peristalsis of the intestine, the excretion of urine, and inflammation should be excluded from the science; that it is ambiguous and undefined and means very different things for Blonsky and Pavlov, Watson and Koffka; then we will not hesitate to throw it away.

I would, further, consider it incorrect to define psychology as "Marxist." I have already said that it is unacceptable to write textbooks from the viewpoint of dialectical materialism (Struminsky, 1923; Kornilov, 1925); but also "Outline of Marxist Psychology," as Rejsner translated the title of Jameson's booklet [73], I regard as improper word usage. Even such word combinations as "reflexology and Marxism," when one is dealing with different concrete currents within physiology, I consider to be incorrect and risky. Not because I doubt the possibility of such an evaluation, but because one takes incommensurable quantities, because the intermediate terms which alone make such an evaluation possible are missing. The scale is lost and distorted. After all, the author passes judgment upon the *whole* of reflexology not from the viewpoint of the *whole* of Marxism, but on the basis of different pronouncements by different groups of Marxists-psychologists. It would not be correct, for instance, to raise the problem of the district soviet [74] and Marxism, although the theory of Marxism has undoubtedly no fewer resources to shed light upon the question of the district soviet than upon reflexology and although the district soviet is a directly Marxist idea which is logically connected with the entire whole. And nevertheless we make use of other scales, we utilize intermediate, more concrete and less universal concepts. We talk about the Soviet power and the district soviet, about the dictatorship of the proletariat and the district soviet, about class struggle and the district soviet. Not everything which is connected with Marxism should be called Marxist. Often this goes without saying. When we add to this that what psychologists usually appeal to in Marxism is dialectical materialism, i.e., its most universal and generalized part, then the disparity of the scales becomes still clearer.

Finally, there is a special difficulty in the application of Marxism to new areas. The present concrete state of this theory, the enormous responsibility in using this term, the political and ideological speculation with it—all this prevents good taste from saying "Marxist psychology" *now*. We had better let others say of our psychology that it is Marxist than call it that ourselves. We put it into practice and wait a little with the term. In the final analysis, Marxist psychology *does not yet exist*. It must be understood as a historical goal, not as something already given. And in the contemporary state of affairs it is difficult to get rid of the impression that this name is used in an unserious and irresponsible manner.

An argument against its use is also the circumstance that a synthesis between psychology and Marxism is being accomplished by more than one school and that this name can easily give rise to confusion in Europe. Not many people know that Adler's individual psychology links itself to Marxism. In order to understand what kind of psychology this is, we should remember its methodological foundations. When it argued its right to be a science it referred to Rickert, who says that the word "psychology" applied by the natural-scientist and the historian has two different meanings and therefore distinguishes natural-scientific and historical psychology. If one would not do this, then the psychology of the historian and the poet could not be called psychology, because it has nothing in common with psychology. And the theorists of the new school assumed that Rickert's historical psychology and individual psychology were one and the same thing [cf. Binswanger, 1922, p. 333].

Psychology has been divided into two parts and the debate is only about the name and the theoretical possibility of the new independent branch. Psychology is impossible as a natural science, the individual factor cannot be subsumed under any law; it does not want to explain, but to understand (ibid.). This division was introduced into psychology by Jaspers, but by understanding psychology he meant Husserl's phenomenology. As the basis of any psychology it is very important, even irreplaceable, but it is not itself and does not want to be, individual psychology. Understanding psychology can only proceed from teleology. Stern founded such a psychology; personalism is but another name for understanding psychology. But he attempts to study the personality in differential psychology with the means of experimental psychology, of the natural sciences: both explanation and understanding remain equally unsatisfactory. Only intuition and not discursive-causal thinking can lead to the goal. The title "philosophy of the ego" it considers to be honorary. It is no psychology at all, but philosophy, and wishes to be so. And *such* a psychology, about whose nature there can be no doubt, refers in its constructions, for example in the theory of mass psychology, to Marxism, to the theory of the base and superstructure, as to its natural foundation. In *social* psychology it has yielded the hitherto best and most interesting project of a synthesis of Marxism and individual psychology in the theory of class struggle: Marxism and individual psychology must and are called upon to extend and impregnate each other. The Hegelian triad is applicable to both mental life and economics (just as in Russia). This project evoked an interesting polemic which showed in the defense of this idea a sound, critical and—in a number of questions—entirely Marxist approach. While Marx taught us to understand the economic foundations of the class struggle, Adler did the same for its psychological foundations. [75]

This not only illustrates the entire complexity of the current situation in psychology, where the most unexpected and paradoxical combinations are possible, but also the danger of this epithet (incidentally, talking about paradoxes: this very psychology contests Russian reflexology's right to a theory of relativity). When the eclectic and unprincipled, superficial and semi-scientific theory of Jameson is called Marxist psychology, when also the majority of the influential Gestalt psychologists regard themselves as Marxists in their scientific work, then this name loses precision with respect to the beginning psychological schools which have not yet won the right to "Marxism." I remember how extremely amazed I was when I realized this during an informal conversation. I had the following conversation with one of the most educated psychologists [76]:

> What kind of psychology do you have in Russia? That you are Marxists does not yet tell what kind of psychologists you are. Knowing of Freud's popularity in Russia, I at first thought of the Adlerians. After all, these are also Marxists. But you have a totally different psychology. We are also social-democrats and Marxists, but at the same time we are Darwinists and followers of Copernicus as well.

I am convinced that he was right because of one, in my view decisive, consideration. After all, we would indeed not call our biology "Darwinian." This is included in the concept of *science* itself. It implies the acceptance of all great conceptions. A Marxist historian would never use the title "A Marxist History of Russia." He would regard this as self-evident. "Marxist" is for him synonymous with "truthful" and "scientific." Another *history* than a Marxist one he does not acknowledge. And for us it should be the same. Our science will become Marxist to the degree that it becomes truthful and scientific. And we will work precisely on making it truthful and to make it agree with Marx's theory. According to the very meaning of the word and the essence of the matter we cannot use "Marxist psychology" in the sense we use associative, experimental, empirical, or eidetic psychology. Marxist psychology is not a school amidst schools, but the only genuine psychology as a science. A psychology other than this cannot exist. And the other way around: *everything* that was and is genuinely scientific belongs to Marxist psychology. This concept is broader than the concept of school or even current. It coincides with the concept *scientific* per se, no matter where and by whom it may have been developed.

Blonsky (1921) uses the term "scientific psychology" in this sense. And he is entirely right. What we wanted to do, the meaning of our reform, the crux of our divergence with the empiricists, the basic character of our science, our goal and the size of our task, its content and the method of its fulfillment—is all expressed by this epithet. It would fully satisfy me if only it were not unnecessary. Expressed in its most correct form it clearly revealed that it cannot express anything more than is already contained in the word it predicates. After all, "psychology" is the name of a *science and not of a theater piece or a movie*. It cannot be anything other than scientific. Nobody would call the description of the sky in a novel "astronomy." The name "psychology" is as little suited for the description of the thoughts of Raskol'nikov or the ravings of Lady Macbeth. Whatever describes the mind in a nonscientific way is not psychology, but something else—whatever you like: advertising, review, chronicle, fiction, lyric poetry, philosophy, philistinism, gossip and a thousand other things besides. After all, the epithet "scientific" is not only applicable to Blonsky's outline [77], but also to Müller's investigations of memory, Köhler's experiments with apes, Weber–Fechner's theory about thresholds, Groos' theory of play, Thorndike's theory of training, Aristotle's association theory, i.e., to *everything* in history and contemporaneity which belongs to science. I would be prepared to argue that theories which are known to be incorrect, which have been falsified or are doubtful, can also be scientific, for being scientific is not the same as being valid. A ticket for the theater can be absolutely valid and nonscientific. Herbart's theory about feelings as the relations between ideas is absolutely false, but equally absolutely scientific. The goal and means determine whether a theory is scientific and no other factors. That is why to say "scientific psychology" is equal to saying nothing or, more correctly, to saying simply "psychology."

It remains for us to accept this name. It perfectly well stresses what we want— the size and the content of our task. And it does not reside in the creation of a school next to other schools; it does not cover some part or aspect, or problem, or method of interpretation of psychology alongside analogous parts, schools, etc. We are talking about *all* of psychology, *in its full capacity*; about the only psychology which does not admit of another one. We are talking about the realization of psychology as a science.

That is why we will simply say: psychology. We will do better to explain other currents and schools with epithets and to distinguish what is scientific from what is nonscientific in them, psychology from empiricism, from theology, from *eidos* and from everything which has stuck to it in the centuries of its existence as to the side of an ocean-going ship.

Epithets we need for other things: for the systematic, *consistently logical, methodological division* of disciplines within psychology. Thus, we will speak about general and child psychology, zoo- and pathopsychology, differential and comparative psychology. Psychology will be the common name for an entire family of sciences. After all, our task is not at all to *isolate* our work from the general psychological work of the past, but to *unite* our work with all the scientific achievements of psychology into one whole, and on a new basis. We do not want to distinguish our school from science, but science from nonscience, psychology from nonpsychology. The psychology about which we are talking does not yet exist. It still has to be created—and by more than one school. Many generations of psychologists will still work on it, as James said [see p. 401 of Burkhardt, 1984]. Psychology *will have* its geniuses and its ordinary investigators. But what will emerge from the joint work of the generations, of both the geniuses and the simple skilled workmen of science, will be psychology. With this name our science will enter the new society on the threshold of which it begins to take shape. Our science could not and cannot develop in the old society. We cannot master the truth about personality and personality itself so long as mankind has not mastered the truth about society and society itself. In contrast, in the new society our science will take a central place in life. "The leap from the kingdom of necessity into the kingdom of freedom" [78] inevitably puts the question of the mastery of our own being, of its subjection to the self, on the agenda. In this sense Pavlov is right when he calls our science the last science about man himself. It will indeed be the last science in the historical or prehistorical period of mankind. The new society will create the new man. When one mentions the remolding of man as an indisputable trait of the new mankind and the artificial creation of a new biological type, then this will be the only and first species in biology which will create itself . . . [79]

In the future society, psychology will indeed be the science of the new man. Without this the perspective of Marxism and the history of science would not be complete. But this science of the new man will still remain psychology. Now we hold its thread in our hands. There is no necessity for this psychology to correspond as little to the present one as—in the words of Spinoza [1677/1955, p. 61]—the constellation Dog corresponds to a dog, a barking animal.

EPILOGUE

M. G. Yaroshevsky and G. S. Gurgenidze

1

L. S. Vygotsky was a brilliant theoretician of Soviet psychology. One associates his name above all with the cultural-historical theory of the development of the higher mental functions. But the richness of the ideas which Vygotsky contributed to the conceptual tissue of the organism of scientific psychology is by no means limited to this theory. For an adequate understanding of his views on the mind, we must examine them in their dynamics and development, as a constant search for new solutions. The cultural-historical theory was but one of those solutions. The strength of the conceptions developed by Vygotsky is determined by their methodological basis and their direction. As no other of the Soviet psychologists of his time, Vygotsky had mastered the methodological principles of Marxism applied to the problems of one of the concrete sciences. He emphasized that "psychology needs its own *Das Kapital.*" His did not want to gather psychological illustrations to the well-known theses of materialistic dialectics, but to apply these theses as tools which allow us to reform the investigative process from inside and compared to which other methods of obtaining and organizing knowledge are powerless.

This theoretical methodological work of Vygotsky is inseparable from his historical scientific work. And it is not just a matter of a sense for historicism, which never left him no matter what subject he studied. Vygotsky left us brilliant examples of the analysis of psychological thought—from the 17th century (the analysis of Descartes' and Spinoza's theories) to modern times, and it is impossible to draw the boundary between what has now become history and what has become part of what we consider the present body of knowledge of the science. To the latter category belong his prefaces to the Russian translations of the books of eminent Western investigators. He examined his contemporary psychological currents and took positions which represented a new level in the development of the methodology of scientific knowledge compared to the positions occupied by those whose views he subjected to critical analysis.

When he becomes acquainted with the broad cycle of works of Vygotsky in which an analysis is given of the main psychological currents in the West of the first third of our century (behaviorism, Gestalt psychology, psychoanalysis, etc.) and also with the general characteristics of the crisis in this science given in them, the reader can convince himself (particularly after his acquaintance with such a work by Vygotsky as "The Historical Meaning of the Crisis in Psychology") that his attention was drawn by such key questions for the methodology of contem-

345

porary scientific knowledge as the lawfulness of the development of science, its periods of crisis and revolution, its social determinants, structural reforms, the relation between scientific concepts and facts, methical procedures and intellectual operations, etc. Everything that regarded science as a special developing system and form of activity was investigated by Vygotsky according to its nature and in the historical context. Thanks to this, the knowledge of science grew from the analysis of the world of certain historical contexts, and this world itself appeared as an internally connected dynamic whole and not as a catalogue of events which replace each other in time. Although the indicated directions in Vygotsky's investigations are hard to distinguish, for his theoretical voice was constantly connected with the historical one, each of them had nevertheless its own aspects, which was the reason we grouped the different works representing these directions into two sections.

We have maintained the chronology in the compositions of the volumes, which allows us to better understand the development of Vygotsky's thought, its direction and the principal points of the route of his scientific search. Only in one case did we diverge from the chronological order. The exception was made for Vygotsky's work "The Historical Meaning of the Crisis in Psychology," which had not been published before. Although it was written before several other critical studies, it provided a general picture of the developmental paths of scientific psychology and the principles of orientation in its basic currents and developing tendencies. Because of this, the indicated work can be regarded as a synthesis of the main ideas of Vygotsky concerning the special methodology (or particular methodology, derived from philosophical methodology, but not identical to it) of psychological knowledge which forms the supreme organizing instance with respect to the whole variety of manifestations and forms of this knowledge.

We can distinguish several periods in Vygotsky's investigative activity. And although there is no sharp boundary between them, each of them is distinguished by characteristic details. A comparison of these periods not only allows us to reveal a certain logic in the development of Vygotsky's psychological ideas. It is of more general importance as it sheds light upon the developmental path of our psychology as a whole.

As is well known, his initial interests were devoted to the psychology of art. The years of work on them have been published in *The Psychology of Art*, finished in 1925. This work was not published during the author's lifetime. It was first published 40 years after it was written. It is assumed that Vygotsky did not want to publish it because he felt the analysis of the mechanisms of artistic creation and the specific functions of art was incomplete, unfinished (cf. Leont'ev's preface in *The Psychology of Art*, Moscow, 1968). [1]

The above-mentioned work set itself the goal of solving psychological tasks, but it was also a work of literary criticism. It provides an original treatment of a number of literary works both in the plane of their construction and from the viewpoint of their perception, which Vygotsky explained starting from the assumption that art is the "social technique of feeling" (*The Psychology of Art*, p. 5). [2] Vygotsky considered his main task to be revealing the psychological mechanisms of the aesthetical reaction. According to Vygotsky, this goal cannot be reached when the subject (the author, or reader), with his unique, immediately experienced inner world, fulfills the role of the explanatory principle of the processes of the creation and perception of products of artistic creation. According to Vygotsky's project, the inner world of the subject with its inalienable forms, motives, drives, etc. must be eliminated, just like the psychologist isolates a pure reaction, sensory or motor, selection or distinction, and studies it as an impersonal reaction (ibid., p. 5).

Thus, Vygotsky's idea about the union of art criticism with psychology presumed, according to the author's basic idea, a radical reform of psychology, i.e., it should be transformed from subjective into objective, from individual into social psychology. Vygotsky's attempts to approach the problem of "personality and culture" in a new way are worthy of our attention. He tried to overcome the conceptions of those who counted on solving this problem on the basis of an idealistic understanding of man as being secluded in the world of his creations.

But the reform did not take place.

Vygotsky did not succeed in creating an objective psychology of art. It is this circumstance, we assume, which motivated the author to refrain from publishing a work which contains a number of statements that attract attention even in our time (first and foremost in connection with the development of semiotics).

The idea that objective psychology is the only current which meets the requirements of scientific knowledge (its exactness, freedom from arbitrary interpretations, etc.) continued to live in Vygotsky's consciousness, but acquired a totally different meaning when he turned from cultural topics to the real behavior of living beings which in that period had become the object of investigation in the new currents of psychology—American behaviorism and Russian reflexology.

The second period in Vygotsky's creative career takes shape in connection with his orientation to the investigation of the dependency of mental phenomena upon the biological mechanisms of behavior. When he worked on the problems of the psychology of art, Vygotsky viewed the concepts and explanatory principles of traditional empirical psychology as the main danger for the scientific understanding of the mind. The latter was no unified, homogeneous formation. It combined elements and tendencies of various systems, both materialistic and idealistic ones. But despite all the divergences, its adherents shared the conviction that the subject matter of psychology, the plane where it must search for the lawful connections of its phenomena, is the area of consciousness immediately given to the subject in his inner vision. Both Wundt with his ideas about psychology as a science which studies the immediate experience of the subject and Brentano, who counterbalanced Wundt with his claim that the area of psychology, in contrast to other sciences, must be formed by particular intentional acts of consciousness, as well as the adherents of faculty psychology who proceeded from the theory of faculties as primary forces of the mind—all of them agreed that by their nature and by the way they are known, the facts of psychological life fundamentally differ from other phenomena of being. Vygotsky first tried to overcome this presumption that the subject has immediate access to the mental sphere on the basis of the objective psychology of art and later by linking up with natural scientific psychology.

At the same time, empirical psychology, along with the methodological positions mentioned, experienced a strong and spontaneously materialistic current which conditioned the accumulation of concrete data about the unique mental world of people and the individual differences between them.

One of the best representatives of the spontaneously materialistic current was the Russian psychologist A. F. Lazursky. It was his idea to transform the laboratory experiment into a natural one, bringing scientific psychology closer to life, and also to create a differential psychology which he considered a scientific characterology with important practical importance.

In international science no one, except for Lazursky (1908, p. 73), thought that the study of individual properties of people can only change psychology from being descriptive into being explanatory when the link with "different sides of the activity of various nervous centers" has been established. Lazursky arrived at the conclusion that it is necessary to explain the properties of the personality neurodynamically under the influence of his collaboration with Bekhterev, who founded the Psychoneurological Institute where Lazursky conducted his experimental investigations.

In 1912, Lazursky published the course of lectures *General and Experimental Psychology*. This book was notable for its progressive orientation, which clearly manifested itself in comparison with the courses of lectures by psychologist-idealists such as, for example, Chelpanov. Lazursky's course of lectures in psychology was republished in the first years of Soviet power as a textbook. How can we explain this? Why did the collaborators at the Moscow Psychological Institute, who set themselves the task to "reconsider the foundations and principles in the light of dialectical materialism" (p. 51; this volume), select Lazursky's book from the multitude of different courses and textbooks? The answer to this question is the preface to the book written by Vygotsky, who emphasizes that the advantage of Lazursky's course is that he defends a general biological viewpoint on the mind and examines all questions of psychology as problems of a biological order.

It would seem that such an approach should become the basis for a union between the variant of empirical psychology represented by Lazursky and the achievements of Russian reflexology, which, after all, was as consistent in its biological orientation. Vygotsky contrasts the "natural scientist and realist" Lazursky with the representatives of the objective psychology of various currents, above all Pavlov and Bekhterev. The psychology of consciousness is contrasted with the psychology of behavior. However, Vygotsky assumed that neither Bekhterev's nor Pavlov's objective psychology can lay claim to the name of scientific psychology which

> will not arise out of the ruins of empirical psychology or in the laboratories of the reflexologists (p. 61, this volume).

He thinks that "it will come as a broad biosocial synthesis of the theory of animal behavior and societal man" (ibid.). Vygotsky's creative work of this period is distinguished by its reflections about a new psychology.

Consequently, the characteristic properties of this second period are the acceptance of the advantage of objective psychology of the reflexological type over the traditional, empirical psychology, the conviction that we can never reach an integral theory of the human mind by the simple addition of the achievements of these two currents, and also the conviction that the "new psychology will be a branch of general biology and at the same time the basis of all sociological sciences" (ibid.).

Vygotsky's position is inconsistent because his views are close to those of Bekhterev, on the one hand, while he clearly sees their limited nature, on the other hand. He had not yet found his own positive solution. The word "consciousness" had not yet been pronounced.

An important landmark in Vygotsky's search for the unique nature of the mental regulation of human vital activity, as distinguished from the reflex acts of animals, was his work "Consciousness as a problem for the psychology of behavior" (1925). Vygotsky regarded it as reflexology's error (both in the Bekhterevian and the Pavlovian variant) to ignore the problem of the psychological nature of consciousness. In his understanding of the specific character of consciousness, he proceeded from Marx's well-known thesis that man in the process of labor, before he has the final product, already possesses a model of this product, a model which as a goal determines the character of his bodily actions with the natural substance. This general characteristic of labor guided the psychologist to search for the mechanisms by which the conscious goal gives human behavior its unique properties. As can be seen from his first attempt to explain the psychological nature of consciousness, Vygotsky criticized a number of the theses of reflexology, but at the same time remained within the boundaries of the reflexological categories. He assumed that for consciousness

> we must find a place . . .in one series . . .with all the reactions of the organism. . . Consciousness is the problem of the structure of behavior (p. 67, this volume).

If the result obtained as the result of labor was present in ideal form before the beginning of the process, this means that the subject must somewhere acquire a schema for the future actions of his hands with the natural substance. According to Vygotsky's suggestion, such a schema, or, as he said, model, is born in the system of mutually interacting reflexes. One reflex is transmitted to another without the indispensable interference of a new external stimulus.

Imperceptible to the objective observer, in the human organism reflexes are constantly being replaced by others. When these reflexes provoke each other, it is not only the external signals that evoke them which are imperceptible, but also the final executive parts as the latter are inhibited.

Without referring to Sechenov, Vygotsky uses his famous statement about thought as a reflex "interrupted after two-thirds." [3] Thought cannot be separated from speech, from the speech motor reaction combined with it. In this period it seemed to Vygotsky that the study of such inhibited reactions by means of objective methods was the main path toward the discovery of the secrets of the conscious regulation of human behavior.

Although he had not yet torn himself away from reflexology at the time, Vygotsky nevertheless took a number of steps in a direction which eventually led him to a radical revision of his previous views on the role of consciousness in the organization and guidance of behavior. The most important of these steps were connected with the treatment of the word as a reflex phenomenon of a special nature, which differs from other acts both according to the character of the stimulus which elicits it and according to the character of the influence of the effector, executive part of this act upon the further activity of the person.

The word was characterized by Vygotsky as a "reversible reflex-stimulus." It is in the first place directed toward the other person and only in the second place toward the person who generates it. To the extent that the word is a mechanism of consciousness, it follows that this mechanism is identical with social contact. That is why Vygotsky defines consciousness as the "social contact with oneself." For Vygotsky the selection of the word as a special stimulus which plays the role of regulator of human behavior meant that when the speech signal is included in the guidance of this behavior an intellectual, logical aspect is included as well. This implied essential amendments not only to the traditional treatment of the conditional reflex associations on the level of human behavior, but also to the explanation of speech associations by the principle of the frequency of repetitions popular at the time.

Vygotsky observed that words can be combined according to the law of association, but in those cases where a logical association is established between them the result of the combination of the words-reflexes will be entirely different. We thus see that, despite his general reflexological orientation, Vygotsky accentuated the specific content and communicative properties of the word and moved to a new border in the explanation of human consciousness as an integral component of behavior.

The first border revealed itself when Vygotsky distinguished the word from the immediate reflex reaction of the speech apparatus produced by the organism and began examining the word as a special phenomenon of culture. As a result, human behavior became included in the context of cultural-historical determination.

The general thesis about the dependency of consciousness upon social factors was made more concrete in the theory of the higher mental functions (Vygotsky often called them psychological), which is usually given a central place in Vygotsky's legacy. It is discussed in more detail in Leont'ev's introductory article to which we refer the reader. Here we remark that the elaboration of the cultural-historical theory was based on the introduction into the conceptual apparatus of psychology of the concept of the cultural sign, which played a decisive role in the transition from the pre-human forms of behavior to the specifically human ones. Vygotsky includes in the category of cultural signs not only language forms, but also different bearers of a significative function—schemes, maps, algebraic formulas, works of art, etc. These signs are special psychological tools by means of which the individual organizes his behavior and learns to direct them voluntarily. Just like tools of labor, they act as an intermediate link between the activity of the person and the external object and mediate the relationships between them. But whereas the tools of labor are directed toward the object and change it according to a consciously set goal, the signs change nothing in the object, but serve as a means by which the subject can influence himself, his own mind. Thanks to the signs the psychological structure of the personality becomes radically transformed and acquires a qualitatively new character. What was involuntary in the pre-sign period of the regulation of behavior (perception, attention, memory) becomes increasingly more voluntary in the process of sign use.

In this way, two levels of the organization of mental functions develop. On top of the natural, lower, involuntary functions (shared by animals and humans), cultural, higher, voluntary functions develop. Vygotsky treated the appearance of this second level as the product of societal-historical development, as the creation of a special social milieu under the influence of which the human being finds itself from birth.

Education, as a specific form of social influence, determines the process of the child's mastery of the psychological tools-signs; being at first external, independent of the individual consciousness (but absolutely social), these signs are mastered by the subject and become transformed from external to internal ones (are internalized). Thereby they guarantee the self-regulation, or in Vygotsky's terms, the autoregulation of behavior.

Vygotsky clearly realized that this split of psychology's phenomena into two spheres that are supposedly subject to fundamentally different regularities—the natural scientific and the cultural-historical one—was very dangerous for psychology and for its future. Before his eyes was the picture of a crisis in psychology which was engendered, as he wrote more than once, by the confrontation of the "biotropic" (oriented to the natural sciences) and the "sociotropic" (oriented to the world of culture) currents. The problem of the synthesis of these currents was constantly on his mind.

Vygotsky concentrated on the study of the specific nature of the instrumental forms and functions of behavior (i.e., those whose organizing principle is the psychological tool or word), and in his work "The instrumental method in psychology" he resolutely argued against their separation from the natural ones.

> We should not conceive of artificial (instrumental) acts as supernatural or meta-natural, acts constructed in accordance with some new, special laws. Artificial acts are natural as well; they can, without remainder, to the very end, be decomposed and reduced to natural ones, just like any machine (or technical tool) can without remainder be decomposed into a system of natural forces and processes (pp. 85-86, this volume).

By insisting on the fact that artificial things are composed of the same forces and processes as natural ones, Vygotsky attempted to avoid dualism. And although his comparisons do not always sound convincing, we must not forget the main line of his search. He viewed the danger of contrasting the higher and lower levels of the organization of behavior and at the same time he felt the need to explain the qualitative distinctions between these levels. He regarded it as his main task in this case to penetrate into the mechanism of the emergence of new structures.

At first he searched for this mechanism in the reform of different functions, for example, the transformation of involuntary or mechanical memory into voluntary or logical memory, etc. Later he regarded this approach as unsatisfactory for explaining the regularities of the development of mind. He proposed the thesis that in the course of the historical formation of human behavior the interfunctional connections and relationships are changed and interfunctional systems are formed due to psychological tools.

The clarification of the way that these systems develop and become transformed became a new task of psychological investigation which Vygotsky above all tried to solve for the problem he knew best: the problem of the relationship between thinking and speech. But here we see a turnaround in his psychological views connected with the fact that speech acted as a factor which regulates not only the thinking process, but also the activity of consciousness as a whole as a specifically human form of mind.

The question of the relationship between consciousness and behavior appeared in a new perspective. This question had been at the center of Vygotsky's interests since the time from which, in his search for ways to build an objective psychology, he turned from the study of aesthetical reactions to the elucidation of the possibilities which the reflexological current opens in the plane of scientific knowledge of the mind.

At first he attached a special role to the speech reflex (which differs, as the reader recalls, from the other reflex reactions both according to its stimulus and according to its executive, motor part). Then the word, viewed as one of the main variants of the cultural sign, acquired the meaning of a psychological tool whose interference changes (along with other signs) the natural, involuntary mental process into a voluntarily guided process or, more exactly, a self-guided process. The attempt to understand the character of the interrelations between the different mental processes made Vygotsky think about the instrumental role of the word in the formation of the functional systems. But the question about the bearer, the "boss" of these systems, about the single mental "substrate" in which perception, memory, feeling, and will are rooted, remained unsolved as before. It was assumed that on the level of human beings such a "substrate" is formed by consciousness.

The next period in Vygotsky's scientific search was connected with the program he developed to study consciousness as a systemic and semantic structure. Now he defines the area he is elaborating as "height psychology," which is contrasted with two other psychologies: "surface psychology" and "depth psychology." By "surface psychology" he meant the whole variety of schools and currents which proceeded from the postulate that mental phenomena are immediately given to the subject who experiences them. In this view psychology is a descriptive, or, as Vygotsky said, "observational" science, which confines its subject to the circle of phenomena that can be detected by the inner eye of the subject (by "observation") as he moves his eye along the surface of consciousness conceived of as a sort of kaleidoscope of images, acts, Gestalten, etc. In such an approach phenomenon and essence are equated. In other words, psychology found itself in a position opposite to the goals of other sciences, which saw it as their task to discover the regularities behind the surface of the phenomena that determine them.

In contrast to such a "surface" psychology, the so-called "depth" psychology (psychoanalysis) attempted to penetrate behind the screen of consciousness into the sphere of action of the hidden irrational forces. It attached a key role to the unconscious. In what regards the treatment of consciousness as such, its position was in no way different from that of the "surface" psychology. Consciousness was identified with an "inner stage" where different phenomena replace each other. That is why it lacked its own qualitative characteristic nature and appeared as an immutable, nondeveloping entity.

In contrast to the "surface" psychology, the new conception of consciousness, the elaboration of which became Vygotsky's main task, proposed to transcend the boundaries of the immediately given mental phenomena, not into the sphere of the unconscious mind, but to a fundamentally different mental mechanism which determines what appears before the "inner eye" of the subject. Vygotsky calls this mechanism the functional system.

This concept, which subsequently appeared in our psychology in connection with new physiological approaches, had long before been established by Vygotsky as a special psychological approach. It presumed a radical revision of the traditional understanding of function, an understanding which could be traced, as Vygotsky rightfully emphasized, to classic faculty psychology. The mental "organism" was conceived of as a bodily one. And the faculties of the mind were conceived of as bodily functions—perception, memory, thinking, etc. Vygotsky considered that the weakness of functionalism was that it could explain neither the character of the relationships between the functions (the problem of the system) nor the relationship of the function with the external phenomenon (the problem of intentionality, the orientation upon an object outside consciousness) and with the image of this phenomenon as experienced by the subject (the problem of meaning).

Vygotsky outlines several directions to overcome the weaknesses of functionalism. He suggests speaking about activities of consciousness instead of functions. These activities are not realized separately but in a mutual connection which forms the functional system as a dynamic whole. Dynamic means changeable, developing. The development of the system, its history—this is still another of the very important principles put forward by Vygotsky.[1] The organizing principle of the development of consciousness is its special structural unit, which Vygotsky denoted by the term "meaning." Not the image, not experiencing, not the act (as in previous ideas about consciousness), but meaning. The idea according to which meaning forms an organic component of individual consciousness had far-reaching consequences. This is the turning point which separates the preceding period of Vygotsky's creative career from what we are examining now.

> In older works, we ignored that the sign has meaning . . .. We proceeded from the principle of the constancy of meaning, we discounted meaning . . .. Whereas before our task was to demonstrate what "the knot" and logical memory have in *common*, now our task is to demonstrate the difference that exists between them (see pp. 130-131, this volume).

"The knot" is a sign, admittedly a "cultural sign," and as such it is different from the signal-stimulus as the regulator of behavior at the pre-human level. But the function of the sign as the bearer of objective meaning (in the system of the culture) was discounted in the period of the development of the cultural-historical theory (as the author himself admits). Of course, this hindered Vygotsky from revealing the specific qualitative characteristic nature of consciousness, which neither could the previous investigators lay bare, and thereby prevented him from explaining consciousness from the position of the system approach and historicism.

Such a perspective revealed the idea that the tissue of consciousness is built from meanings, that it is in the sphere of meanings and not signs that the factors which change the interfunctional relationships are operative.

The thesis that meanings (as distinct from signs, on the one hand, and concepts as logical forms, on the other hand) become transformed in the process of the individual development of the subject introduced an idea of tremendous importance to the psychological interpretation of consciousness. It offered new perspectives for the investigation of consciousness according to the plan for the construction of a "height" psychology.

Just like in "depth" psychology (Freudian theory, etc.), the phenomena that were directly before the subject (in his field or stream of consciousness) were not viewed as a primary datum, but as something derived from mechanisms which could only be penetrated indirectly, revealing the strata inaccessible to introspection. But whereas "depth" psychology searched for these strata in a quasi-biological underground, Vygotsky proceeded from the assumption that the new approach would not uncover the "depths" but the "heights" of the personality, its intimate connections with the supra-individual world of developing human culture. After all, meaning cannot be separated from the word (although it is not identical with it), and the word as a component of language concentrates in itself the richness of the social development of its creator—the people. The word lives in communication, and in his new program when he answers the question "what moves the meanings, what determines their development," Vygotsky emphasizes that due to this the "cooperation of consciousnesses" becomes possible.

Here the last period in Vygotsky's search in the area of theoretical psychology ended. It stopped at ideas whose great promise can be acutely felt after half a century, perhaps even more so than in the times in which they were born in yet immature, unfinished form in the head of their generator.

When psychology declared itself to be an independent science, it pretended to be a science about consciousness. But, as Vygotsky demonstrated, when psychology defined itself as the science of consciousness it hardly knew anything about consciousness. Can its conclusions about the identity, continuity and vividness of consciousness really be considered as having serious scientific meaning? These conclusions were called laws. But their formal nature was obvious. Psychology stood for the task of explaining the objective mechanisms of the construction and development of consciousness as functional systems which were inaccessible to self-observation and whose components were special units—meanings, which connect the subject with the world of culture and with the people who create this world in the process of communication.

2

There is no theoretical work by Vygotsky in which he does not connect his reflections about the problems of psychology with the situation in international science. These works are a never-ending dialogue with the representatives of various currents, directions, and schools. In a number of cases, the critical analysis of currents became a special task for Vygotsky. Then the emphasis was shifted. Special stress was laid on tracing the historical roots of some conception and also on the functions which it fulfilled in the complex relationships of the ideological-scientific forces in a certain period of the development of psychological knowledge. In these studies, Vygotsky's theoretical search became, as it were, concealed, but they constantly influenced the general course of his critical analysis of the given direction.

The critical studies mentioned were usually prefaces to the works of Western psychologists. The second part of this volume acquaints the reader with the majority of these prefaces. Vygotsky wrote them in various years and each of them is stamped, of course, by the corresponding stage of his creative career (which was, as the reader already knows, a very dynamic one). That is why we can establish a certain correspondence between the ideas which determined the outlook of Vygotsky's special theoretical talks and publications and the nature of his articles which contain an analysis and evaluation of the works of Western psychologists. We have arranged his critical studies in chronological order and offer the reader the opportunity to convince himself of this.

Vygotsky thought that the new system of psychological knowledge cannot but develop in the channel of the objective analysis of behavior, and he had a high opinion of the conception of the first leader of American behaviorism, Thorndike (see the preface to the latter's book *Principles of Teaching Based on Psychology*). In this conception, the mind was no longer contrasted with other phenomena of being either according to its essence or according to the way it is known. Thorndike characterized it as a system of bodily reactions of the organism which developed in problem situations which can be objectively observed, guided and controlled. Following an openly reductionist style of thinking, Thorndike saw no differences in principle between the reactions of animals and humans. But Vygotsky did not consider this aspect of the matter important at the time. He saw the decisive advantage of Thorndike's theory in the fact that it demolished the dogmas of the older psychology which was constrained by the idea that the only "witness" of mental phenomena is the subject who has immediate access to them in his inner perception. As a result, the formation of the child's mind, about whose nature self-observation can say nothing, remained outside the reach of scientific analysis. From the viewpoint of the theory of reactions, which develop before the eyes of the objective investigator who can construct these reactions according to some agreed upon program, the picture became radically changed. The mechanisms of the development of child behavior were uncovered, and a perspective was outlined for the guidance of the processes of this development by the educator or pedagogue.

Subsequently, Vygotsky rejected Thorndike's theory as being "mechanistic" (reducing the process of the human acquisition of new forms of behavior to blind trial and error), "atomistic" (taking separate elements and not integral structures for its point of departure), and for ignoring the importance of the biological maturation of the organism as a factor in mental development and the qualitative steps ("stages") in this development. But such a re-evaluation by Vygotsky of Thorndike's conception took place later under the influence of the discussion between various psychological schools, notably the critique of behaviorism by the adherents of Gestalt psychology. [4]

Vygotsky analyzed Thorndike's conception of educational psychology and distinguished a pedagogical and a psychological part. He emphasized that for Thorndike the fundamentally new understanding of the factors of behavior and the laws ruling them is meant to assist the practice and needs of the American school system with its individualistic foundations and its goals and norms foreign to Soviet pedagogy. Vygotsky rejected this pedagogical theory and considered Thorndike's treatment of the mechanism of the formation of reactions that were not present in the previous experience of the individual to be progressive. However, Vygotsky does not so much explain this mechanism itself according to Thorndike, as according to Pavlov. He conceives of education as the process of accumulation and elaboration of conditional reactions, as the formation of new associations between organism and environment. A decisive role is attached to the environment, by which he means not the sum-total of biologically significant stimuli (as in Pavlov's system), but the social environment. To the extent that it is social it is historical as well, i.e., it is changeable from period to period.

Thus, while he remained within the confines of the behavioristic (reflexological) approach, Vygotsky had already tried to combine the concept of environmental stimuli with a content other than the adherents of behaviorism and reflexology did. He viewed these stimuli, which play a decisive role in the development of the response reactions of the organism, as special determinants, determinants of a societal-historical order.

Another important correction which Vygotsky introduced into the conditional reflex schema applied to the development of behavior was the emphasis upon the internal dynamics of the reflexes. In contrast to the conception of the simple determination of the organism's response action by the immediate influences of environmental stimuli, stress was laid on the "struggle between man and the world which does not stop for a second," on the dialectics of the internal processes. In Vygotsky's description, the organism is far from being a control panel where external signals are automatically relayed from some channels to others and the construction of stable associations between impulses and the response reactions to them is established.

Vygotsky's thesis about the "organism's very complex strategy" in the struggle with the immediate influences of the environment sounds amazingly modern. This was combined with ideas about children's activity which introduced conditions into the characteristics of their behavior which were ignored by the traditional conditional reflex conception. Here we can see the sprouts of the ideas which later allowed Vygotsky to re-interpret from a new angle both Thorndike's behavioristic position and Pavlov's theory of higher nervous activity.

Both behaviorism and reflexology, although they were based on biological and not social-cultural foundations, attached a decisive role to the formative influence of the external environment. But Vygotsky, as we have seen, did not confine himself to an abstract conception of the environment and attempted to re-interpret it. In this process he was guided by a general methodological position that assumes a qualitative difference between the conditions and determinants of human behavior and the living environment of other living beings. But this does not exhaust the originality of his attempts to explain the specifically human regulation of behavior. He persistently searched for the actual internal regularities of development, i.e., for the solution of a problem which had been raised by neither the behaviorists nor the Russian reflexologists. In the West, most important in the treatment of this problem were the adherents of the view according to which the basic factors of the development of forms of behavior can be nothing other than biological. This view was held for both the elementary and the higher mental functions. This was, in particular, the position of the well-known Austrian psychologist Bühler, whose theory of mental development Vygotsky criticized in the preface to the Russian translation of his work "Abriss der geistigen Entwicklung des Kindes" (see Chapter 12, this volume).

While he acknowledges Bühler's important merit for the clarification of the biological foundations of the child's mind and his intention to understand the biological functions as a whole in the united rhythm of their development, Vygotsky views as an error of this psychologist the fact that he removes the social functions and the social rhythm from the field of attention of the investigator. As a result, the distinction between innate and cultural disappeared and the concept of the development of the human mind lost meaning. It appeared abstract and absorbed all forms of change. No distinction was made between higher and lower, elementary and intricately organized, and as the final cause of these forms acted biological maturation or, in modern terms, their unfolding according to the genetic program. As Vygotsky emphasized, such a conception of mental development is linked with reactionary social conclusions about the pre-determination of persons' behavior by determinants hidden in their genes.

We can say without exaggeration that the problem of development, and above all the "drama of the mental development of the child," becomes the focus of Vygotsky's reflections during the most intensive and, unfortunately, last decade of his creative career. His critical analysis of the two currents which had by then become the most important ones on the psychological scene, Gestalt psychology and Piaget's theory, was above all concentrated upon this problem.

Of course, Gestalt psychology, behaviorism, and psychoanalysis (which Vygotsky knew extremely well) were all general psychological conceptions and directions and not special theories about the development of the mind, not to mention the early childhood or school period. But each of the above-mentioned directions widely drew upon empirical material in the area of child psychology and gave this material an interpretation which was meant to strengthen and confirm the correctness of the "big" theory which pretended to provide a scientific explanation of the mechanisms of human activity as a whole. Vygotsky, in turn, examined in the problems of the development of the child's mind its cardinal knot: having untangled it, we can test the strength of the conceptual threads from which the methodological tissue of the new currents in Western psychology is woven.

In preparing this tissue, he connected his analyses with ideas worked out on the basis of the Marxist conception of humans. Here Vygotsky felt his major buttress. At the same time an adequate theoretical orientation was important for those empirical investigations whose data might be contrasted with the data of the Western psychologists, on the one hand, and might strengthen the union between the scientific investigation of the mechanism of development of mental functions and the practice of education and instruction, on the other hand.

In the article "The problem of development in structural psychology," Vygotsky above all dwells upon the critique by one of the major Gestalt psychologists, Koffka, of the two conceptions of the development of the mind mentioned above: the conceptions of Thorndike and Bühler. According to Thorndike, instruction is equivalent to the selection and reinforcement of reactions according to the formula "trial, error, and accidental success." According to Koffka, it consists of the elaboration of new structures. As regards Bühler, his schema assumed three levels of development: instinct, training (behavior of the habit type), and intellect. The weakness of such a schema was its incapability of covering the different forms of development of the mind with a single principle which, according to Koffka, is again a structure. Bühler contrasts Thorndike's mechanistic "unitarian" idea, which ignores the dialectics of the process of development, the qualitative changes and transformations in this process, with the "pluralistic" idea of three different psychological apparatuses which are built upon each other, but lack, however, an inner connection.

Koffka claimed that the principle of structure allows us to overcome the limitation of these approaches which are to an unequal extent impotent before the unique nature of the development of the mind. He used the term structure to refer to the integrated and meaningful nature of behavior. The meaning of these two features of the basic explanatory concept of Gestalt psychology becomes clear in the context of its general methodological orientation which was directed against two ways of treating behavior: the mechanistic one (of the type of Thorndike's conception of trial and error) and the vitalistic one (of the type of Bühler's conception of the three levels).

The principle of trial and error attributes the development of new actions (and, consequently, development as well) to the mechanical selection of a multitude of different reactions, among which successful ones can be found by accident. The conception of the three levels transforms the highest of these levels, intellect (which was reduced by the behaviorists to the accidental coupling of uncoordinated movements), into a special mental form which is self-contained and has no connections with the preceding levels of development. We can call such an approach psychovitalism, insofar as the unique nature of the mental (intellect) is explained by a force which is inherent to it and which has no basis in something external to it—whether biological or social. Using Koffka's critique of the above-mentioned currents, Vygotsky uncovered the shakiness of Koffka's own position and of Gestalt theory as a whole.

When we treat the concept of structure as a universal concept we lose the possibility of explaining the qualitatively distinct stages of development and erase the boundaries between them.

With regard to the evolution of the mind in phylo- and ontogenesis, the Gestalt psychologists stop distinguishing the unique nature of the human mind and identify it with the germs of the intellectual regulation of behavior in anthropoids. The psychological nature of animals and children is placed on an equal footing and reduced to a common denominator. Structure becomes the primary phenomenon and principle which is capable of explaining everything and itself needs no explanation. And insofar as this principle is generalized to the whole of human mental development, this refutes the claim about the development of some qualitatively new elements beforehand. The Gestalt movement took the concept of structure as its credo and could not explain how some structures change into others. As a result, it proved as impotent with respect to the problem of development as the theories it criticized.

Another matter is the critique of Gestalt theory by Vygotsky himself. It was made from the position of his ideas about the higher mental functions, which by then had already developed and which, as the reader knows, took shape under the influence of the new dialectical-materialistic guidelines. The search for the unique nature of these functions, which emerge as the result of the radical transformation (due to special psychological tools) of innate ("natural") ways of interaction between the individual and the world, sharpened Vygotsky's sensitivity to the deep methodological gaps in the psychological schools of the West. This applies also to Vygotsky's analysis of Piaget's innovative investigations which immediately drew the attention of the psychological world. While he emphasized the advantage of Piaget's conception, which rested upon an enormous amount of empirical material that had been painstakingly verified in clinical conversations with the young subjects, Vygotsky demonstrated that although this conception uncovered the qualitatively unique nature of the mental organization of the child in a number of important points, it could not, considered as a whole, reconstruct an adequate picture of the development of this organization.

The sources of this inadequacy were hidden, as in the case of Thorndike, Bühler, and Koffka, in the difficulties of elaborating the problem of the determination of the mind, the fact of its being conditioned by the interaction between innate and social factors.

The principle of practice entered Vygotsky's thinking from Lenin's theory of reflection, from Lenin's "Philosophical Notebooks," where it was emphasized that human practice builds the "formulas" which are "repeated billions of times and become stamped in human consciousness as the figures of logic" (*Complete Works*, Vol. 29, p. 198). It is this statement by Lenin which Vygotsky uses as the decisive argument in his critical analysis of Piaget's conception.

When we follow the path Vygotsky pursued to elaborate the problem of mental development, we can discern several central points in it. When we turn to them we can connect his search in the field of theory with the critical interpretations of the systems which at the time determined the outlook of scientific psychology. At first he assumed that psychology might from the traditional-subjective become objective, from the empirical-descriptive become explanatory and genuinely deterministic if it took the new theory of behavior as the foundations of its structure. Russian reflexology (above all Pavlov's investigations) and American behaviorism of the Thorndike type were perceived as the most promising variants of this current. This promise was viewed in their natural scientific orientation, which put an end to the view of the mind as a special self-sufficient essence given to the subject in introspection.

The main task to which Vygotsky devoted his efforts was to understand the mind as a developing process. He first tried to solve it proceeding from the principle of the interaction of the organism with the environment and the elaboration of new forms of reactions in the course of this interaction. The "atomism" (mechanicism) of the behavioristic and reflexological ideas about the development of behavior was subjected to sharp criticism by the Gestalt psychologists, whose conception was carefully studied and, in turn, critically analyzed by Vygotsky. He was sympathetic to the idea of structure which the Gestalt theorists defended. There is reason to suppose that it (as the distinguishing characteristic of the general "systemic" style of thinking which developed at the beginning of the century) also appealed to him in the early—philological—period of his scientific endeavors.

While he saw its advantage, Vygotsky at the same time demonstrated its incapacity to cope with the problem of the qualitative shifts in mental development both in the plane of the transition from the intellect of higher animals to human consciousness and in the plane of the transformations which this consciousness itself undergoes in different age periods (particularly, thinking and speech). The Gestalt concept not only proclaimed the integrative nature of the mental structures (and the physical structures isomorphic with them) in contrast to the idea of mental "atoms," but it also contained the idea that the "field of behavior" is saturated with semantic (form) content in contrast to the idea that behavior develops through a blind selection of reactions.

Behind the Gestalt concept stood the category of the form as the permanent regulator of mental activity. Gestalt theory changed this concept into a universal explanatory principle and could not, as Vygotsky showed, indicate a productive approach to the mechanism of mental development. No matter how strongly the structural and integrative nature of the semantic (form) content of the mental acts was emphasized, in order to understand their genesis, development, and reform, it was necessary to transcend the boundaries of the Gestalten as such and turn to the forces (above all to the social ones) which determine the mental organization of humans.

The turn to sociality undertaken by Piaget introduced a new spirit in the investigation of thinking and speech. But the treatment of sociality as the "communication of consciousnesses" separated the subject of the epistemic activity from the real, practical actions due to which this activity acquires its direction and content. "Social practice"—this was the term which Vygotsky took from Lenin and which became the last in the brilliant Soviet psychologist's search for the factors determining the development of the mind.

3

A special place in Vygotsky's theoretical-historical works belongs to the investigation of the crisis which took possession of scientific psychology in the first quarter of the 20th century. Worried voices on this occasion were heard everywhere, both in Russia and abroad. In the Russian literature, Lange, Vagner, and others wrote about it. One year after Vygotsky finished his manuscript "The historical meaning of the crisis in psychology," the well-known Austrian psychologist Bühler published his book *Die Krise der Psychologie*. But the first attempt to investigate and scientifically explain this phenomenon from a Marxist position belongs to Vygotsky.

An external sign of this crisis was the appearance of new schools and directions. The concept of school is ambiguous. In the present case, we mean the split of the science into currents or systems whose adherents operated with various facts and ideas and did not accept each other's facts and ideas.

Freudian theory, behaviorism, Gestalt theory, personalism—each of these systems demanded to put an end to the previous conceptions of consciousness and the methods of studying it. Each laid claim to a turnaround, a discovery of a new era in scientific psychology. The young Soviet psychology faced the question: with whom and following which path shall we proceed in our efforts to solve the problem of psychology?

As he stood on Marxist grounds, Vygotsky inevitably diverged radically from those who followed an idealistic methodological line in his scientific reflective analysis. The divergences are important and instructive for the theory of science, for the solution of the question of how to build it.

In this connection, his polemic with the Swiss psychologist Binswanger is of special interest. Binswanger proposed a plan for a "critique of psychology" by which he meant the examination of the basic concepts of the science, its logic, and the methods of its internal organization. The plan was to create a special science about the ultimate foundations and general principles of psychological knowledge. In the atmosphere of the crisis, this plan was associated with the hope of rising above the contradictions of the schools and systems and establishing the unity of the science through methodological generalizations. The idealistic approach gave this striving for unity in psychology a false direction.

In modern terms, Binswanger conceived of the general science as a meta-theory which studied the structure and connections of the concepts in themselves, irrespective of the reality they reconstruct. The fact that the logical structure and the intellectual structures of the science were isolated from objective reality implied that they were isolated from the historical process as well. After all, it is only by the fact that it is immersed in it and only due to it that human consciousness is connected with the world. Thus, idealism was combined with a-historicism. From such principles developed the version of the methodology of science as a special area which has no other basis than itself and which prescribes the rules for the construction of theories and brings order to the concrete disciplines.

Vygotsky considered that for psychology the creation of a "general science" was the most important task of the century. In contrast with the idealistic method, he sketched this theory proceeding from the Marxist interpretation of theoretical knowledge, from the principles of reflection and historicism. No matter how abstract a statement is, it always contains a clot of the concrete real reality, "albeit in a very weak solution" (p. 248, this volume). That is why the "general science," which synthesizes scientific knowledge and isolates its foundations and regulative principles, does not deal with "pure" concepts, but with concepts which picture aspects of mental reality for whose understanding the conceptual apparatus of the particular psychological disciplines is insufficient.

A general science was born, as we learn from the experience of the highly developed disciplines of the type of physics and biology, in the stage of maturity. Psychology reached a historical moment when its further development without a general science became impossible.[2] This demand for a general science does not express the needs of the logic for the development of knowledge itself, but above all the needs of practice. Psychology will be helpless before the practical tasks that surround it from all sides as long as it has not created its own logical methodological infrastructure.

The general science can be defined as a science which receives its material from a number of scientific disciplines and which further elaborates and generalizes material which cannot be elaborated within each different discipline. The general science operates with fundamental concepts (categories) and explanatory principles and fulfills the role of methodology with respect to the concrete empirical investigation. The general science remains the highest, but nevertheless inalienable, part of concrete scientific knowledge. It is critical, but in a different sense than was assumed by the adherents of a-priorism.

In contrast to Binswanger, for whom the criticism of concepts was to be a special logical methodological discipline, Vygotsky proceeded from the assumption that concepts are being constantly criticized in practice, in the daily work of the scientist, as they are connected with the real facts, the empirical data. Each step presupposes a critique of the concept from the viewpoint of the fact and the critique of the fact from the viewpoint of the concept. Vygotsky assumed that each discovery in science is always at the same time an act of criticism of the concept.

Such an interaction of concept and fact, of the theoretical and empirical components of knowledge, constantly takes place in science. At a higher level, where the concepts (the facts of the particular disciplines) become the material for further criticism and elaboration, which creates the abstractions that are most general and (insofar as reality in them is "clotted") richest in content, this interaction forms the subject of the general science. It can also be called methodology in the sense of a theory about the ways, paths, and methods of concrete scientific knowledge, but again we must take into account that "toolness" (a method to process the empirical material) is intrinsic to even the most elementary concept.

The general science "copies," elevates this operation with concepts to a higher rank; now they are already—corresponding to its subject—the most general concepts (categories). It thus determines the subject and method of any forms of scientific psychological investigations, no matter what objects it covers.

The methodology of a concrete science develops under the influence of philosophy, but it has its own status which is determined by the nature of the subject of this science and the historical development of its categorical structures. The methodological investigation of psychological concepts, methods, and explanatory principles is, therefore, not a philosophical "attic" built on the science. It is born in connection with the demands of the concrete science and forms its inalienable part.

The idea that the two methods of investigating science—the logical and the historical one—cannot be separated, became the cornerstone of Vygotsky's whole theoretical construction.

A scientific methodology on a historical basis is possible, because regularity, repeatability, and correctness are intrinsic to the process of knowledge acquisition itself, to its historical being. From the objective logic of the development of the process, a logic hidden behind the unrepeatability of the events registered in the memory of science, we distill general formulas which are used to deduce and predict these events. Vygotsky (p. 241, this volume) says that

> The regularity in the replacement and development of ideas, the development and downfall of concepts, even the replacement of classifications, etc.—all this can be scientifically explained by the links of the science in question with (1) the general socio-cultural context of the era; (2) the general conditions and laws of scientific knowledge; (3) the objective demands upon the scientific knowledge that follow from the nature of the phenomena studied in a given stage of investigation, i.e., in the final analysis, the requirements of the objective reality that is studied by the given science.

The fact that psychology already realized the need for a general science (a methodology), but was not yet ready to bring it to light, was considered by Vygotsky to be a sign of the crisis in psychology. The acute need for a methodology motivates different structural parts of the science to carry out "vicarious actions." The particular sciences (child psychology, pathopsychology, zoopsychology, etc.) try to appropriate the role that general psychology—and only general psychology—should play by rights, by elevating their concepts-facts, which are true only for a limited circle of phenomena, to the rank of general psychological categories.

One can observe an amazing similarity in the evolution of the most diverse psychological conceptions—from a particular discovery in a special discipline to the subsequent extension of its ideas to all psychology and then to human knowledge as a whole. This was the case for Freudian theory, reflexology, Gestalt theory, and personalism. They went this path with surprising uniformity and thereby expressed in an inadequate form that the need for a general science had ripened. Through its fundamental abstractions, this general science should give unity and inner coherence to the concepts and facts of psychology and determine its subject as a unified science and not as a disorderly conglomerate of phenomena.

In contrast to those who in the crisis saw merely loss, merely the collapse of all foundations, who felt themselves, in the words of the well-known Russian psychologist Lange, to be "in the position of Priam sitting on the ruins of Troy," Vygotsky believed that the crisis contained not only a destructive, but also a constructive principle.

Those who are directly involved with the practice of scientific knowledge and change of humans feel more acutely than any others the need for a critical analysis of the heterogeneous facts, hypotheses and empirical generalizations, the need to "pull the beginnings and ends of our knowledge together."

The difficulties in solving this task are intensified by the fact that the organism of science is "fused" with heterogeneous components—causal, natural scientific psychology and indeterministic, teleological psychology. The crisis showed that their existence is intolerable, that they have to be "cut off," that a productive study of the mental regulation of behavior can only be causal. History passed its sentence—it showed the poverty and lack of promise of indeterminism. Great perspicacity was needed to see the two main directions, causal and indeterministic psychology, behind the swarm of big and small schools which jostle one another on the psychological scene and to establish that the second one is doomed.

The crisis showed that the only candidate for a scientific psychology is deterministic psychology. This is its deep historical meaning. The limited nature of previous determinism was due to the fact that it had no resources to rise to the level of a natural scientific treatment of human consciousness which is societal-historical by its nature. This made the flowering of teleological views possible, which acted under the name of various psychologies: descriptive (Dilthey), intentional (Brentano), phenomenological (Husserl, Pfänder), axiological (Münsterberg), personalism (Stern), and others.

Historicism was also foreign to the conceptions which had a natural scientific spirit—behaviorism, Gestalt psychology, and functionalism. Their philosophical orientation prevented a way out of the crisis situation, which requires, as has been observed, the creation of a general science as the methodology for psychological investigation. According to Vygotsky, such a concrete scientific methodology, which is the only legitimate heir to one of the two tendencies, and notably the natural scientific one, which determined psychology's path in all of the preceding centuries, can only be developed on the foundation which the previous builders "despised," the foundation of dialectical materialism.

Vygotsky regarded Marxist psychology not as one of the schools (just as one spoke of, for example, the associationist, experimental, eidetic and other schools), but as the only scientific psychology. In contrast to other authors who had lost the feeling of historicism and required that psychology "finish with the past" and "start from scratch," Vygotsky did not think that the reformation of psychology on the basis of Marxism implies that we need to throw away all previous work. Every effort of free thought to master the mind, every attempt at deterministic investigation paved the way for the future psychology and that is why they (in a transformed form) will inevitably form part of it.

The natural scientific current in psychology which spontaneously developed under the pressure of social practice stopped at the threshold of the deterministic explanation of the human mind insofar as its determination has a social-historical character. In keeping with this, the explanatory concepts of the natural sciences were insufficient for the building of a new psychology whose task is to uncover laws that are valid for all levels of the mind, including its highest forms, which are determined by the interconnection of the human person with the world of historically developing culture. At the same time, being the immediate heir to the achievements of the preceding natural scientific psychology, a psychology based upon Marxism can, according to Vygotsky, be seen as a natural science in the broad sense of the word. It is obvious that in the present context Vygotsky not only considers the phenomena studied by the sciences about nature (inorganic and organic) to be natural phenomena. Both the development of societal-economical formations in Marx's theory and the development of the mind must be regarded as a natural historical process. Such an approach permits us to bring the investigation of the determination of the phenomena of the mind to a new level while preserving psychology's organic connections with natural science. Vygotsky's subsequent creative work showed the fruitfulness of such a methodological approach for the elaboration of concrete scientific ideas about the determination of genuinely human mental acts—attention, memory, imagination, thinking. It must be observed, however, that in the work under consideration Vygotsky merely stated the question of the need to re-orient psychology along new paths. Later, many Soviet psychologists would move further along these new paths.

The philosophy of Marxism is treated by Vygotsky as being adequate for the actual needs of scientific psychology which seeks a way out of the crisis and not as something which was introduced from outside by persons who planned the reform of psychology for political or ideological reasons (this was, in particular, Chelpanov's opinion). Vygotsky's explanation of the crisis developed under the influence of Lenin's analysis of the critical situation which developed around the turn of the century in the natural sciences. The development of these sciences required new methodological solutions of a dialectical-materialistic nature. In the works of the classics of Marxism, Vygotsky saw a model for applying this philosophical doctrine to a concrete science which in its historically developing concepts reflects a certain aspect of natural and (or) social being.

This task could not be solved by direct diffusion of the universal categories and laws of materialistic dialectics to the field of concrete scientific knowledge. It was also fruitless to follow the other path of attempting to find a ready-made psychology in the various statements of the classics, i.e., to search for the solution of the specific nature and regularities of the mind in these statements. In order to apply Marxism to some science, it is necessary to elaborate a methodology—a system of intermediate, concrete methods of organizing knowledge which can be applied on the scale of this very science.

The dialectics (methodology) of psychological knowledge is called upon to reconstruct the objective dialectic of the mind in the forms of knowledge. This is the core of the science which is common to the multitude of individual psychological disciplines. In this way, a hierarchy of levels of investigation evolves: the highest level is represented by philosophy, the next highest level is the methodology of the general science. Its resources are supplied on the next level of the hierarchy by the individual psychological disciplines. The latter, in turn, are directly connected with the practice of influencing and transforming persons, with various forms of education and instruction, the elaboration of working habits, the organization of activity, medical treatment, etc. One can see not only a movement "top–down"—from philosophy via the general science and the individual disciplines to practice, but also in the opposite direction—"bottom–up"—from practice, generalized and integrated in the individual sciences, to the general psychology whose categorical apparatus summarizes their "sovereignty."

The decisive factor, the beginning and the end in this "cycle," is practice. It directly enters psychological knowledge and does not merely function as the means of its verification. Vygotsky regards scientific investigation itself as a practical activity derived from man's other methods of influencing nature or other people, but at the same time capable of giving this influence, now already "guided" by science, incomparably more effectiveness than at the pre-scientific level.

4

According to Vygotsky, a science is an internally connected system. Each of its components (facts, terms, methods, theoretical constructs) receives its meaning from the whole which goes through a number of stages which replace each other with an inevitability comparable to that of the transition of one societal-economic formation into another.

In Vygotsky's opinion, the problem of the language of science, the problem of words or terminology acquires fundamental importance in methodological investigations.

> The language reveals as it were the molecular changes that the science goes through. It reflects the internal processes that take shape—the tendencies of development, reform, and growth [p. 282, this volume].

The language of science is an instrument of analysis, a tool of thought. It can only be developed by someone who is involved in research and who discovers new things in science. The discovery of new facts and the development of new viewpoints concerning the facts requires new terms. Thus, we are not talking about the creation of new words for phenomena which are already known—this is attaching labels to finished products—but about words which are born in the process of scientific creation.

To the extent that psychology is an experimental science, it uses for the solution of its tasks different apparatuses, instruments or equipment which perform the function of tools. But the development of experimental technique hides the danger of its becoming a fetish and may engender the hope that the application of this technique by itself is capable of discovering new scientific facts. Such a passion for the technique of the equipment without theoretical assumptions, without the understanding that it plays merely an auxiliary role, brings harm to scientific creation and engenders, in Vygotsky's words, "feldsherizm in science." [5] "Feldsherizm in science," in Vygotsky's view, is the separation of the technical, executive function of the investigation (the maintenance of the equipment according to a certain routine) from scientific thinking. Such a separation has a negative influence upon thinking itself, as the whole burden of the investigative work is transferred from the operation with words and terms to the operation with equipment. As a result, the words are not filled with new content and become impoverished; they stop fulfilling their role as the most important instruments of thinking.

We see that for Vygotsky the bases of the analysis of the methodological problems of scientific investigation were not speculative constructions, but the "molecular" work with the word, concept, instrument, and scientific fact which takes place daily in laboratory research.

Several decades before it was confirmed by the contemporary system approach, Vygotsky already realized it in his analysis of science following the Marxist principles according to which the system nature and historicism are inseparable. Vygotsky connected the idea of the system nature of science, which permits us to uncover the unique nature of its structure, with the principle of its social determination.

The theory of the crisis in science which Vygotsky developed is not only of historical interest. It is topical even today in the plane of the elaboration of a Marxist theory of scientific knowledge as a socially determined and dialectically contradictory process with its peaks and lows, its critical and revolutionary situations.

Nowadays the question of the nature of the crises and the ways of solving them also attracts the attention of methodologists of science in capitalistic countries. Well known, for example, is the treatment of crisis phenomena in science by the American historian of science Kuhn. According to Kuhn, a crisis flares up when enough anomalous facts have been gathered which are incompatible with the ruling paradigm. By eroding it they pave the way for a revolution in the science. In the end, the previous paradigm breaks down and the scientific community unites on the basis of a new paradigm.

Vygotsky analyzed the development of psychology and uncovered other determinants of the crisis phenomena. He rejected the positivistic idea of "pure" facts (behind them was the theory that sensory data are the source of knowledge and not objective reality reflected in sensory experience and interpreted by means of consciousness). After all, scientific investigation can only operate with facts which were first conceptually elaborated. Already by naming an object, we classify it and isolate by means of words-tools the essential features in a certain context from the multitude of others.

Insofar as the "elaborating force" comes from thinking immersed in the object existing independently of it, the conceptual elaboration is nothing other than a more adequate, richer (than on the preconceptual level) epistemic reconstruction of this object.

According to Vygotsky, the crisis is engendered not by the collision of new facts with the ruling structure of knowledge, but by practice which engenders and stimulates the needs for a transition from individual theoretical schemes to more general ones, which introduce these individual schemes into a context in which their concepts-facts display their deep categorical meaning. In the period in which the general schema has not yet developed, although the time for this has already come, individual conceptions strive to take its place, as we have seen. The external picture of the crisis which above all strikes the eye is characterized by this struggle.

According to Kuhn, the old and the new paradigm have nothing in common. The one cannot include the other. They exclude each other.

Vygotsky's approach allows us to understand the dialectics of the evolutionary (cumulative) and revolutionary moments in the development of positive knowledge. According to Vygotsky, in order to understand the nature and meaning of the crisis in science it is necessary to transcend the boundaries of the interrelations between theories and facts in the development of scientific knowledge. It is not the disagreement between the theoretical and the empirical as such which stimulates and guides this development. The forces which operate within the science itself and function on the level of applied investigations are directly connected with practice—whether educational, industrial, medical, etc. It is practice which requires the construction of a methodology without which the practical scientific influence upon the person cannot be effective.

Vygotsky's criticism of the schools which pretended to be strictly empirical and supposedly independent of any speculative, philosophical assumptions was not declarative. Vygotsky deeply and carefully analyzed the development of these schools and their historical fate and showed convincingly that behind these schools which seemed empirical and free of assumptions certain social-philosophical forces were operative. These led the mentioned schools from making empirical statements, via the establishment of relationships between psychology and other individual disciplines, to the pretense of being all-embracing world views.

The work which we examined stamped the development of Vygotsky's thought before he developed the concrete scientific program of his investigations which was based on the cultural-historical, or instrumental conception. According to this conception, the psychologist is called upon to study the instruments (tools, signs) by means of which the "natural" mental processes turn into cultural ones. The external operations "go inside," become internalized and form the structure which is usually seen as primordially given to the individual and inalienable from his subjective world. It is customary to begin Vygotsky's genealogy with these ideas. Tradition counts them as the first page of the chronicle of his school.

The appeal to the so-far unpublished work about the crisis in psychology radically changes this retrospective and sheds new light upon the enormous methodological work which preceded the special scientific achievements with which Vygotsky's name became associated later on. Vygotsky the philosopher, methodologist, and theorist of science spoke his word before the apparition of Vygotsky the investigator of the higher mental functions, the author of the cultural-historical conception in psychology and the leader of one of the most important Soviet psychological schools. Was this word heard? The manuscript lay unpublished. There is no doubt, however, that its ideas did not remain "unemployed." There are historical examples of ideas that were ahead of their time and became committed to paper, but did not become part of science. The unpublished notebooks of Leonardo da Vinci and Diderot's notes refuting Helvétius' tractate "De l'homme" [6] are interesting as documents of great prognostic value. But they did not influence the ideological atmosphere of their time. Such a conclusion is hardly justified with respect to Vygotsky's manuscript. The author was surrounded by comrades-in-arms and numerous students in his struggle for a new psychology. There is no doubt that in communicating with them he developed the theses which we know now. He taught them his appraisal and analysis of the nature of scientific knowledge and this became the hidden methodological meaning of the subsequent activity.

Vygotsky's endeavors form an example of reflections which belong to what we now call the philosophy of science and which prepare the way for the construction of a positive system. It is a unique "critique of psychological reason," but a critique based on an "x-ray" of its historical vicissitudes, on the analysis of real facts. It is perfectly understandable that here we speak of facts in a totally different sense than when we have the usual scientific empiricism in mind.

In this connection, theoretical conceptions, the rise and fall of scientific truths and whole systems, crisis situations, etc. function as the facts. Such "metafacts" require their own theories, which are different from concrete scientific ones. Vygotsky understood this well when he wrote about the scientific investigation of science itself. Without the risk of exaggeration, we may say that the philosophy of science reflection, the historically oriented analysis of the problems of logic and methodology of science, became the essential pre-requisite of all of Vygotsky's subsequent work.

He did not proceed from a priori considerations regarding the possibility of scientific psychology, but from an in-depth investigation of historically reliable forms of the realization of this possibility. For him, history was an enormous laboratory, a gigantic experimental structure where hypotheses, theories and schools are being tested.

Before he became involved in experimental psychology, he studied the experiences and operation of this laboratory. Before he made the child's thinking and speech his object, he examined the fruits of the mental activity of people in its highest manifestation, the construction of scientific knowledge. He was, as it were, guided by the well-known Marxist thesis that highly developed forms provide the key to the discovery of the secrets of the elementary ones. He says, for instance, that the word is the "embryo of science" and studies not this embryonic form, but the function of a scientific term-word which carries the highest semantic load. He discusses the question of "the circulation of concepts and facts with a conceptual return" [p. 252, this volume] with respect to the evolution of science. Subsequently the scales are changed. What has been clarified at the macro-level leads to the explanation of the development of concepts in children.

The systemic treatment of collective scientific reason was followed by the theory of the systemic structure of individual consciousness. The comparison of scientific concepts with tools of labor which become worn out by their use was followed by instrumental psychology with its postulate about tools—the means to master the world and to build an internal image of it.

All radical questions of human epistemic activity—the relation between the theoretical and empirical, the word and the concept, the methods of operating with the concept as a special tool due to which its objective content is changed, the real practical action and its intellectual correlate—were first examined on the material of developing scientific knowledge. Only after they had been verified in this special culture did Vygotsky turn from historical experience to psychological experience.

As we have seen, Vygotsky did not conceive of the dialectic of knowledge—the principles of historicism and reflection—in a speculative way, but on the special empirical historical basis which became the beachhead for the methodological offensive against the stronghold which the previous deterministic, natural scientific psychology could not seize.

Since Vygotsky's time, Soviet psychologists have done tremendous work in the theoretical reconstruction of psychological knowledge on the basis of the principles of Marxist-Leninist philosophy. But the need for a general psychology and its understanding, i.e., a special methodology for concrete psychological investigations, which Vygotsky defended, has not been adequately met. Being indivisibly connected with philosophy, this special methodology must have its own principles, tasks and structure and must be the integrative center of the whole variety of psychological knowledge and the main linchpin of its construction.

5

We conclude with some final words about the circumstances determining Vygotsky's achievements.

To everyone who had personal contact with him it was immediately obvious that this person was extremely talented. But no personal characteristics can in themselves explain the appearance of a new leader. For Vygotsky, the central idea in his analysis of science and any of its phenomena was that behind the back of the different figures of the historical process objective laws were operative "with the force of a steel spring." On their behest and not by the whims of the heros of the historical process the conceptions, schools and currents develop and perish, rise and replace each other.

It is expedient to extend this approach which Vygotsky realized in his construction of the dynamics of scientific ideas to the evaluation of his own creative work. It developed under the influence of new social conditions and a new world view. These factors motivated him to interpret the historical limitation of the psychological schools which were born in another social-ideological atmosphere and to give an impulse to the current which permitted researchers to find new answers to problems of the logic of the development of scientific knowledge.

Vygotsky [p. 342, this volume] wrote that

> Our science could not and cannot develop in the old society. We cannot master the truth about personality and personality itself as long as mankind has not mastered the truth about society and society itself.

As Vygotsky said, Marxism spoke the truth about society. The explanatory principles of this philosophy—historicism and system thinking, the unity of theory and practice and the determining role of the latter, the primacy of being with respect to the mental image of it—guided Vygotsky, together with the collective of the Soviet psychologists, to the reformation of the ultimate bases of the study of humans. And if Vygotsky, according to the historical evidence, became the avant-garde figure in this collective, the explanation for this must, presumably, be sought in the following.

First of all, in the high philosophical culture of his investigations. He perceived the correctness of Marxism in the context of the development of international philosophical thought. Descartes, Spinoza, Hegel, and Feuerbach, the whole great philosophical tradition is present between the lines (and sometimes in the text) of his investigations of the human mind from a dialectical materialistic position. Nothing was more foreign to him than the naive positivistic belief in "pure," a-theoretical science, in the capacity of experimental or mathematical procedures to master mental reality by themselves, without the creative work of theoretical thought.

At the same time, the flight of Vygotsky's thought had been impossible without the support of the tradition which developed in the concrete scientific study of mental phenomena. It was only he who perceived them organically, who absorbed the tremendous efforts of the previous searches.

Before the reader's eyes, Vygotsky's works pass through the broad panorama of the development of international psychology, its basic directions, the knowledge of which became the prerequisite of the new theoretical synthesis. But Vygotsky did not only intently and penetratingly look at the events in that part of the scientific front where the study of mental phenomena took place. He had the capacity to comprehend the processes and tendencies of development in the sciences related with psychology—the natural and the humanitarian ones. This capacity to think in an interdisciplinary way worked out beneficially for the special psychological analysis, as the objects of such an analysis by their very nature form part of the system of relations with the objects of biological and social knowledge.

Among the important features of Vygotsky's creative work we must also count his persistent attempt to connect the progress in psychological problems with the imperious demands of practice. Behind this was the methodological credo which he made his own: practice not only checks the results of the process of knowledge, it constitutes this process.

We cannot understand Vygotsky's psychological conception disregarding its evolution.

In the literature on Vygotsky one often encounters an inadequate assessment of his theoretical positions. The source of this inadequacy is hidden, particularly, in the fact that the evolution in Vygotsky's position concerning the nature of the mental is ignored and that ideas from different periods of his creative career are heaped together.

As is well known, in the examination of the creative work of a scholar, Marxist methodology requires us to follow a method for the historical reconstruction of his influence in the basic stock of scientific knowledge which does not admit of either an apologetic or a nihilistic approach. Unfortunately, the traces of such approaches can be seen in the whole course of the history of Soviet psychology and nowadays manifest themselves in the evaluations of some contemporary authors. In these cases the appeal to the genuine Vygotsky is replaced by arbitrary interpretations which inevitably displace the historical perspective.

Vygotsky's creative work must be examined and assessed in the social-cultural context in which it was born. His theory took shape in the postrevolutionary years, in the era of the breaking of the old world, of the radical reform of the ideas about human personality and the perspectives for societal development. In this atmosphere, Vygotsky's psychological views, just like those of other eminent Soviet psychologists, were oriented toward a dialectical-materialistic methodology for scientific knowledge. The best traditions of our native psychological thought were developed on a new methodological basis through the prism of this methodology: the natural scientific tradition which goes back to Sechenov and the cultural-historical tradition which goes back to Potebnya.

Vygotsky did not create some finished psychological system. In his intensive search he constantly generated new ideas. He gave up his ideas without regret, proposed other ones, and at times abruptly changed the course of his thinking. He was, perhaps, the most agitated figure in our psychology. And the fruitfulness of this agitation we feel until this very day.

Much of what he gained through suffering has lost its topicality. But much preserved its theoretical potential as before. Submerging in the past and reconstructing the problems which captured Vygotsky, the sharp polemics around these problems, the complex upheaval of the struggle for a new psychology, we vividly feel the connection with those times, the dependence of our present-day research upon what was created in that era.

NOTES TO THE ENGLISH EDITION

On Vygotsky's Creative Development

[1] This introduction was written in the late 1970s. The selection and editing of Vygotsky's *Collected Works*—which in actual fact cover only about half of his writings—took many years and much political maneuvering. Leont'ev's relationship with Vygotsky was problematic in the final years of the latter's life, and the assessment of Vygotsky's work by Leont'ev should be seen against the background of Leont'ev's sharp criticisms of Vygotsky's writings in the 1930s. It was only in the late 1950s when the ban on Vygotsky's writings became gradually lifted that Leont'ev became involved in the promotion of Vygotsky's writings and that the myth about the troika consisting of Vygotsky, Leont'ev, and Luria developed. Leont'ev became so successful in describing himself as the legitimate heir and co-developer of Vygotsky's ideas that Luria, who in actual fact cooperated with Vygotsky on a much more intimate basis, came to be seen as a theoretically second-rate figure.

[2] These figures are very approximate and imply both an over- and an underestimation. An overestimation because Vygotsky used to publish the same text with slight alterations over and over again. An underestimation because Vygotsky's literary reviews have not been taken into account.

[3] It is funny that someone would make this remark about Vygotsky's writings. If ever a psychologist was sloppy in referring to his sources it was Vygotsky.

[4] It is interesting to note that Leont'ev in his (incomplete) overview of the Institute's research activities mentions that several people were using psychoanalytic· ideas, but fails to mention that Luria was one of the most prominent members of the psychoanalytic movement in Russia.

[5] One should realize that Leont'ev's knowledge of Vygotsky's youth and the first part of his intellectual development is a reconstruction based on the scarce knowledge available at the time. The reader does well to compare his account with the more direct accounts provided by Dobkin (in Levitin, 1990) and Vygotsky's daughter G. L. Vygodskaya (forthcoming).

[6] Some years ago approximately 50 of Vygotsky's literary reviews, published in a Gomel newspaper in the late 1910s, were unearthed by Tamara Lifanova. They still await publication.

[7] But not in the English translation of this book, which is based upon some abridged Russian edition. See Vygotsky (1971).

[8] This is a somewhat simplified account of the complex changes that took place in Vygotsky's views over the years. The contemporary ideological gate-keepers certainly sensed some non-materialistic views in his dissertation and it was never published during his lifetime.

[9] This is incorrect. Vygotsky did try to publish his book. See Van der Veer and Valsiner (1991).

[10] It is essential to note that already in 1920 Blonsky in his book *The Reform of Science* voiced the idea of the importance of labor activity for the analysis of the psychology of the person. Somewhat later than Vygotsky, Basov (1927) in his *General Foundations of Pedology* stated deep ideas about the meaning of external and labor activity for psychology. However, Vygotsky's and Basov's concrete analyses of activity were different. It is important to remark that both tied the meaning of the investigations of practical, labor activity of humans directly to the task of building a Marxist psychology. Among the foreign psychologists it was the great French scholar Janet who in the 1920s developed interesting ideas about the meaning of work and labor activity for psychology. [Original footnote]

[11] Vygotsky more than once wrote about two methods of analysis—into elements (atomistic analysis) and into units. The analysis into elements breaks down a whole into its simplest component parts which, however, have lost the properties of the whole (e.g., breaking down water into hydrogen and oxygen atoms). The analysis into units breaks down a whole into the smallest possible component parts which still retain the properties of the whole (e.g., the breaking down of water into molecules). In psychology Vygotsky counted the breaking down of mental processes into reflexes as well as the bipartite system of the behaviorists (S—R) as analysis into elements. [Original footnote]

[12] We must understand that such a use of the word "stimulus" was very unusual. It suffices to compare it with the way the behaviorists, reflexologists, etc. dealt with the stimulus. Such terminological "sloppiness" by Vygotsky formed one of the difficulties of the proper understanding of his work, and it can be explained first and foremost by the unfinished state of his conception. He was in a great hurry—in a hurry to realize his ideas, to complete, albeit in rough outlines, his theory. In this process terminological precision was a matter of secondary importance. [Original footnote]

[13] A more detailed description of Vygotsky's (vague) distinctions can be found in Chapter 9 of Van der Veer and Valsiner (1991).

[14] In this discussion of Goethe's words, Vygotsky was actually following Gutzmann (1922). See Van der Veer & Valsiner (1994).

[15] Whether Piaget already read Vygotsky's criticism of his work in the 1930s is still unclear. A copy of the combined Russian edition of two of his books, which contained Vygotsky's lengthy critical discussion of his thinking, has been found in his library and he certainly was capable of finding adequate translators.

[16] An annotated translation of Sakharov's paper can be found in Van der Veer and Valsiner (1994).

[17] "Family indication" is used as in Wittgenstein's "family concept." Such concepts were seen by Vygotsky as immature forms of real (academic or scientific) concepts. Modern research has shown that most concepts are of the natural or family type.

[18] Leont'ev is being somewhat unfair to "traditional" psychology. The concept and term "pseudoconcept" were not original with Vygotsky and can already be found in Groos (1921), but more important were Werner's (1925) elaborate discussions of the various stages in concept formation. See also Chapter 11 of Van der Veer and Valsiner (1991).

[19] It is interesting that Jaensch's research is just mentioned without indicating why it would be relevant in this context. The reason for this might be Jaensch's nasty role under the Nazi regime. See Van der Veer and Valsiner (1994) for more information.

[20] Vygotsky uses the term "obuchenie," which is often best translated as "teaching/learning."

[21] References are to Volume 1 of this edition.

[22] See Volume 1 of this edition.

[23] At approximately the same time, Bernstein arrived at a similar concept following a different route. This was the concept of the dynamic motor systems (one and the same movement can be taken care of by various mutually interchangeable physiological organizations). [Original footnote]

[24] This is a rather sinister remark to make. Talankin and (especially) Razmyslov were instruments in the hands of the Communist Party who viciously and unfairly attacked both Vygotsky's ideas and his person. See Chapter 16 of Van der Veer and Valsiner (1991).

[25] See Volume 1 of this edition.

[26] This and other remarks should be seen against the background of Leont'ev's attempts to present his own "activity theory" as the legitimate heir and logical continuation of Vygotsky's ideas.

PART I: PROBLEMS OF THE THEORY AND METHODS OF PSYCHOLOGY

Chapter 1

[1] This paper is based on a talk presented at the combined session of the psychological and reflexological sections of the 2nd All-Russian Congress on Psychoneurology in Leningrad, January 6, 1924. [Original footnote]

[2] Correlative activity (*sootnositel'naja dejatel'nost'*). A term introduced by Bekhterev to designate any activities bound up with the establishment of the relation of an organism to its environment and which replaced such "subjective" terms as "mental" or "neuro-psychical" functions. See Bekhterev's explanation of the term on p. 17 of Bekhterev (1932).

[3] The fourth edition was translated into English as Bekhterev (1932). The page numbers refer to this edition.

[4] In the report about the conference, published in the volume "Recent developments in reflexology," Giz, 1925, in the commentary to my talk it is said with respect to this thought that the author "again attempted to erase the border between the reflexological and psychological approach and even made some remarks concerning reflexology that had fallen into intrinsic contradictions," p. 359). Instead of refuting this thought, the reviewer refers to the fact that "the speaker is a psychologist, who, apart from that, also attempts to assimilate the reflexological approach. The results speak for themselves." A very eloquent passing over in silence! Although an accurate phrasing of my error would have been more appropriate and more needed. [Original footnote]

[5] See pp. 3-19 of Burkhardt (1976). In contrast to Vygotsky, James did not refer to the reflex concept in his analysis.

[6] Bekhterev was inclined to equate consciousness with the subjective states that accompany the inculcation of an association reflex. It followed that wherever the formation of association reflexes proved possible (e.g., in protozoa) one had to accept the existence of subjective processes. He also said that the irritability of tissue in general is associated with subjective processes, which led to the same result,

that is, the hypothesis that unicellar organisms manifest a subjective aspect (cf. pp. 70-75 of Bekhterev, 1932).

[7] K. Koffka (1924). "Introspection and the method of psychology," *The British Journal of Psychology*, *15*, [149-161]. [Original footnote]

[8] Cf. V. Ivanovsky, "Methodological introduction to science and philosophy," 1923, pp. 199-200. The author points out that some psychologists objected to the introduction of the unconscious in psychology on the grounds that it cannot be directly observed. The psychologist-objectivist studies the phenomena of consciousness as indirectly as the previous psychologists studied the unconscious, by its traces, its manifestations, influences, etc. [Original footnote]

Chapter 2

[1] The Psycho-Neurological Institute.

[2] Artemov, Dobrynin, Luria, and Vygotsky all worked at the Institute of Experimental Psychology of Moscow University headed by K. N. Kornilov.

[3] Judging by the 1912 edition of the book, the section on religious feelings was short, but not uninteresting. Lazursky defined a religious feeling as "an emotion, connected with a belief in the existence of a certain value, and also in the existence of a relation between this value and man" (Lazursky, 1912; p. 210). He distinguished several types of believers and historical stages in religion, and noticed the strong need for concrete images of the deity in believers. He claimed that this need was also at the basis of the popularity of materialist doctrines, "despite the numerous epistemological and other arguments that may be raised against them" (ibid., pp. 211-212). Lazursky believed that scientific knowledge had not weakened, but rather strengthened religious beliefs by purifying them from superstition. He saw no fundamental distinction between religious beliefs and other world views, claiming that no world view (materialism, atheism) can be logically proved and all rest to some degree on belief. Of course, by 1925 this was not what the authorities wanted professors to teach at the universities.

[4] A dubious metaphor in view of the fact that vaccination works by injecting (dead) bacteria into a sound body.

[5] Potassium chloride. See also Chapter 2 of Vygotsky, L. S. (1926d).

[6] See his "The methods of reflexological and psychological investigation" (p. 46) and "Consciousness as a problem for the psychology of behavior" (p. 65).

Chapter 3

[1] The fourth edition was translated into English as Bekhterev (1932). Added page numbers refer to this edition.

[2] Blonsky, P. P. (1921). *Outline of a Scientific Psychology*. [Moscow: GIZ; Chapter 1, p. 9]. [Original footnote]

[3] Academician I. P. Pavlov (1923), *Twenty Years of Experience with the Objective Study of Higher Nervous Activity of Animals* (Chapter 19 and others) [Original footnote. In the following, page numbers refer to the translated enlarged edition of this book, that is, Pavlov (1928/1963)].

[4] Ukhtomsky, A. A. (1923). "The dominant as the working principle of the nervous centers." *Russkyj Fiziologicheskyj Zhurnal*, *6*. [Original footnote]

[5] Bekhterev, V. M. (1923). *General Foundations of the Reflexology of Man*. [Moscow: Gosudarstvennoe Izdatel'stvo]; Chapter 3. [Original footnote]

[6] This criticism was not original and was considered unfair by Bekhterev (1932, p. 87). In the fourth edition of his book he changed the sentence Vygotsky refers to into "Do not forget that reflexology, generally speaking, does not exclude any hypothesis of consciousness and of the mind" and added the following footnote: "In the second edition, as a result of such inattention as may occur in any work, the words "of the soul" were used instead of "of the mind." This must be noted here, for some subjectivist psychologists, for instance, Basov (and, I regret to say, Kornilov also) have made appropriate use of the slip, and imagined that, by utilizing isolated passages from a work saturated with mechanistic views, they could minimize the importance of reflexology in the study of human personality and so enhance their own position. Futile defense!"

[7] Ibid.; Chapter 7 [1932, p. 133] and others. Cf. also his *Mind and Life*. [Original footnote]

[8] Ibid.; Chapter 46; [1932, p. 380]. [Original footnote]

[9] Here and in several of the following pages Vygotsky (often literally) borrows from his paper "The methods of reflexological and psychological investigation."

[10] Ibid.; Chapter 4. [Original footnote]

[11] Vygotsky is criticizing a metaphor which Bukharin, the Party's chief ideologist in the 1920s, used to ridicule the individualist approach in psychology. Bukharin's claim was that individuals are no more than "sausage skins stuffed with the influences of the environment." See Yoravsky (1989, pp. 213-215/260) for details.

[12] Cf. the article by Ukhtomsky, A. A., Vinogradov, M. I., & Kaplan, I. I. (1923). *Russkyj Fiziologicheskyj Zhurnal*, 6. [Original footnote]

[13] Sherrington, C. S. (1906). *The Integrative Action of the Nervous System*. [New York: Charles Scribner's Sons]. [Original footnote]

[14] Kannitfershtan. Distorted Dutch. "Kan niet verstaan," i.e., "Cannot hear."

[15] V. M. Bekhterev. *General Foundations of the Reflexology of Man*; Chapters 50 and 51. [Original footnote]

[16] Vagner, V. A. (1923). *Biopsychology and Related Sciences*. Petrograd; Chapter 4. [Original footnote]

[17] The problem of the conservation of energy was widely discussed in this connection. Assuming that the principle of the conservation of energy holds for the phenomenon of consciousness, one should explain its production and expenditure of energy. See p. 35 of Dennett (1991) for a recent statement of the claim that the principle of the conservation of energy is violated by dualism.

[18] This reasoning and the concept of doubled experience introduced below can also be found in Vygotsky (1926d).

[19] K. Marx. *Das Kapital*. Vol. I; Part 3; Chapter 5. [Original footnote]

[20] Academician Pavlov (1928/1963). *Twenty Years of Experience*. [Original footnote]

[21] See p. 259 of Pavlov (1928/1963).

[22] Academician Pavlov (1928/1963). *Twenty Years of Experience*; Chapter XXV [p. 257]. [Original footnote]

[23] Sherrington, C. S. (1912). "The correlation of spinal-brain reflexes and the principle of the common path." Russian translation in the volume *Successes of Biology*. Odessa, 1912. [Original footnote]

[Several versions of this paper exist. Cf. Sherrington (1904) and lecture IV of Sherrington (1906). In the following, page numbers refer to one of these two publications]

[24] The expression is Hering's. [Original footnote]

[25] C. S. Sherrington. "The correlation of spinal-brain reflexes." [Original footnote]

[26] C. S. Sherrington. "The correlation of spinal-brain reflexes." [Original footnote]

[27] Academician Pavlov (1928/1963). *Twenty Years of Experience*; [p. 123]. [Original footnote]

[28] C. S. Sherrington. "The correlation of spinal-brain reflexes." [Original footnote]

[29] Academician I. P. Pavlov (1928/1963). *Twenty Years of Experience*; Chapter 25. [Original footnote]

[30] Dr. T. Zelenyj (1923), "On rhythmic muscle movements," *Russkyj Fiziologicheskyj Zhurnal*, 6. In Pavlov's school the same term is also used to indicate several other mechanisms for the combination of reflexes into a chain. Cf. D. S. Fursikov (1922), "On conditional chain reflexes," *Russkyj Fiziologicheskyj Zhurnal*, 4. [Original footnote]

[31] Cf., for example, Lange, N. N. (1914), "Psychology," *Itogi Nauki*, 8. (Publisher Mir). [Original footnote]

In Varshava and Vygotsky (1931, p. 94) it is explained that a circular reaction consists of 6 (rather than 3) parts: (1) an external stimulus; (2) central processing; (3) the reaction; (4) a kinaesthetic (proprioceptive) stimulus that serves to perceive the organism's own reaction; (5) the processing of this stimulus: (6) repetition (strengthened or weakened) of the original reaction.

[32] C. S. Sherrington, "The correlation of spinal-brain reflexes." [Original footnote]

[33] Academician I. P. Pavlov (1928/1963). *Twenty Years of Experience;* Chapter 23 [p. 247]. [Original footnote]

[34] V. M. Bekhterev, *Foundations of the General Reflexology of Man*; Chapter 2. [Original footnote]

[35] Sechenov's definition. [Original footnote]

[36] Prof. V. Protopopov (1923). "The methods of the reflexological investigation of man." *Zhurnal Psikhologii, Nevrologii, i Psikhiatrii*, 3; [p. 22]. [Original footnote]

[37] James, W. (1911). *Psychology*. [St. Petersburg]. Transl. by Lapshin; Chapter XXIV [Original footnote] [Translation of *Psychology: Briefer Course*. See Burkhardt, 1984].

[38] Külpe, O. (1922) Über die Bedeutung der modernen Denkpsychologie]. In O. Külpe, *Vorlesungen über Psychologie*. Russian transl. in *New Ideas in Philosophy*, 16. [Original footnote]

[39] M. B. Krol' (1922). "Thinking and speech." *Trudy Belorusskogo Gosudarstvennogo Universiteta*, 1. [Original footnote]

[40] Cf. the analysis of the voluntary act by Münsterberg, H., (1909), *Psychology and the Teacher* and Ebbinghaus, G., (1902), *Grundzüge der Psychologie*. Vol. II.; Chapter IV. [Original footnote]

[41] Zalkind, A. (1924). *Sketches of the Culture of a Revolutionary Time*. [Original footnote]

[42] Vvedensky, A. (1917). *Psychology Without Any Metaphysics* [p. 71 ff.]; *On the Boundaries and Indications of Being Animated* (1892). [Original footnote]

[43] Theories from analogy, i.e., theories which attribute to other persons feelings, thoughts, etc. which are similar or analogous to those that we experience ourselves. They were critically analyzed in Lipps' book to which Vygotsky refers but also, for instance, in Bekhterev's (1932, pp. 47-53) book earlier referred to and in Binswanger (1922). Lipps' own theory was a theory of *Einfühlung*.

[44] Lipps, Th. (1907). *Das Wissen von fremden Ichen.* Cf. also Lapshin, I. I. (1910). *The Problem of the Other Person's "Ego" in the Newest Philosophy.* [Original footnote]

[45] Cf. Natorp, P. (1899/1974), *Sozialpädagogik.* [p. 95]: "There is no understanding of the self without the understanding of others as its basis." He also says: "Even in solitude, when we silently think to ourselves, we constantly use the words of language and, consequently, retain at least the fiction of communication." Consciousness, in our opinion, indeed is "the fiction of communication." [Original footnote]

[46] Freud, S. (1923/1973), *The Ego and the Id*; Chapter 2, [p. 25]. [Original footnote]

[47] W. Jerusalem (*Laura Bridgman*, V, pp. 54-55), analyzing the processes of thought and consciousness in the deaf-mute Laura Bridgman, remarks: "Für sie gehörte also das Denken zu den Sinnesorganen, zunächst natürlich, weil es Kenntnisse vermittelt, dan aber auch, weil sie die Arbeit des Denkens auch sinnlich empfand." Laura herself considered that she had four sense-organs: "Denken und Nase und Mund und Finger (think and nose and mouth and fingers" (Lamson, p 56 ff.). Here it is perfectly obvious that thinking is placed in one series with the work of analyzers [Original footnote; cf. Jerusalem, 1890; the English words are from one of Jerusalem's main sources: *Life and Education of Laura Dewey Bridgman, the Deaf and Dumb Girl*, by Mayr Swift-Lamson, Boston, 1878.]

[48] Epilogue. [See p. 400 of Burkhardt, 1984] [Original footnote]

[49] "Does consciousness exist?" Russian translation in *Novye Idei v Filosofii*, 1913, 4. [See p. 19 of Burkhardt, 1976] [Original footnote]

[50] This article was already in proofs when I came across several works written by psychologists-behaviorists concerning this problem. The problem of consciousness is stated and solved by these authors in a way that comes close to the thoughts developed here, [that is,] as the problem of *the relation between reactions.* Cf. the "verbalized behavior" in Watson, J. B. (1924), "The unverbalized in human behavior." *Psychological Review*, [31, 273-280]; and also Lashley, K. S. (1923), "The behavioristic interpretation of consciousness." *Psychological Review*, [30, 237-272; 329-353]. [Original footnote]

Chapter 4

[1] "Everything is quiet at the Shipka." Words of Radetzky, hero of the war of the Russians and Bulgarians with Turkey, who held out (from August 21 to August 26 in 1887) against the ferocious attacks of superior numbers of Turks headed by Soliman and reported daily that "everything was quiet at the Shipka." The battle was fought at the Shipka Pass in the Balkan Mountains (Stara Planina) in Bulgaria. See p. 90 of Vitte (1991). Radetzky also excelled in the army of what is now called Austria and became extremely popular in this country. In fact, Johann Strauss Sr. made him the subject of his Radetzky march.

[2] Meinong, A. (1853-1920). Austrian philosopher. Author of works on the psychology of perception, thinking and imagination.

[3] *After Empiricism.* Leningrad, 1925. [Original footnote] I. V. Evergetov was the director of the Institute of Pedology in Leningrad. Published, among other things, a reader with contributions by Bekhterev, Basov, and others. See Evergetov (ed.) (1924). We haven't been able to locate the paper referred to.

[4] Prof. Evergetov was completely right when he called his overview "After empiricism." [Original footnote]

[5] "What is internal is external as well" is the translation of Goethe's words "Denn was innen, das ist aussen" quoted in Köhler (1920) and Köhler (1933).

Chapter 5

[1] Richard Thurnwald was the author of a book on ethnographic psychology which exerted a great influence on Vygotsky. See Thurnwald (1922).

[2] The so-called method of double stimulation consisted of introducing two series of stimuli into the situation. One series, the stimulus-means, could be used by the subject to aid performance with the other series, the stimulus-objects. For example, if the goal was to memorize a series of pictures (stimulus-objects), then the subject might be provided with a series of words (stimulus-means) which could be associated with the pictures to facilitate performance. For an extensive discussion of the concept of double stimulation, see Valsiner (1988) and Van der Veer & Valsiner (1991).

[3] Vygotsky is paraphrasing Marx's famous passage on the same page.

[4] Refers to Dewey's ideas on the logic of empirical research as first presented in Dewey (1910) and further elaborated in Dewey (1938).

[5] Modern scholarship has a more favorable opinion of Binet's theorizing. The view of mental giftedness as a natural, immutable, inherited property of the child was not advanced by Binet, but by American scholars such as Goddard, Terman, and Yerkes, who basically perverted Binet's views. See Gould (1981).

[6] In the case of memory, "natural memory" would be the capacity to memorize and retain an image not making use of any mnemotechnical device (including language). This capacity for "natural memory" was presumably shared by animal and man and supposedly did not improve with age. Indeed, like many of his contemporaries Vygotsky suggested that it deteriorated with age, referring to cases of eidetic memory which are much more prevalent in children than in adults. "Artificial memory" referred to memory based on culturally variable mnemotechnical systems (including language) and was supposed to be specifically human. For a critical discussion of this view, see Van der Veer & Valsiner (1991).

[7] Examples of Vygotsky's method of double stimulation applied to various tasks can be found in Cole (1978), Van der Veer & Valsiner (1991; 1994), and Van der Veer, Van IJzendoorn, & Valsiner (1994).

Chapter 6

[1] Judging by the content and style, this talk was addressed to a group of researchers and students who regularly gathered with Vygotsky to discuss research matters and, in particular, Vygotsky's own cultural-historical investigations carried out at the Academy for Communist Education.

[2] "turn the problem into a postulate." Refers to Goethe's words "Die grösste Kunst im Lehr- und Weltleben besteht darin, das Problem in ein Postulat zu verwandeln, damit kommt man durch" in a letter dated August 9, 1828 to Carl Friedrich Zelter. See p. 296 of Mandelkow (1967).

[3] The word "division" ("razdelenie") is not in the manuscript. It has "razmerenie" ("measurement"), which does not make sense in the given context.

[4] Judging by a note of the editors in the sixth volume of the Russian edition, this description probably refers to the work of the American child psychologist Samuel Kohs.

[5] "Speech as a means to understand oneself." The reference is to Potebnya (1913/1993), who claimed that "the word is as much a means to understand the other as a means to understand oneself" (p. 97) and "language is the means to understand oneself" (p. 102).

[6] Piaget (1923) referred to Janet and Rignano, who had "shown that all reflexion is the outcome of an internal debate in which a conclusion is reached, just as though the individual reproduced towards himself an attitude which he had previously adopted towards others. Our research confirms this view." For the origin of this idea in the work of Royce, Baldwin, Mead, and Janet, see Valsiner and Van der Veer (1988).

[7] "Man orders and obeys himself." The example is Janet's. See Van der Veer and Valsiner (1988).

[8] N. G. Morozova was one of the small group of students devoted to Vygotsky's cause. She later became a defectologist. See Van der Veer and Valsiner (1991).

[9] "Biological evolution was finished before historical development began." Elsewhere Vygotsky claimed that these periods overlapped. See Van der Veer and Valsiner (1991).

[10] We have been unable to establish the identity of this critic of Freud.

[11] "Collective representations." The reference is to Durkheim and his school. See Chapter 9 of Van der Veer and Valsiner (1991).

[12] Thus in the shorthand report. [Note by the Russian editors]

[13] The psychologist was Karl Bühler. See pp. 264-265 of Bühler (1918).

[14] "If this animal has long ears, it is either a donkey or a mule. If it has a shaggy tail, it is either a mule or a horse. Well, it has long ears and a shaggy tail. What kind of animal is it?." See p. 68 of Piaget (1924).

[15] In this connection Piaget spoke of the "juxtaposition" of various elements and the child's "synthetic incapacity." See Chapter 4 of Piaget (1924).

[16] For Vygotsky, thinking in "complexes" was one of three stages which preceded real conceptual thinking. It signified a type of elementary generalization in which groups of objects are taken together on the basis of superficial characteristics and/or on the basis of shifting criteria. See Chapter 11 of Van der Veer & Valsiner (1991) and Chapters 6 and 9 of Van der Veer & Valsiner (1994).

[17] The term "dementia praecox" literally means "premature madness" and was introduced by Kraepelin to indicate what we now call (juvenile) schizophrenia. The term was rejected by Bleuler who introduced the term "schizophrenia." See Bleuler (1911).

[18] The "station" forms part of a metaphor which Vygotsky does not fully develop here. He used to say that the process of the development of the ability to think in concepts and its loss are as similar as two trains which stand at the same station but part in different directions.

[19] This suggests that Vygotsky was thinking of Goldstein and Gelb (1920), but in this book there is no such text. In reality, the reference is to p. 158 and p. 177 of Gelb and Goldstein (1925).

[20] The schema that Vygotsky used to explain his (and Janet's) thinking is not given in the Russian text.

[21] We have been unable to establish the identity of this Russian expert on Parkinson's disease. Possibly it was the same I. D. Sapir mentioned before.

[22] In so-called professiographic analyses of labor processes it was tried to make a "professiogram" which was a kind of formalized description of a certain

profession based on a combination of different parameters, mostly reflecting motor characteristics.

Chapter 7

[1] Throughout his paper Vygotsky uses both subconscious (*podsoznatel'noe*) and unconscious (*bessoznatel'noe*). Although he does not seem to distinguish these concepts in the present context we have opted for a literal translation.

[2] "refined materialism." See p. 45 of Dilthey (1894/1977).

[3] Here and in the following Vygotsky refers to Spranger's (1925) dictum *"psychologica psychologice."* The idea was that psychological phenomena should be explained by psychological concepts and methods.

[4] Elsewhere Vygotsky makes no rigorous or consistent distinction between the terms "mental" and "psychological."

[5] Thus in the text. It is unclear what Vygotsky or the Russian editors omitted.

[6] Here Vygotsky is actually quoting from p. 131 of Bernard Hart's chapter in Münsterberg *et al.* (1910). See also note 31 to Chapter 15.

[7] "In the first case." What is meant is "in the second case."

Chapter 8

[1] The psychology of behavior, i.e., American behaviorism.

[2] Here and in the following citations page numbers refer to Bergson (1896/1939). Vygotsky probably used the Russian edition published in St. Petersburg in 1911.

[3] Possibly Möbius, F. J. (1853-1907), German neurologist and psychiatrist, author of so-called "pathographies" on Goethe, Schopenhauer, Nietzsche, Schumann, and Fechner in which he analyzed the allegedly pathological traits of their personality.

[4] *Psychologica psychologice."* See note 3 to Chapter 7.

Chapter 9

[1] Vygotsky quotes Lipps' statement several times in this volume. The source is p. 146 of Lipps (1897).

[2] Husserl's and Dilthey's "geometrical" psychologies are discussed in Chapters 7 and 15.

[3] William James' letter to Stumpf is not in the two-volume edition of his correspondence edited by his son Henry (see James, 1920), nor can it be found in Stumpf's (1928) booklet about James.

[4] See the Bible, Ecclesiastes, book 3, verse 5.

[5] The knot. Refers to the mnemonic device of tying knots in strings to remember something. Vygotsky argued that such material devices ontogenetically precede the "immaterial," verbal strategies used by adults.

[6] For a discussion of Vagner's conception of mixed and pure lines, see Vagner (1923) and Valsiner (1988). The page numbers apparently refer to Vagner's book.

[7] The swallow refers to pp. 64-66 of Koffka (1925a), where it is said that swallows build their nests as closed integral wholes in accordance with the structure of the environment. See Chapter 13.

[8] In Selz (1922), the author gives a lengthy discussion (pp. 610-688) of Köhler's experiments from the viewpoint of his own theory.

[9] See Edinger (1911).

[10] Here the word 'objective' is used as explained in note 17 to Chapter 14.

[11] Buytendijk, F. J. J. (1887-1974). Dutch psychologist. See Buytendijk (1929; 1930).

[12] James' schema can be found in his *Psychology: Briefer Course*. The terms were coined by Romanes ("recept"), Lloyd Morgan ("isolate," "construct"), and James ("influent") to designate the abstract classifications that animals are capable of and that are not equivalent to human concepts. See p. 318 of Burkhardt (1984).

[13] See Paulhan (1928).

[14] See Stern (1927) and Stern & Stern (1928/1981).

[15] Ingenieros, José (1877-1925). Professor of psychology at the University of Buenos Aires and author of seventeen books, some of which were translated into French. Vygotsky probably had access to his *Psicología Genética* (in later editions called *Principios de Psicología Biológica* and *Principios de Psicología* and first published in 1911), which appeared in French translation (Ingenieros, 1914). For information about Ingenieros, see Bagú (1963).

[16] See the 8th chapter of Dostoyevsky's "Diary of a Writer (1873). By now it will have become clear to those acquainted with Vygotsky's work that the theme of his talk largely overlaps with the material presented in the last chapter of his "Thinking and Speech" (see the first volume of this series). Many unclear points will be clarified by reading this chapter.

[17] See for this argument p. 266 of Van der Veer & Valsiner (1991).

[18] See pp. 280-281 of "Thinking and Speech" in Volume 1 of this series. Vygotsky probably was inspired by an early draft of Stanislavsky's notes (written during 1916 to 1920) on Griboedov's play "Woe from Wit" which were posthumously published in Stanislavsky (1981). A petitioner was delegated by a community—usually a village—to ask the central authorities for some favor.

[19] Cf. "We have compared thought to a hovering cloud that gushes a shower of words." See p. 282 of Volume 1 of this edition.

[20] Refers to Head and Hughlings Jackson. See Head (1915; 1926).

[21] Implicit reference to Potebnya (1913/1993), who extensively argued that "language is a means not to express a ready-made thought, but to create it" (p. 120).

[22] See Mill (1843/1904).

[23] See note 17 to Chapter 14.

[24] "The dream of the Kaffir" refers to Lévy-Bruhl's example given in Chapter 6. Masha Bolkonskaya is a figure from Tolstoy's novel "War and Peace."

[25] "For me this knowledge is enough" ("*S menya dovol'no sego soznaniya*"). Words from Pushkin's poem '*Skupoj rycar*' ("The covetous knight") spoken by the baron, who, looking at his gold, considers that he might be a mighty man using it, but concludes that for him "this knowledge is enough." See p. 329 of Pushkin (1984).

[26] See p. 246 of Lenin's *Complete Works*.

Chapter 10

[1] Vygotsky was well acquainted with the work of Goldstein and Head to which he often referred (see the previous chapters). Pötzl was the author of various books on aphasia, apraxia, and related topics. The reference is to Pötzl (1928).

[2] These "laws" were subsequently elaborated by Luria in his neuropsychological work. See Chapter 2 of Luria (1973) for a discussion and some examples.

[3] See note 6 to Chapter 9.

PART II: DEVELOPMENTAL PATHS OF PSYCHOLOGICAL KNOWLEDGE

Chapter 11

[1] This was the translation of Thorndike (1906).

[2] "Cadet." The party of the Cadets (abbreviation of Constitutional Democrats) opposed the October revolution and was eventually outlawed.

[3] This paragraph makes extensive use of Chapter 2 of Vygotsky (1926d).

[4] This paragraph is heavily dependent on Chapters 4 and 5 of Vygotsky (1926d).

[5] This passage is inspired by Marx's analysis in *Das Kapital*. See, for example, p. 455 of Marx (1890/1981a) and Chapter 8 of Van der Veer & Valsiner (1994).

[6] This seems to be some variant of Watson's (1924/1970, p. 104) famous words "Give me a dozen healthy infants, well-formed, and my own specified world to bring them up in, etc.."

Chapter 12

[1] Translation of the fourth and fifth enlarged editions of Bühler (1929). This work was partly based on Bühler's (1918) great *Die geistige Entwicklung des Kindes*, but formed an authoritative book in its own right due to the different organization of the material and the many new insights.

[2] Refers to Bühler (1918).

[3] See K. Bühler (1918, pp. 217-224; 1929, pp. 93-101) and Ch. Bühler (1918). According to the Bühlers, the fairy-tale age began at approximately four years of age and lasted until early adolescence (depending on the social class to which the child belonged), when the Robinson age began. In the latter period children lose interest in fairy tales and become fascinated by more realistic adventure stories in which the protagonists—like Robinson Crusoe—have to think critically to solve real-life problems. The Bühlers were convinced that fairy tales reflect the child's mind in a given age period since over the centuries fairy tales have been gradually adjusted to children's tastes. The fairy tale of Struwwelpeter is a collection of moralistic stories of a German boy who doesn't behave properly and is duly punished. The stories are so close to reality that even very young children can understand them.

[4] Bühler (1929, pp. 10-11) leaves the question of the presence of primitive minds or mind-like factors in animals entirely open. He states that Driesch may well be right, but that we have no reliable evidence.

[5] The three levels of psychological development were instinct, training or dressure (essentially learning through operant conditioning), and intellect.

[6] The last three sentences Vygotsky quotes verbatim.

[7] Chromatin is the protoplasmic substance in the nucleus of the cell that contains the genes.

[8] Bühler refers to Peters (1915) and says that Peters took great pains to avoid the mistake of attributing environmental influences to heredity. Using statistical procedures, Peters came to the curious conclusion that children of one very bright and one very dull parent do not show average intelligence, but tend to have the same intelligence as one of the parents. This leads Bühler to conclude that apparently the hereditary influence of one of the parents wins over the other's. He also surmises that intelligence is no simple quality, that is, is possibly determined by several genes. The whole discussion of his own and Peters' investigation followed a concise exposition of Mendel's law and was intended to show their applicability in humans. It may be doubted whether Vygotsky read Peters' original article.

Chapter 13

[1] The preface was published in the Russian translation of Köhler (1921b), which was translated into English as "The mentality of the great apes." It formed part of a series of publications on Gestalt psychology which were virtually identical or at least showed considerable overlap. These included Vygotsky (1929a; 1929b; 1930a; 1930b/1960; and the first chapter of Vygotsky & Luria, 1930).

[2] Kloach (Cloatsch?). We have not been able to establish the identity of this author and may even have misspelled his name (Russian uses a phonetic transcription of names).

[3] This suggests that the attacked ape would have grabbed a stick to defend itself if only there had been enough time. In reality Köhler (1921b, p. 60) writes that the attacker throws itself on its adversary and has no use for weapons.

[4] "Life in time." The expression is used by Köhler (1921b, p. 192).

[5] In discussing Lindworsky's (and to some extent Bühler's) criticism, Vygotsky is following/paraphrasing Koffka (1925a, pp. 161-177). Koffka analyzed various interpretations of Köhler's experiments, including the one by Lindworsky (1919).

[6] We confine ourselves to the examination of the problems connected with Köhler's experiments, i.e., with zoopsychology, and do not touch upon psychology and *Gestalttheorie* as a whole. [Original footnote]

Chapter 14

[1] The preface was to the Russian translation of Koffka (1921). The page references given here are to the second edition of this text (Koffka, 1925). Throughout the essay "structural psychology" should be read as "the psychology of form" or "Gestalt psychology." Similarly, the "structural principle" is the "principle of form" or the "Gestalt principle."

[2] Paraphrases Spinoza's text "Even as light displays both itself and darkness, so is truth a standard both of itself and falsity" in *The Ethics* (Part 2; Proof of Proposition XLIII).

[3] This whole passage is an almost verbatim quote from Koffka's text.

[4] Vygotsky's abundant use of "osmyslennyj" and "osmyslennost'" which dictionaries translate as "sensible, intelligent" and "intelligence" and which he uses alongside "razumnyj" ("reasonable, intelligent") and "razumnost'" ("intelligence") confronts the translator with a problem. I have followed the dictionary's advice in many cases. It is clear, however, that at times Vygotsky used the term somewhat differently. Thus, when he writes that Köhler's chimpanzees displayed "osmyslennost'" he clearly means "insight." And when he writes about the "osmyslennost'" of a situation he obviously means that the situation is "meaningful" to the observer, i.e., that the observer has interpreted or understood the situation. In addition to this Vygotsky uses "osmyslennyj" at times to convey the meaning of such German words as "sinnvoll" and "singemäss." I therefore decided to translate "osmyslennost'" and "osmyslennyj" in different ways depending on the context.

[5] "One of its critics." We have been unable to identify the critic. See note 2 to Chapter 6 for Goethe's words.

[6] See Koffka (1925, p. 116). Koffka argued that one often views the *repetition* of a successful performance as the proof of learning, whereas he wished to shift the attention to the *first time* ("die erste Leistung") successful performance is demonstrated.

[7] Actually, Koffka (1925, p. 130) does not say that the animal structures the situation *from the beginning* but that there is *a beginning* of a new structure.

[8] "Novel forms." Translation of Vygotsky's "novoobrazovanija," which was in turn based on Koffka's "Neuschöpfungen."

[9] Not in the first or second German edition. See p. 117 of the Russian edition (Koffka, 1934).

[10] See Koffka (1925, pp. 132-135), who discusses Ruger (1910).

[11] The last two sentences are quoted. See Koffka (1925, pp. 151-152).

[12] We have translated Koffka's term "geschlossen" as "closed." For Koffka, problem solving behavior was "closed" if it led to a solution of the problem and the behavior proceeded smoothly from the beginning to the end. As long as the solution had not been found the behavior lacked something and was somehow incomplete, or "open." See p. 76 ff. of Koffka (1925).

[13] Actually, Koffka fully retains Thorndike's position in his attempt—following Thorndike—to build a theory of child development upon the findings and laws of animal learning. Within this position, he very successfully attempts to change the conception of the nature of these laws. But the methodological path from zoopsychology to child psychology remains his path as well. He doesn't even ask himself the question to what extent is it at all possible to apply the word "learning" to animals and children while preserving a single meaning. [Original footnote]

[14] Vygotsky is still paraphrasing the same page of Koffka's text.

[15] Actually Köhler says that the chimpanzee displays behavior which so far *ranked* as specifically human.

[16] Köhler surmised that chimpanzees do not plan ahead and that their mental life is restricted to the here and now.

[17] The terms "predmetnyj" and "predmetnost'" pose a problem to the translator. I chose to translate them as "objective" and "objectivity," although one sees in other translations terms such as "object-relatedness." In this sense of the word the term "objective" in, for instance, "objective perception" does not mean that perception is "not subjective" but that the subject is capable of perceiving objects. This notion was not original with Vygotsky. In fact, in his famous study of spiders, Volkelt (1914) devoted much attention to spiders' incapability of seeing objects or things in our sense of the word. In his words, the spiders' perception is not "dinghaftig" and their perception lacks "Dinghaftigkeit." What he meant was that for a

spider there is no such thing as a fly which retains its properties in various situations. The fly is only perceived and recognized in a very narrowly defined situation. The spider reacts to the total situation of a "moving thing in the web" and does not attack flies outside its web or even immobile flies inside its web. This led Volkelt to argue that "things" in the sense of objects with invariant properties independent of the total context do not exist for the spider and for lower and even higher animals in general. He concludes that animal perception is not "dinghaftig" or "objective." Köhler's experiments with chimpanzees confirmed this hypothesis. In some contexts the notion of "objectivity" comes close to ordinary object constancy in perception.

[18] "Pure and mixed lines." Refers to Vagner (1923).

[19] "Structuralists," that is, the theorists of form, or structure, or Gestalt.

[20] The theories of Koffka and Bühler are, in essence, not as opposite as the author presents it. They are rather two variants of a single model which attempts to understand the whole psychological development of animals and man with a single principle. In this respect the positions of the authors coincide. We have already pointed out that this also unites Koffka's and Thorndike's theories. [Original footnote]

[21] These experiments are described in Vygotsky and Luria's "Tool and sign." See Van der Veer & Valsiner (1994).

[22] We have in mind, essentially, the question stated by Köhler as to the degree to which the chimpanzee may rely in its relationship to the situation and in its behavior upon elements that are not present, not visual, but upon elements that are "just conceivable," just ideas, i.e., upon all that is of the greatest importance in human thinking. This we provisionally call the semantic field by analogy with Köhler's optic field. [Original footnote]

[23] Typical in this respect is Lipmann and Bogen's *Naive Physik*, 1926, which is dedicated to the investigation of the child's practical intellect. [Original footnote]

[24] "Koffka's speech." Refers to a talk delivered on May 29, 1932 at the Institute of Experimental Psychology in Moscow, which was published as Koffka (1932).

[25] "Some quality against a uniform background." Cited from Koffka (1925, p. 108). Koffka argues that the phenomenal world of the newborn child is not a chaos of disconnected sensations, but that some primitive forms (e.g., human faces) are naturally perceived against the background of other forms.

[26] Implicit reference to Spinoza. See note 2.

[27] Refers to a passage in the chapter on emotions in *Principles* and *Briefer Course*. See, for example, p. 326 of Burkhardt (1984).

[28] We are actually dealing with the whole problem of higher psychic functions in structural psychology. Their voluntary and intelligent nature is just one of the features characterizing these higher forms of psychological activity. [Original footnote]

[29] Koffka devoted his "chapter" (actually a paragraph of three pages) to a discussion of some findings that showed that for children and primitive people numerical operations are tied to concrete objects or body parts and cannot easily become "decontextualized," an idea which Vygotsky himself propagated elsewhere.

[30] The last two sentences are quoted.

[31] Refers to Binet (1894). It was said by a chess player who described his mental image of the chess pieces during games of "blind chess," that is, chess without seeing the board and pieces.

[32] That is, in the second edition.

[33] The original paper by Peters dated back to 1915. Vygotsky is following Koffka's account of this paper and paraphrasing his text.

[34] This sentence is quoted from Koffka, who in turn quotes Gelb and Goldstein (1925, p. 152).

[35] The Sterns (1928/1981, p. 239) had claimed that the child's thinking goes through three stages, called the stage of substance (during which the child gradually begins to arrange reality into things—objects or persons—that remain constant), the stage of action (during which the child focuses on the actions objects and persons perform), and the stage of relations (during which the child begins to perceive the properties or qualities of things and their mutual relations; this was referred to as the stage of quality by Vygotsky in the text given above). These stages were inferred from, among other things, children's descriptions of the content of pictures, e.g., young children would list the objects and persons pictured, somewhat older children would convey the actions performed, etc. Vygotsky demonstrated that these findings were to an extent an artefact of the method used by asking some children to describe the content of pictures in words and others to convey their content by acting. See Stern & Stern (1928/1981).

[36] "a piece of phantasy." See p. 330 of Volume 29 of Lenin's *Complete Works*.

[37] "Plus ça change, plus c'est la même chose."

Chapter 15

[1] "Ewen Ma'asoe HaBoniem Hajetah le Rosh Piena." Quoted from Psalm 118; verse 22. Variants can be found in Matthew (21-42), Mark (12-10), Luke (20-17), The Acts (4-11), and 1 Peter (2-7).

[2] "industrial psychologists" is the translation of the term "psychotechnicians" which was widely used at the time. In the sequel we will retain the term when it is clear that Vygotsky is using it in the broader sense advocated by Münsterberg (1920).

[3] "a featherless biped." See Plato's *Definitiones* (415 a 11).

[4] This whole passage reflects Marx's reasoning in *Das Kapital* (1890/1981a, p. 192), but applied to matters of art by Plekhanov (1922).

[5] Chapter 4 of Vygotsky (1925/1986) is devoted to a critical discussion of the application of psychoanalytic ideas to the psychology of art.

[6] Vygotsky is paraphrasing pp. 3-5 of Binswanger (1922).

[7] "The non-existence of something is a specific non-existence." Translation of Engels' text "Das Nichts von irgend Etwas ist eines bestimmtes Nichts." See for the relevant passage pp. 67-68 of Hegel (1812/1948).

[8] The influence of important Russian linguistic thinkers such as Shpet and Potebnya on Vygotsky's thinking has been insufficiently investigated. The reference is to Chapter 9 of Potebnya (1913/1993).

[9] Goethe's words "Das Höchste wäre: zu begreifen, dass alles Faktische schon Theorie ist" can be found in his *Maximen und Reflexionen*. See p. 72 of Morris (MDCXL).

[10] Engels (1925/1978, p. 506) has "chemical (?) beams." He was referring to a review by Romanes of a book by Lubbock, who had claimed that ants are very sensitive to ultraviolet light rays. See note 329 in Engels (1925/1978).

[11] Incidentally, this psychological example demonstrates that in psychology the scientific fact and the fact of immediate experience do not coincide. It turns out that we can study how ants see and even how they see things invisible to us without knowing how these things appear to the ants, i.e., we can establish psychological facts without for a moment proceeding from inner experience, in other words, without proceeding subjectively. Obviously, Engels even considers this latter

factor unimportant for a scientific fact: who deplores this, he says, is beyond help. [Original footnote]

[12] Vygotsky is paraphrasing p. 21 of Binswanger's (1922) text.

[13] It is not clear how this could be a valid criticism of Bekhterev. Bekhterev accepted on the basis of the argumentation of Vvedensky and others that subjective methods cannot lead to reliable knowledge of the external ego (the problem is nowadays known as "the problem of the other mind"). But he criticized Vvedensky for his solipsism and concluded that "if the great lights of subjective psychology are ultimately led to solipsism, it is clear what value the subjective method in general has." Exactly for this reason he proposed to limit ourselves to manifest, objectively measurable behavior. See pp. 47-52 of Bekhterev (1932). The problem of the external ego is also discussed in Chapter 3 (notes 43 and 44) of this volume.

[14] Refers to topics discussed in several chapters (e.g., pp. 297/370) of Bekhterev (1932). The "certain Dr. Schwarzmann" was a co-worker at Bekhterev's laboratory as Vygotsky knew very well.

[15] See p. 411 of Bekhterev (1932).

[16] See p. 413 of Bekhterev (1932).

[17] Curiously, Bekhterev sees the subjective correspondence with the dominant in a totally different area; in his description of the school of Jung and Freud and the complex sets he also finds, of course, a full coincidence with the data of reflexology, but not with the dominant. And the dominant corresponds with the phenomena described by the Würzburg school, that is, it doubtlessly "participates in logical processes" and correlates with the concept of the determining tendency. The range of non-coincidences of different coincidences (the dominant is now equal to the complex, now to the determining tendency, now to attention—in Ukhtomsky) testifies best of all to the emptiness, uselessness, fruitlessness, and complete arbitrariness of such coincidences. [Original footnote]

[18] Refers to Freud's remark in *Beyond the Pleasure Principle* (1920) that "We have unwittingly steered into the harbour of Schopenhauer's philosophy." See pp. 49-50 of Vol. 18 of the Standard Edition. Freud acknowledged more than once that Schopenhauer had anticipated several of his ideas.

[19] It is remarkable that not only Freud's critics create a new social psychology for him, but reflexologists (Zalkind) as well reject the attempts of reflexology to "penetrate into the area of social phenomena, to explain them," like its different general philosophical claims and its method of investigation "here and there" (Zalkind, 1924). [Original footnote]

[20] Probably refers to Freud's words "Psycho-analysis is not, like philosophies, a system starting out from a few sharply defined basic concepts, seeking to grasp the whole universe with the help of these and, once it is completed, having no room for fresh discoveries or better understanding. On the contrary, it keeps close to the facts in its field of study. . . ." See pp. 253-254 of Vol. 18 of the Standard Edition.

[21] "Our views have from the very first been dualistic." See p. 53 of Volume 18 of the Standard Edition.

[22] See pp. 59-64 of Volume 18 of the Standard Edition.

[23] See p. 389 of Volume 16 of the Standard Edition.

[24] "Even when investigation shows that the primary exciting cause of a phenomenon is psychical, deeper research will one day trace the path further and discover an organic basis for the mental event." See pp. 41-42 of Volume 4 of the Standard Edition.

[25] See p. 40 of Molière (1670/1984).

[26] Allusion to Hegel's words. See note 7.

[27] Vygotsky claims to paraphrase the preface in Freud's (1920) *Beyond the Pleasure Principle* written by himself and Luria (Vygotsky & Luria, 1925). It must be said, however, that in that preface he and Luria were rather more positive about Freud's new idea and his thinking as a whole and even defended him against some of the criticism that Vygotsky now raises (e.g., the criticism that Freud subscribed to a philosophy of the Nirvana). See for the text of this preface Van der Veer & Valsiner (1994).

[28] Reference to Marx's famous words that Hegel "stood materialism on its head" ("Sie steht bei ihm auf dem Kopf. Man muss sie umstülpen, um den rationellen Kern in der mystischen Hülle zu entdecken"). See p. 27 of Marx (1890/1981a).

[29] This description of Frolov's experiment probably refers to Frolov (1926). See p. 398 of Pavlov (1928/1963).

[30] Implicit reference to Lipps's remark.

[31] This refers to "A symposium on the subconscious" organized by Morton Prince, the editor of *The Journal of Abnormal Psychology*. Prince asked Münsterberg, Ribot, Jastrow, and Janet to submit a paper about the topic of the subconscious. Together with his own paper on this topic and his prefatory note these constituted the symposium. See *The Journal of Abnormal Psychology*, Vol. 2, 1907-1908; 22-43; 58-80. Subsequently, the contributions were published, with an additional chapter by Bernard Hart, in Münsterberg *et al.* (1910)

[32] We have no other information about this author.

[33] Jerusalem, Wilhelm (1854-1923). Austrian philosopher and psychologist. The reference is probably to the Russian translation (1911) of Jerusalem (1902). See for a complete bibliography of his works Jerusalem (1924).

[34] "causa aequat effectum" (Latin). "The cause equals the effect."

[35] "cum grano salis" (Latin). "With a grain of salt."

[36] Vygotsky is paraphrasing pp. 50-52 of Lalande (1923). The proposals by Claparède (1910b) and Baldwin (1910) were followed by a confused discussion (partly conducted in Esperanto) about the language(s) in which the scientific discussions should be held and about the possibility of introducing a system of abstract signs and symbols. It ended up, of course, with the installation of a committee consisting of Baldwin, Claparède, Ferrari, and Lipmann to come up with a proposal for the unification of terminology. See pp. 482-499 of Claparède (1910a).

[37] Refers to Beer, Bethe, & Von Uexküll (1899).

[38] It was Pavlov (1928/1963) who introduced the reflexes of purpose and freedom.

[39] "Es denkt, sollte man sagen, so wie man sagt: es blitzt." Literally this would translate as "One should say 'It is thinking', just like one says 'It is thundering'." In the sequel I have rendered the passive sense ("It is thinking") as "It comes to my mind."

[40] Vygotsky is paraphrasing another passage of the same page of Engels (1925/1978).

[41] See paragraph 7 of this chapter.

[42] In view of the uncertainties concerning the reliability of this text, sketched in the introduction to this volume, it is unclear whether these periods are simply a rhetorical device or whether they indicate some gap in the manuscript.

[43] Translated into English as Lamarck (1809/1914).

[44] In the Russian edition this paragraph is somehow numbered "13." This mistake is continued until the final section, where another number is skipped. See also note 42.

[45] Vygotsky is referring to such plays as *Le médecin malgré lui* (1666) and *Le malade imaginaire* (1673).

[46] Vygotsky uses the expression "dachnaya" psychology, from "dacha" or "holiday cottage."

[47] The Russian text has "but applied in practice," which is not in agreement with Münsterberg's text which Vygotsky is closely following. Also, the transition to the next sentence is somewhat awkward as Vygotsky suddenly leaves out part of Münsterberg's text. The reader should add "but in psychology this paradoxical situation did take place and" and then continue reading the next sentence "Education and law etc." The "movement" referred to in this sentence is empirical psychology.

[48] Vygotsky is paraphrasing pp. 19-20 of Münsterberg (1920).

[49] "phases." Thus in the text, but "camps" (as in the Spanish translation) would perhaps make more sense.

[50] Paraphrases Marx's well-known words in his "Der achtzehnte Brumaire des Louis Bonaparte": "Hegel bemerkt irgendwo, daß alle großen weltgeschichtlichen Tatsachen und Personen sich zosuzagen zweimal ereignen. Er hat vergessen hinzuzufügen: das eine Mal als Tragödie, das andere Mal als Farce" ["Hegel remarks somewhere that all great facts and persons in world history happen so to speak twice. He forgot to add: the first time as a tragedy, the second time as a farce"]. See p. 115 of Marx (1852/1972). The words were not original with Marx. He repeated a similar observation made by his friend Engels one year before. See p. 381 of Marx & Engels (1970).

[51] "science before science itself." Allusion to an idea of Hegel (that one cannot study the activity of knowing without engaging in this activity) which he voiced on several occasions, e.g., in his "Wissenschaft der Logik," in "Phänomenologie des Geistes," "Vorlesungen über die Geschichte der Philosophie," etc. See, for example, pp. 52-53 of Hegel (1812/1948).

[52] "Pia desiderata," actually "pia desideria" (Latin). "Pious desires." The sentence that results after translating the Latin text is of course ungrammatical.

[53] "Coefficient of specification." The expression was taken from Hegel.

[54] Utitz, Emil (1883-1956). Author of such works as *Die Ueberwindung der Expressionismus: Charakterologische Studien zur Kultur der Gegenwart* (Stuttgart, 1927), *Jahrbuch der Charakterologie* (Berlin, 1924-29), and *Die Sendung der Philosophie in Unsere Zeit* (Leiden, 1935). In the present case Vygotsky probably refers to Utitz (1925).

[55] "as obvious as a simple scale." Implicit reference to Salieri's words ["jasno, kak prostaja gamma"] in Pushkin's "Mozart i Salieri" (1830). See p. 332 of Pushkin (1984).

[56] The "God-seekers" and the "God-builders" were two religious currents which emerged in the Soviet Union at the beginning of this century. Among the God-seekers we find such important philosophers as Berdiaev, Bulgakov, and Merezhkovsky. They proposed to reconstruct society and human life on the basis of a renewed Christianity. The God-builders included Lunacharsky, Bazarov, and Gorky. They wished to create a Marxist proletarian religion without a God. In actual fact they worshipped the collective and progress. Both currents were repeatedly attacked by Lenin.

[57] Machism, i.e., following the ideas of Ernst Mach. Lenin and other Marxists particularly disliked his *Die Analyse der Empfindungen* (1886) in which Mach identified experience with sensations, making sensations into the observational data of both physics and psychology.

[58] Quote from the Bible. "And, behold, the veil of the temple was rent in twain from the top to the bottom." See Matthew (27-51).

[59] Vygotsky uses the word "perezhivanie" which means "experience" or "interpretation." "Perezhivanie" covers both the way an event is emotionally experienced and the way it is cognitively understood by the subjects.

[60] This is our translation of Vygotsky's strange phrase "Eto prekrasno do jasnosti."

[61] Elsewhere Vygotsky ascribed the metaphor to Stern. Stern himself and other sources (e.g., Høffding, 1908) also designate Fechner as its author.

[62] In his preface to the first edition of *Das Kapital* Marx explains that he regards the stages in economic history as stages in an objective, "natural-historical" (*naturgeschichtlich*) process and that individual persons ("capitalists," etc.) are merely representatives (*Träger*) or products of these objective stages.

[63] (Inexact) quote from the Bible. "And he said unto them. The sabbath was made for man, and not man for the sabbath." See Mark (2-27).

[64] In the Russian edition this paragraph is somehow numbered "16." See also note 42.

[65] Again there may have been a gap in the manuscript. See also note 42.

[66] The 8th Congress on Experimental Psychology was held in Leipzig in April 1923. See p. 201 of Spearman (1924).

[67] Frank mentioned, among others, Dostoyevsky, Tolstoy, de Maupassant, Ibsen, Flaubert, and Carlyle.

[68] This is not entirely correct. Actually, Dilthey criticized the people who held the view given in the quoted sentence.

[69] The first congress on individual psychology was held December 1922 in München. Oppenheim dealt with the question as to whether one can become a good judge of human character by reading Shakespeare. See Oppenheim (1923).

[70] "Blue ink." The Russian word for ink ("chernila") is linked with the word "black" ("chernyj").

[71] "like a dead dog." Allusion to Marx's words on p. 27 of Marx (1890/1981a).

[72] The information about Goclenius, Casmann, and Melanchthon is taken from a footnote in Lalande (1923, p. 1) to whom Vygotsky referred in the above.

[73] We have been unable to trace the original of Jameson's book.

[74] The Russian term is "volsoviet" which is a compound of "volostnoj soviet."

[75] For some time Vygotsky was quite impressed by the work of Adler. See Van der Veer and Valsiner (1991).

[76] The reference may be to Koffka or Lewin. In later years he would have personal meetings with both of them, but it seems that contacts started earlier. See Van der Veer and Valsiner (1991).

[77] Blonsky's (1921) book was called "An outline of scientific psychology."

[78] "The leap from the kingdom of necessity . . ." Quoted from p. 264 of Engels' (1878/1978) *Anti-Dühring*.

[79] See note 42. Etkind (1993) has argued that this and other passages of the "Crisis" were clearly inspired by the work of Trotsky and that Vygotsky at this time was some sort of a follower of Trotsky. His claims have been contested by Jaroshevsky (1993).

Epilogue

[1] See note 9 to Leont'ev's introductory article to this volume. Leont'ev's preface to *The Psychology of Art* can be found in the English translation of this book. See pp. v-xi of Vygotsky (1925/1971).

[2] The references here and in the following are to the English translation indicated in note 1.

[3] Vygotsky does refer to Sechenov. See footnote 28 to Chapter 3 of this volume.

[4] The authors simplify the picture somewhat. In his *Educational Psychology*, published in the same year as the preface to Thorndike, Vygotsky voiced ideas critical of Thorndike and explicitly condemned reductionist ideas. It is true that at this time Vygotsky felt the spell of behaviorism and reactology, but he never was and never became a behaviorist or reactologist.

[5] A "feldsher" was a medical practitioner lacking graduate qualification. "Feldsherizm" has the connotation of "nonprofessional work, a botch job."

[6] The authors refer to Diderot's "Réfutation d'Helvétius" (1774), in which he criticized Helvétius' (1772) treatise "De l'homme, de ses facultés intellectuels et de son éducation." See Diderot (1971).

NOTES TO THE RUSSIAN EDITION

PART I: PROBLEMS OF THE THEORY AND METHODS OF PSYCHOLOGY

Chapter 1

1. Published in Kornilov, K. N. (ed.) (1926). *Problemy sovremennoj psikhologii* [Problems of contemporary psychology (pp. 26-46)]. Leningrad: Gosudarstvennoe Izdatel'stvo.

2. By reflexology Vygotsky meant (in accordance with the views accepted at that time) Bekhterev's theory of the synthesizing reflexes as experimentally created response reactions of the organism to external stimuli and Pavlov's theory of the conditional reflexes.

3. Experimental psychology. A term that originally signified the investigations of mental phenomena through experimental methods. These methods were first applied to the investigation of sensory thresholds, reaction time, associations, etc. The use of the experiment played an important role in the establishment of psychology as an independent science.

4. *Protopopov, Viktor Pavlovich* (1880-1957). A Soviet psychiatrist. Elaborated principles and methods for the protective regimen and a series of other methods for the prevention and cure of psychoses. Protopopov's investigations in the field of the physiology and pathology of the higher nervous activity of man facilitated the introduction into psychiatry of Pavlov's theory of conditional reflexes.

5. *Pavlov, Ivan Petrovich* (1849-1936). Russian and Soviet physiologist. Founder of the theory of the higher nervous activity, which caused radical reforms in the investigation of the physiological substratum and the determination of mental phenomena.

6. Secondary conditional reflex. A particular type of conditional reflex elicited by the signal that replaced the original stimulus.

7. Associative experiment. A method proposed by Jung to detect unconscious tendencies of the person via the study of the nature of his reactions to a series of "neutral" words. An inhibited or inadequate reaction was considered to be a symptom of the action of unconscious mental forces.

8. *Bekhterev, Vladimir Mikhajlovich* (1867-1927). Russian and Soviet physiologist, neurologist, and psychologist. Founder of the theory of behavior as a system of reflexes which is at the basis of both the mental and the social activity of persons. This theory he first called objective psychology, then psychoreflexology, and finally reflexology. The latter he considered to be the antithesis of empirical, subjective psychology.

9. *Sechenov, Ivan Mikhajlovich* (1829-1905). Russian physiologist and psychologist. Founder of a new current in the investigation of the higher nervous centers on which a program for the creation of an objective psychology was based. He exerted a tremendous influence on the deterministic study of behavior through natural scientific concepts and objective methods.

10. Inhibited reflex. The concept of the reflex act as "broken off" in its final ("third") part was put forward by Sechenov. It was used to explain the origin of the process of thinking not manifested in external behavior.

11. The Würzburg school. One of the currents in the experimental study of higher mental processes (thought, volition). It was based on idealistic assumptions about consciousness as the sum-total of special mental acts which can be studied through controlled introspection. It claimed the qualitative uniqueness of thinking as a process which is not reducible to sensory images and regulated by the subject's set. The Würzburg school originated at the beginning of the 20th century. Its main representatives were O. Külpe, N. Ach, K. Bühler, and K. Marbe.

12. *Krol', Mikhail Borisovich* (1869-1939). Soviet neurologist.

13. *Zalkind, Aron Borisovich* (1888-1936). Soviet pedagogue and psychologist.

14. *James, William* (1842-1910). American physiologist, psychologist, and philosopher. Founder of the functional current in psychology, which considered the mental processes from the point of view of the role (function) they played in the adaptation of the organism to the environment.

15. *Lange, Nikolaj Nikolaevich* (1858-1921). Russian psychologist. Professor at the New Russian University (Odessa). Important representative of the natural scientific current in the study of mental functions (perception, attention). Defended a genetic and biological approach to these functions.

16. *Watson, John* (1878-1958). American psychologist. Founder of behaviorism.

17. *Weiss, Albert* (1879-1931). American psychologist. Supporter of behaviorism. Considered psychology to be a part of physics.

18. Gestalt psychology. A current that considered whole structures (*Gestalten*) and their transformations to be the subject and main explanatory principle of consciousness and behavior. Gestalt psychology originated before World War I but became well known and influential in the twenties due to the works of Wertheimer, Köhler, Koffka, and Lewin. The university of Berlin became the center of its elaboration, the journal *Psychologische Forschung* its main publication outlet.

19. *Köhler, Wolfgang* (1887-1967). German psychologist. One of the leaders of Gestalt psychology. Author of experimental works on the study of perception and the behavior of anthropoids.

20. *Koffka, Kurt* (1887-1941). German psychologist. One of the leaders of Gestalt psychology. Vygotsky subjected his conception of the development of the mind to a critical analysis in a special article which is published in this volume.

21. *Wertheimer, Max* (1980-1943). German psychologist. His main works are in the field of perception and thinking. One of Gestalt psychology's theorists.

22. Empirical psychology. A series of currents that considered it to be psychology's task to study various phenomena of mental life in an empirical way. Its idea was first put forward by Christian Wolff (1679-1754), who in the book *Empirische Psychologie* (1732) contrasted it as a science that describes facts to rational psychology which deductively deduces these facts from the essence of the soul. Later all currents that attempted to found psychology on the data of experience were traced to empirical psychology. Chief importance was given to the methods of introspection. Other methods were considered auxiliary.

23. Behaviorism (from the English "behavior"). The representatives of behaviorism, which originated at the beginning of the century in the USA, considered

the externally observable bodily reactions of the organism to stimuli to be the subject of scientific psychology. They considered it their main task to study the process of learning as the obtaining of new forms of reactions. They did not distinguish between animals and man concerning the regularities of this process. They dismissed consciousness as a subject of psychology.

24. *Ivanovsky, Vladimir Nikolaevich* (1867-1931). Russian philosopher and psychologist. Studied the history of associationism. Criticized from the position of associationism the concepts of spiritual activity and apperception of Leibnitz, Herbart, and primarily Wundt. Actively participated in the development of Russian educational psychology.

Chapter 2

1. Preface to A. F. Lazursky's book *General and Experimental Psychology*, written in 1924. Published in the third edition of the mentioned book (Leningrad, 1925).

2. *Lazursky, Aleksandr Fedorovich* (1874-1917). Russian psychologist. Initiator of the elaboration of the theory of individual psychological differences which adhered to a natural scientific orientation.

3. *Artemov, Vladimir Aleksandrovich* (born 1897). Soviet psychologist. One of the leading collaborators at the Psychological Institute of Moscow State University in the years 1920-30. Main works in the area of the psychology of speech.

4. *Dobrynin, Nikolaj Fedorovich* (1890-1981). Soviet psychologist. One of the leading collaborators at the Psychological Institute of Moscow State University in the years 1920-30. Main works in the area of the psychology of attention.

5. *Luria, Aleksandr Romanovich* (1902-1977). Soviet psychologist. Close collaborator of Vygotsky on whose conception he relied working in the area of general and child psychology, neuropsychology, psycholinguistics, pathopsychology, etc.

6. *Thorndike, Edward* (1874-1949). American psychologist. Initiator of the experimental investigation of behavior with the help of objective methods. His works stimulated the development of behaviorism.

7. Rational psychology. A current starting from the assumption that the laws of mental life are established through their deduction from theoretical ideas about the soul as a special essence. The concept of rational psychology as opposed to empirical psychology was introduced by H. Wolff.

8. *Locke, John* (1632-1704). English philosopher. He considered experience acquired through sensation and reflection (the observation of the activity of one's own spirit) to be the basis of mental development. He played an important role in the development of the materialistic current in psychology through his theory that the impressions received by the sense organs form the foundation of man's cognitive work. He introduced the term "association" in psychology.

9. *Ebbinghaus, Hermann* (1850-1909). German scholar, one of the founders of experimental psychology. Elaborated methods for the study of memory on the basis of the associationist conception.

10. *Wundt, Wilhelm* (1832-1920). German physiologist, philosopher, and psychologist. Initiator of the elaboration of experimental psychology (called physiological by him) as a separate discipline. Organized (1879) the first laboratory for the study of elementary psychological functions (sensations, reaction time, etc.), which served as a model for the creation of laboratories in other countries. Regarded psychology as the science of the subject's immediate experience and especially trained self-observation as its basic method.

11. *Stumpf, Carl* (1848-1936). German psychologist. Author of experimental works on the psychology of auditory and spatial sensations and perception. Under the influence of Brentano he proposed a theory of psychological functions as distinguished from psychological phenomena.

12. *Avenarius, Richard* (1843-1896). Swiss philosopher. Defender of a subjective idealist conception of experience as "neutral" with respect to the difference between the physical and the mental. Thereby, as was shown by Lenin (*Complete Works*, Vol. 18), he rejected the idea that the mental is secondary with respect to external reality and forms its reflection in the brain.

13. *Meinong, Alexius* (1853-1920). Austrian psychologist and idealist philosopher. Headed a psychological school in Graz. Demonstrated that sensory structures are formed in the act of perception whose integral nature is determined by that act and not by the combination of the sensations in themselves. This thesis influenced Gestalt psychology.

14. *Binet, Alfred* (1857-1911). French psychologist. Main investigations in the area of the psychology of thinking and the study of individual differences (psychometrics, test theory).

15. *Müller, Georg Elias* (1850-1934). German psychologist. Main investigations in the area of psychophysics and psychophysiology. The axioms he proposed about the correlation between mental and nervous processes exerted influence on Gestalt psychology.

16. *Darwin, Charles* (1809-1882). Founder of the evolutionary theory in biology, which exerted tremendous influence on the development of genetic and objective methods in psychology and new ideas about the determination of mental functions.

17. *Lazarev, Petr Petrovich* (1878-1942). Soviet physicist, biophysicist, and geophysicist. Elaborated a physicochemical theory of excitation (the so-called ion theory of excitation) and a theory of the adaptation of the central nervous system to external stimuli.

Chapter 3

1. The article was written in 1925 [and based on a talk with the same title presented at Vygotsky's own Institute on October 19, 1924; see Luria, A. R. (1926). Moskovskij gosudarstvennyj institut eksperimental'noj psikhologii v 1924 godu. In K. N. Kornilov (Ed.), Problems of Contemporary Psychology (pp. 244-252). Leningrad: Gosudarstvennoe Izdatel'stvo.]. Published in Kornilov, K. N. (Ed.) (1925). Psychology and Marxism [pp. 175-198]. Leningrad: Gosudarstvennoe Izdatel'stvo.

2. *Blonsky, Pavel Petrovich* (1884-1941). Soviet pedagogue and psychologist. Active participant in the reform of psychological science in the USSR on the basis of dialectical materialism. Main works in the area of child psychology and the problem of the development of memory and thinking.

3. *Ukhtomsky, Aleksej Alekseevich* (1875-1942). Soviet physiologist. Elaborated the theory of the dominant as a special functional system (a constellation of processes in the nervous centers) which formed the physiological mechanism of the organization and regulation of behavior.

4. *Sherrington, Charles* (1857-1952). English physiologist. Created the theory of the integrative nature of the activity of the central nervous system. At the basis of this conception lay the notion of the reflex arc as an integrative process which served an adaptive function. The mind, however, he considered to be a particular phenomenon not subject to the regularities of the brain's action.

5. The concepts of the "reflex of purpose" and the "reflex of freedom" were introduced by Pavlov [(1928/1963). *Lectures on Conditioned Reflexes.* New York: International Publishers; Chapters XXVII and XXVIII]. However, they did not fit in the fundamental deterministic scheme of the formation of the conditional reflex. Vygotsky agitated against the generalization of this scheme, because its positive meaning would be lost in the process. It can only be retained when we confine the mentioned scheme to a limited circle of phenomena [Cf. "The historical significance of the crisis in psychology"].

6. *Freud, Sigmund* (1856-1939). Austrian physician and psychologist. Founder of psychoanalysis.

7. *Vagner, Vladimir Aleksandrovich* (1889-1934). Founder of zoopsychology in Russia. Investigated instincts in animals using objective methods and starting from Darwin's theory. Proved that the unique character of the psychological regulation of behavior is revealed in comparative historical studies.

8. *Zelenyj, Georgij Pavlovich* (1878-1951). Soviet physiologist, pupil of Pavlov.

9. Psychoanalysis. A current that starts from the assumption that the basis of mental life is formed by unconscious forces (drives, in particular sexual, aggressive, etc. impulses), which are in conflict with the processes of consciousness and capable of deforming these processes, thereby giving behavior an inadequate character, causing neuroses, mental traumas, disturbances, etc. It is assumed that with the help of special methods (free association, clinical conversations, various types of psychotherapeutic devices) the person can be liberated from the pressure of the traumatizing unconscious complexes. The action of the mentioned psychological systems is also explained by social processes and the development of culture. The founder of psychoanalysis was Freud, whose ideas exerted influence on other varieties of this current (Adler, Jung, the neo-Freudians, etc.):

10. The theory of the "three-dimensionality of the feeling" put forward by Wundt assumed that feelings vary in a system of three dimensions: (a) pleasantness–unpleasantness; (b) strain–relaxation (slackening); (c) excitement–calm.

11. *Külpe, Oswald* (1862-1915). German philosopher and psychologist. Leader of the Würzburg school. Proposed the conception of thinking as a process not connected to the sensory images and determined by the determining tendencies. He considered introspection to be the only method of the experimental investigation of the mind.

12. *Münsterberg, Hugo* (1863-1916). German psychologist. One of the pioneers of applied psychology.

13. *Vvedenskyj, Aleksandr Ivanovich* (1865-1925). Professor at the University of Petersburg, idealist philosopher. Mental life, in his opinion, has no objective characteristics and therefore another person's mind is unknowable. Considered it the task of psychology to confine itself to the description of mental phenomena for which introspection served as the only means of comprehension.

Chapter 4

1. Written in 1926. Published as a preface to the work of Koffka, which was printed in Kornilov, K. N. (Ed.) (1926). *Problems of Contemporary Psychology* [pp. 176-178]. [Leningrad: Gosudarstvennoe Izdatel'stvo]. [In a section dedicated to the "new foreign literature," Vygotsky's introduction preceded the translation by O. N. Gardner of Koffka (1924). See also Chapter 1].

2. *Husserl, Edmund* (1849-1938). German philosopher, founder of the phenomenological current in philosophy which sought to build a theory of "pure" mental

essences which were understood with the help of a special set of consciousness—intellectual intuition. This view influenced the development in German psychology of a tendency to describe the phenomena of consciousness (the experiences of the subject) in their immediate givenness.

3. By descriptive, or descriptive–introspective psychology, Vygotsky meant the analysis of the phenomena of consciousness through specially organized self-observation (introspection). This current has to be distinguished from the descriptive (or "understanding") psychology in Dilthey's interpretation. Vygotsky supposed that Gestaltism allows one to combine the descriptive–introspective method of studying the mind with the functional, objective reactological one.

Chapter 5

1. Theses of a talk read in 1930 at the N. K. Krupskaya Academy of Communist Education. From the private archives of Vygotsky. Published for the first time.

2. *Claparède, Edouard* (1873-1940). Swiss psychologist. Main works in the area of child and genetic psychology. Exerted influence on Piaget.

3. *Dewey, John* (1859-1952). American philosopher, psychologist, and pedagogue. In psychology a representative of the functional school, which assumes that consciousness is a function which serves the process of the adaptation of the organism to the environment. Opponent of the materialistic explanation of the mind.

Chapter 6

1. Polished shorthand report of a talk read at the Clinic of Nervous Diseases I of Moscow State University on October 9, 1930. From Vygotsky's private archives. Published for the first time.

2. *Goethe, Johann Wolfgang* (1749-1832). German poet, thinker, natural scientist. Investigator of the problems of visual perception.

3. *Goldstein, Kurt* (1878-1965). German psychiatrist and psychologist. Close to Gestalt psychology, whose ideas he extended to the treatment of the organism as a whole, driven by the need for self-actualization.

4. *Jaensch, Erik* (1883-1940). German psychologist. Known for his works on the study of eidetics.

5. *Stern, William* (1871-1938). German psychologist. Main works in the area of child and differential psychology. Proposed a theory of the person as a particular, unique essence.

6. *Leont'ev, Aleksej Nikolaevich* (1903-1979). Soviet psychologist. Close collaborator of Vygotsky. Elaborated the problem of the origin and development of the mind, proposed the thesis of the common structure of the external, practical and the internal, theoretical activity of the person.

7. *Zankov, Leonid Vladimirovich* (1901-1977). Soviet defectologist and psychologist.

8. *Piaget, Jean* (1896-1980). Swiss psychologist. Author of many experimental and theoretical works in the area of child and genetic psychology which exerted great influence on the development of this current.

9. *Groos, Karl* (1861-1946). German psychologist. Main works in the area of genetic psychology. Author of a theory of play, according to which play serves as a school that prepares the organism for the trials of life.

10. *Morozova, Natal'ja Grigor'evna* (1906-?). Soviet defectologist.

11. *Lévy-Bruhl, Lucien* (1857-1939). French philosopher, sociologist, and ethnographer.

12. *Tacitus, Cornelius* (55-120). Roman historian.

13. *Bühler, Charlotte* (1893-?). Austrian psychologist, who worked on problems of child and genetic psychology.

14. *Galton, Francis* (1822-1911). English anthropologist and psychologist. Exerted great influence on the elaboration of experimental and quantitative methods in psychology. Attached a decisive role to hereditary factors, underestimating the influence of the social environment.

15. *Hegel, Georg Wilhelm Friedrich* (1770-1831). German philosopher who completed the development of German classical idealist philosophy.

16. *Bergson, Henri* (1859-1941). French idealist philosopher. The primary basis of everything he considered to be the "pure" (that is, nonmaterial) duration [*dureé*], of which memory, instinct, consciousness, freedom, and spirit represented aspects. The understanding of duration is accomplished through intuition [conceived of] as a mystical act of direct understanding opposed to the intellect.

17. *Kretschmer, Ernst* (1888-1964). German psychiatrist and psychologist. The author of investigations into the relations between the body build and the mental properties of the person. On this basis he suggested a typology of characters.

18. *Bleuler, Eugen* (1859-1939). Swiss psychiatrist. Proposed the concept of autism (or autistic thinking) as a condition in which the patient (the schizophrenic) loses contact with reality, fully concentrating on his own drives and ideas.

19. *Blondel, Charles* (1876-1939). French psychiatrist.

20. *Spinoza (Spinosa d'Espinosa), Benedict* (1633-1677). Dutch materialist philosopher. His works exerted great influence upon Vygotsky.

21. *Sapir, Isaj Davidovich* (1897-1937). Soviet psychiatrist.

22. *Sombart, Werner* (1863-1941). German bourgeois economist and sociologist. Distinguished "psychological sociology," which analyzed psycho-biological facts—feelings, instincts, drives—as the basis of human culture, and "zoological sociology," which studied the spiritual factors of culture—religion, ethics, rights, etc. Under the influence of Freud he distinguished biological and spiritual foundations of culture.

23. *Lewin, Kurt* (1890-1947). German psychologist. Elaborated a theory of the motivation of behavior that was close to Gestalt psychology.

Chapter 7

1. Time of writing unknown. First published in the reader *Elements of General Psychology* (Moscow, 1930).

2. *Lipps, Theodor* (1851-1914). German philosopher and psychologist. Regarded psychology as the science of the experiences felt by the subject. Proposed the theory of empathy (*Einfühlung*) according to which the person projects his feelings onto the object he perceives.

3. Descriptive, or understanding psychology. A conception according to which the task of psychology should not be the explanation of its phenomena on the basis of natural scientific concepts and methods, but a special reconstruction of these phenomena as components of the integral spirit imbedded in a system of cultural

values. This conception was put forward by the German philosopher Dilthey and developed by Spranger.

4. Eidetic psychology. In the present context Vygotsky understands by eidetic psychology not the study of visual representations that are similar in brightness and perception, but Husserl's conception of the comprehension by the subject of the pure forms (*eidea*) of his own consciousness.

5. *Dilthey, Wilhelm* (1833-1911). German philosopher who suggested a plan for the creation of a descriptive, or understanding psychology.

6. *Spranger, Eduard* (1882-1939). German philosopher and psychologist. Follower of Dilthey.

7. *Mach, Ernst* (1838-1916). Austrian physicist and philosopher, subjective idealist. Denying the difference between the physical and the mental he considered that nature must be described in neutral "elements" of experience, by which he, essentially, understood sensations. The influence of his philosophy on psychology (Wundt, James, Gestalt psychology) promoted the deepening of the crisis phenomena in this science. A critique of his subjective idealistic views is given in Lenin's book *Materialism and Empiriocriticism*.

8. *Bühler, Karl* (1879-1963). Austrian psychologist. Main works in the area of the psychology of thinking and the development of the mind. Provided an analysis of psychology's critical situation in the 1920s.

9. *Plekhanov, Georgyj Valentinovich* (1856-1918). Eminent theorist of Marxism in Russia.

10. *Severcov, Aleksej Nikolaevich* (1866-1936). Soviet biologist. In the work *Evolution and Mind* (1922) he analyzed the way organisms adapt to the environment by changing their behavior without changing their structure. The individual mechanisms of behavior which reach the highest level of development in man guarantee his adaptation to whatever conditions of existence and lead to the creation of so-called artificial environments—the environments of culture and civilization.

11. *Feuerbach, Ludwig* (1804-1872). German materialist philosopher.

12. *Brentano, Franz* (1838-1917). Austrian idealist philosopher. Proposed a program for the construction of psychology as a science of the acts of consciousness. His theory exerted great influence on German and English psychology (Stumpf, Husserl, Külpe, Stout, and others).

13. *Bain, Alexander* (1818-1903). English psychologist, representative of the associative current. Considered that the elaboration of psychology should conform to the achievements of the physiology of the nervous system.

14. *Herbart, Johann* (1776-1841). German philosopher, psychologist, and pedagogue. Having criticized faculty psychology and Kant's theory, he proposed to modify psychology into a theory of "the statics and dynamics" of representations as primary elements of consciousness, whose interaction could be calculated by means of mathematical methods.

15. *Hartmann, Eduard* (1848-1906). German irrationalistic philosopher who considered that the basis of being is the unconscious spiritual principle.

16. *Bernheim, Hippolyt* (1840-1919). French doctor, investigator of hypnotism, which he considered to be based on suggestion. His data on posthypnotic suggestion exerted influence upon Freud's ideas concerning the unconscious mind.

Chapter 8

1. Written and published in 1931.

2. *Hering, Ewald* (1834-1918). German physiologist and psychologist. Author of works in the area of sensation and perception. In 1870 he presented a talk "Memory as a special function of organized matter" ["Über das Gedächtnis als eine allgemeine Funktion der organisierten Materie," a lecture given on May 30, 1870, to a session of the Kaiserliche Akademie der Wissenschaften in Vienna. See Boring, E. G. (1950). *A History of Experimental Psychology*. New York: Appleton-Century-Crofts; p. 379].

3. *Comte, August* (1798-1857). French philosopher, one of the founders of positivism and bourgeois sociology. Proposed a new classification of the sciences in which psychology was absent. The mental phenomena as the object of positivistic investigation were divided between physiology and sociology. Considered that the internal world can only become the subject of scientific analysis through the observation of the facts of social life of which the interaction between people is the first principle.

Chapter 9

1. The first publication of this material was in the book *The Psychology of Grammar* (Moscow, 1968). The publication was preceded by a foreword by A. A. Leont'ev and an introduction by A. N. Leont'ev. We reprint their text.

Foreword to the publication

The notes of Vygotsky's talks are published on the basis of the manuscript copybooks preserved in the archives of A. N. Leont'ev. In these notebooks the main text is written on the right (odd) pages, while the insertions and additions which were particularly made by Zaporozhec are on the opposite left (even) pages. All notes (except for some that we ignored as they were obviously added later and only summarized what Vygotsky said in more modern wordings) were written with a pen.

Naturally, in our publication we first of all made use of the basic text. It is supplemented with the corresponding insertions from the even pages of the notebooks, which are given in angle brackets < >. We did not cut the material. Following the original, halfway through the notes we added the notes of Vygotsky's speech on the occasion of Luria's talk, which according to its theme corresponds to the specific part of the talk "The problem of consciousness."

All highlightings in the manuscript made by A. N. Leont'ev have been preserved.

All parentheses and square brackets belong to the original. The passages in quotation marks are direct quotes from Vygotsky's oral speech. In the published excerpt from the record of Vygotsky's speech about the theses for the debates in 1933-1934, we have followed the same principles with the only difference being that between the angle brackets are given the insertions made with the same ink by A. N. Leont'ev himself.

Introduction

Toward the end of the twenties, a small group of young psychologists had gathered around Vygotsky and began to work under his guidance. Apart from the discussions of scientific problems that were systematically conducted at the meetings of the department and the laboratory where we carried out our investigations at the time and during private talks, Vygotsky now and then gathered his closest collaborators and students in meetings which we called internal conferences. Their purpose was to theoretically think through what had been accomplished, to discuss problems that had arisen in the discussions, to plan future work. Usually such internal conferences proceeded in the form of a free exchange of opinions about the issues that had been raised; in other cases we listened to and discussed full-blown talks especially prepared for the occasion. No minutes were taken in either the first or the second case. For that reason only some of Vygotsky's presentations have been preserved in the personal notes of the participants in these conferences.

The notes of Vygotsky's talk relate to the moment when the inner necessity arose to sum up the results of the investigations of the higher mental processes thus far carried out from the perspective of the theory of human consciousness, to present an analysis of its inner structure. This talk, which was written down by me in a very condensed thesis-like form, rested on an overview of many investigations carried out under the supervision of Vygotsky and with his participation. Therefore, its exposition by the author took tremendous time—with a pause of approximately two hours it lasted more than seven hours, and another day was devoted to its discussion.

As far as I remember, apart from Leont'ev and Luria in this internal conference Bozhovic, Zaporozhec, Levina, Morozova and Slavina also participated.

Some clarification is required about the notes of Vygotsky's talk at the internal conference where the problem of the theses was discussed which had been prepared for a public debate about the works of Vygotsky and his school. Such a debate was expected in 1933 or 1934, but before Vygotsky's death it did not take place. What was left was the unfinished and provisional work prepared for this debate. The published fragments of the notes concern only those questions which coincide with those raised in his talk about the problem of consciousness.

2. *Selz, Otto* (1881-1944). German psychologist. Investigated the problems of thinking.

3. *Watt, Henri* (1879-1925). English psychologist. Representative of the Würzburg school.

Chapter 10

1. Summary of a talk presented at the First All-Ukrainian Congress on Psychoneurology (June 1934). Published in the book *The First All-Ukrainian Conference of Neuropathologists and Psychiatrists* (Summary of the talks, Kharkov, 1934).

2. *Lashley, Karl* (1890-1958). American psychologist. Proponent of behaviorism. Studied the dependency of behavior on the organization of the brain.

3. *Head, Henry* (1861-1940). English neurologist. Investigated the nervous mechanisms of sensibility and the higher mental functions (speech, in particular).

PART II: DEVELOPMENTAL PATHS OF PSYCHOLOGICAL KNOWLEDGE

Chapter 11

1. A preface written by Vygotsky to the Russian translation of Thorndike's book *The Principles of Teaching, Based on Psychology*. Highly regarding Thorndike as a representative of the new objective psychology, Vygotsky makes some critical remarks primarily about the fact that Thorndike provides the psychological foun-

dation to a pedagogical practice that is foreign to the Soviet school system as it ignores the social factor in education.

Chapter 12

1. The Russian translation of Bühler's book *Outline of the Mental Development of the Child* was published in 1930 in Moscow.

2. Vygotsky refers to the Würzburg school because Bühler in his time was one of its prominent representatives. Having overcome the subjectivism of this school, Bühler, however, continued to defend its teleological claims, which in his conception of the development of the child's mind acquired a biological tendency.

3. Bühler's book *The Crisis in Psychology* (1927), after an analysis of the crisis-like situation in psychology, attempted to argue that its solution could be found in the synthesis of the positive components of three currents: the introspective conception of consciousness, the behaviorist conception of behavior, and the theory of the realization [embodiment] of the mind in cultural products.

4. *Driesch, Hans* (1867-1941). German biologist, founder of neovitalism.

5. *Rickert, Henrich* (1863-1936). German idealist philosopher, one of the founders of the so-called Baden school of neo-Kantianism.

6. *Pearson, Karl* (1857-1936). English scholar, who developed statistical methods for the investigation of mental phenomena.

Chapter 13

1. The article was written as a preface to Köhler's book *The Investigation of the Intellect of Anthropoid Apes*, published in the Russian language in 1930. In the book, the eminent representative of Gestalt psychology, Köhler, develops, starting from an evolutionary position, the thesis of the uniqueness of the intellectual behavior of the higher animals. Vygotsky saw the advantage of this approach in the struggle against the mechanicism of Thorndike and other behaviorists. Meanwhile Vygotsky emphasized that the deep qualitative difference of human activity, which has a conscious character, rests on the use of tools, and marks the transition to sociohistoric forms of life.

Chapter 14

1. Vygotsky's article "The problem of development in structural psychology" was first published as a foreword to the Russian translation of Koffka's *Foundations of Mental Development* (Moscow–Leningrad, 1934).

2. *Brunswik, Egon* (1903-1955). Austrian psychologist.

3. *Kries, Johann* (1853-1928). German psychophysiologist.

4. *Volkelt, Hans*. German psychologist-idealist.

Chapter 15

1. Vygotsky's work "The historical meaning of the crisis in psychology" (written in 1927) is a fundamental investigation into the psychology of the radical problems of the structure and regularities of the development of scientific thinking and the roads of psychology as a science. It is published for the first time.

The epigraph to the work (taken from the Gospel according to St. Matthew) indicates its main idea: "The stone which the builders rejected is become the head stone of the corner." This stone was, according to Vygotsky, practice and philosophy in their unity.

Relying on the Marxist principle of historicism Vygotsky explains the crisis as a specific stage which inevitably emerged in the development of psychological knowledge, reveals the confrontation of the main directions behind the many-colored pattern of schools, and sketches the road toward a way out to a new science of the human mind.

2. *Adler, Alfred* (1870-1937). Austrian psychologist. One of the prominent representatives of psychoanalysis who called his conception "individual psychology." In contrast to Freud he considered that the main source of unconscious motivation is not the sexual impulse, but the inferiority complex, which leads to compensatory (and over-compensatory) reactions, to the personality's aspiration to be superior to others.

3. *Binswanger, Ludwig* (1881-1966). Swiss psychiatrist and psychologist. In the early period of his career a follower of psychoanalysis. Later one of the leaders of the so-called existential (or humanistic) psychology which considers the person as a special whole, who can be known through the analysis of his significant experiences. One of Binswanger's early works became the starting point for Vygotsky's critique of the idealistic explanation of the reasons for the psychological crisis.

4. The actualistic conception. The theory of the Austrian philosopher Brentano according to which the subject of psychology is not formed by the phenomena of consciousness, but by its acts (imagining, and not the image as a form, judging, emotional evaluations). The intention (directionality) of the subject toward the object is expressed in the act, co-exists in this act and is, therefore, an immaterial entity.

5. Faculty theory. By this term is meant the conception proposed in the 18th century to counterbalance the associative psychology of the so-called Scottish school. According to this conception the soul is not a "tabula rasa," but is endowed with a great number of intrinsic mental forces or faculties.

6. *Jung, Karl* (1875-1961). Swiss psychologist. Was affiliated with psychoanalysis, but rejected its pan-sexualism. Proposed the reactionary theory of the collective unconscious and the "archetypes" of thinking inherited by the person.

7. Personalism. A current in psychology, which proceeds from the concept of personality (person) as a unique system. The causes of the activity of the system are hidden in the system itself. The main representative of this current was W. Stern.

8. Refers to Freud's work "Totem and taboo."

9. Freud undertook the attempt to explain the creative work of the great Italian artist Leonardo da Vinci (1452-1519) from the position of psychoanalysis.

10. Differential psychology. A branch of psychology that studies individual and typological differences between people by means of experimental and mathematical methods.

11. *Lamarck, Jean-Baptist* (1744-1829). French biologist.

12. *Einstein, Albert* (1879-1955). German physicist, reformer of contemporary physics.

13. *Schopenhauer, Arthur* (1788-1860). German idealist philosopher. Contrasted rational knowledge with the will as a blind and autonomous force. This doctrine influenced Wundt, James, Bergson, Freud, and others.

14. Mass psychology. One of the currents of social psychology studying the particularities of the behavior and consciousness of large groups of people.

15. *Shchelovanov, Nikolaj Matveevich* (1892-?). Soviet physiologist, student of Bekhterev, investigator of the behavior of young children.

16. *Fechner, Gustav Theodor* (1801-1887). German physicist, physiologist, and psychologist. Founder of psychophysics as the doctrine of the lawful relations between the physical and the mental.

17. *Preyer, Wilhelm* (1841-1897). German physiologist. Author of works on the child's mind.

18. *Petzoldt, Josef* (1862-1929). German philosopher-empiriocritic. Considered the external world as the sum-total of sensory images that may be different for different subjects. Reduced epistemology to psychology and treated the subject acquiring knowledge as an individual who is isolated and has no social ties.

19. *Planck, Max* (1858-1947). German physicist. Subjected Mach's idealistic philosophical and psychological views as well as his works on various questions of the history and methodology of physics to sharp criticism.

20. *Chelpanov, Georgij Ivanovich* (1862-1936). Russian psychologist and idealist philosopher. Founder (1912) and director (until 1923) of the first psychological institute in Russia in Moscow. Proceeded from the principle of the so-called empirical parallelism between mind and body. He considered self-observation to be the single source of knowledge of mental phenomena and assigned an auxiliary role to the experiment considering after Wundt that its main significance is to make self-observation more precise.

21. *Kravkov, Sergej Vasil'evich* (1893-1951). Soviet psychologist, specialist in the field of the investigation of the psychophysiology of the sense organs. Vygotsky criticized him for his work "Self-observation," which saw the light in 1922.

22. *Portugalov, Jurij Ven'jaminovich* (1876-?). Psychiatrist, psychologist.

23. *Shcherbina, Aleksandr Moiseevich* (1887-?). Soviet psychologist and pedagogue.

24. *Kornilov, Konstantin Nikolaevich* (1879-1957). Soviet psychologist. Initiator of the reform of the system of psychological knowledge on the basis of Marxism. Reacted against the subjectivism of Chelpanov, Bekhterev's reflexology and American behaviorism. Proclaimed reactology as the Marxist conception in psychology, which was intended to deal with the one-sidedness of subjective (empirical) and objective psychology (reflexology) by synthesizing these two currents. Later he relinquished these ideas. He worked on problems of pedagogical psychology and personality psychology.

25. *Ach, Narziss* (1871-1946). German psychologist.

26. *Leibnitz, Gotfried Wilhelm* (1646-1716). German idealist philosopher. In his theory of the mind he was a critic of Locke's associationism, defended the idea of the activity of the soul, and introduced into psychology the concepts of apperception and the unconsciousness.

27. *Ptolemy, Claudius* (2nd century B.C.). Greek astronomer and geographer. Elaborated the so-called geocentric theory.

28. *Copernicus (Kopernik), Nikolaj* (1473-1543). Polish astronomer. Founder of the so-called heliocentric theory.

29. *Hall, Stanley* (1844-1924). American psychologist. Main works in the area of educational psychology. Wished to extend the biogenetic law to the development of children's behavior.

30. *Spengler, Oswald* (1880-1936). German idealist philosopher.

31. *Dumas, Georges* (1866-1936). French psychologist and pathopsychologist, student of Ribot. Founded in 1904 together with Janet the first French psychological journal. Specialist in the area of the psychophysiology of the emotions of healthy and sick people.

32. *Plato* (428/7-348/7 B.C.). Classic Greek philosopher. Founder of idealism.

33. *Lichtenberg, Georg Christoph* (1742-1799). German educator, physicist, art critic.

34. *Duhem, Pierre* (1861-1916). French theoretical physicist, philosopher and historian of science.

35. *Wolf (Wolff), Christian* (1679-1754). German philosopher. Distinguished rational and empirical psychology. Adherent of the theory of faculties as primary forces of the mind.

36. *Sarab'janov, Vladimir Nikolaevich* (1886-1952). Soviet philosopher.

37. *Descartes, René* (1596-1650). French philosopher. Founder of the theory of consciousness as direct knowledge of one's own inner mental states and of the reflex as an automatic reaction of the organism to some external stimulus mediated by the brain.

38. *Spencer, Herbert* (1820-1903). English philosopher and psychologist. One of the founders of positivism. Extended evolutionary theory to the area of the organism's behavior and its mental functions.

39. *Paulsen, Friedrich* (1846-1908). German idealist philosopher. Considered the bodily system to be a manifestation of inner mental life whose basis is volition.

40. *Frank, Semyon Ljudvigovich* (1877-1950). Russian religious philosopher.

41. *Titchener, Edward* (1867-1927). American psychologist. Adherent of structuralist introspectionist psychology as a theory of the elements of consciousness and their connections.

42. *Lotze, Herman* (1817-1881). German philosopher and psychologist. Attempted to use the achievements of neurophysiology to strengthen the idealist conception of the mind.

43. *Euclid* (ca. Third Century B.C.). Classic Greek mathematician.

44. *Lobachevsky, Nikolaj Ivanovich* (1792-1856). Russian mathematician, one of the founders of the non-Euclidean geometry.

45. *Riemann, Georg Friedrich Bernhard* (1826-1866). German mathematician, one of the founders of non-Euclidean geometry.

46. *Linné (Linnaeus), Karl* (1707-1778). Swedish natural scientist, who created a classificatory system for the plant and animal world. He included man into his system, which subsequently stimulated the investigation of the similarity, difference, and links existing between man and the animal world.

47. *Cuvier, Georges* (1769-1832). French scholar, zoologist, and paleontologist. Rejected the idea of the evolutionary development of the species.

48. *Natorp, Paul* (1854-1924). German neo-Kantian philosopher. Thought that the object of knowledge is constructed by the activity of the subject.

49. Intentional psychology. See actualistic psychology.

50. *Windelband, Wilhelm* (1848-1915). German neo-Kantian philosopher. Divided the sciences into nomothetic (natural) and idiographic (cultural-historical) ones. The former deal with what is general, repeatable and lawful in the phenomena; the latter study individual phenomena in their unrepeatable and exclusive nature.

51. *Galilei, Galileo* (1564-1642). Italian physicist whose theory played a prominent role in the scientific revolution of the 17th century.

52. *Buffon, George* (1706-1788). French natural scientist, who proposed the idea of the unity of the world of plants and animals and about the changeability of species under the influence of environmental conditions (climate, food, etc.). Was closely tied to the French materialists.

53. *Stout, George* (1860-1944). English psychologist with an idealistic orientation. Criticized the natural scientific tendencies of associationism.

54. *Pfänder, Alexander* (1870-1941). German psychologist and idealist philosopher. Treated man as the trinity of body, soul and spirit, and the spirit as the soul returning to itself.

55. *Jaspers, Karl* (1883-1969). German extentialistic philosopher. Saw psychopathological phenomena not as the expression of the disintegration of the personality, but as an intensification of the person's search for his individuality. Elaborated a theory about extreme situations according to which the genuine meaning of life is revealed to the person in periods of deep turmoil. Exactly during these moments the person is liberated from the burden of everyday concerns and scientific ideas about reality. His most intimate existence (the insight into true existence) and his true experience of God (the transcendent) are revealed to him.

56. Vygotsky's remarks about Marxist psychology must be seen in the context of the debates of the 1920s, when some psychologists understood this task as the direct deduction of concrete scientific conclusions from the laws of materialistic dialectics. Vygotsky's work is polemically directed against such an approach.

57. Here by methodology Vygotsky means not a general philosophical, but a concrete scientific method of organization of knowledge. Vygotsky saw the elaboration of a methodology of psychology as a concrete discipline as the key task of Soviet scientists.

58. The remark about the allegedly "haphazard" pronouncements about psychological problems by the founders of Marxism was on the one hand polemically directed against attempts to reduce a Marxist orientation in psychology to an arbitrary choice of quotations; on the other hand, it reflected the level of mastery of the wealth of psychological ideas contained in dialectical materialistic philosophy typical of the 1920s.

59. Here Vygotsky is mixing up the philosophical theory of knowledge (epistemology) elaborated in Marxism with the means which psychology as a concrete science works out for the study of its subject matter.

60. Vygotsky has in mind his work "The psychology of art," written in 1924.

61. In his polemic with the vulgarizers of the idea of the construction of a Marxist psychology, Vygotsky, in emphasizing the role of method, does not explain the meaning of the statements about the nature of the mental advanced by Marxism as a theoretical world view.

Epilogue

1. The concept of the development of systems was completely new. Its novelty can be easily grasped when we compare it with the treatment of systems in Gestalt psychology, to which the principle of development was foreign. The advantage of Vygotsky's approach is clearly visible when we compare it with several contemporary variants of the "system approach" which were not capable of understanding the connection between the system and historicism. It is not without interest to note

that in the same period Ukhtomsky developed the concept of the functional system and the history of the system in physiology. It is unknown whether Vygotsky was acquainted with these elaborations.

2. According to Vygotsky, the concept of general psychology did not coincide with the concept of theoretical psychology. Theoretical psychology is "in essence the psychology of the adult normal person and should be considered to be one of the special disciplines alongside zoopsychology and psychopathology. That it so far has played and to some extent still plays the role of a generalizing factor, which to a certain extent forms the structure and system of the special disciplines and furnishes them with their main concepts and brings them into line with their own structure, is explained by the history of the development of the science, rather than by logical necessity. This is the way things have been and to some extent still are, but they should not and will not remain this way; this situation does not follow from the very nature of the science, but is determined by external, extraneous circumstances. As soon as they change, the psychology of the normal person will lose its leading role" (pp. 233-234, this volume).

REFERENCES

Bagú, S. (1963). *Vida de José Ingenieros*. Buenos Aires: Editorial Universitaria de Buenos Aires.
Baldwin, J. M. (1910). Report on terminology. In E. Claparède (Ed.), *VIme Congrès International de Psychologie* (pp. 480-481). Genève: Kündig.
Beer, T., Bethe, A., & Von Uexküll, J. J. (1899). Vorschläge zu einer objektivierender Nomenklatur in der Physiologie des Nervensystems. *Biologisches Centralblatt, 19*, 517-521.
Beilin, H. (1993). Mechanisms in the explanation of cognitive development. In J. Montangero, A. Cornu-Wells, A. Tryphon, & J. Vonèche (Eds.), *Conceptions of Change over Time* (pp. 137-157). Genève: Fondation Archives Jean Piaget.
Bekhterev, V. M. (1921). *Kollektivnaja refleksologija*. Petersburg.
Bekhterev, V. M. (1923). *Obshchie osnovy refleksologii cheloveka*. Moscow–Petersburg.
Bekhterev, V. M. (1926). *Rabota golovnogo mozga*. Leningrad.
Bekhterev, V. M. (1932). *General principles of human reflexology*. New York: International Publishers.
Bekhterev, V. M. (1904). *Mind and life*. St. Petersburg: K. L. Rikker.
Bergson, H. (1896/1939). *Matière et mémoire. Essai sur la relation ducorps à l'esprit*. Paris: Alcan (seventh edition) (Russian translation 1911).
Binet, A. (1890). Perception d'enfants. *Revue Philosophique, 30*, 582-611.
Binet, A. (1894). *Psychologie des grands calculateurs et joueurs d'échecs*. Paris: Librairie Hachette et Cie.
Binswanger, L. (1922). *Einführung in die Probleme der allgemeinen Psychologie*. Berlin: Springer.
Bleuler, E. (1911). *Dementia praecox oder Gruppe der Schizophrenien*. Leipzig and Wien: Deuticke.
Blondel, Ch. (1914). *La conscience morbide. Essaide psychologie générale*. Paris: Alcan.
Blonsky, P. P. (1921). *Ocherk nauchnoj psikhologii*. Moscow: Gosudarstvennoe Izdatel'stvo.
Blonsky, P. P. (1925a). Psikhologija kak nauka o povedenii. In K. N. Kornilov (Ed.), *Psikhologija i marksizm* (pp. 225-229). Leningrad: Gosudarstvennoe Izdatel'stvo.
Blonsky, P. P. (1925b). *Pedologija*. Moscow: Rabotnik Prosveshchenija.
Borovsky, V. M. (1927). *Vvedenie v sravnitel'nuju psikhologiju*. Moscow: Gosizdat.
Bühler, Ch. (1918), Das Märchen und die Phantasie des Kindes. *Zeitschrift für angewandte Psychologie (Beiheft 17)*.
Bühler, Ch. (1928/1967). *Kindheit und Jugend*. Göttingen: Hogrefe (4th edition).
Bühler, K. (1918). *Die geistige Entwicklung des Kindes*. Jena: Verlag von Gustav Fischer.
Bühler, K. (1919/1929). *Abriss der geistigen Entwicklung des Kindes*. Leipzig: Verlag von Quelle und Meyer (Russian translation 1930).
Bühler, K. (1927/1978). *Die Krise der Psychologie*. Frankfurt/M: Ullstein.
Bühler, K. (1930). *Ocherk dukhovnogo razvitija rebenka*. Moscow: Rabotnik Prosveshchenija.
Burkhardt, F. H. (Ed.) (1976). *The works of William James. Essays in radical empiricism*. Cambridge, MA: Harvard University Press.
Burkhardt, F. H. (Ed.) (1984). *The works of William James. Psychology: Briefer Course*. Cambridge, MA: Harvard University Press.
Buytendijk, F. J. J. (1929). Zur untersuchung des Wesensunterschieds von Mensch und Tier. *Bl. deutsche Philos., 3*, 33-66.
Buytendijk, F. J. J. (1930). Les différences essentielles des fonctions psychiques de l'homme et des animaux. *Cahiers Philos. Nat., 4*, 1-60.
Chelpanov, G. I. (1917). Ob analitcheskom metode v psikhologii. *Psikhologicheskoe Obozrenie, 1*.
Chelpanov, G. I. (1924). *Psikhologija i marksizm*. Moscow: A. V. Dumnov and Co.
Chelpanov, G. I. (1925). *Ob'ektivnaja psikhologija v Rossii i Amerike*. Moscow.
Chelpanov, G. I. (1926). *Social'naja psikhologija ili uslovnye refleksy?* Moscow–Leningrad.
Claparède, E. (1910a) (Ed.), *VIme Congrès International de Psychologie*. Genève: Kündig.
Claparède, E. (1910b). L'unification et la fixation de la terminologie psychologique. In E. Claparède, (Ed.), *VIme Congrès International de Psychologie* (pp. 467-479). Genève: Kündig.
Cole, M. (Ed.) (1978), *The selected writings of A. R. Luria*. White Plains: Merle Sharpe.

Darwin, Ch. (1871/1981). *The descent of man*. Princeton, NJ: Princeton University Press.

Deborin, A. M. (1923). *Vvedenie v filosofiju dialekticheskogo materializma*. Moscow.

Deborin, A. M. (1929). *Dialektika i estestvoznanie*. Moscow–Leningrad.

Dennett, D. C. (1991). *Consciousness Explained*. London: The Penguin Press.

Dessoir, M. (1911). *Abriss einer Geschichte der Psychologie*. Heidelberg: Carl Winter's Universitätsbuchhandlung (Russian translation 1912).

Dewey, J. (1910/1933). *How we think*. Boston: Heath and Company.

Dewey, J. (1938/1982). *Logic. The theory of inquiry*. New York: Irvington.

Diderot, D. (1971). Réfutation d'Helvétius. *Oeuvres Complètes. Tome XI*. (pp. 465-653). Paris: Le Club Français du Livre.

Dilthey, W. (1894/1977). *Descriptive psychology and historical understanding* (pp. 21-120). The Hague: Martinus Nijhoff (Russian translation 1924).

Duhem, P. (1906). *La théorie physique. Son objet et sa structure*. Paris: Alcan (Russian translation 1910).

Dumas, G. (1924). Conclusion. In G. Dumas (Ed.), *Traité de psychologie. Vol. II* (pp. 1121-1158). Paris: Alcan.

Ebbinghaus, G. (1902). *Grundzüge der Psychologie*. Leipzig: Verlag von Veit & Comp (Russian translation 1912).

Edinger, L. (1911). *Vorlesungen über den Bau der nervösen Zentralorgane der Menschen und der Tiere*. Leipzig: Quelle & Meyer.

Eldredge, N. (1993). Stability and change in biological systems. In J. Montangero, A. Cornu-Wells, A. Tryphon, & J. Vonèche (Eds.), *Conceptions of Change over Time* (pp. 33-43). Genève: Fondation Archives Jean Piaget.

Engels, F. (1925/1978). *Dialektik der Natur*. Berlin: Dietz Verlag.

Etkind, A. M. (1993). Eshe o L. S. Vygotskom: Zabytye teksty i nenaidennye konteksty. *Voprosy Psikhologii*, 4, 37-55.

Evergetov, I. V. (1924). *Posle empirizma*. Leningrad.

Evergetov, I. V. (Ed.) (1924). *Methods for the Objective Investigation of the Child*. Leningrad: Publishing House of the Leningrad Institute of Pedology.

Feuerbach, L. (1955). Protiv dualizma dushi i tela, ploti i dukha. In L. Feuerbach, *Izbrannye filosofskie proizvedenija*. Moscow.

Feuerbach, L. (1971). *Werke. Bd. 10*. Berlin.

Frank, S. L. (1917/1964). *Dusha cheloveka*. Paris: YMCA Press.

Frankfurt, Ju. V. (1926). Plekhanov o psikhofiziologicheskoj probleme. *Pod Znamenem Marksizma*, 6.

Freud, S. (1900/1973). The interpretation of dreams. In J. Strachey (Ed.), *The Standard Edition of the Complete Works of Sigmund Freud. Vol. IV. The Interpretation of Dreams (First Part)*. London: The Hogarth Press.

Freud, S. (1906/1973). Three essays on the theory of sexuality. In J. Strachey (Ed.), *The Standard Edition of the Complete Psychological Works of Sigmund Freud. Vol. VII. A Case of Hysteria, Three Essays on Sexuality, and Other Works*. London: The Hogarth Press (Russian translation 1924).

Freud, S. (1917/1973). Introductory lectures on psycho-analysis. In J. Strachey (Ed.), *The Standard Edition of the Complete Psychological Works of Sigmund Freud. Vol. XVI. Introductory Lectures on Psycho-Analysis (Part III)*. London: The Hogarth Press (Russian translation 1923).

Freud, S. (1920/1973). Beyond the pleasure principle. In J. Strachey (Ed.), *The Standard Edition of the Complete Psychological Works of Sigmund Freud. Vol. XVIII. Beyond the Pleasure Principle, Group Psychology, and Other Works*. London: The Hogarth Press (Russian translation 1925).

Freud, S. (1923/1973). The ego and the id. In J. Strachey (Ed.), *The Standard Edition of the Complete Psychological Works of Sigmund Freud. Vol. XIX. The Ego and the Id and Other Works*. London: The Hogarth Press (Russian translation 1924).

Fridman, B. D. (1925). Osnovnye psikhologicheskie vozrenija Frejda i teorija istoricheskogo materializma. In K. N. Kornilov (Ed.), *Psikhologija i marksizm* (pp. 113-159). Leningrad: Gosudarstvennoe Izdatel'stvo.

Frolov, U. P. (1926). Transformation of conditioned trace-stimuli and trace-conditioned inhibitors into non-trace stimuli. *Collected Papers of the Physiological Laboratory of I. P. Pavlov*, Vol. I, no. 2-3.

Fursikov, D. S. (1922). About conditional chain reflexes. *Russkij Fiziologicheskij Zhurnal*, 4.

Gelb, A. & Goldstein, K. (1925). Ueber Farbennamenamnesie. *Psychologische Forschung*, 6, 127-186.

Goldstein, K., & Gelb, A. (1920). *Psychologische Analysen hirnpathologischer Fälle*. Leipzig: Barth.

Gould, S. J. (1981), *The Mismeasure of Man*. Harmondsworth: Penguin.

Groos, K. (1899). *Die Spiele der Menschen*. Jena: Fischer.

Groos, K. (1904/1921). *Das Seelenleben des Kindes*. Berlin: Verlag von Reuther & Reichard (Russian translation 1906).

Guillaume, P., & Meyerson, I. (1930). Recherches sur l'usage de l'instrument chez les singes I: Le probleme du détour. *Journal de Psychologie*, 27, 177-236.

Guillaume, P., & Meyerson, I. (1931). Recherches sur l'usage de l'instrument chez les singes II: L'intermédiaire lié á l'objet. *Journal de Psychologie*, 28, 481-555.

Hamlyn, D. W. (1969). *The Psychology of Perception. A Philosophical Examination of Gestalt Theory and Derivative Theories of Perception.* London: Routledge & Kegan Paul.

Head, H. (1915). Hughlings Jackson on aphasia and kindred affections of speech. *Brain, 38,* 1-190.

Head, H. (1926). *Aphasia and kindred disorders of speech. 2 Vols.* Cambridge: Cambridge University Press.

Hegel, G. W. F. (1812/1948). *Wissenschaft der Logik. Vol. 1.* Leipzig: Felix Meiner.

Hetzer, H., & Wiehemeyer, E. (1929). Optische Rezeption und Bilderfassen im zweiten Lebensjahr. *Zeitschrift für Psychologie, 113,* 268-286.

Høffding, H. (1908). *Psychologie in Umrissen auf Grundlage der Erfahrung.* Leipzig: O. R. Reisland (4th German edition after the 5th Danish edition; Russian translation 1908).

Husserl, E. (1911/1965). *Philosophie als strenge Wissenschaft.* Frankfurt am Main: Vittorio Klostermann (Russian translation 1911).

Ingenieros, J. (1910). *Principios de Psicología.* Buenos Aires: Ediciones L. J. Rosso.

Ingenieros, J. (1914). *Principes de psychologie biologique.* Paris: Alcan.

Ivanovsky, V. N. (1923). *Metodologicheskoe vvedenie v nauku i filosofiju.* Minsk.

Jaensch, E. R. (1923). *Über den Aufbau der Wahrnemungswelt und ihre Struktur im Jugendalter.* Leipzig: Barth (second edition 1927).

James, H. (1920). *The letters of William James.* London: Longmans, Green, and Co.

James, W. (1899/1920). *Talks to teachers on psychology and to students on some of life's ideals.* London: Longmans, Green and Co. (Russian edition 1905).

James, W. (1904/1976). Does consciousness exist? In F. H. Burkhardt (Ed.), *The works of William James. Essays in radical empiricism* (pp. 3-19). Cambridge, MA: Harvard University Press.

Jameson, L. (1925). *Outline of a Marxist psychology* (Russian translation 1925).

Jaroshevsky, M. G. (1993). L. S. Vygotsky—zhertva "opticheskogo obmana". *Voprosy Psikhologii, 4,* 55-60.

Jerusalem, W. (1890). *Laura Bridgman. Erziehung einer Taubstummblinden. Eine psychologische Studie.* Vienna: A. Pichlers Witwe & Sohn.

Jerusalem, W. (1902). *Lehrbuch der Psychologie.* Vienna-Leipzig: Braumüller.

Jerusalem, W. (1924). *Gedanken und Denker. Neue Folge.* Vienna-Leipzig: Braumüller.

Koffka, K. (1922). Perception: An introduction to the Gestalt-theorie. *Psychologically Bulletin, 19,* 531-585.

Koffka, K. (1924). Introspection and the method of psychology. *British Journal of Psychology, 15,* 149-161 (Russian translation 1926).

Koffka, K. (1925a). *Die Grundlagen der psychischen Entwicklung.* Osterwieck am Harz: A. W. Zickfeldt (Russian translation 1934).

Koffka, K. (1925b). Psychologie. In M. Dessoir (Ed.), *Lehrbuch der Philosophie. Band II. Die Philosophie in ihren Einzelgebieten* (pp. 495-603). Berlin: Ullstein.

Koffka, K. (1932). Preodolenie mekhanisticheskikh i vitalisticheskikh techenij v sovremennoj psikhologii. *Psikhologija, 5,* 1-2, 59-69.

Koffka, K. (1934). *Osnovy psikhicheskogo razvitija.* Moscow-Leningrad: Gosudarstvennoe Social'no-Ekonomicheskoe Izdatel'stvo.

Köhler, W. (1917). *Intelligenzprüfungen an Anthropoiden.* Berlin: Königliche Akademie der Wissenschaften.

Köhler, W. (1920). *Die physischen Gestalten in Ruhe und imstationären Zustand: Eine naturphilosophische Untersuchung.* Erlangen: Verlag der Philosophischen Akademie.

Köhler, W. (1921a). Die Methoden der psychologischen Forschung an Affen. In E. Abderhalden (Ed.), *Handbuch der biologischen Arbeitsmethoden* (Abt. 6, Teil D) (pp. 69-120). Berlin: Urban & Schwarzenberg.

Köhler, W. (1921b). *Intelligenzprüfungen an Menschenaffen.* Berlin: Julius Springer (Russian translation 1930).

Köhler, W. (1922). Zur Psychologie des Schimpansen. *Psychologische Forschung, 1,* 2-46.

Köhler, W. (1924). *Gestalt psychology.* New York: Liveright Publishing Corporation.

Köhler, W. (1929). La perception humaine. *Journal de psychologie, 27,* 5-30.

Köhler, W. (1930). *Issledovanie intellekta chelovekopodobnykh obez'jan.* Moscow: Izdatel'stvo Kommunisticheskoj Akademii.

Köhler, W. (1933). *Psychologische Probleme.* Berlin: Verlag von Julius Springer.

Kornilov, K. N. (1922). *Uchenie o reakcijakh cheloveka s psikhologicheskoj tochki zrenija ("reaktologija").* Moscow: Gosudarstvennoe Izdatel'stvo.

Kornilov, K. N. (1925). Psikhologija i marksizm. In K. N. Kornilov (Ed.), *Psikhologija i marksizm* (pp. 231-242). Moscow-Leningrad: Gosudarstvennoe Izdatel'stvo.

Kravkov, S. V. (1922). *Samonabljudenie.* Moscow.

Kretschmer, E. (1929). *Körperbau und Character.* Berlin: Verlag von Julius Springer (Russian translation 1924).

Krol', M. B. (1922). Myshlenie i rech'. *Trudy Belorusskogo Gosudarstvennogo Universiteta, 11,* 1.

Külpe, O. (1916). Sovremennaja psikhologija myshlenija. *Novye Idei v Filosofii, 16.*

Külpe, O. (1922). Über die Bedeutung der modernen Denkpsychologie. In O. Külpe, *Vorlesungen über Psychologie* (pp. 297-331). Leipzig: S. Hirzel.

Lalande, A. (1923). Introduction. La psychologie, ses divers objets et ses méthodes. In Dumas, G. (1923). *Traité de psychologie. Vol. I* (pp. 1-56). Paris: Alcan.

Lamarck, J. B. (1809/1914). *Zoological philosophy.* London: Macmillan.

Lange, N. N. (1914). Psikhologija. *Itogi Nauki, 8.*

Lange, F. A. (1866/1974). *Geschichte des Materialismus und Kritik seiner Bedeutung in der Gegenwart. Bd. 2. Geschichte des Materialismus seit Kant.* Frankfurt am Main: Suhrkamp.

Lapshin, I. I. (1910). *The problem of the other person's "Ego" in the newest philosophy.* Petersburg.

Lashley, K. S. (1923). The behavioristic interpretation of consciousness. *Psychological Review, 30,* 237-272; 329-353.

Lazursky, A. F. (1925). *Psikhologija obshchaja i eksperimental'naja.* Moscow.

Leibniz, G. W. (1908). *Izbrannye filosofskie sochinenija.* Moscow.

Lenin, V. I. (1909/1984). *Materializm i empiriokriticism.* Moscow: Izdatel'stvo Politicheskoj Literatury.

Lenin, V. I. (1929/1978). *Filosofskie tetradi.* Moscow: Izdatel'stvo Politicheskoj Literatury.

Lenin, V. I. (1973). *Werke. Bd. 38.* Berlin: Dietz Verlag.

Lenin, V. I. (1975). *Werke. Bd. 14.* Berlin: Dietz Verlag.

Lenz, A. G. (1922). Ob osnovakh fiziologicheskoj teorii chelovecheskogo povedenija. *Priroda,* 6/7.

Leont'ev, A. N. (1931). *Razvitie pamjati. Eksperimental'noe issledovanie vysshikh psikhologicheskikh funkcij.* Moscow-Leningrad: Uchpedgiz.

Lévy-Bruhl, L. (1922/1976). *La mentalité primitive.* Paris: Alcan.

Lindworsky, J. (1919). Referat über Köhler. *Stimmen der Zeit, 97,* 62-68.

Lipps, Th. (1897). Der Begriff des Unbewussten in der Psychologie. In *Bericht des III Internationalen Psychologie Kongresses* (pp. 146-164). Munich: Verlag von J. F. Lehmann.

Lipps, Th. (1907). Das Wissen von fremden Ichen. In Th. Lipps (Ed.), *Psychologische Untersuchungen. Vol. I* (pp. 694-722). Leipzig: Verlag von Wilhelm Engelmann.

Luria, A. R. (1925). Psikhoanaliz, kak sistema monisticheskoj psikhologii. In K. N. Kornilov (Ed.), *Psikhologija i marksizm* (pp. 47-80). Leningrad: Gosudarstvennoe Izdatel'stvo.

Luria, A. R. (1926). Moskovskij Gosudarstvennyj Institut Eksperimental'noj Psikhologii v 1924 godu. In K. N. Kornilov (Ed.), *Problemy Sovremennoj Psikhologii* (pp. 244-252). Leningrad: Gosudarstvennoe Izdatel'stvo.

Luria, A. R. (1928a). Soprjazhennaja motornaja metodika v issledovanii affektivnykh reakcij. *Trudy Gosudarstvennogo Instituta Eksperimental'noj Psikhologii. Vol. III.* Moscow.

Luria, A. R. (1928b). Soprjazhennaja motornaja metodika i ee primenenie v issledovanii effektivnykh reakcij. In K. N. Kornilov (Ed.), *Problemy sovremennoj psikhologii.* Leningrad: Gosudarstvennoe Izdatel'stvo.

Luria, A. R. (1973). *The Working Brain: An Introduction to Neuropsychology.* Harmondsworth: Penguin.

Mandelkow, K. R. (Ed.) (1967). *Goethes Briefe. Band IV.* Hamburg: Christian Wegner Verlag.

Marx, K. (1904). *Critique of Political Economy.* Chicago: Charles Kerr, Co.

Marx, K. (1852/1972). Der achtzehnte Brumaire des Louis Bonaparte. In *Marx, K./ Engels, F. Werke. Bd. 8* (pp. 111-207). Berlin: Dietz Verlag.

Marx, K. (1890/1981a). Das Kapital. Bd. 1. In *Marx, K./ Engels, F. Werke. Bd. 23.* Berlin: Dietz Verlag.

Marx, K. (1890/1981b). Das Kapital. Bd. 3. In *Marx, K./ Engels, F. Werke. Bd. 25.* Berlin: Dietz Verlag.

Marx, K., & Engels, F. (1970). Briefe. Februar 1842—Dezember 1851. In *Marx, K./ Engels, F. Werke. Marx, K. (1978) Bd. 27.* Berlin: Dietz Verlag.

Michotte, A. E. (1927). Rapport sur la perception des formes. In *VIIIth International Congress of Psychology* (pp. 166-174). Groningen: Noordhoff.

Mill, J. S. (1843/1904). *A System of Logic, ratiocinative and inductive: being a connected view of the principles of evidence and the methods of scientific investigation.* London: Longmans, Green & Co.

Molière, J. B. (1670/1984). *Le bourgeois gentilhomme.* Paris: Bordas.

Morris, M. (Ed.) (MDCXL). *Goethes Sämtliche Werke. Band 39.* Stuttgart/Berlin: Gotta'sche Buchhandlung Nachfolger.

Mourelatos, A. P. D. (Ed.) (1974). *The Pre-Socratics. A Collection of Critical Essays.* Garden City, NY: Anchor Books.

Münsterberg, H. (1900). *Grundzüge der Psychologie. Band I. Der Prinzipien der Psychologie.* Leipzig: Verlag von Johann Ambrosius Barth (Russian translation 1922).

Münsterberg, H. (1909). *Psychology and the teacher.* New York: D. Appleton.

Münsterberg, H., Ribot, Th., Janet, P., Jastrow, J., Hart, B., & Prince, M. (1910). *Subconscious Phenomena,* Boston: Richard G. Badger.

Münsterberg, H. (1920). *Grundzüge der Psychotechnik.* Leipzig: Barth.

Natorp, P. (1899/1974). *Sozialpädagogik.* Paderborn: Ferdinand Schöningh.

Natorp, P. (1904). *Logik.* Marburg: Elwert'sche Verlagbuchhandlung. (Russian translation 1909)

Oppenheim, D. E. (1923). Shakespeares Menschenkenntnis. *Internationale Zeitschrift für Individualpsychologie, 1,* 37-39.

Overton, W. F. (1993). The arrow of time and cycles of time: Implications for change in cognitive development. In J. Montangero, A. Cornu-Wells, A. Tryphon, & J. Vonèche (Eds.), *Conceptions of Change over Time* (pp. 159-180). Genève: Fondation Archives Jean Piaget.

Paulhan, J. (1928). Qu'est-ce que le sens des mots? *Journal de Psychologie, 25*, 289-329.

Pavlov, I. P. (1926/1960). *Conditioned reflexes. An investigation of the physiological activity of the cerebral cortex.* New York: Dover Publications.

Pavlov, I. P. (1928/1963). *Lectures on conditioned reflexes.* New York: International Publishers.

Pearson, K. (1900). *The grammar of science.* London: J. M. Dent & Sons Ltd. (Russian translation 1911)

Peters, W. (1915). Über Vererbung psychischer Fähigkeiten. *Fortschritte der Psychologie und ihrer Anwendungen, 3.*

Pfänder, A. (1904). *Einführung in die Psychologie.* Leipzig: Johann Ambrosius Barth. (Russian translation 1909)

Piaget, J. (1923). *Le langage et la penseé chez l'enfant.* Neuchatel: Delachaux et Niestlé. (Russian translation 1932)

Piaget, J. (1924). *Le jugement et le raisonnement chez l'enfant.* Neuchatel: Delachaux et Niestlé. (Russian translation 1932)

Planck, M. (1919/1970). Das Wesen des Lichts. In M. Planck, *Vorträge und Erinnerungen* (pp. 112-124). Darmstadt: Wissenschaftliche Buchgesellschaft.

Plekhanov, G. V. (1922a). *Ocherki po istorii materializma* (3d edition).*

Plekhanov, G. V. (1922b). *Iskusstvo.* Moscow.

Plekhanov, G. V. (1922c). *Osnovnye voprosy marksizma.* Moscow.

Plekhanov, G. V. (1956). *Izbrannye filosofskie proizvedenija.* Moscow.

Pillsbury, W. B. (1917). *The fundamentals of psychology.* New York: The Macmillan Company.

Portugalov, Ju. V. (1925). Kak issledovat' psikhiku. In *Detskaja psikhologija i antropologija. Vypusk I.* Samara.

Potebnya, A. A. (1913/1993). *Mysl' i yazyk.* Kiev: SINTO.

Pötzl, O. (1928). *Die Aphasielehre vom Standpunkt der klinischen Psychiatrie. Die optisch-agnostischen Störungen.* Leipzig: Deuticke.

Protopopov, V. P. (1923). The methods of the reflexological investigation of man. *Zhurnal Psikhologii, Nevrologii, i Psikhiatrii, 3*, 1-2.

Pushkin, A. S. (1984). *Sobranie Sochinenij v Odnom Tome.* Moscow: Khudozhestvennaya Literatura.

Ribot, Th. (1888). *La psychologie de l'attention.* Paris: Alcan.

Ribot, Th. (1923). Préface. In G. Dumas (Ed.), *Traité de psychologie.Vol. I* (pp. v-xiv). Paris: Alcan.

Rubakin, N. A. (1929). *Psikhologija chitatelja i knigi.* Moscow.

Ruger, H. A. (1910). The psychology of efficiency. *Archives of Psychology*, No. 15.

Samukhin, N. V., Birenbaum, G. V., & Vygotsky, L. S. (1934). K voprosu o demencii pri bolezni Pika. *Sovetskaja Nevropatologija, Psikhiatrija, Psikhologija, 6*, 97-136.

Sander, F. (1927). Ueber Gestaltwahrnehmung. In *VIIIth International Congress of Psychology* (pp. 183-189). Groningen: Noordhoff.

Sechenov, I. (1866/1965). *Reflexes of the brain.* Cambridge, MA: The M.I.T. Press.

Selz, O. (1922). *Ueber die Gesetze des geordneten Denkverlaufs. Bd. II. Zur Psychologie des produktiven Denkens und des Irrtums.* Bonn: Verlag von Friedrich Cohen.

Semon, R. (1920). *Die Mneme als erhaltendes Prinzip im Wechsel des organischen Geschehens.* Leipzig: Verlag von Wilhelm Engelmann.

Severcov, A. N. (1922). *Evoljucija i psikhika.* Moscow.

Shchelovanov, N. M. (1929). Metodika geneticheskoj refleksologii. In *Novoe v refleksologii i fiziologii.* Moscow-Leningrad.

Shcherbina, A. M. (1908). Vozmozhna li psikhologija bez samonabljudenija? *Voprosy Filosofii i Psikhologii, 4* (94).

Sherrington, Ch. S. (1904). The correlation of spinal-brain reflexes and the principle of the common path. *Nature*, September 8, 460-466. (Russian translation 1912)

Sherrington, Ch. S. (1906). *The integrative action of the nervous system.* New York: Charles Scribner's Sons.

Sombart, W. (1913). *Der Bourgeois. Zur Geistesgeschichte des modernen Wirtschaftsmenschen.* München-Leipzig: Duncker & Humblot.

Spearman, C. (1924). Ueber psychische Gesetzmässigkeiten. In K. Bühler (Ed.), *Bericht über den VIII. Kongress für experimentelle Psychologie in Leipzig* (pp. 201-202). Jena: Verlag von Gustav Fischer.

Spinoza, B. de (1677/1955). *On the improvement of the understanding. The ethics. Correspondence.* New York: Dover.

Spranger, E. (1925). *Psychologie des Jugendalters.* Leipzig: Quelle und Meyer.

Stanislavsky, K. S. (1981). *Creating A Role.* London: Eyre Methuen.

Stepanov, I. I. (1924). *Istoricheskij materializm i sovremennoe estestvoznanie.* Moscow.

Stern, W. (1913). Die Anwendung der Psychoanalyse auf Kindheit und Jugend. Ein Protest. *Zeitschrift für angewandte Psychologie, 8*, 71-101.

Stern, W. (1919). *Die menschliche Persönlichkeit*. Leipzig: Verlag von Johann Ambrosius Barth.
Stern, W. (1924). *Person und Sache. Bd. III. Wertphilosophie*. Leipzig: Verlag von Johan Ambrosius Barth.
Stern, W. (1927). *Psychologie der frühen Kindheit*. Leipzig: Verlag von Quelle & Meyer. (Russian translation 1922)
Stern, Cl., & Stern, W. (1928/1981). *Die Kindersprache*. Darmstadt: Wissenschaftliche Buchgesellschaft.
Storch, A. (1922). *Das archaisch-primitive Erleben und Denken der Schizophrenen*. Berlin: Verlag von Julius Springer.
Stout, G. F. (1909). *Analytic psychology. Vol. 1*. London: Swan Sonnenschein & Co. (Russian translation 1923)
Struminsky, V. Ja. (1923). *Psikhologija*. Orenburg.
Struminsky, V. Ja. (1926). Marksizm v sovremennoj psikhologii. *Pod Znamenem Marksizma*, 3/4/5.
Stumpf, K. (1928). *William James nach seinen Briefen. Leben. Charakter. Lehre*. Berlin: Pan Bücherei.
Thorndike, E. L. (1906). *The Principles of Teaching Based on Psychology*. New York: A. G. Seiler. (Russian translation 1925)
Thorndike, E. L. (1911). *Animal intelligence*. New York: The Macmillan Company.
Thorndike, E. L. (1920). *The Elements of Psychology*. New York: A. G. Seiler.
Thorndike, E. L. (1925). *Principy obuchenija, osnovannye na psikhologii*. Moscow: Rabotnik Prosveshchenija.
Thurnwald, R. (1922). Psychologie des primitiven Menschen. In G. Kafka (Ed.). *Handbuch der vergleichenden Psychologie. Vol. I*. (pp. 145-320). Munchen: Verlag von Ernst Reinhardt.
Titchener, E. (1910/1980). *A textbook of psychology*. Delmar, NY: Scholars' Facsimiles & Reprints. (Russian translation 1914)
Ukhtomsky, A. A. (1923). The dominant as the working principle of the nervous centers. *Russkij Fiziologicheskij Zhurnal*, 6, 1-3.
Ukhtomsky, A. A., Vinogradov, M. I., & Kaplan, I.I. (1923). [unknown title]. *Russkij Fiziologicheskij Zhurnal*, 6.
Uspensky, G. (1949). *Izbrannye Proizvedenija*. Moscow.
Utitz, E. (1925). Aesthetik und Philosophie der Kunst. In M. Dessoir (Ed.), *Lehrbuch der Philosophie. Band II. Die Philosophie in ihren Einzelgebieten* (pp. 607-711). Berlin: Ullstein.
Vagner, V. A. (1923). *Biopsikhologija i smezhnye nauki*. Petrograd: Obrazovanie.
Vagner, V. A. (1928). *Vozniknovenie i razvitie psikhicheskikh sposobnostej. Vol. 5*. Leningrad: Nachatki Znanij.
Valsiner, J. (1988). *Developmental Psychology in the Soviet Union*. Brighton: The Harvester Press.
Valsiner, J., & Van der Veer, R. (1988). On the social nature of human cognition. *Journal for the Theory of the Behavioral Sciences*, 18, 117-135.
Van der Veer, R. (1994). The concept of development and the development of concepts. *European Journal of Psychology of Education*, 9, 293-300.
Van der Veer, R., Van IJzendoorn, M. H., & Valsiner, J. (1994). *Reconstructing the Mind. Replicability in the Social Sciences*. Norwood, NJ: Ablex Publishing Corporation.
Van der Veer, R., & Valsiner, J. (1988). Lev Vygotsky and Pierre Janet. On the origin of the concept of sociogenesis. *Developmental Review*, 8, 52-65.
Van der Veer, R., & Valsiner, J. (1991). *Understanding Vygotsky. The quest for synthesis*. Oxford: Blackwell.
Van der Veer, R., & Valsiner, J. (1994). *The Vygotsky Reader*. Oxford: Blackwell.
Vishnevsky, V. A. (1925). V zashchitu materialisticheskoj dialektiki. *Pod Znamenem Marksizma*, 8/9.
Vitte, S. Yu. (1991). *Izbrannye vospominanija 1848-1911 godov*. Moscow: Mysl.
Volkelt, H. (1914). Ueber die Vorstellungen der Tiere. Ein Beitrag zur Entwicklungspsychologie. In F. Krueger (Ed.), *Arbeiten zur Entwicklungspsychologie. Band I. Heft 2* (pp. 1-126). Leipzig-Berlin: Verlag von Wilhelm Engelmann.
Volkelt, H. (1924). Primitive Komplexqualitäten in Kinderzeichnungen. In K. Bühler (Ed.), *Bericht über den VIII. Kongress für experimentelle Psychologie in Leipzig* (pp. 204-208). Jena: Verlag von Gustav Fischer.
Vonèche, J. The mirror and the lamp: The opposition between mechanical and organismic explanations in developmental psychology. A response to Harry Beilin and Willis Overton. In J. Montangero, A. Cornu-Wells, A. Tryphon, & J. Vonèche (Eds.), *Conceptions of Change over Time* (pp. 181-194). Genève: Fondation Archives Jean Piaget.
Von Glasersfeld, E. (1993). Notes on the concept of change. In J. Montangero, A. Cornu-Wells, A. Tryphon, & J. Vonèche (Eds.), *Conceptions of Change over Time* (pp. 91-96). Genève: Fondation Archives Jean Piaget.
Von Hartmann, E. (1869). *Philosophie des Unbewussten*. Berlin: Carl Duncker's Verlag.
Vvedensky, A. I. (1892). *On the boundaries and indications of being animated*.
Vvedensky, A. I. (1917). *Psikhologija bez vsjakoj metafisiki*. Petersburg.
Vygotsky, L. S. (1925a). Predislovie. In A. F. Lazursky, *Psikhologija obshchaja i eksperimental'naja* (pp. 5-26). Leningrad: Izdatel'stvo M. K. Kostina. (3d edition)

Vygotsky, L. S. (1925b). Soznanie kak problema psikhologija povedenija. In K. N. Kornilov (Ed.), *Psikhologija i marksizm* (pp. 175-198). Leningrad: Gosudarstvennoe Izdatel'stvo.

Vygotsky, L. S. (1925/1971) *The psychology of art*. Cambridge, MA: The MIT Press.

Vygotsky, L. S. (1926a). Metodika refleksologicheskogo i psikhologicheskogo issledovanija. In K. N. Kornilov (Ed.), *Problemy sovremennoj psikhologii* (pp. 26-46). Leningrad: Gosudarstvennoe Izdatel'stvo.

Vygotsky, L. S. (1926b). Po povodu stat'i K. Koffka o samonabljudenii (vmesto predislovija). In K. N. Kornilov (Ed.), *Problemy sovremennoj psikhologii* (pp. 176-178). Leningrad: Gosudarstvennoe Izdatel'stvo.

Vygotsky, L. S. (1926c). Predislovie. In E. L. Thorndike, *Principy obuchenija, osnovannye na psikhologii* (pp. 5-23). Moscow: Rabotnik Prosveshchenija.

Vygotsky, L. S. (1926d). *Pedagogicheskaja Psikhologija* Moscow: Rabotnik Prosveshchenija.

Vygotsky, L. S. (1929a). Geneticheskie korni myshlenija i rechi. *Estvestvoznanie i Marksizm, 1,* 106-133.

Vygotsky, L. S. (1929b). K voprosu ob intellekte antropoidov v svjazi s rabotami V. Kolera. *Estvestvoznanie i Marksizm, 2,* 131-153.

Vygotsky, L. S. (1930a). Strukturnaja psikhologija. In L. Vygotsky, S. Gellershtejn, B. Fingert, & M. Shirvindt (Eds.), *Osnovnye techenija sovremennoj psikhologii* (pp. 84-125). Moscow: Gosudarstvennoe Izdatel'stvo.

Vygotsky, L. S. (1930b/1960). Povedenie zhivotnykh i cheloveka. In L. S. Vygotsky, *Razvitie vysshikh psikhicheskikh funkcij* (pp. 397-457). Moscow: Izdatel'stvo Pedagogicheskikh Nauk.

Vygotsky, L. S. (1930c). Predislovie. In W. Köhler, *Issledovanie intellekta chelovekopodobnykh obez'jan* (pp. i-xxix). Moscow: Izdatel'stvo Kommunisticheskoj Akademii.

Vygotsky, L. S. (1930d). Predislovie. In K. Bühler, *Ocherk dukhovnogo razvitija rebenka* (pp. 5-26). Moscow: Rabotnik Prosveshchenija.

Vygotsky, L. S. (1930e). Psikhika, soznanie, bessoznatel'noe. In *Elementy obshchej psikhologii* (pp. 48-61). Moscow: Izdatel'stvo BZO pri Pedfake 2-go MGU.

Vygotsky, L. S. (1931). Predislovie. In A. N. Leont'ev, *Razvitie pamjati*(pp. 6-13). Moscow-Leningrad: Uchpedgiz.

Vygotsky, L. S. (1934a). Psikhologija i uchenie o lokalizacii psikhicheskikh funkcij. In *Pervyj Vseukrainskij s'ezd nevropatologov i psikhiatrov* (pp. 34-41). Kharkov.

Vygotsky, L. S. (1934b). Problema razvitija v strukturnoj psikhologii. Kriticheskoe issledovanie. In K. Koffka, *Osnovy psikhicheskogo razvitija* (pp. ix-lvi). Moscow–Leningrad: Gosudarstvennoe Social'no-Ekonomicheskoe Izdatel'stvo.

Vygotsky, L. S. (1934c). Thought in schizophrenia. *Archives of Neurology and Psychiatry, 31,* 1063-1077.

Vygotsky, L. S. (1985). *Ausgewählte Schriften. Band I. Arbeiten zu theoretischen und methodologischen Problemen der Psychologie.* Köln: Pahl-Rugenstein Verlag.

Vygotsky, L. S. (1991). *Obras Escogidas. I. Problemas teóricos y metodológicos de la psicología.* Madrid: Visor Distribuciones.

Vygotsky, L. S., & Luria, A. R. (1925). Predislovie. In S. Freud, *Po tu storonu principa udovol'stvija* (pp. 3-16). Moscow: Sovremennye Problemy.

Vygotsky, L. S., & Luria, A. R. (1930). *Etjudy po istorii povedenija. Obez'jana. Primitiv. Rebenok.* Moscow–Leningrad: Gosudarstvennoe Izdatel'stvo.

Watson, J. B. (1924). The unverbalized in human behavior. *Psychological Review, 31,* 273-280.

Watson, J. B. (1924/1970). *Behaviorism.* New York: W. W. Norton & Company Inc.

Watson, J. B. (1926). *Psikhologija kak nauka o povedenii.* Moscow: Gosudarstvennoe Izdatel'stvo.

Wertheimer, M. (1912). Experimentelle Studien über das Sehen von Bewegungen. *Zeitschrift für experimentelle Psychologie, 61,* 161-265.

Wertheimer, M. (1925). *Drei Abhandlungen zur Gestaltheorie.* Erlangen: Verlag der philosophischen Akademie.

Yerkes, R. M., & Yerkes, A. (1929). *The great apes.* New Haven: Yale University Press.

Yoravsky, D. (1989). *Russian Psychology. A Critical History.* Oxford: Blackwell.

Zalkind, A. B. (1924). *Ocherki kul'tury revoljucionnogo vremeni.* Moscow.

Zankov, L. V. (1935). *Ocherki psikhologii umstvennogo-otstalogo rebenka.* Moscow: Gosudarstvennoe Uchebno-Pedagogicheskoe Izdatel'stvo.

Zelyenyj, G. P. (1923). O ritmicheskikh myshechnykh dvizhenijakh [About rhythmic muscle movements]. *Russkij Fiziologicheskij Zhurnal, 6,* 1-3.

AUTHOR INDEX

SUBJECT INDEX

Abstraction 6, 27, 28, 99, 113, 131, 132, 220, 224, 239, 248, 249, 297, 320, 326

Action
instrumental 85-87, 89
intellectual 164, 183, 200-204, 206, 207, 231
structural 192, 204

Activity
higher forms of 214, 216
human 21, 191, 219, 356, 403
labor (see also Labor) 15-18, 21, 31, 179, 180, 372
lower forms of 216
practical 15, 17, 25, 31, 32, 363
psychological 385

Adolescent 98, 99, 101

Aesthetic reaction—see Reaction

Affective processes 93, 102-104

Agnosia 141, 143

Agnosticism 293

Amnesia 135, 136, 223

Analysis
the "cell" of psychology 320
in elements 24, 143, 372
in units 24, 27, 87, 110, 139, 142, 143, 194, 221, 352, 353, 372

Anthropoid apes (chimpanzee) 3, 4, 17, 20, 131, 164, 165, 168, 170, 176-189, 191, 198, 200, 201, 203-213, 216, 217, 219, 231, 384, 385, 403

Aphasia 92, 94, 133, 134, 141-143, 208, 382

Applied psychology, psychotechnics—see Psychological science, branches

Apraxia 141-143, 382

Art—see Psychological science; psychology of art

Association 38, 40, 71, 74, 130, 139, 177, 182, 183, 185, 187-190, 197, 200, 203, 222, 260, 283, 336, 342, 349, 355, 373, 393, 395, 397

Association psychology, associationism—see Psychological science, currents

Associative connection 86

Atomism (in the analysis of mind) 18, 19, 61, 130, 139, 167, 197, 222, 225, 230, 300, 354, 358, 372

Attention
involuntary 18, 85
voluntary 18, 85, 91, 94, 98, 99, 127

Behavior
acquired 58, 155
animal 4, 58, 64, 68, 110, 168, 169, 175-177, 183, 185, 192, 205, 207, 235-237, 284, 287, 348
external 83, 98, 394
higher forms 164, 170, 176
human 4, 35-39, 43, 44, 46, 57, 59, 60, 63-69, 74, 75, 78, 107, 113, 152, 161, 169, 175-177, 202, 349-351, 355, 377
innate 199, 357
internal 93, 98
lower forms 202
personal 95, 157
as a psychophysiological process 93, 113
system 35, 44
structure 66, 67, 79, 87, 349

Behaviorism—see Psychological science

Being and thinking 256, 322, 324, 328

Biogenetic law 20, 270, 406

Brain 5, 31, 60, 66, 69, 70, 86, 95-97, 104-106, 110, 113-115, 117, 124, 125, 131, 139,